For Donya Feuer
who provided the occasion and encouragement
and for Peter Brook
who provided the key to the key
and for Roy Davids
who provided the moral support and the books

Contents

CHAPTER 6 The Dismantling of the Tragic Equation:
The Tempest

POSTSCRIPT: the Boar with a Flower in its Mouth, 501

APPENDICES

Foreword

Years ago, in a brief note to an anthology of Shakespeare's verse,* I made an observation about a basic structural pattern, a fundamental dramatic idea, which seemed to recur in fourteen of the mature plays, beginning in *All's Well that Ends Well* and ending in *The Tempest*. I called this pattern Shakespeare's 'myth'. The recurrence of various themes, motifs, situations and character types in the plays is familiar to all who know them. But this particular configuration seemed to operate at the level of the poetic vision itself, almost like the DNA, as it were, of his poetic organism. That was my impression.

I came upon this myth inadvertently, via the anthology. Picking out the most intense passages of verse had the incidental effect of isolating and – to my eye, at least – spotlighting those tirades of seeming misogyny in the mature plays. This prompted me, as editor, to look for some concise, explanatory image of that larger, balancing context from which my excerpts had been plucked. I was guided by two fortuitous circumstances in my own life. The first of these was my sustained interest in the mythologies and folklores of the world, which had long preceded my interest in poetry and had in a way led me to poetry. The second was the work I did with Peter Brook, beginning at the Old Vic with actors of the National Theatre, back in 1968, then later with the international group of actors at his Centre for Theatre Research in Paris, where I served as – among other things – an ideas man, providing germs of plots and suggestive dramatic situations which the actors then explored, in improvisation (for many hours a day), under Peter Brook's eye. Some days we got through five or six of my 'plots'. From my notes, it seems that I produced hundreds. Occasionally, we developed them into productions and performed the results to a range of audiences – from primitive village to royal court. During this work, as can be imagined, the materials, as well as the actors, were put to strange tests. Meanwhile, in my constant search for galvanic, nuclear dramatic ideas, I became far more aware than I had been of the diverse repertoires of

*A Choice of Shakespeare's Verse, Faber and Faber, 1971, new and revised edition 1991.

[xi]

basic plot schemata that have evolved, under their camouflage, in the various traditions of drama. As a matter of course I developed a hunter's eye for such things. Accordingly, when I lined up those Shakespearean tirades in my selection, I recognized that all were the same organ – as they might be specimens of hearts in the four-chambered evolutionary line. The basic physiology of the schema within which this heart worked then simply stepped out, 'wrapp'd in a player's hide', as a combination of the myths behind the two long narrative poems, *Venus and Adonis* and *Lucrece*, which, as I was already aware, secreted the two fundamental myths of Christianity. That gave me the essential equation – Shakespeare's 'myth'.

I realized that a full treatment would require a long book, and this I was reluctant to undertake at the time. In the end I tried to suggest the idea in that brief note appended to my selection from Shakespeare's verse. One reader, Donya Feuer of the Royal Theatre in Stockholm, found a hint in my remarks, and eventually, in 1978, put together a full-length performance of interlinked verse extracts in which a solo actress relived her Shakespearean earlier incarnations, following the evolution of one of the myth's figures from play to play.

Well aware that almost anything can be projected into Shakespeare, nevertheless, as time passed, I could not help but become more convinced that what I had described as his myth was not entirely imported by me, but did have objective life, and in fact evolved from play to play with riveting consistency. I began to see those mature plays, from *As You Like It* (the overture to *All's Well that Ends Well*) to *The Tempest*, as a single, tightly integrated cyclic work. This work dramatized a myth which expressed a particular temperament, which in turn reflected, even in a sense embodied, a daemonic, decisive crisis in the history of England.

When the opportunity came, recently, to clarify what I had said in my old introduction, I made the attempt. That inclusive, subterranean pattern of unity in the plays might be suggested, I thought, to a reader who had patience, if I could only find a simple diagrammatic form. While I was thinking about this, Donya Feuer contacted me again, out of the blue, wanting to know if anything could be done with our old notion of the last fifteen plays, hugely shuffled and rearranged to make a *perpetuum mobile* maze of metamorphic episodes, play dissolving into play, characters going through their transformations, in and out of each other's worlds, like supernatural, dying and resurrected entities in a real myth.

I had no clear idea how such a thing might ever be practicable, but the thought of it would intrigue anybody. However, it did occur to me that if I anatomized what I had identified as Shakespeare's myth, as it revealed itself in each work, and followed through what are to me its fascinating evolutions, and set it all out in letters to Donya Feuer, bit by bit, as simply as possible, who knows, maybe something would emerge. Those letters became this book.

10 January 1992

Acknowledgements

My thanks are due to all the authors on whose work I have drawn in writing this book. My special thanks are due to Peter Brook. Any practical knowledge of working in the theatre that I may have derives from the work I did with him over several years. I see this book as a continuation in many ways of my close association with his dream (which was also mine) of a theatre simultaneously sacred and profane, simultaneously a revelation of spiritual being and an explosive image of life's infinite animal power and psychological abundance, where the tacit ideal, for both of us I think, was Shakespeare.

My thanks are also due to the Revd Moelwyn Merchant who understood the basic idea when I first sketched it in 1970 and urged me to go on with an early draft of this later version, to Keith Sagar who played devil's advocate to some effect (I trust) while giving the main theme his absolute support, and to Ann Pasternak Slater who, with her husband, Craig Raine (my former editor at Faber and Faber), made such crucial suggestions after reading an early draft that I rewrote the whole thing more fully (although even with drastic simplifications that meant lengthening the book a little). I am also indebted to Richard Proudfoot who gave generous time and raised several important points that I have tried to take account of – though I have not managed, I fear, to do justice to his more radical suggestions. I am grateful to Donya Feuer whose dream of exploring the possibilities on stage actually prompted this exposition in the first place, and Roy Davids who opened to me his library of books on and from the period, and from beginning to end supplied comments and suggestions. Finally, I would like to thank Judith O'Connor and Julie Armstrong who set the pages out in readable form, and my telepathic copy editor, Gillian Bate, for her skill in helping to find the easiest direct route for a reader through the multiple helix of this particular pattern in the great carpet.

The Greeks, a certain scholar has told me, considered that myths are the activities of the Daimons, and that the Daimons shape our characters and our lives. I have often had the fancy that there is some one myth for every man, which, if we but knew it, would make us understand all he did and thought.

W. B. Yeats,
'At Stratford-on-Avon: Ideas of Good And Evil'

One of these men is Genius to the other;
And so of these: which is the natural man,
And which the spirit?

The Comedy of Errors, v. i. 3 3 4–6

I have seen a just and mighty vision . . .

Black Elk

But Cordelia is the quiet absolute . . . her very silence
is the still centre of this turning world.

Ann Pasternak Slater, *Shakespeare The Director*

That nature, which contemns its origin,
Cannot be border'd certain in itself;
[He] that [him]self will sliver and disbranch
From [his] material sap, perforce must wither
And come to deadly use.

King Lear, IV. ii. 3 2–6

There is only one history, and that is the soul's.

W. B. Yeats

Thunder is the honey of all beings; all beings the
honey of thunder. The bright eternal Self that is in
thunder, the bright eternal Self that lives in the voice,
are one and the same: that is immortality, that is spirit,
that is all!

Brihadaranyaka-Upanishad

SHAKESPEARE
AND THE GODDESS OF
COMPLETE BEING

INTRODUCTION

Shakespeare's 'myth' is made up of two actual myths. Since his way of combining them takes the form of an equation where the first half, by its own inherent dynamics, produces the second half, and where the constants and variables work quite a bit like algebra (as they generally do in the life of myth), always producing the tragic explosion by the same chemistry, and eventually always producing the rebirth into transcendence by the same chemistry, I have called it Shakespeare's Equation or, more often, his Tragic Equation, and sometimes his Mythic Equation, though occasionally it is more convenient to call it simply his myth. And I have called that particular dynamic event, by which the energies of the first half of the Equation explode, transformed, into the second, 'the Shakespearean moment'.

The immediate practical function of this equation is simply to produce, with unfailing success, an inexhaustibly interesting dramatic action. From *Hamlet* onwards it produces, as I say, tragic action, and from *Cymbeline* onwards, the redemption of tragic action. In this way, it works as a basic flexible formula, a prototype plot model.

Would Shakespeare descend to such a device? Every reader will answer differently, according to what they know of modern instruction manuals for professional writers or of the actual working habits of professional writers harnessed to a demanding production line (whether in Athens's great, competitive century or in the modern TV drama and pulp fiction markets), or perhaps according to their sense of Shakespeare's attitude to his trade. He was, after all, part theatre owner, part manager, part worker, part supplier of raw materials, and full-time entrepreneur in a precarious yet fiercely demanding industry. Whether it was an old play rejigged or a new piece, it had to work. Maybe, under those pressures, it was inevitable that he should do as other hack professionals have always done, and develop one or two basic reliable kits of the dynamics that make a story move on the stage.*

*Discussing the purpose of a practical course for playwrights, a modern dramatist recently remarked that dramatists waste 80 per cent of their productive life on unworkable ideas that have to be abandoned.

On the other hand, if he approached his plays in the careful spirit of a watchmaker or a detective-story writer, where every slightest detail is subtly adjusted, albeit for the simple practical job of gripping the ordinary public, he would be just as likely to appreciate the built-in advantages of the perfect archetypal plot, one that would guarantee basic drive.

In the end, of course, all this is speculation. But the circumstances of Shakespeare's working life, in the thirty-year boom of the Elizabethan/Jacobean drama, and the way he manipulated and developed the various factors of his Equation from play to play, suggest that he knew exactly what a successful piece of stage equipment he had invented, and what a useful skeleton key, also, to his own deepest resources (such as every writer dreams of finding).

The other main function of this formula, once it becomes mythic, is, like myth itself, metaphysical. I shall say more about this when I come to deal with each play in more detail. Here it is enough to say that Shakespeare uses myth in (at least) three broadly distinctive ways.

In the first he uses it as decorative reference, as in:

> For valour, is not Love a Hercules,
> Still climbing trees in the Hesperides?
> *Love's Labour's Lost*, IV. iii. 340–1

In the second he uses it, sporadically, as a structural device, but retaining the original mythic terms, as when Jupiter descends, as Jupiter, hurling thunderbolts, on an eagle's back, in the dream of Posthumus in *Cymbeline*; or as when Diana, as Diana, speaks to Pericles in that play; or, more intricately, as in the Masque of *The Tempest*, where the account of Venus and her 'waspish-headed son' being repulsed from the betrothal of Ferdinand and Miranda draws together the threads of the whole tragic series of fourteen dramas.

In the third he strips the myth of all identifiably mythic features, and secretes its mechanism within his plot, as he does with the two myths — of the Great Goddess and of the Goddess-destroying god — which are the theme of my argument here. However, though he secularizes these two myths and translates them into the terms of his Equation, he continues to draw on their specifically mythic resources. And this is the crucial circumstance in the role they play: the mythic terminology appears in the finished work no more than the mathematics (without which it would have been unthinkable and impossible) appear in the nuclear reaction and flash of the bomb.

This is the point I shall try to establish. By constructing his basic Equation out of living myth, he is able to create dramas which, no matter how secular they seem, or how real in the dimension of external historic event and of psychology, nevertheless embody and communicate a very particular 'mythic' dimension, which is to say a 'divine' or 'daemonic' dimension. His 'mythic' Equation operates at mid-level in each work, as a controlling, patterned field of force, open internally to the 'divine', the 'daemonic', the 'supernatural' (of which the constituent myths were the original symbolic expression), but externally to the profane, physical form and individualities of the action, to the words of the actors, and the local habitation and burden of the plot.

An example of what I mean, to anticipate a little, appears in his use of the myth of *Venus and Adonis*. Basically, this is the most familiar variant of the myth of the Great Goddess and her consort, the sacrificed god, the myth of one of the most widespread and profoundly rooted religions of the archaic world. Shakespeare appropriates it by adapting it to his peculiar needs, making Adonis a chaste, rational, moralizing, self-preoccupied young man who rejects the infinite passion of the Great Goddess (instead of responding in kind, as in the original myth).

Stripped of mythic frippery and 'secularized', these two figures reappear in *All's Well that Ends Well* as Helena, hopelessly in love, pursuing the scornful Bertram, who coldly and angrily rejects her. Again, they reappear in *Measure for Measure*, as Isabella, the passionately obstinate, eloquent advocate (albeit to her own surprise) for sexual licence – her plea rejected by the ice-cold Angelo, who has been appointed to purge the seething, venereal stews of Vienna and to pass sentence of death on sexual offenders.

In both these uneasy examples Shakespeare seems to have difficulty in making his women real – something that has hardly happened to him before. One is more than a little aware that a new, much bigger, extra dimension has opened behind them. They both produce an uncomfortable impression, like a double exposure. Both seem wilfully committed to awkwardly superhuman roles. The truth is, perhaps, that the secularized characters of Helena and Isabella, with their human histories which the audience observes from the outside, are inadequately insulated from their mythic roles, which continue to galvanize them from the inside. In other words, Shakespeare has some difficulty in bringing these women down to earth. This is evident in what they say, but it is visible too in various details. To perform her part, Isabella is snatched from the very gates of the nunnery, a creature 'ensky'd and sainted', just about to become (like mythic Venus) a 'bride' of the sacrificed god no less. And Helena, who, having declared from the opening scene that her passion for Bertram is a 'holy' matter, goes on a pilgrimage, and materializes as Diana, in a shrine to consummate it.

At this point, in these first two experiments with his new invention, Shakespeare has not quite assimilated the Venus figure of the requisitioned inner myth to the human frailty and complexity of the characters in his visible outer plots. But it should not be surprising that he met a problem here, and that Helena and Isabella are flawed, as I say, by supernatural gleams from their mythic existence. This existence enfolds, after all, the highest idea of the Divine.

This same Great Goddess — female sexuality as a symbol of the Mother of Creation — in a Christianized form opened to Dante the ultimate vision of his *Paradiso*. To assert that his vision descended on Dante exclusively from Catholic iconography and religious feeling would be as mistaken as to argue that he nursed it into being solely from the erotic impact of Beatrice on the nine-year-old nervous system of a motherless boy. Both extremes are inseparably active, and the continuum between them is the subjective life of Dante. In a similar way, Helena and Isabella, these prototypical Shakespearean heroines (perhaps like the Beatrice of *La Vita Nuova*), blushing into hectic, sexual life, are only just touching earth with their toes.

Shakespeare soon brings these heavenly daemons solidly into their palpitating, temporal names and fates, not by exorcizing their mythic inner being, but by packing their hearts and voices with livelier human weight. The hidden myth continues to supply their superhuman dramatic force and resonance — in fact it intensifies its transmissions — but the faces through which that force field communicates itself become more and more vulnerably, intimately human. This presence of the living myth and the mythic dimension is what distinguishes Shakespeare's work from that of all his contemporaries. It puts into his power the forces, the great music, of a new kind of tragedy. Which does not mean that any myth would have served.

The two myths which he combined, in his Equation, were the myths of the two religions* which between them dominated English life in the sixteenth and seventeenth centuries. His first long poem, *Venus and Adonis*, incorporates the first of these. His second long poem, *Lucrece*, incorporates the second. The myth behind *Venus and Adonis*, as I shall attempt to show, operated as the 'myth' of Catholicism, while the myth behind *Lucrece* operated as that of Puritanism. In the life of Shakespeare's time, these two complexes of religious fanaticism were deadlocked in a holy war, albeit suspended and in a sense arrested by Elizabeth I's religious policy. Within Shakespeare's drama one finds them deadlocked and arrested in the same way. Yet not absolutely arrested: in both history and his drama they were inching towards a catastrophe. In this sense the equation into which he combined the two myths was the composite myth of the English Reformation itself.

Interesting as that is, Shakespeare's attention seems to have been focused on this theme by some obsessive private experience† – something to do with his peculiar (one might say abnormal) dramatic genius – which, when he turned to writing the two long poems, went straight to these two myths. I will come back to this. But first, a brief account of the myths.

Shakespeare knew the myth of Venus and Adonis from Greek and Latin contexts, though his feeling for it seems to have been coloured by what he knew, through Roman sources, of the closely related cult of Attis and Cybele. Again through Roman sources, he was familiar with other manifestations of the Great Goddess, both in her triple forms and in her various aspects. Some sense of yet other forms and cults of the Goddess reached him, indirectly and fragmentarily, in the context of the Bible. Again, he knew of the related Egyptian myth of Horus, Isis and Osiris through Roman sources, and was familiar with the mythographer's game of interrelating these deities. For Shakespeare, as for Plutarch, Venus was a token in the vast Goddess complex, behind the various religions, where his aptitude for symbolic language and metaphor played with great ease.

*For my argument it is convenient to speak of them as separate religions.

†A modern parallel would be T. S. Eliot's early, well-recorded obsession with the image of St Sebastian. This vision, behind his 'juvenile' poem, *The Death of St Narcissus*, provides a key to the inner mythic unity of the cycle of his poems in much the same way that *Venus and Adonis* provides a key to the inner mythic unity of Shakespeare's dramas. In fact, both poets saw the death of the same god (or demi-god), but from slightly different angles.

Adonis's home was originally the lands east of the eastern coast of the Mediterranean. He appeared everywhere as the son and consort of the Great Goddess who, under many different names, can be seen as the creative womb of the inchoate waters, gradually refining herself into human form, and everywhere tending to be fish-tailed. The most typical primordial representative of the type, and maybe the most influential in the tradition that filters through, eventually, to Shakespeare's Equation, is Tiamat, the monstrous Mother of First Created Things in the Babylonian creation myth. In her later forms, throughout the Middle East, she takes on a double existence as Inanna (Ishtar, Astarte, Athtar, etc.), who is Goddess of Love and Reproduction, and as Ereshkigal (Allatu, etc.), who is Goddess of the Underworld. Her consort was Thammuz, or Dumuzi, 'the son of the deep waters', who spent one part of the year in the upper world, with the Love Goddess, and the other part in the Underworld with the Queen of Hell. In the Babylon known to the Hebrew prophets she was Ishtar, whose consort was Thammuz. In Jerusalem, down to the sixth century BC, as the lover of Astoreth, Asherah, or Anath, for whom the Temple was first built, her consort was Thammuz or Baal (Ezekiel heard the woman mourning Thammuz at the north gate). His title was Adonis, 'Lord'.

Around 900–700 BC, Phoenicians brought this god and goddess, under the names Adonis and Aphrodite, to Paphos in Cyprus, which became their cult centre in the Greek world. Under these and other names they were installed here and there around the Mediterranean. (In Libya one of the Goddess's names was Dido – the phonetic radical of Aphrodite.)

Throughout Adonis's range his story was basically the same, with local variations of detail. Aphrodite was originally born from the sea. In the Cyprian version, she compelled the virgin Smyrna to seduce her drunken father. Learning that he had sired her unborn child, he chased his daughter to kill her. As his sword descended, Aphrodite transformed the girl into a myrrh tree. The blade split the trunk and out tumbled baby Adonis, the Divine Child, the god of the earth's flowering.

This overture to the myth is the vestige of a grander event, more fully dramatized in other variants, where the god is released or reborn from the tree, as if by Caesarean birth. It has no structural relevance to Shakespeare's basic Tragic Equation, but great relevance to what he made of it in the last four plays. It places Adonis in the lineage descending to Ariel, whom Prospero released from the pine and who thereafter lived in a cowslip. Again, I will come back to this.

The sinister peculiarity of Aphrodite is that, like Inanna before her, she has a 'double' in the Underworld, who shares with her the dying and resurrected god. In effect, the two goddesses are the two poles of the one Great Goddess. In Tiamat they were united. In every epiphany of the Goddess the two aspects are present – one latent behind the other. In the foreground they appear to be two, and opposites, but in the background they are one.

These two aspects are the most regular manifestations of the great triple Goddess's three aspects: the Mother, the Sacred Bride, and the Queen of the Underworld. Generally, Mother and Sacred Bride appear as a single being, as in Venus, Ishtar, Inanna, etc., in polar opposition to the Queen of the Underworld. This is not irrelevant, as far as Shakespeare is concerned. The triple form of this figure, with Mother and Bride clearly defined but linked, appears quite distinctly in *All's Well that Ends Well*, *Troilus and Cressida*, *Hamlet*, *Coriolanus*, *Pericles*, and *The Winter's Tale*. The same triple being, with different aspects of Queen of the Underworld, Mother and Bride shifting enigmatically but clearly identified in a way that bewilders and maddens the hero, appears also in *Measure for Measure*, *Othello*, *Macbeth*, *King Lear*, *Antony and Cleopatra*, *Cymbeline*, and *The Tempest*. That accounts for all but one of the plays in the tragic series. And in *Timon of Athens* the hero behaves as if the whole complex of women were present.

Adonis's myth proper begins where Aphrodite hides the Divine Child in a chest and gives him into the care of Persephone, Goddess of the Underworld. As he grows, Persephone falls in love with him and refuses to give him back to Aphrodite, even though the Goddess of Love descends into the Underworld to beg for him. Aphrodite appeals to Zeus for justice, and it is finally arranged that she shall have Adonis for one part of the year, and Persephone shall have him for another part.

Now it is Aphrodite's turn to refuse to hand Adonis over to Persephone. Persephone, enraged, emerges in her animal form as a wild boar, and reclaims him by killing him. After that, he alternates between the two goddesses.

The two sacred festivals of Adonis's year are his divine birth, when he returns amid ecstatic jubilation to the upper world, and his sacrificial death by a boar, amid cries and mourning, when he passes to the lower world.

Through the practice of the cult, these two deities imprinted history in various ways. Since the business of the Goddess was fertility, reproduction, and renewal of life, everywhere her worship involved ritual prostitution: obligatory premarital or occasional prostitution of all women, and institutionalized prostitution within the Temple itself. At Jerusalem, the priestesses were prostitutes, and the priests 'dog prostitutes', which is how their Goddess came to be characterized in the sacred books of the Jehovan reformers as 'the Great Whore of abominations and adulteries'.

Another no less dramatic and influential feature of her cult was the incarnation of the god in the king, and the consequent identity of their fates – to be sacrificed and reborn. This ritual murder of the Goddess's consort, the god-king, by his successor, eventually produced the sacrificial substitute and other refinements, but also modified the myth with the extra figure of the god's murderous double, who emerged, somehow at the behest of the Goddess, to usurp the reigning consort. In the Adonis myth, this fatal double emerged as Mars, Aphrodite's jealous lover, who took on the form of a wild boar and killed Adonis. So it comes about that two versions of Adonis's death exist side by side. In the first, he is killed by Persephone in the form of a boar. In the second, he is killed by the one who will replace him – in the form of a boar. In other words, the Boar is simultaneously the Queen of the Underworld in her enraged animal form, and Adonis's usurping double, a murderous martial warrior in enraged animal form.

This could be explained as an accidental superimposition or conflation of two different myths. However that may be, the double identity of the Boar is consistent throughout the fourteen lives of Shakespeare's tragic hero, as I hope to make clear. It is the origin of the two forms of the Equation. In the first form, the tragic form, the hero rejects the Goddess and is 'killed' by the Boar (arriving as a madness), which is to say that he is transformed by it. In the second form, the Boar is incarnated in the 'irrational', inferior one of two 'rival brothers'. He usurps his 'rational' brother, either by dispossessing or killing him. In both forms, the Boar (whether as the madness, or as the usurping brother) seems to emerge from a female who incarnates the Queen of Hell. Both forms, clearly, are dramatizations of the same event: the overthrow of the rational by the irrational, though this bald simplification hardly helps to explain the wealth of drama that Shakespeare draws from the conflict.

The documentation of the pervasive, formative influence of these Goddess religions on early Christianity is a vast literature. A few details are enough to indicate that this influence was not so much formative as a substantial continuation under changed names.*

Roman culture was resistant to the virus of the Great Goddess in the form carried by the Greek Aphrodite and Adonis, but helpless before the bizarre and shocking variant that came by way of Phrygia (Turkey), carried by Attis and Cybele. The inner life of this cult is better known than that of Venus and Adonis, perhaps because it was officially adopted by Rome (204 BC) and spread vigorously through much of the Empire until Christianity officially suppressed it (partly absorbing it) in the fourth century AD. Certain features of these rites, including the more gruesome, are one way or another familiar from the Christian inheritance.

The ritual death and resurrection of Attis was celebrated in Rome between 22 and 26 March. On the first day, a pine tree trunk was carried, swathed with wool and violets, and with an effigy of Attis bound to it. On the third day, her worshippers, by this time in an ecstatic frenzy, castrated themselves and hurled the amputated parts at the image of the Goddess.

The fifth day, when the god was thought to have risen, was the day of universal Saturnalian licence. On the sixth day, the Goddess's image, with its black meteorite face, was washed in a stream near the Tiber. At the same time, in a secret sacrament, initiates in a pit were washed under the cascading blood of freshly slaughtered bulls, and emerged 'sinless' and new-born to be clothed, and for some days fed, as new-born babies. Cybele's temple in Rome, where these rites were performed, was on the site of St Peter's Basilica on Vatican Hill. Since the resurrection day was regarded as the day on which Cybele conceived the new god, it also decided the nativity date as 25 December, which in many regions of the Great Goddess was already celebrated as the birthday of the Divine Child. (Christ's birthplace, Bethlehem, was a ritual centre of Thammuz and Astarte.)

While Shakespeare absorbed Christianity's massive transmission of

*An extensive account of local survivals of earlier Goddess cults into the cult of Mary is given in Marina Warner's *Alone of All Her* *Sex: the myth and cult of the Virgin Mary*, London: Weidenfeld and Nicolson, 1976.

the more obvious features, he seems to have been especially sensitive to some of the archaic details. While Adonis was simply killed by a boar, Attis was killed by a boar under a pine tree, and the fatal wound was also castration. In other words, the Goddess in the form of the Boar removed her consort from sexual life in the world and claimed all his 'love' for herself, by castration. This image stirs alarmingly, and confusedly, in the strange 'Adonis' sonnet (*The Passionate Pilgrim*, no.9), and on this count alone one might suspect it to be Shakespeare's. The same image fuses, quite violently, in the long poem *Venus and Adonis*, with the absolute, dedicated temper of Adonis's chastity, and later, in the plays, with the idealization of 'chaste' love dedicated to a 'sacred' beloved, and the hero's positive terror of female sexuality that reaches its climax in *King Lear*.

This 'meaning' of the Boar becomes more intricately clarified in the evolution of Shakespeare's Equation, where the Boar's charge, as a big spark leaping a gap, is in every case the detonator of the tragic explosion.

In the Christianized Empire, repeated attempts were made to obliterate the visible pagan forms of the Goddess religion. At the same time, the early Christian theologians anathematized it as a great heresy. They fought to extricate Christ's mother from the archaic mantle of the Great Whore, and to dissociate their new love god in every way from the erotic Attis, Thammuz, Adonis and the rest. Temples, priesthoods, priestesses and religious ceremonies could be expunged fairly easily. The instincts or even the habits of inner life were not so accessible. The signs are that the old religion merely went underground. In any case the deities that had been adopted by the Empire – Attis and Cybele, Horus and Isis, among others – were already part of the psychic inheritance of the Evangelists themselves. And so the Divine Child, Horus Harpocrates in Isis's arms, provided Christianity with its icon ready made, not to speak of the sacrificed god on the tree. Even more important than these, maybe, was the immense moral prestige and pervasive influence, throughout both Greek and Roman worlds, of the Greek Eleusinian Mysteries, in which ritual death, coinciding with the sacred marriage and rebirth, revolved around the Great Goddess, as Demeter, and her Divine Child, Iacchos – a form of Dionysus.

In the circumstances, the fanatic Puritanism of those early Christians accommodated itself, gradually, to the inevitable, as the Goddess reasserted herself in her own religion. When the mystical ecstatic adoration of the Divine Beloved streamed into eleventh- and twelfth-century Europe from the Sufi poet-saints of Islam, it was appropriated, as a matter of course, for Mary, who had become the beneficiary of all the innate Goddess worship of the masses that had survived into the Christianized world. The Puritan reformers of the sixteenth century did not have to search the Old Testament to stir their indignation against what came with the Goddess. Even into modern times Cyprian peasants adored the Mother of Christ as Panaghia Aphroditessa, and were anointing the stones of her great temple in Paphos in honour of 'the maid of Bethlehem'.

In the light of all this it seems likely that Shakespeare would be acutely aware of the theological implications of the myth of Venus and Adonis.

Meanwhile the essential ideas that he instinctively appropriated from the Venus and Adonis myth include the following motifs:

The Great Goddess is divided into two antithetical figures – the Goddess of Benign Love and the Goddess of the Underworld, though the benign aspect can divide further into Mother and Sacred Bride.

The Boar is also the Goddess of the Underworld.*

*The Boar's peculiarly hermaphroditic nature is almost universally recognized in mythology. This presumably derives from our long and intimate acquaintance with the unique bodily character of this most impressive, dangerous, fascinating and human of the animals that are both domesticated and hunted. As a matriarch equally well known, the cow has been given the benign, spiritual role of the nursing mother. But the sow has attracted different associations. Her combination of gross whiskery nakedness and riotous carnality is seized by the mythic imagination, evidently, as a sort of uterus on the loose – upholstered with breasts, not so much many-breasted as a mobile tub entirely made of female sexual parts, a woman-sized, multiple udder on trotters. Most alarming of all is that elephantine, lolling mouth under her great ear-flaps, like a Breughelesque nightmare vagina, baggy with over-production, famous for gobbling her piglets, magnified and shameless, exuberantly omnivorous and insatiable, swamping the senses. This sow has supplanted all other beasts as the elemental mother (even Zeus was born of a sow, even Demeter, Mother of Iacchos/Dionysus and Persephone, was a sow (cf. page 73)). But she fulfils an ambiguous lunar role. Her variable dark part is sinister, not only because she incorporates more shocking physical familiarity, more radical enterprise, more rapturous appetite, cruder travesties of infantile memory, wilder nostalgias, than the cow, but because she is inseparable from the lethal factor of the Boar, who carries the same vaginal grin yet is prodigiously virile – that same swinging, earth-searching, root-ripping mouth but equipped with moon-sickle tusks – and who incarnates the most determined, sudden and murderous temperament. (As a country boy, and the nephew of several farmers, Shakespeare enjoyed a familiarity with pigs that is not irrelevant to his myth. The imagination's symbols are based on subliminal perception. The male, aphrodisiac, pheromone scent spray, sold in modern sex shops, is commonly based on a hormone extract from the wild boar.) This figure of the Boar has

The Boar is also the martial 'twin' or 'brother' who displaces the god in a frenzy of jealousy.

The wound that the Boar inflicts is sexual, and is the means by which the 'dark' Goddess lays claim.

The flowers from the god's blood are 'blood flowers' of various kinds, sometimes violets.

The god is reborn through this flower which the Goddess cherishes and carries into her Heaven.

The death of the god is accompanied by terrific uproar of lamentation.

Shakespeare's awareness of the greater matrix of the myth manifested itself gradually, as his Equation developed. But in 1593, for *Venus and Adonis*, he used one simple source: the half-secularized, domesticated version in Ovid's *Metamorphoses*.

This Roman tale has lost Persephone, Mars and any sense of religious sexual terror. Venus's passion for the hunter is returned in kind. She fears that his dangerous prey might injure him, but he ignores her foreboding and carries on hunting until her worst fears are fulfilled and a boar kills him. She mourns him, turns him into a flower, and flies back to Paphos. As I will show, Shakespeare took this ornamental anecdote and, with a single twist, brought all the mythic demons bursting out of its cupboards.

There is little difficulty in recognizing in the myth behind Catholicism the myth of Venus and Adonis. Both are obviously variants of the myth of the Love and Mother Goddess and her dying, resurrected god: in other words, there is little difficulty in accepting that these figures belong to an archaic, albeit still-evolving, myth. But Puritanism tends to

---

assimilated the magical birth-source of the Sow to create a symbol that emerges, in a man's eyes, from everything about female sexuality that is awesome, alien, terrifying and 'beyond' the reaches of his soul. So the Boar becomes the animal form of the Queen of Hell, the Black Witch, the Terrible Mother, bringing the crippling wound in the thigh, wherever he enters man's fantasy. In his role in this myth of the god who dies for and by the Goddess, and who is reborn to destroy her, he appears at the centre of religious mysteries, and Shakespeare could have found him, in the same role, as easily in England (for instance, as the Twrch Trwyth, the terrible Boar King, who is hunted through the Celtic world in the great Welsh myth of Culhwch and Olwen) as in classical mythology (see page 465).

resist the mythic interpretation. It is not so easy to accept that Jehovah, or the Jehovan Christ of what might be called fundamentalist Protestantism, is a figure belonging to an archaic, evolving myth. In Protestant societies, whether He is regarded as unchanging, unchangeable Almighty God, or as a human illusion of unchanging Almighty God, or as a still-misunderstood and not yet properly defined Almighty God, or wears the aura of the individual conscience, or of absolute moral goodness, or of any combination of similar, abstract, infinitely flexible notions, He seems far removed from the sensational, dramatic adventure of what is thought of as 'myth'. In the historical record, however, Jehovah (or Jehovan Christ) does have a myth, ancient and modern, in which He always performs quite specific sensational, dramatic actions, and is always more or less the same personality. And this is the myth out of which Shakespeare formed the second part of his Equation, and which lies, as I have suggested, behind his long poem *Lucrece*.

The story of Tarquin and Lucrece is a historical anecdote, with little suggestion, superficially, of any mythic dimension. It tells how Prince Tarquin, the son of the Roman King Tarquin, became suddenly possessed by uncontrollable lust for Lucrece, the chaste wife of his fellow Roman commander, Collatine. Arriving, by design, as a surprise guest at the house where he knows her to be alone, he rapes her and flees. She calls the Roman nobility to hear her account of the crime, then kills herself, whereupon Tarquin is banished and the Roman monarchy brought to an end. A reader might look no further into this weirdly obsessed narration of the ultimate sexual crime if it were not for what Shakespeare went on to do with it.

The mythic-religious nature of the story of Venus and Adonis is self-evident. But I indicated how Shakespeare secularized it, in his Equation, for the first part of *All's Well that Ends Well* and *Measure for Measure*, concealing its mythic power circuit within the human and perhaps contradictory psychology of the plot. In *Lucrece*, this process has already occurred. To identify the mythic power circuit here, therefore, one has to resacralize the character and sequence of events. This produces the account of a martial, uncontrollable god ravishing a goddess or half-deity or nymph. That might resemble one of Jupiter's escapades if it were not for the ending – where because she is destroyed (destroys herself) he is banished from his rule.

Still, that is as far as one can go until the story reappears as the second half of the Equation in the plays. To begin with, then, in *All's Well that Ends Well* it supplies the design for Bertram's forceful seduction of Diana (who at the crucial moment is replaced by Helena, the wife he is trying to escape). This is neither particularly impressive nor very dramatic (though it has a tightly worked out logic as a mechanism of ritual), and one might consider it a little far-fetched to cite the possessed Tarquin for Bertram's seedy piece of philandering. But the subsequent career of the Equation in the later plays proves that Tarquin is indeed here, though in low profile. And yet this first occasion adds little to one's idea of what Tarquin's source myth might be.

In *Measure for Measure*, which is the next play in the sequence (according to the Equation, see page 98), Tarquin's rape is represented by Angelo's ravishment of Isabella (though here again at the crucial moment she is replaced by the woman the ravisher has deserted). But on this occasion the dramatic situation begins to identify the myth behind Tarquin. It does so in so far as in this play all the values of the basic relationship are shifted, much as in the preceding long poem the values of the relationship between Venus and Adonis were shifted, into the context of Reformation theology. Isabella, in fact, is a brilliantly articulated symbol of the paradoxical double nature of the Goddess's role in Reformation England. Her single yet two-sided figure bears the projection from both Catholic and Puritan extremes. Pleading for the sanctity – the natural holy innocence – of sexual licence (of total surrender to love) in a city of orgiastic promiscuity where

> corruption boil[s] and bubble[s]
> Till it o'errun[s] the stew . . .
> *Measure for Measure*, v. i. 316–17

she is a high priestess, as it were, of Astarte in the Jerusalem of the Goddess, seen through the eyes of a reforming Calvinist – a latter-day Hezekiah. Simultaneously, as a Catholic votaress about to enter her novitiate and become a bride of the sacrificed god, her love dedicated, with absolute chastity, to him alone, she is manifestly consecrated by the Divine in the most sacred Catholic sense. From both points of view she is an avatar of the Goddess.

Angelo's point of view, meanwhile, is exclusively that of the reformer – of Calvin/Hezekiah/Jehovah. That is to say, his pitiless suppression of sexuality finds its mythic template in the myth of Jehovah. Yet his sudden volte-face – that amazing reversal, in which his whole nature capsizes and he is possessed by uncontrollable lust to ravish Isabella, and is ready to kill rather than be denied – does not seem very Jehovan. Again one can get no further until one follows the Equation into later plays. In *Hamlet*, things become clearer, and in *Othello*, clear. In *Hamlet*, the second part of the Equation mutates, and the factor of 'rape' is modified, becoming simply 'killing by some means' indirectly. In *Othello*, the rape has become straight murder. In *King Lear*, it becomes banishment, which results indirectly in death. From there it reverts to 'intent to murder' and evolves thereafter consistently, as I will show, but never again reverts to rape.

From that point, then, the hero in the second part of the Equation is, on the mythic plane, an uncontrollably enraged Jehovan God, who annihilates, or attempts somehow to annihilate, the Goddess; and his motive, in every case, far from being lust to rape the female, is exactly the opposite: it is abhorrence of what he imagines to be the Goddess's whorishness, or at least her treachery in love. (For an interpretation of the mechanism behind this apparent reversal, see pages 220–1.) It is a 'madness' of the Puritan fear of female sexuality – where female sexuality has become identified with the infernal. That this 'madness' of the hero's is usually based on a delusion has much to do with Shakespeare's ultimate judgement of the conflict – in whatever context it occurs – but does not alter the fact that the 'myth' behind this 'madness', in his formulation of it, is the myth behind the Calvinist attitude to sexuality, which is the myth behind the conflict of Jehovah and the Great Goddess of seventh-century BC Jerusalem as it was enshrined in the Holy Bible. In this way the behaviour of the hero, in the plays of the tragic sequence, retrospectively identifies the myth behind Tarquin's rape of Lucrece. This myth, like that of the Great Goddess, has many variants. The most impressive (and as I said earlier the most germane for the specific tradition that came through the Bible into the European Reformation and to Shakespeare) was the Assyrian-Babylonian creation myth of Marduk's destruction of Tiamat.

Like the Greek Eurynome, Tiamat was a First Mother, and her children were all the gods. She was the monster of the oceanic abyss (in Hebrew, Tehomat – whom Jehovah dealt with as Marduk dealt with Tiamat). Her offspring, the gods, aspired to usurp her power and control the universe. After some opening skirmishes, she exalts her son

Kingu, making him her viceroy, and giving him the tablets of Fate.*

The gods are duly terrorized. They send a succession of champions against Tiamat, who, one after the other, are paralysed with fear and overcome by her powers.

Finally, Marduk is elected and armed. He has the panoply of a storm god: behind him are the storm gods of the Indian subcontinent, in particular the Vedic Mitra Varuna. He destroys Tiamat, forcing tempests down her throat until she bursts. He then splits her 'like a shellfish' and creates the heavens from her upper half, and earth, and everything on it except man, from her lower half. Finally he binds and sacrifices Kingu, and makes mankind out of his blood.

Shakespeare was aware of the feelings behind this myth through the Bible, by its indirect effects on the reforming expurgators of Hebrew history and their prophets, who were overwhelmingly aware of it – in the sense that their Jehovah is a later and more absolute development of the Marduk type of martial Goddess-destroyer. Jehovah's fulminations against the Goddess and her worshippers drew mythic authority from Marduk's defeat of Tiamat, which established that dominance of the pattern in the Babylonian/Hebrew (Reformation/Shakespeare) succession.

A single further detail highlights another curious point. Marduk himself seems to have been, originally, a god of the Adonis type – a sacrificed, reborn consort of the Goddess. Somehow, it seems, he became independent, and rejected her – finally destroying her. And Kingu, too, is obviously a god of the Adonis type. The fact that Marduk sacrifices him, and creates mankind out of his blood, sets him centrally in the lineal descent to the part performed later by Christ and Christ's blood. From this it appears that the sacrificed god can pupate – and become a Goddess-destroyer.

This actual moment of pupation was preserved, and annually re-enacted, in the Babylonian New Year festival, where it appears as two fossil rituals from the *earlier* phase embedded in and subordinated to the drama of a larger ritual from the *later* phase. On the shortest day of the year the sacred King (the earthly Marduk) pretended to be killed (at sunset, like Shakespeare's Hector in *Troilus and Cressida*) and entered

*This is another example of the emergence of a champion of the embattled Goddess, out of the Goddess's rage. The roles are, as it were, reversed exactly as in *Antony and Cleopatra*. Kingu is a prototype 'rival brother', advancing the cause of the infernalized Goddess against the pitiless warrior Marduk – the Goddess-destroyer.

his tomb, whereupon a young substitute was invested with his titles and married to his Queen. This is one 'fossil' of the death of the 'sacrificed god' and his replacement, as consort of the Goddess, by a usurper or new-born other self. On the following day this substitute was killed by being dragged at the tail of a chariot pulled by runaway horses (elsewhere, in more primitive forms of the same rite, he was torn to pieces by women disguised as horses). This is a second 'fossil' of the mode in which the sacred King, as consort of the Goddess, was originally, and actually, killed – i.e. it was enacted here as a more fully ritualized dramatization of what had supposedly happened to him the previous day. This second death would also take place at sunset, after the 'deputy' had reigned for a single day. The larger ritual was now completed, by the sacred King emerging from his tomb, fitting the two fossils into place, as follows. The 'death' of the sacred King on the first day had been regarded as Marduk's descent into the Underworld to do battle with Tiamat – a re-enactment of that creation myth. During his absence, or rather during his struggle with the hitherto invincible Goddess (i.e. during his hiding in the tomb), the world was in 'chaos'. So, just as elsewhere the world mourned the Boar's dismemberment of Adonis/Thammuz, here the world mourned what was being torn to pieces by that sudden irruption of the horses of Tiamat. Finally the sacred King's emergence from the tomb on that third day became the return of the gloriously triumphant Marduk after his terrific otherworld fight with Tiamat in which he had once again destroyed her: so he resumed his throne as the victorious Goddess-destroyer who is also, at the same time, somehow, the new-born god. In this way the (earlier) ritual of the Goddess's consort being torn to pieces by the Goddess herself in animal form was incorporated, as a sub-set, within the (later) ritual of the god fighting and destroying the Goddess.

And after that, it seems, the two forms can coexist. The Goddess-destroyer presides, in Heaven, over the continuing, recurrent 'sacrifice' of his former self, the consort of the Goddess whom he has destroyed.

Jehovah recreated a similar situation. Having destroyed the Goddess, he presides, in Heaven, over the annually repeated blood sacrifice of the consort of the Goddess whom he has destroyed. That is, he does so in so far as Christ is son and consort – like Thammuz and Adonis, before him – of the Great Goddess.

Christ is called God's son. It is only logical, therefore, that in due course he should grow up and, like his father, reject his mother. Just so, in the Reformation, it is not Jehovah who attempts to destroy the Great Goddess, but the militant, Puritan, Jehovan Christ, the new Christ.

This cycle reveals what Shakespeare rediscovered in such a mysterious fashion when he combined these myths in his Equation: the two stories are two phases of a single story. The adoring beloved of the Goddess pupates and destroys her. What Shakespeare goes on to reveal is that in destroying her he destroys himself and brings down Heaven and Earth in ruins.

I do not mean to suggest that Shakespeare's mature plays (the sequence based on the Mythic Equation) are first and foremost allegories of this religious conflict. Even from what I have said it can be seen that those two myths, and even the vast religious system of which they are the nuclei, are Western man's greatest image of a fundamental polarity in human existence. Presumably, the crisis that preoccupied England throughout Shakespeare's lifetime, defining and formulating this duality in painfully specific and religious terms, simultaneously imposed it, painfully, on the moment-by-moment crises of daily life. All it needed then was the peculiarity of Shakespeare's nervous system to make him the dial finger (or the dial panel) of the historic surge of those potentials.

At a certain point, in *King Lear*, he either reinvents by some feat of clairvoyant anamnesis (not so rare in the annals of psychoanalysis) or introduces in a learned but highly idiosyncratic fashion another major lineage of myth: the ancient Egyptian. Again, at that point, I give an outline of as much as seems necessary (pages 268–71).

That third myth helps him to a fourth: the Gnostic myth of Sophia. This fourth major myth, as it happens, develops, historically, out of the other three, and with his usual divinatory instinct Shakespeare brings it naturally and logically out of his Equation as a whole extra development, which provides him with the means (the vehicle, the spacecraft), to penetrate the further regions of the last plays. I give an account of this myth, too, in its place (pages 349–53).

What Shakespeare's attitude to this mythic material was it is impossible to know. Perhaps the clue lies somewhere in that elusive religious-philosophical movement known as Occult Neoplatonism. This, again, is a vast subject, but unless one takes into account its pervasive influence on the intellectual life of England at the end of the sixteenth century, it is not really possible to see Shakespeare's use of mythology in perspective.

The movement began in Italy in the early sixteenth century. It was a response, consciously devised and directed, to the deepening schism of the Reformation. At that time a strange collection of ancient writings was translated, attributed to Hermes Trismegistus, who was thought to have been an Egyptian sage from the period of Moses;* and whose visionary ideas seemed to anticipate both Plato and Christ. The possibility that this work seemed to offer, of returning to the fount and origin of all spiritual revelations, and of finding the genetic common denominator, so to speak, of them all, in some grand universal synthesis centred on a Christ figure, created immense excitement. Somehow this book of wisdom made available everything in man's psychological history that Catholic orthodoxy and Protestant militancy excluded. The new synthesis, therefore, was open on principle to the religious, spiritual and philosophical systems of the earlier world, and of the world outside Christianity. Wherever appropriated, these were reduced to a single system of symbolic correspondences. All known mythologies, that is, were reduced to a single but inexhaustibly rich and compendious language of metaphorical terms, or images – the vast thesaurus of a new language of signs, precisely defined by their histories, in which the new cosmology could be expressed. What remained was to give this cosmology a structure and to find a means of integrating it with an active spiritual life.

Rather than presume to convey the breadth and sweep of Hermetic Occult Neoplatonism† through the sixteenth century (which it barely survived), I will pick out the salient features of the movement as it came within the orbit of Shakespeare's known social and literary world, and as it can be seen to relate to his imaginative life, his treatment of the theme of the Reformation, and his relationship, in particular, to Prospero. But a general idea of the scope of the movement as a whole emerges from this account by Mircea Eliade:

A most surprising result of contemporary scholarship was the discovery of the important role magic and Hermetic esotericism played, not only in the Italian Renaissance, but also in the triumph of Copernicus' new astronomy, i.e., the heliocentric theory of the solar system. In a recent book, *Giordano Bruno and the Hermetic Tradition*, Frances A. Yates has brilliantly analysed the deep implications of the passionate interest in Hermeticism in this period. This

---

*Actually a compilation of treatises, partly Gnostic, from the first and second centuries AD.

†The series of books by Frances Yates, published by Routledge, covers the subject exhaustively.

interest discloses the Renaissance man's longing for a 'primordial' revelation which could include not only Moses and Plato but also *Magia* and *Cabbala* and, first and foremost, the mysterious religions of Egypt and Persia. It reveals also a profound dissatisfaction with medieval theology and the medieval conception of man and the universe, a reaction against what we may call 'provincial', that is, purely *Western* civilization, and a longing for a universalistic, transhistorical, 'mythical' religion. For almost two centuries Egypt and Hermeticism, that is, Egyptian magic and esotericism, obsessed innumerable theologians and philosophers – believers as well as sceptics and crypto-atheists.*

In effect, the Hermetic Occult Neoplatonist vision of the universe and of man was given a structure, and was psychologically activated, by a combination of memory systems and Cabbala. Memory systems were already naturalized in classical and theological tradition. Basically these were mental maps, fixed in imagination, on which the whole summa of knowledge and speculation could be arranged, with each item anchored to its place on the map by a mnemonic visual image. Usually the map took the form of a stairway from the lower Hell, through the intermediate worlds, to the Divine Source. St Thomas Aquinas had authorized devices of this kind, partly through the prodigious example of his own colossal memory, and partly through his dispensation (later annulled by the Puritans): 'Man cannot understand without images.' He was regarded as the patron saint of memory maps of the Catholic spiritual cosmology, and Frances Yates suggests that Dante's *Commedia* is virtually a memory map of the *Inferno*, *Purgatorio* and *Paradiso*, furnished with a sequence of charged images, historically defined figures and self-evident, graphic episodes which become the mnemonic symbols, and the lexicon, of the poet's vision, encompassing his entire intellectual and spiritual universe. The whole work serves as a complete Catholic meditation, formulated like a liturgy, raising Dante (or the reader) from a commonplace, profane condition (the worldly fear of the call) to ecstatic contemplation of the Divine Source.

Cabbala was introduced to Occult Neoplatonism by its founding father, Pico della Mirandola. The Cabbalist's Tree of Life is a pattern of ten ascending stations (Sephiroth – Angelic Powers) positioned on and between the pillars of Justice and Mercy, mounting from the lowest Hells to the Divine Source. These ten stations form a graded system of symbolic correspondences, each station being like a file in a filing

*Mircea Eliade, in 'The Occult and the   *Cultural Fashions*, University of Chicago
Modern World', *Occultism, Witchcraft and*   Press, 1976.

cabinet, or like one of the chakras in the body of a yogi, the ganglion of a whole realm of being, from the lowest in the tenth to the highest in the first. The ten stations encompass all the possibilities of existence. Everything in the universe, attached to its symbol, can be given its proper place on the Tree, according to its spiritual quality and significance. So the Tree becomes a model of the nested hierarchies of the universe, a contrivance for imagining the ordered universe – in other words, a means of organizing the psyche by internalizing the knowable universe as a stairway of God. Climbing in meditation through the stations, on the path of the Serpent of Wisdom, the practitioner endeavours to raise his consciousness, step by step, towards union with the Divine Source.

Because the language of Cabbala is Hebrew, the language of biblical God and the angels, and because the structural imagery of the Tree of Life is biblical and Talmudic, and because this strange apparatus for contemplation of the Divine Creation was thought to be the very Temple that Christ would build again in three days, and because it was, coincidentally, the most formidably established and sophisticated, the most awesome in occult reputation, of all memory maps, and because it was operated by techniques of meditation that at the very lowest were like devout prayer while at the highest they resembled communion with supernatural beings, if not with the Divine Emanation itself, it provided Pico della Mirandola with what appeared to be the natural framework, syntax and psychic discipline for his new system of symbolic correspondences, by which he hoped to renovate and refashion the disintegrating Christian spirituality of Western man. All that was required was for him to lift Cabbala out of Judaism, and recentre it on Christ, which he did. In this way he created the Christian Cabbala that became the nervous system (or the prototypical model for it) of all variations of Hermetic Occult Neoplatonism.

Attempts have been made to trace the presence of Cabbala in Shakespeare's plays, particularly in *The Merchant of Venice*. But there is much about Cabbala that a dramatist could use without him being a serious occultist. On the other hand, the assiduous practice of Cabbala, for some period of his life at least, could help to explain (as it does with Yeats) several aspects of Shakespeare's imaginative development, quite apart from his apparent attitude to religion and his handling of myths.

The main currents of Occult Neoplatonism converged, in one sense even came to a climax, in England, during the last two decades of the sixteenth century. The great, formative figures of this final phase of the movement were Giordano Bruno and John Dee, then both at the height of their powers.

Dee was Queen Elizabeth's mathematician, consultant to navigators and the builders of the navy, and the most celebrated English philosopher of the day: a man of prestige and influence. His Occult Neoplatonism was imperialist, messianic, Christian Cabbalist, moving towards a deepening preoccupation with the conjuration of spirits and angels that eventually almost swallowed him up. He had been tutor to Sir Philip Sidney, the admired luminary of the intellectual, literary circle from which the Elizabethan poetic renaissance sprang, and which was inherited, after his early death, by the Earl of Essex, patron to Sir Francis Bacon and the closest friend of Shakespeare's patron, the Earl of Southampton. Dee had also been tutor to Fulke Greville, the Warwickshire nobleman who so famously declared himself 'friend to Sir Philip Sidney' and in the same paragraph, for some reason not so famously, 'master to William Shakespeare'. So is seems likely that Shakespeare knew plenty about Dee and his Christian Cabbala.

Bruno came to England in 1583. This Italian, impassioned, combative evangelist of the new vision made an impact. His brand of Occult Neoplatonism was a combination of Ancient Egyptian religion, a Copernican universe that was also a gigantic image of the spiritual creation, and a phenomenal cultivation of memory systems. All these systems of his were based on principles similar to the Cabbalist's Tree of Life; in other words each was based on some form of a ladder of symbolic correspondences, every correspondence fixed with its mnemonic image, ascending from the lowest orders of existence, through the angelic powers of the planets (which functioned as Sephiroth), to the Divine Source which, in Bruno's system (as in Dee's) was Divine Love. The practitioner operated any of these systems like the Cabbalist, mounting the ladder, locking his meditation into overdrive (the *furor* of Love) by various procedures of ritual magic (that would now be called techniques of self-hypnosis). On the way, like the Cabbalist, Bruno strove to open 'the black diamond doors' of the psyche, releasing visions, revelations of divine understanding, and even supernatural intelligences and powers. This 'magically animated imagination', as he described it, was the key to his teachings. He called his mnemonic images 'seals', meaning 'sigils', a sigil being the signature of a daemonic being. These entities of Bruno's, like Dee's angels, did not exist as scholastic abstractions, crowding on to the point of a needle. Just as for the Cabbalist, they had personality and were open to human negotiation, accessible to the attuned mind of the magically trained adept, susceptible to his manipulative will, and were able, properly handled, to raise him to near god-like awareness and being. So it was claimed. Bruno stayed in England for three years, writing several books, lecturing and disputing on his system. He published his major work on memory maps, *Seals*, in England in 1583, and dedicated two other works, during his stay, to Sir Philip Sidney. With all religions and all mythologies conscripted into his giant synthesis, this 'awakener of sleeping souls' (his own term for himself) looked down on the savage conflicts of the Reformation as on the 'squabbling of children', and created a cyclone of controversy (at one point he had to take refuge in the Italian Embassy) in the superheated atmosphere of this small society that secreted Shakespeare just coming of age and Sir Francis Bacon in his mid-twenties.

Bruno's ideas had their effect, presumably, within the already established magnetic field of Dee's, but the extent of Bruno's influence in particular can be judged, maybe, by the degree to which certain prominent features in his version of Occult Neoplatonism now seem, in retrospect, characteristically Elizabethan, not to say Shakespearean. Shakespeare's mystical deification of love has been linked to Bruno's *eroici furori*, and Berowne's great rhapsody about the divine power of love, in *Love's Labour's Lost* (IV. iii. 324–45), is a direct response, it has been suggested, to Bruno's teachings – and almost a direct expression of them. One of the most famous speeches in the plays, Ulysses's great exposition of cosmic, social and psychological order in *Troilus and Cressida* (I. iii. 85–124), could be drawn directly from Bruno's vision of a Copernican cosmos physically, morally and spiritually centred on the sun. Bruno's universe, as I have indicated, is simultaneously an assemblage of spiritual powers; everything in it is an image, or *umbra*, or *sigil*, or *hieroglyph*, of a spiritual entity. In his inner theatre of meditation these images, taking on daemonic autonomy (the vitality of powers from beyond them), revealed a universe of which, on occasion, he might conceivably have said:

> These our actors,
> As I foretold you, were all spirits and
> Are melted into air, into thin air:

And, like the baseless fabric of this vision,
The cloud-capp'd towers, the gorgeous palaces,
The solemn temples, the great globe itself,
Yea, all which it inherit, shall dissolve
And, like this insubstantial pageant faded,
Leave not a rack behind. We are such stuff
As dreams are made on, and our little life
Is rounded with a sleep.

The Tempest, IV. i. 148–58

This agglomeration of forces, adaptable to every human mask, essentially innocent and amoral until embroiled in the moralizing, distorting passions of human limitation and polarity, unfathomable in existential being, at bottom simply the *prima materia* of creation and inseparable from it, is for Bruno, and, as I shall argue, for Shakespeare too, Divine Love – the ectoplasmic or magnetic, vital substance of the Goddess of Complete Being herself.

Bruno first and foremost propounded his system (and sought royal sponsorship for it throughout Europe) as a solution to the political and spiritual dilemma of the Reformation. In some quarters, on that level it penetrated deeply (Shakespeare's ethical design can be seen, as I shall attempt to illustrate, partly as an Occult Neoplatonist and perhaps even a Bruno-esque solution to that dilemma). But Bruno's most potent and immediate influence, like the most potent influence of Dee, radiated from his magical 'technology' – the methods developed for gaining access to and control over the spiritual powers. It is not difficult to see why Hermetic Occult Neoplatonism exerted such fascination, offering, as it did, psychic release from the claustrophobic cells of Catholicism and Protestantism, and seeming to promise limitless computer power of thought and knowledge. But early in the development of the movement that heady openness to all spiritual paths took a sinister turn. The example of Cabbala, and the authorization of magical practices given by Hermes Trismegistus himself, prompted Cornelius Agrippa to revive the whole ancient corpus of ceremonial magic, sorcery and necromancy, and to incorporate it into the system. This cast a terrific spell on a certain susceptibility in the spirit of the times, in England. Agrippa became a revered authority on occult operations (as Marlowe's Faust acknowledges, when he determines to be

as cunning as Agrippa was
Whose shadow made all Europe honour him).
Doctor Faustus, I. i. 144–5

After this (although the holy discipline of Jewish Cabbala, and the strenuously Christian ethical controls of Christian Cabbalists, protected the movement for a while), as far as his many and powerful enemies were concerned, the Hermetic Occult Neoplatonist trafficked with the devil. In particular, he trod a knife edge between the increasingly turbulent, buffeting opposition of Catholic and Protestant. In some way the outlawed, imperilled idealism of such practitioners, and the violence of the reaction against them, became terms of the greater religious conflict. This is powerfully illustrated by two notable results, two of the most luminous acts by which that explosive epoch declares its inner nature to our own: Marlowe's *Doctor Faustus* and Shakespeare's *The Tempest*.

In the 1580s and even in the 1590s, evidently, in some circles (for instance, the group for whom Shakespeare wrote *Love's Labour's Lost*) Bruno was regarded as a realist. One of the most significant elements in his teaching (and the same could be said of Dee's) was that he presented himself not as the high priest of a new religion, nor even as a philosophical theologian, but as an empirical investigator – as if he were exploring the real anatomy of the divine universe for the first time (albeit finding himself spiritually transfigured in the process). His theme is still the nature of the soul, and the unified spirituality of creation, but everything now happens in a laboratory which is also a mental gymnasium, and the entire operation is pervaded by a new pragmatic spirit – the scientific spirit.

One might recognize this spirit in Shakespeare too, in his analysis – so extraordinarily objective and methodically thorough – of human subjectivity. And it is certainly possible to recognize it in the group which included, on the one hand, Chapman, whose works are saturated with the occultist's magical outlook, and on the other hand the hard-headed sceptic Ralegh and the mathematician Hariot, whose combined enterprise opened North America to English settlement. It also touched Sir Francis Bacon, whose own shrewdly covert and rationalized Occult Neoplatonism found belated expression (posthumously published in 1627) in his *The New Atlantis*, which, though later claimed as one of the holy books of Rosicrucianism (with Bacon himself claimed as one of the founding fathers), was the acknowledged inspiration (almost the first draft of their constitution) for the Royal Society eventually formed in 1660, which in turn founded the English tradition of practical science and pragmatic philosophy.

Bacon reveals a familiarity with the Hermetic, alchemical and Rosicrucian texts, as well as with the work of Bruno and Dee. Several curious questions in the Shakespeare/Bacon debate would become simpler, perhaps, if one could accept that Shakespeare and Bacon might well have been as close as Bacon and Ben Jonson undoubtedly were. And there is abundant evidence that Bacon was the intimate confidant and adviser of his noble patron, the Earl of Essex, and was also close to Essex's constant companion and Shakespeare's patron, Henry Wriothesley, the 3rd Earl of Southampton. In other words, Bacon was a likely member of the group for which *Love's Labour's Lost* was written. This would help to explain the fact, pointed out by Jean Overton Fuller in her book about Sir Francis Bacon,* that the names of that play's three principal Lords, attendants to the King of Navarre, and of the Lord attendant on the Princess of France, are all but identical to the names on the passports of Anthony Bacon (Sir Francis's brother) and his entourage during their visit to Navarre some years earlier: namely, Biron (which becomes in the play Berowne), Dumain (which becomes Dumaine), Longaville (unchanged) and Boyesse (becoming Boyet). The anecdote would be regarded as an in-joke of the group. *Love's Labour's Lost*, apart from its generalized Bruno-esque Neoplatonism, contains more particular indications of what become, eventually, specifically Rosicrucian features. Its plot is less likely to have been the result of one man's influence and special interests – whether Bacon's or Shakespeare's – than a situation projected from the shared preoccupation of the whole group: an excited and perhaps argumentative preoccupation with different kinds (Dee's versus Bruno's, perhaps) of Occult Neoplatonism, tending towards a deliberate plan of common study, in a retreat, withdrawn from society, with the beginnings of a manifesto and rules of conduct. This immediate, social background makes the whole drama a highly topical and meaningfully instructive joke that is also serious (but that is inevitably rather obscure, forced, irrelevant, to

Sir Francis Bacon: a biography, London and The Hague: East-West Publications, 1981

anyone not in on the peculiar situation). The opening speech of the play, by the King of Navarre to his three Lords, plants this situation dead centre:

> Let fame, that all hunt after in their lives,
> Live register'd upon our brazen tombs,
> And then grace us in the disgrace of death;
> When, spite of cormorant devouring Time,
> The endeavour of this present breath may buy
> That honour which shall bate his scythe's keen edge,
> And make us heirs of all eternity . . .
> Navarre shall be the wonder of the world;
> Our court shall be a little academe,
> Still and contemplative in living art.
> You three, Berowne, Dumaine, and Longaville,
> Have sworn for three years' term to live with me,
> My fellow-scholars, and to keep these statutes
> That are recorded in this schedule here . . .
>
> *Love's Labour's Lost*, I. i. 1–18

Longaville instantly vows obedience, with a line:

> The mind shall banquet, though the body pine
>
> I. i. 25

that Shakespeare took more seriously in Sonnet 146:

> Poor soul . . .
> Why so large cost, having so short a lease,
> Dost thou upon thy fading mansion spend?
> Shall worms, inheritors of this excess,
> Eat up thy charge? Is this thy body's end?
> Then, soul, live thou upon thy servant's loss,
> And let that pine to aggravate thy store;
> Buy terms divine in selling hours of dross;
> Within be fed, without be rich no more . . .

But this proposal, in the drama, as Berowne points out with dismay, excludes woman and the love of women. The plot that follows is the machinery by which this wrong-headed project is corrected – to include the love of women. Where the Puritan mode of Occult Neoplatonism, in which magical studies were adapted to investigate creation in Baconian resolutely objective style, excluding the subjective love-creation of the Goddess, was forcibly corrected by the Goddess herself. The Princess of the great kingdom of France, and her three aspects, her three Ladies, impose on the King of the petty realm of Navarre and his three Lords a new mode of Occult Neoplatonism, one that not only includes her but is centred on her and her love. This correction is the occasion for Berowne's passionate conversion to the divinity of love, when he delivers his long, Bruno-esque rhapsody to love's power.

> Other slow arts entirely keep the brain,
> And therefore, finding barren practisers,
> Scarce show a harvest of their heavy toil;
> But love, first learned in a lady's eyes,
> Lives not alone immured in the brain,
> But, with the motion of all elements,
> Courses as swift as thought in every power,
> And gives to every power a double power,
> Above their functions and their offices.
> It adds a precious seeing to the eye;
> A lover's eyes will gaze an eagle blind;
> A lover's ear will hear the lowest sound,
> When the suspicious head of theft is stopp'd:
> Love's feeling is more soft and sensible
> Than are the tender horns of cockled snails:
> Love's tongue proves dainty Bacchus gross in taste.
> For valour, is not Love a Hercules,
> Still climbing trees in the Hesperides?
> Subtle as Sphinx; as sweet and musical
> As bright Apollo's lute, strung with his hair;
> And when Love speaks, the voice of all the gods
> Makes heaven drowsy with the harmony.
>
> *Love's Labour's Lost*, IV. iii. 324–45

The rest are converted with him. But this does not mean that their grand, ambitious plan for a prolonged course of self-transformation, in some retreat, withdrawn from society, is abandoned. On the contrary, the Goddess and her three selves present the convertites with a reformed plan, which includes the Hermetic Rosicrucian discipline of austerity:

[In] some forlorn and naked hermitage,
Remote from all the pleasures of the world;

v. ii. 803–4

and of visiting the sick:

A twelvemonth shall you spend, and never rest,
But seek the weary beds of people sick

v. ii. 829–30

and again, specifically for Berowne, the Shakespearean Bruno of this ritual instruction by the Diotima-like female:

to win me, if you please,
Without the which I am not to be won,
You shall this twelvemonth term, from day to day,
Visit the speechless sick, and still converse
With groaning wretches; and your task shall be
With all the fierce endeavour of your wit
To enforce the pained impotent to smile.

v. ii. 856–62

She continues:

then, if sickly ears
Deaf'd with the clamours of their own dear groans,
Will hear your idle scorns, continue them,
And I will have you, and that fault withal;
But if they will not, throw away that spirit,
And I shall find you empty of that fault,
Right joyful of your reformation.

v. ii. 871–7

In these early lines, the Rosicrucian *dulia* of helping the sick with active love, selflessly, in the crowded busyness of life, while at the same time cultivating the ambitious soul in solitude, prefigures that 'pity, like a naked new-born babe', which becomes incarnate in the reborn saintly self of the tragic hero, at the ultimate point of self-transformation that still, for Shakespeare, lies ahead. In this way, *Love's Labour's Lost* is an image of the Occult Neoplatonist's ethos in its Shakespearean mode – which also, at this point, turns out to be a Rosicrucian mode. It maps out Shakespeare's own self-directing future course, sketched in Sonnet

146, ritually undergone (see pages 108–116 and 117–23) in *As You Like It* and *All's Well that Ends Well*, and realized in full through the complete development of the Tragic Equation. But at this point, in terms which later became, as I say, historically, Rosicrucian.

It can be seen here, maybe, why Bruno's 'technology' fitted so helpfully into the English conflict in its early Shakespearean phase – in what might be called its *Venus and Adonis* phase. By Newton's day (whose secret alchemy and astrology persisted like a vestigial reflex), which was the aged Milton's day (whose Christian Cabbalism died between the pillars of the Temple), the conception of 'Truth' had radically purged itself of any taint of human subjectivity, emerging like a new, brassy sun as stern cosmic dualism, a supernal *conjunctio* of atomic materialism and mathematical law. The Goddess, in other words, had been violently and finally defeated, Marduk-style, and converted, Tiamat-style, into the inert, material domain of her conqueror, while her 'magical' and 'divine' creative powers had been expropriated, aboriginal-style, as his 'science'.

Long before this moment, however, in England Occult Neoplatonism's dealings with the supernatural had proved suicidal. Since the movement aspired so openly to dissolve both Catholicism and Protestantism in its own greater synthesis, they combined effectively to liquidate it. The magical theory and practice, so easily seen as diabolism, was the exposed underbelly. For Catholicism this 'most imaginative idea of the Renaissance' became devil worship and heresy (Bruno was burned at the stake in Rome in 1600). For Protestantism it became plain devil worship (John Dee was discredited, and died rejected and destitute in 1608). For Puritanism it was devil worship and idolatry (hence the pictographic imagery of memory systems – and the divine faculty of the Occult Neoplatonist, imagination itself – became anathema, even as an educational technique, in the Puritan society). For materialist, rational philosophy it was a superstition. For science, an absurdity. It disappeared from the intellectually respectable range of ideas and was pushed so deep into Hell (with the witches) that sensible men soon feared to be associated with it. In the works of Shakespeare, or anywhere else, it ceased to be visible (and much of Shakespeare, accordingly, ceased to be visible). In later centuries it stirred occasionally, where revolution cracked the crust of suppression, and reached up an arm to embrace Goethe – who was wondered at. And Blake – who was deplored. And Yeats – who was ridiculed.

While Shakespeare was still alive, it had retreated into various more or less secret societies and brotherhoods, modelled on Islamic Dervish orders, and strongly coloured by Sufi influences, as with the Masons and Rosicrucians.*

Frances Yates refers to contemporary suggestions that English acting groups were involved in the Rosicrucian movement. She surveys the Catholic Ben Jonson's familiarity with German Rosicrucian writings (he had served as amanuensis to Sir Francis Bacon), and with their alchemical interpretation of 'the fables of the poets, Jason's Fleece, the Garden of the Hesperides

> Thousands more
> All abstract riddles of our stone.'

She interprets *The Alchemist* (1611) as Jonson's Catholic, derisive 'counterblast' to *The Tempest* (1611),† where Prospero is so thoroughly an Occult Neoplatonist magus that he is commonly regarded as a portrait of John Dee (when he is not regarded as a portrait of Shakespeare himself). Dee's writings are known to have been a formative influence on the Rosicrucian movement, but it is a curious fact that the main sacred book of European Rosicrucianism, *The Chemical Wedding of Christian Rosenkreutz* was composed (published 1616) by a German author, Andreae, who had devised plays 'in imitation of the English dramatists' (his own words) and who in *The Chemical Wedding* seems to be sleepwalking through a phantasmagoric reminiscence of Shakespeare's last dramas.

One of the most peculiar memory systems to influence Bruno was associated with theatre. This was Camillo's Memory Theatre, an actual theatre-like structure, which seems to have resembled a gigantic filing

*Shakespeare's mysterious lifeline link of affinity with the Sufism of Islam may be partly explained by these Hermetic Occult Neoplatonist secret societies. Idries Shah (in *The Sufis*, London: W. H. Allen, 1964) has explained the term 'Rosicrucian' – a Christian-seeming image of the Rose at the centre of the Cross – as a 'translation' of a composite term in Arabic meaning 'a particular (Dervish) discipline – to extract the marrow (of spiritual meaning)', and used by Sufis as a general term for their spiritual exercises. The Occult Neoplatonist societies took over the mistranslation as a name (as they also took over the name 'Masons') – as they certainly took over other symbolism, procedures and doctrine from the Dervish orders.

†Since *The Alchemist* was registered in October 1610, the 'counterblast' could have blown in the opposite direction.

cabinet of token images. Again, after Bruno's death, the most famous was the Memory Theatre of the Occult Neoplatonist Robert Fludd, a self-proclaimed Rosicrucian and Hermetic philosopher, active in the first decades of the seventeenth century. Frances Yates argues that this Memory Theatre (described and illustrated in Fludd's works in detail), another gigantic, systematically interlinked hierarchy of images, uniting Heaven and Earth, with an operational ladder of ascent and somehow incorporating the Cabbalist's Tree of Life, was based on Shakespeare's actual Globe Theatre. The metaphor of a theatre for the structured image system and 'magically animated imagination' of the Occult Neoplatonist, where surprising entities emerge from 'the black diamond doors' to make revelatory pronouncements, is apt. But the Tree of Life-style memory map, as a thesaurus of symbolic correspondences, an organized compendium of 'hieroglyphs', each with its family of fixed yet evolving connotations, has obvious implications for an organically unified cycle of symbolic dramas, and also for a unified poetic imagination. Bruno's version of Hermetic Occult Neoplatonism was founded on his notion of the Ancient Egyptian religion (and I hope to show how uncannily familiar with this particular mythology Shakespeare himself was, too), and his use of internally structured emblems, his 'seals', owed a good deal to his idea of Egyptian hieroglyphs. He understood the poetic possibilities of this type of image (as did Aquinas) and adapted them to specifically poetic use, with deliberate method, as an illustration of these possibilities, in the sonnet sequence that he dedicated to Sir Philip Sidney, rather as Pound made the attempt to naturalize the principle behind the internally structured ideograms of Chinese characters to English poetry three hundred years later.

Without assuming that Shakespeare was a devout Occult Neoplatonist, or was more than amused by the ingenuities, curious about the claims, and intrigued by some of the concepts, one can suppose that out of this vast complex of archaic, magical, religious ideas and methods, the following items caught his attention:

The idea of an inclusive system, a grand spiritual synthesis, reconciling Protestant and Catholic extremes in an integrated vision of union with the Divine Love.

The idea of a syncretic mythology, in which all archaic mythological figures and events are available as a thesaurus of glyphs or token symbols — the personal language of the new metaphysical system.

The idea of this concordance of mythological (and historical) figures simply as a Memory System, a tabulated chart of all that can be known, of history, of the other world, and of the inner worlds, and in particular of spiritual conditions and moral types.

The idea of this system as a theatre.

The idea of these images as internally structured poetic images — the idea of the single image as a package of precisely folded, multiple meanings, consistent with the meanings of a unified system.

The idea of as-if-actual visualization as the first practical essential for effective meditation (as in St Ignatius Loyola's *Spiritual Disciplines*, as well as in Cabbala).

The idea of meditation as a conjuring, by ritual magic, of hallucinatory figures — with whom conversations can be held, and who communicate intuitive, imaginative vision and clairvoyance.

The idea of drama as a ritual for the manipulation of the soul.

It might or it might not be too much to add to this list the four ethical aims fundamental to Cabbala. They could just as easily be cited as the four fundamental aims (and achievements) of Shakespeare's cycle of dramas, becoming more refined and pronounced with each successive work.

The first is to achieve harmony between the fixed and the free, between the severe formal powers of Judgement and the flowing spontaneous powers of Mercy: the second is to achieve the sacred marriage, the conjunction of masculine and feminine; the third is to redeem the Shekina from the abyss of the demons, where the Shekina is the Divine Spirit (originally the soul of Israel (Ariel), imagined as female, the soul as God's bride) immersed in material existence; and the fourth is to attain mastery over — or defence against — the demonic powers of the abyss. These four principles are also the cornerstones of the Gnostic myth of Sophia which rises so forcibly into the substructure of the 'romances' (cf. pages 349–53).

In spite of his polyglot fluency in that international current of metaphysical systems, within the plays Shakespeare's own radical myth remained true to itself, almost with the integrity of an organism, as it evolved.

Following the organism of the Equation, I shall be rather dogged on the narrow trail (though to my mind nothing like dogged enough: a more scholarly method along the track I take could only (it seems to me) make my overall suggestion even more self-evident). I do not profess to be an Occult Neoplatonist, but my own approach, I should say, is if anything from that point of view, rather than through literary studies. I reduce my references to such arcana to the absolute minimum.

Fortunately, none of that Hermetic cultural meteorology is essential to understanding the biological, therefore timeless and universal, integrity of Shakespeare's Tragic Equation. It is only necessary if one cannot otherwise understand how he came to use mythology and the language of mythic hieroglyphs as he did and if one doubts the fundamentally 'religious' implications of his vision. Following the Equation, inevitably I move through a great deal of generalization and speculation. That is the tropic, *matto grosso* tangle of my route, for which I am making my own crude map. As you will see, I rely on hand-torch and divining rod through the tunnels of the wild pig – which does not mean to say that at some (many) important junctures I do not find myself treading a well-worn track and, in one stretch at least, through the last four plays, I trudge within a stone's throw of a ten-lane highway. But my whole point is to explore the Equation, and its variants, and to stick with it to the bitter end.

I am conscious of another problem. Any remark about Shakespeare comes to its senses in a submarine world of weird echoes, where everything is gobbling everything else and thriving on it. His reputation corresponds to the evolution of life along this reef. It would certainly be proper for me to make acknowledgement of specific concrete pieces of information, such as A. J. Akrigg's account* of John Clapham's allegorical poem about the young Wriothesley that directly preceded Shakespeare's *Venus and Adonis* dedicated to the same Lord. And it would be a natural development of my argument to borrow the whole of Ann Pasternak Slater's† observations about the meta-language of the plays, the greater (and truer) 'silent' vocabulary behind the words. Her

*Shakespeare and the Earl of Southampton, London: Hamish Hamilton, 1968.　†Shakespeare The Director, Brighton: Harvester Press, 1982.

essential insight, that the axis of Shakespeare's universe is the silence of Cordelia, is so close to what the Tragic Equation reveals that until I read her book I had thought of titling these pages 'The Silence of Cordelia'. More generally, though I came at it late in the day, and though it surveys the vision from a very different and exclusively Catholic, learned standpoint, Peter Milward's *Shakespeare's Religious Background** coincides in its conclusions with much that I have to say about the religious nature and formulation of Shakespeare's tragic idea.

The fact that Milward does not extend his argument into the mythic substratum, and does not go so far as to postulate an autonomous mythic organism in the animate vigour of the drama, does not weaken his distinct map of the invisible field of force within which that organism seems to operate. Many other things, such as the presence of the Osiris myth in *Antony and Cleopatra*, and of the Demeter myth of the Eleusinian Mysteries in the 'romances', have been well turned over elsewhere and are by now the common property of readers to take or leave as they wish, though the responsibility for commandeering such items to the service of the Tragic Equation is mine alone.

If my argument is to be understood, the main assumption on which I base it will have to be accepted – even if only provisionally. This assumption is: that there exists in Shakespeare two different personalities (they could almost be called two different poets): the 'mythic' and the 'realist'.

Typical poetic works that are 'mythic' in the way I mean are Milton's *Paradise Lost*, Blake's *Prophetic Books*, Coleridge's *Ancient Mariner* and *Christabel* Part I, Keats' *Endymion*, *Lamia* and *La Belle Dame Sans Merci*, Yeats' *Wanderings of Oisin* and the poems (and plays) about Cuchulain, and Eliot's *The Death of St Narcissus* (which, it can be argued, matured into *The Waste Land*).

Nobody to my knowledge has defined the term 'mythic' satisfactorily, but in these poems, and in poetry generally, most of us know well enough what it means. It does not necessarily mean that the subject matter of the poem is taken from the mythology of some historical culture, but that it constitutes an image of a particular kind. In each of those poems listed, the whole subject matter is the image of a subjective event of visionary intensity. Obviously many poems take myths as their subject matter, or make an image of a *subjective* event, without earning

*London: Sidgwick and Jackson, 1973.

the description 'visionary', let alone 'mythic'. It is only when the image opens inwardly towards what we recognize as a first-hand as-if religious experience, or mystical revelation, that we call it 'visionary', and when 'personalities' or creatures are involved, we call it 'mythic'. All the poems cited are of this kind.

The mythic and realist personalities exist, in different proportions, in each writer, but in extreme types one or other can be almost wholly dominant. In the poems above, the only contribution made by the realist in their author is in descriptive touches and in the common comprehensibility of the grammar. Otherwise, each poem creates a self-contained, self-consistent world, utterly other and separate from the shared reality of our external world, and obeying quite different laws. What is also distinctive about these examples is how fully dramatized they are, how unselfconsciously preoccupied they are with the life and death urgency of their business. We do not feel any lack of a realist scaffolding or support system. That is to say, the world of the mythic poem, drawn from a mystical apprehension of something fundamentally internal and subjective, is a self-validating world. Few readers will have any difficulty in conceding that, in spite of the immense prestige of realism in modern literature.

A list of writers in whom the realist is dominant, to set opposite those mythic writers, might include Balzac, Dickens, Tolstoy, Chekhov, Flaubert. Again, readers know well enough how 'realist', in this sense, differs from 'mythic'. While the mythic writer turns inward, facing what Eliot called 'the higher dream', interpreting that mystical vision in imagery wholly commandeered by the subjective meanings of the vision, the realist faces in the opposite direction, interpreting our shared, external reality through the creation of human characters who seem in every way like real people in real circumstances. Because of Shakespeare's power to create such characters, it is customary to set him among these realists, as one of the very greatest.

These extreme types, the mythic and the realist, are to a degree antagonistic, each towards the other. Precisely this antagonism is dramatized by the relationship between the spirit of Treplev's inspiration and that of Trigorin's in Chekhov's play *The Seagull*. Yeats was a more evolved Treplev, and his abhorrence, in his drama, of any touch of naturalism that would break 'the higher dream' was notorious, but typical of the hieratic, sacramental instinct of the mythic operation. At the other extreme, the demands of Tolstoy's realism were so severe that even Shakespeare's was suspect – was in fact condemned and thrown out. Of Shakespeare, Tolstoy rejected everything that did not fit, without distortion, into observable, 'real' human behaviour, and, notoriously, very little remained. Yet this was the same argument, basically, with which modern literary realism asserts and promotes its own documentary truth. In spite of this, Shakespeare's position among the great realists remains unshaken.

At the same time, this raises the question of his position, generally granted without demur, as the greatest of our poets. He is not only a great realist poet – who can challenge Chaucer, Dryden, Pope, Frost at their own speciality – he is obviously something else as well. He can more than challenge Milton, Coleridge, Keats, Yeats at theirs. The actors and directors of his plays are fully aware of this. Immersed in the psychological realism of Lear, they know that the tiny, realistic remark, 'Pray you, undo this button', has to be placed at the centre of an event somehow as unearthly, awesome, wild, metaphysically grand, as Blake's *Prophetic Books* and *The Book of Job* combined. They are aware that when Macbeth stalks out, drugged with his wife's domestic will, to kill King Duncan, it is a more momentous shifting of Heaven and Hell than when Satan lifts off in Milton's inferno. Everybody recognizes how all this gigantic accompaniment emerges from some-thing other than realistic characterization. The effect is attributed to the ritualizing power of Shakespeare's polyphonic verse, the suggestiveness of the imagery, the choreographic and choral shaping of the scenes, the musical counterpointing and symmetry of the plots – all that massive, mesmeric activity of the writing which occupies the stage even more obtrusively than the realism of the characters. It is recognized as a charisma strobing from everything the characters say and do – a radiant medium in which they move, like Yeats' Sages 'in God's holy fire, As in the gold mosaic of a wall'. To describe this effect, without which the most realistic staging of Shakespeare is simply not Shakespeare, we use the word 'poetic'; we readily call it 'visionary', and often, when it wholly overpowers us, 'mythic'. Nevertheless, because Shakespeare's status as the great realist is so officially established, this extra-realist glory of his has to be defined as some particular aspect of his realism, a unique burnish on the metal of it – as if, while Balzac's realism is wrought iron, and Dickens' bronze, and Tolstoy's phosphor-bronze, and Joyce's steel, each giving off, as it certainly does, its own unique poetry of burnish, Shakespeare's realism is some not-yet-identified

[37]

metal melted from a chunk of meteor – but still a metal of true realism.

On the other hand, if we recognize that his affinity with those mythic poets is at least as striking as his affinity with the realists, we might easily suspect that this bigger effect comes from something more profoundly organized and substantial than a poetic effulgence from his electrified realism. Perhaps, if the realist is lifted away, we might find a mythic writer, a narrator of some subjective, visionary event, as different from Dickens and the rest as the writer of *The Death of St Narcissus* or *La Belle Dame Sans Merci*.

Accordingly, I propose to do just that, and separate the two Shakespeares. That is to say I am temporarily lifting away everything that might have been written by a kind of Dickens, everything that Tolstoy might have approved. This leaves everything that a Dickens could not have written, everything that Tolstoy hated. It turns out, indeed, that what I am left with is, as I suggested, 'profoundly organized and substantial' and yet of the same family as *Paradise Lost*, *The Ancient Mariner*, *Christabel* Part I, *Lamia*, *Endymion*, etc. In other words, having removed the realist psychologist and impersonator, I am left with the mythic poet.

If the reader insists that the realist in Shakespeare cannot be separated in this way – in imagination, playfully – then my book must remain closed. This act of separating the two Shakespeares is, as it were, the first rule of the game that I am inviting the reader to play. Obviously, anybody curious to play the game will accept the rules – even if only provisionally. However, those who accept the rules must beware of what has proved to be a common difficulty. Quite a few have sat down to my game with me only to find the sheer stubbornness of their mental conditioning obstructing their efforts to play. Suddenly they find it impossible to see Shakespeare's works as anything but incarnations of the psychology of realism. They balk at the radical yet simple shift that Wittgenstein illustrated with the rough drawing of a bird's head with open beak which can also be seen as a baby rabbit's head with its ears back. My game requires the player to see both together and then, while still seeing both together, to suspend the one (in this case, the bird's head). This is what seems to be difficult. Before these jibbing players are aware of it, they have forgotten my rules for, say, Three Card Brag, which they had so smilingly accepted, and start crying in great distress (and even rage), 'But this isn't how you play Bridge – what on earth's going on here?'; they insist thereafter on playing the hands I deal as if this were a game of Bridge, before throwing down the cards altogether and storming off in exasperation.

To mix and change the metaphor slightly, it is a tendency of such players to leap to the conclusion that I am denying the existence of the upper temple complex of the realistic Shakespeare while I present him as a creature exclusively of underground tunnels and chambers. Those who keep my rules in mind, however, and play patiently, will understand that I am simply exploring something else altogether, in an attempt to open up the crypts and catacombs that have been – in our cultural enthusiasm for the upper architectural marvels of the realistic Shakespeare – somewhat ignored and neglected. Once entered, this underground system becomes self-evident. In this book I map out what can be found fairly readily, and say something about what appears to be happening down there – to be observed by anybody who will play the game.

It is implicit in my first rule that I am not denying the existence of any part of Shakespeare. Fair players must agree that, in so far as I succeed, I open up a more or less forgotten piece of real estate, which can now be added to the entire property holding – possibly not as salubrious as the main buildings above but still useful to those who know how to value it.

Having said that, I must alert my reader to another rule of the game. A firm grasp of this rule entails, I realize, accepting another assumption – an assumption about the structure of mythic imagination and about the vital link, the umbilical link, between that structure and the evolving nature of the author's own psyche.

Shakespeare's attitude to myth was obviously not pedagogic. As with his plots, he seized on what he recognized as a good image for what he had to say – and then let what he had to say take possession of it and reshape it, 'swing and sing' it as Frost said. If he was like other outstanding poets, he was susceptible to obsession by certain images – fixation on images that promised release to the unique dark embryo-like something that he felt compelled to express. With Wordsworth it was the mountains, cataracts, rocks and gloomy woods, and their elusive inhabitant Lucy, that 'haunted [him] like a passion'. With Eliot, it was the image of St Sebastian – tied to a stake and pierced with arrows. (Mishima, in his autobiography, describes his overmastering early obsession with a similar image.) Since Shakespeare only ever chose one mythic subject – Venus and Adonis – and since he chose it for his first

[39]

and (considering *Lucrece* as an automatic sequel) only long poem, one can believe that the image of the beautiful youth Adonis, rejecting the voluptuous, besotted Goddess, then being bloodily, sumptuously slain by the Boar, before being restored as a flower between the breasts of the Goddess as she flies to heaven, was an obsessive nexus of images to which he was drawn by irresistible fascination. One can feel the luxury of his fascination. Setting aside the question of why he should be so overwhelmingly obsessed by that particular image (which I deal with later), the point I wish to make is that once he had focused on it, laboured to give it form, relived it in an excited, even rapt, imaginative creation, his mythic creative subjectivity was thereafter imprinted by it, just as the mother-need (the mythic personality, so to speak) of baby ducklings is imprinted by whatever serves, at the right moment, as mother, even though it may be a human being. Adonis' metamorphic death was the image of 'the higher dream' that his mythic personality seized on at this 'right moment' – this first effort at full, direct self-representation in mythic terms.

This imprinting of the creative subjectivity, which often seems accidental, is how mythic imaginations acquire their peculiar symbolic systems: as Yeats said of himself, 'I have no speech / But the pagan speech I made, amid the dreams of youth'. In one sense, the imprinting is irreversible and final: it cannot be superseded or truly abandoned – it can only evolve. In Emily Dickinson's words: 'The soul selects her own society / Then shuts the door.'

The imprinted image complex can have propitious implications or sinister ones, presumably because the mythic personality, in choosing its image, finds what corresponds to its own character – which includes its fate. The mythic works of art which it then projects in the sign-language of that image, throughout life, are 'self-portraits' of the successive stages of that unfolding. The propitious, infinitely positive (but costly) future programme of Shakespeare's image (and Eliot's) is inherent in the fact that his slaughtered Adonis was always a god, who died only to be reborn, and was in fact the universal god of deathless, spiritual renewal.

Elsewhere I have described in some detail the role of two obsessive but minatory images (actually two related myths) in Sylvia Plath's basically mythic *oeuvre*. She was obsessed by the story of Phaeton (the earthly son of the Sun-God, who takes the reins of his father's Sun-chariot, loses control and is wrecked) and the story of Icarus (the son of the wizard artificer Daedalus. Escaping from Crete on wings constructed by his father, Icarus flew too near the sun, which melted the fixing wax and plunged him into the sea.) Breughel's picture of Icarus falling was on her wall. The capstone of the *Ariel* poems is the poem titled 'Ariel'. Behind that poem is the myth of Phaeton – Phaeton hopeful: a mythic image of her relationship with her inaccessible, worshipped father, which was a subjective experience, going back to her childhood, with a strong visionary and mystical core (the core of her mythic personality). The 'reverse' of that poem came five weeks later. She titled it 'Sheep in Fog', but at the time gave it what turned out to be a makeshift, hopeful ending. Two months later again, and a few days before her death, she corrected this ending, and gave it its final form. Externally, both these poems have the same plot: they describe riding on the same horse over the same moor at the same time of day – dawn. The difference in mood, exultant in the first, mournful in the second, seems to change everything. But there is more to it. The drafts reveal, with explicit literalness, that the later poem is the funeral lament for the earlier one, and indeed for the whole surge of inspiration that had produced the *Ariel* poems. (It was, in fact, the last one of them that she wrote, after which for two months she wrote nothing. When she started writing her last small group of poems, her first act was to make the final correction to this poem.) On the mythic level, 'Sheep in Fog' is a lament for Phaeton. In the draft corrections of this later poem, descriptions of the vast wreckage of a mythic chariot repeatedly emerge and are repeatedly suppressed, finally settling into the realistic 'train' and the 'rust' colour of her horse. At the same time the startling corpse of the charioteer, who appears in these drafts as a blackening 'dead man' lying across the landscape, is transformed (much as in Shakespeare's *Venus and Adonis*, curiously enough) into 'a flower left out'. In her final correction of the last three lines, the speaker, who in 'Ariel' had been the Phaeton figure urging the flying horse into the sun (triumphant, albeit 'suicidal' and doomed to fall), suddenly becomes an Icarus, whose melting world threatens to let her through 'into a heaven', not of the sun and freedom, but 'starless, fatherless, a dark water'.

None of this, in these two poems, could be called pedagogic culture ornament, or a dip into the myth-kitty. Nothing in the drafts of the earlier poem, 'Ariel', suggests that Plath was even conscious of the Phaeton myth's working presence while she wrote, and nothing in her simple, final correction of the last three lines of 'Sheep in Fog' suggests that she was conscious there of the Icarus myth that supplied both verbs, both nouns and all three adjectives, as well as the situation. But in the drafts of this later poem those specific details of the scrapped chariot and the dead man lying on the moor are evidence that by then, at least, she understood all the connections, and that the mythic personality was in charge of the realistic plot of the poem – the ride on the moor. Clearly, by this point in her career these two myths, her early obsessions, had lost their Greek settings, their name, gone down the full five fathoms, and had become the expressive symbols of her own soul's story. One could say, especially in the case of the later poem, that the realist in her (arduously worked at and developed) suppressed those myths absolutely, and translated them to beautifully precise, lucid, realistic if impressionist images. These realistic details are all that most readers see (since they cannot see the drafts, and are conditioned to discount myth). Nevertheless, the quite extraordinary power to move the reader that this short, obscure poem, 'Sheep in Fog', has is obviously drawn from that subjective, visionary, mystical experience, her mythic personality's relationship to her father, which was then in crisis. And, just as obviously, it exerts this power through the dramatic form and the vocabulary of the stories of Phaeton and Icarus, which in her imagination had become truly mythic in the sense I have been trying to define.

If one were to imagine that mythic hinterland removed from these poems, they would not disappear entirely. They would be reduced to sequences of descriptive details of the sharp, objective, evocative kind that Treplev toiled for in despair but that Trigorin (and Sylvia Plath) could produce with miraculous ease. Or of the kind that would characterize a short poem by William Carlos Williams or, closer, Elizabeth Bishop. As it is, in both poems, Sylvia Plath's mythic personality had moved into total dominance, and her metamorphosis of Phaeton into Icarus, which a realist might notice as a pretty piece of myth-kitty counterpoint, and use as an illustrative, clever metaphor, was for her the crucial episode of her soul's myth – in the most literal sense a life-and-death emergency trying to communicate itself. There is no getting round the fact that these poems are valued as they are because it was so. Which tells us why an author's 'myth' is worth searching out. This blood-jet, autobiographical truth is what decides the difference in value between a myth (or any other image) as used by the realist and the mythic image as it appears in a truly mythic work.

What I have done above, temporarily, in two short poems, is to separate the realist contribution from the mythic. Any reader will see how easy it is to do this, and how the experimental removal of the realist does not leave a gulf. If the logical positivist feels compelled, even so, to reject what it does leave, we know what he (like Adonis!) is rejecting.

Clearly, these two poems, as successive 'self-portraits' of Sylvia Plath's mythic personality, are very tightly related – by the umbilical link that I mentioned – to the evolving struggle in her own psyche. Throughout this book, I interpret Shakespeare's successive mature plays in just this way.

The second rule of my game, then, requires the reader to accept that the myth of *Venus and Adonis* (hospitably open to all mythic developments connected with it, and all parallels), having imprinted Shakespeare's creative subjectivity, evolves thereafter, step by step, as the expressive mechanism, the changing 'self-portrait', of his mythic personality. For the reader, this has one important consequence. It means that the sections of my book, which follow this step-by-step development, *have to be read in order and nothing can be missed*. In effect, my argument resembles the serial instructions for the stage-by-stage assembly of what is quite an intricate piece of machinery – a flying machine, perhaps. That Shakespeare's development should be so true to itself and organic, and that his works should interdepend in such a tight concatenation within the sequential unfolding, is perhaps an unfamiliar idea, but again it is one that my reader will have to accept, if only provisionally, as a mind-game. In other words, my argument cannot be sampled by dipping. Such a wary scanning approach will find my book incomprehensible except for the few separable digressions.

The length of the book is deceptive, even so. It is actually about twenty short books – though each book, as I say, is rather densely connected with what goes before and after, like the chapters in the investigation of a crime. In fact, it does constitute the investigation of a crime – the inevitable crime of Civilization, or even the inevitable crime of consciousness. Certainly the crime of the Reformation – the 'offense / From Luther until now / That has driven a culture mad' as Auden phrased it. In Court, the cultural tradition behind the 'tragic error' of the Adonis figure is in the dock, accused, and Justice is being sought (by Shakespeare) for the different cultural tradition behind the outcry of his victim, the plaintiff, who speaks for the rejected (assaulted, murdered, escaped from murder) Goddess. Even though Shakespeare, finally, divines how the two might be reconciled in understanding and love, the reader should beware of identifying too briskly and narrowly with the man in the dock (and therefore with his uncomprehending attack on what I present as the nature and sufferings of his victim) or even with his victim (and therefore with her accusations against what I present as the behaviour and nature of the man in the dock). In either case, the reader will feel to be in Court, against my argument. Since this great Court Case is, as it were, still unfinished, the reader (like Shakespeare, and like my book, I trust) will have to make efforts to surmount the quarrel, and embrace Shakespeare's final judgement. But once my basic assumptions are accepted, everything follows, logical and consistent, like a detective story.

The ideal reader would regard my idea as a sort of musical adaptation, a song. The only justification for it, perhaps, is that it might form a preliminary outline for a new kind of Shakespearean production. After all, I am addressing the whole thing to the stage, not to anybody's study. I shall keep reminding myself that the main point is to project the fourteen plays and their overture (*As You Like It*) as a single titanic work, like an Indian epic, the same gods battling through their reincarnations, in a vast, cyclic Tragedy of Divine Love. That is the way to think of it: two great deities appear. They subdivide, in pain – there's the opening movement. Like fighters choosing weapons, they take up their first masks (all the other future masks are dangling on threads from the heavens). They pull on second-hand shirts. Blouses, dresses, pants. They squeeze into shoes that don't quite fit, and take a few hobbling steps. Suddenly they begin to hear the noises of earth . . .

PART I

The Immature Phase
of the Tragic Equation

———

CHAPTER I

CONCEPTION AND GESTATION
OF THE EQUATION'S TRAGIC MYTH:
the *Sonnets, Venus and Adonis,
Lucrece*

━━━━━

Shakespeare turns to poetry

The *Sonnets* as the matrix of *Venus and Adonis*

Venus and Adonis as theology

The *Sonnets* and Shakespeare's love

The Dark Lady and the Goddess

Venus and Adonis: the Tragic Equation's moment of conception

Venus and Adonis and the *Hippolytus* of Euripides

Historical background of the Tragic Equation

Lucrece as a metaphysical poem

The contrapuntal symmetry of *Venus and Adonis* and *Lucrece*

Shakespeare's vision as prophecy

Venus and Adonis as a shamanic initiation dream

Shakespeare turns to poetry

By the time he emerged into history – announced, in typically English fashion, by a howl of indignation from an older writer (Greene's diatribe against the 'upstart Crow') – Shakespeare had written the *Henry VI* trilogy, *Titus Andronicus* and two or three successful comedies. His foothold on the stage, as can be seen now in hindsight, was firm. But he must have been aware that at any moment the stage itself could founder. A troubled, barely twenty-year-old experiment, under constant threat of closure from the city authorities, and frequently closed by plague, the theatre's continued survival must always have seemed precarious. In that autumn of 1592, when an unusually severe outbreak of plague had closed all theatres since summer, it could well have seemed they might never open again.

During these times of plague, it was customary for the lordly patrons to carry their poets off to their country houses. On this occasion, perhaps, the precocious young Henry Wriothesley, 3rd Earl of Southampton, seized the opportunity to carry off Shakespeare. However it happened, by April 1593 Wriothesley had become Shakespeare's patron.

Throughout his life, notoriously, the money-lending, corn-chandler-ing, property-speculating, wheeling and dealing dramatist displayed a flexible opportunism, nimbly attuned to market forces. Perhaps at this point Shakespeare had a shrewd premonition of the gap in income that lay ahead. Anyway, Wriothesley presented a new kind of opportunity, which he took. As if he had put the stage firmly behind him, during this winter of 1592–3 Shakespeare made a determined bid (denying any earlier offspring of his pen, and describing this as the 'first heir' of his invention) to establish an alternative career as a respectable poet of the classical, high court culture, with his long narrative poem (as long as a play) *Venus and Adonis*, dedicated to Wriothesley and published in 1593.

It seems unlikely that he would have gone on writing new plays for the popular stage without contract and without confidence that the market would even exist. Maybe *Richard III*, planned earlier as a sequel to the *Henry VI* trilogy, was written about this time – forced into existence, one could believe, by the terrific Gloucester himself, already born 'legs forward' and with all his teeth (his tusks) in the last act of *Henry VI Part III*. And several bits of evidence combine to suggest that *Love's Labour's Lost* was composed during this period, not for the popular stage but as a private country-house entertainment. What is sure is that immediately after the huge success of *Venus and Adonis*, Shakespeare applied himself to consolidating his new status as an admired poetic ornament of the high culture with a stream of sonnets (automatically stepping into a tradition of quasi-feminine subjection to the patron that went back into prehistory, and that, right up to Shakespeare's day, was the only ecological niche – apart from the stage – in which a poet could hope to survive), and by the following year had completed *Lucrece*, again dedicated to Wriothesley.

What he might have gone on to do in that line was aborted by the reopening of the theatres in the spring of 1594, and by the simultaneous formation of the Chamberlain's Company (in which he was to work for the rest of his life), with Shakespeare and his leading actor – and theatre builder – Burbage as the principal members. From that point, he gave his patron only more sonnets, and refocused his imagination exclusively on the stage.

In Chapter 1 I trace connections between the *Sonnets* and *Venus and Adonis*, and between *Venus and Adonis* and *Lucrece*, suggesting how this group of works came to be the foundation of the mythic form of the Tragic Equation as it appears in his mature plays.

The *Sonnets* as the matrix of *Venus and Adonis*

My starting point is to suggest that there is a real subjective link between the love expressed in Sonnets 18 to 126 and the love expressed by the figure of Venus – embodied in her as well as declared by her – in the long narrative poem *Venus and Adonis*. At the same time, I want to suggest that there is a similar real subjective link between Shakespeare's attitude to the woman in Sonnets 127 to 154 and the attitude of Adonis to Venus in the same long poem.

The point of emphasizing this link is to show how the pronounced characteristics of Shakespeare's way of loving – his very peculiar subjectivity in this respect – which he analyses in detail in the *Sonnets*, are converted, in the long poem, into two particular dramatis personae and into a specific dramatic situation.

Everything that I want to say in the subsequent pages will concern what Shakespeare did with these two figures and this basic situation. They are the genetic nucleus of my whole argument. In other words, *Venus and Adonis* is the key to the tragic myth which emerges in the mature plays and evolves through each one of them to the end.

It is not absolutely necessary, for what I have to say about this evolution, that I make this link between Venus and Adonis (as personifications) and Shakespeare's own subjectivity (as he portrays it, first-hand, in the *Sonnets*). But it makes the idea of the tragic myth as a living organism – as something that lived inside Shakespeare – more vivid and easier to grasp. It also helps to explain how his plays, so objective in their worldly existence, come to be so subjective in their essence, and how his public language comes to carry such a naked, intimate current of private feeling, such a constant charge of urgent apprehension and inner crisis.

There is a great deal of evidence connecting the earliest of the *Sonnets* to this long poem, but I will outline simply the main points.

Venus and Adonis, which was registered for publication in April 1593 (just before Christopher Marlowe was murdered), is prefaced by a letter dedicating it to the powerful 3rd Earl of Southampton, Henry Wriothesley. When this letter is compared with a second letter, a year later, dedicating his second long poem, *Lucrece*, to the same Lord it becomes clear that the earlier poem belongs to the very beginning of their relationship. At this time Wriothesley was nineteen years old and Shakespeare had just turned twenty-nine.

Wriothesley, the only son of a widow, had as guardian (who brought him up and educated him from the age of about eight) the great Lord Burghley, Queen Elizabeth's chief minister and the most powerful man in the land. It was the guardian's responsibility to arrange a suitable marriage for the ward, one that would strengthen his fortunes and alliances. If the ward disliked the proposal, and rejected it, he became liable for a very heavy fine. When the young Earl reached seventeen, Burghley proposed such a marriage between him and Burghley's own granddaughter Elizabeth de Vere, daughter of the Earl of Oxford. Wriothesley rejected it. Displeased, Burghley continued to press the match. Wriothesley went on rejecting it in spite of the immense debts that cumbered the large estates he was due to inherit, and even though his stubbornness would eventually cost him a fine of £5,000, a fortune in itself.* In 1591 one of Burghley's secretaries, John Clapham, presumably to please his master, wrote and dedicated an allegorical poem to Wriothesley. Titled *Narcissus*, it tells a strikingly familiar story. Wriothesley/Narcissus enjoys the love of the Goddess Venus, but is carried away on a horse called Lust, which pitches him into a pool called Self-Love. Drinking of this water, he falls in love with his own image, drowns in it, and is transformed by Venus into a flower.

Not much more than a year later, Shakespeare is writing his long narrative poem, dedicated likewise to Wriothesley, using very similar elements and virtually the same theme, but with a difference. The god Adonis is wooed passionately by the Goddess Venus, and when he rejects her love, calling it lust, she accuses him – at great length and with great eloquence – of self-love. Preferring his solitary hunting to dalliance with Venus, Adonis is killed by a boar, whereupon he is transformed by Venus into a flower. The earlier poem, by Clapham, was evidently part of Burghley's campaign of persuasion. Shakespeare's poem, while the same campaign was still in full swing, could well be seen as a continuation of Clapham's brief, almost as if it had been commissioned for the purpose. It has been pointed out that one possible explanation for the fact that this daringly erotic poem was approved and licensed by one of the most morally severe theological censors of the age, Whitgift, the Archbishop of Canterbury, was that Burghley somehow authorized it.

In the circumstances it does seem that Shakespeare's poem, like Clapham's, is allegorical. In that case, the main obstacle to Burghley's marital plan was not that Wriothesley was averse to womankind, but that he was too fond of it. Clapham's poem, concentrating on Narcissus's selfish, reckless lust, is to be read as a cautionary tale for one who too heedlessly prefers sexual liberty to marriage. Shakespeare's apparently complementary approach is more ambiguous. In his poem, Venus is lust and Adonis's self-love not an erotic self-indulgence but devotion to an ideal of true love, i.e. the chaste and faithful love of marriage. Yet if the intention was to present a corrective model of exemplary behaviour, it is oddly contradicted by the violent death which is then visited on Adonis, perhaps as an accident (part of the old story, a colourful ending) but resembling a punishment.

As seems clear from the dedicatory letter, Shakespeare's relationship

*A day's takings at the Globe was about £7.

[52]

to the Earl was already in some way established – still tentative and diffident, but dutiful and even affectionate. If that is so, it is not easy to imagine how a poem urging his patron to do what he clearly did not want to do came to be written, let alone commissioned, or how Shakespeare came to occupy the Polonius-like role of avuncular exhortation. Unless the poem has a deeper, different motive.

What seems much more unambiguously consistent with Burghley's wishes, and Clapham's example, is the group of seventeen sonnets that open Shakespeare's sequence of 154. His sole argument, throughout this group, is concerned with persuading the recipient to cast off self-love, to marry and to beget an heir. They are addressed to the man who, from internal evidence in the later sonnets, can only have been Shakespeare's patron and who therefore must have been Wriothesley. Other more material links between the *Sonnets* and the long poem confirm that the poem and the early sonnets belong to the same moment and the same situation, some time late in 1592. And in fact the first seventeen sonnets powerfully suggest how the poem came to be written, with just that particular theme, while the later sonnets suggest how it came to be such a maelstrom of undercurrents.

At some point during the first seventeen sonnets, Shakespeare seems to have seen the opportunity for a handsome witticism. Prompted by Clapham's own example, by Burghley's steady pressure to which, as those first sonnets suggest, he was already lending his obedient voice, and possibly by Wriothesley's mother (whom Shakespeare mentions, and whose interests were the same), the poet simply lifted the argument of his sonnets into the parable of the long poem. Wriothesley now becomes the Adonis who perversely rejects procreation, and prefers his bachelorhood, while Shakespeare has handed his own brief to no less an advocate than the Great Goddess of Love herself.

Shakespeare was playing with fire. Reincarnating Wriothesley as Adonis, he reincarnates himself as Venus. The Goddess takes up his appeal, on a divine scale, and Adonis continues to play Wriothesley's part of stony indifference. Shakespeare has identified himself, that is, at what was evidently a most inflammable moment of his life, with the Great Goddess of Love possessed by a hopeless passion for Adonis/Wriothesley.

Possibly Shakespeare's magnificent jest backfired. Or perhaps the idea only occurred to him because it was already too late, and he needed to disguise a passion that could not be silenced.

[53]

However it came about, Shakespeare lost control, internally. The 'commissioned' aspect of the poem, the level on which it continues the drift of Clapham's poem, pleading the case for Burghley and for Wriothesley's mother, was violently overtaken by an altogether more private emergency, and the first barely manages to retain its composure as it smuggles through the contraband of the second.

The evidence for what happened is clear enough in the *Sonnets*. Between Sonnets 17 and 18 Shakespeare has fallen in love with this powerful, unstable, tempestuous, ambitious, unpredictable, extravagant nobleman, who, as a possible Queen's favourite and Essex's best friend, living a life of splendid, wanton prodigality far beyond his considerable means, was for the next eight or nine years at the very eye of the storm of Elizabeth's final decade.

And from this moment Shakespeare no longer urges Wriothesley to take advantage of one of those 'uneared wombs' that are craving to bear his children. In fact he never mentions begetting heirs again in any subsequent sonnet. Instead he offers his poetry alone as the sole perpetuator, to all succeeding generations, of the young man's beauty, worth and truth, as if these sonnets were some altogether superior kind, some divine, immortal kind, perhaps, of female reproductive system.

Meanwhile, in the long poem he has shifted his private, subjective situation into the giant step-up transformer of this mythic narrative, where the collision of private attitudes and feelings has become the drama of a god and goddess.

Venus is the only deity to whom Shakespeare ever openly gave a major part. And he gives it to her here, in what is, as I shall show, the first, seminal formulation of the tragic myth from which he will eventually shape the great plays of his maturity. (Her significance becomes yet more evident when he stages her once again, in a slightly different form and in a more human guise, in *Antony and Cleopatra*.)

Venus and Adonis as theology

When Shakespeare chose the myth of Venus and Adonis for his long poem, he did four things. The first was, as I suggest, to embody his own passion for Wriothesley in the form of the Great Goddess of Love. (And I further suggest that this had consequences for the permanent structure of his imaginative system.) But the second thing he did also had large consequences. By making Adonis, as Wriothesley, reject Venus

[54]

(whether as one who resisted procreation or as an exemplar of chastity, or as both), Shakespeare answered the needs of the occasion by adjusting one of the most potent of archaic myths. This was the joke. The god, who, throughout history and prehistory, had loved the Goddess of Love as totally and unconditionally as she loved him, had suddenly – because he was incarnate in Wriothesley – rejected her. This abrupt innovation crackles with outrage. The ancient momentum of the great myth has been brought to a dead halt by Adonis/Wriothesley.

In spite of the fact that it turns on such a private reference, the poem struck a deep chord in Elizabethan readers. It was a best-seller. It seems to have pleased and fascinated everybody. And it made Shakespeare famous in a way far beyond his reputation as a dramatist.

For the immediate social requirement, he had acquitted himself in splendid style. He had flattered and glorified his new patron, as the most beautiful of the gods, without blunting the ticklish point of his brief. He had exalted him, too, as the darling of the Divine Love. And by setting his own words between the lips of the Great Goddess herself, he had given his commissioned role, pleading on behalf of all lovesick woman-kind, supernatural amplification. Finally, he had brought the whole thing off as a sumptuous, erotic, Renaissance witticism.

And he had done something else, that had a broader significance.

By the adroit modification of Adonis's attitude to Venus he had converted a straightforward tale of idyllic love and unlucky accident into vibrant drama. As I say, his poem becomes a collision of divine wills. And what could well have begun as a sophisticated joke teeters out along the brink of authentic tragedy.

But in the longer perspective, he had done something momentous. (The word is appropriate because his use of this story turns out, eventually, to be just that.) Out of all the countless myths and legends available to him he had selected, for the theme of his first long narrative poem, the one source myth of Catholic Christianity.

It might be said, so what? But reading the poem as, say, the theologian censor Whitgift must have read it, for its religious appli-cation, it is clear that Shakespeare had not only appropriated this Catholic myth of the sacrificed god and the Great Goddess in its prototypical form, he had also updated it. With that same little joke, that little adjustment to the character of Adonis, by which the god to be sacrificed rejects the Great Goddess, Shakespeare had lifted the myth out of its leafy recess in Ovid and planted it, as his own poem, squarely centre stage, in the tragic theological conflict of the English Reformation.

By modern secular definition, myth is something not to be taken seriously. This is so rooted in the popular point of view, and this point of view has so thoroughly naturalized Shakespeare as a secular author, that it is almost impossible for a modern reader to consider the myth of Venus and Adonis, as Shakespeare adapts it, as anything but a picturesque fable, a Renaissance ornamental fantasy, sensationalized to amuse an idle lord. Forcibly desacralizing his poem in this way, we somehow exempt him, by a kind of arbitrary secular warrant, from the world of feeling in which he lived, where at his birth two-thirds of the country (including his mother and most probably his father too) had been worshippers of the cult of the sacrificed god and the Great Goddess, taking the myth absolutely seriously, and where numbers of them, even in the 1590s (including one of his own distant relatives), were evidently ready to be half-hanged, castrated, disembowelled, quartered and to have their heads stuck on prominent spikes, all for taking this myth – of the sacrificed god and the Great Goddess – too seriously.

Not even the most secular mind can suppose that, even though the religion itself may be important to them, the worshippers cannot be serious about the myth. Obviously what may seem to be two things in language, in reality are only one thing. If the myth of the sacrificed god and the Great Goddess is removed from modern Catholicism, or from the pre-Christian worship of the god Adonis and the Great Goddess, or from the Catholicism for which English Elizabethan priests were half-hanged, castrated, disembowelled, etc., absolutely nothing is left.

So how could Shakespeare write this poem without triggering a seismic response in the suppressed Catholicism and indeed in the suppressed Puritanism of the Elizabethan nightmare?

It might be argued that for the Elizabethan (even more decisively than for the devout modern Catholic or the strongly believing Protestant or the modern agnostic who, like Freud, regards all religion as a form of self-delusion) those pagan names, Venus and Adonis, would insulate the archaic myth from any short circuit with the deadly serious, explosive religious feeling of their own times. Though Southwell (a Catholic, later executed) could deplore Shakespeare's poem as a 'paynim toy', and call for a more serious 'Christian Work', the evidence suggests that many Elizabethans were not so naive. The continuity of deities, traditions and ideas behind the different names, and through different cultures, was taken for granted by learned Englishmen of the 1590s as naturally as by the mythographers of the classical era – or by the modern secular anthropologist with the common reader's access to the history of religions. Perhaps it is easy to underestimate Shakespeare's Elizabethan facility, his purposeful dexterity, in that code made of the codes of religions. And perhaps that is why it is so easy to see his attitude to religion as secular. Because he uses all his mythological references as a poet's argot (as Ben Jonson does), they can resemble articles of stage costume with little behind them but a dramatist's opportunism. Exploiting all, he seems to take none seriously. But that is a shallow impression. In Shakespeare's case that argot is, as I say, a sacred symbolic language in itself, and proves to be phenomenally consistent. It is a code, and much of it can be cracked.

Venus and Adonis is the simplest example of his method. Even though Burghley may have fostered the poem as a worthy successor to Clapham's *Narcissus*, it seems doubtful whether it could have got past the official eye of Archbishop Whitgift if Shakespeare had interpreted the myth in a sense overtly indulgent to Catholicism. In so far as it is a theological work, it seems to favour a Protestant (actually a Puritan) idealism. The new Christ, Adonis, seems to be rejecting the Catholic Church, personified in the poem by the Great Love Goddess as a whore. This is how Shakespeare seems to have updated and retheologized the archaic myth.

Had Whitgift read it thirty years later, he might have thought again. In the context of the later tragedies, the poem is a judgement not of Venus but of Adonis. Adonis's rejection of the Great Goddess of Divine Love turns out to be an error, for which he pays. Eventually, say the tragedies, it turns out to be an error that brings down the kingdoms of both Heaven and Earth. In tracing the course of the tragic myth, the nature of this error is what I hope to make clear.

Shakespeare's is the only version of the myth (to my knowledge) in which Adonis (in the name of Adonis) rejects Venus. Adonis's love for the Goddess is, as it were, by definition absolute, and even in Ovid's degenerate sentimentalization of the myth in the *Metamorphoses*, which was Shakespeare's immediate source, Adonis's love is still absolute.

[57]

I noted in the Introduction that, in Ovid, the myth has been reduced to an anecdote in which the Goddess Venus, doting on the bold hunter Adonis, lives in dread of what his dangerous prey might do to him. Having her worst fears realized when a wild boar kills him, she mourns him, and turns him into a blood-coloured flower. This is the myth as a woeful, prettified legend. But the mythic essentials are there: the Goddess of Love, the Boar, the slain consort, the Flower.

Shakespeare's curiosity about narrative raw materials was inexhaustible. He must have known what was common knowledge: the earlier Greek version of this myth in which Adonis is shared by the two different Goddesses – Aphrodite, on Earth, and Persephone, beneath it – where the two lives, and the two Goddesses, were of equal importance. And the whole mystery of Adonis is that he is the god of this double existence which in its full cycle is a single existence: Adonis lives two lives.

Shakespeare's innovation had the effect of reawakening, in Ovid's simplified little tale, the tremendous living presence of this whole original myth – but with a difference.

It is generally assumed that he lifted the motif of Adonis's rejecting Venus from the story in which Hermaphroditus rejects the passion of the nymph Salmacis (also in Ovid's *Metamorphoses*). In fact, as the course of the Equation proves, he fused the two stories together, demonstrating incidentally that Salmacis, as a Persephone, carried the missing half of the myth, Venus's missing alter ego, the Queen of Hell who, in the shape of a boar, claimed Adonis for herself. A more potent source, maybe, for Shakespeare's innovation was the tragedy of *Hippolytus* (Euripides and Seneca).

But before I say any more about this I want to go back to what happened in the *Sonnets* when, after Sonnet 17, Shakespeare had shifted his labour of hired persuasion into parable form, giving his patron the role of the reluctant Divine Beloved and himself the role of the uncontrollably besotted Goddess of Love.

The *Sonnets* and Shakespeare's love

A modern reader of the *Sonnets* will naturally ask how far this extravagant declaration of love is a literary convention. If the poet's love is serious, how can he be so unselfconscious about it, unless the poems were written as absolutely private love letters? Again, since we know that at least some of them were passed around among his 'private friends', and since he was aware that 'mocking' comments might be made, damaging to his noble recipient, how could he go on being so unguarded?

His love is of an altogether peculiar kind. He submits it quite nakedly to the caprice of this powerful, unpredictable, spoiled young aristocrat. He never makes the slightest attempt to shield it from hurt. Rather the opposite: he exposes it almost wilfully to abuse, and embraces every pain. He almost welcomes the rebuffs, the betrayals – not masochistically, but as opportunities to reaffirm, in new sonnets, renewed love. Not just renewed love, either, but absolute, indestructible love. He transforms every pang, every petty humiliation, into fresh proofs of total love – unconditional love.

The strange humility of it all looks even stranger when one compares it with the love expressed by other admired love poets. Donne's love, for instance, is certainly more familiar. Donne always comes out of it so dashingly. Auden was embarrassed by the abject self-prostration of Shakespeare's sonnets, but it seems unlikely that he was embarrassed by Donne's, whose defences are all brilliant, even when he adopts the prostrate and stricken posture of the helplessly loving lover. He always wins, always masters the pose, in a coiled sort of containment, and escapes with a flourish or a swagger – scaled with wit. The genuine anguish is there, the turbulent electrical storm, and it glints on the scales, but it is involved, at some other depth, with different matters. Wyatt is more authentically disabled by love. Yet he too protects himself. His guarded, mourning, wounded wisdom is a sort of immunity. After Donne, English love poetry succumbed to courtly accomplishment, an institutionalized dishonesty, a series of conquests in one supercilious form of heartlessness or another, and hardly recovered before Wordsworth's Lucy poems. Quite soon after his death, Shakespeare's kind of love seems to have become incomprehensible. As late as 1766 it was being asserted confidently that if nothing of his work had survived but these sonnets, then he too would have been forgotten.

Even now there is something incredible about it. The only poet in the whole canon who perhaps comes near the same defenceless self-surrender and self-exposure is Clare. Shakespeare's attitude to his audience, and to his verses, may have something to do with it. He is not wanting to make a poetic artefact. The poetry is in the urgency of that need to make himself understood. And it is incidental. He has no interest, therefore, in the distancings, the objectifications, the obliquities, sacred to modern aesthetic theory — and monumentally exemplified in his other work. In these sonnets he never shows the slightest anxiety to present the admirable, shapely object that communicates the feeling but reserves the secret. Never attempts to transmute private hurt to public triumph. In sonnet after sonnet, in 'true plain words by thy true telling friend', he deploys great art and no small ingenuity to be artless and simple, to proclaim his secret, to surrender himself, and to bare his wounds without making any move to protect them. He never reserves for himself any escape clause, or waiver of irony. If there is irony, it is always a further surgery into the intricacies of his own pain.

The only voices in our literature that truly resemble Shakespeare's in his sonnets are those of his own love-smitten heroines declaring their 'total, unconditional love', ignoring any apparent change in their beloved, ready to immolate themselves on the subjective truth and loyalty of their love. That sort of thing on a stage, in the voice of an heroic girl, is one thing. But seriously meant, in real life, off the stage, by a grown man . . . No wonder that scholars who find it as embarrassing as Auden did speculate how mortified the author must have been when the whole collection was published in 1609.

Shakespeare's weakness (or genius) for total, unconditional, self-sacrificial love seems a little abnormal in the suite of English poets. On the other hand, it is quite at home in other literatures, where the medieval tradition of romantic love was almost inseparable from religious adoration of the Virgin eroticized. This 'total, unconditional love', wilfully subjecting itself to hardship and pain, worshipping the physical beloved (whether she likes it or not) as an incarnation of the Divine, animates the troubadours and Dante. Something of the same burns in the *Sonnets*, but with a difference, a rawness, an untheologized, surprised, private pain.

The tradition flows directly into the troubadours, and into Dante, from the Sufi poets of Islam. The Sufi originals at their best have a savage abandon, a frenzy of self-dedication. One can imagine those lovers rending not only their garments but their bodies too, lying in the gutter and howling like dogs for a glimpse of the lost beloved as in some Sufi fables they do. That is not quite Dante's style. But Shakespeare's tragic heroes tend that way — Othello, Lear. And that same current can be felt behind the naked shock of the *Sonnets*.

Compared to the inexhaustibly inspired incantations of Rumi, which revolved around a succession of three male avatars of the Divine Beloved, Shakespeare's rhymed love letters seem parochial, personal, tight-waisted. Yet that Sufi link might not be so fanciful. The philosophical and religious system that produced those poet-saints regarded the schismatic bigotry of medieval Christian theology with pity, as Christ himself might have done. This lofty breadth of overview is what comes through from Sufism into Occult Neoplatonism, and into the Hermetic fraternities that, as I mentioned, were direct imitations of the Dervish orders and proliferated in the Occult Neoplatonist excitement as it swept through Reformation Europe. If Yeats in the 1920s could pretend to receive the explanation of *A Vision* from a Sufi of the Judwali Order (who expounded to him an Occult Neoplatonist book supposedly published in 1594), it is not so impossible that a similar spirit touched Shakespeare. In later chapters I argue that Aaron, the daemonic power supply of his first 'tragic' play *Titus Andronicus*, is the first manifestation of an elemental being that takes possession of each of the tragic heroes in turn, and that appears for the last time in Caliban, in *The Tempest*. It is more than a coincidence, presumably, that these two figures, Aaron and Caliban, the beginning and ending of the greatest sequence in our literature, should both be Moors.

The Dark Lady and the Goddess

Whoever the temperamental, promiscuous, musical, white-faced, black-haired, black-eyed, diabolical woman was, who prompted the last twenty-eight sonnets, she seems to have bestowed on Shakespeare some venereal disease. The last two sonnets of all – 153 and 154 – convoluted as they are, give the evidence. Much as the beautiful six couplets, Sonnet 126, conclude the sequence to the man, positioned as if with some deliberation and care, these conclude the sequence to the woman, standing as ironic, macabre finials on this little shrine of Venus the Torturer. They read like two drafts of different adaptations of the same fable. Perhaps the first is the later of the two. In both, Shakespeare, as 'love's vassal', betakes his pox to the warm spa waters at Bath (an Elizabethan cure), which he supposes were heated when a virgin quenched Cupid's fiery arrow in the spring. But Shakespeare finds, by experience, in the second (154), that though love's fire may have warmed the water, the water cannot quench his love – for the woman who gave him the disease. Sonnet 153 is even more specific; after the virgin had warmed the water by quenching in it Cupid's fiery arrow, Cupid lit his arrow again at the eyes of Shakespeare's mistress, then touched the poet's breast with it – which gave him his disease. Soaking himself in the warm springs as 'a sad, distempered guest', Shakespeare finds himself uncured, and realizes there is no help for him except in a different kind of bath – that bath of fire in the eyes of his mistress who gave him the disease.

The contortions of this are of a piece with his all-suffering forbearance towards his patron. He is still busily converting the beloved's bad behaviour into occasions for new avowals of his own intensified love. But the patron's petty treacheries were nothing to what comes now. Shakespeare suddenly finds himself dragged out of his depth, or into new depths, by what emerges from this woman's 'lust' or seems to emerge from it. He calls his helplessness 'frantic madness', but as he states literally, and as the future cataclysms that develop out of it will prove, this new revelation is as metaphysical as it is carnally real:

> For I have sworn thee fair, and thought thee bright,
> Who art as black as hell, as dark as night.
>
> Sonnet 147, 13–14

Without relaxing its hold, his 'total, unconditional love' has been split into two, as his lady's body is possessed by two different women. One is the beloved of his 'true soul', the other a demoness. These two figures either confront him simultaneously, in one body, as a sort of double exposure, or they alternate in rapid oscillation, each looking out through the eyes of the other. The anguish of these poems is the anguish of his effort, and failure, to separate the two women behind the one pair of eyes. Considering what a role it came to play, eventually, in his tragedies, this 'double vision' must have risen from a great depth. It emerges like a sphinx fully formed. He projects it on to his lady just as Hamlet will project it on to his mother (and on to Ophelia), as Othello will project it on to Desdemona. The fact that this particular individual seems to have justified his fears is only partly relevant.

The effective power of the vision comes direct from what must have been his helpless inner exposure to the metaphysical equivalent of these polar opposites. It originates, in other words, in a peculiarity of his nervous system, his sheer susceptibility to any epiphany of the Great double-natured Goddess.

Sonnet 127 seems to be the earliest of the group, and is especially fascinating, since it shows the whole complex breaking the surface. It registers the complicated shock of his first impression of this paradoxical creature. What he is actually doing, or failing to do, in the poem's busy working, is to disentangle his hope of winning her love from his evil forebodings.

He sets out to persuade himself that her blackness – black eyes, black eyebrows – are authentic beauty. His argument is strained. He claims that, contrary to the judgement of an earlier day, black hair has now become the fashionable distinction of true beauty. But then he laments that this is no problem to those – 'the foul' – who lack the real thing, since they simply don the black wigs made from the hair of the dead – 'Art's false borrow'd face' – and no doubt blacken their eyebrows. This 'bastard's shame' brings such real slander and disgrace on real beauty (the genuinely black haired) that his lady's genuinely black hair, black eyebrows and black eyes are in mourning.

Throughout the sonnet he labours this conceit to heighten the beauty of his lady's real blackness by working at the distinction between it and the imitations that compel it to mourn. But the more he labours the less of a distinction there seems to be. His prophetic soul, perhaps, overwhelms his pen with negatives. The poem seethes with 'black . . . not counted fair' (first line), with 'bore not beauty's name' (second line), 'beauty slander'd' and 'bastard's shame' (fourth line), 'Fairing the foul with Art's false borrow'd face' (sixth line), 'Sweet beauty hath no name, no holy bower' (seventh line), 'but is profan'd' and 'lives in disgrace' (eighth line). In the ninth line all this is drawn to a startling centre, 'Therefore my mistress' brows are raven black'. Then follows a huddle of 'mourners' of 'such who, not born fair, no beauty lack', 'Sland'ring creation with a false esteem', more mourning and woe.

When he concludes that 'every tongue says beauty should look so' he is too late. His 'beauty' stares out at him from a wreath of coiling premonitions. He has materialized the image of a Medusa. Most ominous of all, he has defined her beauty, its authenticity, in terms of the curling vapours of Hell-mouth.

In Sonnet 128, he is still undisillusioned, still hopeful, diffident, even innocent, blushing beside her as she plays music. This is a brief idyllic prelude. But, as I have suggested, from what follows it seems likely that her music opened for him the same door that a woman's music opened for Tolstoy when he stepped into *The Kreutzer Sonata*.

Shakespeare spells this out in the next sonnet, the great 129th, where he anatomizes 'lust'. In its way, this poem is the key (with Sonnet 116) to the entire 154. Just as the two together are the key to the tragedies. But his words have to be taken literally. When he says 'lust' is perjured he means, literally, that it is without any scruple, capable of every treachery – as, for example, in Hamlet's mother who colludes in her husband's murder by marrying the murderer. When he says that 'lust' is 'murderous, bloody' he means that it is straining to be incarnated in a Tarquin who will kill. And the whole tragic myth, which I am approaching slowly, unfolds from the Tarquinian incarnation. When he says that the consciousness of 'lust' is a 'madness' he means it literally. The supranormal dramatic momentum of his tragic myth (Hamlet's torment, Othello's tortured frenzy, Macbeth's possessed horror, Lear's rage, etc., etc.) rides the kinetic power of precisely that madness.

Finally, when he calls 'lust' the path to Hell he means Hell literally not figuratively – unless the sufferings of his later heroes are figurative. He means the kingdom of damnation, the concentric circles of the utmost possible horror.

Apart from two or three moments of respite and the single episode where Shakespeare's patron and his mistress seduce each other (anticipating some of his stage situations), in the rest of this group of sonnets he wrestles with that 'double vision'. In each one he attempts to separate his beloved from that Queen of Hell, as they alternate within the single body.

The Sonnets, then, are a sketch of this Goddess, and of Shakespeare's relationship to her. They make a simplified but strongly marked map of his erotic subjectivity. The two basic attitudes are extremely consistent. He looks at his patron, through Sonnet 116, with the eyes of Helena looking at Bertram, Desdemona looking at Othello, Cordelia looking at Lear – in so far as their love is total, unconditional, and not to be removed. But he looks at his lady, through Sonnet 129, with the eyes of his tragic heroes in that moment just before their madness, that moment of the double vision which detonates the tragic action as Hamlet looks at his mother (and at Ophelia), while hearing the Ghost's whisper; as Othello looks at Desdemona, while hearing Iago's whisper. In this sense, the Sonnets are the vestibule to the bloody temple of the tragedies. Or, to put it more positively, they disclose the begetting of the tragic myth, which will be conceived, and will become a full embryo, in the two long narrative poems.

Venus and Adonis: the Tragic Equation's moment of conception

For three-quarters of *Venus and Adonis*, 768 lines, the love-sick Goddess is trying to wring some affectionate word from the stubbornly indifferent, beautiful young hunter. She batters him physically as well as verbally, wrestles him to the ground, faints, half-strangles him, exasperates him to the point at which, finally, he can stand it no longer and protests. He needs only thirty lines, but his words leave her crushed.

Her appeal, as I said, amplifies the brief of the first seventeen sonnets, but with wilder licence:

> 'Fie! lifeless picture, cold and senseless stone,
> Well-painted idol, image dull and dead,
> Statue contenting but the eye alone,
> Thing like a man, but of no woman bred . . .'
>
> *Venus and Adonis*, 211–14

Obviously Shakespeare has to find some very powerful argument for Adonis's strange, unnatural rejection of the Goddess. At this point, his model, Wriothesley, couldn't help him, chiefly because, though the young Lord was so adamant against marriage, he was not averse to women. In context, Shakespeare's solution, which is the turning point of the poem, seems forced, pedagogic, oddly out of place. He makes Adonis a prudish, Puritan idealist and his decisive lines are:

> 'I hate not love, but your device in love,
> That lends embracements unto every stranger.
>   You do it for increase: O strange excuse!
>   When reason is the bawd to lust's abuse.
>
> 'Call it not love, for Love to heaven is fled,
> Since sweating Lust on earth usurp'd his name;
> Under whose simple semblance he hath fed
> Upon fresh beauty, blotting it with blame;
>   Which the hot tyrant stains and soon bereaves,
>   As caterpillars do the tender leaves.'
>
> 789–98

In retrospect, one could call this the Tragic Equation's very moment of conception. Venus lies stunned:

upon her back deeply distressed.
Look how a bright star shooteth from the sky,
So glides he in the night from Venus' eye.

814–16

She laments all night, but rouses herself at dawn to search for him again. Straight away she hears that his hounds have found a wild boar. Then she meets the boar, its frothy mouth bloodied, 'Like milk and blood being mingled both together' (902). Searching desperately, she finds wounded and frightened hounds, and at last the body of Adonis.

Once she recovers her wits, she performs two acts that will have large consequences in the works that are still to come. First, she prophesies over his corpse:

'Since thou art dead, lo, here I prophesy:
Sorrow on love hereafter shall attend.
It shall be waited on with jealousy,
Find sweet beginning, but unsavoury end.'

1135–8

Which is to say, the Goddess of Love condemns all love, hereafter, to certain tragedy – caused by jealousy. As she speaks, she transforms Adonis. His corpse vanishes, and a purple flower 'chequer'd with white' (1168) springs out of his blood. Venus now plucks this flower, settles it between her breasts, and flies back to her heavenly home in Paphos.

In the Christianized version of the Adonis myth, surface features had been changed. And in Ovid's version of the legend, too, certain things had been lost. As I mentioned earlier, Ovid's rendering lacked the double form of the Goddess. Catholicism, too, had lost that Queen of Hell (or had displaced her major role, rather, on to Satan). Catholicism had kept, however, the main thing – the religious world in which the death of Adonis is a sacred event, expressing a mystery. Ovid had lost any sense of this world.

As Shakespeare takes up the story it looks like a secular, cheerfully desacralized fantasia, where the team of doves that draws Venus through the air back to Paphos, and the magical flower between her breasts, are the memory of a painted Italian ceiling, or a Tudor wall-hanging. Nevertheless, as I say, by his little adjustment to the figure of Adonis, he has wired the legend back into its mythic generator. And with that same small adjustment, he has switched it back into its live

[66]

religious context, as an image of the great myth's Christianized contemporary form.

The vital mythic feature, which Shakespeare resuscitated by making that change in Adonis, was the nature of the Boar.

As I recounted before, at a certain point in the original Greek myth Aphrodite decided to keep Adonis for herself for ever, and never again to let him go down into the Underworld. Enraged with jealousy, Persephone emerged as a wild boar and killed him. In other words, the Queen of Hell, in her animal form, took him for herself, by violence. That is the inside story of Adonis's death by the Boar.

In Ovid's story of Hermaphroditus and Salmacis the rejected nymph ends up uniting with her chosen male so violently that the two become one body – a hermaphrodite. As I will demonstrate, this is actually what happens in *Venus and Adonis* or rather, it is what happened (in a modified fashion) in what Shakespeare went on to make of it later, in the plays. The rejected Venus becomes the Boar, and the Boar combines with Adonis to make a third figure – the Shakespearean tragic hero. This anticipates my argument a little, though the steps do begin here.

And these first steps lead at this point to another closely related myth which Shakespeare knew well — the story of Hippolytus and Phaedra. By looking more closely at this story, in the form used by Euripides and Seneca, one can see what is going on in the circuitry behind the dancing coloured lights of *Venus and Adonis*.

Venus and Adonis and the *Hippolytus* of Euripides

The dramatizations by Euripides and Seneca had made common knowledge of the incestuous passion of Theseus's Queen Phaedra (sister of the Minotaur, which Theseus had killed) for her stepson Hippolytus, who was a devotee of Diana, goddess of chastity and hunting.*

The two classical dramatic versions handle the forces involved somewhat differently, but from the point of view of the characters the story in both reaches the same end. Shakespeare seems to be aware of the Euripides, certainly of its mythic implications, but is more directly influenced, perhaps, by the Seneca, which simplifies and conceals them.

*Hippolytus was later resurrected as Virbius, the god of the Golden Bough, at the grove at Aricia, in Italy, where he was consort to Diana, as Adonis was to Venus, and where his priest was periodically slain and supplanted by a 'usurping brother'. This tradition supplied the thread-end by which Sir James Frazer unravelled the pre-Christian system of dying gods, consorts of the Great Goddess.

In the Euripides, Aphrodite complains that of all men only Hippolytus refuses to worship her, and instead bestows his devotion on her rival Artemis (Diana). She vows to avenge herself by destroying him – but in a roundabout way, through his father Theseus and his stepmother Phaedra.

While Theseus is away, the Goddess maddens Phaedra with intolerable lust for Hippolytus. Phaedra, loyal to Theseus or at any rate afraid of revealing her condition, prefers to die rather than declare her incestuous love. Her nurse, thinking to procure gratification for the Queen's passion and so cure it, solicits Hippolytus's compliance. She underestimates him. He responds with raging, horrified disgust, and Phaedra, overhearing this outburst, hangs herself for shame, but first inscribes a tablet accusing Hippolytus of raping her. Theseus arrives, reads the tablet, curses Hippolytus his son, and using the last of three wishes calls on Neptune to kill him. As Hippolytus drives his chariot along the beach, an immense wave rears out of the sea and heaves ashore a monstrous sea bull that attacks his equipage. His horses panic, the chariot is shattered, and he is dragged to death among the rocks.

In the Seneca, Aphrodite makes no appearance. In Theseus's absence, Queen Phaedra has simply fallen uncontrollably in love with her stepson: her passion is her own, not visited on her, against her will, by the Goddess. When she tells her love, Hippolytus's first reaction (as a fanatic devotee of Diana, goddess of chastity) is to draw his sword as if to kill her, but thinking better of it he flings the sword aside and rushes away. With differences in plot, everything then follows essentially as in Euripides. The sea bull emerges and Hippolytus is dragged to death by his horses.

As can be seen, the mythic situation in Euripides is stated simply. Hippolytus has rejected Aphrodite, goddess of sexual passion, and preferred Artemis, goddess of chastity. As a result, Aphrodite has vowed to teach him a lesson, i.e. to correct him. The bull from the sea then kills him in a ritual death. This is a clear and complete transposition of the myth of Aphrodite's and Persephone's quarrel over who should have Adonis. The names have to be watched here: Euripides' Artemis corresponds to the mythic (heavenly) Aphrodite, while his Aphrodite corresponds to the mythic (infernal) Persephone. Hippolytus's fidelity to Artemis is, in effect, a form of the mythic Aphrodite's refusal to let Adonis pass to Persephone when her turn comes round. Euripides's play begins where, in the myth, Persephone's jealous fury begins, and the action is an account – translated into dramatic detail and human puppetry – of just how the rejected Goddess comes to emerge in her animal form, claiming in violence what she has been denied in love.

The situation is exactly the same as that created by the hero's 'double vision' in Shakespeare's poem (and later, in the Equation, in all the tragedies), with the one all-important difference: here in Euripides the Goddess's chaste Artemis aspect and her loving Aphrodite aspect (as, in the myth, the Goddess's loving Aphrodite aspect and her infernal Persephone aspect) are distinctly formulated in two different characters in the background, whereas in Shakespeare's poem they are combined in the one woman.

Shakespeare begins, in other words, from the beginning – where the Goddess is complete and undivided. Rejecting Venus's 'lust' (which, as in Sonnet 129, and as everywhere in Shakespeare, lives in Hell), Adonis splits her – as if into two separate deities, the loathed, lustful Queen of Hell, and the cherished, loving Sacred Bride/Divine Mother, Queen of Heaven. But since both aspects inhabit the one woman (the one body of the poem's very substantial Venus), in rejecting the one he must reject both. This is the key to Shakespeare's tragic hero, and much of my argument will concern his reaction to this dilemma and its consequences.

The two (or rather three) aspects of the Goddess are combined in this same way, of course, in Euripides's Phaedra. His Phaedra, in fact, recapitulates, in the action of the drama, the whole course of Aphrodite's feelings about Hippolytus – from before the Goddess's announcement of her revenge with which the play starts. Aphrodite's jealousy must originally have been love – becoming a jealous revenging frenzy (extreme in proportion to the love) only when it was rejected. Phaedra re-enacts this original love, and in doing so displays the three component parts of the Goddess: the Phaedra who loves Hippolytus and needs his love is the Sacred Bride; the Phaedra who is his 'mother' is the Divine Mother; the Phaedra whose love is incestuous, a violation of moral law, and who will destroy him if he rejects her, is the Queen of Hell.

Like Adonis, what Hippolytus rejects, in Phaedra, is this Queen of Hell. But as in Shakespeare's Venus, all the components are fused behind the single human face and cannot be separated on the natural plane. And like Adonis, when Hippolytus rejects one, in horror and loathing, he must reject all, whereupon the human Phaedra kills herself.

That would be the end of it if these characters were not the masks of mythic powers (in which case, this would not be sacred tragedy). As it is, the death of the temporary human vehicle, Phaedra, is irrelevant. The possessing Goddess has been split, and the rejected Queen of Hell emerges in her animal form.

The audience understands the mythic, poetic truth: the sea bull is not an accident, not an arbitrary marvel or the tangled end of some nonsense fable about three wishes, as if Theseus might just as easily have asked for Hippolytus to be turned into a mouse. Theseus is merely an unwitting link in the mythic circuit. The sea bull is Divine Love completing its circuit by breaking violently through the obstruction of Hippolytus's self-enclosing resistance. And lustful Aphrodite (the Persephone aspect of the Goddess), rejected, enraged, but still possessive, is now claiming in her infernal animal form what she was denied in the person of Queen Phaedra. Exactly as in Shakespeare the Goddess's rejected 'lust', splitting off on the mythic plane, as Queen of Hell, emerges to claim, in the form of a wild boar, what she was denied in the person of Venus.

In this way, the combination of mythic pattern and human dramatic action in Euripides's *Hippolytus* provides the cipher and the logbook for the mythic working of Shakespeare's *Venus and Adonis*.

In both the Phaedra story and the Venus and Adonis story, the animal form of the infernalized Goddess is male: the sea bull and the Boar.

This sea bull, as a sea monster, an alternative form of the Boar, resurfaces at intervals through the tragedies, until in *The Tempest* Stephano recognizes the family features in Caliban, a lineally descended 'moon-calf'.

Phaedra's mother became a cow (with the ingenious help of Daedalus) to satisfy her passion for the sea bull that Neptune had provided, for sacrifice, but that Cretan Minos, her husband, had covetously withheld (and the result of the congress was the Minotaur). Aphrodite's animal form was 'translated' in this way, through the totemic nature of Phaedra, to a sea bull.

Phaedra's link to this cow/bull lineage is combined with another, less overt but – especially in Shakespeare – equally relevant mythic inheritance. The name Hippolytus means 'torn to pieces by horses'. The animal form of the infernalized half of the Goddess incarnated in Phaedra was both the sea-bull monster that frightened his horses *and* the horses that actually dragged him to death. This particular personification of the 'sacrificed god' – torn to pieces by horses, either directly or at the tail of the chariot – is the nucleus of other myths, including those of Phaeton, Hector and (see page 17) that lineal original of the Tarquin who had been Adonis – the Babylonian Marduk. The man-killing aspect of Phaedra/Aphrodite is descended (like the horse aspect of the Sow Goddess, Demeter) from the teeming mythic cosmologies of India, where the two poles of the Goddess are consistently associated with the cow (maternal, wifely, nurturing, benign) and the horse (sexually insatiable, whorish, devouring, destructive). According to his name, in the original myth of Hippolytus the Goddess must have been embodied exclusively in his horses (again, page 17). The sea bull came in, perhaps, like the other half of a coat of arms, at a marriage of two myths. Or – a transformation common in the Indian myths – the Goddess who, as a horse, kills her consort appeared formerly as a cow who nursed and loved him, and who now sends the sea bull, as her official representative, to supervise his killing by her other self.

It is worth noting, if coincidental, that in Shakespeare's *Venus and Adonis* the uncontrollable erotic energy of Venus is projected first (as a demonstration) into a sexually excited and therefore uncontrollable stallion before – frustrated – it materializes in the fatal form of the Boar:

> But lo! from forth a copse that neighbours by,
> A breeding jennet, lusty, young, and proud,
> Adonis' trampling courser doth espy,
> And forth she rushes, snorts and neighs aloud:
>> The strong-neck'd steed, being tied unto a tree,
>> Breaketh his rein, and to her straight goes he.
>
> Imperiously he leaps, he neighs, he bounds,
> And now his woven girths he breaks asunder;
> The bearing earth with his hard hoof he wounds,
> Whose hollow womb resounds like heaven's thunder;
>> The iron bit he crushes 'tween his teeth,
>> Controlling what he was controlled with.

His ears up-prick'd; his braided hanging mane
Upon his compass'd crest now stand on end;
His nostrils drink the air, and forth again,
As from a furnace, vapours doth he send:
    His eye, which scornfully glisters like fire,
    Shows his hot courage and his high desire.

Sometime he trots, as if he told the steps,
With gentle majesty and modest pride;
Anon he rears upright, curvets and leaps,
As who should say, 'Lo! thus my strength is tried;
    And this I do to captivate the eye
    Of the fair breeder that is standing by.'

What recketh he his rider's angry stir,
His flattering 'Holla,' or his 'Stand, I say?'
What cares he now for curb or pricking spur?
For rich caparisons or trapping gay?
    He sees his love, and nothing else he sees,
    Nor nothing else with his proud sight agrees.

Look, when a painter would surpass the life,
In limning out a well-proportion'd steed,
His art with nature's workmanship at strife,
As if the dead the living should exceed;
    So did this horse excel a common one,
    In shape, in courage, colour, pace and bone.

Round-hoof'd, short-jointed, fetlocks shag and long,
Broad breast, full eye, small head, and nostril wide,
High crest, short ears, straight legs and passing strong,
Thin mane, thick tail, broad buttock, tender hide:
    Look, what a horse should have he did not lack,
    Save a proud rider on so proud a back.

Sometimes he scuds far off, and there he stares;
Anon he starts at stirring of a feather;
To bid the wind a base he now prepares,
And whe'r he run or fly they know not whether;
    For through his mane and tail the high wind sings,
    Fanning the hairs, who wave like feather'd wings.

He looks upon his love, and neighs unto her;
She answers him as if she knew his mind;
Being proud, as females are, to see him woo her,
She puts on outward strangeness, seems unkind,
    Spurns at his love and scorns the heat he feels,
    Beating his kind embracements with her heels.

Then, like a melancholy malcontent,
He vails his tail that, like a falling plume
Cool shadow to his melting buttock lent:
He stamps, and bites the poor flies in his fume.
    His love, perceiving how he is enrag'd,
    Grew kinder, and his fury was assuag'd.
               Venus and Adonis, 259–318

Shakespeare's sensitivity to the dream-lexicon of sexual myth contrasts this stallion (Venus's irresistible sexual appetite) with Venus's own portrait of the hare which she begs Adonis to hunt instead of the lethal boar. The hare, in all mythologies and in spontaneous dream life, is the mythic animal of the menstrual cycle, the self-sacrificial victim and divinity of the womb's ritual of reproduction, the moon's own magical love creature, in oestrus, passive, appealing. Here she is Venus's prophetic image of herself as she will be, a 'dew-bedabbled wretch', searching distractedly for the hunter whom her other self – her own rejected 'lust', who was a horse and is now a boar – has already killed. The same stallion that appears here at the beginning of the tragic sequence will reappear at the very end in *Two Noble Kinsmen*, still uncontrollable, once more possessed, as here, by the fury of rejected Venus, and will transform itself (within a single speech), whining 'pig-like', into the animal mass that crushes and kills Arcite, the Goddess-rejector.

As I remarked earlier, the Boar always has the double role of being both the Goddess, infernalized and enraged, and her infernal consort (Mars in boar form) who supplants Adonis, and who is, therefore, always some 'usurping brother'. This sequence (rejected and inferna-lized Goddess = Boar = Hot Tyrant who overthrows Adonis) is the essential formula in the algebra of the Tragic Equation, as it emerges eventually.

Shakespeare's design, in *Venus and Adonis*, has a mythic complete-ness lacking in Euripides's, Seneca's and Racine's versions of the story. In *Venus and Adonis*, once the Queen of Hell has split off, as the Boar, to find Adonis and kill him, the Divine Mother/Sacred Bride aspect does not simply evaporate (kill herself) like Phaedra. Her part in events is by no means over. One of the most powerful episodes in Shakespeare's poem recounts her panic anxiety as she hurries 'she knows not whither' – like that hunted hare, tearing the brambles, and

> Like a milch doe, whose swollen dugs do ache,
> Hasting to feed her fawn hid in some brake.
>
> 875–6

When she finds his body, Shakespeare settles with what is presumably deep satisfaction on the ominous icon of the mater dolorosa mourning over the corpse of the sacrificed god.

At this point he has already gone some way beyond Euripides and Seneca before him (and Racine after him). These three took the tragic possibilities of the myth no further. What I want to show is how, for Shakespeare, *Venus and Adonis* was only the opening phase – of the real tragedy.

But first, just to align my argument in its context, I need to highlight a few features in the historical background.

Historical background of the Tragic Equation

In all the turmoil of sixteenth- and seventeenth-century England one broad pattern emerges which will help to lift into relief Shakespeare's tragic myth and which may, to a degree, validate it.

Such a vast complication as the crisis of religious belief at this time, which was also a crisis of political, intellectual, economic and social life, can be spoken of only in the largest kind of generalization. But it can perhaps be said that between the Catholic regime (repressive terror, executions, martyrs) of Queen Mary, who died six years before Shakespeare was born, and the Puritan regime that executed Charles I thirty-three years after Shakespeare died, England went through the final phase of its Reformation and was transformed.

These two historical points were extreme opposites in that events immediately preceding Mary's reign pushed her Catholic fanaticism to a ferocity beyond anything that England had ever suffered before, while the momentum of the passions of the Civil War carried Cromwell's victorious Puritans to a severity beyond what the country would ever tolerate again. The conditions that prevailed, between these two episodes, were also, at every point, one way or another, extreme. And peculiar – in being so uniquely productive.

It is not really possible to separate, except artificially, this energy wave from the convergence on England of various other tidal global movements, from Europe and America, over and above the tectonic shifts of the Reformation, that lifted everything from its old foundations and simultaneously opened all horizons, physical and mental. But the decisive factor in England – the factor which perhaps more than any other determines the nature and evolution of Shakespeare's Tragic Equation – was that the process of religious change was arrested, or rather held in suspense, by the historical accident of Elizabeth I. Those two savage competitors for the English soul, which were the new Puritan spirit and the old Catholic spirit, each intending to exterminate the other, both uncertain of the outcome, were deadlocked, and in a sense spellbound, by her deliberate policy throughout her very long reign. They were not openly deadlocked, as on the Continent, with embattled cities and occasional massacre of populations. They were deadlocked out of sight, forcibly disarmed, and forbidden any physical, direct expression whatsoever, inside Elizabeth's crucible.

As the daughter of Henry VIII she had no alternative but to keep them there. The Papacy had already condemned her as 'the bastard of a heretic', and denounced her claim to the throne as illegitimate. The revolutionary Puritan doctrine, that had so frightened Queen Mary, ultimately opposed monarchy and pressed towards what could only be civil war. Elizabeth's solution, reaffirming her father's ideal of a middle way between the two extremes, was to outlaw and suppress both.

She needed a police state to do it. Even so, though she could anchor her ship of state she could not anchor the tides beneath it. Behind the new Puritan, the *tsunami* of the Continental Reformation piled like a tidal bore into the narrow haven of England. And it carried within it the frenzies of a jihad. And behind the old Catholic, in an intermittent campaign of war that lasted through Elizabeth's life, the international might of the Catholic Empire went on gathering itself to bring England back into the fold by any means. The ghostly front line of the deadlocked spirit armies of these two giant historical forces was drawn through the solar plexus of each of Elizabeth's subjects.

What she suppressed, then, when she suppressed those furies in England, was virtually an internationalized civil war. She pushed it down into that subterranean region as a controlled explosion, and sealed it there, in the black hole of the Englishman's nervous system, for the forty-five years of her reign. And after her death in 1603 King James contrived, by one accident or another, to raise the pressures and temperatures inside it even further.

Down there it became the inner life of that epoch. It created the psychodrama, the internationalized proscenium of a struggle – civil war conducted by other means – that forced England through what has since turned out to be her decisive mutation, towards the day, twenty-six years after Shakespeare's death (in the lifetime of his daughter), when it would erupt into the apocalypse of the actual war.

The psychoanalyst of this prolonged trauma would want to see the dreams. England's permanent state of war, the unrelenting threat of the armies and armadas of the Papacy, had two effects in particular that had consequences for those dreams. It created, for the first time in England's quite young history as a single state, an heroic, exalted, defiant sense of national identity. But in doing so it pushed that national identity towards a fusion with the Puritan hardcore – whose religious loathing of the common enemy could be relied on. Inevitably, a Puritan inclination came to feel like patriotic fervour and a Catholic inclination like a proclivity for high treason. This phenomenon helps to explain the total inner confidence of a man such as Ralegh, as well as Elizabeth's confidence in him. Though he himself was unusually (dangerously, as it turned out) free of bigotry, his Puritan credentials were nevertheless fundamental and intact. His mother, like Sir Francis Bacon's mother, had been a militant enough Puritan to have left her mark on history. But the effect on those with Catholic mothers must have been of another kind.

Shakespeare's mother was an Arden – a family known to have been strongly Catholic. John Somerville, a mentally unbalanced 'cousin' of the main branch of Warwickshire Ardens, was in 1583 convicted of an attempt to assassinate Queen Elizabeth. Edward Arden, head of the family, was implicated and also executed. This prompted renewed official persecution of Catholics in the area, but particularly of those related to the Ardens, with orders to apprehend 'such as shall be in any way akin to all touched, and to search their houses'. The recusancy (persistent failure to attend church) of John Shakespeare, the poet's father, has been attributed to a stubborn Catholicism (as has his financial ruin). One of the 'Spiritual Testaments' (declaration of loyalty to the Catholic faith) distributed in the region in 1580 by the Jesuit priests Edmund Campion and Robert Persons (both executed later), and drawn up in John Shakespeare's name, was found by a bricklayer in 1784 stuffed under the roof of the Shakespeare birthplace in Henley Street. First doubted as a forgery, it has since been accepted as genuine. The persecution following the Arden convictions, it has been suggested, would be the occasion for John Shakespeare to cache the incriminating evidence. Shakespeare's father's family came from the neighbourhood of Wroxhall, just north of Stratford, where up to the dissolution under Henry VIII there was a large convent whose prioress in the early sixteenth century was one Isabella Shakespeare. At the time of the dissolution, a little later, the sub-prioress was a Joan Shakespeare, who lived till 1576. Apart from the coincidence of this prioress's Christian name with that of the heroine of *Measure for Measure*, these stray hints from Shakespeare's extended family suggest what a secret and passionate (even fanatic) cell of illicit, fearful religious loyalty his early home could well have been.*

One can imagine the nightmares of these Catholic sons. One hardly needs to imagine them: they parade the Elizabethan stage in a dense gas of suspicion and guilt. During that reign every man knew himself to be, or could suspect his neighbour of being, at heart, officially a traitor. Elizabeth could reasonably persuade herself that any of her subjects – even her nearest and dearest such as Essex – was her potential assassin. The theatre itself had materialized (only fifteen years or so before Shakespeare found it) from the sheer uncontainable excess of this national struggle with conscience, this internal Inquisition in perpetual session. Even Ralegh, at his trial, was accused of having 'the soul of a Spaniard'. And though he was reprieved for a few years, he was sentenced to the death of a Catholic activist and traitor, to be half-hanged, castrated, disembowelled and the rest, his only consolation being that his rank would limit the event to a simple beheading.

*See Peter Milward, *Shakespeare's Religious Background*.

Flashes of this sort give a taste of the paranoia that served for air in the crucible. But Shakespeare's phantasmagoria is the thing itself. His susceptibility to large, cataclysmic visions, and the fact that his plays emerged as poetry, inspirationally, suggests how much of his life, too, was underground, and concealed, perhaps, even from himself, as with the poet who planned a work on a life like Timon's:

> the fire i'the flint
> Shows not till it be struck.
> *Timon of Athens*, I. i. 23–4

And that is what I would like to bring into alignment: the Elizabethan/Jacobean dream not as it appears in the historian's archive, but as it appeared – the 'form and pressure' of the 'very age and body of the time' – in the tragedies. Not the mirrored image of the civic procedures, but the processes of the inner explosion, behind the faces of both judges and accused – the controlled slowness of that explosion. First, the religious substance of it, the mass and depth and pressure. Then the retardation, the deferred release, as everything inched towards a conclusion that could only be frightful.

Since Shakespeare was born, lived and died within the crucible, his art evolved as a kind of salamander. It had time to develop the means to thrive on and to deal with the conditions and forces that had brought it into being. The elements of the creative chemistry did not blow off in a single blissful dawn, as with most revolutions, leaving him and a few other lyrical prophets to make what they could of the ringing in their ears. Within that crucible, the conditions and forces that shaped him were also, inevitably, the very substance of his vision. What I want to suggest is that the equation of his tragic myth was, in a real sense, the equation of the chemical process within that 'controlled explosion'.

Lucrece as a metaphysical poem

After contemplating the role of Venus as the ancestral mother of Christ, a reader might well be alerted, when Shakespeare sets Rome so boldly at the centre of his next poem, *Lucrece*. Even to such a historian as Ralegh, Rome meant first the Antichrist, the Whore of Babylon, and only then Caesar and the Empire.

Tarquin is a lawless, irreligious figure at first sight. And the whole poem is solidly knotted in the turmoil and cries of real bodies, on real earth. But the prose historical note that prefaces the poem gives the clue. Just as Prince Hamlet is the son of another Hamlet, Prince Tarquin is the son of another Tarquin (titled Superbus for his outrageous pride), who had seized the crown of Rome by murdering his father-in-law in defiance of the popular will. Prince Tarquin's father, that is, was not only a Claudius, but a Macbeth. He ravishes the crown, so to speak: the crown of Rome.

Once again briefly: the Roman army is besieging Ardea. On a wager, the Roman commanders leave the siege to see what their wives are up to in their absence. It turns out that all are making merry, in a variety of licentious ways, except for Collatine's wife, Lucrece. She alone is dutifully tending the shrine of her wifely chastity and virtue. Prince Tarquin is instantly possessed with uncontrollable lust for this unique, inaccessible treasure. He returns unaccompanied to her house, where Lucrece entertains him royally, as a friend of her husband and a prince. There is no reason to suppose that Shakespeare means less than what he says when he makes the basic position clear:

> This earthly saint, adored by this devil,
> Little suspecteth the false worshipper.
>
> *Lucrece*, 85–6

Nowadays, he would be reproved for dealing in metaphysical stereotypes a little too glibly, but there it is. That night Tarquin breaks into Lucrece's bedroom and rapes her.

In one of the most fascinating passages, between Tarquin's leaving his own bed and arriving at the side of Lucrece's, he debates in full, hideous awareness the madness of what he is about to do:

> pale with fear he doth premeditate
> The dangers of his loathsome enterprise.
>
> 183–4

Tarquin is walking down a familiar corridor. The locks and thresholds 'prate' of his whereabouts, just as the stones do under Macbeth's feet as he goes 'with Tarquin's ravishing strides' to murder King Duncan. His torch argues against him, and – just as Othello's does when he stands over Desdemona's bed – puts in a clear, strong word. Everything intensifies Tarquin's horror of his own act. And when he finally stands over Lucrece he stops her wild reproaches with his own even wilder self-condemnations:

[79]

'I have debated, even in my soul,
What wrong, what shame, what sorrow I shall breed . . .
Yet strive I to embrace mine infamy.'

                                        498–9, 504

But then he plunges in deeper, as Macbeth speaks through him again, with familiar words. Unless she surrenders to him, he will kill her, carry her to the bed of some 'base groom', then proclaim that he murdered both in a fit of revulsion at their crime.

At each step, in spite of the steady, naked shock of primitive human emotion, Shakespeare keeps reasserting, with slight touches, the sacred context. Lucrece lies there,

the picture of pure piety . . .
Pleads in a wilderness where are no laws,
To the rough beast that knows no gentle right,
Nor aught obeys but his foul appetite,

                                        542, 544–6

and yet Tarquin's worst violence cannot break out of the sacramental web of responses that are recording every thought and move. In a poem of nearly two thousand lines the actual rape slips past in only six of them, which contain, respectively, the words 'piteous', 'chastity', 'modest', 'so pure', 'purifying' and 'tears'.

Shakespeare is interested not in the act but only in making sure that the reader understands it in a certain way:

O! deeper sin than bottomless conceit
Can comprehend in still imagination.

                                        701–2

And in his powerful portrait of the post-coital Tarquin he puts his finger on what, for him, is the main point:

his soul's fair temple is defaced;
To whose weak ruins muster troops of cares,
To ask the spotted princess how she fares.

                                        719–21

That 'spotted' is the indicator.

She says, her subjects with foul insurrection
Have batter'd down her consecrated wall,

And by their mortal fault brought in subjection
Her immortality, and made her thrall
To living death . . .

722–6

In other words, Tarquin's rape of Lucrece is also the violation of his own soul, who is evidently a divine, immortal, royal female, now dethroned and imprisoned by depraved, damned, mortal appetites and powers. This integral simultaneity of external and internal event, where the hero's action against the real female is the visible, physical aspect of an inner act against his own soul ('in so far as ye do it unto the least of these, ye do it unto me') is consistent throughout the tragedies.

The first half of the poem concerns Tarquin's state of mind before the rape, and then, very briefly, the state of his soul (those lines above) as he 'creeps sadly' away 'like a thievish dog', and a 'heavy convertite'. In the rest of the poem Lucrece attempts to fathom what has happened to her. This longest lament, by far, in Shakespeare's works, bewails the violation of her chastity.

Venus and Adonis turned on Adonis's chastity. And the real subject of this second poem is Lucrece's chastity. It is her chastity that marks her out for Tarquin as a projection of his soul, from which he is – for reasons I shall look at later – estranged. And which he therefore needs to reclaim by force. In exactly the same way, Angelo in *Measure for Measure* will be inflamed not by Isabella's beauty (though it helps) but by her chastity.

In so far as the Lucrece figure and the hero's soul are aspects of each other, Shakespeare's metaphysical concern with 'chastity' is actually a concern with the most sacred quality of the soul. The weight and tenacity of his preoccupation with chastity seem exaggerated only if one fails to accept that wherever it appears in his work, as in these two poems, he is dramatizing it in this way, on the mythic plane, as a quality of the soul. His idea of 'chastity' is inherent in his idea of the 'true soul' and of 'sacred truth' (see page 218), and is centred on his concept of the Cordelia at the heart of his ethical system.

Another typical cadenza on the mythology of the idea of rape occurs later in the poem where Lucrece translates her own rape into the sack of Troy. Helen becomes the sexual defaulter, that part of Lucrece which had to take the consequences and guilt of her ravishment. Royal Priam is the soul of Lucrece, corresponding to Tarquin's 'spotted princess'.

Queen Hecuba is the more overtly feminine aspect of the 'crown and soul' complex, who lives long enough, like Lucrece, to lament its destruction. On this occasion, Lucrece translates Tarquin as Sinon. Hamlet will make a much more logical translation (in Lucrece's own terms) when he calls for that ferocious description of the regicide Pyrrhus, a passage that resembles a compact replay of the rape of Lucrece taken to the umpteenth power.

Finally, having revealed Tarquin's crime, Lucrece stabs herself. Mythically, this removes Tarquin's last hope of reprieve (of forgiveness); the external pattern then completes itself inevitably: in destroying his soul he has destroyed not only his own succession to the throne, but monarchy itself; and is banished 'everlastingly'.

No matter how one tries to read *Lucrece* as a secular poem, it can only justify its own extreme terms by being read as a mythic, a metaphysical poem. Having followed it that far, there is no way of denying its function as a religious poem.

The contrapuntal symmetry of *Venus and Adonis* and *Lucrece*

Composing *Lucrece*, Shakespeare inverted all the main features of *Venus and Adonis* in a crisply symmetrical counterpoint.

Where the first poem was dashed off lightheartedly, a half-joke, this graver labour is presented seriously. The divine and fantastic world of the first has become a secular and real world in the second. The uncontrollably passionate lover, formerly female, is now male. The sexual victim, formerly male, is now female. The sexual purpose, formerly accomplished only in symbolic, mythic form, is now completed in earnest. Death that came to the victim by a supernatural animal now comes to her by her own human hand. The survivor, formerly returning to mourn, heartbroken, in Heaven, is now banished from his own country, broken by guilt. The setting, formerly Arcadian woodland, is now a claustrophobic bedchamber. And so on. All these points are nicely judged, in the choreographic spirit of the plays.

This symmetry at the surface reveals a deeper symmetry beneath: *Lucrece* is the same event as *Venus and Adonis* on a different level; it is also the second half of a binary whole; and it manages to be both these things at the same time.

In the Introduction, I identified the myth behind *Lucrece* as the archaic myth of the Goddess-destroyer who from the infancy and through the adolescence of Western religious history had overtaken, again and again, the myth of the Great Goddess and her sacrificed god.

As I noted before, the difference between the motive of Tarquin's raping and indirectly destroying the chaste Lucrece and the motive of Jehovah, attempting to annihilate Asherah, the great serpentine Goddess of orgiastic love whose priestesses were sacred prostitutes, might seem irreconcilable. In fact, Shakespeare reconciled them without difficulty. Or rather he divined how both were images of the same act — the destruction of the soul: the tragic 'crime' of the Puritan hero. (The mechanism of this 'reconciliation' is discussed on pages 220–2.) What I want to concentrate on here is the curious fact that out of all the countless available narratives Shakespeare, having picked the source-myth of Catholicism for his first long poem, now picked the source-myth of Puritanism for his second. Somehow he had identified and appropriated the opposed archetypal forces of the Reformation, the two terrible brothers that Elizabeth had pushed down into her crucible, under the navel of England, to fight there like the original two dragons of the island. And having appropriated them, as his imaginative capital, he locked them together so deeply, with dovetailed forms and contrapuntal music, that they seem like the two halves of one brain.

But he has done something even more unlikely. Having found that Catholic source-myth, Venus and Adonis, he has interpreted it from the Puritan point of view. And then having found the Puritan source-myth, he has interpreted it from the Catholic point of view.

In the first poem, which exploits the Catholic myth, he presents the uncontrollable Love Goddess through the eyes of the Puritan young god who is rejecting her with his scholastic distinction between 'love' and 'lust', and who sees in her what the Puritan sees in the Goddess of Love — the voluptuary demoness who will destroy him. In the second poem, which exploits the Puritan myth, he presents the irresistible warrior god (secularized) through the eyes of the Goddess (secularized), and sees a martial, homicidal, lust-maddened, pitiless rapist, who will destroy her. In the first poem, the god is the perfect young Puritan Christ figure, whom Shakespeare's Puritan and also theological Protestant contemporaries would recognize without difficulty, who fears for his 'soul', not for his life. In the second poem, the Goddess is the perfect, chaste wife and mother (so divinely true in love that she seems virginal, a figure that Shakespeare's theological Catholic contemporaries would recognize without difficulty), who fears, again, not for her life but for her 'soul'. Yet in both cases they are the same Goddess and the same god.

Here the two poems begin to appear as the same event on two different levels. I suggested that they were also the two halves of a whole where the second is an inevitable consequence of the first: the second poem, as a second half, emerges from the first, where what happens to individual human beings, in the real world, in the second half, is a consequence of what has happened to gods, on the mythic plane, in the first half. Exactly how this can be so becomes apparent when the two myths emerge, as a single equation six or seven years later, on to Shakespeare's stage.

Shakespeare's vision as prophecy

If this is the living myth of the Reformation and of the English Reformation in particular, it should supply Shakespeare with a comprehensive, organic image of Elizabethan/Jacobean England's inner life, its spiritual life, in which case it should be prophetic, in a way that a computer model, accurately programmed, simulates the entire future development, and projects an outcome.

I have implied that the apprehensive imagination of the whole age, in England, was prophetic. But Shakespeare's plays do seem immediately prophetic. From the first lines of what might well have been the earliest of his surviving plays:

> Hung be the heavens with black, yield day to night!
> Comets, importing change of times and states,
> Brandish your crystal tresses in the sky . . .
>
> *Henry VI Part I*, i. i. 1–3

the *Complete Works* open a revolutionary vision which is as apocalyptic as Blake's, and much more accurate in detail. Maybe Shakespeare should be viewed against the contemporary epidemic of prophesying or messianic hallucinating madmen – as the one who could handle it (but with a weird light in his eyes). Not only his 'affable familiar ghost', or those spirits that taught his spirit, too, 'to write above a mortal pitch', gulling him 'nightly with intelligence', but the *Zeitgeist* itself, it seems, conscripted Shakespeare's synapses to rehearse all those regicides (malevolent and pitiless like Richard III; possessed yet noble like Macbeth; noble and selfless like Brutus; shrewd and evil like Edmund) before it finally stepped out (after quirkish flashes in the pan – the giddy Essex, its attempts to incriminate Ralegh) into flesh and blood and history. In about the year that Shakespeare wrote *Macbeth*, Oliver Cromwell (another apocalyptic dreamer) dreamed he would be king (and told his master and was whipped for it). But did the plot of *King Lear* occur to Charles I (Shakespeare was one of his favourite authors) the night before his execution? The violent commoner at the head of the English army, the King's hopes in France, the King himself hunted like an animal through the English landscape . . .

In another dimension, a bigger prophecy lifts into a longer perspective, aligned with the tragic age in Greece. To be dense with realistic understanding of secular man, as Shakespeare's tragedies are, isn't enough to earn them a place beside the tragedies of Aeschylus, Sophocles and Euripides, where one does instinctively set them. Presumably they qualify for that fraternity because they operate, as I have said, on the mythic plane, and embody a vision of sacred man, or of falling and fallen man in a sacred universe. Or of rational man confronting and challenging a sacred universe. In both the Greek world and Shakespeare's the archaic reign of the Great Goddess was being put down, finally and decisively, by a pragmatic, sceptical, moralizing, desacralizing spirit: in Greece by the spirit of Socrates, and in England by the spirit of the ascendant, Puritan God of the individual conscience, the Age of Reason cloaked in the Reformation.* For England, as for Greece, it was a supernova moment, which, it seems, can happen only once in a nation, as in a star. And while the Red Giant swelled towards the ultimate explosion, disintegration and collapse, Shakespeare's dramas incarnated the chemistry of the whole process. Maybe this is how the *Complete Works* come to be (with whatever else they may be) modern England's creation story, our sacred book, closer to us than the Bible. As if, since that final phase of the explosion in the Civil War, the spiritual life of England has been a Black Dwarf.

But in that case they should be, in a larger sense – as the Greek tragedies are too – the creation story of civilization. After that explosion, maybe, civilization too is a Black Dwarf, in the dark, turning the wheel of its satanic mill, grinding the neutrons. On the other hand,

*It is relevant, presumably, that both processes climaxed in civil war (or its equivalent) and political tyranny.

[85]

Shakespeare gets beyond his tragedies, and invents, in those last plays, an alternative.

Venus and Adonis as a shamanic initiation dream

I suggested a rationale for the momentous change that Shakespeare made in the traditional character of Adonis when he composed his first long narrative poem. I also suggested that when he lifted this motif (the hero rejecting the deity) from the Ovidian story of Salmacis and Hermaphroditus, the remainder of their story, also, became integral to what he made of the whole complex. I went on to suggest that in doing this what Shakespeare also did (unconsciously or not) was to fashion a timely theological fable, in which the former consort of the Goddess had now become the moral New Puritan, rejecting the old Catholic world. Finally, I made the point that his appropriation of this myth gave him simultaneously the image for the fundamental conflict within his own subjectivity and the key to the spiritual tragedy of the Reformation, which in turn gave him access to the Reformation's inner life as workable material for his art. There is one other source, however, for the all-important change, this fear of the Goddess, that he introduced into the traditional character of Adonis.

It is not too difficult to show how solidly Shakespeare belonged to his times. Or rather, it is comparatively easy to find links between his words and current tradition of the historical record. But it is not so easy to say anything about just what gave his inner illumination that peculiar, not to say extraordinary, power, scope and depth, or just why it expressed itself in poetry, or why his poetic, dramatic activity was of that particular quality. And his creative activity not only resurrected ancient patterns of vision and understanding into urgent, familiar life, and embodied the climactic struggle of the day, it was, as I say, also prophetic. This cannot be discussed in any but the psycho-biological terms of his individuality, of which, it might be thought, we know nothing.

But we do know what he told us. In his psycho-biological make-up he was a type. A rare type, but a type. It would be an interesting and not particularly difficult experiment to narrate the plot and details of *Venus and Adonis* to various primitive groups, or at least to groups that still hang on to their old ways of dealing with the supernatural. Or to narrate it without names to any anthropologist who specializes in such things. They would all recognize this poem as a classic example of the dream of spontaneous shamanic initiation, the dream of 'the call'.* As such, it is a marvellously lucid, complete, powerful specimen.

The dreamer, Adonis, is the uncomprehending, resisting ego, who simply wants to get on with his ordinary life. He is forcibly wooed by

*Records of the shamanic 'call' in dreams of this type are voluminous. The initial reluctance of the 'chosen one' and the spirit's threat of death if he (or she) rejects the call, are standard features. The following account by a Goldi (Siberian) shaman is typical, though the reluctance of the subject here is quite slight, and there is no mention of the most regular episode of all – the dismemberment and remaking, by the supernatural power, of the body and brain. But the alternative animal form of the 'spirit' is standard, as is the retinue of 'assistants' who take different forms at different times.

'Up to the age of twenty I was quite well. Then I felt ill, my whole body ailed me, I had bad headaches . . . Once I was asleep on my sick-bed, when a spirit approached me. It was a very beautiful woman. Her figure was very slight, she was no more than half an arshin [nearly three feet] tall. Her face and attire were quite as those of one of our Goldi women. Her hair fell down to her shoulders in short black tresses. Other shamans say they have had the vision of a woman with one half of her face black, and the other half red. She said: "I am the 'ayami' of your ancestors, the Shamans. I taught them shamaning. Now I am going to teach you. The old shamans have died off, and there is no one to heal people. You are to become a shaman."

'Next she said: "I love you, I have no husband now, you will be my husband and I shall be a wife unto you. I shall give you assistant spirits. You are to heal with their aid, and I shall teach and help you myself. Food will come to us from the people."

'I felt dismayed and tried to resist. Then she said: "If you will not obey me, so much the worse for you. I shall kill you."

'She has been coming to me ever since, and I sleep with her as with my own wife, but we have no children. She lives quite by herself without any relatives in a hut, on a mountain, but she often changes her abode. Sometimes she comes under the aspect of an old woman, and sometimes under that of a wolf, so she is terrible to look at. Sometimes she comes as a winged tiger. I mount it and she takes me to show me different countries . . . She has given me three assistants – the "jarga" (the panther), the "doonto" (the bear) and the "amba" (the tiger). They come to my dreams, and appear whenever I summon them while shamaning. If one of them refuses to come, the "ayami" makes them obey . . . When I am shamaning, the "ayami" and the assistant spirits are possessing me: whether big or small, they penetrate me, as smoke or vapour would. When the "ayami" is within me, it is she who speaks through my mouth, and she does everything herself. When I am eating the "subdu" (the offerings) and drinking pig's blood (the blood of pigs is drunk by shamans alone, lay people are forbidden to touch it), it is not I who eat and drink, it is my "ayami" alone.'

Another example, illustrating the return of the rejected 'Goddess' in enraged, vengeful animal form, comes from a shaman of an aboriginal tribe in India:

'When I was about twelve years old, a tutelary girl called Jangmai came to me in a dream and said, "I am pleased with you; I love you; I love you so much that you must marry me." But I refused, and for a whole year she used to come making love to me and trying to win me. But I always rejected her until at last she got angry and sent her dog (a tiger) to bite me. That frightened me and I agreed to marry her. But almost at once another tutelary girl came and begged me to marry her instead. [Then] the first girl . . . said, 'I was the first to love you and I look on you as my husband. Now your heart is on another woman, but I'll not allow it." So I said "No" to the second girl. But the first in her rage and jealousy made me mad and drove me out into the jungle and robbed me of my memory . . .' This was the beginning of his initiation from which he eventually emerged as a shaman. [Both the Goddess. When he continues to reject her, she appears in animal form, tears his ego-body to pieces, then reassembles it afresh as her obedient servant – the servant of the spirit world. In *Venus and Adonis*, Shakespeare's shamanic animal is the Boar, and his butchered self is reborn symbolically as a purple flower 'chequer'd with white', resembling:

> [the] frothy mouth bepainted all with red,
> Like milk and blood being mingled both together
>
> *Venus and Adonis*, 901–2

of the fatal Boar, in which the red of his own blood and the white of the Goddess are intermixed. In other words, his first long poem enshrines his shamanic rebirth into the service of the Goddess, the dream form of the cataclysmic psychological event which was the source of his poetic inspiration. The Boar would thereafter be his shamanic animal, his link with the supernatural dimension of his vision – the animal form, as it were, of his visionary awareness. As the Tragic Equation demonstrates, this Boar returns, in some shape or other, to deliver the poetic *donnée*, the daemonic power charge, in every play that uses the tragic myth. (It also appeared in some of the earlier plays, before the tragic myth was fully articulated in dramatic form. In each case its presence distinguishes those plays that we think of as poems, or as unfathomable poetic images that have been dramatized, from those plays that we think of as being merely theatrical or rhetorical.)

The Boar is always associated with the Underworld or nocturnal aspect of the Goddess, and through her with the other aspects of the Goddess. It delivers, in fact, the whole myth, and everything comprehended within that system. A consistent family of adjectives would cover its regular attributes. It is present, as I have said, in elemental form, in Aaron the Moor. It is there in Bottom's Ass's head (the Ass, as

---

extracts taken from Mircea Eliade, *Shamanism*, London: Routledge and Kegan Paul, 1964]

Dreams of this type become significant because, when the whole world's contributions are put together, they are so consistent in producing the mythic essentials (familiar as fossils or vital organs in the evolved religions), and because they project the inner experience, consistent and archetypal, of a spontaneous human transform-ation that always tends to produce the same end result: a healer who exercises his power through public, dramatic performances. In the light of this heavily documented shamanic tradition, it is not easy to see Shakespeare's reshaping of his Ovid, and his lifelong obsession with the Goddess's dealings with her chosen one (and his with her), as anything but a preoccupying inner event of this kind.

the Egyptian Set, who was also Typhon, is another form of the Boar, in a mythical system to which, as I hope to show, Shakespeare's tragic myth is intimately connected). It is there in Falstaff, the Bartholomew Boar Pig of the Boar's Head, as it is in Macbeth. And it is there in the child of Sycorax ('swine-crow'), the heir to her kingdom, Caliban. In other words, it stands centre stage in the beginning and at the end, and at the comic extreme and at the tragic extreme, of Shakespeare's series of visions.

The anthropologist would ask, if Shakespeare was indeed, in his psychic temperament, a shaman of this kind, why did he appear just then? It seems to be a rule that the shamanic visitation occurs only where it is desperately needed. Almost all primitive groups are desperately in need of that help 'from the other side', all the time. Within more evolved, historical cultures, it occurs only at certain moments – typical moments of breakdown or crisis. Throughout history, as countless precedents show, wherever a people, or a culture, or a social group, is threatened either with extinction or ultimate persecution and assimilation by the enemy, the great shaman tends to appear. The lesser shamans heal and solve problems with transcendental help. The great shaman, typically, gathers up the whole tradition of the despairing group, especially the very earliest mythic/religious traditions, with all the circumstances of their present sufferings, into a messianic, healing, redemptive vision on the spiritual plane. These figures are not always spiritual warriors of the Christ type. They occasionally come on a lower plane as fanatic, national leaders, simply – like Hitler. Or as artists. A modern casebook specimen would be Isaac Bashevis Singer, a great literary shaman of East European Hasidic Jewry, whose initiation dream is recorded perhaps in his *Satan in Goray*. Another would certainly be Eliot, a great literary shaman of the spiritual tradition of the West where it collided, in particular, with the ultimate demon of desacralization in the scientific materialism of the American economic miracle. His initiation dream is projected successively into *The Waste Land*, *The Hollow Men* and *Ash Wednesday*. Yeats would certainly be another: a great literary shaman, like Eliot, of the spiritual traditions of the West on the more Gnostic and unorthodox wavelength, but in his case fused with his role as shaman of the Irish as a nation emerging from the Irish ultimate humiliation and experience of near annihilation in the mid nineteenth century. As I mentioned before, *The Wanderings of Oisin* can be read as a pure shamanic initiation dream.

The anthropologist might justifiably ask whether the right conditions for the great shaman occurred in Elizabethan England. The prolonged, savage persecution and threatened extermination of the old Catholic tribe, which was virtually the whole tradition of Older England, but which was also the whole tradition of Europe, would seem to provide an answer.

The inner identification of Shakespeare's Goddess with the archaic Goddess of the Catholic world, and with his own mother, suggests that in so far as he was a shaman of that type, for that tradition, he was indeed not merely crypto-Catholic but committed to Catholicism with an instinct that amounted to fanatic heroism. The great shaman is the one who, as if involuntarily, lives a martyrdom to the defeated cause. This explains in just what way the sequence of tragic plays, and even his whole oeuvre, can be seen as Shakespeare's record of the sufferings of the Goddess (very much, as it happens, like the sufferings depicted in *Satan in Goray*), and his heroic, lifelong, patient attempt to rescue the Female – in some way or other to salvage the Goddess.

On the other hand, it is not so simple. There is another shamanic type who rises not out of the defeat of some ancient, rooted culture, some humiliated nationalism, but out of a historically new spirit. He struggles to bring a new vision from beneath an order of things that is felt to be obsolete. This type incarnates a revolutionary sensibility. His vision is an idealized renovation of society, a jolting re-adaptation, like the fault shift of an earthquake, to a fundamentally changed reality. And he locates the new order not on a spiritual plane but on earth, in social forms. In the English tradition, Milton, Blake and Wordsworth have the credentials.

In actuality, each type always contains some admixture of the other: the messianic type always projects a vision of a new world for the sufferers, even if it is not quite on this earth; and the revolutionary type always hearkens back to some golden age of justice, some state of Eden where men loved each other and dealt fairly. But in each case, one type or other is usually so dominant that there is no mistaking it.

The question with Shakespeare is, how far was he a shaman of this other, revolutionary type, as well as of the first type?

As the shaman of Old Catholicism, he registered the suffering of the Goddess and raised a vision of her salvation. But as he dramatized the will, and the militant ferocity, of the Puritan God who attempts to overthrow the Goddess, and make his kingdom out of her ruins –

exactly as in the primal combat of Marduk and Tiamat, or of Jehovah and the Goddess of the Temple — he was a prophet of the Puritan ascendancy. His adjustment of the character of Adonis is a perfect example of that belated fault shift, that seismic, sudden re-adaptation, at the surface, to a fundamentally changed reality.

This becomes quite clear, I think, if one imagines him going on to write *Comus, Paradise Lost* and *Samson Agonistes*. In those three works of Milton's, the Goddess (whom Shakespeare, in every play up to *The Tempest*, tried to save) has been finally condemned and defeated. But apart from that frigid absence of the vast, suffering concern of the Catholic shaman, the Puritan vision is the same — only more tyrannically absolute. *Comus* (written when Milton was twenty-six) is a curious replay of *Venus and Adonis* (written when Shakespeare was twenty-eight). Once again the great theme is chastity. But with a difference. Adonis's chastity, which conceals Tarquin and the tragedies, has been translated, by Milton, to the lady's armour of virginity, which radiates pure and unassailable, triumphant Christ. Venus and her Boar, which again contain Tarquin and the tragedies, have been translated to Circe (who converts men to swine simply) and her servant Comus, whose sexual threat turns out to be a vial of essence soon spilled ineffectually on the ground. The titanic potential of the tragedies, which leaped in the spark (the Boar) from Venus to Adonis, has evaporated. All potential has gone. Nothing remains but for the triumphant Jehovan (Pauline) Christ to consolidate his victory by thrusting the Goddess into Hell (as Satan whispering at the ear of Eve) and sealing her over (as Delilah's divinity, the fish-tailed Dagon, crushed under the ruins of the Temple).

Nevertheless, this was the real, historical conclusion of the revolutionary vision of the Puritan shaman in Shakespeare, who made his first clear prophetic pronouncement in Tarquin's crushing despoliation of Lucrece, and who re-enacted it in every play from *All's Well that Ends Well* onwards.

In other words, Shakespeare was a shaman, a prophet, of the ascendant, revolutionary, Puritan will (in its Elizabethan and Jacobean phase) just as surely as he was a visionary, redemptive shaman of the Catholic defeat. As a prophetic shaman of the Puritan revolution, in opposition to his role as the shaman of Old Catholicism, he experienced a second initiation dream, opposite to the first, and enshrined in his second long narrative poem *Lucrece*. That is presumably how he came to possess the extraordinary faculty of dealing with the visionary revelation of each side of the conflict from the point of view of the other. He was on both sides, simultaneously a major shaman of both types. His incarnation of the Goddess's suffering, and his incarnation of the Puritan that makes her suffer, but destroys himself in the process, are equal and entire. Both these demonic, vatic personalities fight to come to terms inside his head – and inside his heart and throughout his nervous system. Moreover, as I shall demonstrate, he understood their interconnection – the inexorable, as if natural process that brought one out of the other and set them against each other, making a shadow play of that controlled historical explosion above which the English crown floated.*

It might be thought a kind of sacrilege to drag Shakespeare back into capering about in a public arena (on a stage!) to a drum (a jig!), not in a goatskin, like the forerunners of the Greek tragedians, but in the bristly pelt of that holiest of Celtic and Anglo-Saxon beasts – the wild boar. Then again, we have no idea what Prospero got up to, between his books. Any more than we know exactly who that Diotima was, who taught Socrates about the real nature of 'total, unconditional love', and 'the thing itself'.

---

*That second shamanic dream, translated into the rape of Lucrece, has also, like the dismemberment of Adonis, a psycho-biological foundation. Where Adonis' death by the Goddess as a Boar is the nuclear image of shamanic initiation for the resisting male, so Lucrece's (fatal) rape by a Mars-like warrior (who is also the Goddess as a Boar) is the nuclear image of shamanic initiation for the resisting female. The shattering, first-hand authenticity of Shakespeare's experience of this second vision suggests that he was – psychologically at least – as fully female as he was male. In fact, the tendency of the shamanic male to evince a strongly (often predominantly) female psychology – whether based on physical actuality (with strong female characteristics) or simply regular possession by a female 'spirit' – is so usual that all over the world societies have institutionalized it. Just as extreme, and in some cases as obtrusive, is the tendency of the shamanic female to display the psychology of a warrior-like male – or regular possession by a Tarquinian daemon (avatar, as I say, of the Goddess as the Boar), who, in her initiation, subjugated her conventional feminine ego by force. This double psycho-biology in Shakespeare, as I described in the section about the contrapuntal symmetries of *Venus and Adonis* and *Lucrece*, aligns itself behind the hero of the first poem and the heroine of the second, respectively, opening a more rawly existential, visceral dimension behind the magical battle of the two shamans within his single body.

CHAPTER 2

BIRTH, CHILDHOOD AND ADOLESCENCE OF
THE TRAGIC EQUATION:
*As You Like It, All's Well that Ends Well,
A Lover's Complaint, Measure for Measure,
Troilus and Cressida*

━━━━━

Shakespeare takes up the spiritual quest

As You Like It: Jaques

Two kinds of ritual drama

As You Like It: the ritual pattern

Autobiography in *All's Well that Ends Well*

All's Well: the ritual pattern

All's Well: entry of the Mythic Equation

The three sources of *All's Well that Ends Well*

Shakespeare's double language and the verbal device

The evolutionary history of the verbal device

The double language as translation

The double language in *All's Well that Ends Well*

Shakespeare's hieroglyphic system

The verbal device and Tragic Equation as brain maps

A Lover's Complaint: the heroine's guilty secret

Shakespeare takes up the spiritual quest

Having located the two 'Christian' myths in such distinct form, with such fullness of detail, and so precisely aligned with the opposed Catholic and Puritan points of view, Shakespeare seems to have forgotten about them. Six or seven years passed in which he wrote a dozen or more plays that show only indirect evidence, here and there, of the continuing gestation of that particular complex of mythical material.

But then, quite suddenly something changed, it seems, in his attitude to what he was doing. In this chapter I shall argue that this change was prepared for and initiated – by Shakespeare, with conscious purpose – in *As You Like It*, and that it actually happens in the next play (in the sequence), *All's Well that Ends Well*. I shall then attempt to show how, when it happens, his whole imagination becomes accessible to him – in a particular form. This form incorporates the mythic material from the two long poems, but now combined in a single dramatic sequence of cause and effect – making a single, composite myth. Somehow or other the action, symbolism and metaphysical implications of this myth have risen into the plot of *All's Well that Ends Well* and fused with it. Myth, plot and drama have become one indivisible thing.

At this point it becomes clear that Shakespeare's old, workaday plot-schema, his playwright's fail-safe action kit, which appeared quite clearly formulated in *The Two Gentlemen of Verona* (a good candidate for his very earliest surviving play) and thereafter cunningly adapted in other early comedies, is the blueprint, the naked template, of the mythic plot of the two long narrative poems *when they are combined*. In other words, the bald action theorem of the plot that has been jerking his comic characters (and some of his historical characters) about the stage for the first ten years of his career, and the mysterious, archaic double myth of the Western world's grandest religions, first formulated in prehistory, that has been approaching him barely noticed, entering his imagination through the two long narrative poems, and now emerging seven years later into *All's Well*, are in their dramatic form exactly congruent, one with the other. As if the plot (say) of *The Two*

Gentlemen of Verona were the shape in the sand, found by Shakespeare (and dimly recognized in obscure excitement), where the great myth had slept overnight. During its early search, perhaps, for the one who could tell its story.

Wherever Shakespeare uses this action model in the earlier plays the myth tends to gleam through at odd moments.

In *The Comedy of Errors* it activates the city of Ephesus, cult centre of Diana as Hecate, and opens a trap door for Antipholus of Ephesus, as a usurped brother, to fall into madness (even if only imputed) and imprisonment (i.e. outlawed). In *Titus Andronicus* it extrudes Aaron the Moor as the Boar, emerging from the Queen of Hell, Tamora. In *A Midsummer Night's Dream* it opens a magic casement directly on to the fairy doings of Oberon, Titania and Bottom, which anticipate a phase the myth does not attain until *Antony and Cleopatra*. *Richard III*, probably written quite close in time to the two narratives, is the ur-form of the tragic hero in his Macbeth phase, which is to say that he is an Aaron somewhat evolved, the hump-backed Boar itself, a meteoric fragment from the orbit of the myth, plunging through the card-game battlefields of the early histories.

Falstaff is another fragment – an undivided Goddess Venus in masculine, comic phase, besotted with Adonis/Prince Henry (memory of the Henry (Wriothesley) behind the Adonis in the long poem), or rather the undivided Goddess *and* her divine consort combined, like Antony and Cleopatra in a transcendent embrace, as viewed by Octavius Caesar, who saw them as Henry finally sees Falstaff, an 'irrational' brother, inextricably, disreputably, lasciviously entwined with an amoral Queen of Hell, but here (like Bottom and Titania) in comic, infinitely indulged self-indulgence. The knightly Boar of Venus has become an old boozer (instead of a thunderbolt of infernal appetite) and Divine Love rejected (misunderstood) has become universal tolerance, affection, forgiveness, understanding, insuppressible good spirits.

Shylock is another fragment of the myth, another phase of the Boar emerging from the rejected Goddess (while his daughter Jessica splits away from him), in this case from the Shekinah, the chosen people regarded as the Divine Love rejected, emerging vengefully against the (Puritan) anti-Semitism of the Venetians. *Julius Caesar* could almost be included in the tragic sequence. In *Twelfth Night*, Malvolio's startling anguish as the (Puritan in burlesque mode) brother usurped by the 'irrational' brother (Sir Toby) and his Queen of Hell (Maria who plots the mischief) brings into that genial plot the sulphurs of the usurped brother's 'madness' in some imprisoning darkness (outlawry in the wilderness – like Edgar's in *King Lear*), which is an image of the tragic hero's madness (Lear's).

These comments will make more sense I trust, retrospectively, as I expand my argument through the tragic sequence of the mature plays and analyse the working of the mythic Tragic Equation in detail. At a convenient point, later on, I will come back and trace the shadow of the Equation through some of these earlier plays a little more coherently (see pages 488–97).

Once the Mythic Equation has been subsumed into the working plot, in *All's Well*, it evolves, step by step, from play to play, with the determination and logic of a natural process, towards the solution achieved in *The Winter's Tale* and *The Tempest*. The high definition of the algebraic mythic factors that make up the Tragic Equation enables one to follow these steps in some detail. Because this logical progression seems so clear, it is possible to set an order – an ideal or evolutionary or as it were biological order – to the sequence. It can't be claimed that this was the order in which the plays were actually composed: in the oeuvre of most artists there are proleptic inspirations, inexplicable yet apparently necessary regressions.* I shall make no attempt to guess at that

*Since this point, while being crucial to a fair reading of my argument, seems to be an unfamiliar idea and especially open to misunderstanding, I will try to make it a little clearer. Almost every *developing artist* (as distinct from those artists whose work shows no marked development) occasionally produces a work that they recognize immediately as being 'out of phase' – an outrider from some future stage of the inner development. The problem then is to bring the whole level of production up to that point – though by the time that has been achieved some other new herald will have appeared, very likely, from further beyond again. Some artists release nothing but works that express these stages of newness. But most artists produce for a while within a mode, then move more or less suddenly to a new mode which is the next stage of a development: and so on. It is among this second group that 'out of phase' works are most recognizable. But even among the other group artists sometimes produce a

work, or some part of a work, from so far ahead that it sticks out plainly in any survey of their whole oeuvre. In other words, in all artists there are two parallel sequences, with the same works appearing in both sequences but here and there in different order. The outer chronological sequence is the one in which the artist actually finishes the works, while the other goes on at a psychic depth beyond any significant interference from the artist's will or conscious craftsmanship, and could be called the organically alive, as-if-biological development of the Muse's creative process. The artist's own sense is that the inner sequence is always somewhat ahead, but then, on those lucid occasions, so far ahead that the product seems unfamiliar. In many cases the conscious craftsmanship, and perhaps the dogmatic set of the intellectual will, cannot handle these native guides from the artist's own future, so they may emerge into the world 'mistranslated', distorted, or may not emerge at all, may simply be suppressed as undesirable aliens. Perhaps real outer order, about which nobody seems to be sure, but will look at the plays only within this ideal sequence, their order according to the evolutionary development of the Tragic Equation. As it happens, this follows the conventional chronology pretty closely, and goes as follows (though much of *Hamlet*'s verse argues, to my ear, that the final revisions came after *Othello*).

> *All's Well that Ends Well*
> *Measure for Measure*
> *Troilus and Cressida*
> *Hamlet*
> *Othello*
> *Macbeth*

those artists who fail to recognize, or fail to adapt to their own 'out of phase' inspirations in this way are the ones who fail to develop, or whose work simply recycles a fixed style, or fizzles out. This tendency for real inspirations to be ahead of the artist's mind-set and technical equipment of any particular moment is acknowledged by Eliot in:

> For the pattern is new in every moment
> And every moment is a new and shocking
> Valuation of all we have been.
> 'East Coker', II

and again in:

> . . . one has only learnt to get the better
> of words
> For the thing one no longer has to say, or
> the way in which
> One is no longer disposed to say it.
> 'East Coker', V

Where the artist can both recognize a new inspiration and improvise new technical means to express it, we get the work that can seem (depending on his general mode of production at that time) 'out of phase'. Not all such works come from the future. Most artists are aware of the odd work that is in every way a throwback — as if a cat might produce, among the litter of kittens sired by the latest tom, a leftover from two or three toms back. This occasional 'out of sync' mismatch between the outer, visible sequence of artistic production and that

inner, plant-like (with all its surprises) evolutionary development of the Muse's inspiration is, as I say, the norm — one of which most artists are intensely aware. The resulting curious anomalies in the outer sequence are described by Robert Graves as:

> the tourbillions in time made
> By the strong pulling of her bladed mind
> [*the relentless inner sequence*]
> Through that ever-reluctant element.

In a poet such as Shakespeare, who developed with such leaping speed, and over such a distance, those tourbillions must have been notable. For that reason alone the outer sequence, even if it were known, could not be expected to reflect the evolutionary development of the Equation. But added to that is the unlikelihood of Shakespeare finishing one play at a time, and staging each one (making it known to the world) before he finished the next. If he was like most other writers, the odd work would hang around for two or three years, resisting completion, while he wrote others. Others, presumably, he staged then took away and completely or in some essentials rejigged — as most playwrights do. That might explain, for instance, how *Measure for Measure*, in its dealing with the Equation and in almost all of its verse, is only just beyond *All's Well that Ends Well*, yet in two or three passages is beyond the most mature *Hamlet*. Then again, just those passages might have been 'out of phase'. (And see page 479.)

King Lear
Timon of Athens
Coriolanus
Antony and Cleopatra
Cymbeline
Pericles
The Winter's Tale
The Tempest

An explanation for that abrupt change which came with *All's Well* is suggested by the play itself, especially when it is read as a sequel to the play that seems to introduce it, *As You Like It*. Often pointed out is the fact that the plot pattern of the Rival Brothers in *As You Like It*, where the usurped ducal brother ends up outlawed in the forest with his daughter, anticipates the similar pattern in *The Tempest*, where the usurped ducal brother ends up banished with his daughter on Devil's Island. Often remarked, also, is the presence in both plays of a character who vividly suggests, for various reasons, a self-portrait of the author. It is curious that such a figure should be there, in the play that brings the tragic sequence to a close, and likewise in the play that, while being not strictly part of the great mythic cycle of cave dramas, nevertheless stands at the threshold, in the cave mouth. And while in *The Tempest*, as Prospero, this figure judges, repairs and redeems the tragic fraternal crime that has spoiled his life, in *As You Like It*, as Jaques, he resolves to search, i.e. to investigate, 'through and through' man's tragic crime against himself and his brothers.

The nature of *As You Like It* and *All's Well that Ends Well*, by which I mean the category of drama into which they fall, suggests, if it doesn't clearly reveal, what is happening. Both make powerful sense (many of their oddities and loose ends become logical, and strengthen the whole structure) if they are regarded as dramatic rituals of self-transformation. In other words, they dramatize Shakespeare's conscious resolution to commit all his energies to the exploration and development of his own spiritual life. The analogy of this kind of decision in a non-artistic life would be retreat into a religious, contemplative order. This needn't be supposed so alien to his temperament, though in *Love's Labour's Lost* he mocked the more ascetic form of it. In a general way, as I mentioned before, he expresses the attitude behind such a decision in Sonnet 146:

Poor soul, the centre of my sinful earth,
Fool'd by these rebel powers that thee array,
Why dost thou pine within and suffer dearth,
Painting thy outward walls so costly gay?
Why so large cost, having so short a lease,
Dost thou upon thy fading mansion spend?
Shall worms, inheritors of this excess,
Eat up thy charge? Is this thy body's end?
Then, soul, live thou upon thy servant's loss,
And let that pine to aggravate thy store;
Buy terms divine in selling hours of dross;
Within be fed, without be rich no more:
   So shalt thou feed on Death, that feeds on men,
   And Death once dead, there's no more dying then.

Whether this sonnet belongs to this particular crisis or not is less important than the proof it supplies of Shakespeare's preoccupation with the theme. It is the only sonnet in the entire 154 not directly absorbed in one or the other love affair. *As You Like It* and *All's Well that Ends Well* suggest that he saw a way of taking this step not by retiring into a religious order (like the penitent Duke Frederick whom Jaques follows), but within his working life, and especially within his plays. He was neither the first nor the last to do this. The analogy within literature might be Eliot's decision between *The Waste Land* and *Ash Wednesday* or, even closer, Dante's deliberate reinterpretation of his earlier life in *La Vita Nuova* and his subsequent self-transformation through the cantos of *The Divine Comedy*.

In fact there is a strong hint, in the play which stands as the initiation ritual at the threshold of his new life, that Shakespeare has *The Divine Comedy* in mind and knew exactly what he was about to attempt. In this play, *As You Like It*, Shakespeare makes his farewell to his old life (and there is a suggestion that sickness is helping him to decide) and addresses himself to the inward journey. In the second, *All's Well*, he enters the Underworld, and the tragic sequence begins as a resolute self-examination that confronts him with the mythic enigma (the Sphinx in person) of his own nature.

The next play (in the sequence) is *Measure for Measure*. Here Shakespeare seems to have understood what has happened – exactly what mythic form the enigma has taken, and what its psychological dynamics are. But even in *Measure for Measure* the new myth made out of the two old myths is still only in its prototype phase. These first exploratory works of the sequence are not yet tragedies. One essential modification had to be made before the Mythic Equation could become the Tragic Equation, and he makes it in *Troilus and Cressida*. At this point the Tragic Equation so to speak matures. Immediately it produces *Hamlet*, *Othello*, *Macbeth* and the rest.

In the following pages, I will take these developments as far as *Troilus and Cressida*.

As You Like It: Jaques

Shakespeare wrote *As You Like It* in about 1599, when he was thirty-five. It is a play which seems to me to go out of its way to present some intriguing features. The first is the name of the setting: the Forest of Arden. In Shakespeare's source this had been Anglicized from Ardennes.* But it must have struck him oddly, being the name of his mother's family, whose eponymous link with the real English forest of the same name, Arden, was ancient and historic. The main action of the play, then, takes place in a forest that he can only have associated, at every level, with his mother. In the symbolic language of all literatures and traditions, the Mother Forest is the wilderness that guards the mouth of the other world (for better or worse).

Another curious feature, not supplied by Shakespeare's source, is the superfluous and fascinating character Jaques. Scholars have worried every possibility out of this collection of letters. It seems so obvious that most of them look for something more sensible, but the plain meaning of this name to Shakespeare and his contemporaries was not only Jakes = privy = joke, but the fact that it was the first syllable of his own name. Unless he had a very specific reason for using that self-deprecating joke, he would have had no problem avoiding it. He seems to scan it with two syllables, as if he forced into the single syllable Shax (common contemporary spelling of the first syllable of his name) the double syllable of the name it concealed. As a joke, and as a self-mocking pun, it must have operated on his inner ear as the key to that character's place in a pattern – where maybe the pun became serious. This would be a

*The goddess Arduina, a gallicized Diana/ Cybele whose giant statue stood through medieval times at Cavignan, gave her name to the forest of Ardennes, in north-east France.

typically Shakespearean way of coding an individual into the mechanical function of a ritual, and a reading of *As You Like It* as a ritual makes such an interpretation hard to avoid.

Jaques presents himself as one oppressed by the spectacle of the grisly antics of humanity. But he seems to have withdrawn to the forest for a purpose. He asks leave to

> speak my mind, and I will through and through
> Cleanse the foul body of the infected world,
> > *As You Like It*, II. vii. 59–60

and makes it clear that his reclusive contemplation in the forest – without any hint of self-deception or bitterness – is a serious business, and a preliminary, a preparation for something else.

By identifying himself in this role as Jaques, Shakespeare converts his own name into a transitive phrase. He was surely as apt to play this game with his interesting surname as he was, in Sonnets 135, 136 and 143, with his Christian name. No doubt he was mightily fortified, in the depths of his hypersuggestible soul, by the armorial image of himself as the shaker of a spear, of 'a lance, / Brandished at the eyes of ignorance', where the 'spear' is his notably succesful assault on the world. The alternative 'Jaques-pierre' must have been as good, in its way. There the 'pierre' becomes his obdurate, thoroughgoing but inspired determination, the pebble that brings down Goliath. Or it stiffens his Christian name Will to a herm of basalt, proof against every human weakness. The 'Shake' or the 'Jaques' is thereby left to the withheld, secretive self, 'the still and mental parts', which suffers, ponders, weighs alternative courses.

The third possibility, Jaques Père, re-enforces these other two. As the super-ego of authoritarian, moral control, 'Père' is identified with the ruler, the King, the rational brother and Adonis figure, who is both the principle of order and the realistic negotiator with reality. This relegates Jaques again to the turbulent inner realm of the dispossessed, as the irrational man of uncontrollable feeling, the potential Tarquin who is also, as it turns out (in *King Lear* and after), the potential saint.

The biblical original of a usurping brother who nevertheless carries in himself the potential for saintly union with Divine Love is Esau's younger twin, Jacob. Jacob means 'he who holds by the heel': Jacob was born clutching Esau's heel. It also means 'the outwitter', the 'one who supplants', and literally 'the usurper', just as Jacob did usurp Esau from his birthright. But it also means, in its original form Jacob-el, 'God protects' – as God protected Jacob to become Israel, father of the Twelve Tribes. If Shakespeare knew Cabbala (and had a Jewish-Italian Diotima, perhaps), he would very likely know this.

Jacob is a form of James (originally Shamash – literally 'the Sun as the High God'). Apart from the use (through French) of Jaques as a form (via Jacob) of James, Shakespeare knew James as Christ's favoured Apostle, the first to be martyred, who became the Iago of Santiago of Compostela, the patron saint of Spain. And Shakespeare knew this particular St Iago as St Jaques.

From Shakespeare's point of view, Jacob (Jaques) was a very special type of 'inferior' brother. Though he committed the act of usurpation, he showed no sign of the Tarquinian inheritance, that uncontrollably lustful or savage personality – which in Shakespeare's mythos was the inevitable lot of all the usurping, inferior brothers. He lacked this for the good reason that his elder brother, Esau, the red-haired violent hunter, had taken it all for himself, and was indeed the very incarnation of it. Jacob's irrationality took the form of an unwordly devotion to limitless God, rather than an unworldly obedience to limitless Queen of Hell. His grasp of the saintly ethos was intuitive and philosophical, not something alchemized in the fires of existential suffering during the death and rebirth of the soul. He was an intellectual *reflection* of the moral goodness of Divine Love, not (like Shakespeare's authentic 'irrational' brothers) an *incarnation* of its rejected, vengefully distorted, infernalized 'lust'.

As a symbol, therefore, the name 'Jacob' (Jaques) offered Shakespeare an etymologically precise, paradoxical inversion of the usurper of the Rival Brothers: the 'irrational' brother not possessed by the hairy animality of the Boar, but standing back from it, reflecting its hidden divinity and with a long view of its ultimate redemption. And this is how Shakespeare uses Jaques, who excoriates man's evil (especially his usurpations) as he reflects the hidden goodness suffering within it, i.e. within Oliver (the usurping, 'tyrant' brother who is redeemed by love), and within Duke Frederick (the usurping, 'tyrant' brother who is finally converted and retires to a holy life).

There are no successors, in the later plays, to Jaques, perhaps because from this point his ruminative, analytical, melancholy moralizings are internalized, during the next three plays within various characters but from *Hamlet* onwards within the tragic hero himself.

This 'internalized' function is easier to see in his opposite. By retuning the name to a needle on a different dial, Shakespeare finds the wavelength of Jaques's antithesis. Once that name Jaques enters Spain, he becomes Iago. In the Elizabethan lexicon of values, 'Spanish' meant 'diabolical'. By translating Jaques (the critical, 'loving surgeon', the intellectual, ethically inspired nurser of the goodness that suffers within man's wickedness) into the Spanish mode, Shakespeare arrives at the critical, sadistic surgeon, the intellectual, diabolically inspired destroyer of the goodness that suffers within man's wickedness: he arrives, that is, at Iago.

Both Jaques and Iago stand at the same distance from the Boar. Both are non-participating attendants of the sufferings of love. But where Jaques's intellectual ministrations are compassionate, and actively helpful, Iago's are sadistic and actively destructive. Where Jaques is the loving intellectual reflection of Adonis, pitying his torments and those of his beloved, Iago is the prurient, intellectual reflection of the homicidal 'lust' of the Boar, envying the joys of Adonis and his beloved, and rejoicing in their sufferings. These characterizations obviously can never do more than point towards a nexus of qualities, in approximate fashion, but I hope to anatomize Iago a little more closely when I come to *Othello*. As a type he is the culmination of a succession of antitheses to Jaques. And after *Othello* he too is internalized in the tragic hero.

Shakespeare's sensitivity to the connotations of the name Iago is revealed, presumably, in his deliberate avoidance of it when he wishes to name Santiago of Compostela in the next play, *All's Well*, where, at the same time, he corroborates everything I say here about Jaques (footnote to page 431).

Iago as an Antichrist heightens the idea of Jaques as the man of sorrows, pity, infinite understanding, the bottomless receptacle of everything the world tries to deny: the scapegoat of man's unthinking sins, the carrier away of man's corruption, a Jakes cleansing 'the foul body of the corrupted world', the dedicated cathartist. Shakespeare's mythicization of himself as a Christ figure ('blessed Mary's son') seems as evident in this joke-solemn name as was the mythicization of his erotic self into a humanoid phallus, in his joke use of 'Will' in the *Sonnets*. This home-made, talismanic heraldry is typical of the coding of his metaphorical language throughout.

However that might be, by using the interpretation of Jaques that I suggest here, one can unlock a strange ritual in *As You Like It* – a ritual that opens straight into the Tragic Equation of the next play.

Two kinds of ritual drama

At various points, with ingenuity, fine distinctions between 'soul' and 'soul', 'soul' and 'spirit', and 'spirit' and 'spirit', can be worked into Shakespeare's plays. But in general the wide range of meanings that he gives to the word 'soul' – at one extreme the notion of 'spiritedness' in Iago's:

> These fellows have some soul

and at the other the idea of man's immortal essence, in Othello's:

> This look of thine will hurl my soul from heaven,
> And fiends will snatch at it . . .
>
> *Othello*, v. ii. 273–4

are bundled into a single roomy concept that he keeps as baggy and inclusive as possible, capable in Macbeth's case of collecting the blood of his victims, or in Posthumus's case of hanging round his neck, like fruit on a tree, in the shape of Imogen. The pedagoguery of defining this word for so many occasions more meticulously belongs to other contexts.

This old-fashioned soul appears on that stage which I call the mythic plane, where events and figures and images come into focus from beyond consciousness, and where they perform, so to speak, in obedience to the preconscious laws of their association and meaning, or so much in obedience to those laws that they remain mysterious to the observer. The soul is that whole dimension, in its allegiance to the preconscious laws. In another sense the soul lives within that dimension like a creature within a universe full of other creatures. All ritual drama is drama about this 'soul'.

Speaking very generally, ritual drama falls into two broadly different categories. The first kind is passive towards the mythic world, the second kind is actively manipulative towards it – though the first kind is always tending to become the second, and the second kind reaffirms the metaphysical assumptions of the first.

Passive ritual gives form to figures and events observed – in visionary imagination – on the mythic plane. Then it simply re-enacts them. The simplest, most spontaneous form of this type of drama is the elaborate acting out, in detail as faithful to the original as possible, and sometimes using large numbers of people and taking immense trouble, of the great dreams of shamans among the North American Indians – as described by Black Elk. As a rule the figures and events of these dramas are part of the mythology or set of metaphysical ideas shared by the group – which is both audience and actors. And one can see that the performance reactivates, re-enforces and reaffirms what the whole group shares in its spiritual life. This kind of drama, in some form, arises spontaneously wherever beliefs on the mythic plane are shared. It arises with great force and, as it were, authority, presumably for good reasons (reasons connected with survival).

The unstated assumption of passive ritual drama is that controlled re-enactment of those phenomena on the mythic plane is necessary – is somehow an essential nutrient – for external life on the realistic plane. In this way, passive ritual drama serves as something more than a communally organized social bonding at the normally preconscious level, though it does that too. It acts as a natural form of deep therapy, where the mythic plane holds the keys to health, vitality, meaningful-ness and psychic freedom on the outer plane. For those keys to be turned in the locks, releasing the benefits, the doings of the mythic plane need to be externalized and shared. The historic experience of all peoples is like that of modern therapists: it confirms the truth of the assumption.

The deeper understanding, the instinctive prompting, of ritual drama recognizes, presumably, that a human being is only half alive if their life on the realistic, outer plane does not have the full assent and co-operation of their life on the mythic plane. The whole business of art, which even at its most naturalistic is some kind of attempt at 'ritualization', is to reopen negotiations with the mythic plane. The artistic problem is to objectify the mythic plane satisfactorily – so that it produces those benefits of therapeutic catharsis, social bonding and psychological renewal – without becoming unintelligible, and without spoiling the audience for adaptive, practical life on the realistic plane. The human problem is that life evolves at different speeds on the two planes. Only where the two planes are synchronized can there be fully effective ritual drama. This obtains in static societies, before they enter the historical torrent. And it obtains in those societies where the mythic plane itself tilts and pours down the historical cataract, as in religious revolutions. The society then seems to be changing very fast, but it is still controlled by the mythic plane. When evolution on the outer, realistic plane wrenches a society away from its allegiance to the mythic plane there is a psychological explosion – ritual drama goes into convulsions: as in fifth-century BC Athens and Elizabethan/Jacobean England. Once the dissociation is complete, and the mythic plane makes demands which the individual life on the realistic plane refuses to meet, ritual drama becomes difficult. Perhaps this is another way of describing what Eliot called the 'dissociation of sensibility' that occurred, according to the testimony of art and literature, in seventeenth-century England. After that, ritual art, in any medium, becomes more and more fragmentary, experimental, provisional, primitive, as it searches deeper and deeper into the primordial levels of the psyche for any scraps of mythic experience that still might be shared, and that might still produce a trickle of the old benefits.

The second kind of ritual drama, active ritual drama, works on the same premise as the first, but with a different purpose. This is the kind of drama relevant to *As You Like It* and *All's Well that Ends Well*. It is invented by proselytizing religions, or Hermetic societies, or magicians, as a large-scale application of the technology of making a spell, working on the assumption (archetypal and instinctive) that a deliberately shaped ritual can reactivate energies on the mythic plane so powerfully that they can recapture and reshape an ego that seems to have escaped them on the realistic plane.

The familiar example of this kind of sympathetic magic as actively manipulative ritual drama is the Mass. Materialists grant the technique some validity and explain it by hypnosis. However its functioning was understood, Hermetic alchemical ritualists, which is to say Occult Neoplatonist ritualists, went to work just as mystery religions always have done in the past, and as orders such as the Golden Dawn have done in the present, attempting to transform the personality by manipulating the mind or 'soul' on the mythic plane.

Various aspects of *As You Like It* suggest that, on one level, it is a manipulative ritual of this kind. Active ritual drama always begins with a psychic malaise, usually a failure in the link between the personality on the realistic plane and the spiritual self or soul on the mythic plane. This breakdown of communications between ego and soul is always brought about by a 'sin' – usually some more or less extreme form of the ego's neglect or injury to the soul. The result is like the primitive's 'loss of the soul'. In this sense, active ritual drama begins where the traditional shaman's healing drama begins, and its purpose is the same: to recover the soul and reconnect it to the ego. The basic mythical form of its operation is also the same.

It is on this level that *As You Like It* begins, with Shakespeare's ailing ego personified by the dispossessed Orlando. The play dismantles his entire being into its component parts, rearranges them correctly, as if rearranging disordered chromosomes, then reassembles the whole, with ego and soul reunited in perfect love. This means: with ego illuminated and transfigured by new spiritual understanding and in harmony with the universe – of which the elemental soul is an emanation.

In effect, two different dramas are being performed simultaneously. One for the public who wants to be entertained, and one for Shakespeare himself – and, it may be, a small circle of initiates. The first audience enjoys a romantic comedy and accepts the confusing details (the fact that there are two characters called Jaques, for instance) as part of the rich complexity of general effect. The second audience watches an active ritual in which a shattered individual is put back together again on the realistic plane, and is simultaneously, on the mythic plane, committed to the spiritual quest.

As You Like It: the ritual pattern

Assuming for a little while longer that Jaques is something of a self-portrait (not so much a self-portrait as a way of Shakespeare having a self-representative in the ritual) in *As You Like It*, and Prospero the same in *The Tempest*, one looks for a connection between them. But though the theme of the Rival Brothers shapes both plays, Prospero's place in the pattern is obviously very different from that of Jaques, or at least it seems so. Prospero, at the end of the tragic series, is the banished Duke, as if Shakespeare were making some statement about his career in general (and, as James Joyce has suggested, about his brother in particular). But Jaques, on the threshold of the tragic series, seems quite unrelated to either of the Dukes in *As You Like It*. To make 'ritual' sense of Jaques, one needs, as I say, to read *As You Like It* as a 'double' play: the outer entertainment, the comedy, conceals (yet reveals) the inner soul-drama, the ritual.

There is another Jaques. In all Shakespeare's work there appear only two characters called Jaques, and for some peculiar reason or by some unimaginable oversight (not corrected in many performances?) both are in this play. He found neither of them in his sources.

In the dance of the two pairs of brothers, the two Dukes keep to the background, while the foreground is taken up by Oliver and Orlando, the heirs of a rich estate. In the second sentence of the play, Orlando describes a third brother: Jaques. This Jaques, older than Orlando, younger than Oliver, is still at school, where 'report speaks goldenly of his profit'. But this brainy Jaques is not the Jaques who later ruminates in the Forest of Arden, and is no relation of his either. He seems to have no link with him whatsoever except that they happen to appear in the same play and share that unusual name.

In such a polished and musically shaped drama, it is not easy to imagine that Shakespeare could duplicate such an odd name, except to secure, very carefully, a meaning which was important for him. He can only have intended that if his audience did notice the duplication of the name they would be alerted to some shared identity in the two characters. Which is what happens. The listener who does register that first use of the name, and that particular relationship, and that scholarly prowess, automatically assumes, when Melancholy Jaques first appears in the forest, that this is the aforementioned brother of Orlando, now playing truant, his academic precocity sunk into moody contemplation of the corruption and pathos of man. He sounds a little more travelled and seasoned than might have been expected. But at this point in the play that is a gnat easily swallowed. Generally, there is no confusion, because few have registered the first fleeting mention of the name, or if they have, they put it down, perhaps, to Shakespeare's carelessness. Likewise, at the very end of the play, where that student brother of Oliver and Orlando finally emerges on to the stage, for the very first time, to make an announcement, there is still no confusion, because he is not introduced by name. He specifically avoids using his name Jaques (at this point it certainly would be confusing). The audience merely hears that he is the 'second son of old Sir Rowland'. It is only the close reader of the text of the play who, seeing the stage directions, is sharply reminded that this is no other than Jaques de Boys, that mysterious third brother, apparently even more superfluous to the play than Melancholy Jaques, and never mentioned since that first scene's second sentence. And now one looks again at the curious surname of the three brothers, de Boys.

Like the name Jaques, that de Boys is also Shakespeare's invention.

Here again, he presumably picked the surname 'of the Forest' because in a play set in the Forest of Arden he wanted to indicate something in particular – namely that these three de Boys brothers are intimately and internally linked with Arden Forest, which, as I suggested, can only mean the 'Mother' Forest. That they are lineally somehow hers. Their names are virtually Oliver, Orlando and Jaques (i.e. Shax-père) Arden. (Maybe it's a coincidence that in this same year, 1599, Shakespeare was applying for the right to impale his mother's family arms with the Shakespeare arms that he had procured in 1596.)

It now becomes possible to see the framework of verbal connections and parallel circuits by which Shakespeare conducted the current of meanings to illuminate his coded ritual. Externally, his purposeful ingenuity seems purely architectonic, without metaphysical intent, because the ritual which he so carefully constructs is one whose existence no casual theatre audience could possibly divine, if only because such details as the name *de Boys*, and the fact that the Jaques are synonymous, hardly break into consciousness and have no function, except on that covert level of the esoteric ritual. Different names would not damage in the slightest the popular appreciation of the play as a charming confusion of romantic changes of fortune which seem, somehow, mysteriously, inevitable and right. In other words, the two Jaques become the key to the inner ritual only to an audience of initiates.

In alchemical allegories of this kind (as in Gnostic narratives or dramas) the theme of the Rival Brothers is a standard motif. The ruling principle, because it is weakened in some way, is violently displaced by an immoral impulse, which takes the throne. Suffering and calamity result, in which the dislodged ruling principle, exposed to the primitive elements, is spiritually enlightened, by divine help, whereupon order is restored in greater understanding and strength.

In *As You Like It*, the central figure, the figure who contains, as it were, all the others, Orlando, is morally the natural, virtuous sovereign of himself – but in trouble. His trouble is that he is divided from his soul no less. At least he is so according to the ritual. This makes sense, obviously, only in terms of the ritual, only in terms of the movement of the figures in the ritual game or dance.

Orlando's lack weakens him and exposes him to takeover from the inside, by his 'dark' brother. In this 'primal, eldest' crime the evil, usurping brother, who is a composite of all that the rational principle, the lawfully ruling brother, has necessarily rejected, is, in Freudian terms, Lord of the Id and of all misrule. As Lord of the Id he is prince of the Underworld, consort of the Goddess of Hell. In this way, he is always a kind of Tarquin. Claudius in *Hamlet*, Macbeth (where King Duncan is his 'kinsman'), Edmund in *King Lear*, Antonio in *The Tempest*, are only four. Each of these Tarquins commits a rape on the soul of order, i.e. displaces the ruling figure violently. The displaced brother collapses into the abyss, the infernal darkness, the blasted heath, the islet in the ocean, the Mother Forest, where he disintegrates. Eventually, reconstituted in some superior, enlightened, avenging form, he returns. Murdered King Hamlet returns as Prince Hamlet, Duncan returns as Banquo's ghost plus Macduff, Edgar returns as Edgar invincible, Prospero returns as Master of the Elements.

Orlando's double emerges into dramatic, realistic form as his ruthless brother Oliver. Oliver is 'older' because, though morally inferior, he is temporarily, circumstantially stronger. Orlando, disinherited by his brother and banished, falls into the abyss – the Mother Forest. The conflict between the two human brothers – the two selves of Orlando – cannot be resolved on the human or realistic plane because that is where it is entrenched. It can be resolved only by resort to the mythic plane: their brotherhood – Orlando's unity – can only be repaired where they might find mythic, supernatural help.

Their conflict is itself projected on to the mythic plane. In this way the two Dukes appear as the mythic selves of Oliver and Orlando (royalty, sanctity of rule, etc., being phenomena of the mythic plane, hieroglyphic symbols, invented spontaneously on the mythic plane and operating there, manipulating transcendent solutions to what is happening on the realistic plane).

Older Oliver's family cruelty exercised against younger Orlando is expressed, on the mythic plane, by Duke Frederick's (mythically younger because morally less evolved) usurping and banishing of his brother the lawful Duke Senior. (Shakespeare establishes his position in the mythic pattern by what would be otherwise a feebly perfunctory name.) The revolutionary coup and displacement of Duke Senior is therefore the same event, on the mythic plane, as Oliver's usurping and disinheriting of Orlando on the realistic plane. Displaced, Duke Senior falls, like his real self, Orlando, on to the dance floor of the mythic plane, the maze of the Mother Forest, where real and mythic selves meet. This makes the role of Rosalind clear. She is the Lucrece figure corresponding to the soul of lawful rule: the spirit of the Crown of order. (More about this a little later.) She remains with (or rather quickly rejoins) her banished father Duke Senior as inevitably as Miranda grew up beside the banished lawful Duke Prospero. According to this, she is the feminine aspect of Orlando's mythic self – which is to say, she is Orlando's 'soul'. She is what Orlando was lacking at the beginning of the play. The two recognize each other automatically, on first sight. The end of the play and the mending of all the other fractures will come when Orlando and Rosalind are betrothed.

Celia is clearly subordinate to Rosalind, but her closest friend. She is the feminine aspect of the usurping Duke, who is Oliver's mythic self. She is therefore Oliver's 'soul', as Rosalind is Orlando's. As I say, the quarrel of the two Dukes reflects in passive, mythical representation the quarrel of the two brothers or Orlando's two selves. But the mutual loyalty of the two women expresses the deeper mythic circumstance that the two selves of Orlando belong together in mutual support and love.

The play opens with every relationship falling apart or in difficulties (and the lower characters are figures in the same dance). Orlando is separated from his soul and therefore from Oliver, Duke Senior from Duke Frederick, Rosalind from her father, then Celia from her father, and both women from their sex. But the moment that Rosalind and Orlando begin to move, indirectly, towards each other, all these relationships begin to move, somehow, towards unity and enlightenment, though with apparent reversals and new delays, which nevertheless all have their mythic logic according to the mechanism of the pattern. This process makes up the body of the play.

The two Jaques still have to be accounted for. The closed square of the two pairs of brothers left that middle brother, Jaques de Boys, as the odd man out. Between Orlando and Oliver he seems to be the invisible third, belonging equally to both. Because such pointed emphasis was placed on his mental ability, one supposes that he is a factor of understanding. He is the principle of the single awareness, in some way, of Orlando's divided mind.

In a system of such tidy symmetry one looks towards the two Dukes for some equivalent of this intermediate brother. And of course the moment the banished Duke Senior enters the play, in the Forest of Arden, there he is – Melancholy Jaques. After an introductory word or two, the Duke will hear of nobody but Jaques. And he leaves the stage only to search for Jaques and to learn what he can from him:

> I love to cope him in these sullen fits,
> For then he's full of matter.
>
> *As You Like It*, II. i. 67–8

Melancholy Jaques, it appears, occupies a position between the two Dukes, in some way a counterpoise to that of Jaques de Boys between Oliver and Orlando. And like Jaques de Boys he is the mental type. He is a summarizing, unifying intelligence. But he is not, like his namesake, wrapped in abstract studies. His study is the world. He suffers the usurper's conscience as keenly as he suffers the pains of the usurped. He is the interrogator of the real nature and cost of the quarrel of brothers. The anomalous and in a way disruptive aspect of Jaques is that he seems not to belong to the mythic world of the Dukes. And he is no part of the healing dance in the Mother Forest. He is a gloomy wallflower there, a gatecrasher from the real world, who has brought the real world with him. Pondering the mythic quarrel of the Dukes, he makes it real. He belongs, rather, to the world of the opening scene, the hard-edged realism of the conflict between Oliver and Orlando, and Charles the Wrestler.

Now it is possible to find a place for him in the design. Still considering the worlds of the two pairs of brothers as two distinct planes, one can see that Melancholy Jaques, the unifying intelligence from the human or realistic plane, is operating, as a kind of investigator, on the mythic plane. And Jaques de Boys, though he is positioned on the realistic plane (as brother of Oliver and Orlando) never actively operates there: he is buried in studies (like young Prospero, perhaps), which is to say that he actually belongs to the mythic plane. The realistic intelligence is on the mythic plane: the mythic intelligence is on the realistic plane. Jaques de Boys, in other words, is the mythic double of Melancholy Jaques, and this mortise-and-tenon interlocking joint of the mythic and the realistic intelligence binds the two planes together. The exchange expresses the accessibility of each plane to the other, and is what makes it possible – in a mythic sense – for Orlando on the realistic plane to find Rosalind on the mythic plane. That is presumably why Jaques de Boys and his cleverness is almost the first thought that occurs to Orlando in the play.

When all the fractured relationships, except one, have been repaired, suddenly from the depths of the Mother Forest comes the news that the usurping Duke Frederick, en route to find his banished brother and put him 'to the sword', has met an old religious man in the forest and has been converted, on the spot, to such extraordinary effect that he has relinquished his crown to his banished brother, its rightful owner Duke Senior, has 'Thrown into neglect the pompous court' and has 'put on a religious life' (v. iv. 188–9).

According to the play as a romantic comedy, this news, which solves every last problem, could as well be brought by almost anybody. It might have looked much neater, for instance, if Monsieur le Beau had brought it. We know him, though not very well, as Duke Frederick's man, and he is otherwise left dangling somewhere at a loose end. But le Beau's role bears no load in the ritual structure. According to the play as a ritual structure, only one person can bring good news from the mythic plane: it has to be the mythic intelligence, Jaques de Boys.

Once that news has arrived, it is inevitable that it should be Melancholy Jaques, the unifying intelligence of the realistic dimension, who solemnizes the repair of Orlando's whole being, returning the Duke to his dukedom and each of the selves to his soul, and all to Orlando, in a formal ceremony. This small but very clear instance indicates just how it is the mythic pattern alone which dictates the moves of the pieces in the ritual game. The human motivation may often seem arbitrary or inexplicable, but that is because the characters are moving in this way, according to mythic, not human, logic. But maybe this is how a surface effect of apparent confusion and irrational sequences, resembling life, nevertheless completes a pattern that seems, on the deepest level, inevitable and right.

But now, as far as the play's position in relationship to the tragic sequence is concerned, the most important thing of all happens. The pattern of the play is complete, but, as in a Persian carpet, at the end of the pattern a thread leaks out into a great mystery – the unpatterned.

Orlando and Oliver, the divided mind, like an ego of consciousness and another in subconsciousness, are both intent on the life struggle, and the play has temporarily healed their division. But if the two Dukes are the same divided mind on the mythic level, and if Duke Senior, corresponding to Orlando, has now returned to a sovereign control, which corresponds to Orlando's healed unity of mind, what about Duke Frederick?

If one now shifts the whole play on to the stage of autobiography, as if it were a visionary dream that Shakespeare happened to write out in dramatic form, one might say the following. Jaques de Boys, the invisible student, represents the mythic intelligence, alias the unifying, healing intelligence of the Mother Forest, alias the creative intelligence or spiritual intellect. This figure now brings news that the mythic, irrational self, the former usurper (Duke Frederick), has abjured all earthly ambitions and committed himself to the spiritual quest. If this were indeed happening in a visionary dream, the dreamer would have to take this news seriously. What the rational self decides depends on the support of the irrational self and the precarious apparatus of the conscious will. What the irrational self decides is generally a foregone conclusion, and will be carried out whether the conscious rational self approves or not, as a rule. But in this case, it seems, Shakespeare's rational self approves: Melancholy Jaques, the unifying intelligence of his rational consciousness, determines to join the convertite Duke. In other words, Shakespeare commits himself consciously to the quest on which his irrational self has already decided. Melancholy Jaques dismisses the pursuit of social happiness:

> So, to your pleasures:
> I am for other than for dancing measures.
>
> v. iv. 199–200

This solemn playfulness at the end of *As You Like It* might seem like the truest poetry which is the most feigning if it were not immediately followed by *All's Well that Ends Well, Troilus and Cressida, Measure for Measure, Hamlet, Othello, Macbeth* and *King Lear* all within the next five or six years.

Jaques de Boys, then, appears as a kind of Hermes, the guide to the mysteries of the Underworld. He is the voice of the mouth of the Underworld which opens through the cave in the Mother Forest. He has announced the call. And Shakespeare, as Melancholy Jaques, has answered and willingly started towards it. One sees that the two Jaques coalesce like the diver entering his image. And the two pairs of warring brothers, and the two daughters who are now to be wives, coalesce into each other and into the Jaques who sinks into the Underworld as (twelve years before *The Tempest*) Prospero climbs, with his baby daughter, into 'the rotten carcass of a butt'.

And Jaques is Shakespeare himself, thirty-five years old, *nel mezzo del cammin*, awake in the depth of the Mother Forest, about to enter (there is even a lion!) his *Divina Commedia*.

Autobiography in *All's Well that Ends Well*

According to his received biography, Shakespeare probably left Stratford and his wife in about 1585, and did not return to live with her permanently until she was fifty-four.

On the other hand, when she was forty-one, he moved her and his two daughters into the second largest house in Stratford. He went on buying other properties in and around the town. Tradition tells that he returned home every year, finally coming back there for good in about 1610. In other words, his tie to her – or at least to his family – was evidently strong. Then again, the impulse that had been insistent enough to establish him so famously on the London stage by the time he was twenty-eight had been, for years, much stronger. This suggests big upheavals in the early days. And the periodic aftershocks can be imagined. Not to speak of the curious complications that might have developed later, of the kind fantasized by Stephen Dedalus.

One thing that cannot be imagined is that he was unaware, when he came to plot *All's Well that Ends Well*, just how closely the story tracked his own domestic life, and particularly that most decisive move he ever made – his first flight from his wife (for whatever reason). And his continuing to stay away, except for those visits.

If he had happened to scribble on some (surviving) page of a notebook an account of being pursued by an infatuated woman, forced into marrying her by her powerful guardian, and then, after having escaped from her again, and thinking himself free, finding her in his arms when he was, as he thought, enjoying some adulterous conquest, it can be imagined what volumes of speculation would have been written about it. But the volumes would be equally divided. Though half would point out drily that it was clearly a note for the main theme of *All's Well*, the other half would find it much more interesting as a revealing and indeed obvious dream, the routine dream of countless men in his predicament.

The point seems simple and human enough, even if scholars do have to set it aside. When Shakespeare was writing *All's Well that Ends Well* the autobiographical secret sharer must have been breathing down his neck. To avoid it with a different plot, if he had wished to, would have been the simplest thing. But he must have searched out that specific plot for that specific reason – to deal in some way with that heavy breather.

Once this is accepted, then some points can be made – about his treatment of the characters and even the nature of the play – that cannot be made otherwise. And several features which otherwise seem strained or arbitrary become natural and perhaps inevitable.

All's Well: the ritual pattern

The relevant externals of the plot of *All's Well that Ends Well* are:

Helena, the daughter of the great physician now dead, adopted by Count Bertram's mother, is in love – 'total, unconditional love' – with Bertram, and has the consent and support of Bertram's mother in her hopeful passion. Young Count Bertram is impatient to be away to the French court and to life in the world. He is unaware of Helena's love, and gives her hardly a thought. The Count's companion, Parolles, recites to Helena the devil's catechism on chastity – a surreal demolition of the virtues of virginity.

The French King is dying of an incurable fistula. Helena, who possesses the near-magical cure for this, bequeathed to her by her late father, sees her opportunity to win the gratitude of the King, and thereby, maybe, Count Bertram as a husband – though she keeps her ultimate motive to herself. For this enterprise too, she wins the support and help of Bertram's mother.

At court, she cures the King. When he offers her as her reward anything in his gift, she chooses Bertram as a husband. The King enforces his word on Bertram, and Helena is married to the outraged, furiously resisting but finally obedient Count.

Bertram instantly flees to the wars in Italy, as an adventurer, among other lords, but notably in the company of Parolles, who urges him to defy both wife and King. In this passage, Bertram comes out with some heartfelt phrases:

> War is no strife
> To the dark house and the detested wife.
> *All's Well that Ends Well*, II. iii. 308–9

He calls his new bride his 'clog', and refusing her a first and parting kiss commands her:

Go thou toward home: where I will never come
While I can shake my sword or hear the drum.

II. v. 96–7

(He almost said 'shake my spear'.) Later he sends her a letter: he will never be her husband till she wears his ring and bears his child.

In Italy, Bertram espies a desirable beauty and lays plans to seduce her. He is, apparently, more intent on a conquest than infatuated, especially since this beauty (named after the goddess of chastity, Diana) is unassailably chaste – like Lucrece in *Lucrece* and like Isabella in *Measure for Measure*.

Meanwhile, in the guise of a pilgrim, Helena pursues Bertram to Italy. She meets this same Diana and her mother, at whose hostelry the pilgrims lodge, and hears of the Count's courtship. On the mother's own hint she contrives a way to consummate and seal her marriage to Bertram. Diana seems to surrender to Bertram's will, on the condition that he will give her his family ring and that their meeting shall take place in complete darkness, with no word spoken. Helena then takes her place in the bed, receives his ring and is impregnated by him.

Simultaneously, Bertram's bosom companion, Parolles, having lost the company's drum in a skirmish, is unmasked for the totally false and worthless fellow that he is.

Back at the French court everything is resolved. In front of the French King and the whole court, Helena reveals to Bertram the ring from his finger, her pregnancy, sired by him, and the entire story. Bertram is transformed, and vows that he will

love her dearly, ever, ever dearly.

v. iii. 321

If one sticks to the hypothesis that Shakespeare's self-dedication to the inward journey, which he seemed to make at the end of *As You Like It*, was absolutely serious, then *All's Well that Ends Well* fulfils the criteria for the next step.

Shakespeare starts his new life in orthodox fashion (like a resolute *sadhaka* – a beginner on the Holy Path) with an examination of his old one. Bertram becomes the token representative of that earlier self. This character's empty values, his callow wrongheadedness, are allegorized in his misvaluation of Helena and his petulant flight from her. Considering what this rejection of Helena becomes in later plays, it is interesting to notice just how Shakespeare portrays it here, in these lucid, opening moves, before the flames and smoke begin to obscure the basic issues. Bertram appears as an arrogant, aristocratic puppy, gadding and jigging, with sword and plume and codpiece, under the baleful, corrupt star of Parolles. The ethical character of his rejection of Helena, in other words, is objectified in the character of Parolles.

None of Shakespeare's later heroes, not even Angelo in *Measure for Measure*, seems so unlikeable, so utterly without any redeeming quality, as Bertram. If the portrait is a self-analysis, even allowing for the strong characterization and mythicization, it displays a remorseless kind of temper in Shakespeare's anatomization of his own doings. But since it is also a self-purgation, from which Bertram (as Shakespeare's persona) has to be rescued, his sins are externalized – into that figure of Parolles.

The real punishment is therefore reserved for Parolles. Everything that Shakespeare identifies as native to the counterfeit world of the lie is embodied in Parolles. As the man of the ostentatious, corrupt, glib word he is the natural opposite to what, in Helena, will eventually become the woman of the hidden, true, unutterable word in Cordelia. This 'jackanapes with scarves' is stripped, in that ritual humiliation and riddance which is so unforgettably painful, to the traumatized animal: 'simply the thing I am / Shall make me live' (IV. iii. 373–4). At that point Lafeu – the alchemical fire that has smoked and tried and now at a remove burned away this baseness from the true metal of the true Bertram – helps him up with 'you shall eat'. Few characters in the plays receive as little shrift as Bertram and Parolles, but maybe no other play reflects such a direct examination, by Shakespeare, of his own conscience, and such a decisive change in the direction of his inner life. This same scheme of self-correction helps to explain his treatment of Helena.

Shakespeare's guilt concerning his wife back in Stratford, which I projected earlier into a likely nightmare, might have been moon-dead or volcanic, or merely the attenuated concern of a practical necessity, but the situation alone, as I say, would be enough to suggest the role of Helena in a scheme of self-renovation. She incarnates the new spiritualized level from which Shakespeare conducts his correction of his own outgrown ego, Bertram. And reunion with her, at the end of the play, will thereby become the new spiritualized life. Everything in the text points Helena in that direction.

Her love, for instance, is the 'total, unconditional' love of Venus from the long poem – lacking only the 'lust'. She incorporates the Sacred

Bride rejected, the Divine Mother abandoned by son and consort, and the miracle-working Divine Love itself. That is to say, she incarnates Bertram's all-forgiving soul – searching for him to correct him and to redeem him into his new life, whether he likes it or not.

This aspect of Helena explains what – from a human point of view – might seem unattractive about her. Shakespeare treads a fine line. Her relentless pursuit of Bertram can only seem unscrupulous, unless we accept that, as his soul, she belongs to him, and he to her, and that unless she can outmanoeuvre his false indentity, they are both lost. This is a price paid for the carefully rigged ritual dimension of the play.

Her Divine nature also explains how, when she comes to wind her arms around him finally, she lifts him on to a plane where a miracle can happen. She transforms him in spite of himself, and in fact uses his most material act of infidelity to work the transformation. In her arms the theatrical mechanism of the bed trick becomes a sacrament. Bertram's heartless (Tarquinian) conquest of Diana, which is the nadir of his life of wilful error, becomes on the immediate level the consummation of his marriage with his never before embraced true wife, but on another level his breakthrough, her impregnation, into a new spiritual existence, and on that same level his reunion with his true self and his soul.

The scapegoat role of Parolles makes this clear. The unmasking of Parolles, which begins before Bertram's encounter with Helena in the dark, and ends after it, enacts, in cruel burlesque, the flaying of Bertram's false identity – the exorcism of his ignorance of his true self (a 'stripping' which anticipates the 'stripping' that precedes the rebirth in *King Lear*). It takes a little time, in the densely naturalized world of the play, for the revelation to clarify, but on seeing Parolles plucked naked, like a foolish cockerel, Bertram sees through his own moral stupor. His rejection of the phantasmagoria of the lie seems so suspiciously effortless because, in ritual terms, it has been done for him. And his 'total and unconditional' love of Helena, which on the naturalistic plane of the drama sounds more than a little hollow, if not incredible, on the ritual plane is revealed, quite simply, as inevitable.

In this sense, *All's Well that Ends Well* is like the first vision of Jaques/ Duke Frederick's quest, seen by the Duke, perhaps, and recorded by Jaques: an alchemical vision (the quasi-mythical psychology of alchemy is obtrusively visible here for the first time in the plays) unfolding in the higher dream, where the ailing King and the errant Bertram are two aspects of the one individual (the outgrown personality), and where

Helena, the divine corrector and truth of the soul, works on both the evil of the Bertram/Parolles compound and on the King's evil through the mediation of her alchemical fire – literally Lafeu. Fontibell/Diana becomes, so to speak, her crucible. The old self is corrected, the old evil identified, purged, banished and the new spiritual life embraced.

As such, *All's Well that Ends Well* inadvertently diagnoses, maybe, the real reason for Jaques's withdrawing into the forest in *As You Like It*. It illuminates that vivid sympathy between Jaques and the wounded stag which, like him, has withdrawn its horns from the herd, and over whose fate he weeps and ponders.

This is the place to remember (and take seriously) the arrow with which Cupid touched Shakespeare's breast in Sonnet 153. It made him 'sick withal' and drove him, 'a sad, distempered guest', to seek a cure in a spring that a 'maid of Diana's' had magically transformed into a healing fount – much as the solitary stag (sobbing, like Jaques) had brought its arrow wound to the forest brook. *All's Well that Ends Well* is the last play which is free from sexual disgust and it immediately precedes plays that are overwhelmed with a horror of sexual disease. At the same time it is notably the play with the strange theme of a semi-divine women who is also a doctor. She searches out the hero's mythic self – the soul-stricken Duke Frederick now evolved into an ailing monarch – to cure the disease of the French crown. (In the next play, *Measure for Measure*, 'French crown' means venereal disease.) Simultaneously, with the same recipe, this divine doctor rescues Jaques, now transmuted to Bertram/Parolles, the hero's real self, from the dissolute life and its consequences, and restores him through 'Fontibell' (the 'bath' or fountain of beauty who is actually Diana) to spiritual wholeness.

On this level, *All's Well that Ends Well* is an incantatory ritual, calling on the help of Divine Healing. Beneath the theological allegory of Helena's pursuit of Bertram as the soul's search for the lost or fallen ego runs the shamanic origin of the folktale – the healer's difficult transcendental journey. After this comes the boiling stew of sexual corruption in *Measure for Measure*, which bears the imprint of a desperate effort to be rid of sexual disease, and *Troilus and Cressida*, which swamps a painfully raw first-hand love affair beneath a mythic battle over 'the contaminated carrion weight' of the Renaissance ideal of feminine beauty, Helen, and signs off by bequeathing to the audience the sexual diseases of the man who brought Troilus and Cressida together, and whose last word is 'diseases'.

Whichever viewpoint one chooses, Shakespeare's ritual structure in *All's Well that Ends Well* dictates the details of the action, the patterned relationship of the characters, and the motivation of the characters themselves, to shape a magical operation which is continuous with that ritual closing scene of *As You Like It*.

I will make only one other point about the ritual aspect because once the key has been identified and turned, the rest opens. The point I want to make is exactly that – the nature of the key. Then I will get down to the Tragic Equation.

As I mentioned, the two Jaques in *As You Like It* are the only two figures in all the plays with that name. I suggested that they are in fact two aspects of one figure, being the two planes of Shakespeare's own unifying creative intelligence. But there is, of course, a third Jaques – in *All's Well that Ends Well*. He never appears. Only his name enters. But it enters at such a point, and in such a role, that it discloses the ritual meaning of the whole play. Shakespeare leaves this single key in the lock.

When Helena follows Bertram to Italy, intending to secure her husband's family ring and to conceive his child, in some magical fashion, against his will, she professes to be making a pilgrimage. If she succeeds, the consummation will be, as I say, the spiritual transformation of Bertram. And in so far as Bertram represents Shakespeare's own self, the ritual consummation of the play will be the spiritual transformation of Shakespeare himself, or at least the spiritual enlightenment of his 'Jaquesian' understanding. That Shakespeare devised the play with just this purpose in mind seems confirmed by that key. Helena's pilgrimage brings her towards two shrines. She claims to be heading for the one, Saint Jaques le Grand, but she actually arrives at the other. Both in fact are aspects of the *temenos* within which the sacramental transformation of Bertram is to take place. The shrine at which she arrives is that of Diana. Shakespeare takes pains to wire in that connection between the goddess of chastity and the quarry marked down by the sexual predator with Bertram's curious mistaking of her name, surprisingly pronounced in the first line of a scene, at their first meeting on stage, where he asks if she is not, as he thought, called 'Fontibell'. And when she corrects him with 'Diana', he exclaims: 'Titled goddess', as if the last thing on his mind were his plan to ravish her. In association with the titled goddess Diana, Fontibell can only mean 'fountain goddess', or 'the beauty in Diana's fountain', an ominous name for any Actaeon who should peep at her naked, as Bertram intends to.* By taking the place of this surrogate goddess of chastity, Helena conceives Bertram's child while he, his old self torn to tatters (like Actaeon and like Parolles), is reborn into the new spiritual life. That is to say, he is rechristened in Diana's font, into that greater or so to speak primary aspect of the shrine – that of Saint Jaques le Grand. The carefully constructed ritual purpose of *All's Well that Ends Well*, in other words, is to transform whoever corresponds to Jaques, and to deliver him into the *Vita Nuova* of a spiritualized life, pointedly identified by that anticipatory canonization of Jaques into spiritual greatness.

This is how the mind works in occult ritual. The figures are each precisely coded, before the programme is run through on the mythic plane, in ritual performance. This elaborate procedure, as a practical method of piloting himself across the high seas of the soul's journey, would be as familiar to Shakespeare as to Yeats.

If it sounds unlikely and a little fantastic, once again, one can only remember how much more unlikely and fantastic was the unprecedented, never to be repeated spiritual illumination which Shakespeare's mythic and realistic understanding, his 'Jaquesian' understanding, did attain within the next two or three years, and in fact with the first draft of Hamlet, probably within the next year. Perhaps such a method of soul-making seems unlikely only because the cultural context of his ritual operations was so utterly lost when the ultimately victorious orthodoxy of the Restoration swept Occult Neoplatonism and Prospero into the pit, with Sycorax.

All's Well: entry of the Mythic Equation

In *All's Well that Ends Well* the myth appears as a single sequence of events, but the two parts of it – the first corresponding to *Venus and Adonis* and the second to *Lucrece* – are still only loosely connected. Not until the following play, *Measure for Measure*, does Shakespeare integrate the two parts dynamically with explosive (though not yet

*Actaeon, the hunter, watched Diana bathing naked in a fountain. Lest he should boast of the sight, she changed him into a stag, whereupon his own hounds hunted him down and tore him to pieces.

tragic) effect, into what is recognizably the Equation. And in that play the factors of the Equation begin to reveal their algebraic or mythic values fairly distinctly. The working of the myth in the preceding play, *All's Well*, therefore, will be seen more clearly in retrospect, once the discussion of *Measure for Measure* has been read.

Meanwhile, however (though it will mean repeating one or two things later), I will sketch the working skeleton of the myth – or the cartilaginous rudiments of it – as it operates in the plot of *All's Well*, while the outline is still fresh.

The two parts of the myth divide the play into two parts. Bertram's flight from Helena, alias his petulant rejection of her 'total, uncon- ditional love', of his soul (Divine Love), recapitulates Adonis's rejection of Venus, producing the first movement of the play. His determined, forceful, heartless despoliation of the chaste woman Diana (as he thinks) recapitulates Tarquin's assault on Lucrece, and produces the second movement of the play. The pattern, it might be said, especially in the Tarquin episode, is rather faint. And there seems to be no organic connection, no inevitable connection, between the two halves. The young man who will blankly neglect the woman who dotes on him yet desperately pursue the woman who rejects him is a proverbial common- place, at worst the mechanical reversal that supplied the symmetry for Shakespeare's old plot-schema, at best a human truth that gave his schema its simple strength and authentic feeling.

Certain details begin to identify it. As I have said, the fact that Bertram's mother is, so to speak, incorporated within Helena's infatu- ated pursuit completes the Divine Mother/Sacred Bride fusion with the figure of Aphrodite/Venus. And Helena's healing gift – her ability to heal the King who should heal others – is a ray breaking through from her hidden divinity.

Adonis's mania for hunting corresponds, as a manly pursuit, to Bertram's light-headed mania for adventures in war. The absence, in Bertram, of Adonis's Puritan rigour is consistent, maybe, with his role as a self-portrait of the author (up to a point) and with the harmless, disarming face of the myth in this first, tentative emergence (the dangerous point is concealed). Even so Bertram finds himself going through the motions. If anything he is more vehement and absolute in rejecting Helena than Adonis was in rejecting Venus, as if he truly did see something that threatened his life.

Because there is no doctrinal razor of the Puritan manifesto in

Bertram's act of rejection, there is no Queen of Hell, and therefore no 'double vision', therefore no charge of the Boar, therefore no convulsive transformation of personality, no madness – and as a result, almost no drama.

Nevertheless, the Equation's magnetic field is already taking control. If in Helena's passion there is no rustle of a voluptuously sexual threat – no hint in the underbrush of infernal lust – still the Queen of Hell, biding her time, has sent Parolles to reconnoitre. He appears, like Mephistopheles – out of nowhere – the moment Helena announces her idolatrous passion for Bertram. He simply pops up as the unholy *doppelgänger* of her holy love – the Queen of Hell's proxy. From the first moment he is fully in character. He promptly establishes his infernal relationship to female chastity, to sacred, female, faithful love, to the truth and integrity of the loving aspect of the Goddess, so eloquently, with such sudden ferocity, one might almost say so rabidly, in his magnificent gasconade against virginity, that nothing could possibly justify it, here in the play (or at this point in the play), except as a metaphysical requirement of the newly emerged myth – presenting that third component, the absent Queen of Hell's near presence, to make up the totality of the Goddess. This is a sharp enough instance of just how, at every doubtful point, and even here where, as I say, it had hardly broken through into consciousness, that subterranean magnetic field of the Tragic Myth imposes its design. Parolles is a free-floating, cynical reflection of the Queen of Hell, much as Lucio will be in *Measure for Measure*, as Thersites will be in *Troilus and Cressida* and Iago in *Othello* – a peculiarly sinister form of the irrational 'usurping brother' who operates by suggestion and osmosis rather than by forthright assault. Meanwhile the Queen of Hell remains invisible to Bertram because the factors of the Equation are still so loosely articulated and muted, and Shakespeare himself is still uncertain perhaps what to make of it.

In a similar loose and muted form, the constituents of the second half of the Equation, corresponding to *Lucrece*, are present in the latter half of the play. Bertram swings from the Adonis phase into the Tarquin not by becoming possessed and transformed, but simply by subordinating his judgement and attuning his life to the wavelength of Parolles. He does change his behaviour but in unsurprising fashion. The Tarquin in him is not a madness, rigidly suppressed and denied, then just as violently succumbed to. It could be said that the 'hot tyrant' is there all the time, or at least a cold reflection of his existence is there, like a detached component of his irrational self, the 'irrational brother' who does not so much usurp him as coerce him without effort – the rascal Parolles, trotting along beside him, lewd, lying and treacherous, not a formidable wild boar but a tawdry minor bailiff of Persephone. And Helena as suppliant Venus becomes, without dramatic recoil, Helena as violated Diana/Lucrece.

At this apparently inadvertent discovery of what will be the Tragic Equation, Shakespeare has not located its explosive potential, or worked out how to detonate it, let alone how to contain the consequences.

The symbolic implications and substance of both myths – the two plots of the long poems – have emerged completely enough to make themselves felt, to decide interpretations, and to tax the language to its utmost, yet they are still only juxtaposed, entangled rather than dramatically connected. They function as a single, symmetrical design, and as a mythic template for Helena's sacred mission and for Bertram's sin, purgation and redemption. They stop short of formulating the Equation because, for one thing, that would have disrupted the focal self-portrait necessary for the play's ritual function, destroying its potency as a planned magical operation for the author's own benefit. And he needs Bertram's lust to be repulsively cool and deliberate, an act of conceit, if it is to characterize the antithesis of love, the sin without one redeeming feature. At this point, Shakespeare might possibly say, it was more important to get the ritual right than to be overcome by the premature excitement of a coincidental artistic revelation. He could save that for the next plays, *Measure for Measure* and *Troilus and Cressida*.

The three sources of *All's Well that Ends Well*

Once the mythic form of the Equation becomes quite clear, some Shakespeareans will notice a multiple coincidence, which seems worth a comment.

I have traced the Equation's mythic lineage back from *All's Well*, through the two long narratives, to its sources in the two great early myths. I took particular note of the fact that the crucial event in the collision of the two myths, in modern or ancient history, was the same as in Shakespeare's Equation – the rejection of the Goddess by the god.

And I pointed out how the demonization of the Goddess, or of one half of her, as a result of this rejection, was fully anticipated in the original mythic splitting of the Great Goddess into an Aphrodite figure (Mother and Sacred Bride) and a Persephone figure (Queen of Hell), in the various traditions. (Elsewhere I refer to an even earlier, aboriginal source of this combat with the Great Witch, see pages 327–8). According to this lineage, the Equation is itself a primordial mythic structure, like an elemental law in physics. Shakespeare somehow picked it out of the electrified Elizabethan atmosphere, and conducted it through his two long poems into his drama at *All's Well that Ends Well*.

Then again, I suggested that he unearthed the main complex of this equation from his own subjectivity, as he analysed it in the *Sonnets*. According to this, it would seem that the Equation, or the main active elements of it at least, originated not only in prehistoric myth but there too, inborn, within his own nature.

And again, in the discussion of *All's Well*, I made the observation that Bertram's rejection of Helena (with all its consequences), while it sketches out the first complete mythic outline of the Equation, can be read at the same time as Shakespeare's examination and correction of his own life, assuming that his flight from his wife, and his prolonged separation from her, was one of the dominant unsettled questions of his solitary existence.

Here are three different sources of the Equation: one in historical myth and religious conflict, one in the accidents of his biography, and one innate, all turning on that same perverse event – the hero's compulsive rejection of the love-consecrated female.

It could be said that the three sources are not really so different, but are actually three aspects of the one source. Innate temperament is biography: the subjective requirements simply work out in linear form through time. And it seems likely that a particular innate temperament comes to full artistic expression only where it is in some way a microcosmic image of the age, or of the moment perhaps. As if the unique psychic configuration of Shakespeare's nature, and the unique psychic configuration of the English Reformation between 1590 and 1610, were by chance images of each other – and of the Equation.

Something of the kind would explain why Shakespeare, as a very young man, a very young dramatist, when he wanted a good idea for a plot, went straight to the Equation even in those earliest plays – *The Two Gentlemen of Verona, The Comedy of Errors, The Taming of the*

Shrew, long before the mythic blood suddenly flushes through the veins of *All's Well that Ends Well*.

The practical explanation of this can only be that somehow, by the time he came to those first surviving plays, he was already experienced enough, as a practical dramatist, to have hit on his own first-class prototype design for a basic plot. But he can have had little idea, in those early days, just what he had discovered, or what its potentials were. Although, as he went on to prove, it was precisely this Equation, this key, that (when the double myth had given him the combination) unlocked the tragic vision, sealed for two thousand years, yet those early plays demonstrate quite clearly that it occurred to him, first of all (and *already combined* with the Rival Brothers), as a windfall comic idea. Right up to *Twelfth Night* it worked hard and well for him – as the formula for an unfailing (but slightly cruel, somewhat disturbing) joke.

Throughout these early plays it remains abstract, schematic, exploratory – as he permutates its variations, and tests its effects on the increasing abundance of his love conflicts and comic realism. It resembles a physicist's mathematical hypothesis – which predicts, anticipates in some detail, and finally guides him to the real structure and the real laws of matter and space. From beginning to end of his career, that is, the Equation is consistent with itself, and its development is a continuum. It goes through only the one substantial metamorphosis, there in *All's Well*, where theory, so to speak, becomes practice, where the elegant choreography of the known becomes an astrolabe plunging into the unknown, and where the playwright's workaday plot-schema is suddenly possessed by the Equation of archaic religious war, the Equation of domestic fate, the Equation out of the spinal cord: the Equation as a psycho-biological tragic myth.

The Equation, in other words, led him straight to his subject, and indeed finally gave him his subject, which might be called, generally, the fate of love. But even though it takes him twenty plays to get to the mythic core of the real thing (apart from those isolated outcrops of Aaron, Richard III, Shylock, Falstaff, Bottom and Titania, etc.), the subject, like the Equation and the Rival Brothers, is centrally there from the outset. And like the Equation, it goes through the one big change, and at the same point. Always setting the Histories slightly to one side, the fate of this love, up to *As You Like It*, could be described as love's tribulations in the world of misfortune, malice and morality. And throughout those plays the delights and difficulties are moulded out of a

Renaissance erotic sensibility that seems familiar and, in a sense, conventional – abnormal only in the absolute intensity of its declarations. After the big change in *All's Well that Ends Well* the tribulations of love are still tribulations. But now they could be described as the Tragedy of Divine Love in the fallen world of the 'Puritan' ego. And the sufferings are hacked out of the unearthly substance of the Goddess. Yet it is still the Equation that forces this tragedy, through sheer spiritual stress, into transformation and its own redemption, where the Goddess is made whole – albeit only provisionally (in *The Winter's Tale*). And finally it is the Equation which, in *The Tempest*, returns that transformation to elemental reality, restates the tragedy, and salvages what can be salvaged.

It would certainly be interesting to know Shakespeare's impressions of what exactly was happening in his imagination as he composed *All's Well that Ends Well*. There must be some explanation for the mismatch between the cool, coolly planned exterior and the unprecedented, subterranean turbulence. Perhaps his attention was so purposefully fixed on this work as a soul-making ritual that he was not altogether aware of what figures were rising out of the depth – trying on his old plot pattern, and maybe that parable of his marriage, like second-hand clothes. On the other hand, as I have argued, all the signs are that he knew exactly what he was doing. And yet he shows no awareness, at this point, of just where it might lead – if he combined the two violent, antithetical heroes of the two violent myths into the one hero in the one story. Possibly he thought he was updating Proteus, from *The Two Gentlemen of Verona*. He seems to have had no inkling, in other words, of the daemonic potential within the Equation's new mythic form. That was the new factor, after all: the *mythic* dimension. *All's Well* remains an introverted, self-enclosed, self-absorbed play. When the finished article turned out to be so disturbingly radiant, and yet such a cold fish on stage, he probably had little idea what a prodigious new form of life had 'slipped idly from him'.

Shakespeare's double language and the verbal device

Just as the opposed forms of the two myths have combined in the plot of *All's Well*, so their antithetical worlds have combined in the play's language, which suddenly becomes – in a way peculiar to the verse from now onwards – double.

Eliot's remark, that Shakespeare did the work of at least two poets – one who simplified the language and another who then elaborated it into patterns of increasing complexity of sound and sense – can be applied to the abrupt division in the oeuvre which comes where the Tragic Equation enters at *All's Well*.

The first poet evolves, in a steady progress of simplification, from the rigid, hectic rhetoric of the common dramatic pool of the late 1580s, which characterizes *Henry VI*, to the limpid music of the middle plays: the humble, relaxed, scrupulous, clear-eyed service of the matter in hand, with its open, smooth-bodied warmth, which characterizes *Twelfth Night* and *As You Like It*.

The second poet is certainly there, quite suddenly, in *All's Well*. From this point, the dicotyledon of the new language swiftly ramifies, oak-fashion, almost convulsively. Sound and sense become more tortuous and robust: and within two or three plays the music has fully adapted itself to the abnormal emotion and thunderbolts of high tragedy.

Eliot's remark says nothing of the fact that the earlier process of simplification continues even after the second process of complication has taken over. While the second poet now produces constantly richer compounds, the first poet – as obedient assistant – continues to work away, refining the basic elements. Eventually that process of simplification emerges again – beyond the complications. Or rather, at a certain point – a very curious and significant point – the complexity and simplicity melt into each other (like Hermaphroditus and Salmacis) in a language more intricately fluid and musically subtle, and yet at the same time more simple and direct, as dramatic statement, than anything before it in the plays. There again, that later change also corresponds to a decisively new phase in the evolution of the Tragic Equation, and enters almost abruptly with the growing point of what could be called, almost literally, a final flowering.

The ultimate 'simplicity' of the first poet was a momentous invention in English poetry. Milton, in *Comus*, requisitions it as directly as his temperament permitted. And ever since, it has reappeared, as a prototype norm, wherever English poets have tried to find that presumably natural yet evidently elusive vocal pitch of 'a man speaking to men'. Its protean durability and resource have survived every social change. But with *All's Well*, Shakespeare seems to have invented a kind of verse, and mounted on a flight, that no poet in English has managed to follow.

At its first appearance here, in *All's Well*, the composite myth of the Equation is like 'an unlicked bear-cub', and barely breathing. But apparently that is enough. And the upheavals in the depths begin to boil at the surface.

The effect is instantaneous. The complexity of all his operations takes a quantum leap. The massive new polyphony emerges in surprising swells, to overwhelm and almost smother the soloists. When the King suddenly bursts out with:

> We thank you, maiden,
> But may not be so credulous of cure,
> When our most learned doctors leave us, and
> The congregated college have concluded
> That labouring art can never ransom nature
> From her inaidable estate; I say we must not
> So stain our judgement, or corrupt our hope,
> To prostitute our past-cure malady
> To empirics, or to dissever so
> Our great self and our credit . . .
> *All's Well that Ends Well*, II. i. 117–26

more is suddenly happening than Shakespeare was quite ready for. As if to take forcible control of it, he writes the rest of that scene – seventy lines or more – in rhymed couplets.

At the same time, generally, there enters a sense of widely disparate and even incompatible worlds of discourse and association being yoked quite violently together within single figures of speech – a simultaneity of conflicting effects. The uniquely hyperactive mechanisms of his mature poetry can almost be seen assembling themselves. This crush of sudden innovations is epitomized in particular by a Shakespearean verbal device which now takes on an emergency function, and becomes, in a sense, characteristic of the language from this play onwards.

Since this 'device' is conscripted, at this point, by the Tragic Equation, I will say a little more about it. It crystallizes the direct influences – on his language – of the Equation, but also of much more, and the simplest way to anatomize it, probably, is to look at some of these other factors. The most striking example of the 'device', in the livery of its new office, here in *All's Well*, occurs where the mortally sick French King is reminiscing to the young Count Bertram about the youth of Bertram's father, who was the King's close friend:

'Let me not live,' –
Thus his good melancholy oft began,
On the catastrophe and heel of pastime,
When it was out, – 'Let me not live,' quoth he,
'After my flame lacks oil, to be the snuff
Of younger spirits . . .'

I. ii. 55–60

That third line brings one to a halt. Here is the uniquely Shakespearean effect, concentrated in all its mature idiosyncrasy – his very signature.

That little formula – two nouns linked by an 'and' (or it can be two adjectives) directing their combined and contrasting meanings on to a third word, always a noun, in a way that startles all three words into odd metaphorical life – has been often enough discussed. What I want to define is just how this 'odd, metaphorical life' is suddenly, in *All's Well*, recognizably different from anything before. It is impossible to imagine this line occurring in any earlier play. It would simply rip the fabric. Yet something like it occurs from quite early on.

The evolutionary history of the verbal device

In *Titus Andronicus* Tamora is creating atmosphere for a murder:

They told me, here, at the dead time of the night,
A thousand fiends, a thousand hissing snakes,
Ten thousand swelling toads, as many urchins,
Would make such fearful and confused cries,
As any mortal body hearing it
Should straight fall mad, or else die suddenly.

Titus Andronicus, II. iii. 99–104

The fourth line is common stock, and 'fearful and confused cries' looks like a piece of journeyman's filler, making up the full pentameter. He could have switched plan and written:

Would make such cries, that any hearing it
Should straight fall mad, or else die suddenly.

But obviously he needed the full line, better the two full lines, to lift the long crescendo, after those three units of heavy caesura, and bring the whole lot full tilt on to the Marlovian line that he was really trying to drive into the back wall of the theatre:

[132]

Should straight fall mad, or else die suddenly.

So the fourth line had to be a full pentameter – therefore filler.

He also needed something spittingly adjectival – a slight frothing at the lips – to convert those fiends, snakes, toads and urchins into subjective horror, something mouth-filling, but not so much as to gag her or distract her with anything too thoughtful as she raced through the Hecate horrors that she was conjuring around her head. As Yeats said, 'some words have to be numb'. And if one replaces the 'and' with an extra adjectival syllable one sees a justification for that gnomic little dictum.

Would make such fearful, soul-confounding cries

makes Tamora stumble. The line simply loses vernacular, throw-away pace, falters out of character (different adjectives might do better) and loses realism – loses, that is, natural, subjective fury, tilting ever so slightly towards analysis and description – not because more adjective has come in but because something has gone.

The 'and', it seems, is not only filler, but a symbol – or vehicle – of the impassioned, headlong flight of the communicating voice, which is looking beyond words, wants only to unburden itself, and may find other words later. It oxygenates the bulk of verbal meaning with a spirit of pure, naked expressiveness – the naked tone, between signals, of the urgent human carrier wave.

At the same time, the two adjectives begin to look less perfunctory. 'Fearful' bears the two opposite meanings of 'full of fear' and 'causing fear'; 'confused' means only 'suffering from confusion'. When the two words are combined in this way – that is, separated for distinction and comparison to be made by that 'and' – while the context evokes the active sense of 'fearful', the participle 'confused' activates its passive sense. The line then creates a dramatic scene, in which fiends, snakes, toads and urchins are making noises so frightful that they themselves are terrified by them and so are crying worse – in a howl-back amplification of their own cries, an especially diabolical idea of infinite terror in a dark wood: existence terrified by its own existence.

On the other hand, maybe that effect was pure chance, and the words were jammed in as filler. But very soon after, the formula begins to find its feet.

In *Richard III*, there occur:

> A beauty-waning and distressed widow
>
> *Richard III*, III. vii. 184

and:

> Seduc'd the pitch and height of his degree
>
> III. vii. 187

and, perhaps within the same year, in *Richard II*:

> Be judg'd by subject and inferior breath
>
> *Richard II*, IV. i. 128

and:

> The tediousness and process of my travel.
>
> II. iii. 12

Supposing that the example from *Titus Andronicus* (and many others, similar, elsewhere) was filler, it is evident that something more purposeful is going on in the examples above. The most evident effect is of a sort of regal gesture, a ritualized flurry of the stately, a small 'grand' moment.

It was more than a stage mannerism. There is little doubt that Shakespeare delighted in 'stateliness' – to the point of infatuation. The huge proportion of his work devoted to kings and their courts being 'stately' and 'ceremonious' was satisfying a powerful hunger. It touched those 'strong shudders' and 'heavenly agues' that stirred in the base of his spine. His addiction to the 'grand' was like a permanent psychological pressure. It is one aspect of his sheer sense of theatre, of what suddenly hushes the groundlings and makes the gods listen, but was no small part of the tremendous sense of 'things high and working, full of state and woe' for which he was able eventually to create a whole new kind of drama. These lines speak directly for that ear.

Having said this much, one can feel in these examples, from the two *Richards*, even in this still fairly low category of function, that there is more to it. In each case, it seems clear enough that the two qualifiers are being weighed against each other – across the fulcrum of that 'and' – with conscious deliberation.

In general, each word supplies a different point of view, usually the objective and subjective in some sense. In the first example:

A beauty-waning and distressed widow,

the first 'beauty-waning' is the observer's contribution, the second the widow's own. The interesting result of this, however, is that the phrase becomes a mini dumb dialogue of the outer widow and the inner – two figures fixed in a somewhat hieratic pose, strongly lit – the 'and' representing the space of stage between them, and their angle of confrontation.

In the second example, the two qualifiers seem tautologous enough to resemble a cut and a slash, or the right barrel then the left for good measure (and for filler). Yet 'pitch' carries the idea of the height from which a falcon might dangerously stoop – might pitch, in fact. In other words it brings 'height' as a threat into hovering balance with 'height' as a dignity – a fateful uncertainty everywhere in these plays about pathological kings.

In the third example, in a straightforward way 'subject' and 'inferior' are the king's view of the outside and the inside of the breather – what ought to be his formal, servile relationship to the king, and what ought to be his inner, slavish reality. But the opening words of:

Be judg'd by subject and inferior breath

having already introduced the idea of the breather as the king's judge, adds to the word 'subject' the idea of a sword of justice, and to the word 'inferior' the idea of 'superior'. The first half of the combination now presents an inversion of social hierarchy, the second an inversion of psychological values. Without being complicated or obscure – being, in fact, fairly obvious and open – this line has nevertheless become the essential Shakespearean scene, the king's confrontation with the victorious rebel.

The fact that those opening words 'Be judg'd by' are no integral part of the device, yet incorporate it and are incorporated (are dramatically analysed and amplified) so naturally by it, begins to reveal just how the rigging of the device and the whole structure of Shakespeare's dramatic imagination, his 'system', are based on the same architectonics – the same cat's cradle of antithetical values. The fact already suggests how any big structural change in that geometry of his system (as when the Tragic Equation arrives) will be expressed directly and precisely in the terms of the device.

The fourth example:

The tediousness and process of my travel,

slightly affected, maybe, by the dreariness of its freight (miming its meaning), nevertheless shows the same instinct – to render the wholeness of the scene by dramatizing two contrasting points of view. 'Tediousness' takes care of the inside point of view, the subjective impression of what had to be undergone, while 'process' accounts for the external record, the actual onerous sequence of obstacles, logistical problems, inconvenience, and so on.

In all these instances, what strikes one is how the work of the 'and' is vital to the dramatic life of the phrase. Where the two qualifiers are nouns, there is no way to avoid it. But where they are adjectives, when it could conceivably be removed, its removal is always fatal. 'A beauty-waning, distressed widow' is vivid in her way – but she is no longer two formal figures facing each other, and the audience, across a vibrant space of squared stage: she is a crumpled heap, and 'beauty-waning', deprived of its formality, has become awkwardly self-conscious, she seems overdressed, the tension of drama has evaporated.

That his 'system' and what we know as 'Shakespeare' are one thing becomes evident when the system is almost absent. Since the 'system' is the drama of his drama, the driving conflict within his work, this pressure can slacken noticeably when the mode is narrative. In the Act Four opening chorus of *Henry V*, the following lines occur:

Proud of their numbers, and secure in soul,
The confident and over-lusty French
Do the low-rated English play at dice;
And chide the cripple tardy-gaited night,
Who, like a foul and ugly witch, doth limp
So tediously away.

Henry V, IV. Ch. 17–22

There is some but not much dramatic activity between the two adjectives of the second line, less between the two of the fourth line. The tautologous cliché of the fifth line is like the last gasp of exhaustion. Words here, one could say, are being used as filler. Mime of meaning, maybe, has got the upper hand. But what is missing from the whole passage is any aspect of the hidden geometrical relationships (which everywhere in the dialogue are expressed by that naked drama in each

[136]

line) of the tensed ethical system of the play, which in turn is an image of some aspect of Shakespeare's total, metaphysical system.

One more example, to illustrate again this last point in particular, out of that same play, *Henry V*, comes when Henry exhorts his men to manic fury before the assault on Harfleur:

> Then lend the eye a terrible aspect;
> Let it pry through the portage of the head
> Like the brass cannon; let the brow o'erwhelm it
> As fearfully as doth a galled rock
> O'erhang and jutty his confounded base,
> Swill'd with the wild and wasteful ocean.
>
> III. i. 9–14

Here 'wild and wasteful' tumble past without exciting special attention – and might do so only to be suspected of being filler. But the line has a technical oddity of its own: it contains three 'wills' – the first two intact, the third overturned and broken, with a wail, on the rocks (as the assault will disintegrate in the confusion of the sacked city). Looking then at 'wild and wasteful' one sees that while Henry, in trumpet tones, urges his men to battle frenzy, Shakespeare is making a homiletic point contrabasso: 'wild equals wasteful'. The two words twinned by that 'and' reach forward to the later speech which threatens his next assault on the same city:

> And the flesh'd soldier, rough and hard of heart,
> In liberty of bloody hand shall range,
> With conscience wide as hell, mowing like grass
> Your fresh fair virgins and your flowering infants.
> What is it then to me, if impious war,
> Array'd in flames like to the prince of fiends,
> Do, with his smirch'd complexion, all fell feats
> Enlink'd to waste and desolation?
>
> III. iii. 11–18

And via that image's little formula, 'wild equals wasteful' reaches directly through into every corner of Shakespeare's apocalyptic vision of civil chaos and 'blood and destruction'.

What appears with muted but firm insistence in this example is that the 'and' is a symbol for 'equals' or 'means'. That is to say, he is presenting 'wild' as a new or not commonly understood word, and saying: 'What this actually means is – "wasteful"', i.e. massacre of children, rape and massacre of virgins.

In this sense, the device has found a new model of possible use. In those earlier examples, this kind of use, it might be said, was latent: 'Beauty-waning' means (for the widow) 'distressed'. But here it is more active, more instructive. The model is that of the word primer, the dictionary.

The double language as translation

Shakespeare's vocabulary is around 25,000 words. The nearest, among English classical authors, is Milton with 12,000. Shakespeare as a word collector – as a successful naturalizer of words to his own use – was in a class of his own. One supposes words simply stuck to him, like tunes to an Irish piper. But he states his own experience, that a strange word had to be 'looked upon and learned', and he clearly worked upon his vocabulary in some systematic way.

There is plenty of evidence that the popular appetite for a new language among Shakespeare's contemporaries was euphorically intense, as never before or since. Presumably this was one aspect of the shared avidity of frustrated religious passions, the suppressed Reformation search for the ultimate argument, plus the sudden opening of new, strange worlds, which constituted being an Elizabethan.

During those decades the language expanded at enormous speed. Words from the classical languages, in particular, poured into learned use, and from there into popular literature. Thousands aborted, thousands strutted and fretted their hour, but a great many got a hold. With some authors this liking for new words became a mania, a collector's craze. And Shakespeare, according to the evidence, was more susceptible to this craze than any other.

The 'craze' had social forms: the educated elite introduced and brandished the new words, as a style of distinction and superiority, and keenly appreciated skilled performance, while the middle classes strove to appropriate them, and the groundlings coveted them. Shakespeare observed and made use of these humours, each with its foible. In other words, this passion for language, like the passion for passion, was something he could rely on, across the whole gamut of his audience, that famous, Globe audience – a microcosm of the English population of his day. It was a situation which created, for those dramatists, a unique opportunity, but also a unique problem, such as no other generation of English authors has ever had to face in quite such urgent form. The problem was compounded by the simultaneous double dependence of the Elizabethan theatre on the highest and lowest levels of this microcosmic audience.

Since the patronage of the educated aristocracy and the court was crucial, in that they defended and kept the theatres open against the incessant efforts of the London Council (with its Puritan tendency) to close them, the jury of sophisticated nobility that assembled daily at the Globe, demanding intellectual gratification, had to be satisfied. Shakespeare (as anxious theatre manager, theatre co-owner, actor and dramatist) wrote first and foremost for these essential patrons.

This noble section of his audience was not only besotted with language, and addicted to new verbal forms and expressions, it was the most imaginatively excited and most formidably educated elite that England has ever possessed. Shakespeare's achievement must be in some way a measure of their cultural tastes, their capacity and their experience. As it happened, he was inclined of his own bent to give them what they wanted. The spiritual conflict of the age, which so preoccupied his imagination, was exactly what determined their supercharged, perilous, occasionally spectacular lives. In this sense these lives were a product of the 'common dream', the buried conflict of the whole population, that I described earlier. They were another kind of symbol, emerging into social, political reality, of the same historical pressures that produced the symbols of Shakespeare's drama. And by seeming to draw his plays, at their most intellectually sophisticated level, from the autobiographical self-preoccupation of the nobility (and of the most sensitive and ambitious of his own kind), Shakespeare was actually dealing with the violent and smothered dream of the entire population, down to the lowest pickpocket's 'trug'. The all-inclusive scope and inexhaustible, rooted depth of his vision was drawing therefore not on any particular part of his audience but on all of it simultaneously. This inclusive wholeness is presumably what prompted his instinct, in the first place, to find 'a local habitation and a name' for it, in a language that was somehow common to all. But it was practical necessity that converted the instinct into a motive, and the motive into a priority. While the 'high' audience controlled the legislation that kept the theatres open, and provided the living gallery of types and fates for the kind of theatre that interested him, clearly he needed the 'low' and middle audience to make it pay. From the way he dealt with them (and from the way some of his colleagues complained about them), it would seem that he recognized the problems as problems. Ideally, the play-wright who rose to the demands of the nobility had to dive, simultaneously, to the demands of the groundlings. With such a mediumistic author as Shakespeare, whose compelling theme happened to be an extreme case of the common psychic conflict, the commercial dilemma became a national opportunity. A true 'language of the common bond' in drama, at every level of theme, action and speech, became essential. And, in finding it, Shakespeare invented, as if incidentally and inadvertently, a new kind of drama and a new poetic vernacular.

His solution, especially obvious at the verbal level, was a response to his predicament, purely and simply. And in this sense the situation created the man. But he did make his predicament uniquely acute – far more acute, for instance, than Jonson made his – by his perverse insistence on using such a huge number of the new words. Dramatists tend to limit their vocabulary, in the interest of immediacy, as a short cut to a common language. They know, as any public speaker knows, that an unfamiliar, recherché word can lose an audience unless something is done about it very quickly. The problem is so real that all writers or speakers who hope for a popular audience obey the rule as a law: avoid strange, complicated, new words, except as technical terms (when they carry a certain chic thrill) or as in-group slang or for comic effect. Yet Shakespeare managed to introduce a steady flow of new words, a large proportion of which would be novelties and utterly foreign to most of his audience, and most of which he used only once or twice, in what turned out to be massively successful 'language of the common bond'. We might well wonder how he did it. However much that lower (essential) audience thrilled to the voguish glamour of a splendid new word, the problem was there – the new word had to communicate something somehow. He could rely on the nobility to give it instant meaning: they would simply translate it through Latin or Greek. But what about the rest?

Up to *Twelfth Night* and *As You Like It*, composed just before *All's Well that Ends Well*, the vocabulary is large but not adventurous or unorthodox. At that time Shakespeare was still responding to those pressures for a comprehensible common language by refining his gifts of simplicity and intimate directness. But then – under whatever abrupt compulsion – the passion to share his passion for the new words seized him with a vengeance. Perhaps he thought to gratify the noble patrons as nobody else could, in that competitive business. Already, in *Twelfth Night*, the stirrings of this become intrusive and in the same play he airs his solution to the problem.

His solution is, in a sense, almost makeshift in its extempore self-adaptation to the need. He does what every public speaker does when that over-recondite word slips out. He interprets it, or translates it, with one or two better-known synonyms, or an explanatory simple phrase, or even a metaphor. With normal resources this can only be done now and again, or it becomes ridiculous. But Shakespeare converts what might have become – with so many new words – a disaster into the richest element of his speech. To do this he requisitions what is already uniquely his own: he adapts his 'device', and patents a little mechanism of translation. This gave him all he needed: he could now speak the high language and the low language, simultaneously, at top speed, as if they were one vividly comprehensible language.

Most of the verse in *Twelfth Night* displays the ultimate mastery of that first simplifying Shakespeare. But the famous opening passage, one of the most carefully written in the whole play, moves through a limpid musicality to a sudden lexicographical flourish at the end:

> If music be the food of love, play on;
> Give me excess of it, that surfeiting,
> The appetite may sicken and so die.
> That strain again, it had a dying fall;
> O, it came o'er my ear like the sweet sound
> That breathes upon a bank of violets,
> Stealing and giving odour. Enough, no more,
> 'Tis not so sweet now as it was before.
> O spirit of love, how quick and fresh art thou,
> That, notwithstanding thy capacity
> Receiveth as the sea, nought enters there,
> Of what validity and pitch soe'er
> But falls into abatement and low price,
> Even in a minute.
>
> *Twelfth Night*, I. i. 1–14

The three words here that might have given his groundlings pause are 'capacity', 'validity' and 'abatement'. Shakespeare provides each one with special treatment. 'Capacity' is immediately reduced to a plain image: 'Receiveth as the sea'. In other words, it is translated: 'capacity' = wider horizons, unfathomed roominess, ability to contain an infinite amount. In a similar way, 'validity', which was probably a new word to most, used only in law, is translated by 'pitch', which was a common word meaning height, or calibrated position on a scale. 'Validity' becomes thereby, immediately, 'place on a scale of values'. He deals with 'abatement' even more plainly. While he tosses the fine word to the Lords' box, he bends to the groundlings and quite shamelessly adds 'that means a cutback to . . . "low price" '. None of these are full-blown specimens of his 'device', where the two balanced words qualify a third, but all demonstrate the new principle that now goes through his usage like a new common law: 'any unfamiliar word from the "high" language shall be balanced, interpreted and translated by an old word (or words, or image made up of old words) from the "low" '.

At this point the second poet, the complicator, arrives in *All's Well that Ends Well*, and Shakespeare's new, double 'language of the common bond' suddenly needs all its ingenuity.

The double language in *All's Well that Ends Well*

The following passage from the French King's speech to Bertram in *All's Well* is enough to illustrate how the sudden influx of complexity and the principle of translation now pervade every phrase.

> Methinks I hear him now; his plausive words
> He scatter'd not in ears, but grafted them,
> To grow there and to bear – 'Let me not live,' –
> Thus his good melancholy oft began,
> On the catastrophe and heel of pastime,
> When it was out, – 'Let me not live,' quoth he,
> 'After my flame lacks oil, to be the snuff
> Of younger spirits, whose apprehensive senses
> All but new things disdain; whose judgements are
> Mere fathers of their garments; whose constancies
> Expire before their fashions.'
> *All's Well that Ends Well*, I. ii. 53–63

At each line a novel concept is introduced, usually with a not altogether familiar word, and then translated into a familiar image, in familiar words, simultaneously creating a total and self-enclosed scene.

[142]

'Plausive', in the first line, was a new word. The *OED* gives priority to the dramatist Heywood, in 1600, but even if this is correct, it was a word that, under Shakespeare's new law, needs translation – which he gives in the next line and a half as 'admirably productive of superior fruit', in a single image that could not be misunderstood. This same image creates a world in which wise words, deliberately planted (even, perhaps, a little against the listener's will), eventually bless the listener – which is an image of what the King is actually doing here, planting in Bertram's ears an unwelcome homily about headstrong, empty-headed youth, which he will, in the future, suddenly understand. And that, in turn, is an image of one aspect of the play, as a parable of the Prodigal Son's belated awakening.

As a new-style example of the 'device', the line 'On the catastrophe and heel of pastime' (I.ii.57) seems almost unassimilated in its rawness. 'Catastrophe', clearly, was a word he culled with pleasure. ('Fine word, catastrophe'!) He tosses 'catastrophe of pastime' to the Lords' enclosure, where it was probably in favour and anyway easily translated and then, to the nut-cracking crowd on the floor of the house, 'that is to say the "heel of pastime"', adding – just as a further guide to the interpretation of this difficult novelty ('heel' is not quite explicit enough although it anchors things) – 'When it was out' (I.i.58), i.e. when it was over, done with. But that line is remarkable, first and foremost, for its lack of syntactic controls. Every possibility of relationship between the three elements is not only left wide open, but all are simultaneously energized. Every possible relationship presents itself as a riddle – with the difference that there can be no final answer (there are too many answers) and therefore no end to the questioning provoked: each of the three components – the two qualifiers and the noun – is liberated into inexhaustible figurative new life.

One is forced to ask exactly what 'catastrophe and heel' mean in this oddly empty yet teeming context. Literally 'catastrophe' means the turn-down to the end, or the change which produces the closing event, generally disastrous, and the word was specifically related to that point in classical drama. (Shakespeare knew it in this sense, as in *King Lear*, I.ii.150 – 'and pat, he comes, like the catastrophe of the old comedy'.) More loosely it means the final disaster itself.

In the phrase 'catastrophe of pastime' the idea of 'pastime', which is the pleasant, unforced, amusing sport which displaces what might otherwise be boredom, has become a drama with a tragic end – a self-contradiction, itself a little comedy concluding in sudden distress – without ceasing to be 'idle play'. Pastime, that is, has become a metaphor for the life which is let go by, foolishly, because the owner cannot waken up to the fact that it is his serious role, his only opportunity to perform and live, until it is on the point of ending. Then, too late, he grasps that it has been, because he wasted it in error, a tragedy, of which the end is therefore a 'catastrophe'. And this overshadowing of an idle bout of pastime with the ominous implication of a life wasted in error is strengthened by the context of the whole speech, which develops further images of wasteful youth and the end of a life ill-spent.

The words are spoken by the mortally sick King to the young Bertram, who is about to embark, though the King does not know it, on a life of error and waste, under the illusion that it is what he desperately wants, but for which he will be sharply corrected. This error and its correction are the substance of the play, in which Bertram is saved by Helena from the 'catastrophe' he will fully have deserved. The 'catastrophe of pastime' is therefore the minatory image of a tragedy which Bertram strives – up to the very last moment – unwittingly to complete. It is the possibility of which the actual play, by dint of Helena's triumph, becomes the happy counter-truth.

But this enriched activity of the first half of the phrase is plunged into new mystery by that odd, anomalous 'heel'.

One set of riddles is already in the air: how is a catastrophe a pastime, and vice versa? The possible answers are now multiplied, amplified: how is a catastrophe like a heel which is like some part of a pastime? How is a heel like a pastime which is a catastrophe? But first of all how is a catastrophe like a heel, simply? And how is a heel like a catastrophe?

'Heel' being the rearmost and lowest part of the body as catastrophe is of the action, 'heel' and 'catastrophe' are synonymous enough for the spark of likeness to leap, which is the life of the gadget. That spark sets both words spinning around 'pastime' like electrons round a nucleus, and each is suddenly alive with all the properties of the others. As if the 'heel', that intimate part of the self, could experience a nightmare, and like some kind of aerial receive and transmit all the tragedies possible to man. Simultaneously, the crowded, howling universal concept of 'catastrophe' orbits there, in surreal form, as a human heel. The suggestive power of these ideas is already explosive. But the 'heel of pastime' is more particular.

[144]

The Achilles' heel is proverbially a strong man's weak spot. The Achilles tendon was the only point at which death could take hold of the great hero, being the part nipped between his mother Thetis's finger and thumb, and which therefore remained dry, vulnerable and mortal, when she dipped him into the immortalizing Styx. In general, damage to this mainspring of the body is the most disabling of athletes' injuries. And it carries in itself a primal fear, being the tendon slashed by hunters and predators from the beginning of time.

Achilles was a sacred king (like the speaker) and died when a poisoned arrow pierced his heel – as the speaker is dying of the toxins of a fistula, which is 'a long, narrow, suppurating canal of morbid origin' like the wound of a poisoned arrow. Through this route, well known to Shakespeare, the 'catastrophic heel' returns to the King's own sickness, which corresponds in the plot to Bertram's moral blindness. So 'heel of pastime', also, becomes itself another image of the inmost theme of the play. In these various ways, the line becomes a crystal of the entire play, faceted for different angles of inspection. On this tiny stage of the three words (plus that all-important 'and') the King is performing several different productions simultaneously.

All this and probably much more, it might be said, can be teased out of that line. But in the moment of hearing it, how much can anyone be expected to receive?

The line is typical, first of all, of Shakespeare's 'new language' in that it does deliver a surging sense of supercharged yet generalized poetic excitement. In fact, it delivers, as I say, a small explosion. This sense of immediate poetic excitement can be deceptive, or authentic, according to whether the flare of poetic suggestion can substantiate itself logically.

In Hamlet's lines:

> To be or not to be? That is the question.
> Whether 'tis nobler in the mind to suffer
> The slings and arrows of outrageous fortune,
> Or to take arms against a sea of troubles
> And, by opposing, end them.
>
> *Hamlet*, III. i. 56–60

'sea of troubles' produces a 'flare' of poetic excitement which turns out to be bogus – it cannot authenticate itself. It brings understanding to a halt – the brain thereupon produces an 'explosion' of possible, dimly apprehended answers, which register in the consciousness as a blip of liberation and delight — the poetic effect. But it cannot stand up to serious inquiry, and in fact it disables the preceding and following lines.

When Cuchulain took arms against the sea, after being tricked into killing his own son, it was a symbolic action of utter despair and deeper self-delusion. He had no way of ending their waves of attack. In any circumstances, taking arms against a sea can only mean: with no hope of ending the assault. One automatically applies this commonplace to validate that 'sea of troubles' as a concise suggestion that (a) the troubles are cosmic and insuperable, and (b) any effort to end them is futile. The image of the pathetically finite life assaulting elemental infinity has its poetic aspect, but it can only be received here in a blur of interfering wavelengths. When Shakespeare wanted to use a related idea in *The Tempest*, he dramatized it clearly:

> the elements
> Of whom your swords are temper'd, may as well
> Wound the loud winds, or with bemock'd-at stabs
> Kill the still-closing waters, as diminish
> One dowle that's in my plume . . .
>
> *The Tempest*, III. iii. 61–5

To patch 'sea of troubles' into the image as it stands in *Hamlet* not only ignores the clear *mise-en-scène* of 'slings and arrows', 'take arms against' and 'And, by opposing, end them', it also contradicts or rather disintegrates the form of the proposition: whether to suffer and endure the troubles, or to oppose and overcome them, where 'they' are physical being itself, the condition of being alive. 'Slings and arrows' are the pestering ordnance of siege. Traditionally, sieges can only be broken by 'taking arms' and sallying out through the gates, and routing the besiegers with a frontal attack. Hamlet's closing phrase, 'And, by opposing, end them', unambiguously offers him this course of action as one that will definitely free him from the troubles. For Shakespeare's line to fulfil the balance of the proposition and to fit the logical integrity of the rest of his imagery (not only here, but elsewhere in the play), the word 'sea' ought evidently to be 'siege'. It does not produce quite such a poetic flare-up, but it is authentic and restores the surrounding lines to health.

'On the catastrophe and heel of pastime' not only delivers an extraordinary flare-up of the poetic effect, but, as I have shown, it authenticates the effect with logical meaning drawn in unbelievable detail from all corners of Shakespeare's system, within *All's Well*.

After this concentrated explosion of the device, Shakespeare moves on to a series of metaphors, each of which develops the same argument, translating into a plain image some difficult concept. To begin with, the speaker wishes to say that he does not want to live after his youthful vigour, burning out, leaves him exhausted, to depress and discourage younger new spirits with obsolete, unseasonable admonishments. Shakespeare translates that instantly in the clear, concise, familiar image of the oil lamp, where each word is likewise simple and familiar. Simultaneously, he creates a scene – the old, used-up person as a burned-up blockage between the flame of vigorous new living and the oil of new life, which again is an image of the play, where the sick King is himself like an image of the false self of Bertram, the Bertram who rejects Helena and prefers folly. Both the King and Bertram are the 'snuff'. When the King is healed, and Bertram's offending self whipped out of him, the 'snuff' will have been removed – and the new oil will flow to the flame in new life.

In the next line, the judgement of young men is good for nothing but to sire not new selves (the theme of the play is the search for, and the finding of, that new self for both the ailing speaker and the one spoken to), but merely the latest garments in fashion (the one to whom the King is speaking, Bertram, is being led astray by Parolles, the 'jackanapes with scarves', a creature of mere words and showy externals, the *doppelgänger* who will be stripped naked finally). The 'constancies' of young men are a form of mental garment (a falsity put on, a mortally sick promise) that cannot live as long as the fleeting fashion in which they dress their bodies.

At each step one sees Shakespeare doubling back over the complexity of his high language, to mix and amalgamate the meaning thoroughly with the simplest language of the lowest.

This incessant busyness of translation, where each unfamiliar word or idea is expounded in a clear and familiar metaphor, which is also a separate, autonomous, total scene, is, as I say, the new mode. What is particularly new is that aspect of 'translation' – of high language and image – occurring in every fresh idea or unit of sense, and the jostling density with which these units of sense, which are also 'whole scenes', are juxtaposed.

Throughout Shakespeare, as was clear in those examples of the device from the earlier plays, the illustrative images tend to be images of the play itself, or of some prominent aspect of it. Now these images arrive not at leisurely intervals, but as a dense, hieroglyphic continuum parallel to, but separate from, the actual immediate meaning of the speech. Yet each of them is a total image of the play from one urgent point of view or another. In these lines the play itself is thinking, defining itself, turning itself this way and that, searching among all possible images for new images of itself, and trying them on. As the voice touches each new idea, the whole drama lights up. Phrase by phrase, the King's voice moves through a flickering succession of holograms of the entire play. But at the same time, facing Bertram, he is saying clearly and directly what has to be said – translating each strange word, nailing down every corner of his ideas with plain words and familiar images, as for the simplest listener.

In general, then, this magnesium, pulsing glow of a constant metaphorical enthralment, a continuous play of riddle, a continuous simultaneity of at least two worlds, at least two aspects of the total play, focused on each unit of verbal meaning, and controlled within the geometrical or musical (there is no word for it) articulation of his sacred, mythic system, is the *coincidental* gain of Shakespeare's new 'language of the common bond' having arrived at the same moment as the Mythic Equation.

In responding to the public need for that language, Shakespeare has invented, as if accidentally, an extraordinary new form of communication. And his democratization of high language and low, with what amounts to an enforced system of intermarriage that goes right through his usage, reflects his inter-fertilization of high seriousness and low comedy on the plane of action. In the subsequent dramas – *Measure for Measure, Troilus and Cressida* and thereafter – he welds the contrasts and conflicting extremes of his new material simultaneously, on all planes – theme, action and words – into his composite, multi-dimensional stage 'language of the common bond'. But he simultaneously opens new worlds of referential possibility for his private 'system'. He has created an idiom which is at the same time a condensed algebra in which his system can formulate itself and a public language in which it can make itself understood.

Something of this can be seen in three other specimens of the new style 'device' from *All's Well*.

Or I will throw thee from my care for ever
Into the staggers and the careless lapse
Of youth and ignorance;

II. iii. 169–71

I know I love in vain, strive against hope;
Yet, in this captious and intenible sieve
I still pour in the waters of my love,
And lack not to lose still.

I. iii. 209–12

The inaudible and noiseless foot of time

V. iii. 41

In each of these, Shakespeare's intermarriage of high and low means the intermarriage of two different linguistic stocks, which represent two different complexes of views of the world.

Granting Shakespeare all his negative capability, it is easy to read into the contractual terms of each one the family branches of the two myths, as represented by the individuals in the plot of *All's Well*, and to see how the large, momentous conflict, in the depths of the Equation, is registered immediately and sensitively within the peculiar poetic life at the surface of the line.

In the first example, 'youth and ignorance' opens generally into the two 'error' myths of the early poems. 'Staggers' goes back through the desperately searching Helena, in this play, to her original, the rejected Venus 'madly hurrying she knows not whither', to find her lost Adonis in a Catholic nightmare. 'Careless lapse' goes back through the hot-headed, self-ignorant Bertram, in this play, to his original, the reckless rapist Tarquin, in the heedless iconoclasm of a Puritan fantasy. The old, autochthonous word 'staggers' is caught in the arms of the not quite naturalized centurion 'lapse'.

In the second quotation two Latinate wanderers with wobbly accents have been coupled to that blonde kitchen 'sieve'. The meaning 'capacious' in the *OED* is given to 'captious' solely on the precedent of its assumed meaning here. The *OED* gives 'intenible' the meaning of 'incapable of holding or containing', again solely on the precedent of the assumed meaning here, and finds the word nowhere else in literature.

Both words, that is, facing each other over that 'and', come to the reader or listener as a new cryptoglyph – they can mean whatever the

[149]

context suggests as likely: a little team of meanings on the loose. 'Captious' is only lightly held by the Latinate 'capt' – which runs with the basic notions of 'hold, holding, held, able to hold, catching, caught, made captive', etc., indifferently. The *OED* has decided to reject, in Shakespeare's case, the common meanings of 'captious': 'apt to take one in, fallacious, sophistical', and 'disposed to find fault, cavilling, carping', though as it happens these meanings are working painfully on the rejected, insulted Helena, who gets her man only against his will. It opts for that 'capacious' which serves, in fact, mainly as an acceptable pacemaker for the dark horses behind.

The point is, all these meanings are electrified and held in a shifty field of resonance around the basically mystifying 'captious'. One expects the balancing partner 'intenible' to select and set an order of precedence among them, rather as Chinese words are defined by their neighbours, but it merely compounds the variables. Shakespeare uses 'tenable' (*Hamlet*) with the distinct meaning of 'what may be held under control, held against attack'. 'Intenible' then becomes not so much 'incapable of holding' which, for a sieve, goes without saying, but 'incapable of being held, impossible to hold' – both against attack and because of its own nature. These meanings perform their dance, with the meanings of 'captious', to hypnotize the idea of 'sieve' with suggestions of a trap, treachery, something too painful to hold even though it has to be held – something that does not simply let love through in unending loss but is the cupped hands full of a sort of napalm. And this little solar system of suggestion and counter-suggestion is held in unstable stability by the magnetic, empty but powerful centre of gravity located in that 'and'. The density of signals and hints of pain released in this way, from the two indeterminate Latinisms, attracts into them the anguished fleshiness of the homely, desperate noun they qualify, that kitchen sieve in Helena's hand, which is also her heart, and which now may remind one of Troilus's description of his heart as an open ulcer into which all the wounding beauties of Cressida were poured (written a year after this).

Because 'captious' and 'intenible' are so odd something drastic needs to be done – if they are to be used at all – to liberate meaning from them, to *translate* them.

The basic novelty, 'captious and intenible', offered to the classicists in the aristocrats' seats, would be interpreted – maybe not without differences, with a rich confusion of possibilities, but all meaningful. To the rest, however, the phrase would be impenetrable. No two modern readers, classicists or no, could ever agree on the meaning.

To begin to extract clear meaning out of those two words, Shakespeare definitely needs that sieve — to activate, direct and focus their possible definition.

The first stage of the 'translation', then, is to pour their meanings through the plain word 'sieve'. But that leaves various ends dangling.

To have said:

> I know I love in vain, where all my hope
> Is but a captious and intenible sieve,

apart from its lameness of emphasis, might yet have suggested, to the classicists, the gist of the following line and a half. That is not enough for the author, who wants to make everything both immediately clear and dramatically full to *all* of his audience. Shakespeare thereupon adds the translation:

> Yet, in this captious and intenible sieve
> I still pour in the waters of my love.

This brings all the properties of the sieve into graphic familiar action, in the plainest kitchen language.

But he wishes to unfold the paradox nestled in his two adjectives: though the sieve, like a sieve, lets everything through, nevertheless, like a true receptacle and *unlike* a sieve, it never depletes her supply. He wishes to use the word 'sieve' to suggest at the same time the very opposite of a 'sieve', something which, while seeming to lose everything, loses nothing. And so he adds, again in simplest kitchen terms:

> And lack not to lose still.

The device has now produced a scene in which the forlorn Helena performs her high distress as in the middle of a poor kitchen. And this scene is an image of the play, where Bertram himself is the sieve — who squanders her love and is, at the same time, the infinite receptacle of it, large as the universe itself, which Helena has filled with her love. Which, again, is an image of the ultimate form of the Tragic Equation *and* the Theophany that eventually resolves it.

In the last quote of all, 'inaudible' and 'noiseless' seem almost too synonymous to be justified. Yet they observe the 'foot of time' from opposed viewpoints — from within the noiselessness of the foot itself and from within the ear that cannot hear it. They not only make a little scene in the way of the earlier examples, they make a miniature of the myth itself. The association test sends the mind running steeply back through 'inaudible', through the insensitive, case-hardened heedlessness of Bertram, to the deaf resolution of Adonis/Tarquin and the defensive, aggressive alienation of the Puritan ego: and back through 'noiseless' to Helena's dogged but vain efforts to overtake Bertram and make herself heard, and beyond that to Venus/Lucrece, who cannot make her plea heard, and finally to the Catholic despair that felt itself to be already, perhaps, a ghost.

These broad suggestions and yet occasional piercing precisions emerge from the essential vitality of the device which is basically an extraordinary fertility of metaphor.

Shakespeare's hieroglyphic system

On the one hand, this verbal language of the common bond, as a crisis improvisation, is a kind of prodigiously virtuoso pidgin. It never loses this extempore, unpredictable quality of something being put together, out of everything within reach, in an emergency – snatched and grabbed out of the listener's ears, his shirt front, his top pocket, his finger ends, in a brilliant and slightly bewildering conjuring act.

On the other hand, it defines and illuminates that vast inner consistency of Shakespeare's articulated, noble system.

It is curious that this upheaval of a change came in with *All's Well*. As I suggest, it came with the Tragic (the Mythic) Equation. Presumably, this colossal new pattern of incompatible extremes, arriving from the interior, tipped the balance. And when it entered what was already a supersaturated chemical solution, everything suddenly crystallized out.

If Shakespeare's image store had been a miscellaneous heap, as with most poets, the results would have been quite different. They might have been magnificent in their abundance, like Neruda's, or Saint-John Perse. But the identifying feature of the mythic poet is that the image store is preconsciously organized, articulated by the poet's myth.

Again, as I have suggested, Shakespeare's image store was not only organized subconsciously by his myth (the spiritual life of the irrational Duke Frederick) but he shows every sign of having worked at it methodically (the intellectual life of Melancholy Jaques, who had joined

Duke Frederick in his 'quest'). To know what his method was would certainly be interesting.

It is not possible to say anything very definite about it, but working backward from the results, one can make a suggestive guess at the origins, and therefore the character, of Shakespeare's technique of meditation. And from that one can venture to say a little more about the functions of the 'device', from *All's Well* onwards – or rather about the generalized function of his hieroglyphic language which the 'device' epitomizes.

With his references to his 'sessions of sweet silent thought' ('so many hours must I contemplate'), it seems likely, in those days when it was not unusual for men to spend many hours a day in 'contemplation', that Shakespeare used the technique based on a mnemonic system of emblems, or seals, like Giordano Bruno's (see page 22).

His preoccupation with imaginative realization, both as a desirable form of apprehension, and as a spontaneous activity, always indicating the highest degree of awareness and vigour of spirit, pervades the plays: it is the ectoplasm in which they take shape. Whether as the Player's 'conceit' that reduces him to a trembling wreck of a witness of his own imaginings, or Imogen's brothers thrown into paroxysms of involuntary living-out the action of a story told, or King Henry exhorting his men to imagine themselves into berserker frenzy, or the Chorus of *Henry V* beseeching the audience to 'work, work your thoughts', the actualization of imagined scenes is, at every point, Shakespeare's way of thinking: he raises the idea into quasi-physical reality, then lets his feeling respond to it exactly as if it were real:

> O! deeper sin than bottomless conceit
> Can comprehend in still imagination;
> *Lucrece*, 701–2

puts one in mind of Flaubert, so wrapped in the actuality of what he was reading that he slipped from his chair and crumpled to the floor still reading. Or of Dante, or indeed of Goethe, so fixed in imagination that they were virtually in trance, and for long periods inaccessible to any disruption. One cannot suppose Shakespeare was much less given in that direction than those two.

This form of 'thinking' was a technique of well-understood benefits, and deliberately exercised. Originally a Sufi method (Ibn el Arabi, twelfth century, called it 'the ABC of spiritual advancement'), it was systematized, using the aforementioned organized 'memory map' of images, by Thomist theologians (see page 20) and developed, through Occult Neoplatonism, eventually into the 'magically activated imagination' of Bruno and the Christian Cabbalists. Even where occultism was eschewed, but where the virtues of imaginative actualization were understood, that 'intensity' of the visualization of images was still the basic principle. In this 'natural' form it became the fundamental principle of St Ignatius Loyola's *Spiritual Exercises* – and from this source, too, it seems likely that it was known to Shakespeare. Through whichever tributary it arrived (and perhaps through several simultaneously), this technique would have found him an apt pupil, not only in that primitive game of magically activated imagination, but in the sophisticated possibility of a *summa*, an articulated, all-inclusive system of imagery, ascending to the Divine Source.

Shakespeare's temperamental aptitude for the first stage, that of the 'primitive game', appears everywhere in his work from its earliest moment. His serious application to the second appears, I have suggested, in the radically changed approach to his art in *As You Like It*, and in the matter of the Tragic Equation, which emerges in *All's Well*, and evolves through the plays thereafter.

One imagines that up to a certain point Shakespeare's drama and his addiction to systematic imaginative 'serious' thought travelled parallel and somewhat apart. His early drama was opportunistic, as if he wrote those plays, like a by-product, easily and lightly.

With *All's Well* the most obvious change from the preceding dramas is one of sheer psychological weight. Quite suddenly, from this point, the plays incorporated his full frontal struggle with himself, as his whole inner world of feeling became accessible to him, in the form of the Mythic Equation, which, as I have argued, was simultaneously the double myth of the Reformation and of his own deepest subjectivity.

What became accessible, to his art, therefore, with this new dramatic material, was his system of organized images, which was already (I suggest) a sacred, consistent system of cryptoglyphs. His system, moreover – the magnetic field of its framework – was now strongly enough established to organize, automatically, any new information, any new imagery.

As an image-based system it also brought with it that principle of translation downwards – translation from high concept to simple sensuous image – on which he now based his 'language of the common bond'. An example of this 'translation downwards' typical of a Bruno-esque mnemonic system would be the following: Catastrophe (the general concept) = the corpus of Classical Tragedy (the category of real examples) = Achilles' heel (the symbol or 'seal', by which that whole department of 'thought' could be switched into consciousness, like a file opened by a computer code-sign).

Perhaps, as I say, the sudden emergence of the system, in the form of the Equation, in *All's Well*, is closely related, in this way too, to the fact that his new double language appears here for the first time, *systematically* adapted and developed.

But having supplied him with that basic principle – Abstract concept = concrete symbol (unforgettable image) – a Cabbala-like, spiritualizing image system would automatically impose the further development – Abstract concept = *sacred* concrete symbol (unforgettable image belonging to the mythic system) – simply because all images would be 'sacred', since all would be magnetized to their place on the Ladder of Ascent, of which his mythic system and Equation were now the dramatic form.

Somehow or other, that is what happened. In *All's Well*, Shakespeare's makeshift, improvised 'language of the common bond' became simultaneously the sacred language of his hierophany.

Apart from the other evidence suggesting his link to Bruno, Shakespeare's interest in the condensed, emblematic image – over and above his preoccupation with visual actualization and visionary contemplation – suggests the affinity. He simply liked composite symbols.

It is interesting that two of the very few authenticated stories about Shakespeare both concern his preoccupation with symbols of this kind: his pursuit of a heraldic symbol for his father (and so for himself), and his designing an *impresa* – an emblem for a shield – for the Duke of Rutland, who paid him one-third of a day's theatre takings for it (in gold).

This second story suggests that his reputation as an *impresa* designer was exceedingly high. Presumably another lost piece of Shakespeareana was the 'special effects' that he had Burbage paint on the shields of his stage knights. The first story corroborates what was assumed anyway: he was fascinated by heraldic glyphs, the language of lineages. The aesthetic power of the armorial image lies in the wealth of opposed yet intermingled real histories – compacted to a single signature, mysterious, finally, as the sigil of a daemon. It speaks from a potent plane of reality – as in the prophecies of Nostradamus, or in Dante, where popes and emperors are identified, as they might be in the *anima mundi*, by their heraldic symbol.

The image Shakespeare acquired for himself is also curiously apt. The lance is the image of his name, in an obvious sense. But as a weapon in two parts – with the grip in the middle – it is also the image of his name's double form: on the title-page of the *Sonnets* (1609) his name was spelled with a hyphen: Shake-speare, and in that sense (as I mentioned on page 102), an image of his double self – the executive, objective will, the Speare, or Pierre, or Père, and the mass of hidden tortured sensibility behind it, who needs to defend himself, who needs to fathom his own mystery and compensate for all his tremblings, who needs to conquer both himself and the world.

Accordingly that lance becomes an image of his double language as it materializes in the device – in the two balanced qualifiers. The device, therefore, is also an image of his name. As in all examples of a similar form, the two halves of:

> On the catastrophe and heel of pastime

make a spear: the aim is steadied and held by that 'and' at the centre of gravity, as the two-part mass of the implement becomes a single, penetrating weight behind:

> The point and impact of a tempered word

where the basic model is:

> The shock and spear of will.

Once Shakespeare had converted the parts of his name to active images, as in the *Sonnets* and *As You Like It*, finding effective syntactical form for it would become a permanent amusement, in some department of his imagination.

In that case, maybe the 'device' developed on the heraldic model as a structural means of expressing his antithetical selves as a dialectical 'system' in iconic form:

> an union in partition;
> Two lovely berries moulded on one stem;
> So, with two seeming bodies, but one heart;
> Two of the first, like coats in heraldry,

Due but to one, and crowned with one crest.
A Midsummer Night's Dream, III. ii. 210–14

The verbal device and Tragic Equation as brain maps

An explanation for some aspects of the poetic effect of Shakespeare's device is suggested by what is now known of the co-operative inter-activity of the left and right hemispheres of the brain. We are told that, in general, the left side processes verbal language, abstract concepts, linear argument, while the right side is virtually wordless, and processes sensuous imagery, intuitive ideas, spacial patterns of wholeness and simultaneity. One side or other tends to be dominant, but from moment to moment the interplay is variable. This duality accounts for the two main resources of human expression.

By nature the two sides presumably live in a kind of happy marriage. A noisily chattering society is supercharged with right-side partici-pation: music, song, dance, colour, imagery – and a vernacular tending naturally to imagery and musicality.

But, as history demonstrates, the onset of rationality institutes proceedings for a kind of divorce. The electroencephalograph tells the story. At a definite moment, rationality acquires prestige (according to some celebrated examples, this happens where the Goddess-destroying god begins to get the upper hand). Rational philosophy proceeds by swift or groping steps to objective science. That is by the way. What matters inside the head, evidently, is that under the new dispensation of rationality, words (and rationality itself) nurture their innate tenden-cies – to abstraction and logic – in formulations that are increasingly exclusive of all other factors (on the tacit ideal model of mathematical inevitability). This new language, it seems, is the terms of the divorce. In other words, while the verbal reformulations of life, in this new language, become increasingly dominant in all human transactions, they become increasingly exclusive of any contribution from the right side. The result is an automatic suppression of right-side activity. In some enclaves (particularly familiar in Western Protestant society) where the cultural incentives promoting the rational tendencies of language are extreme, the activity of the right side can be discredited and suppressed almost to extinction. The consequences, apparently, go deeper than the atmosphere of general aridity and colourless monotony, which are the obvious, perhaps (for many) tolerable signs.

Behind the fairly visible duality of the left side and the right side of the communication system, the other more secretive dualities of the brain (of the whole animal) tend to align themselves. The limbic system, which is the old mammalian brain governing the basic emotion and monitoring internal conditions, tends to associate itself with the language of sensuous images, intuitive assessments, total patterns. The activity of the cortex, the 'new' brain, which supervises all activities, refines interpretations and controls the behaviour according to 'reason', tends to associate itself with the analytic language of words. This tends to ally the deep subjective life of the animal with the right side, and the objective self-control of the animal with the left side. These are only broad and general tendencies — where 'left' and 'right' are not the physically different two halves of the brain, but simply the modes of communication (abstract, conceptual, verbal symbols versus sensuous or concrete, image-patterned symbols) favoured by left side and right side respectively, according to research. In fact, the operational contrapuntal interplay of different parts of the brain seems to be infinitely complicated — and subject to great variations. But as a generalized working model of the brain's two languages (made visible only by the invention of words) it has a use, and its basic reality is apparent enough in the various forms of literature.

These further alignments of specialized energies behind left side and right side have implications that are only just beginning to be appreciated. Excluding imagery and emotion, and promoting the rational, analytical verbal formulation of life, in other words lifting the left side into dominance literally by suppressing the right, seems desirable in some situations. But where it becomes habitual, it removes the individual from the 'inner life' of the right side, which produces the sensation of living removed from oneself. Not only removed from oneself, but from the real world also, and living in a prison of sorts, since the left side screens out direct experience, establishing its verbal 'system' as a hard ego of repetitive, tested routines, defensive against the chaos of real things, resisting adaptation to them.

Coincidentally, this deprivation of right-side participation lowers the left side's efficiency. It is well proved, for instance, that the left-side performance of certain kinds of scientists is measurably enhanced by regular, deliberate efforts to engage in right-side activity: painting, music, etc.

Any sustained verbal activity, because it stimulates the left side, tends to suppress the right and exclude its participation. As a result, sustained verbal activity tends towards boredom. It oppresses both speaker and listener with the usual left-side atmosphere of constraint, recycled clichés, deprivation of new inner life. That this is so becomes evident the moment the speaker meets a dead end in his train of thought – when the next step escapes him, or his idea is momentarily too difficult to verbalize.

What happens then is poetic. 'At wit's end is God', says the proverb. The moment the left side is brought to a halt, in this way, the loyal old right lobe, unembittered by its owner's officialized neglect, leaps forward with a suggestion in its own language – an image. The left side grabs it with relief, and out it comes as a metaphor. That metaphor is a sudden flinging open of the door into the world of the right side, the world where the animal is not separated from either the spirit or the real world or itself. The curious result is always the same: everybody laughs, or at least smiles, or at least feels a sudden lift, a sudden waft of oxygen. Even if it is a very poor metaphor, everybody is grateful.

The speaker might solve the same problem with a comic remark or a jokey pun of some kind, which again is a sort of metaphor, either of his dilemma, or of what he is trying to say, and again it is supplied by the unfailing right side, who can't come up with the right words because it has none, but is ready to help in any way with an image, its own version of what the left side is searching for among words. And again, of course, the effect – on listener and speaker – is momentary euphoria, a surge of energy, which goes off in a laugh, a sudden sense of escape, of expanded awareness, of all the other points of view briefly showing their faces, of feeling at ease and more like oneself.

Poetic metaphor must work in a similar sort of way. The known, seen as enigmatic, and set down by the left side in words, is interpreted, simultaneously, by the right side as an image. In that phrase from the King's speech:

> whose judgements are
> Mere fathers of their garments
> *All's Well that Ends Well*, I. ii. 61–2

'judgements' is the abstract concept set down by the left side, which then puzzles for a way to express the novel and unexpected interpretation that it wants to develop. In other words, it is brought to a halt. The right side then springs to help with a concrete (wildly irrational) familiar image, seized from the mass of the world's actuality: 'Mere fathers of their garments' i.e. fathers able to beget nothing except (a sort of sartorial hit-and-run paternity) the fashions of their clothes – to which they will deny maintenance. (As Bertram will be happy to seduce Diana for amusement, and give her a child – which he would in no way have acknowledged if Diana's place had not been taken by Helena.)

The result is a moment of total co-operation between the full activity of the left side, and the full activity of the right. 'Judgements' interprets the image of the 'fathers' in the left-side language of abstract, moral, analytical, generalizing control, while the image 'fathers' interprets 'judgements' in the emotion-charged, pain-sensitive, image-world language of the right side, the mother tongue of the body. The effect would presumably register on the encephalograph as a surge of excitement in both hemispheres, united by a unique, shared rhythm of comprehension, as the two activities become one harmonized collaboration, focused on the single (unspoken) idea of a young man's shallowness.

This surge of excitement has a subjective effect, like a joke, over and above the actual interest of the new idea. The balanced and sudden perfect co-operation of both sides of the brain is a momentary restoration of 'perfect consciousness' – felt as a convulsive expansion of awareness, of heightened reality, of the real truth revealed, of obscure joy, of crowding, indefinite marvels, a sudden feeling of solidarity with existence, with oneself, with others, with all the possibilities of being – a momentary effect, which is the 'poetic effect'.

Shakespeare's device takes this 'arranged marriage' of the two sides, this almost compulsory co-operation, much further.

To begin with it is actively shaped on the page like a symbolic map of the brain seen from above: the two hemispheres are the two qualifying words. The qualified noun becomes the object of attention. And the 'and' – one now sees that 'and', maybe, in its true biological function – becomes the corpus callosum, the intermediary between the two halves of the electrifying event.

In that example, 'On the catastrophe and heel of pastime', 'catastrophe' becomes the left side's contribution, 'heel' the right side's, and 'pastime' the object of attention. 'Catastrophe' interprets 'pastime' in the abstract, analytical, categorizing language of the left side, while 'heel' interprets it in the vulnerable, experience-saturated, emotionally apprehensive body language of the right side. Simultaneously, 'catastrophe', in left-side language, interprets 'heel' while 'heel', in right-side language, interprets 'catastrophe'. (And even manages to smuggle in, as an antithetical pun, the forlorn counter-hope 'heal', which is also a prophecy and good omen.) Simultaneously the abstract concept of the whole combination is set in that right-side pattern of wholeness, the elegant verbal unit on the page, in itself as physically distinctive as a heraldic logo, which is in turn countersunk in the musical, metrical right-side pattern of the pentameter line.*

The device becomes a marvellously shapely hologram of a total event, where every left-side component is perfectly realized, illuminated and humanized by its right-side correspondence. And the result is an explosion of 'poetic effect' — a glimpse of 'total awareness' — as the reader's or listener's brain reproduces the event within itself.

The poetic effect, in fact, as in all these successful examples of pairings, from *All's Well* onwards, is a kind of 'satori'. Over and above its intricately logical and literal meanings, which are so dense, the device works like a Zen koan. And this same effect, to a lesser degree, pervades the new 'double' language that has entered with the Equation. This is part of the inimitable mystery of Shakespeare's mature verse.

I mentioned before that the device is like an image of the Equation itself. Having said that, one can see that the Equation — the two myths each interpreting the other — is itself a gigantic map of the attempted co-operation of the brain's two hemispheres. The Goddess myth is in the right side, while the (ultimately rational and secularizing) myth of the Goddess-destroyer is in the left side. Blood sacrifice and archaic, matriarchal religious emotion are in the right, while new, Utopian, militant, rational morality is in the left. The two halves divide the Goddess. In the right side she is always the Queen of the Underworld, inseparable from the womb memory, infant memory, nervous system and the chemistry of the physical body, possessed by all the senses and limitless, while the Female in the left side is the Puritan Lucrece figure, idealized, moralized and chaste. The 'Divine Mother' shifts uneasily between the two. In the right side the male figure is the uncontrollable, primeval Boar, image of the sexual body itself, while the male figure in

---

*Shakespeare must have recognized all its potential in the very earliest example, which seems to have sparked accidentally from the clash of dialogue in Henry VI, Part II, v. i. 131–3:

CLIFFORD: To Bedlam with him! Is the man grown mad?
KING: Aye, Clifford; a bedlam and ambitious humour/Makes him oppose himself against his king.

the left side is the moralized, idealized, intellectualized, Puritan Adonis. The Boar emerges from the right side (from the Goddess in her Underworld) becoming – at the point of breaking the horizon of consciousness – the 'hot tyrant', the 'double', and, uniting with the Adonis figure of the left side, arrives there as Tarquin. The Boar and Adonis meet, that is, in the corpus callosum – which is where the Flower springs, to be reborn on into the Tarquin and tragedy of an irrational crisis in the left side, or to be sublimated as if vertically into the transcendent illumination and 'wholeness' of total consciousness, as the reborn flower child of the Goddess of Complete Being. The Theophany which Shakespeare eventually achieves is a mythic form for this inclusive 'aura' of the perfectly (as possible) achieved co-operation of the two hemispheres. The fact that this gigantic vision of complete human consciousness is set down as drama, rather than as an epic or metaphysical poem, is the ultimate aspect of its completeness: physical acting itself is the language of the right side, the verbal text the language of the left side, and their indivisibility – which is a function of the image and of the musical component of the language – is the seal of the global integrity of the whole operation, like no other created human work.

A Lover's Complaint: the heroine's guilty secret

There is a third long narrative poem (longish – 329 lines), the not much noticed A Lover's Complaint. The Equation reveals this to be a crucial little work. As the roughed-out sketch of a dramatic possibility, it is like a pre-birth auscultation of what had been given living form in the two major long narratives of 1593 and 1594 and would be delivered in All's Well that Ends Well at about the turn of the century.

According to the verse, which seems hasty, provisional, unrevised, it belongs just before All's Well. Such lines as the fourth of:

> Small show of man was yet upon his chin;
> His phoenix down began but to appear
> Like unshorn velvet on that termless skin
> Whose bare out-bragg'd the web it seem'd to wear . . .
> A Lover's Complaint, 92–5

or the second of:

> O! then, advance of yours that phraseless hand,
> Whose white weighs down the airy scale of praise . . .
>
> 225–6

seem further along Shakespeare's rising graph of verbal refinements than anything in the *Sonnets* (except for a few lines of a very different kind), and would be surprising in *Twelfth Night* or *As You Like It.* Among several examples of his device in the poem, the following:

> Thus merely with the garment of a Grace
> The naked and concealed fiend he cover'd . . .
>
> 316–17

is a highly developed, perfect specimen of the adjectival type, directly rooted in the substratum of the Mythic Equation, while the second line of:

> Lo! all these trophies of affections hot,
> Of pensiv'd and subdu'd desires the tender . . .
>
> 218–19

is experimental and 'too curious good' in a fashion very close to the *All's Well* example discussed earlier on pages 149–51, 'Yet, in this captious and intenible sieve', and would not be out of place in the verse of that play, though unimaginable in anything earlier. The texture of several other single lines and sequences of a music that anticipates the new sonic ensemble of the verse of *All's Well* strongly suggest, to one reader's ear at least, a date of composition around that time.

The theme likewise suggests a tentative juxtaposing of the incompatible elements, in particular the mythic and the realistic, that finally come together, though still nervously, in *All's Well.* The 'action' is familiar. It is a variant of Lucrece's lament after being ravished, but in an entirely different mode. The 'I' in the poem takes no more part than the author or 'chorus' opening the scene and disappearing as the action begins, while the 'reverend man who grazed his cattle nigh', and who now sits 'comely-distant' from the bewailing woman at the water's edge, becomes his representative, a ruminative, moral observer of the unfolding event – a recognizable Jaques type,

Sometime a blusterer, that the ruffle knew
Of court, of city, and had let go by
The swiftest hours, observed as they flew . . .

58–60

(which again suggests a post-*As You Like It* date of composition). The main action which then emerges from the 'maid's' account of her seduction by the diabolically fascinating and inveigling Casanova is a translation, a domestication (high metaphysics to low consequences), a reducing to Hardyesque realism, of that episode from the Equation in which, in the past, Tarquin overpowered Lucrece's unyielding chastity, and in which, in the future (in *All's Well*), Bertram will attempt to overpower Diana and (in *Measure for Measure*) Angelo will attempt to overpower Isabella; and in all of which (though in each case the ravisher gets satisfaction of a kind) the maid's chastity remains essentially inviolate and blameless.

Maybe, in the case of *A Lover's Complaint*, this compliant surrender of chastity to lust is what makes many commentators find the poem un-Shakespearean. It happens nowhere else in the *Complete Works*, which permit lecherous seducers to succeed only with characters of low comedy – girls who might return pregnant from the garden where they went to find parsley to stuff a rabbit – or with women who are radically false, like Cressida, and who thereby become for the hero perilous Queens of Hell. In other words, Shakespeare's fallen women are either comic or are part of a system in which chastity is the real axis: up to *All's Well* the real axis of a moral system and after *All's Well* the mythic axis of a moral universe.

In *A Lover's Complaint*, the victim is in no way a Queen of Hell, nor is she comic. She is simply a real woman, and has no other dimension. (She is 'mythic' only in the attenuated sense in which Hardy's heroines are mythic: Hardy's myth shares some general features with Shake-speare's.) In one sense, her 'realism' is the whole point. Her 'real' plight dramatizes – with precision and deftness – the eternal human common-place around which Shakespeare's obsession with chastity revolves. Or rather, if his obsession with chastity, his heroic image of the chaste woman (the woman faithful to her soul's truth), is the axis, then this 'commonplace' is what makes his system and universe revolve around it. Hamlet fears (as Prospero expresses):

when she goes
to be sexual
n *Measure for*
(in all but a

mythic chaste
posed to the
All's Well and
ted) uneasily.
hat 'bomb of
the person of
e real and the
tity is inviol-
cted of being
al.

nforms more
ble seductive
ll: it achieves
ite satisfying
t everybody
f charm and
tion, in the
Wriothesley
conspirator
to death, he
d charm — a
is sentence.)
all passions
d variety of
hind which
tragic myth:
r.

e elemental
iring of the
comedy but
e two were
uality with
e 'problem'

ths are straw
d:

est, IV. i. 52–3

itter experience of her failure to
past cannot protect her in future,

of his eye,
his cheek so glow'd,
m his heart did fly,
ongy lungs bestow'd,
tion seeming ow'd,
the fore-betray'd,
ciled maid.

r's Complaint, 323–9

rds, is the natural detonator that
ability'. It is the basis of that 'hair-
's heroes to see the 'double vision',
eir 'soul') is fundamentally available
. This 'fickle maid' in the poem is
t crucial witnesses. She is the reality
ted to redeem.
ical 'mythic' self hovers close to her,
uring her complaint, she identifies
described in the poem. This figure is
in that my boast is true!') to prove to
one who conquered the unassailable
himself the love of

of holiest note;
suit in court did shun,
s made the blossoms dote;
by spirits of richest coat,
ce, and did thence remove,
in eternal love.

232–8

stity (derided by Parolles) emerges to

[165]

envelop the heroine, and is defined in its sacred purpose
on her pilgrimage to Saint Jaques, which turns out
(redemptive) union with her consecrated husband. Then,
Measure, it is wholly assimilated to Isabella, who is
technicality) a nun.

What one sees in *A Lover's Complaint*, then, is the
heroine (the Sacred Bride of the god) tentatively juxt
infinitely vulnerable sexual nature of woman in reality. In
Measure for Measure they are visibly fused, albeit (as I n
In *Troilus and Cressida* Shakespeare brings together
vulnerability' and this real woman's sexual fallibility in
Cressida, and isolates the 'tragic' detonator. Thereafter, t
mythic woman are perfectly fused in women whose cha
ably (divinely) true to itself, but who will always be susp
false, while their human individuality seems intimately r

The male figure in *A Lover's Complaint* already co
thoroughly to the daemonic entity of the myth. His irresist
power is a variant form of Tarquin's irresistible sexual w
its purpose just as 'heartlessly' and 'cruelly', as an appe
only itself. He is 'real' (like the 'maid') in the sense th
(according to the maid) recognizes him as a phenomenon
sexual allure, somewhat resembling Shakespeare's descr
Sonnets (and the description by others, elsewhere) of youn
his patron. (When he stood on trial with Essex, as the majo
in Essex's rebellion, where Essex himself was condemned
astounded the bench of judges with his grace, eloquence a
fact noted at the time – which helped, maybe, to mitigate
He also resembles, perhaps, the protean daemon ('Catchin
in his craft of will' (126)) that poured out the vivacity a
spirits on to Shakespeare's stage – the elemental genius
was, after all, whatever took possession of the heroes of the
Divine Love, in the irresistible infernalized form of the Bo

In this way, the poem reconnoitres a link between t
power circuit of the religious myth and the home-made
domestic realistic world (from which he drew first his lowe
eventually the 'reality' of all his characters) just before t
interconnected in that confrontation of primal, female se
male, Puritan morality, and of the Boar with the nun, in t
plays.

Measure for Measure: the Mythic Equation comes to consciousness

The assembling of the Mythic Equation can best be seen in *Measure for Measure*. The love plot of this play (the relationship between Angelo and Isabella) is based, like that of *All's Well*, on the plots of the two long poems, but whereas in *All's Well* the plots were juxtaposed end to end, somewhat indistinctly, and spliced together loosely, in *Measure for Measure* they are fitted together tightly, boldly and indivisibly. In fact, they are no longer brought from apparently separate provenances to be coupled by technical skill: they are now so wholly a single thing that it is clear: one has been drawn out of the other. The plot matter of the second poem now, in the play, emerges (erupts) from that of the first, like the larva from the egg. Having clarified this natural piece of evolution, Shakespeare reduces the plot of the first poem to one algebraic formula, and the plot of the second poem to another, and by demonstrating just how the second is a product of the first makes his dynamic (explosive) Mythic Equation. The briefest outline of the plot, as it bears on Isabella and Angelo, provides enough of an X-ray to show what is happening:

> The Duke of Vienna appoints the notoriously strict and exacting Puritan judge, Angelo, to take his own place as Governor of Vienna while he absents himself. Ostensibly the Duke's purpose is to use Angelo's extraordinary moral severity as a violent medicine to purge Vienna of its sexual squalor and corruption, which at every point spills over on to the stage.

> Angelo's Calvinist rigour outlaws the sexual liberties of this city of Venus: the punishment for adultery being death.

> His immediate clampdown catches Claudio, who has impregnated his betrothed Juliet, and who is accordingly sentenced to death.

> On that day, Claudio's sister, Isabella, is about to become a nun. Desperate, Claudio sends his friend Lucio to persuade her to forget the nunnery for a while and plead with the judge, Angelo, for her brother's life.

> Lucio is the cynical, irrepressible Mephistopheles of the sexual underworld, the satyr of Vienna. But Isabella is persuaded by him

to plead for her brother's adultery. With Lucio beside her, prompting her words, she confronts Angelo and pleads, on behalf of fornication, for sexual licence.

In other words, the beautiful Isabella, 'a thing ensky'd and sainted', almost a nun, chastity incarnate, attempts to overwhelm Angelo's Puritan censorious judgement with her plea for procreation and sexual freedom.

After resisting for some time, Angelo, to his amazement and horror, finds himself suddenly possessed by uncontrollable lust for the body of Isabella.

The moment he reveals his desire, Isabella recoils into outraged defence of her sacred chastity.

Angelo thereupon bargains with her. If she will surrender her body, her brother will be allowed to live: otherwise he will surely die.

That is to say, the lust-mad ravisher is ready to murder to satisfy his appetite. And he not only has his will, as he imagines, with Isabella, but he orders Claudio to be executed into the bargain.

This is the nervous system of the play. Without Isabella's desperate plea for the sexual act, and Angelo's Calvinist condemnation of it, there would be no play. Without the virtually insane drive of Angelo's lust, and the horrified opposition of Isabella's radical chastity, there would be no play.

From this, it is easy to see how the plots of the two poems can be recovered from the drama's single plot in which Angelo plays two diametrically opposite parts and where Isabella likewise plays two diametrically opposed parts.

Reduced to the Equation's structural formula, *Venus and Adonis* coincides with the confrontation of Angelo and Isabella up to the point at which Angelo's Puritan self is displaced by the other. More specifically, Isabella's plea for sexual licence corresponds to Venus's plea for the same. Angelo's Puritan, judgemental rejection of her plea corresponds to Adonis's rejection of the same. Other algebraic factors bring the identities closer. Isabella is a double deputy for both extremes of the Goddess. She is a high priestess (in effect) of the goddess of fertility and promiscuity, such as confronted the Jehovan reformers in Jerusalem as

Astoreth, Asherah, Anath, Sacred Bride of the sacrificed god Adonis/ Thammuz. At the same time she is the Diana-like priestess, in all but fact, of a Catholic nunnery.

The obvious drama of her predicament lies in this, that she has to play both roles simultaneously (as if she were, exactly like Venus in the poem, the Goddess of Complete Being, undivided). As one about to become the chaste Bride of Christ (the sacrificed god), she pleads for the sanctity of her brother's impregnating his betrothed Juliet, just as Venus pleads for the divine naturalness of her own impregnation by Adonis. And Shakespeare conjures the Venusian Underworld into her appeal by making her, to a degree, the ventriloquial mouthpiece of Lucio, the priapic demon of the seething brothels of Vienna, who, in the most unlikely fashion (as if he were invisible), is there beside her, prompting her with whispers, like Satan at the ear of Eve, or like the 'lust' (as in Sonnet 129) that Adonis could see behind the importunity of Venus.

What Angelo sees in her words, therefore, is what Adonis sees in the words of Venus. And his reaction is the same, only far more dangerously severe. Even more exclusively than Adonis, Angelo is a personification of the distinction that Adonis made between 'Love', which is now in Heaven, and 'sweating Lust', which is on Earth. In this first part of the play he is little more than an abstract function: the absolute condemnation of sexuality. His blood is 'very snow-broth', his urine 'congealed ice'. So long as Isabella fulfils that role of desperate supplicant, and so long as Angelo resists her, the plot of the play and the plot of Venus and Adonis coincide, in all mythic essentials, to make the first half of the Equation.

Just as closely, the second half of the play, in mythic essentials, recapitulates the confrontation of Tarquin and Lucrece, to make the Equation's second half. Like Tarquin, Angelo suddenly forgets his high office and duties, his reputation, his future, and lets lust overwhelm him. Like Tarquin, he is ready to blackmail and kill to satisfy his appetite. Everything that Tarquin debated with himself, between his bed and Lucrece's, Angelo can now debate likewise, just as horrified by the 'infamy' he is nevertheless determined to 'embrace'.

Angelo fails to follow through quite as fully and disastrously as Tarquin. But in his own mind he goes through to the end and ultimately expects the worst. If the ubiquitous Duke had not contrived the elaborate substitution of Angelo's ex-fiancée's body for Isabella's in the dark bed, and the pirate's head for Claudio's on the executioner's block,

Angelo's fate would be the same as Tarquin's. Only the Duke's legerdemain saves him from his new self.

But who is this new self? His identity could hardly be more unmistakable. At that juncture, where the two poems become one drama, the Angelo who behaved like Adonis has somehow – without blood, without visible rending of the flesh – been abruptly supplanted by the Angelo who behaves like Tarquin. Behind Angelo's face, Adonis has become Tarquin.

It is an awkward moment in the play itself. So sudden, so schematic – from one extreme to the other. Yet this moment, which arrives so nakedly, nevertheless introduces Shakespeare's most vital invention.

It can be seen here (but much more clearly later) that in divining just how the second myth erupts from the first, in other words just how the man who rejects the female, in moral, sexual revulsion, becomes in a moment the man who assaults and tries to destroy her, Shakespeare has divined a natural law. One that presents no mystery to post-Freudians. It is so natural, in fact, that the inevitability of the tragic dramas which follow is based on precisely that law.

To isolate the natural law was no more than an observation. But power of divination is evident in the way he fathomed its key role in the essential, tragic conflict of Reformation man: and power of invention in his constructing, with such precise articulation, the equation that expressed, and through which he could explore, that conflict.

Here in *Measure for Measure* (as in *Lucrece* and *All's Well*) he keeps it to private pathology, where the assault against the female springs from uncontrollable sexual lust and takes the form of rape. It is only later on, when this 'rape' modulates first to murder (in *Othello*) and then to 'banishment' (*King Lear*) or 'attempted but unsuccessful murder' (all the subsequent plays up to *The Winter's Tale*), that Shakespeare shifts his composite Equation into the greater dimension, and incorporates the greater reality of the religious, cultural conflict, as distinct from the narrower, Freudian, individual conflict alone. One could argue that only after that shift has occurred does he move from the comparatively constrained world of the immature work to the open universe of the mature (cf. page 221).

On the level of personal psychology, Angelo has undergone an inversion of personality – easy to understand. But on the mythic level, which supplies the kit of algebraic components out of which Shakespeare assembled his later intricate plots, Adonis has died and is reborn.

This is the main point: the mythic Adonis never dies — without being reincarnated. He only seems to die.

But even in the archaic cycle of the vegetation myth his rebirth had a certain versatility. When jealous Persephone, as a boar, kills him, he is reborn into her Underworld, as the Queen of Hell's consort. That rebirth into the Underworld is then inevitably followed by his rebirth to Aphrodite, in the upper world, as a flower. These two events – death by the Boar which is conversely rebirth as the Queen of Hell's consort, and rebirth in flower form as Aphrodite's consort, are such an automatic sequence that they can be conflated: his death by the Boar (alias his rebirth as the Queen of Hell's consort) was celebrated simultaneously with his rebirth to Aphrodite as a flower.

Because *Measure for Measure* exists and has revealed (as all the subsequent plays confirm) that the two narrative poems are the two basic structural units of Shakespeare's Equation, we know that here too, in the Equation, Adonis's rebirth has the same two options as in the archaic myth – either rebirth into Heaven, with the Goddess, or rebirth into Hell, with the Queen of the Underworld. While Adonis is killed by the Boar only in the first poem, he is reborn in both: in *Venus and Adonis* he is reborn as the Flower, in *Lucrece* as the lust-mad Tarquin.

In each of the two poems (which is to say, in each half of this naked, simplest, fully displayed, unmodified form of the Equation), the rebirth is analysed – the nature of the Flower and the nature of Tarquin are made explicit. In *Venus and Adonis*, the Flower that will be gathered by the Queen of Heaven is presented (exactly as in the later plays) as a *combination* of the triumphant Boar and the slain Adonis. Behind this combination of the rejector and the rejected lies (for those who require a more graphic and literal metaphor of what has happened) the sinuous, male–female coalescence of Hermaphroditus and Salmacis. Or, in the specific terms of the poem, Shakespeare departs from his source in Ovid, where the Flower is 'all of one colour with the blood', and carefully mixes an amalgam of rejected Goddess and slain Adonis to produce a Flower in the likeness of the Boar's murderous

> frothy mouth bepainted all with red,
> Like milk and blood being mingled both together,
>
> 901–2

Like the Boar's mouth, this Flower is 'purple' (the blood of Adonis) and 'checker'd with white' (the milk of the Goddess who

> Like a milch doe, whose swelling dugs do ache,
> Hasting to feed her fawn hid in some brake
>
> 875–6

had sought him so desperately). And equally explicit, viewed retrospectively through the lens of *Measure for Measure* (and in the same way confirmed throughout the later plays), is the similar composite nature of the 'lustful lord' Tarquin, possessed by the Queen of Hell: the 'hot tyrant' 'inflamed with [rejected] Venus'.

Evidently the Flower, there on the trampled deathbed of Adonis, just before Venus plucks it, swells with two futures: it is both the Flower that she will tuck into her cleavage as she flies up through the clouds with her doves, and the Flower that will burst open – in the next poem, *Lucrece* – as the blood-darkened Tarquin: triumphant Boar plus slain Adonis is either or both. And just as the Flower between the breasts of the Goddess secretes Tarquin, like a sleeping gene, so Tarquin, in his 'rage of lust', secretes (as the later plays disclose) the Flower. In other words, as I say, where those two halves of the Equation lie glowing in the moulds of their sparkling stanzas, that double rebirth (in some ways simultaneous, in some ways two alternatives, in some ways a sequence), which always did belong to Adonis, reappears, bold and pivotal, as the Tragic Equation's essential variable factor.

The phenomenal dramatic and metaphysical potential of this contrapuntal option of rebirth (into Heaven or Hell), which Shakespeare explores to every limit later on, is not immediately apparent in *Measure for Measure*. In this drama (as in *All's Well*) that Flower-rebirth into reunion with the Goddess seems to be missing: foreclosed, withdrawn, suppressed, or simply by-passed – torn up and flung aside, one might believe, by the convulsive instantaneity of Angelo's metamorphosis, which actually takes place in full view, on stage. What emerged unsuspected, through the quietly labouring months between summer 1593 (publication of *Venus and Adonis*) and summer 1594 (publication of *Lucrece*), now arrives in a premonitory shiver, an awed whisper. And as Angelo stares at Isabella, astonished, and murmuring:

> She speaks, and 'tis
> Such sense that my sense breeds with it . . .
>
> II. ii. 141–2,

the Boar hits him, slashes open the Puritan ego, pulls him on like a body

[172]

mask and, somersaulting across the gap between the two poems, from Heaven to Earth, from the mythic plane to the real, stands up as Tarquin, still wearing the mask of Angelo, while Isabella, studying his face in vain for some flicker of a sign, has not blinked.

Though far back in the world of *Venus and Adonis*, Venus leans forward to pick the blossom that she will cuddle in her bosom and croon to:

> 'Lo! in this hollow cradle take thy rest,
> My throbbing heart shall rock thee day and night:
>   There shall not be one minute in an hour
>   Wherein I will not kiss my sweet love's flower'
>   *Venus and Adonis*, 1185–8,

here in the play, in the trap of the Equation (as if at the beginning of *Lucrece*), Angelo wakes into Tarquin's obsession, giddy with lust, saturated with the presence and perfume of the Queen of Hell, suddenly, like Macbeth, filled with her flames and already helpless in the momentum of his crime. Nevertheless, the Flower does peep through the text, and even out of Tarquin himself, at exactly this moment.

After Isabella has left Angelo, he questions himself:

> The tempter or the tempted, who sins most?
> Ha!
> Not she; nor doth she tempt: but it is I,
> That, lying by the violet in the sun,
> Do as the carrion does, not as the flower,
> Corrupt with virtuous season.
>   *Measure for Measure*, II. ii. 163–8

Is Angelo comparing himself as the tempted to a carrion corpse that rots in the sun, while a more virtuous man, a nobler self, would in the same sun have grown sweeter and flourished, like the violet? In that case, Isabella is the sun. This seems a little strained, perhaps because one automatically identifies the violet as Isabella, since Angelo is so pointedly the carrion. Perhaps Isabella flourishes in incorruptible sweetness, immune to the contagion of Angelo who rots beside her under the same sun. In that case the sun is presumably God's gift of the freedom to choose between rotting and flowering, which is a major theme of the play, precisely the choice that the Duke gave to Angelo. Yet that is not quite right either, since the carrion has no choice, neither does the violet. While such meanings argue with each other, and strive to co-operate, knowledge of the myth points wordlessly to a more sinister meaning, which arises with this image (the only flower image in the play) from the world beneath the plot, where the purple flower has just sprung from Adonis's blood, and where Tarquin has just 'leap'd from his bed' to rape Lucrece. In this image, therefore, Angelo is also speaking, in self-loathing, directly out of the myth, from the mangled rags of his Adonis ego, while his new Tarquinian ego sprouts up *through his blood*. And both vivid processes, of the decaying corpse, and of the new, opening flower, are induced by the same blessed sun – Isabella's beauty and chastity.

What has happened here is typical of the imagery in all the plays of the Tragic Equation. While the predicament of the speaker in the play employs the image with a contingent, external meaning, relating to the specific matter of the plot, the Equation requisitions it with an internal meaning, relating to the original matter of the two myths. Accordingly, when Angelo next confronts Isabella, he is in all but place and name Tarquin standing over Lucrece's bed.

In this way the Boar carries the energy and meaning of the first half of the Equation into the second, through that explosive Shakespearean moment, as it will do in every subsequent play of the tragic series except *The Tempest*.

What Shakespeare did at this point seems to have been unthinkable until he did it. And nobody has managed to explore it since. As I noted before, neither Euripides nor Racine, who both took the first step, took the second. By fitting the two myths together, Shakespeare opened his own new, greater dimension of tragedy. The tragic error – the ego's rejection of the Divine Love of the Goddess – no longer ends in mythic sudden death as in *Hippolytus* or *Phèdre*. It lurches through into a prolonged consequence of intensifying agonies in which the hero is compelled to understand the full meaning of what he has done, while his whole mental and social universe comes crashing down and chaos erupts.

Moreover, in doing that, Shakespeare demonstrates how the second myth grows out of the first. He shows just how the sacrificed god of the first is only the larval form and will become the Goddess-destroying tyrant of the second, and just how the female who has to be overpow-ered (and perhaps destroyed) in the second is the same figure as the Divine Love of the first.

The mathematical prodigy divines his revelatory equation some time before the age of thirty-five, then spends the rest of his life exploring its implications. Shakespeare had unearthed here the psycho-biological law of the Reformation, in a usable form that captured its energies and anticipated its conclusions. And he incorporated it, whole and alive, as the DNA of his drama's tragic nucleus, where, as I say, it evolved through every play in the tragic cycle. Presumably this is how he brought the oceanic currents of the psychological history of the Western world to turn the wheel of his little mill on the Thames.

Troilus and Cressida: the Mythic Equation becomes the Tragic Equation

According to my reading of the Equation's evolution, the play following *Measure for Measure* should be *Troilus and Cressida*.

In *Measure for Measure*, Shakespeare assembles the device carefully, and explodes it under controlled conditions. He seems to know exactly what he is doing, and works towards that first climax from the play's first word. But the action, though it carries an alarming charge of dangerous energy, is not yet tragic.

He does the same, works towards the explosion with the same precision, in every play following *Troilus and Cressida*. But in *Troilus and Cressida* itself, he seems to take a step back. Stepping back he finds a broader, deeper perspective, a bigger, more inclusive pattern than the one behind *Measure for Measure*. With this, a crucial new element enters. New, at least, in the short history of the *mythic* equation (though not new in the earlier history of the Equation in its pre-mythic phase, cf. pages 488–9). This new element changes the nature of the explosion. And if he works towards that explosive moment here, he now seems to do so in slow motion, almost as if reluctantly. But he gets there at last. And when he gets there, it becomes clear that the new element has made all the difference, and that Troilus, the new hero, unlike Bertram and Angelo, is potentially tragic. Also, in spite of its strange inertia, this is the first *warm* work of the series.

This warmth is noticeable because *All's Well* and *Measure for Measure*, like the two poems, are so strangely frigid. They are cold, maybe, because of what is obviously missing: because their heroes lack love. Adonis rejects love, Tarquin feels lust without love, Bertram rejects love and feels lust without love, Angelo rejects love and feels lust without love.

[175]

This coldness is odd – and unlike anything else in Shakespeare's drama, where every work, even among the dogged early histories, is driven with an exuberant, creative joy, and the 'holiness of the heart's affections'. Even *Titus Andronicus* is driven with a savage sort of glee, a black flame.

And when Shakespeare sank a well directly into his own autobiography in *All's Well*, then things ought to have hotted up further. Instead, the temperature dropped towards zero. And in *Measure for Measure* – sub zero.

Presumably, this signifies that what he had struck was too hot. Too hot for him to handle. It argues that he had broken through to a whole new inner world of molten life – but still had only the old technology to deal with it, which meant that he could observe it only through shatter-proof lenses, and handle carefully limited amounts of it only with asbestos gloves. Even so, it was that ritual approach to his own autobiography in *All's Well*, perhaps, that had done the trick. It had brought him directly to the two myths: his two old long poems that embodied in mythic form the essential stuff of his real subjectivity – his peculiar love nature. Having brought him to that, which he then explored further in *Measure for Measure*, his fixed contemplation of those two myths reactivated, unearthed and conjured afresh the experience that had produced them in the first place: the trauma behind the *Sonnets*: his 'total, unconditional love', and the riddle of the 'double vision': the loved and the loathed woman in the one body. Imaginative play had brought him to the painful secret: exactly as in psychoanalysis.

At that point, clearly (according to the evidence), he discovered that the Mythic Equation did not begin with the Adonis who rejected Venus. It did not begin, either, with the enterprising young man who abandoned Stratford, nor with some projection of his own excessively critical moral intelligence, such as Angelo. It began much earlier, and at a greater, more secret depth, with a figure who worshipped the Goddess, or rather the incarnation of the Goddess, in 'total, helpless, unconditional love', and was worshipped the same by her. A figure who lived somewhere down there in his own unmanageably incandescent nervous system.

Once he grasped this (grasped it afresh) and connected the main artery of the Equation with his own aorta, in other words with the *agon* of his own 'total, unconditional love', everything changed. His drama flushed immediately with his most intimate and subjective life – and his inner world overflowed. Instead of projecting shadows of ritual abstractions, as in those last two plays, he now staged his own living mystery – in *Troilus and Cressida*.

Which meant that he put himself, as they say, on the line. The consequences became real. Once he had invested his own vulnerability in Troilus, the prospect of exploding this bomb, even in a tragic fantasy, became, perhaps, seriously alarming. This is the sort of thing that is meant by saying that a writer needs courage.

And maybe that is why Troilus – and the whole play – moves towards that explosion so slowly, with so much qualifying palaver, so much uncertainty and 'experiment' in every posture, such an efflorescence of style, so much concern for substitute confrontations, such a bed-ridden paralysis of the next decisive step. Every writer would recognize that nightmare, garrulous, circumstantial deferment of the real issue – when the real issue has suddenly reared up. Hamlet will have a similar problem, but will also try harder, knowing better what is at stake.

So, with Troilus, Shakespeare introduced the factor missing from the two preceding plays: that larval phase of Adonis, the phase of 'total, unconditional love'. After that it seems obvious. If the Equation has to tap the reservoirs of authentic passion, and real knowledge, it has to spring from Adonis's original love – the 'dear, religious love' (Sonnet 31,6), 'the madness': if the bomb is to be tragic, it has to be primed with a total vulnerability that has everything to lose.

Troilus and Cressida: the new factor and the different madness

Shakespeare assembles this new, larger and more effective dramatic device with a completeness and precision that argues an extraordinary awareness of just what he was doing. The pattern is worth dismantling in some detail if only to sharpen the eye to his code and his methods, which are less nakedly visible in later works. The foreground features relevant to this new form of the Tragic Equation, and to the hero's new plight, develop as follows:

It is the seventh year of the Greek siege of Troy. Helen, stolen from her husband King Menelaus by the Trojan Prince Paris, is still in Troy, but both sides are beginning to doubt whether she is worth the bloodshed. Nevertheless, on both sides the chieftains are still determined – the Greeks to attack, the Trojans to defend.

Two plots alternate on stage: the war plot, and the love plot. The war plot is suspended because the Greek champion, Achilles, refuses to fight. For four acts the only action in the war plot is prompted by a challenge to single combat, delivered by the Trojan hero Hector but converted, by the Greek chieftains, to a ruse (which fails) to bring Achilles back into the battle. This episode interrupts briefly an atmosphere of more or less constant, indecisive skirmishes. A day of battle is coming to an end, the heroes returning from the field, as the play opens. Another, beginning in the fifth act, is overtaken by the sudden rage of Achilles, and becomes the last great battle, in which the Trojan champion, Hector, is slain.

The love plot develops within the war plot, during those first four acts. Prince Troilus has fallen totally and unconditionally (helplessly and idealistically) in love with Cressida. Cressida convinces him (but not the audience) that she returns his love in kind.

Her father, the prophet Calchas, who has foreseen the outcome of the war, is already in the Greek camp. He begs the Greeks to exchange a captured Trojan for his daughter and, since Calchas has obliged them with his agreeable prophecy, they comply. So Cressida is parted from Troilus and welcomed into the Grecian camp where she is immediately and willingly seduced by Diomed.

Visiting the Grecian camp during a truce, Troilus spies on Cressida and Diomed together, and realizes what has happened: his adored Cressida has become a whore.

The war plot, up to this moment lolling – like Achilles – on its pressed bed, now blazes into action, and Troilus rushes into the fray in a suicidal battle frenzy.

In this combination of Rival Brothers and Tragic Equation, clearly the Equation is not triggered until that moment in Act Five, Scene Two, when Troilus suddenly sees the whore in Cressida and for the first time confronts the 'double vision'.

In the structure of the Equation, Troilus's sudden loathing of

Cressida's lust occupies exactly the same position as Angelo's official loathing of the lust of Vienna. In other words, it takes Shakespeare over four acts of *Troilus and Cressida* to reach the position with which he had opened *Measure for Measure*. These are the four acts that he devotes to establishing the 'new factor'. This new factor, clearly, is not an addition but a backward exploration into the origins of that loathing – Angelo's loathing of the lust of Vienna, Adonis's loathing of the lust of Venus. And the form Shakespeare finds for those origins emerges under accurate analysis. It is organically all of a piece with what now follows. These heroes loathe the Female because they loved her (and love her) too well – too 'totally and unconditionally' – in some other, mythic dimension (in childhood, perhaps). In this perspective, Troilus's case is therefore a much deeper, more radical and complete psychoanalytical portrait of Angelo's case, and Adonis's. It 'explains' the double vision. And it confirms, it traces in more detail, and in slow motion, just how that moment of revelatory loathing, that flash of double vision, is simply the opening phase of the hero's madness – which in mythic terms is the impact of the Boar that transforms him to a Tarquin.

As I implied earlier, this new factor, the larval or introductory phase of the hero's idyllic (idealistic) love, enables Shakespeare to connect his Mythic Equation to the impassioned enigma of his own subjectivity (as the *Sonnets* revealed it) in a way that is impossible to ignore. As if he had replaced the sonnet form with a new superior lens, he now examines that same episode of innocence and experience afresh – bringing it into such full and nakedly raw close-up that it seems to be coming under his attention for the first time. This helps to give *Troilus and Cressida* its autobiographical feel. Exactly like Shakespeare in the *Sonnets*, Troilus needs his beloved to be perfect in true love, though at bottom he fears it to be impossible:

> O! that I thought it could be in a woman –
> As if it can I will presume in you –
> To feed for aye her lamp and flames of love;
> To keep her constancy in plight and youth,
> Outliving beauty's outward, with a mind
> That doth renew swifter than blood decays:
> Or that persuasion could but thus convince me,
> That my integrity and truth to you
> Might be affronted with the match and weight

Of such a winnow'd purity in love;
How were I then uplifted! but, alas!

Troilus and Cressida, III. ii. 165–75

He fears she will betray him, and, exactly as in the *Sonnets*, she does.

Troilus reiterates the *Sonnets*' protestations about love's relationship to time, and to words, and redefines the holy simplicity of its truth. But his words are counterpointed by a running accompaniment on what 'true love' refuses to know – the true nature of sexuality (cf. page 165, *A Lover's Complaint*), and the apparently inevitable fact, accepted with torment in the *Sonnets*, of Cressida's treachery. This cynical realism, which spoke in *All's Well* through the mouth of Parolles, and in *Measure for Measure* through Lucio, and will speak in *Othello* through Iago, speaks here through Thersites (and wise Ulysses), who come into the same world as Troilus, the same scene, only when the idealist Troilus accepts the bitter truth of what Thersites simply knows.

At this point, in Act Five, Scene Two, it becomes evident just how the new factor, the preliminary phase of undisillusioned, exalted love, which charged Troilus's double vision with the bomb of vulnerability that has everything to lose, has produced, out of the impact of the Boar and the fusion of the Boar with the idealist, a different kind of 'madness'. This altered form of the madness is no small consequence. If the new factor connected Shakespeare's enterprise to a new, bottomless resource, this different madness opens for it a vast and it might be said infinite new field of operations. Since both the new factor and the modified madness are from now on integral features of the Equation, through all its future evolution, it is tempting to attribute to them the astonishing new amplitude of material and feeling and the sudden expansion of vision that arrive with *Troilus and Cressida*.

The difference between the old madness and the new is stark enough to be puzzling (cf. page 221), though its inevitability, following on the new factor, is overwhelmingly true to life. Where formerly this madness seized heroes who were previously loveless, and directed them with uncontrollable sexual desire against a woman all but unknown (and even forbidden) to them, now it seizes the hero of 'total and unconditional love' and directs him, not in a sexual but in a homicidal frenzy, against his own beloved.

Obviously it happens in life that a maddened Othello will rape his wife rather than murder her, but on stage, in a symbolic work, that would be pitiably weak and one-dimensional, locked into pathology, without resonance of any kind. Murder, on the other hand, as everybody understands, lifts the situation into a bigger theatre: it expresses the mythic stature of the original love, and of the injury it has suffered, and of its weird justice. The word 'mythic' here spans both poles of mythic being: in one direction it encompasses all possibilities of spiritual complexity in the act (which Othello, for instance, is fully aware of when he wishes to call his killing of Desdemona not a murder but 'a sacrifice'); in the opposite direction it incorporates that even more potent range of being, in which sexuality has commandeered the primordial (pre-heterosexual) instinct of killing to eat, and has sublimated and transformed and adapted it (in the inspired economy of biological life) into the equally compulsory act of reproduction. This universal double perspective opens behind his tragic hero's 'madness', when Shakespeare shifts the act from rape to murder. Even so, the internal mechanism of the shift, in the working of the Equation, is not simply a symbolic or metaphorical upgrading: it is determined by crucial dynamic pressures (this is gone into more fully on page 221 and later) within Shakespeare's myth. Here in *Troilus and Cressida* it shoulders into place seeming, as I say, simply inevitable and 'true to life'. And this is where the tap-root of the Tragic Equation can be seen emerging, aching with sap, from the darkness beneath the *Sonnets* into the giant, oaken ramifications of the tragic sequence of dramas that now follow.

The new field of operation, made accessible by the new form of the hero's 'madness', is of course the potentially tragic dimension. It is still only potential in so far as Troilus – or rather Shakespeare – in this play hesitates. He defers, piles up the shiftless, glittering circumstances, splits every hair – and in the end contrives to put off the final audit. After those first four acts, in which the dramatist carefully assembles the bomb and wakes up to find it ticking, as I say, in the hand that wrote the *Sonnets*, he manages at the last moment to protect himself and Troilus and – most particularly – Cressida from the blast. So when it explodes, Troilus's love for the Cressida who has proved herself a whore remains strangely intact – as does Cressida. As did Shakespeare's love for the faithless woman in the *Sonnets*. Troilus's last words directly about his love for Cressida reaffirm it:

Never did young man fancy
With so eternal and so fix'd a soul.
Hark, Greek: as much as I do Cressid love
So much by weight hate I her Diomed.

v. ii. 162–5

Though her falsity sends him mad – even as he speaks those words – he preserves his love for her by forcibly splitting her falsity from her ('Swagger[ing] himself out on's own eyes', as Thersites comments) and projecting it on to Diomed, which enables him to deflect his madness away from her and on to the Greeks generally but especially on to Diomed.

This noble forbearance, in which the tragic hero protects his beloved from his own Tarquinian madness, is a temporary half-measure. It never appears again after this first, 'soft-shelled' prototype of the Equation's truly tragic form (unless Hamlet's banishing of Ophelia to a nunnery is a more conscious – but vain – attempt to do the same). In *Troilus and Cressida* the absolute logic of his new invention is complete, but Shakespeare is still unwilling to submit to it. Viewed from the following plays, however, this sparing of Cressida is the last stand of an appalled reluctance (dramatized more painfully and consciously in *Hamlet*) to accept the Tragic Equation's remorseless conclusion – that the beloved Female must die.

Nevertheless, in spite of this final inhibition, when Cressida strokes Diomed's cheek, there in Act Five, Scene Two, the Tragic Equation jolts into gear and everything, in what remains of the play, becomes a function of its mechanism. A brief sketch of the engineering of the first four acts shows how clearly this is prepared for.

The Trojan War: the incubation of the Tragic Equation

The more obvious structural tensions of *Troilus and Cressida* depend on the interaction of that public dimension of the suspended war plot, which is desperately striving to make time move, with the private dimension of the love plot, which is desperately striving to make time stop, and which grows almost like an accidental pregnancy within the war plot. Whichever plot takes its turn in the foreground, the other hovers behind it as a contrapuntal metaphorical comment.

At times, the two plots combine more actively: while puppets act out the one in the spotlit foreground, the other looms and leans over as the dark shapes of the manipulating puppeteers. These interactions tighten until – in that Act Five, Scene Two – public and private plots become one, whereupon the puppeteers suddenly emerge, as it were, and perform in full light with their puppets under their arms.

In one sense when this happens the war plot has made a toy of the love plot, breaking it and scattering the pieces – or, rather, has simply destroyed it with the brutality and unconcern of public events, as if that pregnancy had miscarried during a battle. On the other hand, it is the war plot which exposes, as by relentless analysis and experimental proof, the real nature of the lovers and the love plot. Both these interpretations accept the play as a version of as-if-actual happenings. Which is presumably how this play, like most plays, hopes to be accepted. Yet the second approach, reading the war plot as an analysis of the love plot, suggests that the war plot can be seen as a projection of the love plot – an enclosing, matrix-like metaphor of its already corrupted corruptibility, fragility, brevity and inevitable disintegration. Virtually, that would reduce the play to an analysis of female sexuality – a further, more ample, more bitter analysis of the sexuality of that 'maid' (now a little more worldly wise) in A Lover's Complaint (where female sexuality is the ultimate image of sexuality itself – the mirror of amoral Eros).

To take that second approach a shade more seriously, and remembering that Troilus and Cressida has established its character in our imaginations as an inexhaustibly symbolic and wholly artistic (i.e. musical) work, and remembering too that Cressida shares the intimate aspect of the action with Troilus, who is in fact more deeply central than she is, since the drama revolves around and to a degree within his inner life, then the whole play can easily be seen as a symbolic expression of his subjective being, specifically of the pitiless correction and destruction of his idealistic attitude towards love. This view brings sharply into focus Troilus's role as the prototype Shakespearean tragic hero.

In other words, it is in this perspective, which is the mythic perspective, that he stands, in Act Five, Scene Two, facing the double vision of the loved and the loathed woman in the one body, while Diomed, her secret lover, emerging, so to speak, from her skirts, confronts him as the Rival usurping Brother, who is also the Boar. In that same perspective, these two contenders throw back through the play two gigantic, opposed shadows, fixed outlines in the whirling mist, which are in fact the two sides of the war plot: a classic specimen of Shakespeare's Rival Brothers fighting over the Female.

In this inclusive pattern the Greeks – who will sack the sacred city, kill the King, and carry off ('rape') the Female – are the usurping irrational Brother. Conversely, the Trojans – who defend their patrimony in vain, are murdered (as a champion hero and a king: Hector now, Priam later), are usurped (Troilus now, Paris later) from possession of the Female, and are driven into exile (as Aeneas later) – are the rational Brother, in Shakespeare's (retrospectively) well-established scheme.

Within this large format the dramatist keeps operational control over the two clusters of names by – again – a kind of algebra. As I indicate above, he analyses each Rival Brother (Trojan side and Greek side) into its constituent but distinctly characterized parts. Each individual, wherever he appears, can represent his whole team, can be 'boil[ed]', 'As 'twere from forth us all, a man distill'd', becoming the irrational brother (always with the mythic attributes of the 'hot tyrant' or the Boar) if he is Greek, or the rational brother (always with the mythic attributes of Adonis) if he is Trojan. Needless to say (and this must always be understood, throughout all the plays), the personifications of this basic, structural polarity in no obvious way interfere with the individualized life of the characters. All discharge their mythic duties as it were incidentally, in the interplay of the personalities that Shakespeare has bestowed on them.

Trojans with minor parts, such as Priam, Paris, Antenor, go through their paces in the pattern, but the main burden of representative rational brother (and Adonis) passes to and fro between Hector and Troilus – and, to a lesser degree, Aeneas. Each performs a different aspect of that one role. As the action gets under way, in the fifth act, where the Tragic Equation begins to bite, Hector becomes more defined as that aspect of Adonis which is too rational (here too noble) to apprehend the mystery behind the irrational, and which must therefore be destroyed (by the transforming impact of the Boar). Troilus becomes definable as that aspect which is only too susceptible to the mystery, too capable of apprehending and suffering the (rational brother's) full horror and loathing of it, the pain of being transformed by it – of becoming, that is, a Tarquin. Aeneas has a more generalized function as a composite of both: he is the surviving aspect of the rational yet suffering man, who will escape death by fleeing into exile (falling into the wilderness) where he will become, eventually, a saint of some kind (and son of Venus, like Adonis, who will found the Holy Roman Empire). (Even here, in this supernumerary, off-stage deployment of his mythic algebra, Shakespeare anticipates the ultimate final development of his Tragic Equation: Aeneas reappears in *The Tempest*, cf. page 418).

Between the Trojan rational brother and the Greek irrational brother the Female is subjected to a similar analysis and share-out of the Goddess's different aspects. In the public dimension, Helen fulfils a role – in spite of everything – as the sacred principle of Divine Love. That is to say, in this war she is the living palladium of Troy, the queen bee at the heart of the Trojans' coherence and morale, and the motive of their defence. At the same time, obviously she fulfils a similar role for the Greeks. That both sides have such grievous reservations about her, and regard her to a greater or lesser degree as a whore, is in a sense irrelevant in so far as they do not absolutely abjure and reject her, but go on attacking and defending only because of her. They suspend their judgement of her 'contaminated carrion weight' on both sides as if both sides, recognizing the loathed woman in the body of the loved one, acknowledged the 'double vision' but somehow suspended their reaction to it indefinitely – suspending all serious action in the process.

Accordingly, the Goddess's antithetical aspect, that of the Queen of Hell, is also suspended. This condition is perfectly figured in Cassandra – the sybil, the oracle, the mouth of the Underworld whose whole being is temporarily neutralized because (by a curse) she cannot be believed. Possessed by the 'final state' of the Female, in this out-of-gear Tragic Equation, she describes what a Queen of Hell can always see: the death of Hector (Adonis) and the destruction of Troy (chaos), but is simply not listened to, or is dismissed as a shamefully frightened, dream-deluded fantasist. She will not be believed, her infernal viewpoint will not be accorded full reality, till her prophecies come true. (Shakespeare does not mention it, but he was well aware that she would then become a fully qualified Queen of Hell by entering the 'hot tyrant's' and the Boar's otherworld as King Agamemnon's consort and prize. Here again Shakespeare seems to be lifting out of the wealth of his materials precisely that figure, that nexus of historical meaning, which suited his purpose – opening that whole empire of mythic hinterland behind the simple title of Helen's opposite, when he positioned Cassandra in his design.)

Between those two, Cressida's role seems to be adjusted with even more deliberate art, as the key to the whole structure. Her relationship to them resembles that of Aeneas to Hector and Troilus, in that her nature comprehends and is in its way the sum of both theirs. But while his lightly drawn figure eventually fades away (escapes) altogether, Cressida incarnates, in a wholly realistic personality, and brings right into the dead-end, cornered, spotlit forefront of the private dimension, the inflammatory human implication of what Helen somewhat abstractly and remotely represents at one extreme (the primal Goddess for whom India is a bed, in which she lies as a pearl) and what Cassandra infernally and symbolically implies at the other (the Queen of Hell's duplicity, and her vision of the doom of Adonis). In the action, Cressida moves from the one extreme to the other. She appears in the early scenes in her aspect of (a tainted) Helen, compared to Helen, and up to a point identified with her: her own first remarks about Troilus concern Helen's liking for him, and his giving Helen a forked hair from his chin as a stand-in for Paris. Exchanged for Antenor, she slips out of this persona and out of the rational, Trojan world, where she shares the bed of Troilus, reappearing in the irrational Greek world as a full Queen of Hell in the arms of the 'hot tyrant' Diomed the Greek, alias (as far as Troilus/Adonis is concerned) the Boar, who will fulfil Cassandra's prophecies. (How precisely, fully, literally, Diomed carries the mythic credentials of the Boar I will show in a moment.) In this transition from one extreme of her genetic possibilities to the other, Cressida detaches herself from Helen as if she were, in fact, the hidden, whorish elemental emerging from her, as a beautiful demon, to make her secret truth manifest — revealing it in full to Troilus, who thereupon goes mad (his Tarquinian battle frenzy). So Cressida's role in the larger pattern is that of an embodied revelation of the corruption (and Queen of Hellishness) within the divine Helen for whom the war is being fought.

This secret emergence of Cressida from 'the dark and vicious place' (King Lear's phrase) that illuminates Helen's beauty with its irresistible 'mana', and her returning swoop into Diomed's tent, completes a movement of 'fearful symmetry' within the aerobatics of the whole play. While Helen is a beautiful illusion, a sunlit, majestic wonder of the world, stared at by the world, who moves, as it were, externally, in the glaring pomp of the crowded war, from the Greek King's famous bed to the Trojan Prince's equally famous bed, Cressida dives, simultaneously, by night, unseen, as a night-owlish, lunar demon, via her secret Trojan lover's bed, to her secret Greek lover's bed — where the ornithological

Shakespeare's flashlamp camera reveals her. The last line of the play, spoken directly to the audience by Pandarus but as if from behind the play by the author (the author who was already, maybe, avoiding society and when invited out was sending word, for excuse, that he 'was in paine') bequeaths to them his 'diseases', and touches again, obliquely, the 'putrefied core' of the play and the awareness – which was common folklore knowledge – that Cressida died a leper.

Shakespeare's characterization of the Greeks, completing this pattern, has the same long-range, panoramic, mythic (legendary, historic) precision that he touched into focus behind Cassandra and Aeneas.

Agamemnon, Menelaus, and especially Ulysses are weighty components of the conglomerate irrational brother. But this role is performed – in the public dimension of the war plot – mainly by Achilles and Ajax. Achilles carries the Mars-like 'hot tyrant' aspect, Ajax the Boar-like ('Mars his idiot') aspect. The mythic attributes that go with these aspects are buckled and studded thickly upon this pair, wherever they speak or are mentioned. Just as Aeneas comprises both Hector and Troilus, and Cressida both Helen and Cassandra, these two are compounded in Diomed, who transmits their combined impact into the private dimension of the love plot. These individualizations of the representative irrational brother (and the Boar) are defined more and more strongly as the role shifts from one to the other in those final, violent, strobe-like scenes.

The spoor of the myth, within the action of the Tragic Equation, is particularly clear in this play, from Act Five, Scene Two onwards. What I have said so far will have made it easy for readers to follow for themselves. Even so, for any who are still uncertain, I will take this opportunity to point out the Boar's track in some detail: it will sharpen the eyes for the coming encounters in the later plays, where the creature is not always so nakedly visible.

The secret nature of Diomed

The first trick is to scratch a little make-up off Diomed. According to the myth of the Tragic Equation, under this make-up there ought to lie something like Boar bristles.

What does appear is almost uncanny. It emerges by an indirect route, through Cressida's letter. After Troilus has seen and fully understood her infidelity, and has addressed himself to the battle (in which his nobler double Hector will be killed), Pandarus brings him this letter, which he reads. But when Pandarus asks what 'yond poor girl' says there, Troilus simply tears up the letter, making no reply but:

> Words, words, mere words, no matter from the heart;
> The effect doth operate another way.
> Go, wind to wind, there turn and change together.
>
> v. iii. 109–11

He then strides out into the battle where he will perform

> Mad and fantastic execution,
> Engaging and redeeming of himself
> With such a careless force and forceless care
> As if that luck, in very spite of cunning,
> Bade him win all.
>
> v. v. 38–42

And the letter is never mentioned again.

Shakespeare took this letter from Chaucer's long poem *Troilus and Criseyde* (one of his sources), where, in Book Five, Chaucer devotes lines 1500 to 1631 to a 'litera Criseydis', signed 'la vostra C.', in which, in a strangled, forced half-heartedness ('one eye yet looks on thee', as Shakespeare's Cressida tells herself), she makes a feint at reassuring Troilus, promising to come to him but 'in what yer or what day' she cannot say. Soon after this, a Trojan warrior brings into Troy a coat of arms torn from Diomed in battle, and fastened into it Troilus finds a brooch – a love-token that he had given to Criseyde and that she had sworn to keep for ever. Hurling himself into battle – to find Diomed and make 'his sydes blede' – Troilus begins to slay 'thousandes', before he is himself killed by Achilles.

From this it appears that Shakespeare not only switched love-tokens, he also reversed the order of letter and token for dramatic effect. That proof of Cressida's infidelity – the brooch – which seems to come after the letter in Chaucer, in Shakespeare comes before it, as a 'sleeve'. A closer look, however, confirms that in Chaucer too the real revelation comes before this dubious letter. And in both Chaucer and Shakespeare it is exactly the same disclosure. A difference is that while Shakespeare formulated it in those transparent, immediately painful, dramatic terms, where Troilus watches Diomed and Cressida together, Chaucer buries it in deeply rooted, obscure mythic terms, as a cryptic image, and while Shakespeare's Troilus is instantly shattered, Chaucer's Troilus is mystified and needs to inquire further. Yet Chaucer is the one who reveals what Shakespeare hides. He reveals, in a sense, Shakespeare's (conscious, half-conscious, unconscious) method by divulging that elemental mythic power source of the situation, which Shakespeare translates into demythologized human statement and human action (as in every example of the Tragic Equation except the first long poem *Venus and Adonis*).* Though this is only a detail, it is instructive in this way, and worth a pause to bring it fully to light.

In Chaucer, Criseyde sends another letter, earlier. More positive than the second, but only briefly paraphrased by the poet, it promises Troilus that she will come to him, and that she loves him 'best'. After this, waiting for her, Troilus begins to sicken with love and deferred hope:

> He ne eat, ne dronk, ne slep, ne no worde seyde

till finally he sinks into a distracted sleep and has a dream. In this dream, Jove reveals to him Criseyde's 'untrouthe' by showing him the mysterious figure of a wild boar. He wakes baffled, and asks his sister, the 'Sibille' Cassandre, to divine for him the meaning of this 'stronge boor with his tuskes stout'.

Whereupon Cassandre tells him:

> Thow wel this boor shalt knowe, and of what kind
> He comen is, as men in bokes find.
> *Troilus and Criseyde*, Book v, 1462–3

and proceeds to recount the story of how Diana (as Artemis, the Great Goddess), enraged against the Greeks by their neglect of her shrine, sent 'a boor as gret as ox in stalle' — her infernal animal form — to devastate their lands. This was the fabled beast of Calydon, eventually slain by Meleager who (from this famous victory as well as from his divine father, the god Mars) took the Boar as his armorial crest, passing it lineally to Tydeus (one of the seven kings who died at Thebes), who passed it in turn to his son — Diomed. Cassandra then interprets Troilus's dream:

> This ilke boor bitokneth Diomed,
> Tideus sone, that down descended is

*i.e. the 'method' which is the theme of this book.

[189]

Fro Meleagre, that made the boor to blede.
And thy lady, wherso she be, ywis,
This Diomed hire herte hath, and she his.
Wep if thow wilt, or lef! For, out of doute,
This Diomed is in, and thow art oute.

1513–19

In Chaucer's poem, that is, the fact that Diomed is both Troilus's usurping Rival and the Boar of the Goddess is a functional feature of the plot, and not just decoration.* And they now emerge, as one, against Troilus, out of a 'whore', exactly as in the Equation, to kill him in battle, while the news of their approach comes from one whom Troilus now sees as a witch:

'Thow seyth nat sooth' quod he 'thow sorceresse,
With al thy false goost of prophecye!'

Whether Shakespeare pondered this Chaucerian dream much or not, when in Act Five, Scene Two his Ulysses revealed to Troilus the 'untrouthe' of Cressida, and showed her as a Queen of Hell, embracing and wooing his rival Diomed, while Thersites laughed hyena-like in the shadows, he was lifting the same veil that Jove lifted for the sleeping Troilus in Chaucer's poem. In other words, the role of Shakespeare's Diomed as the Boar, in that myth of the Boar as an emissary of the rejected Goddess, does not need to be imported into this play by any Cassandra-like interpreter: it is an integral, historical part of the materials that Shakespeare chooses to fit into this position, in his invention.

So at this point, where the Boar myth enters the play and Troilus sees the 'double vision', the Tragic Equation is sprung, and (according to that 'ideal order' of the plays this is the first time it does so in full) completes its action. Or, to stick to the 'bomb' image, as it explodes here for the first time it does so in slow motion, and Shakespeare registers – as on a computerized simulation – the composite chemical signature of each phase of the process.

Accordingly, as the hero's larval phase, the ticking-time-fuse phase, comes to an end, and the two detonating elements are brought together (which is to say, as the 'divine love' of Sonnet 116 which descended

*This reveals Diomed and Troilus – and Cressida – as weathered outcrops of the archaic myth. Diomed's original mythic title as himself a love-god killed by the Boar is preserved in the Irish myth of Dermot and the Boar.

from Heaven is usurped and chemically transformed by the 'sweating lust' of Sonnet 129 that belongs to Earth) Troilus describes the change in literal terms:

> Instance, O instance! strong as Pluto's gates;
> Cressid is mine, tied with the bonds of heaven:
> Instance, O instance! strong as heaven itself:
> The bonds of heaven are slipp'd, dissolv'd and loos'd;
> And with another knot, five-finger-tied,
> The fractions of her faith, orts of her love,
> The fragments, scraps, the bits, and greasy relics
> Of her o'er-eaten faith, are bound to Diomed.
>
> v. ii. 150–7

The Adonis of the idyll has become the Puritan loather of lust and the explosion has begun. The lowering, diffused glow of indefinite 'double vision', which has held the whole drama suspended in a fog for so long, now condenses, for Troilus, in this dazzling, single flash – as he sees the loved and the loathed woman in the one body. It leaves everything agonizingly clear. Again, the description is literal – so literal that to Thersites it sounds ludicrous:

> Let it not be believ'd for womanhood!
> Think we had mothers; do not give advantage
> To stubborn critics, apt, without a theme,
> For depravation, to square the general sex
> By Cressid's rule: rather think this not Cressid . . .
> This she? no, this is Diomed's Cressida . . .
> This is not she. O madness of discourse . . .
> . . . this is, and is not, Cressid.
> Within my soul there doth conduce a fight
> Of this strange nature that a thing inseparate
> Divides more wider than the sky and earth;
> And yet the spacious breadth of this division
> Admits no orifice for a point as subtle
> As Ariachne's broken woof to enter.
>
> v. ii. 126–49

In a few lines the whole play leaps from Sonnet 128 to 147 taking 129 with it. The speed and economy with which Troilus now becomes Tarquin is itself algebraic, but the whole working out is there in his words: his very next words are pure mythic algebra. When Ulysses, his guide, asks if what he sees — Cressida fondling and pleading with Diomed — affects him, and he cries:

> that shall be divulged well
> In characters as red as Mars his heart
> Inflam'd with Venus:
>
> 160–2

he is fitting together basic factors of the Tragic Equation in their primary terms, where the composition of Tarquin (the full-blaze phase of the explosion) is expressed as the murderous Roman military leader (Mars, the war god of Rome) possessed ('inflamed' = crammed with blood fury) by the infernal aspect of the Goddess (the Boar).

This image, like a *quipu* or knotted code signal from the myth beneath, announces the Boar's charge. It may seem a little forced to call such a routine image of homicidal jealousy a carefully (or effortlessly or automatically) placed anticipation of that precise juncture of the two myths (the two poems) at which the one who was Adonis, slain and possessed by the Boar, will become Tarquin. But there is, of course, still another purely classical precision to this particular reference: the Boar which killed Adonis always was, as I noted earlier, also the Goddess's divine lover, Mars — the 'hot tyrant', emerging from her shadow in animal form as the usurping Rival Brother. Nor has Shakespeare finished here. Troilus goes straight on from that coded declaration of his own mythic transformation to rehearse the 'fatal blow', in which Adonis's attempt to kill the hunted Boar becomes the usurping Rival Brother's death blow (in other words, Adonis's attempt to kill the Boar becomes the Boar's own fatal impact), overthrowing the rational man:

> his helm
> Were it a casque composed by Vulcan's skill
> My sword should bite it.
>
> 166–8

(A reader will recognize, in this, a rehearsal for that moment, in *Hamlet*, where Pyrrhus's sword, in the Player's speech, descends through the same mythic arc:

> And never did the Cyclops' hammers fall
> On Mars's armour, forg'd for proof eterne,

With less remorse than Pyrrhus' bleeding sword
Now falls on Priam . . .

Hamlet, II. ii. 519–22

Troilus then plunges directly into a description of what will accompany every Tarquin's terrible emergence (see page 383) – the storm that lifts the sea above the head:

Not the dreadful spout
Which shipmen do the hurricano call,
Constring'd in mass by the almighty sun,
Shall dizzy with more clamour Neptune's ear
In his descent than shall my prompted sword
Falling on Diomed.

Troilus and Cressida, v. ii. 168–73

(the same storm which becomes, for Pyrrhus's arrested sword, the lightning and thunder that releases its violence). The mysterious dramatic power of Shakespeare's brief pictograms, such as those here, depends as can be seen on his manipulation and control of their massively integrated mythic interiors, which are so tightly wired to his words – as if each word were a switch coded with a glyph, and as if each switch were less a word than a physical feature of the actor, who is therefore, in speaking, not so much recounting a process as performing it, not so much commenting on it as being transformed by it.

So it is here, in the middle of Troilus's rapt vision of his own role in the myth – the 'double vision', the collision with the Boar, the self-transformation, the imminent madness, in the tornado of Tarquin's emergence – that he is interrupted by Aeneas, entering to tell him that Hector is arming himself for what will turn out to be a full dramatization of that very collision with the Boar, but translated from the private, subjective terms of the Tragic Equation in the love-story to the public, objective terms of the Tragic Equation in the battle (for Hector, death; for Troilus, battle-frenzy 'madness') between Greek and Trojan.

This interruption, in other words, lifts the drama on to a different plane. This is where those puppeteers step forward, each a puppet clutching a puppet like itself, and itself manipulated now by the mythic law, like iron filings on a page held over a magnet, on the ritual dance floor of the Tragic Equation.

The Boar's track into the battle

What has happened inside Troilus, as he stared at Cressida, is now enacted by all. While Hector sets out on the hunt, to find the Boar, Aeneas – the free factor of this doomed Adonis – communicates to the still-dreaming Adonis that he must awake and act (i.e. become as Hector).

As Hector sets out – for the encounter in which he will be killed – he meets both aspects of the Female: Cassandra, the temporarily neutralized Queen of Hell, and Andromache – who is both Sacred Bride and Divine Mother. Shakespeare makes no overt use of this composite role of Andromache, but it is famously there. In Virgil's account of Hector setting out for his last battle, the hero's leavetaking from Andromache and their little son Astyanax is one of the most celebrated moments of the *Aeneid*. In Homer's account, as Hector went out to meet Achilles, his mother tried to prevent him by baring her breast, calling him 'my child', and begging him to remember her cares for him when she suckled him as a baby. In the algebraic shorthand of Shakespeare's account it is enough that Andromache should appear (for the first and only time), frightened by premonitory dreams, pleading with him to turn back from the battle. To begin with Cassandra does no more than support her.

Troilus, now as it were thoroughly awake, joins this scene and attempts to persuade Hector to stay at home. Hector's strange response is to ask Troilus to stay at home. This odd exchange seems to have no basis (except as a courtesy with little dramatic point) unless it relates to Shakespeare's ubiquitous vacillation:

> One of these men is Genius to the other;
> And so of these: which is the natural man,
> And which the spirit?
>
> *A Comedy of Errors*, v. i. 334–6

At this point Troilus's words define Hector as that nobler aspect of the Adonis whose destiny they share, the part that refuses to entertain any fear of what is about to happen, or even to take it seriously, while Troilus himself, having been imprinted with the 'double vision', is already feeling the first currents of 'madness'. He sees the costly 'error' of Hector's high-minded, ceremonious rationality:

[194]

> Brother, you have a vice of mercy in you,
> That better fits a lion than a man . . .
> When many times the captive Grecian falls,
> Even in the fan and wind of your fair sword,
> You bid them rise, and live.
>
> *Troilus and Cressida*, v. iii. 37–42

The extraordinary, tight circuitry of Shakespeare's code lights up almost every phrase here. That penultimate line is a practice stroke that will fall perfected when Pyrrhus (Achilles's son), in the Player's speech in *Hamlet*, 'with the whiff and wind of his fell sword' – a sword that was in the 'fair' hand of Adonis somehow now in the 'fell' hand of Tarquin – knocks down none other than King Priam. Whereupon, exactly as Cassandra prophesies will happen when Achilles's sword falls on Hector, Priam and Troy itself ('Thou on him leaning, and all Troy on thee') will fall 'Seeming to feel this blow, with flaming top'.

Here in *Troilus and Cressida* Troilus is identifying Hector's idealist, unrealistic mercy, which will have to pay, with the Greekish pitiless realism, which will exact the full price, and pointedly contrasting it with his own present transformation – into a berserk, Pyrrhus-like Tarquin. That this self-transformation is exactly what he is referring to is confirmed by what he goes on to say next. When Hector rebukes him, calling him a 'savage', and almost ordering him not to fight that day, Troilus cries:

> Who should withhold me?
> Not fate, obedience, nor the hand of Mars
> Beckoning with fiery truncheon my retire;
> Not Priamus and Hecuba on knees,
> Their eyes o'ergalled with recourse of tears;
> Not you, my brother, with your true sword drawn,
> Oppos'd to hinder me, should stop my way,
> But to my ruin.
>
> v. iii. 51–8

Again, at this confrontation of the highest tension, just before the external explosion that will finally release all the pent-up pressures of the drama, these mythic tropes do not seem otiose, or in any way inert – as purely ornamental references of such a kind (as in all post-Shakespearean drama) certainly would be. Once again, with these words he is merely touching the controls of the Tragic Equation which has now taken possession of him. The Mars with 'fiery truncheon' is – once more in primary terms – the 'hot tyrant', the irrational brother, and the Wild Boar. In literal mythic terms, he is precisely the antagonist that meets Adonis – and takes possession of him, and even now, as he speaks, is transforming Troilus into an uncontrollable Tarquin. The view of Priam and Hecuba, weeping on their knees, is notoriously that seen through the eyes of Pyrrhus when in Virgil's account they vainly plead as the sword of Achilles (Pyrrhus had inherited it) begins its descent on Priam's 'milky head'. And the view of Hector, the rational brother, his 'true' (i.e. rational) sword drawn to stop the frenzied Troilus, is clearly that seen by the irrational brother, who is about to kill and supplant him. It is the view Achilles will have of him. These three glimpses, in fact (like Angelo's strange glimpse of the violet growing by the carrion), are all snatched from Troilus's own internal mythic transmogrification into his opposite – in which Hector appears in front of him like a projection on a screen, as his doomed rational self, about to be transformed, as he is destroyed, by the impact of the Boar.

After this, as if speaking now as one, Hector and Troilus defy the restraining pleas of Cassandra, Andromache and Priam too (the rational crown of Troy itself). Hector, with sudden anger, banishes Andromache – and she goes, only to be replaced (as in a mini-fractal of the Tragic Equation) by the sybil Cassandra screaming her vision of his bloody death and Troy's despair:

> O farewell! dear Hector,
> Look! how thou diest; look! how thy eye turns pale;
> Look! how thy wounds do bleed at many vents:
> Hark! how Troy roars: how Hecuba cries out!
> How poor Andromache shrills her dolours forth!
> Behold, distraction, frenzy and amazement,
> Like witless antics, one another meet,
> And all cry Hector! Hector's dead! O Hector!
>
> v. iii. 80–7

which is a feminine, verbal form, like a rehearsal, of the Boar's onslaught.*

As the two heroes exit together to the battle, Troilus shouts a challenge towards Diomed, as if he were hallooing the game in a hunt. In the simplest terms of the myth, after rejecting the Goddess in a greater or lesser degree of intensity in all her manifestations, Adonis, as Hector/Troilus, closes in on the Boar, as if to destroy it.

This transition of the action of the Tragic Equation from the private dimension of the love plot to the public dimension of the battle, and from the hieroglyphic poetry of the hero's subjective account of his transformation to the quasi-historical action of the drama that objectifies it, takes up almost every line of Scenes Two and Three in Act Five. But what follows is if possible even more economical. Any reader who has by now picked up Shakespeare's algebraic method of operating the Equation's electrical currents will be able to follow it through the detail of (again) almost every line, right up to Troilus's closing couplet. For those readers who still have a doubt about the theatrical or existential relevance of this 'mythic dimension', a rapid aerial survey of these final duels might help to illustrate it.

The Hunt staged as the death of Hector

Scene Four opens with Thersites, as if he had materialized like a genie from the scraps of Cressida's letter, announcing that Diomed is out there on the battlefield (like the angry Boar, waiting for Troilus and Hector, tearing the ground), wearing on his helm (where Anglo-Saxon warriors in Beowulf's day wore the Boar-crest of the Great Goddess Freya) Troilus's love-pledge 'sleeve'.

To take another Pole-Star bearing during this tempestuous passage, this 'sleeve', and its crucial role here, in the scene spied on by the hero, ought

---

*Exactly the same combination of maternal/wifely dread and sybilline fateful prophecy tried to restrain Adonis at exactly this same moment in *Venus and Adonis*, lines 662–6, where Achilles is replaced by the

    angry-chafing boar,
Under whose sharp fangs on his back doth lie

An image like thyself, all stain'd with gore;
  Whose blood upon the fresh flowers being
                      shed
Doth make them droop with grief and
                hang the head.

to be compared with the strawberry-embroidered 'handkerchief' in *Othello* (see pages 474–5) and the cowslip-coloured 'mole' under Imogen's left breast in *Cymbeline* (see pages 475–6). All three are reflective forms of the 'flower' – that came into Angelo's head at just this moment in his transformation, and that originally bloomed between the two long poems (and between the breasts of the mourning Venus). In passing, the only two flower images in *Troilus and Cressida* might be noted. The first:

> Hector . . . today was mov'd:
> He chid Andromache, and struck his armourer . . .
> And to the field goes he; where every flower
> Did, as a prophet, weep what it foresaw
> In Hector's wrath.

I. ii. 4–11

which is a preview of the next time we see him 'mov'd', chiding Andromache, and going to the field, when Hector's 'wrath' will become, as prophesied, 'Hector's death' among flowers that hang their heads heavy with his blood. In the second reference Troilus tells Pandarus (Cressida's uncle):

> I stalk about her door,
> Like a strange soul upon the Stygian banks
> Staying for waftage. O! be thou my Charon,
> And give me swift transportance to those fields
> Where I may wallow in the lily beds
> Propos'd for the deserver!

III. ii. 8–13

wherein he plainly sees her as the Queen of the Underworld (with the Styx flowing beneath her threshold), his love for her as a death, and his future a 'wallowing' in those lily beds which are, in the myth behind this prophetic fantasy (which affected Keats like a drug), the death-bed of Adonis – those beds of white blood-splashed flowers in which the only wallowings will be the death throes of the love-god, alias the Boar's wallowings (in his corpse) that will resurrect him as a Tarquin.

The Hunt now pounds across the stage – in the simplest terms as Troilus chasing Diomed, Diomed seeking a place to fight (Adonis bringing the

Boar to bay), while Thersites goads them both like the hormone reek of the excited Boar itself.

Scene Five then opens surprisingly, with Diomed sending Troilus's captured horse to Cressida, as a trophy:

> Tell her I have chastis'd the amorous Trojan,
> And am her knight by proof.

v. v. 4–5

This horse appears in Shakespeare's sources, but it also appeared in *Venus and Adonis* as an incarnation of the lust which Adonis rejected. And as the stallion left him then to join the lust of the mare that resembled (and in the contextual mythology actually was) the erotic, rejected Goddess, so it leaves him now to join, as it were, Cressida. Whether so intended or not, this almost subliminal dramatic signal indicates the departure of the body of lust (in fact, the body of Eros) from the hero (who has in effect rejected it) to the Queen of Hell, from whom it will re-emerge as the vengeful and fatal Boar. This *mythic* meaning swells behind the obvious, immediate dramatic shock. The impression that cocky, lucky Diomed has triumphed again (even if he procured the horse by a trick), and the wrench of Troilus's humiliation, work powerfully. But the larger recognition, that Troilus's *barakha*, the power which was his good fortune, has left him (as when Hercules leaves Antony in *Antony and Cleopatra*) and has joined Diomed, deepens everything else into the real understanding that Troilus is now doomed.

There follow three magnificent descriptive speeches that are virtually three scenes. In the first, the great leader of the irrational horde, Agamemnon, enumerates the prostrating blows being delivered by the Trojans. In simple mythic terms, the thunderous roll call of conquering Trojans and defeated Greeks is the Boar's screech of pain at a maddening wound that Hector and Troilus have managed to inflict upon it. And within this screech can be heard the voice of the specific injury – the death of Patroclus – which will convert the Boar into an irresistible counter-attacker. The cry ends with an appeal to Diomed alone, as if he were the whole Greek host, or – in the myth – the magical real name of the Boar's soul: as if the Boar were now mustering all its spirit and will, to turn and stand at bay.

In the next passage Nestor – the wisdom of the irrational – utters the second 'screech'. Instead of calling on Diomed, he calls directly on the sleeping Achilles and on Ajax. As if the Boar, having summoned will and spirit, should now appeal beyond them to the dormant resources, the Boar strength multiplied by five, the strength of Boar-madness, in the depth of its physical cells: the Achilles who will recognize the death of Patroclus as a blow at his life, and the Ajax who has so far not bestirred himself from his wallow. Nestor now identifies the Greek host with the sole name of Hector, who is performing miraculous battle feats, doing the work of a whole army. In mythic terms, Nestor summons the Boar's Mars-like savagery, Achilles, and its pure physical strength, Ajax, to deal with the hunter, Hector, in the public dimension.

Finally, Ulysses, the practical, impartial intelligence of the irrational horde, utters a third 'screech'. The Boar has commenced its charge, and this is by way of a battle cry. In that public dimension, the Boar, as Achilles, has singled Hector. But in that same public dimension as Ajax it has also singled Troilus. The function of this speech is to identify Troilus as Hector and Hector as Troilus, whose miraculous battle feats, his mad and fantastic execution, are described in the same terms as Hector's and sound like his.

In these three speeches, then, the Boar charges in both private and public dimensions: which is to say in these three speeches the two become securely one. At the same time the Boar's three aspects, Achilles, Ajax and Diomed, share that single aim and momentum, to bring down Hector in the public dimension and Troilus in the private dimension with the one blow: as if Hector and Troilus were simply the outer and inner names of the one hunter, Adonis, which of course they are.

The implications of this are immediately dramatized: Ajax and Diomed enter, like a two-headed Boar, calling not for Hector, or any other Trojans of the rampaging host, but for Troilus alone. They are joined by Achilles – who is roaring only for Hector. And now Nestor, leaning over this war-dance like Shakespeare himself, or like a Prospero, nods fatefully, 'So so, we draw together' (v.v.44). In five lines Hector is aligned with Achilles and, in parallel, as inner to outer, Troilus is aligned with Ajax/Diomed, as the Boar closes on Adonis.

The next scene, Scene Six, takes this process of fusion a little further, binding the two components of Adonis and the three components of the Boar more tightly together, but unexpectedly lurching in a new direction.

Diomed and Ajax almost quarrel about who shall fight Troilus – again like the two selves in the one body, till Troilus drives them out as one. Simultaneously Hector meets Achilles – and is startled. That noblest, most idealist aspect of Adonis suddenly perceives, for the first time, through a crack of battle fatigue, the real situation and his real peril. After this threat, Achilles swings past (intending to limber himself up before coming to grips) as if the Boar had jinked and charged on past. Adonis still has the initiative, in so far as in the aspect of Troilus he is chasing Ajax and Diomed. But in the aspect of Hector he has had a scare, and felt the first chill of premonition.

This sudden loss of confidence is immediately objictified by Troilus's announcing that Ajax has captured that other (minor) aspect of Adonis – Aeneas. It is here, while Troilus rushes away to rescue Aeneas or die in the attempt, that the strange unknown warrior 'in sumptuous armour' enters.

'Sumptuous armour', like luxurious array, or gorgeous externals of any kind wherever they appear in Shakespeare, alerts the listener or reader to the inevitable corollary – a vacant, or vicious, interior, and a failure of judgement in those who value them. It is a sinister moment, therefore, when Hector, as if suddenly forgetting that ominous brush with the planetary Achilles, dashes light-headedly after this newcomer to strip off his alluring tinsel. And it is made all the more so by contrast with Troilus's simultaneous concern to save Aeneas (who is their own aspect of survival and future redemption). Hector – the idealist rationality of the rational man – is now clearly 'fey', and hurrying to his own destruction. With renewed spirits he renews the chase. Here the subterranean myth of the Hunt runs out across the surface – like a decoy. Hector actually calls the figure a 'beast', and when the 'beast' flees he halloos after him, 'I'll hunt thee for thy hide.'

At this point, Achilles assembles his myrmidons (his 'ants', like creatures of the Underworld), and starts looking for Hector alone, now stalking him, as a wounded boar or buffalo will stalk his hunter. Under this 'stillness in the heavens', a peculiar scene inserts itself. The original Rival Brothers, Paris and Menelaus, cross the stage fighting: the original quarrel in its primary, naked terms, the mainspring of the whole situation, the sepsis at the core of the huge inflammation, the bad conscience and the shameful rationale that have cast their compromising shadows on to every remark spoken and every move made: a cuckold and a cuckold-maker fighting, as Thersites says, over a whore. This brief exposure of the root of the disease, at this point, superimposes on the mythic climax the source of *Troilus and Cressida*'s infinite unease. And Thersites follows the two, again hallooing them as if a dog hunted a bull, or a bull tossed a dog – as if one kind of unnatural Boar, in fact, fought another.

This glimpse of the double irrationality – not a rational brother and an irrational, but two trouble-making usurpers – opens queasy perspectives, retrospectively, through every level of the work. I will come back briefly, a little later, to this keyhole peep into the shame of the play's secret chamber.

Meanwhile, this is where Hector discovers that his prey's 'hide', his 'goodly armour', 'so fair without', concealed a 'putrefied core'. As if he had killed the tutelary goblin of the whole war, the 'genius' of those two who have just butted each other across the stage, though in fact he has also, maybe, as in a premonitory dream, killed the image of his own ornate idealism.

Almost as if he were now miming that dream image of his own murder, he proceeds to hang up his shield, lay his sword aside, take off his helmet, beginning that task of dismantling his 'fair' externals, in other words stripping off his 'hide', which Achilles will in a few minutes violently complete. This is purest Shakespearean algebraic concision. As Hector removes his 'rational' defences, Achilles and his swarm from the Underworld suddenly cover the sun, and the Boar hits him. Just to tighten the screws a little, in presenting this death of Hector, one of the most famous deaths in legendary history, Shakespeare avoids the circumstantial details as Homer had established them, and as the whole world knew them. Instead, he requisitions the description of Achilles's killing of Troilus (from Caxton, one of his other sources). He even retains the peculiar method by which Achilles dragged the corpse of Troilus – tied to his horse's tail, though it would have been just as easy (a matter of changing two words) to use the celebrated method by which he dragged Hector behind his chariot. It may be that for some of the reasons I have noted his imagination insisted on the reappearance of that horse. But, more likely, he seems to have been taking pains, in an action that consummates everything, to make sure that Hector and Troilus should both be there, inextricably one, as Adonis falls.

Shakespeare makes sure that Hector and Troilus are inextricably there together from the very start, locked in the repartee between Pandarus and Cressida, in Act One, Scene Two, which includes the following effort to separate them:

PANDARUS: Troilus is the better man of the two.

CRESSIDA: O Jupiter! there's no comparison.

PANDARUS: What! not between Troilus and Hector? Do you know a man if you see him? . . . Well, I say Troilus is Troilus.

CRESSIDA: Then you say as I say: for I am sure he is not Hector.

PANDARUS: No, nor Hector is not Troilus in some degree.

CRESSIDA: 'Tis just to each of them; he is himself.

PANDARUS: Himself! Alas, poor Troilus, I would he were.

CRESSIDA: So he is. . . . He is not Hector.

PANDARUS: Himself! no, he's not himself . . .

I. ii. 62–80

in a conversation that goes on to make the first links of the shared identity, strengthened later, between Cressida and Helen.

The final tableau is revealed – proclaimed – by Diomed, almost in the form of 'The King is dead: long live the King'. Almost like a translation of that image of the flower beside the carrion. His heraldic words are: 'The bruit is, Hector's slain.' This cry, 'Hector is slain', is taken up immediately by the new Troilus. Where Hector, falling fatally wounded, was also Troilus, and Achilles was the Boar, Troilus is now 'total' Tarquin: a Hector combined with an Achilles, a dead Hector dragged 'in beastly sort' behind a runaway stallion. The play ends with this novel figure poised – as if with sword aloft, 'like a painted tyrant' – about to bring it down in 'revenge'.

As I said, neither he nor Shakespeare seems quite sure just where the blow should fall. For the moment he vows endless assault against the 'vile abominable tents' that conceal the lusts of Cressida – as Coriolanus will assault the treacherous Rome and as Timon will hurl his verbal thunderbolts against the treacherous Athens in due course. But between *Troilus and Cressida* and *Timon of Athens* lie the burning circles of *Hamlet*, *Othello*, *Macbeth* and *King Lear*. If the first of these was *Hamlet*, then the sword that seems to be in the hand of Pyrrhus falls on Priam – who turns out to be both Ophelia and Hamlet's mother. If the first of them was *Othello*, then the raised sword is the torch that Othello addresses above the sleeping Desdemona. Which, as I described, is also the torch that Tarquin holds above the sleeping Lucrece. Behind which all those greater, more shadowy spectres loom into position.

The Trojan War as two warped mirrors

Though it is in a way no more than an accompaniment to this first working out of the mechanism of the full Tragic Equation, that 'double irrationality', projected in the confrontation of Paris and Menelaus, contributes to one of the most pervasive and much discussed characteristics of *Troilus and Cressida*. I mentioned that both sides seem to be 'arrested' in a suspended 'double vision' – an awareness of that vision coupled with a paralysed inability to react (and enter the cathartic phase of 'madness'). And I made the point that this is like a generalized, more amorphous form of the inertia that will (in the next play) afflict Hamlet – or like one aspect of it.

As a subject the siege of Troy guaranteed Shakespeare full employment for his well-developed workforce in that it forms the most admired, most familiar, most pondered, most inclusive and culturally significant specimen of the Rival Brothers theme. But it also guaranteed him bottomless difficulties (which he turned to our benefit), since it carries, as a specimen, a peculiar complication. This complication is a big part of the story's fascination – of its insolubility, so to speak. The siege of Troy is basically a dilemma fable: it poses a question to which there can be no possible 'rational' answer.

The complication inheres in the fact that the present raid, in which the Greeks usurp the Trojans and carry off Helen, is a symmetrical reversal and punitive correction of an earlier raid, in which the Trojans usurped the Greeks and carried off Helen. (That is enough to deal with: the fact that this Trojan raid was a response to a still earlier Greek raid and 'rape' against the Trojans has been all but dropped from the accounts.) Helen consolidates the dilemma by transferring her love. Having loved her husband, Menelaus (as he loves her), from whom she was taken by force, she now loves her abductor Paris (as he loves her), from whom she will be taken by force. In a war over the source of love, where the highest value is the holiness of the heart's affections, this willing bestowal on the thief, by Helen, of the love that he stole, does to a degree sanctify the crime. It lifts the judgement out of the worldly courts, since she now belongs, though by slightly different laws, legally to both sides.

Translated into the terms of Shakespeare's Rival Brothers, this situation gives to each character, on both sides (with the sole exception of Thersites), the role of an irrational brother, and therefore, potentially or actually, also the attributes of the Boar. Simultaneously, each is in the same way a rational brother and to some degree an Adonis. The Greek irrational brother, assaulting the city and taking Helen by force, is a Greek rational brother who was formerly usurped and is now exacting Justice. The Trojan rational brother, fighting off the usurper, is the Trojan irrational brother defending the gains of his rape. The dubious enigma, that sickens the motives of both sides, is the worth of Helen. And the single unquestioned value in the play is the sexual cynicism of Thersites, which relates only to the basic 'infidelity' of Helen and the final condition of Cressida. The antithetical value is Troilus's idealistic erotic love for Cressida, which is like an aspect of the noble magnanimity of Hector, who is ready to die defending Helen. Hector's virtue lends to the other Trojans what dignity they have. But like Troilus's love it is maintained only by an heroic defiance of reality and Fate, and sooner or later meets – as if inevitably – tragic destruction.

In this way the story exists, lit by Helen/Cressida, suspended between two face-to-face distorted and distorting mirrors – one showing the rational Greek behind the irrational, the other the irrational Trojan behind the rational. Either direction opens an infinite corridor of superimposed, warped, oscillating perspectives. Both sides are committed to fight for what they have accepted in one way as the highest ideal – 'the mortal Venus, the heart-blood of beauty, love's invisible soul' (III. i. 35–6) – yet know in another way to be worthless. In this gaseous limbo of tortuous relativity the Trojans cannot settle on a definition of honour, while the Greeks become a fermenting heap of deadlocked wills and squabbling egos in the dissolution of hierarchy and order. Finally, the turmoil precipitates out in almost biological terms. Rational and irrational, the loved and the loathed, public and private, war and love, melt into each other, whereupon the Tragic Equation, to the accompaniment of the voice of Thersites, materializes like a combination of primary elements and fundamental law as the nearest thing to Necessity.

Troilus and Cressida as the first Tragedy of Divine Love

What *Troilus and Cressida* contributes, then, to Shakespeare's remodelling of the Equation is that introductory phase, the 'new factor' and the consequently modified form of the hero's 'madness'. With that new factor the hero incarnates 'total, unconditional love', and with that new madness he becomes tragic. In other words, Shakespeare has here invented a kind of tragedy in which the hero incarnates the Tragedy of Divine Love no less than does the surrogate of the Goddess who is his victim.

From the point of view of the Tragic Equation the shape of the play is simple, clear and strong. The first four acts explore multiple variations of the external Rival Brothers theme in a dogged and methodical-seeming effort to find answers to what has no answer: simultaneously the new factor of the internal Tragic Equation is unearthed and explored, in a close-up stillness of magnification that only the four-act outer stasis makes possible. These four acts are like a carefully sealed laboratory of contemplation in which Shakespeare gets full control of his dangerous new materials and his earthshaking new process. It is the last time he will enjoy this kind of leisure. In Act Five, Scenes Two and Three, the Rival Brothers and the Tragic Equation coalesce and explode, internally, in poetic terms, within Troilus's awareness, which is made up of Cressida, Diomed and his own love. In the rest of Act Five the explosion of the Rival Brothers and the Tragic Equation combined (that impact of the Boar) is externalized – blazingly demonstrated in dramatic terms – in the action of the battle. And finally this pageant-like scrimmage and operatic assassination condense on the solitary, demented figure of Troilus, as if he had only just wakened from 'a phantasma or a hideous dream' to perform, alone, the truly 'dreadful thing' – which in fact he will hand on to Hamlet and Othello. In all but this last action, Shakespeare's Tragic Equation now incorporates the whole phylogeny of Christian myth, from the initial Divine Union of Goddess and consort (her son) to the final destruction of the Goddess by her consort estranged and for one reason or another homicidally enraged against her.

Coincidentally, in this first alignment of the Tragic Equation with Shakespeare's own Eros, Troilus's words offer the fullest, plainest statement of what stands at the heart of Shakespeare's universe of values: the simplicity of Holy Love: the simplicity of the divine innocence of Holy Love. Whatever qualifying inflections may cross the actor's face and voice in the chiaroscuro of the text performed, this is 'the native act and figure' of Troilus's heart on the mythic plane. And it is Troilus, too, who makes the connection, or rather consolidates the connection made in the *Sonnets*, between the 'simplicity' of Holy Love and the 'simplicity' of true words, between the nature of Holy Love, that is, and the nature of words (which is still reverberating, in this play, from the collision between Parolles, the man of words who disintegrated in a babel of words, and Helena who bore, in her womb, the word of Bertram's redemption).

In each of the tragedies the Lucrece figures are constant in one thing: each guards the simplicity of Holy 'total, unconditional love'. *Troilus and Cressida* is a portrait of her opposite. But she is not entirely absent from the canvas: she exists, throughout the play, as an abstraction, within Troilus's idealism – disastrously projected on to Cressida. And she exists, in a more general sense, as an abstraction within the idealism of both the Greeks and the Trojans – disastrously projected on to Helen. But she exists in reality as Andromache – the perfect wife of the perfectly noble hero Hector. And when Hector proposes the single-combat mock war, that takes up the whole middle of the war plot, he heroically inverts the real situation, replacing Helen – the Cressida-like 'double vision' that will bring them all to destruction – with this true Lucrece, his own wife Andromache, the composite Sacred Bride and Divine Mother. From this play, then, it is Andromache who joins Shakespeare's circle of Lucreces – at the centre of which stands Cordelia. I shall say more about this in Part II. There, in *King Lear*, the Tragic Equation engages an even stranger, maybe grander myth – which could be called the myth of Cordelia. Or to put it another way, in Cordelia Shakespeare divines that great myth which is like an armature to the religious myths of the Tragic Equation, and which is latent in the nature of all his Sacred Brides.

PART II

The Evolution of the Tragic Equation through the Seven Tragedies

———

INTRODUCTION

The dominance of the mythic plane

What becomes evident, tracing the myth in this way within the plots of the mature dramas, is the dominance of myth over plot. In fact, as I observed earlier, this helplessness of the characters' humanity, under the compulsion of his or her mythic destiny, provides the immediate human pathos of the plays, and helps to explain why their tragedy feels 'secular'.

A comparison of the tragedy of Orestes with that of Hamlet shows Orestes's story to be mythic in that we know he is forced to defy one set of inexorable religious values (the sanctity of Mother, policed by the inescapable and pitiless Furies) under the irresistible compulsion of another (Apollo's command that he avenge his father). We are constantly aware of Orestes's predicament as a human being trapped by two opposed mythic 'supernatural' forces – from neither of which he can escape – but there is never any sense that he wants to be rid of the whole tragic responsibility and live his own simple life as a rational Athenian, listening to Socrates, or growing his figs.

Imagined as demythologized, the same events would occur, but, instead of acting under the compulsion of Apollo, Orestes would act because he has hallucinated the ghostly admonishment of his father, and cannot bear the sexual crime of his mother. And instead of being pursued by the Furies, he would go mad with conscience. But he would still be wholly absorbed by his subjection to the two incompatible sets of values, and the audience would have no sense that he wants to be free of them, or that he has immense yearning simply to live his own life.

To introduce that extra 'private' or 'secular', modern level of tragedy into the story, something needs to be added. Orestes has to be given some vividly dramatized alternative possibility of living his own life, to show how the inhuman compulsion of those other two forces, in conflict, tears the human possibility out of his fingers and destroys it.

This is exactly what Shakespeare does in *Hamlet*. Had Prince Hamlet used a real dagger, instead of only verbal ones, and killed his mother (as he does indirectly kill her), his story would be even closer to that of a demythologized Orestes than it is. But on top of that, he has the whole extra other private, personal life offered to him by Ophelia, and fondly projected, like a life plan, by his own love for her.

Hamlet fights the civil war of the two irresistible mythic compulsions, which is tragedy on the scale of Orestes's. But he also fights the war between that tragic responsibility

(O cursed spite,
That ever I was born to set it right!)
Hamlet, I. v. 188–9

and his need and longing to live his own private secular life. In this way, Hamlet contains a whole extra dimension of demythologized human individuality. And that is the Hamlet whose face fascinates us, even more than that of Orestes.

But no less than Orestes, as I say, Hamlet also contains the two superhuman compulsions in conflict. What the Equation shows is that those compulsions within Hamlet are just as mythic, just as supernatural, as Apollo and the Furies. Shakespeare has concealed the fact, but the history of the Equation reveals it: Hamlet is under the same pressure from the Puritan Jehovan Christ as Orestes was from Apollo, and he is as imperilled by his inescapable allegiance to the Goddess, and is as possessed by the inescapable 'madness' of having judged and rejected her, as Orestes was by his mother's Furies.

Indeed, as I pointed out, the two religious/mythic alignments are the same, and their conflict expresses two very similar moments of historical crisis, when the sacred world of the Goddess (in Athens, the world of Demeter, Kore and Iacchos) was encountering the desacralizing control of the rational ego's sceptical, independent, autocratic intelligence – the ultimate form of the Goddess-destroyer.

Shakespeare's Tragedy recapitulates the Greek in religious intensity and mythic content, mythic scope. But it adds to it, among other historical modifications, that new dimension of the individual's attempt to escape from the mythic, tragic destiny into his own secular freedom – the life of private feeling and self-determined action. Like none of the other Tragedies, *Hamlet* focuses this particular aspect of Shakespeare's vision: the individual's horror at having to take up the old/new mythic struggle and the inevitable tragic fate.

By concealing the identity of the religious forces, and seeming thereby to demythologize and even to secularize the whole dreadful complex, Shakespeare translated the Mother and Father of all mythic conflicts –

conflict between Goddess religion and Goddess-destroyer in all its ramifications – back into psychological terms, or rather back into the psycho-biological human mystery from which the religion and myth spring in the first place. He retained full possession and awareness of this articulated world of inner forces, as I have described, within the generalized factors of his Equation – the abstract, formulaic DNA of his myth. Before I go on to discuss the mature group of plays, therefore, I need to dismantle this Tragic Equation and to lay out, like a kit, as simply as I can, its constants and the variants of those constants. This will give a better idea of what I mean by the algebra of the Equation. It will also make clear how Shakespeare can arrive at such externally different situations as Macbeth's murdering of King Duncan, Lear's banishment of Cordelia, Coriolanus's determination to annihilate Rome, and Prospero's magical control of the ship's wreck and its mariners, while giving full expression to that basic tragic myth, which supplies so much of the primal, psychological energy, the inevitability of design, the universal validity of meaning and tragic significance, in all these plays.

The constant factors of the Shakespearean moment

Shakespeare's tragic myth appears in its prototype and purest form, as I have said, in the two long poems – in spite of the fact that the dramatic crisis, where Adonis becomes Tarquin, happens between the poems and not within them. But even here, as I suggested earlier, Shakespeare implants various options.

For instance, within *Lucrece*, Tarquin's act against Lucrece takes the form of a rape which results in the victim's suicide. I pointed out how this already works as a metaphor of two parallel mythic events which are in turn aspects of each other. The first of these events is in the Jehovah myth, where the victim, the Love Goddess, is cast into Hell and an attempt is made to destroy her physically, or at least to confiscate and deprive her of her thaumaturgic powers. The second is the Gnostic, Neoplatonist or alchemical myth of the Female as the hero's own soul, the Divine Truth of his being, from which he is somehow alienated, and which he tries to repossess, ignorantly, in the external form of a real woman somehow forbidden to him or removed from him, and whom, in his benighted violence on that physical plane, he kills, so bringing about the destruction of his own soul on the mythical plane.

These are not metaphysical fairy tales, in so far as they assume psychological reality in the plays where, as I say, Shakespeare's own basic vision of the myth is the fundamental constant. The main features of this basic constant are (to state them once again in their very simplest form) as follows:

The Female as the Goddess of Divine Love is identified, in occult fashion, with the hero's own soul: this is a fact which the hero both knows and does not know.

He apprehends the truth about the nature of the Goddess, which is that she is herself half (or, strictly speaking, one-third) enigmatic, daemonic animal, but intellectually he rejects the implication that his soul is the same. His intellectual rejection of that unwanted half of the Goddess, and thereby that unwanted half of himself (and of life), is the tragic error from which his (and her) tragic fate explodes.

The Equation needs two compounds and one catalytic additional ingredient:

The first compound is Divine Love, or Venus as the Great Goddess, complete, with her three aspects intact and undivided: she is the Creatrix and Bride of the innocent consort – that traditional form of mythic Adonis. This full form of the Divine Love is portrayed in the Venus of the long narrative poem – as the reader sees her, i.e. not as Shakespeare's Adonis sees her.

Beginning with *All's Well that Ends Well*, she reappears, again in full form, at the opening of each subsequent play. The length of time she is allowed to remain in her full form, undivided, depends on the plot, since in every case she is, one way or another, just as in the long poem, split into her two basic components, Aphrodite and Persephone, though frequently she is split into all three – in which case the Sacred Mother figure also plays a distinct role.

The second compound is that form of Adonis as her loving consort, the pre-Puritan Adonis, who is portrayed first of all in many of the *Sonnets* (his 'total, unconditional love' at all costs, which corresponds to that of the Goddess). He is brought into the drama in the figure of Troilus, and is the larval form of the tragic hero thereafter.

Those innocent forms, of Goddess and Adonis, are the raw materials, the *prima materia*, of the Mythic Equation. But the Equation only becomes active as a process of tragic consequences when the Puritan eye is opened in Adonis, either by the Female's real action (Cressida, Hamlet's mother) or more usually by Adonis becoming deluded (Othello, Macbeth, Lear, Posthumus, Leontes). This is the catalytic ingredient which, after *Measure for Measure*, is unfailingly added in some form or other, always with calamitous or at least highly dramatic results.

The main constants of this inevitable reaction can be itemized as follows:

By some means, that Puritan fear is awakened in the hero. This is the first constant.

Immediately, the Divine Love (or her equivalent) becomes too much for the hero's Puritanized, fearful ego-vision, which thereupon splits her into two parts. One part corresponds to the Sacred Bride/Divine Mother complex (and carries all the Divine attributes, which Shakespeare never ceases to emphasize); the other part corresponds to the Queen of Hell. This 'double vision' is the second constant.

The third constant is that the hero rejects the Queen of Hell — absolutely and with loathing (in fear).

The fourth constant — most important of all — is that the hero cannot separate the loved and the loathed women.

He cannot separate them, as a rule, because — exactly as in the long poem's Venus, or the woman in the *Sonnets* — they inhabit the one body. But even when they inhabit different bodies, he still cannot separate them. Always, like Adonis, he has to reject both. Always (with the sole exception of *The Tempest*) the indivisible unity of the archetypal Goddess is dominant over the struggling analytic rationality of the hero.

The latter type of situation is articulated in great detail in *Hamlet*. There the presence of the Goddess is incarnate not in Hamlet's mother, Gertrude, and not in Ophelia, but in both together. Or rather in all three. The three aspects of the Goddess are distinctly identified. Ophelia is Sacred Bride and loves him; his mother is Divine Mother and loves him; but his father's wife, who committed adultery with his uncle, then colluded in his uncle's murder of his father, her husband, by marrying the murderer and incidentally ratifying his seizure of the throne, is the Queen of Hell and must be loathed and rejected.

[215]

It is understandable that, in loathing this Queen of Hell figure, Hamlet should rave so violently against his mother, but why can't he leave Ophelia out of it? Why does he find her contaminated by the same criminal lust as his incestuous mother? Their hidden mythic unity makes it impossible for Hamlet to prise the women apart and treat them differently. The plot itself finds other motives to justify Hamlet's behaving as he does towards Ophelia, but all of them are provisional, however deeply human. And to say that his mother's incest has horrified him, temporarily, with the sexuality of all women, is only to find different words for the indivisible mythic unity of his mother and this innocent girl, whom, as he makes clear later, when he jumps into her grave, he loves with 'total, unconditional love'.

A similar situation is defined, again very lucidly, in *Coriolanus*. Here, the hidden Goddess is not incarnate in his wife, or in his mother, but in both of them together *plus the City of Rome*. The totality of the Goddess, in the Tragic Equation of this play, is Rome herself, centred on his mother and his wife. But just as Hamlet could not separate Ophelia (or his mother) from his mother's sexual crime, Coriolanus cannot separate his mother and wife from the Roman mob — which he rejects, on instinct, because he suspects (he knows) that its apparently 'total, unconditional love' is worthless and dangerous. When the mob does indeed reveal that all its apparent love is treachery, and wishes only to destroy him, it proves itself to be the Queen of Hell. This sudden threat of the mob, in the city centred on his worshipped mother and wife, constitutes the 'double vision', and the Shakespearean moment occurs. But there seems to be no human reason why, when he marches to punish Rome with the army of Aufidius, he could not pick out and save his mother and wife. And of course there is no human reason. There is only a mythic reason. He is 'like a battery, a thing made for Alexander', a dial hand of the mythic power circuit: a mask of the Tragic Equation. Right up to the last moment he intends to burn the whole city and everybody in it to one heap of ashes. If he were suddenly to find it possible to spare his mother and wife, as a human being might — if, for instance, he had forcibly kidnapped them when they came on their petition, then gone ahead and burned Rome — his action would cease to express mythic necessity, and the tragedy would cease to be divine. It would even cease to be tragic. It would become a Brechtian morality play of political expedience and pragmatic realism.

The fifth constant is the extraordinary, trigger-happy readiness of the hero to see the 'double vision'. Adonis, the chaste hunter, sees it as a premonition before it has hurt him in any way. Hamlet is sick with apprehension of it before the Ghost makes it real and the play, 'The Murder of Gonzago', confirms it. Othello is like a waiting forest to Iago's carefully nursed sparks. Lear explodes with it at a touch. Coriolanus seems to force it to reveal itself, to confirm his cynical expectations. Posthumus needs only a few words from a liar. Leontes forcibly whispers himself into it.

The sixth constant, which springs direct from the third (his loathing) and the fourth (his inability to separate the two figures of the vision), is the hero's madness.

Finally, the seventh constant, most significant of all, is that this madness is always directed against the Female, and results directly or indirectly in her death. At least, it does so up to *Coriolanus*. *Coriolanus* is the first of the tragic series, after *Hamlet*, in which the Female escapes the hero's lethal purpose. His purpose remains a constant, to the end, but in all subsequent plays the Female is rescued.

These are the constant factors of that complex moment – rejection of the Goddess, 'double vision', loathing, horror, madness – which recurs as the mainspring of the tragic action so consistently, in every play from *Measure for Measure* onwards, that it could be called *the* Shakespearean moment.

Variants

In general, the main variants of the main factors of the Equation are pronounced enough to be distinguished fairly easily. Shakespeare produced these variants simply as metaphors of the basic factors, so an eye for metaphor helps. But to score in detail the whole harmonic orchestration of parallels and correspondences to each factor would take, I imagine, a vast work.

1. The female figure who is the heroine is a constant (with only one or two exceptions) as Venus/Lucrece. She is characterized by 'total, unconditional love', but she mutates to variants, of which the most important, and useful to Shakespeare, is the Crown. This particular variant, which can be translated as 'the principle of divinely consecrated order' or simply as 'the truth', is one of the organic links between the two alternative forms of the Equation – that of the Puritan Adonis/

rejected Goddess/Boar/Tarquin/Lucrece pattern, and that of the Rival Brothers.

The Lucrece figure is also, as I have said, the truth of the hero's own soul, the sacred element in his being. When the Lucrece figure is thrown away or lost, the hero proves, by his behaviour, that he has thrown away or lost his 'soul', and suffers now as one of the damned. When she dies, the hero is doomed and cannot survive. After Ophelia's death, Hamlet's actions are in this sense posthumous, and he climbs out of her grave to perform them. Her identity with the hero's own soul explains, as I noted earlier, the intense, mystical significance of 'chastity' in the plays. Chastity signifies the dedicated, spiritual aspect of 'total, unconditional love', the individualized aspect of that infinite love which is due to the Divine Source, and therefore to nobody else, and which is the individual's union with the Divine Source within him or within her. This internal union with the Divine Source is the 'divinity' of the individual's soul. When Desdemona becomes the external repository of this union in Othello, she has his soul in her possession, and has virtually become his soul – as he repeatedly declares. Her apparent infidelity, then, is exactly as if the Divine Source should abandon him internally, hence: 'Chaos is come again.' If this fundamental conception were to depart from the plays – if the supreme role of 'chastity' were to be deleted – the tragedies would automatically lose their metaphysical axis, and the whole ethical system would collapse.

2. The Queen of Hell is a variable. Her most notable variant (consistent throughout the imagery of the plays) is the Boar. In *All's Well that Ends Well* she is the general potential for treachery and sexual licence, reflected in the words of Parolles and in Bertram's philandering. In *Measure for Measure* she is the orgiastic sexuality of the brothel city of Vienna. In *Troilus and Cressida* she is diffused throughout the war over a whore, reflected in the words of Thersites, finally emerging embodied in the true nature of Cressida. In *Timon of Athens*, she appears again as a city, the city of treacherous friends, and in *Coriolanus*, as the Rome of treacherous plebeians. The role of these large surrogates becomes sharply defined in the reactions of the hero.

3. As I pointed out in the Introduction, the two variants of the Equation are different expressions of the one basic event: the usurping of the rational being by the irrational. In the Tragic Equation proper (as I discuss more fully in the pages about *Macbeth* (see pages 239–55)), the

irrational being and the rational are the two selves of the hero: the Adonis who rejects and the Tarquin that he becomes in his madness. In the Rival Brothers, the irrational being and the rational are two different characters, sometimes actual brothers, usually 'kinsmen', but sometimes merely close or lifelong friends. Their 'rivalry' corresponds to the alienation between the Puritan Adonis and the Goddess. The irrational brother's feeling of inferiority and his consequent bid to supplant his rational brother correspond to the Goddess's rage on being rejected and her consequent inspiring of the Boar to destroy the one who rejected her by usurping him. The irrational brother who usurps his rational brother seizes his Crown – usually in a literal sense (Richard III, Duke Frederick, Macbeth, Antonio), but sometimes both his Crown and his Sacred Bride (Claudius), and sometimes only his Sacred Bride (Proteus, Tarquin, Polixenes according to Leontes): in each case the usurpation corresponds to a cataclysmic collapse of order. It parallels, and is an image of, the tragic hero's collapse into Tarquinian madness (the triumph of his murderous irrational self) in the Tragic Equation.

In the early plays, pre-*All's Well that Ends Well*, the Rival Brothers remained external, non-mythic, even in *Julius Caesar*. In *As You Like It*, the theme attained its most ingeniously choreographed completeness of design (in that interplay of one pair of female doubles and three pairs of male) and simultaneously broke through on to the mythic plane and was internalized. When the myth entered in *All's Well*, the Rival Brothers motif automatically assimilated the mythic symbolism of the Adonis and Boar components of the myth. From this point, wherever he appears in the pattern of the Rival Brothers as the usurped one, the rational brother always incorporates the mythic attributes of the Adonis figure, while the usurper, the irrational brother will always incorporate the attributes of the Boar – which is to say that he will seem to emerge from some form of the Queen of Hell (Claudius from the lecherous Gertrude, Macbeth from Lady Macbeth, Edmund from his Goddess 'Nature' and from Goneril and Regan later on, Antony from Cleopatra, Cloten from the Witch Queen). The relationship between the two forms can be seen most simply, maybe, in the parallel between Edmund's usurpation of Edgar, and the irrational Lear's usurpation of King Lear and his throwing away of Cordelia (the Crown – an image of madness seizing the Crown, i.e. plunging the realm into chaos). This inner identity of the two forms of the Equation enables Shakespeare to bind the apparently separate business of two simultaneous plots into a single, mysteriously unified whole — as the Gloucester story and the Lear story, or the political story and the love story in *Antony and Cleopatra*.

The madness itself produces the richest crop of variants.

The tragic madness

The rejection of the Female is always followed by some kind of 'madness' in the hero (that sixth constant), which is always directed against the Female (or her surrogates). But the big shift that Shakespeare makes in the form of this 'madness' requires some kind of explanation.

Once the Equation has become 'mythic', but before it has become 'tragic', which is to say, in the plots of *All's Well* and *Measure for Measure*, the hero first of all rejects the Female's lust, then assaults her sexually — or attempts to.

This sequence of absolute rejection and lustful assault is logical. The hero's hysterical rejection of female sexuality is merely the last-ditch violent resistance before he surrenders to his own lust. His rejection of her, that is, is projected from his initial suppression of his own lust.

Following this principle, Bertram's cold rejection of Helena does not contradict his lustful pursuit of Diana, but is psychologically linked to it. Angelo's frigid, legalistic suppression of sexual licence is a logical overture to his own reckless plunge into sexual crime.

In the 'mature' Equation, in *Hamlet* or *Othello*, this act of lust modulates to what is some form of banishment or else murder, and evolves thereafter through variations of a madness which always ends in the destruction (or the attempted destruction) of the Female.

But here again, there is no difficulty with the psychological curve. What he is doing, in effect, is not surrendering to his own lust (after a last-ditch struggle of resistance against it that manifests itself in rejecting the Female) but mounting an overwhelming counterattack, and demolishing the threat. The Male who hysterically rejects what he regards as the Female's lust enforces his rejection so violently that he kills her.

The two situations, which began the same, seem to end very differently. But they end differently only because the hero's initial moral reaction — to female lust — becomes more absolute. Shakespeare, like the Jehovah myth in history, has simply advanced the timing. The hero pre-empts his own surrender to his own lust by acting promptly and with 'insane' finality: he re-enforces his self-suppression and liquidates the source of disturbance, i.e. of temptation, of erotic domination and sexual suffering. In murdering her, he virtually murders his own sexuality.

In doing this, as I have pointed out, he shifts the Equation from a narrowly personal 'Freudian' psychology, and lifts it into the mythic dimension, where it becomes a comprehensive image of that mythic historic event: Marduk's, Jehovah's and the Reformation's destruction of the dangerously powerful Female.

But it also becomes a more definite image of what is properly tragic in the hero's original crime – which was his rejection of the Goddess.

All the plays of the tragic sequence are a 'proof', so to speak, of the criminality of that rejection. In play after play, from every angle, Shakespeare is focusing his stubborn investigation into the nature of that rejection. In the end, as I will show, in *The Winter's Tale* (page 356) he brings into court this specific act – the rejection – and calls down the God of Truth to judge it in his own words.

This means that everything happened, in a sense, within the first poem, *Venus and Adonis*, where Adonis rejected Venus:

> I hate not love, but your device in love,
> That lends embracements unto every stranger.
> *Venus and Adonis*, 789–90

What the tragedies dramatize is the *inside story* of that rejection. Those words are the expressionless face, the dead voice, of the superhuman madness that is cancelling the Goddess – wiping her from the universe. From Adonis's universe, that is.

The tragedies then follow as a consequence of these words. They are an unfolding into action, the unrolling of all the thunders, and the arrival on heads and chimneys of all the thunderbolts, released internally, in Heaven, by the silent flash of those words.

In that sense, as Adonis speaks, Tarquin rapes Lucrece. When this act of surrender to lust in an act of rape is eventually translated into the suppression of lust in an act of murder, the sexual nature of the act, the sexual charge, remains the same, though the expression of it, obviously, changes from the blind, guilty gratification of an appetite to a true madness (and the extinction of the appetite).

And Shakespeare locates the tragedy of this true madness in the logical conclusion of the mythic situation. The murder of the Goddess is the murder of the source of life: the destruction of mankind. (And of all Nature, and of Earth.)

From there, it is a natural step to the plot which expresses this fundamental truth: the Female whom the hero rejects must be his own beloved (his own soul, his own life).

Accordingly, Tarquin, who rapes and destroys another man's beloved, is not properly tragic. Bertram cannot be tragic: if he destroyed both Diana and Helena, he still would not be properly tragic – merely their misfortune. If Angelo destroyed Isabella in some way, he would be a monster, but not tragic.

Only with Troilus's love for Cressida does Shakespeare finally locate, as I described on pages 181–2, the tragic possibility. When Troilus hurls himself in battle confusion at the whole Greek army, one can feel Shakespeare moving towards the truth difficult to face. And Othello, with a big shock, finds it: the beloved must die.

In answering the question, 'Why must she?' Shakespeare comes directly to his analysis of that rejection which resolves itself into an analysis of the 'double vision', and from there into an analysis of the hero's reaction to the fact that the beloved and the Queen of Hell occupy the one body, or are, at least, inseparable.

The tragic hero always operates in the absolute belief that the Queen of Hell is the 'terror of the earth'. Ideally, in his own understanding, he reacts only against her. But in practice, because of his extraordinary (hysterical? as if already insane?) readiness to assume that she is present, it is as easy for him to see her in his faithful beloved as in a true Queen of Hell. In his paranoia, it is painfully easier. His tragedy is that, in so far as he embodies the Goddess-destroyer, his madness cannot distinguish. One great labour of the plays is to bring the tragic hero to the point where he can distinguish. And *The Tempest* is a play about the almost impossible laboratory precautions that are necessary before the distinction can be made.

The variant passions of the madness, which have been termed conventionally 'revenge' plus indecision in *Hamlet*, 'jealousy' in *Othello*, ambition in *Macbeth*, 'rage against filial ingratitude' in *King Lear*, 'rage against ingratitude generally' in *Timon*, 'injured pride' in *Coriolanus* and so on, which can themselves be varied considerably according to the reader, are adaptations to the specific requirements of each story, at its most naturalistic level. A little deeper, they become instantly more complicated. But a little deeper still they begin to reveal their common root in that 'jealousy' – the lack or loss of what embodies the Divine Love.

Though the tragic hero lives in a Manichean world where the Queen of Hell is the Queen of Terror, the plays operate in a larger universe where Manichean division is an ocular defect and the Queen of Hell is simply a part of the 'divine, complete being', which is Divine Love. And whatever coloration the plot gives to the hero's 'madness', it can always be seen, on the mythic level, to be a variation on the tragic rejection and loss of the Divine Love.

Through the pre-tragic phase of his drama, there seemed to exist no real metaphysical problem in the union of male and female. In his comedies, the difficulties of Bride and Bridegroom typify a perverse but universally instinctive heightening of betrothal negotiations, like the aphrodisiac rebuffs and scuffling pursuits of bird courtship, as if the rapturous pains and agitations were merely a down payment, an indemnity, for the nuptials proper. The all-embracing persistence of this pattern carries the comedies like the Gulf Stream of a grand, ethical purpose.

When the Mythic Equation enters, in *All's Well*, importing the primeval metaphysical conflict between male and female, Shakespeare automatically imposes the old connubial solution – to correct all errors and redeem all wrongs. In *Measure for Measure*, where the potential for death struggle – between male and female – becomes alarming, he calls up the public reserves and fortifies the ritual marital containment with an open show of force, a stern Christian (Catholic) cordon that makes it quite clear, what is at stake is no longer merely brides and grooms, but the soul, Isabella, who is properly not the victim of the false god (the Puritan) but the bride of the true God, of whom the Puritan (god) is the (angel) Deputy – here tested and found wanting.

But with *Hamlet* and *Othello* that pattern becomes useless. The tragic theme takes off, like a Hindu Goddess with a Lutheran seminarist in her talons, her four illuminated wings looking like eight, their every beat like the jolt of a kaleidoscope, towards the Shakespearean catastrophe which through those next seven plays will explode any possibility of containment.

CHAPTER 3

THE TRAGIC EQUATION MATURES AND MUTATES:
Othello, Hamlet, Macbeth, King Lear

═══════

At wit's end

Othello: the Iago factor

Othello: the Tragic Equation in the body

Hamlet: the Tragic Equation in the mind

Macbeth: X-ray of the Shakespearean moment

King Lear: a triple Tragic Equation

King Lear as a reactivation of its mythic sources

Lear, the Fool, Mad Tom and Cordelia

The silence of Cordelia

At wit's end

The seven tragedies divide naturally into two groups. In the first group of four the Equation, now inescapably and fatally tragic, carries Shakespeare as far as the organism can endure it. At that point, under the inhuman pressure, the organism itself mutates and invents a possible mode of survival.

This group of four divides again into two groups of two. The first pair, *Hamlet* and *Othello*, function in one sense as simultaneous and parallel works, in that *Hamlet* can be seen as an image of what I mentioned before: the fully conscious psychological resistance to the terrible 'mythic' fate – which in *Othello* is undergone helplessly and even with a kind of greed. The fate is, at bottom, the same in both: the beloved must die, destroying the hero's world and himself. But where *Othello* records the experience of it at the level of the body and animal feeling, *Hamlet* records it (managing to delay but not escape it) at the level of the rational intelligence.

This is a rough enough correspondence, good only up to a point. But it illustrates what I mean by the simultaneity of the two dramas, as they record the inevitability and completeness of a particular kind of tragic disaster in which the protagonist sees not a glimmer of hope.

The second pair of plays, *Macbeth* and *King Lear*, while they plunge into exponentially more terrible depths, between them conceive and nurse a hope. In the first, *Macbeth*, where the tragic gradient, so fearfully steep in *Hamlet*, seems to have gone over a precipice, a miraculous thing happens – something like a virgin conception, the germinal spark of what will turn out to be, in *King Lear*, a mutation in the womb of the Tragic Equation.

And in *King Lear*, the fourth and last of this group, where the tragic cataclysm, threefold, puts the characters in mind of the 'promised end' or at least the 'image of that horror', the mutation actually breathes and stirs. It seems, for a while, as if it could live and survive and redeem all that has happened – but it fails.

In Chapter 3, I take the development of the Tragic Equation to that point.

Othello: the Iago factor

According to the Equation, *Othello* was planned, if not written, before *Hamlet*. Maybe the writing, the revisions, leap-frogged (as seems possible in some other plays).

Othello is a very clear, almost schematic exposition of the tragic myth in simple form, which breaks down, on examination, into a complicated analysis of two or three factors. The main relevant points of the story are:

> Othello loves Desdemona and she him. This is 'total, unconditional love' on both sides, in spite of all the swirling undercurrents which their love defies. This is the pre-Puritan Venus and Adonis mythic idyll.

> Iago, who seems to be the evil one, the emissary of Hell, pours his sexual cynicism into Othello's as-if-sleeping ear, revealing to him, as in a waking dream, Cassio's whore in Desdemona's body: the 'double vision'. Wiping Othello's eyes with the sibylline handkerchief, Iago makes the double vision seem real. Othello becomes Puritan Adonis, and with tirades of loathing rejects Desdemona.

> Othello faints (Adonis is slain).

> Othello rises mad with his purpose to kill Desdemona (Tarquin rises mad with his purpose to rape (and/or kill) Lucrece).

> He kills Desdemona, in her bed.

> Having smothered her (much as Tarquin gags Lucrece with her own nightdress), Othello is instantly enlightened, realizes the emptiness of his crime, and so kills himself. (As post-coital Tarquin, relieved of his 'load of lust', flees in remorse, is stripped of his royal succession, and banished for ever.)

Othello belongs to this point in the evolution of the Equation in so far as Iago is the culmination of the Parolles, Lucio, Thersites series. In one respect, all these figures are forms of the evil one. But which evil one?

The first three seem to emerge from the penumbra of the Queen of Hell. It is tempting to call them degenerate specimens of her male consort, that hidden 'hot tyrant' which Adonis saw in her lust, her male infernal escort, the gigolo of Hell. They seem related in some way to the sexuality of the Boar, in that their preoccupation is the inevitability of lust, the ubiquity of lust, almost as if they were the intellectual accompaniment of the Boar. At least, this might be suspected. Just as Adonis becomes a Tarquin by fusing with the Boar, on a parallel course Bertram moves into the Tarquin phase, and ravishes (as he thinks) Diana, when he succumbs to Parolles's sexual cynicism. Angelo, in a similar way, ravishes, as he imagines, Isabella, after he has succumbed, inwardly, to the licentious world of permissive suggestion of which Lucio is the mouthpiece. And when Troilus comes to share Thersites's opinion of Cressida, he is possessed with Tarquinian madness against her.

And yet there is something about all these figures – Parolles, Lucio, Thersites and Iago – which disqualifies them from the favours of the Queen of Hell. The Boar, which definitely does emerge from 'that dark and vicious place', and the 'tyrant', which is the Boar in human form, are both 'hot'. Whereas Iago and his friends are cold. What they lack is that frenzied, dark exaltation, the uncontrollable but joyful *terribilitas* of passion, which animates the tragic hero in his Tarquinian phase. Their preoccupation with female whorishness is always prurient, witty, detached, cynically contemptuous. They embody the cold, destructive laughter of the non-participant. In other words, they are not emanations from the infernal source but, as I have said before, cold reflections of it. They are jealous, intellectual reflections of a passion that is apparently inaccessible to them. They view it externally, cerebrally, bitterly, across a gulf.

Evidently, then, there are two 'evils'. There is the infernal and infernalizing lust of the Boar, which is hot, and the intellectual reflection that accompanies it with prurient, destructive envy, which is cold.

Iago is, one might almost say, the apotheosis of this latter activity. Being so much more fully individualized than his predecessors, he divulges more of the real nature of his composition.

What he confirms is that they all personify the mentally playful aspect of the Puritan rejection of the Divine Love. They embody the fanatic but irresponsibly abstract and inhuman intelligence that splits the Goddess, and condemns her sexuality. Their alienation from her 'love' corresponds to their own purely intellectual (even 'theoretical') substance, to their critical absolutism: 'For I am nothing if not critical,' as Iago himself says.

Iago's words infect Othello, so to speak, with this Puritan Manichean outlook, for which the physicality of Desdemona's sex is by definition not merely frail, like the Maid in *A Lover's Complaint*, but treacherous and diabolical – the reptilian face of the Great Goddess, the reproductive system itself, opportunist and impersonal, recognizing no individual bond. Whereupon Othello's eyes open to the 'double vision'.

In other words, Iago is the inhuman aspect of the Puritan intelligence and incarnates the desacralized, rational intelligence with a purpose. He appears here for the last time externalized from the hero. In *Hamlet*, though this entity's role is performed, up to a point, fleetingly and catastrophically, by the Ghost (likewise in a reek of sulphur), this same Ghost is manifestly linked to Hamlet's prophetic soul, and is already to that degree internalized. And for the rest of the play it is thoroughly internalized, as an aspect of Hamlet's self-tormenting, remorseless, critical intelligence. Just so, in all the tragic heroes thereafter, the Iago factor is internalized from the outset, making only a brief external reappearance as Iachimo, in *Cymbeline*, where Shakespeare dismantles the Tragic Equation and puts it together again in a slightly new way.

But while Iago performs this role, as the envious intelligence of the Puritan, inquisitorial outlook, he throws a bigger shadow. It is clear enough in the text that Iago inherits an old morality-play identity as a parody of the devil himself ('I look down towards his feet, but that's a fable'), and that his obsession with the love of Othello and Desdemona resembles Satan's jealousy of Adam and Eve in Paradise – fanatic to manipulate and destroy the blissful reality and relationship that he can never share, and that excludes him. But Shakespeare goes further. Othello is powerless to resist the sheer pragmatic logicality of Iago's suggestions. Iago's conquest is a triumph of pure empirical reason. But as if this identification of loveless intelligence with reason and the scientific method, and all three with the Satan who destroys love, were not enough, Shakespeare uses various means to invest Iago with his full theological credentials. And there is little doubt, when Iago identifies himself with the pointed inversion: 'I am not what I am', that Satan himself has taken on the mantle of Jehovah in the Reformation myth, as the destroyer of the Goddess. In this portrait, where the Jehovah God, the Jehovah Satan, and dogmatic, rational, objective (finally atheistic) intelligence coalesce in a malevolent onslaught on the world of love, Shakespeare passes close to Ivan Karamazov's Grand Inquisitor on the one side and to Blake's Urizen on the other. And the fact that Iago is one of Shakespeare's most densely realized characters gives these theological and mythic elements in the algebra of his make-up the fullness, and the dramatic force, of a mystery of life.

Setting Iago at the centre of attention, one can see the whole play as an apparatus for analysing his role in the Equation. It turns out, as I have already suggested, to be *the* crucial role. In Iago the intelligence behind the tragic error, that error of the Puritan rejection, is defined in depth, just as a word, or a cryptographic sign, might receive its exhaustive definition, with all etymology and variant usages included. Thereafter, whenever a tragic hero makes the tragic error, and sees that double vision (and all do), we shall know that an Iago is whispering in his ear, and that he is taking the whisper as a divine oracle.

That trigger-happy readiness to see the double vision, which I mentioned as one of the constants of the Shakespearean moment, is nothing but a neurotic susceptibility to the Iago factor. It is the sin which every tragic hero commits, and it can be described as a failure of understanding, that alienation from the 'understanding heart' which, as the Equation develops from play to play, has to be exposed, condemned, punished, corrected, and eventually redeemed.

Shakespeare's complete familiarity with Iago must have something to do – more than a little, perhaps – with the extraordinary, playful, manipulative cruelty of his own writing. Whatever one might say about the ethical grandeur of his system in its entirety, nobody ever tortured his characters more, or with more diabolical zest, or with more coolly, thoroughly fascinated curiosity about the outcome.

Looked into from this angle, Iago becomes a lens of sorts into Othello's blackness.

Othello: the Tragic Equation in the body

If Iago is, as I suggested, the intellectualized form of the ascendant, Puritan, Martial Jehovah – the Goddess-destroyer – then the Goddess, in relation to him in this role, is Othello and Desdemona both together, or rather is Othello as he embraces Desdemona. What I mean is clear enough if one imagines Adonis's Puritan intellectuality *externalized* – leaving Adonis as the original idyllic lover of the Goddess. Shakespeare has taken Adonis apart to look at his mentality, and to observe more closely what the effects are, on Adonis himself, of his own Puritanism. In Hamlet he will put them together again – and as I say will leave them together in all subsequent plays except *Cymbeline*.

He will also put them together again, of course, in this play: Iago injects himself into Othello – whereupon Othello becomes a Puritan Adonis, sees the double vision, etc.

But first, Iago's relationship to Othello is like a mini-statement of Othello/Iago's relationship to Desdemona. Evidently those intellectualized reflections of the Queen of Hell (Parolles, Lucio, Thersites) are mini-Tarquins, mercurial Tarquins.

Iago partakes of that other kind of Tarquin, too: the Rival Brother. As usurping brother, his Tarquinian crime is, in its way, as complete as Macbeth's: not satisfied to usurp he utterly destroys. In this role, his irredeemable evil sends a ray through the tempestuous succession of tragedies to light coldly on the fixed wickedness of Prospero's brother, Antonio. As Goddess-destroyer, he belongs to a more complicated pattern. In this mini-set, Desdemona takes on the two aspects of Sacred Bride and Divine Mother, while Othello takes on the aspect of the Queen of Hell.

This is not so ridiculous. It is perfectly consistent with the mythic algebra in which the Equation works. The Queen of Hell, as the texts repeatedly show, is herself a combination of Queen of the Underworld and a male component – who becomes visible as the Boar, of which the human form is the 'hot tyrant'.

In Othello, the feminine component of the Queen of Hell has shrunk to the witchcraft – the sibylline prophetic fury – sewn into his handerchief, while the male component, the 'hot tyrant' (the human form of the Boar who will be Tarquin) has expanded to fill the foreground – Othello's physical self. But instead of charging into violent combination with Adonis (Iago's Puritan, critical words) to become the uncontrollable Tarquin (as he eventually does), he is, so to speak, suspended awhile within the dark underparts of the undifferentiated total love of the Goddess, in the idyllic dawn of the myth (like Antony and Cleopatra).

His blackness, in other words, is his identification with Persephone, the Queen of Hell. It is a magnificent, primal blackness while it is benign, before the Puritan word has touched it, as Persephone or the Queen of Hell is an undifferentiated aspect of the magnificent, primal power of the Goddess's total love, before she is split by the Puritan censorship. But it becomes a terrible, infernal blackness, the blackness of Hell and the Boar, after the Puritan word has done its damage.

In this way Othello's blackness is recognized instantly, by audience or reader, as his susceptibility to becoming possessed by dark and irrational forces from outside the civilized contract.

When Iago's Puritan 'Call it not love, for Love to heaven is fled,/Since sweating Lust on earth usurp'd his name' (*Venus and Adonis*, 793–4) begins to work on him, he becomes almost literally the charging Boar. He cannot combine with Iago physically, but psychically the fusion is complete. He plunges into the skein of Iago's Adonis words, and stands up in them transformed, as Tarquin stood up transformed in the skin of Adonis, over the bed of Lucrece.

This seems to be saying that what destroys the Goddess is the Goddess. It seems to be saying that the Queen of Hell, separating from the Sacred Bride/Divine Mother, becoming the Boar, fusing with Adonis, transforming him to Tarquin, and then destroying the Sacred Bride/Divine Mother under the illusion that she is the Queen of Hell, is the *perpetuum mobile* of the Equation, (cf. Appendix II).

According to the Tragic Equation, so it seems to be. And *Othello* is the most naked statement in the plays of the tragic hero's physical near identity with the Queen of the Underworld. The most naked statement, that is, of just how the Goddess (total life) is blinded into destroying her avatar – by the worm in the apple, the goblin in the critical intelligence of Adonis.

Hamlet: the Tragic Equation in the mind

The plot of *Hamlet* is dominated by a classic specimen of the Tragic Equation and of its other form, the Rival Brothers, intimately inter-related, but it also teems with variants of both.

Once again, I shall resolutely ignore everything but the skeletal essentials of my theme. If the X-ray plate moves even slightly out of focus, everything will disappear in the mass of complications.

> The Ghost, with the information that Hamlet's mother has married his father's murderer (and brother), presents his son with the double vision – the loved and the loathed woman within the one body of his mother, for which the haste of her marriage to his uncle has obviously prepared him. It is something to notice that Hamlet's double vision is, so to speak, doubled, since it instantly assimilates King Hamlet's double vision of the same woman. Hamlet's double vision, that is, sees his mother from both the

loving son's and the loving husband's point of view, and thereafter he carries the reaction of his father as well as his own.

Hamlet cannot separate Ophelia from his mother. He accuses her of possessing the same treacherous nature by virtue of being female, and seems to reject her absolutely. In other words, the hidden magnetic unity of the Goddess is already stronger than his sense of reality. His mythic role, in which he will become a puppet of the Equation, is already to this degree stronger than his human individuality. The situation is exactly as if he knew, on the mythic plane, that he was going to have to destroy Ophelia, while on the human but baffled plane he fights this inevitability and desperately tries to sever her from his mythic destiny, so as to preserve her.

Meanwhile, just as he cannot separate Ophelia from his mother, so he cannot separate the mother he loves from the mother he loathes, since both inhabit the same body. According to the law of the Equation, the hero cannot separate Sacred Bride, Divine Mother and Queen of Hell, and therefore in rejecting one he must reject all.

In both cases, he attempts to separate the beloved woman from the one who stands, as an apparent Queen of Hell, in the remorseless path of the Tragic Equation. He makes a show of rejecting Ophelia, but into the safe keeping of a nunnery, where she will be separated from the Queen of Hell that he sees in her. Similarly, he entreats his mother to shut herself away, to separate herself from the Queen of Hell that Hamlet (and the Ghost) sees in her, by removing herself (into a kind of private nunnery of voluntary abstinence) from the lustful bed of Claudius. But both attempts are like rhetorical flourishes, wild gestures in his general, flailing effort to resist his mythic destiny, as it sweeps him towards his fatal Tarquinian act, where Queens of Hell will be punished.

The concurrent other form of the myth follows the outline of the Rival Brothers. The Ghost's revelation, which presented Hamlet with that double vision of his mother (and, by mythic contamination, of Ophelia too), and plunged him into the tragic torrent of the Tarquin/Lucrece equation, also injects him with the irresistible compulsion – a command from the Underworld – to murder (and usurp) King Claudius, his uncle.

[234]

In this way, the Ghost has bestowed on Hamlet both types of Tarquinian 'madness': the madness induced by the vision of the Queen of Hell in the body of the loved woman, and the 'madness' of the irrational brother's need to kill the King. The first of these, moreover, descends on Hamlet in a far from simple form: he sees a real Queen of Hell in the body of his beloved mother, and an illusory Queen of Hell in Ophelia.

The two madnesses run parallel. His loathing for the Queen of Hell in his mother is inseparable from his need to kill Claudius. But as an Adonis clinging to his sanity, he resists the one, while he strives towards the other.

In the first, in which he has seen the double vision of his mother (and of Ophelia), he resists, desperately, with all his strength, that moment of final metamorphosis, when his madness will undergo the transformation into the fatal, uncontrollable Tarquin. In the second, in which he has to murder and displace the King, he strives, again desperately and with all his strength, *towards* the moment when he will actually be able to accomplish the change into Tarquin, and perform the act.

Between these two he is paralysed. At the point of deadlock, he calls for the vision of what he most dreads, most longs for, and knows will have to arrive: the vision of that moment in which he will have to explode, like 'the dreadful thunder' that rends Heaven, into the Pyrrhus of the Player's speech – a full-blooded, homicidal Tarquin – 'mincing' the King while the shrieking Queen flees for her life.

Eliot pointed out that *Hamlet*, as a work of art, seems to struggle with a mass of highly pressurized, obscure material that cannot be dragged into the light, as if plot and characters were somehow inadequate to express what Hamlet, and behind Hamlet Shakespeare, seem to be aware of and involved with.

The sense of this hidden excess is very strong, and even finds literal expression at several points in the play. The fact that the work was composed at about the time when Shakespeare's father's death (which might have been some time pending) coincided with the first phase of his own deliberately undertaken spiritual renewal (as intimated in *As You Like It* and *All's Well that Ends Well*) must be relevant.

But all the tragedies, to some degree, carry this sense of hidden, unobjectifiable excess, in so far as the characters are motivated and burdened by the Tragic, Mythic Equation – and by the vast, turbulent historical and psycho-biological implications of that – as well as by the immediate, contingent business of the plot.

Yet it is more acutely evident in *Hamlet* than in any of the later plays. Somehow, in *Hamlet*, the tension between the mythic and realistic planes is more mysteriously supercharged. Two factors in particular certainly contribute to this. The first is not only the extraordinary and prolonged suspense, but the means by which Shakespeare has created it. As in no other play, he sets the mythic plane and the human plane in opposition, or rather he sets Hamlet's mythic destiny, and Hamlet's individual will, in opposition. In all the other tragedies, the hero's individual will, his Adonis will, is demolished and taken over by the mythic Tarquinian will. In *Macbeth*, it happens almost before Macbeth himself is aware of it. In *King Lear*, one word from Cordelia is enough, and Lear erupts into Tarquin. But Hamlet does not merely resist change and attempt to defer his destiny: he goes on resisting it for most of the play. The second factor, which hugely intensifies and complicates the mythic pressure against Hamlet's human resistance, is the sheer multiplicity of variants of the Tragic Equation in the machinery of the play. It is as if Hamlet were putting out all his personal strength against what is a kind of mythic overdrive. Like the driver of a bus containing all the characters of the drama, he hurtles towards destruction, in slow motion, with his foot jammed down hard on the brakes.

As I hope my outlines show, most of the tragedies make do with one main variant of the Tragic Equation, as if each play, in turn, analysed some variant, or isolated one variant to examine some particular factor. *Othello* is a clean exposition of the major variant in which Adonis becomes Tarquin, and Venus, loved as Lucrece, is destroyed as Queen of Hell, with special care given to the new modulation (death of Lucrece rather than rape), and special analytical attention given to the real ethical nature of Adonis's error – that Puritan, intellectual rejection of Divine Love – in the character of Iago. *Macbeth* is a concentrated exposition of the Rival Brothers variant, with special attention given to the Tarquin figure as he emerges from the feminine darkness (the moon-tusked cloud) of the Queen of Hell. But in *Hamlet* Shakespeare attempts to engage as many variants of the Tragic Equation as possible, and to make all interdependent. As if, perhaps, after *Troilus and Cressida* and *Measure for Measure*, he had seen a vision – a Piranesi universe constructed entirely of variants of the Tragic Equation, with the characters of *Hamlet* hurtling about the abyssal staircases, lurching through coiling mazes of halls and chambers, out on to balconies that become crypts, dungeons that become parapets over the gulf. Rather as Dante describes seeing the whole of *The Divine Comedy* in a single vision before he attempted to set it into words, maybe *Hamlet* was Shakespeare's despairing attempt to capture something of the fringes of a 'total', proleptic vision of that kind.

Some sense of the real organic complexity of the themes, each of which is nevertheless inevitably some form of the Tragic Equation, can be glimpsed by totting up the roles that Claudius fulfils from Hamlet's point of view. He is (a) his father's murderer and usurper – therefore to be killed, by Hamlet, and usurped; (b) his father the King's surrogate – therefore (being not the sacred original) killable and usurpable; (c) his mother's consort – therefore to be usurped; (d) the usurper of Hamlet's own crown and succession – therefore to be usurped; (e) his mother's Tarquinian ravisher – therefore to be punished by death and Hell; (g) the 'brother' his mother prefers – therefore to be usurped; (h) the self he must become (all Tarquins rolled into one: brother-killer, regicide, violator of the Goddess). And one can see others.

Hamlet's fatal, tragic action can proceed along either of the two lines of madness, but because of their harmonic unity, by concentrating on one, he inevitably activates and involves himself in the other. The plot precludes his reacting against the unjustly accused Ophelia (as Othello did react against Desdemona) – but that does not save her life. No Shakespearean hero reacts against his mother, as such, but that still does not protect Gertrude. Hamlet singles out Claudius. But his murder of Claudius turns out to be the comprehensive action which indirectly – as the Equation demands – destroys both Ophelia and Gertrude.

The Prince's murder of Claudius becomes a replay of Claudius's murder of King Hamlet, but a more complicated example of the type. In this action one catches sight of the weird *perpetuum mobile* that spins the whole drama into a vertiginous other dimension. When King Hamlet's ghost rises out of Purgatory, in the first act, Hamlet sees, as in a mirror, an image of his own mythic self. He sees himself, that is, as his mother's consort, punished for that incestuous crime by death and now by Purgatory. In the same way he sees Claudius as another image of his own mythic self. In this case he is again his mother's consort, not yet punished, but definitely, inevitably to be punished, and to be punished by him, Prince Hamlet. But this punishment, of himself as Claudius, by himself, will make his mythic life a reality. By that punishment and execution of Claudius he, Hamlet, will become King Hamlet, consort of his mother, therefore to be punished by death and Purgatory.

King Hamlet's ghost in Purgatory, Claudius on the throne, Prince Hamlet planning avenging punishment, are like accelerators in a cyclotron, round which Hamlet whirls unendingly in the tunnel of his bond with his mother – from which he can never break to marry Ophelia. This cyclotron effect is one unique result of the variant Equations being combined in just this way, and adds greatly to the sense of something inexpressible in itself and at the same time rooted beneath the foundations of Shakespeare's own nature, and for that reason also inexpressible. And an incidental effect is that this process, where Hamlet is compelled to live out, in reality, the destiny which on the mythic plane he has already gone through, and in the conclusion of which he is already fixed, as the punished, damned, incestuous consort of his mother as the Queen of Hell, seems to take place entirely in Hell.

A shadow play of that same theme of the Rival Brothers flickers over Hamlet and Laertes in so far as they are fighting over their rival claims to the soul of the play, the inner Crown – the love of Ophelia. But this particular duel anticipates another form of the Rival Brothers theme, one which emerges larger and fully formed in *King Lear*, where it reveals a surprising link to yet another metaphysical world. (The basic mythic structure of that other metaphysical world is also present here, as will be clear retrospectively, cf. page 268.)

Hamlet's black suit is a link to Othello and, like the black skin, suggests the immanence of the infernal form of the Goddess. It corresponds in both to the purple fullness of the flower that springs from Adonis's blood after he has combined with the Boar. Shakespeare has it both ways. Since the blackness suggests a state of possession which is already all but overwhelmingly complete, in Othello it adds to our sense of the precariousness of his control (purple spotted with white), while in Hamlet it adds to our sense of the heroic pathos, the human intensity, of his rational defence against losing control (white spotted with purple) (see pages 473–4).

This plethora of hyperactive Equations is enough to account for much of our feeling that Hamlet is charged with something tortuously inexpressible. And Hamlet's role, which is, in one sense, dedicated to keeping that mass of mythic necessity from being expressed, from emerging and revealing itself in completed Tarquinian action, does give dramatic form, in the play, to that very feeling. But the Tragic Equation is, as I said earlier, essentially inexpressible. The living complex of that immense myth, behind its bare symbols, is like the totality of the artist's biological life. It can only be suggested, intimated, peered into, suffered. *Hamlet* is simply a more than usually full suggestion of that inexpressibility, that totality. By comparison, all the other tragic heroes, in becoming the protagonist of the Equation, expend all their powers in bringing some salient feature of it to expression, or in attempting to.

Probably because the human resistance against mythic destiny and the Tragic Equation is one of the all-pervading themes of *Hamlet*, the humanity of the characters is peculiarly enhanced. Their struggles against that overload of tragic inevitability, their bewilderment under it, and the unusual length of stage time in which we can watch their doomed human attempts to escape it, give them all a poignancy unique to this play. The momentous opposition, between mythic compulsion and human frailty, seems to focus with special pathos on Ophelia, in the way that the daemonized, gigantic flywheel of a cosmos created by Hamlet's destiny revolves around her, as if around a fragile axis. Her helplessness is inseparable from the cut and wilting flowers – either drowning with her or scattered on a grave. Her role, like that of the Lucrece figure in each of the tragedies, is to register the human cost and translate it into the most intimate terms, also to register the metaphysical cost, the cost to the soul (to the hero's own soul), which never acts (fails to act or speak when it should), but only loves, and suffers, and is, and to convert this also into the familiar currency of what the heart finally has to pay.

Macbeth: X-ray of the Shakespearean moment

At first sight *Macbeth* is a stark example of the Rival Brothers variant: Macbeth, the irrational inferior, usurps and murders his rational kinsman, the 'holy' King Duncan. The plot line seems to be quite simple.

> As the play opens, Macbeth is an exemplary champion in the King's service, like the martial arm of this sacred ruler (this 'Lord's anointed'). He and his other kinsman, Banquo, are like Duncan's two guardian angels – defending the Crown, successfully, from the rebels.

Returning, with Banquo, from his victory, Macbeth meets the three Witches, who prophesy that he will be King but that Banquo's descendants will be the future Kings.

His wife, Lady Macbeth, persuades him to make the first part of the prophecy real. Possessed by her demonic will, and his own savage inclination (which suddenly appears from nowhere, against his known character), he murders the King and takes his place. Now he remembers the second part of the prophecy, and to complete the act kills Banquo – failing only to kill Banquo's son.

His punishment arrives swiftly and inevitably.

This bald trunk of an anecdote does little to explain how *Macbeth* comes to feel like the most essential expression of Shakespeare's tragic and poetic vision. There is little sign, for instance, of the key episodes of the Tragic Equation, through which, in each of the other tragedies, the tragic and poetic vision is released. There is no heroine of 'total, unconditional love', therefore no rejection of her by the hero, therefore no 'double vision', no tirade against her, no recoil into the Tarquinian madness and the attempt to destroy her.

The fact that the Rival Brothers pattern is so very strong guarantees nothing in itself. Elsewhere, this pattern seems to be incapable of touching tragedy. Tragic stature appears (in Shakespeare) only where the hero destroys his own 'soul' by destroying his beloved, in full awareness of what he is doing, and suffering the whole process while being convinced that it must be done. So Claudius's usurpation of King Hamlet, though it is disastrous for both, is not tragic. Edmund's usurpation of Edgar, though it is highly dramatic, is not tragic. Antony's attempt to 'usurp' Octavius Caesar, in *Antony and Cleopatra*, would never have been tragic if it had succeeded. It precipitates tragedy only because it fails, and in failing plunges Antony into the Tragic Equation – whereupon he destroys himself and Cleopatra. And when the tables are turned in that play, and Octavius Caesar finally 'usurps' Antony in Egypt, that only becomes tragic (as I will try to show) by transforming Antony's Equation-style tragedy into a tragedy of a different and greater kind. (Much as Edmund's murder of Cordelia – and consequently, indirectly, of Lear – lifts Lear's Equation-style tragedy into a greater kind.) In *The Winter's Tale*, King Leontes's attack on his 'brother' Polixenes could never be tragic: only his attempt to destroy his perfect wife Hermione moves towards the tragic. And Antonio's usurpation of Prospero never touches any note of tragedy. But there is no doubt that Macbeth, in murdering Duncan, not only becomes tragic, but becomes perhaps the most grippingly tragic of all Shakespeare's heroes.

Looking more closely, and remembering Shakespeare's metaphoric variants for the different parts of the Equation, one can't help recognizing that there is something about Macbeth's murder of Duncan that reminds one irresistibly of Tarquin's rape of Lucrece: here is the dark warrior, his dreadful apprehension, his uncontrollable 'lust' to commit the crime that he abhors, his approach through the castle, in the night, towards his sleeping victim. In fact, in feeling and atmosphere, and even in such details as the notion of murdering the grooms and putting the blame on them, Macbeth's act is a more grandly orchestrated reprise of Tarquin's. As he crosses the paving stones, appalled at the sound of his own footfalls, he recognizes it in himself:

> Now . . . witchcraft celebrates
> Pale Hecate's offerings; and wither'd murder,
> Alarum'd by his sentinel, the wolf,
> Whose howl's his watch, thus with his stealthy pace,
> With Tarquin's ravishing strides, toward his design
> Moves like a ghost . . .
>
> *Macbeth*, II. i. 51–6

And one sees that within Shakespeare's algebra, where Crown and Lucrece are interchangeable, Macbeth's role perfectly fulfils the second part of the Equation, and in so far as the Crown is the 'soul' of order in this work, Macbeth is a Tarquin, and Duncan incorporates Lucrece.

So he is playing, as it were, two roles. He is the irrational, usurping inferior in the pattern of the Rival Brothers. But he is also, it seems, the Tarquin in at least the second half of the Equation. One now looks for the first half of the Equation, where Adonis meets the Boar, since according to the Equation's basic algebra Tarquin = Adonis + Boar.

And clearly enough, at the opening of the play, Macbeth was an Adonis, an exemplary Adonis, the admired representative of the moral order which united him not only with Banquo and King Duncan, whose virtues are 'angels', but with Malcolm, who stands 'in the right hand of God', with Macduff, who is the touchstone of Malcolm's virtues (and who, saying of Macbeth's transformation,

> Not in the legions
> Of horrid hell can come a devil more damn'd
> In evils to top Macbeth . . .
>
> IV. iii. 55–7

will be the one – 'not born of woman' – to kill him), and with the
English King into whose 'hand' Heaven has given such 'sanctity' that
with a touch he cures 'the Evil'. This great composite Adonis, of whom,
as I say, Macbeth is originally the champion persona, assuredly, like
Adonis in the poem, would reject the Goddess on the least suspicion of
'lust' (and would defiantly set the Tragic Equation ticking thereby).

In spite of the presence of this eminent Adonis, the play still lacks
certain essential factors of the Equation. That rejection of the Female,
for instance, the initial *sine qua non* of the Equation's tragic action,
seems to be missing – not to speak of the double vision which reveals the
Queen of Hell and provokes the Boar's assault, the recoil into madness,
etc. Are these episodes, perhaps, not absolutely necessary after all?

The clue to what has happened lies in the fact that from the very first
moment the Witches and Lady Macbeth (in other words, the Female)
appear as the Queen of Hell in blatant, unmistakable form. According
to every other play in the sequence, within Shakespeare's universe the
Female is the Goddess Complete *until* she is divided by the Adonis
hero's Puritan spectacles, by his loathing terror of that portion of her
which his Reformation lenses separate out as the Queen of Hell. And so,
since here in *Macbeth* the Queen of Hell actually opens the first scene, it
follows that the Female must have been divided *before the play starts*.

The action of the play attests that this is in fact what has happened,
and one can see how it came about. Shakespeare composed *Macbeth*
probably in 1604–5. Following the latest revisions of *Hamlet*, it could
well have been the first play after his acting company, formerly the
Chamberlain's Men, became the King's Men, and the senior members
Grooms of the King's Chamber (they wore the King's livery). Shakespeare can hardly have escaped being caught up in the feverishly excited
atmosphere that surrounded this new ruler – who moreover loved plays
(and wrote verse). One motive for Shakespeare's choice of the theme of
Macbeth, it has been supposed, was to celebrate James's royal Scots
ancestry (Banquo's lineage) and so salute the legitimacy of his claim to
the English throne. But he seems to have been influenced, too, by
James's obsessive concern with witchcraft, on which the King had

written a book (*Daemonologie*, 1599), and which was one of the best-known things about him.

There cannot be much doubt that Shakespeare shaped his play under an arc-light awareness that this Scot was his principal audience. The play's external frame of cultural reference was, therefore, in a sense, both specialized and predetermined, brought to a hard focus by the metaphysical outlook of this theologically minded king, who was not only strongly Protestant but had gone far out of his way to denounce the evil of witches. The absolute rejection of the Goddess, that is, was a basic assumption, and could be taken for granted. It could be assumed almost as a royal edict.

If it were, the play would open not with a loving woman, or her surrogate, representative of the undivided Goddess (as *Hamet, Othello, Lear, Timon, Coriolanus, Antony and Cleopatra, Cymbeline* and *The Winter's Tale* open), but with what Adonis sees after rejecting her – the Queen of Hell preparing her revenge.

Accordingly, the play does open in this way, with the three weird sisters. They are the Goddess as Hecate, Chaos and Hell – the triple form in which she attended Queen Dido's suicide (which Shakespeare will remember again in *The Tempest*), when she cursed Aeneas who had rejected her (*Aeneid*, Book IV). In other words, they are the Queen of Hell in her most virulent aspect, but also in her most homely mode (Celtic rural hags), and prophesying like the three Norns. This interdicted triple being announces herself to the moral world of Duncan/Banquo/Macbeth, etc., and Jacobean audience alike, in classic double vision terms:

Fair is foul, and foul is fair.

I. i. 11

A powerful aura of the double vision then propagates itself in a bewildering rout of images through the next scene, where a compact series of telescoped reports, describing, to King Duncan, the prowess of his noble kinsman Macbeth in the two battles now being fought offstage, bombards him with sinister doubles. From the King's first words: 'What bloody man is that?' ugly questions begin to stick to Macbeth. Impressions of other selves, alternative identities, all villainous, wrestle with our attempt to get a clear picture of him from these bulletins of his deadlocked battle with opposites. In the description of his struggle with the 'merciless Macdonwald', it is oddly difficult to keep track of which is Macbeth, or which is which of the 'two spent swimmers that do cling together/And choke their art', where 'valour's minion' is knotted with the rebel whose whore is Fortune, till the chopped-off head of one of them is fixed on the battlements.

After a joyful exclamation from Duncan, more reflections begin to writhe, discomforts swell out of comforts, yes stands for no, sparrows do or do not dismay eagles and hares lions, cannon are 'overcharged with double cracks' and two battlers, one of which is Macbeth, 'doubly redouble' their strokes – till the narrator faints.

But another messenger, from a different battle, carries straight on, with an account of Bellona's bridegroom, who seems to be Macbeth but is entangled, inevitably, with that rebel whose whore was Fortune, while the Thane of Cawdor, who will be Macbeth (the Witches have said so) and is 'a most disloyal traitor', comes and goes in among, each confronting each with 'self-comparisons', 'point against point, rebellious arm 'gainst arm', till in the end Macbeth has absorbed everything that was the treacherous enemy's:

> What he hath lost noble Macbeth hath won
>
> I. ii. 69

and the scene dissolves to reveal, once more, the three Witches, with Macbeth and Banquo approaching them, Macbeth exclaiming:

> So foul and fair a day I have not seen.
>
> I. iii. 38

This cunningly confused and confusing diplodic vision of the Witches and the battle is, as I say, like the aftershock and refraction of the double vision, which sends its gleams of blood and merging, separating doubles rippling or heaving through the rest of the action, and sets the duelling pair, 'blood' and 'double', reverberating throughout the text. It signifies that the composite Adonis – 'noble' Macbeth, Banquo and King Duncan – has triggered the Tragic Equation.

At this point, the Equation's other missing bits begin to be recognizable. What the audience sees, and what Banquo and Macbeth will soon be aware of, is that a dangerous figure, a 'hot tyrant', is somehow emerging from the garbled account of butchering doubles and from the Witches. In retrospect Banquo will realize that this was the new Macbeth, materializing from the prophecy, and from the honours stripped off the 'self-comparisons' and usurpers that he has recently overpowered. And, within a minute or two, Macbeth himself will recognize, emerging from the promise of the Witches, his new terrible self:

> Whose horrid image doth unfix my hair
> And make my seated heart knock at my ribs
> Against the use of nature . . .
>
> I. iii. 135–7

as Adonis saw the 'hot tyrant' in the Goddess he had rejected. In other words, at this confrontation Macbeth, as Adonis, meets his 'double' who will be Tarquin – or, rather, who will first of all be the Boar. Banquo and Macbeth now resemble the King's two selves – the incorruptible and the corruptible, who are separating into 'rational' and 'irrational' brothers under the magical temptation of the rejected Goddess and her promise of infinite crowning power (which is actually a fatal curse) to be gained by a murder.

As they separate, the shapes of the two patterns begin to come clear. Macbeth descends towards the pattern of the Rival Brothers, advancing, 'rapt', to meet his terrible 'double' and to fuse with it, while Banquo, more and more firmly the repository of Macbeth's Adonis qualities, backs off, critical and self-controlled. Macbeth gabbles eagerly for reassurance that the Witches' promise is true, while Banquo 'chides' them, and having coolly elicited the information that his own descendants, not Macbeth's, will produce the future royal line, dismisses the weird sisters as 'bubbles of the earth', and supposes that he and Macbeth must have

> eaten on the insane root
> That takes the reason prisoner.
>
> I. iii. 84–5

By the end of the scene in which the King, by making him Thane of Cawdor, confirms the first clause of the Witches' promise to Macbeth, the hero has changed worlds. Leaving his old Adonis conscience in the care of Banquo and King Duncan, his self of 'black and deep desires' ducks out of the world of the Equation and emerges in the Underworld of the Rival Brothers. Here in the welcoming embrace of Lady Macbeth he is suddenly transformed into a creature that neither Banquo nor Duncan would recognize, the one that will be the Boar.

The presence of the Mythic Equation now reveals itself in the portrait of Lady Macbeth as a Queen of Hell. Possessed by the powers of the Goddess (who was rejected before the play began), her avenging fury has already marked down the rational 'ruler' of the Adonis world that rejected her. In other words, according to that larger background pattern of the Equation, not only will Macbeth's Adonis persona have to die, but Duncan and Banquo too. The prophecy of the three Witches has effectually taken possession of her and she now incorporates them in her insatiable, inexorable 'lust' to seize the 'crown'. Her will is like the fixed Fate which they merely announced. In this way, Hecate, Chaos and Hell, in full supernatural panoply, have been shunted on to the natural plane, and Macbeth's wife is supercharged with her mythic role. It displaces everything else about her.

> Come, you spirits
> That tend on mortal thoughts, unsex me here,
> And fill me from the crown to the toe, top full
> Of direst cruelty! Make thick my blood,
> Stop up the access and passage to remorse,
> That no compunctious visitings of nature
> Shake my fell purpose, nor make peace between
> The effect and it! Come to my woman's breasts,
> And take my milk for gall, you murthering ministers,
> Wherever in your sightless substances
> You wait on Nature's mischief! Come, thick night,
> And pall thee in the dunnest smoke of hell,
> That my keen knife see not the wound it makes
> Nor heaven peep through the blanket of the dark,
> To cry, 'Hold, hold!'

I. V. 41–55

Banishing her wifely qualities (Sacred Bride and Divine Mother) in these words, she cleanly divides Nature according to the natural divisions of the Goddess. And in this infernalized form takes possession of her husband.

In spite of the increasingly fearful gulf between them, Macbeth's two newly defined selves still have to coexist in the same head. Accordingly, the doomed, rational Adonis, in whose conscience Banquo and King Duncan sit like deities, tries to defend himself against Lady Macbeth's manipulations, with:

> We will proceed no further in this business . . .
>
> I. vii. 3 I

or, when she fears that traces of the old Adonis, 'the milk of human kindness', might weaken the 'man' (i.e. the Boar) in him:

> I dare do all that may become a man;
> Who dares do more is none.
>
> I. vii. 46–7

But there is never any doubt what will happen. In fact, two things are happening simultaneously, one in the pattern of the Tragic Equation, which Macbeth's Adonis self has to suffer, and one in the pattern of the Rival Brothers, which fills him with exultation. In the first, Lady Macbeth resembles Persephone coming at him in the form of a boar – to 'kill' the Adonis/Macbeth and transform him into her infernal consort, in her Underworld, as the 'hot tyrant'. In the second, Persephone is actually recreating him, out of her own 'divine', infernal substance, as the Boar – who will now kill King Duncan.

From this point he lives both lives simultaneously, in the two different worlds. However, because of the consistency of the myth, there is a complication that intensifies the horror experienced by rational Adonis/ Macbeth beyond anything in the rest of the tragic sequence. As both patterns – Equation and Rival Brothers – now move in parallel, the latter in distinct close-up, filling the foreground, the former in less distinct but larger format, enfolding the whole action in the background, Macbeth's peculiar dilemma is that he is the *chief* protagonist in *both* patterns: he is the irrational brother, with the mythic attributes of the Boar, in the Rival Brothers, and he is Adonis, who having seen the 'double vision' must now deal with the Boar's charge, in the Equation. The unique circumstance of this – for Macbeth – diabolical arrangement is that he himself is the Boar. In all the plays of the sequence, Macbeth is the only hero to live the fully aware inner lives of both these opposed figures *simultaneously*.

This fascinating double nature defines itself in front of our eyes. Within the pattern of the Equation, as Lady Macbeth's insane will floods into him, she signals the point they have reached, in the steps of the Equation, by a familiar hieroglyphic token:

[247]

> Look like the innocent flower
> But be the serpent under it.

I. v. 66–7

The same flower peeped through at exactly the same point during Angelo's transformation in *Measure for Measure*. It is the flower that stands between the two long poems. But though it may resemble the flower that Venus gathered back into her love, and carried away to Paphos, Lady Macbeth is here directing Macbeth to be resolute, to accept his Tarquinian destiny, not as the transcendental (innocent) flower that Venus carried off, but as the tragic, blood-filled flower that opens into the second part of the Equation – the flower that is Tarquin and conceals the Queen of Hell, the Serpent.

From that moment, within the pattern of the Equation, Macbeth is a Tarquin. What follows now, on that level, seen from one angle, is the struggle within the flower: Tarquin awakening to the fact that he is possessed, with a ghastly awareness of exactly what he is doing and what he is about to destroy. So he sleepwalks wide awake into the Tarquinian nightmare, and commits the primal Tarquinian crime, 'rape' of the 'crown' – watching the whole process from the agonized point of view of the possessed Adonis.

Meanwhile, in the pattern of Rival Brothers, he is emerging as nakedly himself, the Boar, like some terrible kind of child, out of the magical, ectoplasmic darkness of the Goddess, of whom his wife is the avatar. And he sets out, as the irrational brother, to perform the murder, as the Boar commences its charge.

In this way, two distinct identities, in two different worlds, arrive at the King's bedside. The Boar itself, full of its diabolical will to kill him, in the infernal world of the Rival Brothers, and the Tarquinized Adonis, who has already foresuffered this death, is already the slaughtered but still aware other self of the sacred King, and whose present action is merely the completion, the actualization, of that self-murder already undergone and who now attempts to finalize the crime (but there will be still another step to take – the murder of Banquo, then of Fleance his son, then of Malcolm the other heir to the throne, etc.), in the moral world of Adonis.

The peculiar intensification of Macbeth's horror during this double act is decided by the dominance of the pattern of the Rival Brothers. It is so dominant that it displaces and distorts the pattern of the Tragic

Equation, and disrupts its natural course, squeezing it into a thin, terrified skin of Adonis, an electroshock sweat of self-awareness, over the full, bristling presence of the demonic being that has burst from the darkness of the raving Lady Macbeth, a hair-on-end *frisson* over the enormity of the crime he is about to commit – but it is also more than that. Being so crushed out of its normal shape, his Adonis reaction obviously cannot – like that of the other tragic heroes – discharge his terror and loathing against the Goddess, embodied in some separate but seemingly faithless beloved, because none such exists. These baffled reflexes, therefore, have searched out the Goddess in her dangerous new form, and have found her in the shape of the Boar, which is the demonic force about to destroy him, and which is, he sees, his own uncontrollable insane will. His Adonis terror of the Goddess, in other words, has been short-circuited to an absolute terror of his other self, a loathing horror of his own actions. And so his 'tirades', too, are directed against the infernal, treacherous, Queen-of-Hellish quality of his own actions, as in the great speech 'If it were done when 'tis done, then 'twere well/It were done quickly', and the titanic musical crescendo which begins: 'I have done the deed'.

Following him through the Equation in this way, one begins to see that Macbeth affects the imagination as he does, more disturbingly than any of the other heroes, precisely because of his radical difference in kind – because of his double life, undergoing the Adonis-into-Tarquin tragic fate, like all Shakespeare's tragic heroes, while at the same time living out, as none of the others does, that full subjective awareness of the Boar. It might be said that this is not so much a radical difference as a difference of degree – since all the heroes are, by definition, possessed by the Boar. Suffering possession by the Boar is a very different thing, however, from *being* the Boar, evidently. And to be both – both the one possessed and the Boar that possesses – as Macbeth is, amounts to a radical difference. One could argue that Hamlet ('Now could I drink hot blood' etc.(III. ii. 415)) has something of the same kind of double life, and that he too, like Macbeth, is horrified by what drives him (by the Boar – which reveals itself briefly as Pyrrhus) towards the murder of Claudius. None of the other heroes, as far as the text is concerned, shares this horror of the demonic being driving them on. And in this respect the difference between Hamlet and Macbeth is indeed one of degree. In Hamlet the suffering Adonis factor predominates, resisting the Boar for almost the entire play, keeping the centre of gravity within the Adonis point of view. In Macbeth the uncontrollable Boar pre-dominates and the Adonis factor is helpless almost before Macbeth properly understands what the Witches are saying, letting the centre of gravity drop with a shock to the Boar's point of view.

To grasp more clearly what Macbeth has to contend with, and just how he comes to be under such unique psychic pressure, it might be helpful to compare, very briefly, the antithetically different inner lives of Adonis/Tarquin and of the Boar. Taking the Adonis figures first, it is possible (up to a point) to isolate the experience common to all of them – the complex of feelings, attitudes and happenings that tends to recur with each one.

First, his Puritan-style ideals, and his distrust of the Female. Follow-ing hard on this comes the inevitable double vision, in which the hero sees the Queen of Hell and resists the Boar's approach with outraged incredulity and perhaps horror. This is Hamlet hearing (and remember-ing and being urged again by) the Ghost, Othello listening to Iago, Lear hearing Cordelia's first 'Nothing', Timon beginning to understand his creditors, Coriolanus forced to acknowledge that Rome has risen against him, etc.

Next, he succumbs to the impact in a frenzy of loathing and an agony of lost happiness. This is the moment of the great tirades.

Finally, when the Boar has climbed into his skin, he is rushed away into the Tarquinian madness. But even in this madness he keeps his self-respect. Indeed, once the Equation has matured, in *Hamlet*, the madness can be described as 'total, unconditional' idealism outraged. Though he then destroys the source of his only possible happiness, his soul and his world, it is characteristic of this hero that throughout the whole tragic seizure, right up to the moment in which he comes to his senses and realizes that he has been possessed, he seriously believes he is correcting a wrong, according to the most absolute standards of right. Throughout the plays of the tragic sequence every hero except Macbeth (and his strange relative Antony) speaks from that 'as-if-rational' point of view, the agonized or distorted point of view of the possessed Adonis who is Tarquin. Even after it has been capsized in spectacular fashion by that irrational secret-sharer rising from beneath it, that point of view, of the Adonis ego, though it no longer has any control over its actions, always retains the ability, like a ship's gimbal, to think itself rational (at least, it does so up to the point at which the ego is destroyed, and a new self, neither Adonis nor Tarquin, emerges – as begins to happen in *King*

Lear). This is what I mean by his keeping the centre of gravity within the Adonis point of view. What appears to everybody else as the lucidity of an insane homicide appears to him as the holy logic of a justice that he is bound to serve. So Othello suffocates Desdemona, Lear banishes Cordelia, Timon curses Athens, Coriolanus prepares to reduce Rome and all its occupants to a heap of ashes, Posthumus orders Pisanio to kill Imogen, Leontes strives to condemn Hermione to death – each with the confidence of the Almighty.

What this Adonis/Tarquin never understands is the nature of his attacker. Throughout his rationalized insanity, neither he nor the audience ever gets a glimpse of what is driving him to what he is doing. The possessing demon never reveals its hand. Which is to say that the irrational self, the Boar, never steps out of Adonis's skin on to the stage, to show its own face and tell what it feels like to be not Adonis possessed by the Boar but the Boar alone, seething with its insatiable need – as, for instance, Aaron tells in *Titus Andronicus*, and Richard III, and Edmund in *King Lear*. In Hamlet (except for that glimpse of Pyrrhus), Othello, Lear and the rest, this possessing demon's own inner life remains unknown and unknowable – a savagely active but silent area in the heart of the tragedy.

The subjective life of the Boar is therefore less familiar. In its simple form – in Aaron, Richard III, Edmund – it never regards its actions as 'just'. It starts without moral ideals, and gathers none on the way. It serves only its own will. And yet in each case, as in Macbeth, there is a consistent nature, an integral character, common to every manifestation.

This can best be seen here in *Macbeth* – possibly only here. As I have tried to define it, the Shakespearean moment occurs where the Boar emerges – from the Goddess – and topples Adonis. This terrific inner event detonates each of the tragedies, but it is actually dramatized – externally analysed in dramatic terms – only in *Macbeth*. In *Measure for Measure* it passes in a flash, with Angelo's 'What's this? What's this?' For King Lear, it explodes out of Cordelia's 'Nothing'. For Othello it arrives between his fainting as an Adonis (collapsing in a whirling vision of animals, with the magically embroidered muleta of a handkerchief flapping at his eyes) and his rising as a Tarquin with the murder of Desdemona completed in all but the practical details. But in *Macbeth* it extends in stage time from Macbeth's first sight of the Witches to his shaking off Banquo's ghost in all-out, murderous, hardened tyranny.

Beginning within the containing framework of the Tragic Equation, Shakespeare in *Macbeth* has zoomed in on this moment, where the irrational topples the rational, and finds the Rival Brothers magnifying out of it. This is where one sees quite clearly just how the Shakespearean moment comes to be the fount and origin of the Rival Brothers. But then Shakespeare zooms in deeper, and the irrational brother, filling the whole field of vision, opens into his mythic constituents – the Queen of Hell and the Boar. Acts One to Three of this play now become an X-ray chamber inside the breast of Adonis. The whole zoology of the creation of the Boar is flash-lit, at the precise moment of its emergence and separation from the dark Goddess, and at the instant of its attack, within the chaotic physiology of the rational self under the impact. Or these scenes become an X-ray magnification, slow-motion sequence of the biology of the blood-filled Flower, as it lifts through the disintegration of Adonis and opens – on the tragic plane – into Tarquin.

Accordingly, this is where one can see exactly what stuff the Boar is made of. The metaphysical nature of this elemental being, the algebraic factors of his role in Shakespeare's myth, are more literally and fully articulated here than anywhere else. The whole bizarre process, or chain reaction, is laid wide open. Shakespeare has made this drama out of the Goddess actually turning into the Boar, and the Boar, as Lady Macbeth, actually crawling into Macbeth's skin, and taking him over, whereupon he, now possessed by the Goddess who is also the Boar, crawls into the skin of the King, and takes him over – whereupon the monarch (now Macbeth) goes mad. The mythic literalness of the sequence becomes apparent when one looks at Macbeth from the point of view of Duncan – in the microsecond fright, after the fatal blow. First, he is aware of the dagger – the Boar's tusk. Behind the tusk, he sees the 'hot tyrant' – Macbeth. Behind Macbeth, the Queen of Hell – Lady Macbeth. Behind Lady Macbeth, the full triplicity of the Goddess. He sees, in fact, what Adonis saw in the long poem – looking over the shoulders of the Boar towards the Goddess he had rejected.

Yet again, it can be seen from this that the subjective nature of the Boar is something extraordinary. First and foremost it is the 'beast', the 'irrational' elemental, that 'kills' Adonis and takes possession of him. But the Boar's mythic nature cannot be left at that. Since it is made, as it were, of the stuff of the enraged Goddess, the immediate preoccupation of its inner life is that 'infinite' (she is supernatural, after all) vengeful (jealous) passion of the rejected Goddess – her will to take possession of

Adonis. This depraved mood in which the Boar charges – the Goddess's assault against the hero's Puritan rejection – produces the tragic action but in fact is temporary. Within or behind this distortion, the substance of the Boar, being the stuff of the Goddess, is always what it was – the Divine Love (cf. Postscript, page 504).

It is this massive thunderbolt of Divine Love, albeit in unrecognizable form, which, taking possession of the Adonis figure, makes him suddenly fascinating – when he becomes a Tarquin. Until that happens, Adonis is merely another dramatic character. But once the Boar has arrived, and transformed him, he suddenly embodies the unique thing: Shakespeare's revelation. Immediately he overflows with inner riches. King Lear, for instance, is a mechanical, foolish despot till the Boar arrives. Timon is a deluded, idealistic prodigal till the Boar arrives. Without the Boar, Adonis is simply stuck in his rules of ego behaviour (something like Prospero). Once the Boar has taken possession, and shattered Adonis, the hidden, potential spirituality reveals itself in the poetry (characteristic of all the Tarquins) but also in the other great Shakespearean event – the transformation which, beginning here in *Macbeth*, establishing itself openly in *King Lear*, and emerging as the main concern of the action from *Antony and Cleopatra* onwards, produces out of Tarquin the 'saint' – the spiritually reborn, redeemed one, beloved of the Goddess.

Seeing Macbeth as the Boar, and seeing the Boar in this way, as a phenomenal, dramatic, mythic, poetic, 'biological' creation, helps to explain why *Macbeth* is so often felt to embody the primal statement of Shakespeare's inspiration. This strange creature is the infinite being, inseparable from the Goddess, that lives the inner life of the uncontrollable will itself – the tenant of that silent area at the heart of the tragedies. And this is Macbeth's dominant inner life, which he shares with no other tragic hero, though he shares their Tarquinian fate and the inner life of Adonis. Standing at the centre of each of the two patterns, Macbeth's two selves, as I say, move towards different objects: Tarquin, in self-loathing helplessness, moves towards the 'rape' of the Crown, while the Boar, irresistible, moves to usurp and destroy the rational brother. But their objects coincide in the one victim and the one act: the King's murder, when Tarquin 'rapes' the Crown, and the Boar climbs into Duncan's slashed skin and stands up King of Scotland.

At that point, the two patterns coalesce, and the pattern of the Rival Brothers, dominant so far, is absorbed into the containing pattern of the

Tragic Equation in which the play began, and which now resumes control. Macbeth, who suffered a so to speak preliminary phase of his Tarquinian fate when he moved towards murdering Duncan/Banquo, now steps into the major phase, where his Boar self, combined with (possessing) the Adonis self of Duncan/Banquo (the monarchy in which his own Adonis self was invested), becomes the mad Tarquin – the tyrant who will now rape and destroy Scotland (repeatedly described as his victim, a woman near death, no longer 'our mother, but our grave', etc.). Accordingly these are the two Adonis deaths in the play: the first, personal to Macbeth, where his wife shows him the 'innocent flower', and the second where Duncan/Banquo are murdered, at which point Macbeth sees the 'flower' in a transcendental vision (cf. page 397).

At this level, in the first half of the Equation the dramatis personae have been: Duncan/Banquo/noble Macbeth = Adonis, while Lady Macbeth/Hecate/three Witches = Queen of Hell, and irrational Macbeth = Boar; in the second half of the Equation, King Macbeth = Tarquin, while Scotland (the royal sanctity of Duncan, and the Scotland of wives and children in particular) = Lucrece.

But under that intensification of Macbeth's double role, the psychic pressure on him has been so intolerable that the Equation itself has undergone a change. This change is revealed exactly where (in retrospect) it might be expected: after the 'death' of the Adonis and before the emergence of Tarquin in his 'madness' – in that juncture between the two halves of the Equation, between the two long poems, where the Flower stands. Macbeth's tragic experience, too much for human nature, has forced Heaven, as it were, to relent, or to show a sign of relenting. This is the change that will eventually, in later plays, transform everything. But for the moment, for Macbeth, the signs are merely revealed and withdrawn, in that strange scene, Act Four, Scene One, where Macbeth returns to the Witches to seek knowledge about his future, and is shown three Tarot-like apparitions. (I return to this on pages 394–9, though the intervening sections are probably needed to bring the reader to the full sense of what is said there about it.) These apparitions rise, as I say, at the point in the play corresponding to the gap between the two poems: immediately before this, Banquo has died; immediately after, Macbeth plunges into his Tarquinian 'madness' with:

From this moment,
The very firstlings of my heart shall be
The firstlings of my hand. And even now,
To crown my thoughts with acts, be it thought and done:
The castle of Macduff I will surprise;
Seize upon Fife; give to the edge of the sword
His wife, his babes, and all unfortunate souls
That trace him in his line . . .

IV. i. 146–53

but just here, for a moment, 'heaven' opens and, through the Witches, reveals the future behind his future (cf. page 394). Trying to interpret it to his own advantage on the most benighted level, he mistakes it on every level. After this, Shakespeare plunges him into outer darkness, unredeemable. He does not reappear at all in Act Four. In Act Five he emerges only to endure his death in weary despair, as the last dead leaf, while Lady Macbeth kills herself.

Abandoned by their mythic purpose (which has now completed its programme), Macbeth and Lady Macbeth cannot humanly sustain what the myth compelled them to do. They are easily and naturally overwhelmed by the cyclic resurgence of the Adonis world.

King Lear: a triple Tragic Equation

The plot and sub-plot of *King Lear* are well-defined and powerful examples of the Tragic Equation and the theme of the Rival Brothers respectively. Here again, one sees how they are alternative expressions of the one basic event, where irrational usurps rational and destroys the soul of order in attempting to seize it by violence. The Gloucester story, where Edmund usurps Edgar, is like a nightmare of King Lear's, after he had banished Cordelia. Alternatively, Lear's banishment of Cordelia, and the consequent reign of his 'dog-hearted' daughters, is like a nightmare of Gloucester's during the family struggle of his sons.

Discussing *Venus and Adonis*, I distinguished between the two planes of Adonis's flower death. On the transcendental plane he was reborn, in the Flower, to reunion with the love of the Goddess. On the lower plane, the tragic plane, he was reborn, through the Flower, into the second part of the Equation as Tarquin. The tragic series of dramas, beginning with *All's Well*, then proceeded from his rebirth into Tarquin, along the tragic plane, which I divided – very roughly – into the 'realistic' plane of the plot and the 'mythic' plane of the Tragic Equation behind the plot. And, as I pointed out, through these dramas the transcendental plane remains closed, as if sealed off. One could say the end of *All's Well*, where Bertram returns to the love of Helena, and the end of *Measure for Measure*, where the Duke returns Angelo to the love of Mariana, are lit by rays from the transcendental plane. If that is so, these endings still give no sense of Bertram and Angelo having broken through, psychologically transfigured, into another realm. The hero's spiritual change is symbolized on the mythic or ritual plane, but not actually dramatized and made real on the plane of the plot. The suspicion remains, in both cases, that the contrition is 'lip-service only', and the effect is sour.

I mentioned that *Macbeth* introduces a radical change into the Equation, revealed in the three apparitions, but that the change is quickly reabsorbed back into the Equation's old pattern. And, as I will show later on, this change is actually the first real opening of the transcendental plane in the evolution of the Tragic Equation. It gives Macbeth a fleeting but vivid glimpse of the escape route from his tragic destiny. But Macbeth cannot understand the vision, and in any case is in no position to respond. Nevertheless, it stands in the play as a startling but positive declaration of what is preparing itself in the 'soul' of the Equation's tragic hero. And in the next play, *King Lear*, that change emerges into the substance of the action as the greatest event in Shakespeare's oeuvre.

In *King Lear*, the metaphysical interdependence of the two plots – of the Tragic Equation and of the Rival Brothers – is so profoundly worked out that they seem to develop like a single inevitable system of cause and effect. In fact, neither is physically dependent on the other in any way. The unity is, as I say, metaphysical – wholly poetic and internal. Any evil commander could lead Goneril's forces, and could execute Cordelia. Any madman could have befriended Lear. The sub-plot, with a few loose hangings of intertangled royalty, could have made a play by Fletcher – a sort of *Two Noble Kinsmen* – without being substantially different. And Lear's story was a popular drama, without the sub-plot (Tolstoy preferred it), before Shakespeare touched it.

I will go through the outline of Lear's story separately. Every definable feature seems to intensify the effect of this play. But one obvious mechanism in this effect of intensification is the triple nature of the Tragic Equation. Lear goes through the 'double vision' and rejection and madness not once, but three times, in a cumulative sequence, which, very roughly, runs as follows:

It is assumed – King Lear assumes – that he and his daughters love each other. Lear stages a public declaration of his love for them, so that they can make a public declaration of theirs for him. But he assumes that the mutual love is beyond question. This is equivalent to that pre-tragic, idyllic phase in which, say, Othello and Desdemona love each other (Othello is convinced) 'totally and unconditionally'.

The tragic hero, Lear, now confronts (rather like Shakespeare drafting his own will in 1606) three women, i.e. the Goddess who incorporates, in some form still hidden from him, the Queen of Hell, but who mainly embodies the love on which his sanity depends. On this occasion, he adopts a novel method of gaining reassurance that this love does exist: the love test. This provides the essential opening love crisis. Goneril and Regan win, by their shameless, voluble exaggeration of what will turn out to have been a lie. Cordelia loses by failing to find words that will express her conception of the truth. (I will come back to this theme: the eloquence of the lie, and the dumbness of the truth. It is no accident, presumably, that Shakespeare's most terrific drama revolves around the failure and falsity of words.)
Lear interprets Cordelia's failure to use the unscrupulously false language of her sisters as a flat denial of the 'total, unconditional love' which he demands. In other words, he hears her refusal as the ultimate treachery. The effect on him corresponds to the effect that Iago's description of Desdemona's adultery has on Othello, only it is far more instantaneous. It is a shatteringly explosive instance of the double vision, as Lear sees, in the woman he most loves, something 'more hideous/Than the sea monster'.

In his instant Tarquinian madness he does not destroy Cordelia, but he does throw her away, with savage emphasis on the completeness of the severance, banishing her for ever, across the seas, in marriage to a foreign king.

And so, as far as Lear and Cordelia are concerned, the Tragic Equation is apparently completed by the end of Act One, Scene One.

However, at this point two other circumstances take over the controls. First, Lear finds himself dependent on the love of Goneril, which he still assumes to be 'total and unconditional'. This is like the opening, therefore, of a new and quite different replay of the Tragic Equation, which is just what it turns out to be. And second, Cordelia is still alive.

The new, more sinister tragedy gets under way when Goneril reveals her true nature, as an authentic Queen of Hell. Once again Lear sees the double vision and recoils towards instant Tarquinian madness with the tirade:

Hear, Nature, hear, dear Goddess, hear . . .

I. iv. 299

Before the end of Act One he is beseeching Heaven to save him from going mad. But he still has the love of Regan:

Degenerate bastard! I'll not trouble thee:
Yet have I left a daughter.

I. iv. 277–8

But then Regan presents him with the third replay of the Shakespearean moment. She combines with Goneril, revealing herself to Lear as 'the self-same metal' as her sister. The two women whom, it seems, for a brief moment there, Lear might have been hoping to divide into the loved and the loathed in separate bodies, now become a single, inseparable, two-headed monster. Before the end of Act Two he plunges into absolute Tarquinian frenzy against both:

No, you unnatural hags,
I will have such revenges on you both . . .

II. iv. 281–2

Or rather, he plunges towards it. But at this point, abruptly, something happens that has not happened before in the tragic series of dramas. Lear's spectacular explosion into Tarquin is suddenly arrested. His very words meet a barrier in the air:

I will have such revenges on you both
That all the world shall — I will do such things —
What they are yet I know not —

282–4

The nascent Tarquin finds himself obstructed. He finds it
impossible, that is, to enter on his destiny and destroy the Female.
The customary lightning path of his madness, and his
transformation, is blocked by the sheer power of Goneril and
Regan. Lear suddenly understands that he lacks the physical
strength to make the first move against them. He is too old, and he
has abdicated.

If Lear cannot become a Tarquin, what is his madness? If it is not a
Tarquinian madness — of egomanic destructive fury against the Female
— what is it? According to the Equation, mingled in it are the following:

Lear's madness was Tarquinian when it was directed against
Cordelia, punishing her effectively for what he saw as her failure in
love. He now understands, like Othello over the murdered body of
Desdemona, that his rejection of Cordelia was a mistake, and that
his Adonis ego must be judged for its error, punished, and
corrected. That first Tarquinian madness against Cordelia has
become, therefore, a fierce, penitential remorse. This is one
component of his madness.

Another component is that aborted Tarquinian 'madness' against
Goneril and Regan. Or rather, not aborted. This blocked birth of
Tarquin is, in terms of the Equation, the Boar's takeover
frustrated. The moment that Lear rushes out into the storm
corresponds, say, to the moment in which Othello falls in a faint.
But whereas Othello rises possessed by the Boar, and transformed,
determined to kill Desdemona and fully able to do so, Lear knows
too well that he is physically incapable of making any effective
move against his terrible offspring. And so he cannot rise. This
knowledge of his helplessness to avenge himself, doubled by his
remorse for having so mistakenly revenged himself on Cordelia,
means, as I say, that he cannot free himself from the onslaught of
the Boar by surrendering to it — that is, by combining in
Tarquinian madness with it and discharging it against Goneril and
Regan. One imagines the Boar, having ripped Adonis open, now

[259]

trying to take possession of him – and finding itself blocked. A hideous predicament for Lear. So, from that first roll of thunder, when the old King swooned into the wilderness, the Boar is tossing him up and down the heathery banks in a vain attempt to get inside his skin and inspire him with his mythic destiny as a Tarquin – a destroyer of the Female.

Because he cannot surrender to it, Lear has to go on enduring its attack – untransformed. As if Adonis were clinging to the Boar's head, hanging on its ears, wrestling with it, while it tears at him and flails him about the heath.

This prolonged resistance of the hero, against the Boar, is not absolutely new: Hamlet fought it off in a similar way. But Hamlet always knew that sooner or later he would surrender and let the Boar have its will, since this would be his revenge against Claudius, the moment for which half of him prayed. His resistance against the Boar was not physical inability to become a Tarquin but simple horror of what it would entail – possession by the Boar and destruction of the Female and of himself. But Lear has no such choice. His only options now are to overcome the Boar or be destroyed by it.

One inexorable law of the Equation, evidently, is that once the process has been triggered, then the old personality must die and a new one must be born. If Adonis's rebirth as Tarquin is blocked, he has to be born, says the Equation, in some other way.

Another element of Lear's 'madness', then, is the labour of a new and shattering kind of rebirth – an unprecedented and different kind of rebirth. Not the old kind, an easy leap into a raving Tarquin, but a 'hard and bitter agony' – into something else.

So everything combines – his own pitiless judgement against his old ego, the Boar's relentless onslaught against his old ego, and his last-ditch fight against the Boar with the new strength that he is having to dig up out of nowhere (out of his powerlessness, his age, his outcast humiliation and solitude, his exposure to elemental nature, his despair) – everything combines in the travail of a new, and newly mutated, kind of rebirth. And this component of the 'madness' is new.

Later on, I will trace the lineage and evolution of the Storm (see pages 382–412). Briefly, it has always, up to this point (actually up to the middle of *Macbeth*) accompanied the death of Adonis and the rebirth of Tarquin. It symbolized, so to speak, the charge of the Boar along the tragic plane. But in the middle of *Macbeth* (again, later on I will show in detail just how it happens, pages 394–403) the Storm changes planes and thereafter, through all the subsequent dramas, accompanies the hero's rebirth as a *saint* on the transcendental plane.

The extraordinary, prolonged violence of the storm in *King Lear* is an expression of the difficulty and dreadfulness of this new process, this earthshaking and painful new kind of rebirth.

As I mentioned, this possibility was laid down at the end of *Venus and Adonis*. The charge of the Boar transformed Adonis into the Flower which became Tarquin and produced the Tragic Equation. But the same charge of the same Boar also produced the Flower which Venus plucked and carried away into her transcendental Divine Love.

That second flower, as I said, went into deep hibernation. But now in *King Lear* Shakespeare is forcing it to wake up. The mutilated Adonis cannot be reborn as Tarquin, yet the gestation must go full term and deliver something, and so, under the colossal biological pressure (and it had already begun in *Macbeth*) the old genetic possibility is activated and the chemistry of the Equation is reversed. And it delivers, after hideous labour, not a Tarquin but the opposite of a Tarquin. Not a lustful purple flower springing through the blood of the mangled Adonis, but a crown of flowering, prickly weeds. Not a Jehovan Goddess-killing tyrant, but an infantile, frail, brain-washed idiot savant, the child of his daughter, the transfigured Lear.

This new Lear is a new type in Shakespeare. The upheavals of the fight against the Boar were also this creature's struggles to be born. As if the Boar's destruction of the old Lear, from the outside, and its attempts to climb into him, energized this new creature who was destroying Lear from the inside in its attempts to climb out – flinging off the old karmic royal rags, fighting to come 'into the desolation of reality', under the 'extremity of the skies', as a 'poor, bare, forked animal'.

As the Equation makes clear, the Boar, which is in some way his birth labour, and which is also the Storm of the disintegration of the old ego, is also, as always, the Queen of Hell. In his battling crawl towards his rebirth, Lear seems to be fighting his way into the teeth of the hurricane of her diabolical terrors – as if in some hope of reaching the very source of the Great Witch: the source of the Goddess!

Throughout his disintegration, Cordelia has been on her way towards him. If Lear's battle with the Boar is also an active journey, towards new birth, it can be measured in terms of Cordelia's approach towards him. Just as his battle began, at the end of Act Two, with the first roll of thunder and his 'O fool, I shall go mad!' so Act Three opens with the news that Cordelia is on her way. Thereafter, Cordelia's march to find Lear, with her invading French army, and the resulting war, is another aspect of the Storm, and corresponds to Lear's passive, battling progress towards her.

A curious thing about this raging emergence of Lear's new self, as it inches towards the light, is its as-if-crucified passivity. This double identity of all-suffering helplessness with inevitable progress suggests that the new Lear, the lightning-scalded 'worm', pounded under the downpour, is undergoing a replay of actual birth. Torn from his reign in the womb, battered in the pelvic maelstrom, sustained only by the unconscious patience of survival and the natural process which has behind it – somewhere far off – a divine woman.

Lear is aware that the storm is also the Queen of Hell, but the audience is aware that he himself is being transformed by it, and reborn out if it. His tirades follow an order, the rearguard actions of a controlled retreat towards a last-ditch surrender. In the first, he rebukes the storm for uniting with his daughters against him. In the second, he calls on the storm to expose those sinners who have hidden their crime – exactly as he himself has concealed, even from himself, the greatest crime against his own soul and against Divine Love: the rejection of Cordelia. His third is a spasmodic execration against filial ingratitude – a brief relapse towards becoming a Tarquin, but he instantly sees the futility there, and recovers himself. Finally, he addresses what he calls a prayer to the creatures that his arrogant pomp and pride ignored: the 'poor naked wretches' – clearly the images of himself, the most helpless, fugitive outcast in his own kingdom.

At this moment, the new self appears, running out of the hovel, as Mad Tom. The new self, in other words, is the old deposed 'rational ego', emerging from the wilderness, transfigured, enlightened by exposure to the elemental universe. All the subsequent dialogue between Edgar and Lear confirms that Edgar and Lear are two variants of this new function in the Equation, which is also the clue to the relationship between the saintly imbecile, who is the new Lear, and the despairing, blinded Gloucester, groping towards his Job-like humility; crushed under his 'huge afflictions'. Edgar is the spiritual son of the King on the transcendental plane as he is the physical son of Gloucester on the tragic and natural plane.

But before Lear can be actually reborn, he has to fight the last battle with the Boar, and go through the darkest hour which precedes the brightest. This last battle opens when he cries: 'I pardon that man's life!' (At last, he forgives himself.) The substance of the combat is in the speech which follows. In several ways it is the moment of birth. Gloucester's eyes, on the physical plane, are torn out – as he passes from delusion into reality. Lear's eyes, on the mythic plane, are newly opened, as he passes from delusion into reality.

And at this point Lear sees Shakespeare's ultimate vision of female sexuality, the cosmic source of creation, as a Queen of Hell:

> Down from the waist they are Centaurs,
> Though women all above:
> But to the girdle do the gods inherit,
> Beneath is all the fiends':
> There's hell, there's darkness, there is the sulphurous pit,
> Burning, scalding, stench, consumption; fie! fie! fie! pah! pah! etc.
>
> IV. vi. 127–33

This speech is the mythic climax of the drama, and in a sense the climax of Shakespeare's tragic vision.* It has a significance in the evolution of the Tragic Equation like that of rebirth in the life of a saint.

Lear goes through the speech, as I say, like one actually being born, with a confused terror of the incarceration into flesh (in the grip of the weaver at the womb door), and broken glimpses of the female genitalia as the topography of Hell. But then, immediately after this darkest moment, and after some snatches of 'we came crying hither' and 'the first time that we smell the air/We waul and cry', and 'When we are born we cry that we are come/To this great stage of fools', he emerges, as on the opposite side of a Black Hole, into a new universe, punished,

---

*The Sumerian Goddess Nintu, who was a form of Ma, formerly Tiamat, was described in a fragment of a poem:

From her head to her navel
She has the body of a naked woman.

From her navel to the sole of her foot
Her skin is the scales of a snake.

She was horned, and suckled a baby at her left breast, like a Mermadonna.

corrected, enlightened and transfigured, as a grey-haired babe, and the Goddess embraces him, correspondingly transformed, and wakens him with a kiss, as Cordelia. It is the same tableau that Shakespeare placed at the end of *Venus and Adonis*, but in this case Adonis is not only a flower, and is alive.

This is the new kind of rebirth. Adonis became Tarquin – now Tarquin becomes a saint. The crucial new factor is that when Lear/Adonis became Tarquin he failed to kill the Lucrece figure. Because Cordelia survived, she was able to forgive and redeem him – to lift him, that is, from the tragic plane of his error and its punishment, to the transcendental plane of his redemption. But this new mutation of the old Equation, promising to both Lear and Cordelia a new and happy life, is still not strong enough to decide the outcome. The old law of the Tragic Equation takes its course, swallows the new possibility, and digests it into the old pattern, where the death of the Female entails the death of the hero.

As a major innovation it flowered astonishingly here, then remained recessive for the next two plays, before emerging again in *Antony and Cleopatra* and becoming dominant, thereafter, throughout the last four plays.

If, for a moment, one imagines the drama of Edmund and Edgar as a projection of the usurpation of the King's rational ego by the irrational Lear, then the prize for the winner, the prize over which the two brothers fight, could be assumed to be Lear's soul – which would be Cordelia.

As it happens, that is the story of the original Welsh myth of the sea god, Llyr, and his daughter, Creiddylad, from which the quasi-historical legend of King Lear descends. A closer look at that myth opens a curious perspective into Shakespeare's play.

King Lear as a reactivation of its mythic sources

One of the masterstrokes of Shakespeare's mythic intuition was what he did with the two brothers in *King Lear*. And it points directly towards the greatest mythic intuition of all.

In his most immediate source – the anonymous verse play *King Leir* that was performed in the early 1590s and published in 1605 (Shakespeare's play was first staged the day after Christmas Day, 1606), the two brothers are absent. In his two best-known historical sources –

Geoffrey of Monmouth's *History* and Holinshed's *Chronicles* — the sons of Goneril and Regan, called Margan and Cunedag, appear in a sequel to the main story. After the deaths of her father and two sisters, Cordeilla (as she is named in both accounts) reigns as Queen of Britain. Several years pass before her two nephews combine and remove her in a coup, throwing her into prison where she kills herself. Cunedag then slays Margan in a battle for possession of the kingdom. Among other versions probably known to Shakespeare, none makes more than this of the two rival kinsmen, if they are noticed at all. Many folktales, in many variants, some of which would certainly be known to Shakespeare, tell of a king who banishes his youngest, dearest and most loving daughter for some trifling fault and is then eventually rescued from destitution by her. But these tales say nothing of the two brothers.

His obvious source for the story of Edmund, Edgar and their father Gloucester is the story of the Paphlagonian King and his two sons, narrated in Sidney's *Arcadia*. Once Shakespeare had chosen the family history of Lear as the theme of a play, he could hardly fail to connect that shocking anecdote with it. Not only are the two situations strikingly similar, but just as the first is a clear example of the opening of the Tragic Equation, the second is a classic case of the Rival Brothers. His own imagination, enlightened by his earlier works, showed him exactly how to combine them, without any nudging from Margan and Cunedag. In the process, this imagination revealed the quality of its mythic intuition.

It is generally assumed that Shakespeare cannot have known of the most immediate *mythic* source of King Lear's story, which is the Welsh myth of the sea god Llyr and his daughter Creiddylad, mentioned briefly in *The Mabinogion*. Two brothers, the white one (Gwyn) and the black one (Gwythur), fought annually for Creiddylad (on May day, the day on which the rivals challenge each other for possession of Emilia, in *Two Noble Kinsmen* (cf. page 507)). As a form of the Goddess, Creiddylad must have had two other aspects. These are not named or mentioned in *The Mabinogion*'s cursory account, but after the myth had filtered down through cultural upheavals to find a place, eventually, as a historicized legend, in the demythologized history of British kings, Creiddylad's lost aspects emerged as Goneril and Regan, while Gwyn and Gwythur, the two supernatural brothers, had become the worldly cousins, Margan and Cunedag, tagging along, displaced and disconnected, as belated contenders for the royal succession. Whatever

prompted him to do so, Shakespeare ignored these historical suggestions and put the two brothers tightly back into the mythic pattern,
virtually restoring the Lear story to the archaic wholeness of the myth.
Mythic intuition could explain that, but it could be, too, that he had
simply heard the myth of the sea god Llyr, in its original form, long ago,
from his Welsh schoolmaster, Thomas Jenkins, who had taught him
between the ages of twelve and fifteen. The traditional Celtic institution
of the poetic schools, where the corpus of myth (a giant body of
material) was part of the required learning, was still alive, and Jenkins
would without any doubt have been familiar with some of it, possibly
with a good deal of it – as many a Welsh schoolmaster even today is
familar with a good deal of it. If Jenkins did know the myth, he could
hardly have failed to impart it to the sort of pupil that Shakespeare must
have been.* And the formative, nurturing presence of another Welsh
myth, from the same provenance, in the situation, plot and characters of
The Tempest, a myth which is closely related to the Llyr myth, and
partly duplicates the Cordelia figure (cf. page 458) suggests that he had
early access of some kind to those riches.

However he found that first key of Lear's myth, the truly mysterious
thing is what happened next, as a whole series of larger and deeper
programmes came up on the screen. The Lyr myth had led a vigorous
life in Ireland. One strong ray of light from this source illuminates the
Welsh Llyr and through him the British King Lear. Another strong ray
illuminates the myth's direct ancestry in Greece and Egypt. Both ways, it
lights up Shakespeare's play.

Taking the first of these first. One of Lear's precursors in Ireland was
Nuada, King of the Tuatha de Danaan, who lost his hand in the first
great battle with the Fomorians (a race of demonic giants). Since the
High King had to be physically perfect, Nuada now seceded his rule to
Bres, who was half Fomor and who proceeded to devastate the
kingdom. The watermark mythic pattern, where the irrational (half-
demon) brother displaces the rational brother, is already visible here, as
it is also in the subsequent episode where Nuada's mutilation is repaired
(for his return to the cyclic combat) when he is given a silver hand. In the
various parallel Irish mythic stories, this Rival Brothers form of the
myth is replaced by something more like the Tragic Equation: the King
is usually Lyr, and the episode of the loss of the hand (and loss of rule) is

*Jenkins's known rigorously English training
as a schoolmaster need not have rooted
out an inherited familiarity with Welsh
curiosities.

replaced by his banishing his beloved daughter (rejection of the Female) in the form of a sea bird, whereupon, true to the mythic pattern, the kingdom is devastated. Nuada became, in Wales, Llud Llawereint, who was also Llyr, father of Creiddylad. But when this sea god Llyr (*Lear*, in Irish, means 'sea') emerged in the succession of British kings as King Lear, he brought with him a father – King Bladud.

In Geoffrey of Monmouth's *History* Bladud's story immediately precedes Lear's, and contains enough to have intrigued Shakespeare. What Shakespeare would have picked up from popular tradition (especially considering his interest in the city of Bath, the home of the Lord Chamberlain, patron of the acting company to which he belonged) would intrigue him more. King Bladud and King Lear are like the two separated halves of the Welsh sea god. Or rather Bladud's story descends from the Nuada lineage of the myth, while Lear's descends from the lineage of Lyr whose daughter was banished out on to the ocean as a sea bird. But while King Lear has been stripped of the sea god's mythic attributes, retaining only his royalty and his strange relationship to his strange daughter, within a despiritualized field of purely political action, King Bladud retains his magical personality, a fascinatingly developed form of 'the silver hand', and operates within a field of almost wholly mythic action. The 'folk' understanding that Bladud and Lear are somehow the same man and yet different men is expressed in Geoffrey's *History* by that relationship of father and son.

In other words, the great magician King Bladud is the suppressed dream self of King Lear. He is Lear's displaced 'magical', supernatural, mythic double – his potentially 'divine' self. Shakespeare's imagination, fascinated by magicians (Prince Hamlet was formerly a powerful, feared magician, as well as Prospero), absorbed this, and mythic intuition knew where it belonged. His Great Work, after all, was to put the secularized ego back into a right relationship with that other, potentially divine self. And in one sense, the 'agonies' of the tragic drama of King Lear are Shakespeare's account of the old egomanic Lear's case-hardened resistance against the enforced reassimilation of his own lost myth, that lost spiritual self incarnated in Bladud. Bladud's eerily lit story moves mysteriously through the nightmare of Lear's unwilling transformation. Briefly, that story runs as follows.

After an encounter with the Underworld (with 'demons'), King Bladud was infected with leprosy. (The leprosy corresponds to Nuada's lost hand, that would be replaced by a silver one, and to Lyr's banishing his beloved daughter out on to the Atlantic as a sea bird.) Compelled by this physical imperfection (like Nuada) to abdicate, Bladud became a swineherd, shunned by men. His pigs then caught his disease (contagion of an earlier myth, in which the pigs would belong to the lunar goddess of the Underworld, or simply to the Underworld), and together the leprous King and his leprous herd of pigs wandered through the pre-Roman wilderness of Middle Britain. Eventually, the pigs found (led him to) a hot swamp in the forest and, wallowing in it, were healed. Bladud did likewise and was healed. He resumed his throne, and at the site of the spring he founded a shrine to Sulis (or Nemetona), the goddess of the healing waters, and around it built the city of Bath. (As an enlightened type, he is said to have visited Greece, and now dedicated his new city to Apollo – the god by whom Shakespeare's King Lear swears. Bladud died, 'shivered like an egg', when he made himself wings and tried to fly from the top of Apollo's temple.) If Shakespeare himself had ever sought the help of these springs (as in Sonnets 153 and 154), it can be imagined how this traumatic jumble of a myth, the despair of the outcast, lamenting, stricken king roaming with his leprous pigs through a Britain that was also an underworld, his horror of the disease that made him untouchable given faces and names in Goneril and Regan, his prayers to the Goddess in the fountain of healing waters (where Bertram too – whose ailing, other self was the French Crown – was reborn) must have seethed around the painful fable of King Lear and Cordelia.

Of the Irish Lyr's ancestry in Greece and Egypt, the Egyptian is the best known and most fully developed, and it is here that the full story behind the Welsh Llyr and Creiddylad and the British King Lear and Cordelia becomes clear, as well as its close family link to the myth of the Goddess and her sacrificed god, and in particular to the myth of Adonis. This is relevant to the poetic and dramatic life of Shakespeare's King Lear in that he was not only aware of this rich Egyptian matrix, from which his Tragic Equation and Rival Brothers emerge so strongly, but seems to have found it especially fascinating. Before this, it had lifted into the structure and themes of *Hamlet*, as will become evident in retrospect, and after this, in *Antony and Cleopatra*, it will give him the apparatus for his most complete and luminous analysis of the limiting, distorting nature of the Reformation world of the Tragic Equation. (Since that play's vision of the Goddess of Complete Being and her divine consort springs directly from King Lear's brief moment of transcendence, it should not be surprising to find patterns of the same pre-Christian mythology behind both dramas.)

Plutarch and others could have told him the basic story of the civil war between the two brothers, Osiris and Set (or Typhon), and about the nature of Isis. From the same sources, he would know about Horus, the son of Osiris and Isis, who attempts to avenge his father and who eventually, but only after a terrible battle with his uncle over one of his own eyes, does triumph. But in King Lear, Shakespeare elaborates these hints into a grand pattern that seems to resuscitate a full context – almost as if he knew what has become generally known only since his day. Perhaps his unusual saturation with this material owes something to Giordano Bruno's obsessive preoccupation with Egyptian religion.

Exactly as in *King Lear*, where the Equation appears as the Tragic Equation in the relationship between Lear and Cordelia, and as the Rival Brothers in the struggle between Edgar and Edmund, so the Egyptian myth appears as two parallel stories, one of them a classic case of the Rival Brothers, the other of the Tragic Equation, the one concerning that struggle between the brothers Osiris and Set, which devolves into a cyclic struggle between Horus and Set, and the other concerning the sun god, Re, and his daughter, the Eye.

The first of these stories, about Re and the Eye, was archaic and lay behind Egyptian mythology through all its three or four thousand years of multitudinous transformations. The second evolved fairly late, and finally, assimilating all that it could of what had gone before, became the official religion in Ptolemaic times, centred in Alexandria. In this form, mainly under the figure of Isis, who was recognized everywhere as Demeter/Aphrodite/Ishtar, it became one of the most popular international cults throughout the Graeco-Roman world, until Christianity absorbed or suppressed it around the fourth century.

In the chaotically fluid iconography of late Egyptian religion certain constants remain clear if bizarre. Not the least peculiar aspect of Shakespeare's anamnesis of this grand cosmic drama is that his structure, in *King Lear*, makes use of the same symbolic constants.

A brief outline of the two complementary myths should give some idea of the more striking correspondences. The main events of the first, older myth, are:

The Eye is separated from the sun god, her father. She goes into the desert, where she becomes a raging lioness, devastating the kingdoms, uncontrollable in her fury.

In this phase, she is also the cobra.

Eventually, Thoth, the Ibis god of letters, finds her and brings her back.

In one of the greatest festivals of the Egyptian year, she is restored to her father, who thereby is able to resume his Wisdom, his Crown and his Happiness.

Behind this myth lies what has been called the fundamental equation of Ancient Egyptian religion:

The Great Goddess = the Eye = the Goddess of Destruction = the Cobra = the Crown.

This could almost as easily be called the fundamental equation of Shakespeare's myth where the Great Goddess has two natures: in her benign aspect she is the Crown of Divine Order and the Soul of Wisdom (and the daughter or Sacred Bride as in Cordelia); in her other aspect, banished (or lost), she appears to be a raging lioness, or cobra, brings in suffering and destruction and the dementia of the hero, and the loss of the kingdom (as in Goneril and Regan).

The second myth, greatly simplified, runs as follows: Osiris, the god of vegetation and all arts, was murdered by his evil brother, Set (the beast from the swamp, 'the black pig'). Set launched his brother's corpse down the Nile in a coffin. In the version known to Shakespeare, the coffin ended up incorporated in the trunk of a tree at Byblus, the Mediterranean cult centre of Astarte and Thammuz. The tree trunk, in turn, became a pillar in a palace. Isis found and hid the body but Set discovered it. He tore it into fourteen pieces which he scattered through the land. Isis retrieved all the pieces except the genitals, and reassembled Osiris, replacing the missing part with a wooden substitute that became her cult object. By this body she conceived a Divine Child, Horus, who is Osiris resurrected. While Osiris remains as the god of the dead (King Hamlet), Horus as his living representative (Prince Hamlet) relives the cycle of his death and resurrection in the perpetually repeated battle with his uncle Set (Claudius).

The divine life of Osiris resides in the Eye of Horus. Set tears this Eye from his head, and hurls it beyond the world's edge. Darkness and confusion descend. The Eye is returned to Horus by Thoth, the Ibis god of letters.

In this cyclic battle between Set and Horus, Horus becomes the perpetually sacrificed and reborn god. But the battle recapitulates, in more individualized dramatic form, the sun god Re's loss of the Eye, which is his daughter. Since Osiris is a form of the sun god Re, Horus is also the son of Re, and the brother of the Eye. The falcon Horus, and the Eye, therefore, are aspects of each other.

The two myths correspond, clearly, as in Shakespeare the Tragic Equation and the theme of the Rival Brothers correspond. The god-king's loss of his daughter (the Eye) introduces the time of chaos and suffering. Set's conquest of Horus, tearing out his Eye, and throwing it away, introduces the time of chaos and suffering.

And, exactly as in the Egyptian myth, so in *King Lear*, a lost daughter (Cordelia) and the 'blinded' brother (Edgar) are aspects of each other.

A point which becomes intensely significant later, as far as Shakespeare's occult eavesdropping on all this is concerned, is that in both myths the lost Eye is found, and brought back, amid rejoicing, by Thoth, the Ibis god of letters.

The Ibis is a kind of crane. The Greek variant, which I mentioned earlier, tells of Apollo and his crane priestess who was a representative of the Goddess. Besides being a sun god, like Re, Apollo was also the god of poetry and learning. The mythic origin of his letters was the shapes made by cranes in flight.

That loose Egyptian ritual link, between the Great Goddess and the god of letters who brings her back from savagery to civilization, has in the Greek myth become a single, fused identity. The crane priestess of Apollo is the Goddess in her aspect of goddess of poetry and learning.

So far, then, the daughter of the sun god's daughter, who is the Eye, Wisdom and the Crown of Order, has crossed the sea and become the goddess of poetry and learning – a goddess who is also an Ibis, a Crane.

The genetic fragments recombined with variations in Ireland (the Isis cult took them all over the known world at that time) but the main features persisted as: the daughter of a god-king, for some reason (conflict with rivals, displeasing her father in a love match), is banished to sea as a sea bird – usually as a crane. In her absence, the kingdom is devastated. (Here and there, particular suggestions of the King Lear story peep through.) Eventually, in one potent variant, she falls into the hands of the sea god. When she dies, he skins her, making a medicine bag of her skin, in which he keeps the magic of poetry – the letters of the alphabet as a collection of hieroglyph-like emblems. This is the famous Craneskin Bag.

Finally, in the Welsh variant, the sea god is Llyr, and the Eye and the Crown of his rule is his daughter, Creiddylad. Horus and Set have become Gwyn and Gwythur, the two brothers battling for alternate possession of Creiddylad. Nothing remained in the record of her illustrious past as the Eye and the vessel of poetry except her name, Creiddylad, Heron of the Sea.

It must remain a mystery, and a curiosity, how Shakespeare, having restored the Llyr story to its mythic form by reinserting the motif of the two 'brothers', then went on to recover so much from the original Egyptian complex. For instance, if Edgar is Horus, then he should be both the reborn form of Lear (Osiris/Re) and the male aspect of Cordelia – which is how Shakespeare seems to think of him and is certainly the function he has in the play. In the same way, if Cordelia's banishment over the seas corresponds to the phase in which the Eye of Re rages in the desert, while the kingdom falls into disorder, then Lear should find his realm overturned by a raging lioness or a cobra, which is exactly what happens: Goneril and Regan are the two-headed demoness of Cordelia's absence, the Goddess in her phase of destruction. Again, where Set's act of tearing out the Eye of Horus corresponds to Lear's irrational self usurping his rational self (and casting away Cordelia) this should manifest on the mythic level as the attack of the Boar (Set's attack on the Eye of Horus was ritually described in Ancient Egypt as an attack 'by the black pig'), and on the real level as the destruction of the kingdom. Where the same act corresponds to Edmund's wresting of the dukedom from his father and Edgar, it should manifest on the mythic level (Edgar's level) as a period of 'deprivation' and darkness, and on the realistic level (Gloucester's level) as physical blinding – which is exactly how it works out. But the mystery Shakespeare goes on to draw from Cordelia, in particular, is even stranger.

Lear, the Fool, Mad Tom and Cordelia

The Equation supplies a clear pattern for the relationship between Cordelia, Lear, the Fool and Mad Tom. Banishing Cordelia, Lear has banished his soul, and is sleepwalking in the soulless, 'mad' kingdom of his Tarquinian pride, ruled by Goneril and Regan. (He has thrown away the Eye – in the terms of the Egyptian myth – which was the divine sanction of his own kingliness, as well as Wisdom, Truth, Peace.)

The moment he becomes vaguely aware of what has happened, at Goneril's first hint of her true nature, the Fool flies in like a familiar. He arrives from the world that Lear has banished – 'the region of his heart'. He is the victim of Lear's crime against himself, the voice of the banished Cordelia (coeur de Lear).*

The shell of Lear's Tarquinian 'pride' in his error, already fractured by Goneril's 'boarish fangs', is now stripped away gradually by the Fool's jests and the lightning.

*An Elizabethan form of Cordelia as a Christian name was Cordell. The Occult Neoplatonist with even minimal knowledge of the Hebrew terms used in Christian Cabbala (and Hebrew was the third language, after Greek and Latin, in an English classical education) would be familiar with El as the name for God. Shakespearean etymology would instantly reduce the 'cord' of the word to mean 'heart' as in the Latin 'cordis', and as in *The Winter's Tale*:

> I have *tremor cordis* on me: my heart
> dances;
> But not for joy; not joy . . .
>   I. ii. 110–11

Though already, two or three years earlier, in *King Lear* Shakespeare had identified 'distress of the heart' with 'mother' (which also had the general meaning of 'hysteria' and 'desperate turmoil') and specifically with the absent Cordelia and his guilt, as in:

> O! how this mother swells up toward my
> heart;
> *Hysterica passio*! down, thou climbing
> sorrow!
> Thy element's below . . .
>   *King Lear*, II. iv. 56–8

To this he would add 'El' meaning God, making a sort of Latin-Hebraic compound meaning 'the heart of God', on the pattern of Ari-el meaning 'Light of God' or 'Lion of God' (which Shakespeare also seems to be clearly aware of, cf. page 478). The 'Cordel' part of Cordelia makes her the heart of God, while her full name Cordelia makes her simultaneously the heart of Lear: she is the intermediary (the soul, in fact) between Lear and God, and as far as Lear is concerned she is therefore the face of God (or the Goddess). This relationship between tragic hero and the Lucrece figure holds good in all the plays of the tragic sequence. Shakespeare makes it literally clear in *Measure for Measure*. As Lear rejects Cordelia for the truth of her love (which he misunderstands), Angelo rejects Isabella's plea on behalf of love (which he regards as a crime punishable by death). Both King Lear in his rage against Cordelia and Angelo in his rejection of Isabella's plea are 'deputies' (Angelo is appointed, by the Duke, literally as a deputy; that is, they are Puritan Jehovan Christs temporarily standing in for the true God. The true God, when he returns, will turn out to be the Duke who marries Isabella – as the loving consort of the Goddess, and the reborn Lear who is united in bliss with Cordelia.

Another link confirms this even more distinctly. I mentioned earlier, describing *As You Like It* as a ritual work quite consciously and purposefully related to the

As I said earlier, the lightnings are the heavenly fires and suffering of the rejected Divine Love, alias the rage of the Boar. In the new circumstances, they are also the struggling of Lear's new self to be born, alias the labour pangs of the old Lear in the parturition of the new, alias the approach of Cordelia. In this way, everything comprehended in the storm, but especially the return of Cordelia and the agonizing emergence of the new Lear, are inseparable from the Fool, who is, as it were, their implement. He is the midwife, their agent. When he has coaxed forth the 'poor, bare, forked animal' that crawls out like a worm – and identifies itself with the sudden appearance of Mad Tom, who will be the new hero – his work is completed. Lear is now effectively reborn.

Mad Tom is the new Lear, corresponding to Lear's rebirth in the arms of Cordelia, and in this sense is the masculine form of the returned Cordelia.

Once this has happened the Fool's work as Lear's fool, as I say, is completed. Since he existed only in that space of separation between Lear and Cordelia, or between Lear and his banished soul, now the two are reunited, in this meeting with Mad Tom, the Fool does not hang around like a 'real' person in an ordinary play, who still has to be accommodated somehow. He simply evaporates. That is to say, the Fool disappears equally into the new Lear, Mad Tom and Cordelia, in so far as the three are aspects of each other.

———

opening of the *Inferno* (pages 115–6), Shakespeare's awareness of Dante. Here it emerges again, where the symbolic equivalence of Beatrice in Dante's system to the Lucrece figure, epitomized in Cordelia, in Shakespeare's system, is made quite clear. Coeur de Lear (or Cor di Lear) is like Cor di Dante in Dante's famous vision, which he records in *La Vita Nuova*:

'I fell asleep and a marvellous vision appeared to me. In my room I seemed to see a cloud the colour of fire, and in the cloud a lordly figure, frightening to behold, yet in himself, it seemed to me, he was filled with a marvellous joy. He said many things, of which I understood only a few; among them were the words: *Ego dominus tuus* [I am your master]. In his arms I seemed to see a naked figure, sleeping, wrapped lightly in a crimson cloth. Gazing intently, I saw it was she who had bestowed her greeting on me earlier that day [Beatrice]. In one hand the

standing figure held a fiery object, and he seemed to say, *Vide cor tuum* [Behold your heart]. After a little while I thought he wakened her who slept and prevailed on her to eat the glowing object in his hand. Reluctantly and hesitantly she did so. A few moments later his happiness turned to bitter grief, and, weeping, he gathered the figure in his arms and together they seemed to ascend into the heavens. I felt such anguish at their departure that my light sleep was broken, and I awoke . . .'

Dante, *La Vita Nuova*, III

This dream can be read in various ways (and possibly as a record of the moment in which Dante transferred his childhood memory of the death of his mother to the figure of Beatrice, foreseeing her own death as he did so) but all are subsumed into what he went on to make of this woman who had devoured his heart, and had become his heart, in *La Divina Commedia*.

Lear's actual reunion with Cordelia is delayed until Gloucester's condition is synchronized with his. In the ritual pattern of correspondences, Gloucester's experience on the mundane level reflects what is happening to Lear on the transcendental level – serving the function, almost, of the chorus in an Athenian tragedy. At this point in the play, the control of these ritual parallels is transparent. The reason that Edgar does not do the sensible thing and tell his blind father who he is at the outset, instead of acting the yokel, leading him to an imaginary cliff and letting him jump over, is that he is performing for his father the service that the Fool performed for Lear and is, so to speak, the Fool on the Gloucester plane of action. Once Gloucester has broken through (by his virtual 'shivered like an egg' death in the imaginary fall) to the all-acceptance that corresponds to Lear's rebirth, the yokel, like the Fool, evaporates. From this point, Edgar ceases to talk madly to Lear, or clownishly to his father, and is only himself.

This 'Equation's eye view' of these complications explains so much, of course, that it becomes suspect. Still, it is interesting to see how far it will go without losing its own consistency. And it is a characteristic of Hermetic drama, where everything serves the ritual, that each tiniest detail of text has a place in the metaphysical design – nothing is accidental.

A Hermetic dramatist would have no difficulty, for instance, in explaining why the Fool's last words, 'I'll go to bed at noon', should be spoken where they are, late at night, in response to Lear's 'We'll go to supper i' the morning'. There are many fewer words in this Act Three than there are notes in a movement of a Beethoven symphony, and there is no reason to suppose that any of them were originally less artfully placed in the total pattern. Both Lear and the Fool will go to bed right now, which is actually midnight (or very near it) and the mid-point of the play (or very near it). But Lear will go to 'supper' (a sacrament at the end of his old life) 'i' the morning' (to solemnize the beginning of his new life). The Fool, however, whose crazy, renovating spirit is now passing into Mad Tom, who will be the new Edgar (Lear's spiritual 'son'), knows that this actual midnight and mid-point of the play, this absolute nadir of the sufferer's journey, the darkest, bottommost *imo caelus*, opposite the sun's zenith, is also the hour of Lear's rebirth, the moment of his highest, spiritual illumination, which is therefore paradoxically 'noon' – where the Fool's role will evaporate in the great light of Lear and Cordelia's reunion. Therefore the Fool goes to bed 'at noon'.

The silence of Cordelia

Cordelia's 'Nothing' is a reply to Lear's 'What can you say about your love for me, using the language of your sisters?' Refusing to play this game according to the rules set by her sisters, Cordelia tries to establish new rules, her own rules. But her attempt to be honest about her love falls foul of the inadequacy of her words. She comes to a halt, tangled in pedantic distinctions, that express nothing but a quibbling will to forestall all misunderstanding – while Lear explodes.

Refusing to use the 'glib and oily' language of false flattery, her love finds itself without any language at all that would truly express it.

According to her archaic myth, Cordelia is the vessel containing the magical alphabet of poetry. As if she were the living pyx of Shakespeare's poetic word. Yet she turns out to be wordless.

The whole titanic drama turns on this 'Nothing' and the bizarre fact that Cordelia's true love cannot find words to declare itself. And it is whirled on this axis by the fact that the treacherous, loveless ones possess an inexhaustible wealth of plausible language.

This speechlessness was a recurrent theme in the *Sonnets*. There, when Shakespeare in his own person was trying to communicate – and to prove – his own love, he found no satisfactory way to do it. It remained a stubborn problem, that time and again reduced his argument to a tautological near dumbness. But he experienced this difficulty as something more than a philosophical impasse. His sense of it, his sense of the truth as something ineffable, as a word locked up (the 'word within a word, unable to speak a word' – maybe he went out of his way to listen to Lancelot Andrewes), is like a mystical apprehension. The *Sonnets* revolve around it as around a plain, self-evident enigma.

The particular kinds of truth that seem to give him this problem are the truth of love, and the truth which is the essence of beauty. This truth of beauty is not far off, maybe, from his notion of the truth of reality.

The solution that he reaches towards, instinctively, is the artist's solution: a blunt invocation of the thing itself.

Who is it that says most? which can say more
Than this rich praise – that you alone are you?

Sonnet 84, 1–2

It is also the dramatist's solution. Nothing can pretend to express the truth, he is saying, but the whole existential presence of the person, the man or woman, in all their living complexity. As if human beings, and their actions, were the only valid lexicon. As if anything short of that were 'words, mere words'.

At its most genial, this apprehension roots him in a pragmatic stolidity, in those 'true, plain words by thy true-telling friend'. It is more than a disinclination to speak for effect.

My mistress' eyes are nothing like the sun;
Coral is far more red than her lips' red:
If snow be white, why then, her breasts are dun;
If hairs be wires, black wires grow on her head.

Sonnet 130, 1–4

That is a joke, but it exploits his natural unease with anything but the thing as it is in life. And, as I say, at its most severe this apprehension locks him up altogether, as it does Cordelia.

Drama gave him the language of this silence. The words of immobilized actors convince nobody, except of the pathos of words without action, the pathos of fantasy. To convince the observer, truth needs actions. All the possible meanings of a developing action can be contemplated, and any verbal accompaniment can be interpreted, but the truth will only appear when the action is in some way completed. Then it becomes clear that the words played their usual role – the role played by deceptive or protective coloration, form and behaviour in the dumb kingdom of flora and fauna. Shakespeare's sensitivity to this dissembling function of language was proportionate to the awe that he felt for the ineffability of the truth.

Considering Shakespeare as a moralist who would

through and through
Cleanse the foul body of the infected world,

As You Like It, II. vii. 59–60

one can see that his starting point had to be some revelation of the truth, of the purity of the truth. The voluble evils that serve any denial of the truth (of Divine Love) are to be measured, and revealed, only against the radiant dumbness of the truth. Conversely, the silent truth (of Divine Love) cannot be dramatized and demonstrated at all, except as a creature suffering in a world where the egomanic voices of the tragic error reject it, violate it, exploit it. Again, this is a Manichean vision, but one can see how in Shakespeare's case it is made manifest within a revelation of the truth which is not ideological but first-hand and mystical, and establishes the poles of a supercharged dramatic vision, which evolves within the larger vision of Divine Complete Being.

As the tragedy of the Divine poetic word and the dramatic parable of the poetic word's role and fate in the world, *King Lear* has a special place in Shakespeare's oeuvre.

Since ordinary words, in this vision, are inherently false, and relieved of any responsibility for Divine Truth, they are given a Saturnalian freedom. The tragic hero demands the Divine Truth – and receives only the mockery of words. At the moment in which Cressida's treachery is proved, and the poetic persona of the *Sonnets* becomes the protagonist of the tragedies, Troilus's cry 'Words, words, mere words, no matter from the heart' (v. iii. 109) emerges from that very axis of Shakespeare's universe.

But these words can encompass the truth in their fashion, on the right tongue. Their inability to declare the truth directly gives them licence to sing about it obliquely, and to glance towards it crookedly, as the hidden meaning, the irony, in the joke. The ultimate personification of this appears again in *King Lear*, as the Fool. His paradoxes and riddles are the only communication possible for Cordelia's (the heart's) banished, speechless truth – until Cordelia herself appears in person.

When the tragedies are read as rituals of the Mythic Equation, each of the Lucrece figures reveals a Cordelia: afflicted, abused, misunderstood, but inviolate. She is the silence at the source of their simplicity. And each of them embodies Shakespeare's worship – I don't think the word is too strong, in the circumstances – of simplicity. Not 'simplicity', as in 'simple truth miscalled simplicity', but the simplicity closest to the dumb speech of action, the simplicity that Shakespeare always presents as the natural path towards the heart's truth, that 'matter from the heart' which will finally reject words. Simplicity as the breath of the locked-up word of Divine Truth. This consecration of simplicity establishes his point of view. It provides the absolute zero, perhaps, for his calibration of all the degrees of devilish dissimulation and tragic self-deception, all those demon-infested registers of garrulity. And maybe it stands behind his godlike judgement of the whole ensemble:

> I am as true as truth's simplicity,
> And simpler than the infancy of truth.
> *Troilus and Cressida*, III. ii. 176–7

CHAPTER 4

THE TRAGIC EQUATION MAKES ITS SOUL:
Timon of Athens, Coriolanus, Antony and Cleopatra

———

Subterranean transition

Timon of Athens: the Tragic Equation without the Female

Coriolanus: the Female survives the Tragic Equation

The tragic hero as the Rival Brother

Antony and Cleopatra as a bridging work

Antony and Cleopatra: the new factors

Antony and Cleopatra as a tragedy

Antony and Cleopatra as a theophany

Subterranean transition

The second group of tragedies contains *Timon of Athens, Coriolanus* and *Antony and Cleopatra*.

According to the Equation, *Timon* and *Coriolanus* are the dramas of a period of transition. They mask the gestation of the Equation's new development – the Gnostic redemption of hero and heroine together, which was so violently conceived in *Macbeth*, so violently and prematurely born to brief life in *King Lear*, and which will emerge again to take the remaining plays of the sequence in its own direction, quite self-consciously, with *Cymbeline*.

Between *Coriolanus* and *Cymbeline* stands *Antony and Cleopatra*. As I shall argue, this play is the natural, perfect full culmination of the evolution of the tragedies proper, in the sense that it dramatizes the spiritual solution of the Tragic Equation in what might be called an organic way, within the terms of the real, tragic world – without Shakespeare lifting the story on to any other symbolic plane of action. With *Cymbeline* the Tragic Equation evolves a whole new tail section – a coda – in which the Tragic Equation finds a spiritual solution on the transcendental plane.

Meanwhile, *Timon* and *Coriolanus* prepare the ground for *Antony and Cleopatra*.

Timon of Athens: the Tragic Equation without the Female

Timon of Athens seems to be such an evident failure as a stage play that most critics have supposed it to be unfinished – an abandoned, half-modelled torso. At the same time, it is a good candidate for Shakespeare's most tremendous poem. What prompted him, at the very height of his powers, to commit himself to a subject that proved so refractory?

Some have supposed a conflict of motives. His wish to write another play, according to the rule* that he had not broken in fifteen years, was

---

*His productivity was no doubt irregular, but if he started in 1588 and stopped in 1612, and if the two long poems are counted in, then he averaged a major work about every seven months for twenty-four years.

somehow requisitioned, they suggest, by his private need to deliver a curse against mankind in general, and against 'the city' in particular. Perhaps the theme touched that traumatic public humiliation of his adolescence – his father's bankruptcy. After three acts of preparation, his Jeremiad bursts the dam, overwhelms all dramatic controls or concerns, and simply floods the audience, for the rest of the play, with execrations so vehement there is nothing like it in the language. If a modern dramatist did anything similar, it would be condemned as an intolerable self-indulgence.

Perhaps the play as it stands gives some clue to Shakespeare's method of composition. If the whole work were as rough as the latter half, one might guess he had planned it freely, but mentally, and then written it out at great heat, encountering all the surprises of inspiration, but also the surprises of the various logics that reveal their inconvenient laws only under trial –

> Sith every action that hath gone before
> Whereof we have record, trial did draw
> Bias and thwart, not answering the aim,
> And that unbodied figure of the thought
> That gave't surmised shape.
>
> *Troilus and Cressida*, I. iii. 13–17

Returning, then, to his glowing draft, he managed to bring the first scenes into order, but soon saw that what had erupted out of them was irredeemable as stage action – and simply dropped the whole manuscript into one of his trunks of foul papers, where Heminge and Condell, editing the 1623 Folio edition, found it.

Having made his choice, and committed himself to the writing, Shakespeare had to deal with the problem: how to find his kind of tragedy in a story that has no Female, in other words in a story that lacks the Equation's essential component: the Goddess incarnated in an actual woman or women?

Timon is the only play of the tragic series not centred on the hero's love relationship to a woman or, as in *Macbeth*, to the Crown which is Lucrece's variant form.

He solved the problem, provisionally, with his usual resource: metaphor. He simply developed what was in effect a new algebraic variant for the Female. Athens itself becomes the surrogate of the Goddess. The populace of Athens. Or rather, in particular, Timon's business friends – where the system of gifts and borrowings is a system of commerce, or barter. The system works in the play as a metaphor for institutionalized brotherly love – a prudent, basically selfish, but necessary and interesting arrangement, on which society depends. Timon's generosity, so 'total and unconditional', bears the same relationship to this judicious, rational system as Christ's love bears to the common or garden social bond. He bestows his loving generosity on the Athenians as Troilus bestows his love on Cressida – or as the idyllic, pre-Puritan god Adonis bestows his love on the Goddess, his Mother and Bride.

One can see the position. And one can see that the bomb of Timon's vulnerability has been set in place, exactly as if he were lavishing his passion on a woman.

Having established his makeshift situation, with Timon as the tragic hero in his larval, innocent phase, Shakespeare gets on with his play, drawing current through that metaphor of Timon's 'total, unconditional love' for the Athenians, as if from the full Tragic Equation. But certain power failures, as one can see straight away, are built in.

A very brief survey of the mismatch between the control of the Equation and the action of the plot will show what I mean:

1. Timon's infinitely generous love to his friends may be psychologically interesting from various angles, but it is dramatically poor in potential. As bombs of vulnerability go, one can foresee that this one will explode with a peculiarly thin, forced and in some ways false note. His need for the social love of these friends is very different from a man's need for the love of the woman who represents the Goddess. That fact already demotes his generous love from the registers of primordial physical and spiritual passion to perhaps that of quirky pathology or neurotic compulsion. Meanwhile the shallow politics of friendship, which his friends play, manipulating his idealism, or whatever else his favour may be based on, is a paltry alternative to the authentic, uncontrollable, wholly natural, unpredictable demands of the Goddess. Where the Goddess, as a character, grips our imagination and stirs our apprehension at the deepest level, these friends merely prompt us to critical impatience with his naivety.

2. Timon's money runs out. When he calls on his friends for credit, they turn against him and none will help him.

According to the Equation, this is the moment of 'double vision': the Queen of Hell reveals herself in the treachery of his friends.

Again, this fails, in dramatic terms, in so far as the revelation of the disloyalty of business associates is a vacuous symbol or substitute for the primal terror of the revelation of the Queen of Hell in the body of the beloved woman. Where Othello projected the Queen of Hell on to Desdemona, and Hamlet projected her on to Ophelia and on to his mother, and Lear projected her on to Cordelia, Timon can project her on to nobody but the detestable knaves who deserve everything he says about them.

At a single stroke, he has been deprived of the tragic status of the hero who set out to destroy the one who absolutely loves him, and whom he loves absolutely. He is reduced to a frenzy against someone who has merely disappointed an unrealistic expectation. The loved and the loathed have not come together in a single person. Reality has merely demonstrated, in its brute language, what happens when the whole heart is invested in an unnatural ideal.

One can see the symbolic meaning of Timon's great love and its betrayal, and a grand architecture of ethical design, where Timon sees through, and rejects, and is rejected by, civilization itself, but the dramatic circumstances prevent us from feeling this, and in fact fill the stage with a mass of petty evidence that confuses and almost chokes any symbolic resonance.

3. The Shakespearean moment has arrived, however, and Timon duly recoils into Tarquinian madness.

This 'madness' arrives on two levels. One of these is inadequate for saving the play. The other is too much for the play to handle. The first is the one that Shakespeare dramatizes with some care. The other seems to overtake him. The first is Timon's moral fury. Measured against Apemantus's brutish cynicism, this fury is titanic and noble – but not tragic. Founded in the ruins of that unrealistic, perhaps foolish ideal, it could still be thought unrealistic, just as Apemantus points out, and if there were no more to it Timon would seem as foolish now as he was before his disillusion: noble but foolish. What saves the situation as a tragic poem, though still not as a play, is our realization that his rage and pain come from a deeper source than he admits to Apemantus. And it is the easy, unearned cynicism of Apemantus that gives us its scale. Timon's great curse erupts from a shock of nihilism. It pours from a vision, newly confirmed, of a mankind without love. Presumably this vision has something to do with the mercantile, atheist, secularized society that was already opening in Jacobean England, in so far as submission to the Divine Love (and therefore any dependence on love in each other) was being supplanted by more pragmatic resorts. When Timon searches in the hearts of his friends for anything resembling the Divine Love, for any human substitute, this ideology is what confronts him – the apelike aspect of a mankind whose heart is, as the proverb says, where its purse is, a mankind that has lost, in fact, the Goddess, and is plunging towards the heartless monkeyland of Swift and Pope, and beyond them towards *The Waste Land* and the dustbins of Beckett's refuse-eating hominids. Timon's volcanic eruption, in these terms, is the fountainhead of the desert of black cinders which now covers the inheritance of secular man and his works – where 'the dead tree gives no shelter, the cricket no relief'.

Looking at it from this angle, one could argue that *Timon* is Shakespeare's most concentrated and justified prophetic vision of the consequences of that 'sin' behind the Tragic Equation – that rejection (and death) not of God (to begin with) but of the totality of Divine Love: the ultimate statement of the true tragedy of Christ within formal Christianity. Shakespeare's is the most agonized of such prophecies, presumably because, being born when he was, he was among the last to be nursed by the universal assurance of the Goddess's eternal love and the first to feel the apparent certainty of her destruction, and because what cries out, in his tragedy, in that Tarquinian madness, is the agony and despair of the Goddess herself.

Perhaps this view of it helps to explain how Shakespeare came to make what seems to be, from the audience's point of view, an artistic mistake. It suggests how that absence of the Goddess (or rather of her female representative, which is as calamitous for the work as a play as it is for Timon as a man of 'total, unconditional love') might well be the most deliberate feature of Shakespeare's design. And it enables one to argue that this Book of Job without God (without Goddess – the God of Job, in his impartial distribution of blessings and terrors, is a masculine form of the undivided glory of the Great Goddess) comes in Shakespeare's career exactly where one ought to expect it – at the very peak of his visionary, penetrative power. By removing that essential, divine *prima materia*, the Goddess, from his Equation, he makes what proves to be his clearest and in some ways most prophetic exposition of its deepest metaphysical implication.

But from the audience's point of view, by removing the Goddess and therefore the Tarquinian victim, he has removed, to a degree, Timon's sexuality and soul. This, as I say, intensifies the bleak force of the poem, as a vision of the meaninglessly absurd appetites of despiritualized mankind, but it maims the drama. It supplants human conflict and apprehension with the numbing spectacle of a natural calamity, like the extinction of a species. The grappling embrace or death struggle of male and female in which all the other tragedies find their universal and, so to speak, biological centre of gravity has become a vast emptiness, through which, like the last man, Timon howls.

His 'madness' can only hurl itself against the whole of Athens, the polis of the Great Goddess as the Goddess of Wisdom, now populated, in his eyes, by a kind of baboon.

4. In spite of such a grievous power crisis in the dynamism of the drama, the Equation struggles to bring the material to order. This is revealed in the fascinating confusion of the text at this point. It is a lucid sort of confusion, and worth looking at closely. Recognizing that his plot cannot provide the dramatic effect he needs, Shakespeare simply suggests it, with a naked display of sleight of hand, creating an impression far in excess of the facts of the plot, and even contradicting them.

By Act Four he needs to get Timon outside Athens, as if banished, or at least a fugitive, looking back on the city and cursing it, and since the full, tragic nature of the Equation demands that the hero destroy the source of his madness, or what he sees as the Queen of Hell, Athens must seem to be in some danger from him -- if the Equation is to work. Shakespeare attempts to solve these problems in the following ways:

Act Three, Scene Four: Timon's friends, panicked by his bankruptcy, having refused to help him, send their servants to reclaim old borrowings. He faces them (the 'double vision') going mad (surrendering to the Tarquinian frenzy) with:

> TIMON: Cut my heart in sums.
> TITUS: Mine, fifty talents.
> TIMON: Tell out my blood.
> LUCIUS'S SERVANT: Five thousand crowns, my lord.

TIMON: Five thousand drops pays that. What yours? And yours? . . .
    Tear me, take me; and the gods fall upon you!

And yet this scene ends with him inviting everybody to a last, splendid banquet.

Act Three, Scene Five: Absolutely new business, wholly unprepared for: the Athenian senators are condemning to death a man who, by his description, is another Timon. At a riotous banquet in his home, this man, notorious for his high, extravagant living, has killed a guest. His name is never mentioned, but after the previous scene we assume that Timon in his extreme rage has killed one of the erstwhile friends. When Alcibiades, the great and popular Athenian general, pleads this man's case, the senators banish him, the defender of Athens, on pain of death, for daring to defend such a monster.

Act Three, Scene Six: Timon is giving the banquet he promised. His guests, his old friends, speak in amazement of his earlier lapse into crazy rage, and they also mention, as a startling piece of news, Alcibiades's banishment.

    At this point we half correct our other impression (if we are listening keenly). Nevertheless, that impression has been made. Somebody who can only be Timon (surely!) in an uncontrollable rage has killed one of his treacherous, formerly beloved friends. And because that impression is not entirely explained away, it remains all the more intrusive for being uncertain.

    Timon's banquet is hot water only. He hurls it in his guests' faces, drives them out with curses, and exits with:

> henceforth hated be
> Of Timon man and all humanity!

115–16

Whereupon Act Four opens with Timon outside the city walls, cursing the whole city.

    What has happened, essentially, is that while Timon is outraged beyond human endurance and is going mad on one part of the stage, on another part of the stage somebody exactly like him, and like him outraged beyond human endurance, has committed murder in noble, indignant fury. Shakespeare lets that double exposure pass subliminally across his audience. Simultaneously, he has planted the ominous

[289]

consequence that the dangerous military commander Alcibiades has been unjustly banished on pain of death – for defending that other Timon. Alcibiades and Timon now have the same cause.

The operation of the Equation, behind the scenes, can be observed here, switching its naked algebra to shunt the dramatic freight across the points. If Timon is to become a thoroughgoing Tarquin, one who can rise to tragic stature by doing the tragic deed (destroying Athens, the Queen of Hell), he needs some extra physical re-enforcement. As far as the Equation is concerned, somebody like Alcibiades had to be conscripted – to guarantee Timon's ability to deal with a Queen of Hell as powerful as Athens. The Equation, in other words, is going through its inevitable procedure, even though Shakespeare might decide to defy it, and use the components in some other way to illustrate some other point.

The Equation now has Act Four primed for a tragic development. Alcibiades, on the political plane, like Timon on the social plane, reels from Athens in a Tarquinian madness. They are like the two aspects of one figure, and our impression is strengthened that Timon must have been judged for that mysterious murder, and banished, like Alcibiades, under threat of execution. This impression is so strong, Shakespeare's conjuring trick was so successful, that some commentators have supposed that a scene or two must be lost, or that in this middle section the text conflates two different drafts. But more likely it is Shakespeare's impressionism at work – creating the effect he needs with broad, suggestive strokes.

What the Equation is now insisting on, beneath the refractory materials of this plot, is that Alcibiades and Timon join forces. When the two do meet, the Equation seems to be offering the play this opportunity. They could combine, like Aufidius and Coriolanus. Timon could pay Alcibiades's soldiers with the gold he has discovered while digging for the roots of the simple life, and both could fulfil their Tarquinian destiny by destroying their mother city, their former beloved.

One can imagine what a different speech Timon could deliver at the close of the play, in that case. He could rise to the most complete, Shakespearean-style, tragic self-understanding, gazing out over Athens from the calcined ruins of the Parthenon, a scorched, soot-blackened, red-eyed Caliban of a Pyrrhus, resuming the form of an ennobled Hamlet.

Perhaps the facts of classical history, guarded by the mockery of Ben Jonson, were too obdurate even for Shakespeare's will. Perhaps he consoled himself with those other possibilities, to be explored, for instance, in the contrast between Alcibiades and Timon, rather than in their fusion, as he searched for the altogether other wavelength that would release Timon's much more appalling news. But there again, whatever the gains, in so far as the separation of the two meant that he had to abandon the Tragic Equation, and spare Athens, it meant the collapse of the drama as a vehicle for his usual kind of tragedy, and even as a drama. Alcibiades goes off to make expedient peace, and Timon remains to die in an infinite waste of invective, the last resort of the powerless. He blazes out in dragonish but ineffectual gouts of flame, and quenches his ashes under the sea's edge – as if he were indeed the last man.

The Equation has done its best to carry the play through all its phases, yet the simple absence of the female focus, the embodiment of Timon's love and soul, as a hostage within the city, has sabotaged its engineering as a stage work. The fortuitous appearance of Alcibiades's whores might be just enough to give us a glimpse of the target that Timon has been missing. And yet this Goddess-less variant of the Equation is logically, as I say, one of its most extreme forms – in one direction an ultimate limit, in that her total absence, her as-if-non-existence, is her most cruel treachery of all, her ultimate faithlessness.

Timon's famous grave, and the words he adds to it:

> Timon hath made his everlasting mansion
> Upon the beached verge of the salt flood;
> Who once a day with his embossed froth
> The turbulent surge shall cover . . .

v. i. 220–3

and the words of the simple illiterate soldier who mourns him:

> Timon is dead;
> Entomb'd upon the very hem o' the sea . . .
> . . . rich conceit
> Taught thee to make vast Neptune weep for aye
> On thy low grave, on faults forgiven,

v. iv. 66–79

compose a forlorn substitute for the pietà deaths, and rebirth into the embrace of the Goddess, that await Shakespeare's luckier heroes. Neptune is the name given here to the great fish-tailed goddess of the sea, the Aphrodite born of the sea, just as the male Athenians in the city represented the Goddess abscondita. Since her love was totally absent in his life, Timon does not expect to be acknowledged by her in his death – though he buries himself under her very hem (creeps under the outermost fringe of her garment). But in fact, belatedly, this ocean does embrace him and weep over his 'faults forgiven'.

Timon's magnificence as a poem emerges, perhaps inadvertently, from the misfire, in this case, of the Equation, and from Shakespeare's failure to hit on other effective dramatic means: poetry has to perform where action fails. Its great power as a parable, a new vision of secular man in his desacralized universe, or of the sufferings of religious man forcibly thrust into a desacralized universe, emerges in the same way. What Shakespeare's *drama* could express, of this fundamental vision, was expressed, perhaps, in *King Lear*. *Timon* resembles the afterbirth of *King Lear* – the placenta (of insane rage against the withdrawal of the Goddess, expressed as a rage against ingratitude), within which *King Lear* was gestated. Timon's helplessness against unconcerned Athens is reminiscent of Lear's helplessness against Goneril and Regan. But here again, lack of the 'soul' figure, the Lucrece, the bond of 'one flesh', precludes any inner transformation for Timon's generalized 'madness', his all-inclusive hatred. As a play, nevertheless, *Timon* served as an experimental prototype for a new model in the evolution of the Equation. As a poetic vision of secularized religious man it was a dead end – or at least a new beginning that Shakespeare himself was not given time to take further. But as a Tragedy of Divine Love, though an apparent stage failure, it served for the first draft of one of his most perfect images of the theme. Maybe such a thorough preliminary exploration of the problem – of a play about a hero betrayed by his own city – explains the unstrained perfection of *Coriolanus*, which recapitulates *Timon* in so many features but (more perfectly obedient to the Tragic Equation) takes care to introduce a real female, who thereupon brings the immense power of the event to a blistering, dramatic focus.

Coriolanus: the Female survives the Tragic Equation

Setting aside all other content (so far as that's possible), and concentrating on the Equation alone, one can see how some of the particular strengths of *Coriolanus* are repairs of what were points of dislocation in *Timon*. Shakespeare makes two principal readjustments. He combines the military force, and cause, of the banished Alcibiades with the implacable fury of Timon, in the single figure of Coriolanus. And he carefully positions the Female at the centre of everything.

The move to Rome in itself brings the tragic myth home in two ways. First, the patron god of Rome is the war god Mars, who, as I mentioned before, in one of his myths became a boar that slew Adonis (and, in Shakespeare, became Tarquin). He is accordingly resuscitated in Coriolanus's very name – Martius.

On another level, the simple central theme – the war god's assault on Rome, who turns into the Mother with the silent Wife and her infant son beside her – is a plain allegory of the great Reformation theme behind the Equation: the Holy Warrior's assault on Catholic Rome. The powerfully realized political drama of events in pre-imperial Rome smuggles this glaring image through uncontested. And the far more prominent (to contemporary audiences) analogy of Essex's relationship to Elizabeth – as her adored, spoiled 'son' who finally led a mad rebellion against her (in which Shakespeare's patron was deeply involved) – would possibly absorb the attention of most. Yet one can hardly imagine that it went unnoticed, in those religion-racked days, that Rome has become, in this play, the Mother of the destroying 'god'.

The unusual fullness and simplicity of this symbol, in *Coriolanus*, is brought out by following the Equation through the plot:

1. Coriolanus's Rome contains the essential nucleus that Timon's Athens lacked: the female embodiment of the hero's soul and love. The city itself is centred on his mother Volumnia's 'total, unconditional' son-worship. Enshrined, so to speak, within Volumnia's love, is his wife Virgilia's husband-worship. Shakespeare pushes the divine role of these two women to the limit. Volumnia and Virgilia, as if in turn, attend Coriolanus's son, who is described, pointedly, as another Coriolanus, his infant self, the god to be sacrificed.

Surrounding the two women, like a dark corona, is the ominous third aspect of the Goddess, the people of Rome, whose passion for their hero Coriolanus is total, but unreliable, suffused with treachery and eruptive animality, and secreting Mars, their god, as the Boar.

2. At the opening of the play, Coriolanus is on the point of seeing the double vision; he anticipates the treachery of the Roman mob that seems to adore him; he loathes it, but he sees no reason yet to fear it. Meanwhile he worships his mother and (as if she were merely some aspect of his mother) his wife. These two women are never seen apart except once, when his mother alone is able to do what nobody else can do – persuade Coriolanus to act humbly in canvassing the votes of the plebeians.

This situation prepares him for the double vision. On the one side he performs his dazzling feats of battle 'for his mother', and on the other he rejects and pours contempt over the Roman mob that claims his victories and worships him for them. At his first entrance he addresses them:

> What's the matter, you dissentious rogues,
> That, rubbing the poor itch of your opinion,
> Make yourselves scabs?
>
> *Coriolanus*, I. i. 170–2

If he really had been 'made by some other deity than Nature/That shapes men better' (a description of the idealist, Puritan attitude), the mob, or some democratic revolutionary (they have their tribune, Brutus), could simply assassinate him, and Shakespeare would have avoided a plot too like *Julius Caesar* and gone on searching for something else, closer to his Equation. But though he is described as 'the oak not to be wind-shaken', Coriolanus is precariously rooted in his mother – this woman who regards herself as the soul of noble Rome. His primitive, idealized devotion to her, therefore, has placed the bomb of vulnerability in his very roots. And his outspoken enmity against the ignoble body of Rome – the mob – sets this bomb ticking out the tragic inevitability. Shakespeare lifts the certainty of this primal pain to come into a sort of appalled dread, by emphasizing Coriolanus's infantile susceptibility, casting him as a Herculean brat hypnotized in the fool's paradise of his mother's love, the boy's soul at the mercy of the terrible abstraction created by his mother's idealism. The vivid presence of his own little son keeps this perspective open until, in the last scene, it swallows the action and Coriolanus with it, as his mother, by sheer maternal power, shrinks him back into the child of himself, as if she were spellbinding the genie back into the bottle, and so saves Rome from him.

3. When the Roman mob that had adored him rises to kill him he confronts the Boar: the Shakespearean moment. He recoils from this double vision with a tirade – the formal declaration of his Tarquinian madness – which is the equivalent of the misogynist eruptions that Shakespeare's other tragic heroes pour over the Female at this point.

4. His next step demonstrates Shakespeare's huge correction of Timon's ineffectuality. The loosely parallel, poorly concerted, anti-Athenian efforts of Timon and Alcibiades seem, in retrospect, like a sketchy rehearsal for the tigerlike co-ordination of Coriolanus and Aufidius against Rome.

5. Coriolanus's advance against Rome is in some ways a massively armoured replay of Tarquin's advance on Lucrece's bedchamber. His 'pause' before destroying Rome recalls, at various points, Tarquin's dreadful threatenings – as a predatory animal, a machine, a batterer down of the city – over Lucrece's prostrate body described as a city about to be sacked.

Likewise, his mother's (and wife's) appeal for mercy in many points resembles Lucrece's, and very clearly in terms of the Equation they correspond to her exactly.

This confrontation between Coriolanus and his mother and wife, outside Rome, brings all the religious and mythic associations to a single focus. Coriolanus appears, as Angelo appeared in the beginning of *Measure for Measure*, as an inhuman abstraction, but much more actively pitiless and destructive – inimical to all flesh and blood, to all individual lives, to all human feeling, to his own nature, to his own mother, wife and child. It is a marvellously formidable embodiment of the tragic error – that Puritan absolutism and severity, the martial judgement against the 'wholeness' of the Goddess. He is the Goddess-destroying god as 'a thing made for Alexander', whose 'hum is a battery', a dragon who inevitably ends up 'tearing his country's bowels out', treading 'on his mother's womb', destroying his wife and child and himself. Likewise his mother, who points all this out to him, is the avatar of that 'total, unconditional love' which created him and which is now trying to protect her world from his insanity.

6. If Coriolanus were to go ahead and destroy Rome, not sparing mother, wife or son, but reducing the whole city to flames, as he had intended, the Equation would be complete.

The fact that at this climax his 'madness' suddenly melts away in tears, and that he withdraws, letting his mother, wife and child survive, is significant – for the Equation.

His weeping, and that sudden relinquishing of his tragic purpose, is as if he understood, while his mother speaks, what Lear did not understand until he woke to find Cordelia bending over him. He understands, by surrendering to his infantile bond with his mother, his tragic error – and separates himself from it.

In *King Lear*, the Tragic Equation reasserted its pattern, and Cordelia had to die. But here, perhaps because Lear's experience has radically modified it, though Coriolanus has to die, this is the first play in the tragic sequence proper (since *Hamlet*) where the Female survives.

The tragic hero as the Rival Brother

Inside their separate category, *Macbeth*, *Antony and Cleopatra*, and *The Tempest*, fall into an odd sequence of their own. Not quite thesis, antithesis, synthesis, but something like.

Because in all three plays the pattern of the Rival Brothers is so dominant, the 'rational' self and the 'irrational' self are personified in two separate characters. And since these two brothers now incorporate the attributes of their equivalents in the composite myth, in each play one chief character must be the Adonis figure, and the other must be the Boar.

Out of all fourteen plays, *Macbeth* and *Antony and Cleopatra* are the only two in which the Boar who makes the assault is also the hero.

In *The Tempest* the Adonis figure – Prospero – is the hero. (As I hope to demonstrate later, he is the same type of Adonis figure as the hero in the other eleven plays.) But in the whole tragic sequence, he is the only Adonis figure who, being the hero, retains control from beginning to end of the play.

That is to say, in *The Tempest* the assault of the Boar fails. But in *Antony and Cleopatra*, also, the assault of the Boar fails. So these two are the only plays in the whole sequence in which the assault of the Boar fails. (In *Antony and Cleopatra* there is a complication to this, which I will come to.)

As a trinity these plays are outstanding, in the sequence, in all kinds of ways, but it is curious to see that it is the dominant role of the Rival Brothers that enables Shakespeare to lift the Tragic Equation into such close focus and magnification, to form three such final statements, where *Macbeth* reveals the full meaning of the Boar's triumph, *Antony and Cleopatra* the full meaning of the Boar's failure, and *The Tempest*, the full – no less disturbing – meaning of the triumph of Adonis.

In the text, as I say, all manner of qualifying circumstances press for acknowledgement, and some of them – such as Caliban's claim to hero status, or Octavius Caesar's role as a Boar (a sub-species in another pantheon) among others – suggest the hovering antithetical drama, a *trompe-l'oeil* reversal of patterns and perspectives, which, in fact, in *Antony and Cleopatra*, finally deposes the other.

One could press a little further and point out the strong (collapsing) Adonis features in *Macbeth*, already converted to Tarquin by the time he stalks towards the murder, and the even more pronounced Adonis features in Antony when he sees the double vision in Cleopatra after her battle fleet has betrayed him and joined Caesar's. But these motifs of the Tragic Equation are counterpointed within the major main theme of the Rival Brothers – in which both heroes are the Boar: Macbeth (triumphing) against holy Duncan, and Antony (failing) against Octavius Caesar.

It is exactly this double role which distinguishes Macbeth and Antony from the heroes of those plays dominated by the Tragic Equation, in each of which the two selves are contained behind the one face – the face of the Adonis who, when the Boar attacks, becomes Tarquin. That is to say, in all those plays, the dramatic elemental being which in *Macbeth* is embodied by Macbeth, and in *Antony and Cleopatra* by Antony, and in *The Tempest* by Caliban, namely the Boar, is invisible.

This double role is made possible, obviously, by the brilliantly integrated double structure of the plays, and the fact that Shakespeare not only sets the Rival Brothers in the foreground, and the Tragic Equation in the background, but gives his hero the role of the 'rational' self in the one and the 'irrational' self in the other. The strong rational self in the Rival Brothers pattern – Duncan/Banquo/Macduff, in *Macbeth*, and Caesar in *Antony and Cleopatra* – then becomes a fortifying, externalized image of the rational self in the coexistent Tragic Equation, i.e. of the weak Adonis in both Macbeth and Antony.

The distance the Equation has travelled, between *Macbeth* and *Antony and Cleopatra*, becomes evident if one considers Cleopatra as an updating of Lady Macbeth (in her role as Queen of Hell) and Antony as an updating of Macbeth (in his role as the Boar).

Antony and Cleopatra as a bridging work

If *Antony and Cleopatra* did not exist, one could say confidently that after *Coriolanus* all Shakespeare's heroines survive. In fact, one could say after this, his tragic heroes survive also.

The evolution of the Equation, however, suggests that *Antony and Cleopatra* comes after *Coriolanus* and before the first of the 'romances'. *Coriolanus* is the last of the tragedies proper, integral with the preceding five, in which the tragic hero and heroine die, unredeemed, within the Tragic Equation. And though, in *Coriolanus*, the Female survives, she does so unredeemed. Though she escapes the Tragic Equation, she remains to mourn on the tragic plane. The action fails to break through on to the plane of transcendence (as Lear and Cordelia did briefly).

One radical difference of the 'romances', as a group – *Cymbeline*, *Pericles*, *The Winter's Tale* and *The Tempest* – is that in each of them (whichever came first), Shakespeare has reshaped the Tragic Equation, adapting it to a 'theophany' which lifts hero and heroine out of their tragedy, alive and reborn, on to the plane of transcendence.

Between the two groups, *Antony and Cleopatra* appears as a bridging work. Though Antony and Cleopatra die, physically, within the Tragic Equation, Antony killing himself – like Othello – when he believes his Tarquinian frenzy has killed Cleopatra, and Cleopatra killing herself because his death leaves her no life, nevertheless, at the same time, in the most resplendent and undeniable fashion, both Antony and Cleopatra transcend their tragic fates (and their deaths) by rising together above the Tragic Equation (and the Rival Brothers), on to a sharply defined, higher, metaphysical plane, where such worldly sufferings are redeemed.

Shakespeare does this not as in the romances, where he hoists his hero and heroine, quite suddenly, in the middle of the play, off the realistic tragic plane on to a symbolic, redemptive plane. Instead, he does it by making the realistic, tragic plane an irreducible image of the human suffering exacted by the divine demands of the transcendental plane. (I hope to make this clearer in the following pages.)

In this sense, then, though both Antony and Cleopatra physically die, spiritually they are reborn, their tragic errors are redeemed – not just briefly at the end of the play, but throughout, in intermittent, glowing epiphanies of increasing intensity. In this way, *Antony and Cleopatra* is psychologically a more evolved work than *Coriolanus*, and must be one of Shakespeare's ultimate achievements – in which tragic and transcendental are objectified by each other, each in the terms of the other, as nowhere else in any earlier play, while in the following plays (the romances), tragic and transcendental have split apart, and in each work require two different kinds of treatment.

In other words, though Volumnia/Virgilia's survival, at the end of *Coriolanus*, indicates an irreversible mutation in the closing segment of the Tragic Equation, *Antony and Cleopatra* introduces the gigantic next step. Shakespeare here devotes a whole play to the discovery he glimpsed in *King Lear*. He outmanoeuvres the hero's Tarquinian madness, painfully destroys the Puritan ego, and unites both hero and Female on the transcendental plane of Divine Love.

He then goes on to consolidate this development in the last four plays of the sequence.

Antony and Cleopatra: the new factors

The interplay of the two patterns – that of the Tragic Equation and that of the Rival Brothers – is more intricate and even more intricately interdependent in *Antony and Cleopatra* than in any of the other tragedies. But the fates of Antony and Cleopatra are lifted into that third pattern, which transcends those other two, by a wholly new factor. This new factor is obvious in the nature of Cleopatra, not quite so obvious in the nature of Antony.

In Cleopatra's case, exactly what the new factor is becomes more visible when her role is compared with Lady Macbeth's. I outlined the general similarity of design (distinct from that of all the other plays in the sequence except *The Tempest*) in these two plays, where Antony and Macbeth, up to a point, perform similar double roles, as simultaneously Adonis and the Boar. Macbeth detaches himself from the rational realm of King Duncan (where he is Adonis) and reveals his true being as the emanation of Lady Macbeth's lust (for power), where he is the Boar and 'hot tyrant'. Antony, with more difficulty, detaches himself likewise from the rational realm of Octavius Caesar and Rome (where he is an Adonis), and reveals his true being as the emanation of Cleopatra's lust (actually the 'love' – like Venus's in *Venus and Adonis* – of the undivided Goddess of Complete Being), where he attempts to be the Boar and the 'hot tyrant'.

That 'attempts to be' (since he fails) is crucial. It is connected with that extra dimension, the new factor, which Cleopatra incorporates but which Lady Macbeth altogether lacks. In the design common to both plays, isolated above, both Cleopatra and Lady Macbeth have the roles of Queen of Hell. As such, Lady Macbeth is highly defined, the near apotheosis of that Goddess's human representative. Her ferocious determination, which is more truly a homicidal greed, to seize what she regards as properly hers, and to topple the royal Adonis figure who keeps her from it, presents almost a biological study of the mythic type. When she invokes the elemental spirits of nature to fill her up from the crown to the toe 'top full of direst cruelty', she makes literal her self-identification with the Medea-like nocturnal Hecate in her most malignant form. Accordingly, her emanation Macbeth, made of the same ectoplasm, becomes the Boar in its most violent, concentrated, authentic form.

It is less easy to characterize Cleopatra as a Queen of Hell, yet from the Roman point of view she obviously is one: not only the black African Queen of serpents, witchcraft, magicians, poisons, the river of the dead and the Underworld, but also a 'gypsy', a 'trull', a 'whore', a 'boggler', 'filth', 'errors', 'confusion'. When the 'double vision' is finally (so belatedly!) triggered in Antony's Roman, Herculean, Adonis ego, these are the terms that he pours over her in his Tarquinian tirade – before she flees, to escape what she recognizes as a murderous fury. On the other hand, at the same time, the audience is aware, and Antony is aware, that this Queen of Hell aspect is only part of Cleopatra's 'infinite variety' – just as, in the Great Goddess, it is only part of her undivided being, which incorporates also Divine Mother, Sacred Bride, the whole of the Goddess.

Antony's nature corresponds to Cleopatra's. Just as she is not narrowly confined to the role of Queen of Hell, so there is more to him than the supreme Roman commander whose ancestor and tutelary god is Hercules. Antony was also, notoriously, the 'ne'er lust-wearied' 'libertine', devoted to riotous feasting and love. Historically (and in the play – overtly and obliquely) he liked to identify himself with Dionysus, the god of orgiastic frenzy (divine drunkenness), who was, of course, the child of the Great Goddess (identified in pre-Christian history with Osiris in particular, and with Adonis, and eventually, in Christian history, with Christ). Again, this extra 'divine' dimension is in Antony's case the new factor. It is what he possesses that Macbeth notably lacks (though he glimpses it, in the three apparitions).

These extra factors are new in so far as the great undivided Goddess of Complete Being has not been incarnated in any earlier Shakespearean heroine (except Venus in the poem), and that Osirian/Dionysian Eros has not been incarnated in any earlier tragic hero except briefly, in infant, helpless form, in the reborn King Lear.

And these 'new' Egyptian 'divine' factors clearly exist in a metaphysical world quite different from the Roman political world, which remains the familiar Shakespearean tragic world, where the Herculean general Antony deserts the 'Puritan' morality of Rome, as the victorious general Macbeth deserted King Duncan.

They exist in a divine love world in which the Goddess and her consort are united. This very much resembles the transcendental plane that Shakespeare established and put into cold storage at the end of *Venus and Adonis*, and that reopened in *King Lear* at Lear's rebirth. It helps if one regards their love world as just this – at least for the purpose of anatomizing the play and tracing out the patterns of Rival Brothers and Tragic Equation.

Apart from Antony and, to a degree, Enobarbus (who is like the deputy of Antony's Herculean, confident self-indulgence), this transcendental world is invisible to the Romans. To them, in the friction and heat of their churning imperial realm – embroiled with Rival Brothers and Tragic Equation – Antony's Egyptian self appears (as Macbeth's murderous self appears to the Scots Lords) merely irrational. They see it only as the regrettable, even contemptible, perhaps pitiable antics of a 'strumpet's fool'. The Roman view, then, of Antony's Osirian 'divine' self is that it is merely the 'not Antony', 'which comes too short of that great property/Which still should go with Antony'. In other words, they see it as a manifestation of the inferiority of Caesar's brother-in-law. From Caesar's point of view, the Osirian world does not exist: for him, the action of the play is confined within the same metaphysical circumference as *Macbeth*: his irrational kinsman Antony has combined with a turbulent foreign witch, made a push to disrupt the Roman order and usurp the imperial power, has failed and is destroyed.

The 'divine' world of Antony and Cleopatra's love is invisible because it is subjective. It is confined entirely to their true feelings – in Antony's case hidden much of the time from himself – which are occasionally reflected in the words of such as Enobarbus (as in his great description of Cleopatra as Isis/Venus, Goddess of Love). Being subjective, this world does not imprint itself on the play in a definable shape of action. At the same time, it very much determines the pace and emphasis, in the development of the action, of the Rival Brothers and the Tragic Equation – to the point, in fact, of debilitating them. Their mechanism seems baffled, and has difficulty getting to grips with, or bringing to a dramatic confrontation, or driving into an inescapable tragic corner, the hero and heroine who, whenever the action snaps at them, somehow float out of its jaws, into their greater, nobler, more magnificent transcendental dimension – where Rome and its arid absolutes become meaningless. Though the action does finally manage to destroy them physically, and makes their love suffer much of what mortal love can suffer, nevertheless, again and again, and finally too, they transcend it.

In this way, as I say, the story of their tragedy becomes the story of their transcendence. The play opens as a double exposure, where the tragic Roman plane and the transcendental Egyptian plane are fused in a mixed image. The two planes tear painfully apart (as the two mutually incompatible gods in Antony tear painfully apart), scene by scene, and in the end present two separate revelations. The nature of the difference between the two planes means that as far as the physical life of the drama goes, the tragic plane is projected in action, whereas the transcendental plane finds palpable expression exclusively in the dramatic poetry. In this way, the action says one thing: the play is a tragedy, the ineluctable, dead-end destruction of the noble Herculean Roman general by his infatuation for an opportunist African queen. But the dramatic poetry says the opposite: the play is a theophany and enacts a love god's liberation from the armoured confinements of the Roman/Puritan ego, and his reunion with the Love Goddess beyond tragic division.

This also means that in anatomizing the action of the play, extricating the pattern of Rival Brothers and Tragic Equation, it is possible to ignore the transcendental plane (at least to begin with).

Then, by superimposing the transcendental plane, like a filter lens, one can see the tragic pattern of the Rival Brothers inverted – into its opposite.

Antony and Cleopatra as a tragedy

If one isolates the essential action as it operates on the tragic plane, and identifies the Antony who loves Cleopatra as the 'irrational' Antony, and the Antony who seeks to preserve his personal Roman integrity as the 'rational' Antony, one finds both Rival Brothers and Tragic Equation, in distinct and classic forms, responsible for most of what happens. A brief sketch helps to outline the two patterns on this lower plane:

Antony, while swearing 'total, unconditional' love to Cleopatra, in her palace in Egypt, hears that his martial wife, Fulvia, has died, after waking 'garboils' in Rome that demand his immediate presence and attention.

Antony is already clearly divided into at least two selves, each well aware of the character of the other. On the one hand, his irrational self swears absolute loyalty to Cleopatra, with a sacred Egyptian oath:

> By the fire
> That quickens Nilus' slime, I go from hence
> Thy soldier, servant, making peace or war
> As thou affect'st
>   *Antony and Cleopatra*, I. iii. 68–71

as if he were nothing but the agent of her will, defying the rest of the world. On the other hand, he can say to Enobarbus:

> I must from this enchanting queen break off
>   I. ii. 137

and more bitterly:

> Would I had never seen her!
>   I. ii. 163

He believes, it seems, that however he indulges his irrational self, his rational Roman self is still in easy control. At the same time, the plot signals ominously that he is deceiving himself, and that he is too late: the balance has already tipped towards the 'strumpet's fool', and his 'dotage', however his Roman rational ego may determine to break with it, already has the upper hand. The clue to this, in Shakespearean terms, is that Fulvia – the 'soul' of his Roman military self – has died, i.e., his Roman ego, whatever desperate efforts it may make to reassert itself, is already somehow obsolete.

The rest of the action of the drama, here on the tragic plane, as far as the Roman Antony is concerned, illustrates his own disintegration. His extravagant reaffirmation of his love for Cleopatra: 'Let Rome in Tiber melt', is like a divine pronouncement – 'let the Herculean Antony melt'. And from that first line of the play, the trickling dissolution can be heard:

Nay, but this dotage of our general's
O'erflows the measure;

I. i. 1–2

until in the end he will partly dissolve into the slime of the Nile and partly evaporate.

Still restricting my account to the tragic plane, both the Tragic Equation and the Rival Brothers are launched in this opening scene.

According to his first declaration of love to Cleopatra, like Othello before Iago's suggestion or King Lear before Cordelia's 'Nothing', Antony is an Adonis in the pre-Puritan phase. Yet he realizes as a (Puritan) Roman that from the Roman point of view she is a cunning witch, with a history of adulterous opportunism. The new circumstance here is that he accepts this knowledge: he sees the double vision but (unlike any tragic hero before him) he does not recoil into madness – yet. Within the confines of the tragic plane, this forbearance, unique in all Shakespeare's tragic heroes, can be put down to his Herculean self-confidence, and to the fact that he is deceiving himself. This tolerance of the double vision keeps the Equation in neutral gear. But only temporarily. In fact, here too the mechanism is standard issue, and whenever he does find that he loves this 'gypsy' 'totally, unconditionally', and is helplessly dependent on her love for him, it will crash into its only other gear – which is top. And that will happen. But it is some way off in the future. Before he can become aware of his true feeling

[304]

for Cleopatra, he will need to be divested of the fool's paradise of his Herculean immunity. Meanwhile, the pattern of the Rival Brothers is bared in a few words, by Cleopatra. She has detected the weakness in Antony's Roman ego. She has sniffed out that in so far as Caesar and Antony (ignoring the temporary Lepidus) share the Empire between them – as brothers – Antony is the inferior. She has divined, in other words, that in asserting his Roman dignity as Caesar's equal, he is deceiving himself, and that Antony the triumvir, or duumvir, rather, is not the true Antony. Her banter needles through his armour:

> Who knows
> If the scarce-bearded Caesar have not sent
> His powerful mandate to you, 'Do this, or this;
> Take in that kingdom, and enfranchise that;
> Perform't, or else we damn thee.'
>
> I. i. 20–4

and when he blushes to hear her words:

> Thou blushest, Antony, and that blood of thine
> Is Caesar's homager.
>
> I. i. 30–1

And as it turns out, he knows she is right. He knows that his rival for control of the Roman world is somehow his superior, while his own role, in so far as they are brothers, is that of the inferior, the 'irrational' one.

Antony returns to Rome, but continues to receive, in Rome, Cleopatra's passionate letters, and he sends his own renewed avowals of love in return.

Nevertheless, once back among his Roman competitors, he sets about repairing the political damage caused by his long absence. Attempting to re-establish his Roman life, and to secure his Roman power base, and to remove the antagonism between Caesar and himself, he leaps at the chance to marry Caesar's sister – the 'holy, cold and still', Diana-like Octavia.

This action, the one juncture in the play at which he has the opportunity to put his rational self in control, and start his life afresh, reveals itself immediately as his most calamitous act of

[305]

self-deception. It reveals itself even to him in this way. He sees at once that his attempt to confirm his Roman ego is an empty gesture, that he has no affinity whatsoever with the Roman virtues of Octavia, that his Roman career is meaningless and that his marriage can only shatter the alliance it was meant to secure. In the very next scene, an Egyptian magician and soothsayer, who rises like a genie from the occult Egyptian world right there in Caesar's house, declares openly what Cleopatra hinted: Antony, in spite of being Rome's supreme military commander, is not a real Roman. And the Roman Caesar is his enemy.

> Therefore, O Antony! stay not by his side;
> Thy demon – that's thy spirit which keeps thee – is
> Noble, courageous, high, unmatchable,
> Where Caesar's is not. But near him, thy angel
> Becomes a fear, as being o'erpowered; therefore
> Make space enough between you.
>
> II. iii. 18–23

At this point, at last, Antony understands this much about himself. And the scene closes with him handing his Roman military command (in the Parthian campaign on which he was about to embark) to a subordinate officer.

Act Two ends with a scene which in a dream would be explicit. On a barge reminiscent of Cleopatra's, as guests of Pompey, their former and future enemy, Caesar and Lepidus are given a taste of Antony's 'Egyptian Bacchanals'. Openly, in his Bacchic or Dionysiac phase, what the Romans would regard as his old degenerate self, Antony, almost as Bacchus himself, leads them in a drunken dance, singing a song to Bacchus, while Pompey contemplates cutting the boat adrift and liquidating them all.

Inwardly, Antony has accepted his place in the Rival Brothers pattern, exactly as Cleopatra divined it, and now he follows its law, as formulated in *Macbeth*. He separates from Octavia, giving her his reasons for his sudden quarrel with her (and now his) brother Caesar, and returns to Egypt to 'make preparations for war'. This corresponds to the point at which Macbeth abandoned King Duncan, assumed fully the role of the irrational, 'inferior' brother, becoming the Boar and 'hot tyrant' in the 'lust' of Lady Macbeth planning the murder of Duncan. It also corresponds, in subtler ways, to the point at which Coriolanus took command of the army of Aufidius against Rome. Antony sets himself at the head of Cleopatra's army and allies, the kings of the earth (who sound, when Caesar recites the roll call of their names, more like a barbaric assembly of demons in Pandemonium), intending to depose that model of his own rational self, Octavius Caesar. In other words, what he formerly declared lightly, as little more than a flattering piece of gallantry, when he titled himself:

Thy soldier, servant, making peace or war
As thou affect'st

I. iii. 70–1

he now accepts seriously, as his true feelings and his fate.

All this time, the Tragic Equation, which should have gone into action from his fully aware double vision of Cleopatra, remains suspended – and seems now more definitely arrested by his simultaneous role in the more urgent pattern of the Rival Brothers.

In its suspended condition, nevertheless, the Equation's action has been, in a sense, galvanized, by his marriage to Octavia. That was a clear, strong statement, if only temporary, of his moral, Adonis-like rejection of Cleopatra. And she duly reacted with savage fury. That vigilant spasm of the Equation, like the kick of a foetus, indicates what is developing – behind the screening action of the Rival Brothers.

As commander of Cleopatra's fleet, Antony now sails into battle against Caesar, at Actium, with Cleopatra's hand on the tiller of his flagship, as Lady Macbeth's hand rested, in effect, on Macbeth's shoulder when he set off across the paving stones, in the dark, 'with Tarquin's ravishing strides', to murder Duncan. This is Antony embarking on his mythic role, on the tragic plane, in the pattern of the Rival Brothers, as the Boar.

But it turns out to be one of those moments when the action of the tragic myth closes its jaws – only to find that both Antony and Cleopatra have somehow slipped into some other dimension. Cleopatra reveals that she is not after all an enraged Queen of Hell, with infinite, malevolent will, and Antony, it now appears, is not a Boar or a 'hot tyrant'.

When Cleopatra turns and flees at the very sight of Caesar's embattled fleet, Antony, 'his heart to [her] rudder tied by strings', turns and follows. The confrontation that was to prove Antony a true and dangerous Roman, even if as the irrational, rebellious, usurping brother leagued with the occult powers, now makes his self-deception manifest. He cracks, and shows the world that he is something else altogether. He creeps out of his Herculean ego, out of his 'experience, manhood and honour', and openly flees after the Queen – like a child after its mother.

This revelation of what he truly is, and of what his true feelings nakedly are, has taken Antony himself (as it took Coriolanus) by surprise. In despair, he has to acknowledge to Cleopatra:

> o'er my spirit
> Thy full supremacy thou knew'st, and that
> Thy beck might from the bidding of the gods
> Command me.
>
> III. ix. 58–61

and he accepts, in the shock of the self-exposure and the shame, that he is no longer the warrior champion of the god Hercules. He sends a schoolmaster (as if he himself were no longer a military general but a boy), asking Caesar to let him live quietly in Egypt, or as a private man in Athens.

In other words, he has renounced his claim to be any part of the tragic world of the Roman power struggle, and of Roman values. But it is not clear yet what else he might be. From the Roman point of view he is simply a washed-up old 'ruffian', a great Roman gone to the dogs, who has let Cleopatra destroy him. He has resoundingly confirmed their lowest opinion of him as a 'strumpet's fool'.

At this point it seems that Antony might have dropped out of the Roman tragic plane altogether, and escaped its consequences by becoming a nobody. But when he rallies, and suddenly resumes his Herculean self, sending a challenge to the victorious Caesar to meet him in single combat, his aide-de-camp Enobarbus is aghast:

> I see men's judgements are
> A parcel of their fortunes. . .
>
> III. xi. 31–2

and recognizing the emptiness of Antony's old Roman self, begins to think of deserting him.

But as Antony's spirits recover, he wakes up to his new situation. Because the shattering of his Herculean self-confidence has exposed him to what he truly feels, and therefore to his helpless dependence on Cleopatra's love, for the first time in the play, the Tragic Equation begins to move, as the bomb of his vulnerability begins to tick. Everything that he knows of Cleopatra's licentious past, of her cunning, and — so painfully confirmed by her flight at Actium — of her self-serving inconstancy, now gathers to a head, like an inflammation. And his Roman self-respect, his awareness of what he has forgone for her sake, beginning to hurt him,

> Have I my pillow left unpress'd in Rome,
> Foreborne the getting of a lawful race
> And by a gem of women . . . ?
>
> III. xi. 106–8

muster like the white cells, the phagocytes. Since his part in the Rival Brothers has collapsed so strangely, and his assault, as the Boar, has not merely failed but has been transmogrified, so ludicrously, to the scurrying of a 'doting mallard', now at last — towards the end of Act Three — he falls into the jaws of the Tragic Equation.

Accordingly, the play jumps into action. Surprising her as she allows Caesar's envoy to kiss her hand, the Roman Antony can no longer protect himself from the double vision. The madness overwhelms him, and, right on cue, the tirade begins to batter Cleopatra:

> You have been a boggler ever,
> But when we in our viciousness grow hard —
> O misery on't — the wise gods seal our eyes,
> In our own filth drop our clear judgements; make us
> Adore our errors; laugh at us while we strut
> To our confusion . . .
> I found you as a morsel, cold upon
> Dead Caesar's trencher: nay, you were a fragment
> Of Gnaeus Pompey's, besides what hotter hours
> Unregister'd in vulgar fame, you have

Luxuriously pick'd out. For I am sure
Though you can guess what temperance should be,
You know not what it is

III. xi. 110–22

The apocalyptic horrors begin to break through, as usual.

my good stars, that were my fomer guides,
Have empty left their orbs, and shot their fires
Into the abysm of hell . . .

III. xi. 145–7

Alack! our terrene moon
Is now eclips'd; and it portends alone
The fall of Antony.

III. xi. 153–5

This is still not quite the real thing however. As the Tragic
Equation seizes Cleopatra – as a Queen of Hell – in these words of
Antony's, she manages to elude it. By sheer sexual magic, and a
shrewd understanding (an Isis-like understanding, which no earlier
Shakespearean heroine has possessed) of the need behind his
outburst, Cleopatra is able to defuse his frenzy. Within moments,
like a reassured child, Antony is promising what the audience (and
Cleopatra, and Enobarbus) realize is now impossible: that he will
this time take on the role of the Boar in earnest, and be 'treble-
sinewed', etc. Cleopatra pretends to rejoice that Antony is 'himself
again', but Enobarbus, seeing that the 'noble ruin of her magic' is
no longer recognizable as the Herculean Antony he served
formerly, decides to leave him.

Meanwhile, in spite of his shallow euphoria, the Tragic Equation
still has Antony in its grip. Though he seems to have escaped it, he
has merely ceased for a while to feel it – under Cleopatra's
anaesthetic touch. In fact, this momentary opening of the jaws is
only turning him – to be swallowed.

The next three scenes dramatize the further, now vertiginous,
dissolution of Antony's Roman ego. Most of his army, melting
from him, has gone over to Caesar, which is to say that most of his
external Roman integrity has returned to Rome.

In the next scene, his valedictory farewell to 'three or four

[310]

servitors', which reduces them to tears, ritualizes the bankruptcy of both his past and his future, and the premonitions of his ultimate disintegration. It decides Enobarbus, who now leaves him. And finally, most ominously, his tutelary god, Hercules himself, leaves him.*

The second battle seems like a fresh start – but obviously it takes place in a changed world. Antony is armed by his servant Eros and by Cleopatra. His victory surprises both sides. On this tragic plane, however, it resembles the cruel playfulness of Fortune, reassuring him with a last success before crushing him utterly.

It has the immediate effect, however, of releasing his 'total, unconditional' love for Cleopatra, in an exultant outburst of adoration. After that preceding misfire of the Tragic Equation, where she spellbound his Tarquinian frenzy, this sets Antony up again for a new (and at last uncontrollable) double vision.

Having relinquished the Herculean Roman 'absolute soldiership' that he has by land, and once more committing his fortunes to Cleopatra's fleet (which has already been adopted by the swallows that love summer, the bird that Isis became when she mourned the slain Osiris), he is betrayed again, this time irrevocably. Her fleet simply joins Caesar's. Then the Tragic Equation closes on Antony. He re-enters his frenzy against Cleopatra, and his tirade erupts with the authentic lava:

>   All is lost!
> The foul Egyptian has betrayed me . . .
>
> IV. X. 22–3

>   Triple-turned whore, 'tis thou
> Hast sold me to this novice, and my heart
> Makes only wars on thee . . .
>
> 26–8

>   when I am reveng'd upon my charm
> I have done all . . .
>
> 29–30

---

*In Shakespeare's source, Plutarch's *Life of Antony*, it is the god Dionysus who forsakes Antony. Shakespeare's manipulative aware- ness of the role of these gods in his design is revealed by his substitution of Hercules for Dionysus at this point.

> Betray'd I am
> O this false soul of Egypt! This grave charm
> Whose eyes beck'd forth my wars, and call'd them home,
> Whose bosom was my crownet, my chief end,
> Like a right gipsy, hath, at fast and loose,
> Beguil'd me to the very heart of loss . . .
>
> 37–42

> The witch shall die:
> To the young Roman boy she hath sold me, and I fall
> Under this plot: she dies for it . . .
>
> 60–2

> She hath betray'd me, and shall die the death.
>
> IV. xii. 26

Cleopatra recognizes the fatal character of the real thing, and even identifies it,

> the boar of Thessaly
> Was never so emboss'd . . .
>
> IV. xi. 2–3

as she flees for her life. The Tragic Equation, inherent in his Roman Adonis ego from the beginning of the play, now completes its course by burning out the Roman Antony and itself together (in the image of Hercules dying in the flames of the shirt given to him by his wife).

Cleopatra flees to her tomb (as if – according to the Equation's law – he had killed her), and sends him word that she has killed herself. Thereupon Antony – like Othello – kills himself.

Cleopatra's death, as required by the Tragic Equation, then follows.

The deferred Equation begins and completes itself within about a fifth of the play (end of Act Three plus Act Four). The *Macbeth*-like pattern of the Rival Brothers, in which Antony fails to perform his part, also begins and ends essentially within about a fifth of the play (end of Act Two, plus most of Act Three, though it revives, spasmodically, through Act Four). The success of the play acted as Antony's tragedy depends largely on how powerfully these two mechanisms can be vitalized. In practice, the rest of the drama is comparatively inactive and even, as I remarked, operates in such a way that it seems to baffle or relax the tension of the parts that are active. It does this, I suggested, by lifting Antony and Cleopatra clear of the bite of the action, at crucial moments. And perhaps, even more effectively, by pervading the Roman tragic world with the light of a transcendental world, in which those imperative values of the Roman (Puritan) world, the world of the Rival Brothers and the Equation, become meaningless.

If one now approaches this drama from another direction, and isolates (as far as possible) the transcendental plane – that 'inactive' plane which floats within a particular waveband of the dramatic poetry – one sees that in regarding *Antony and Cleopatra* as the tragedy of the Herculean Roman commander one is looking at the wrong play, or, at least, at only half the play, the half which, according to the plays he now went on to write, was for Shakespeare already of secondary concern.

Antony and Cleopatra as a theophany

When the action of the tragic plane is examined through the transforming poetry of the transcendental plane the most significant change appears in what the Romans regard as Antony's irrational self, the lecher who had

> become the bellows and the fan
> To cool a gipsy's lust.
> *Antony and Cleopatra*, I. i. 9–10

At his first appearance, this 'strumpet's fool' declares a different kind of love. This is neither the Herculean ego, who is the supreme warrior of Rome, and one of the triumvirate, nor the irrational philanderer who neglects his political career, revelling in Egypt. This is a third Antony, who simply sweeps aside Rome, together with Rival Brother and Tragic Equation:

> Let Rome in Tiber melt, and the wide arch
> Of the rang'd empire fall! Here is my space.
> Kingdoms are clay; our dungy earth alike
> Feeds beast as man; the nobleness of life
> Is to do thus; when such a noble pair
> And such a twain can do't,
>
> I. i. 33–8

as if nothing mattered but Cleopatra's love for him and his for her, which he declares infinite.* This could sound a little hollow, like a prodigal amorist's facile hyperbole, nothing more than a form of sexual display — and indeed Antony himself (who wishes he had never seen her) seems to regard it as not much more, while Cleopatra teases him for the indulgent hypocrisy of it. It turns out, however, to be the speech of his elemental being — the self that chooses and lives out his ultimate fate, the speech of the 'divine' Antony who not only sweeps aside the Roman Antony but eventually, in the very end, throws him away, and, accepting all the failings (betrayals, etc.) of the human Cleopatra as an aspect of the 'divine' Cleopatra, loves her, in spite of everything, with 'total, unconditional' love. In other words, it turns out to be the 'divine' love language of the consort of the Great Goddess. Antony is the pre-Puritan adoring and adored Adonis, in so far as Cleopatra is Venus, the undivided Great Goddess as she is portrayed in the sumptuous description that Enobarbus gives of her (II. ii. 199–248). And in so far as she is more specifically Isis, the Great Goddess of the Egyptian pantheon, with whom she identifies herself, Antony becomes Osiris. In that inner world, their love is beyond moral division, and transcends tragedy. It is this which lifts them, subjectively, out of the tragic fate in which they are physically involved.

Without describing the unfolding of this transcendental nature, which they share, through each epiphany, it is enough (for the sake of the limited argument which I am following) to show how it modifies Antony's roles in the Tragic Equation and the Rival Brothers on the tragic plane.

I noted how the two planes, fused together in the opening scene, gradually tear apart as Antony's Osirian/Dionysian nature becomes more aware of itself and emerges into the open, is forced into the open. Immersed, as he is, in his narrow Roman conception of his two selves — as the Herculean admired champion on the one hand, and the irrational betrayer of his Roman honour on the other — this happens without Antony being clearly aware of it. Though his true love nature decided, for instance, the moment he married Octavia, that he must leave her and return to Egypt, he obeys without any conscious understanding of the real character of his love for the Egyptian Queen. He translates it crudely into Roman terms: 'I' the east my pleasure lies' — as if he were,

*Unmistakably, this speech takes up where the reborn Lear left off in: 'Come, let's away   to prison . . .' (King Lear, v. iii. 8–19).

[314]

indeed, nothing more than a self-indulgent, besotted wastrel, winking at his own irresponsibility. In fact he is obviously in the grip of that other self, the divine self which, by 'diminishing' his rational brain, blinding him to all consequences, seizing every pretext not merely to quarrel with Caesar but to find reason to declare war on him, now takes control of his fate.

In effect, this is the first decisive separation of the two planes, and the beginning of the inversion of values which transforms everything.

When Antony rejects Octavia, it is a curious reversal of the usual Tragic Equation's Adonis-like rejection. In this case, rather than the rational Adonis rejecting the Queen of Hell, the irrational Boar is rejecting the chaste Lucrece figure. Yet this is more than a minor, contrapuntal harmonic of the usual pattern, as appears in what follows. Strictly according to the Tragic Equation's law, there promptly emerges from the rejected Octavia's humiliation an enraged attacker, as if her brother Caesar were a kind of rational albino Boar, charging Antony, and as if Antony had become some kind of irrational black Adonis.

Which is exactly what he has become. Before he deserted Octavia, Antony revealed himself in his Egyptian Bacchus persona, in the Bacchanals with his fellow triumvirs on Pompey's barge. Now, having finally cast off his Roman allegiance, and emerged against Caesar, openly in command of the forces of one whom Caesar and Rome regard as a pure Queen of Hell, he has, as I described, assumed the Macbeth-like role of the Boar — determined to topple the Roman Adonis figure. But by the same change of worlds, from Roman to Egyptian, he has also decisively changed something in himself. He is no longer merely the despised, self-indulgent lover of Cleopatra the witch. He has declared himself as the reigning consort of the Queen of a great, sacred kingdom, her

> soldier, servant, making peace or war
> As [she] affect'st.
>
> I. iii. 70–1

And because Cleopatra is the avatar of Isis, as she presents herself and is understood to be, Antony has become the avatar of Osiris — the Egyptian Dionysus, the African Bacchus, the black Adonis.

Antony himself is not aware of his mythic change, until Cleopatra deserts from the sea battle. He thought he was still within the Roman world. He thought he was the Boar, so to speak, in mid-charge against

Adonis Caesar, with the Queen of Hell at his shoulder. But when she flees, and reveals herself as something other than a remorseless, enraged Queen of Hell, he finds that his Roman martial substantiality melts away with her. Having, as a rebellious, irrational brother, provoked and now become embroiled in the conflict of the Rival Brothers of the Roman world, he finds he can no longer live up to it. To his own astonishment, and that of his whole army, he finds he is no longer a Hercules.

For a while, he has no idea what is happening to him. What he is experiencing, in fact, is the tearing apart, within himself, of the two gods. In his bewildered dismay, he is a little like the 'swan's down feather' stuck on the full tide, that 'neither way inclines', between the two mutually incompatible roles, in the meeting and mixing zone of the two mythologies.

Then, as he turns and follows Cleopatra, he understands that he has become something else, whose element is water, like the dolphin who showed his back for a moment in that first scene of the play, with its 'Let Rome in Tiber melt', and its 'new heaven, new earth', and who later sent Cleopatra the treasure of an 'orient pearl'.

What emerges now, like a new country from under the waves, is the transcendental Egyptian world, where the Rival Brothers have changed places. Antony is now the black Adonis, surrogate of the streaming Osiris, the god of the living water and the green leaf, the one who has to be slain, while Caesar approaches with a speed 'beyond belief', as Set, the malignant, inferior brother, 'the black pig', whose assault will succeed.

What now remains, for this Osirian Antony, is for him to free himself, wholly and finally, from that obsolete Herculean Roman Antony, and emerge as his true self, the universal love god, consort of the Goddess of Complete Being, in so far as that can be incarnated in the body of the middle-aged Roman warrior, lover of a middle-aged, reckless, fearful queen.

In this way, as I remarked, while the drama portrays the self-destruction of the great Roman Antony on the tragic plane, it becomes, on the transcendental plane, a theophany, the liberation of Antony's Osirian Divine Love nature, under the 'magical' influence of the completeness of Cleopatra's. The play is shaped like one of Yeats's gyres. It begins with the love god fully formed but unacknowledged, trapped within the self-ignorant, military Herculean *bon viveur*, who is still confidently wrestling for political control of the Roman world. It ends with the crushed, empty armour of the former Herculean warrior, like an empty chrysalis, while the liberated love god, like an iridescent new winged being, lies in the lap of the Goddess, his love 'total and unconditional', reunited beyond life and death (in the high tomb) with the adoring Goddess.

The point of cross-over, the 'waist' of the gyre, occurs in the scene division between the mysterious departure of the god Hercules from Antony's camp and Antony's rousing Eros to arm him for the second battle.

Shakespeare found Eros in Plutarch, where he appears at this point in the story, fulfilling the same role as in the play. Shakespeare (unlike Plutarch) had introduced him to the audience once earlier on. Eros is to Antony's Osirian self rather what Enobarbus is to his Herculean self. He enters here, as Antony's sole remaining servant, in an episode that brings the news of Enobarbus's desertion to Caesar. On his earlier appearance, Eros brought the news – to Enobarbus – of Caesar's deposing of Lepidus, which left the Empire between Caesar and Antony. By precipitating the quarrel between Caesar and Antony, this exposed the incompatibility, within Antony, between Hercules and Osiris (and incidentally defined the opposite roles of Enobarbus and Eros).

Accordingly, immediately after the god Hercules's departure, it is left to Eros to prepare the new god for war. The scene opens with Antony's cry:

Eros! Mine armour, Eros!

IV. iv. I

Eros then arms Antony, helped by Cleopatra, who does not know which bit of armour goes where, and wishes Antony had stayed in bed. From the point of view of this new deity – this new controller of Antony's life – the unexpected, easy victory of this second battle is less the demonstration of Fate's deceitful giving a little before taking everything, than a symbolic manifestation of the miraculous power of Divine Love, simply. The realistic Cleopatra is pityingly aware that Antony is no longer a warrior. But in their supernatural-seeming victory, they rise once more together above the Roman world. Cleopatra becomes the 'great fairy', the 'day o' the world' that rides 'triumphing' on Antony's heart, while he has become 'Lord of lords, O infinite virtue', and they bestow on a common soldier the royal armour that resembles the sun's chariot – like high gods, making their servants kings.

After his subsequent defeat, Antony, raging against Cleopatra, is alone with Eros. He punctuates his fury with repeated despairing cries – as if into the abyss – to Eros. He repeats the name twenty times in some 150 lines, wringing every inflection out of it. As if, in these last torments of shedding his Herculean shirt of Nessus, he were calling for divine help from that new, greater, immortal self. Eros stands helpless beside him, while Antony burns and melts, smokes and evaporates into 'a rack', indistinct

> As water is in water,
>
> IV. xii. 11

flinging off the last shards of his red-hot Roman karma, with:

> Unarm Eros, the long day's task is done,
>
> IV. xii. 34

as his heart, enlarging to its divine dimension, 'cracks' its 'frail case' (though even in the first speech of the play it was bursting 'the buckles on his breast').

This moment corresponds to Lear's stripping off in the storm. And like a Hermes, Eros then leads Antony into the afterlife, dying first (showing the way), where he will be reunited with the Goddess whom the last convulsions of his Roman ego rejected.

Shakespeare nowhere else found an image of such perfect fullness for the simultaneity of the tragic and the transcendental in the unworldliness of erotic love. Looking speculatively back to *Romeo and Juliet* (that other bookend), one sees how the symmetrical opposition of the two plays enhances this theme of transcendence in *Antony and Cleopatra*. The middle age of Antony and Cleopatra, the leathery toughness and battle-scarred wariness of their imperious egos, are themselves irreducible symbols of the incompatibility between the 'human' nature of personal life and the elemental nature of 'total, unconditional' love. Romeo and Juliet, though their love was hunted out of the world through a double suicide in a tomb, might have lived on to even more spectacular passions than the one they died for: almost as if they were too young to have personal lives, still egoless, as if they had nothing yet to transcend. As if they died, like an image of the sexual act, in a biological, rather than a transcendental, exaltation.

If Antony and Cleopatra had died confined to the tragic plane, within that Roman tragic dimension of their actions – in other words, if Cleopatra's role as Isis had been no part of Shakespeare's imagination, and if Antony's expression of his love had been limited to secular, rhetorical terms – this entire dimension of transcendence would have been absent from the play, as it is absent from *Timon* and *Coriolanus*. Or it would have had to be introduced by some death–rebirth mechanism within the plot, as it is in *The Tempest* (and as in *Pericles*, *Cymbeline* and *The Winter's Tale*). But the unique historical actuality of Cleopatra's role as the incarnation of Isis, and of Egypt's King as the incarnation of Osiris, enabled Shakespeare to do the impossible.

The final 'double' tableau (the slain god in the arms of the mourning Goddess, and the Goddess with a sacred 'infant' at her breast), which first appeared at the end of *Venus and Adonis*, is the Shakespearean *pietà* which Antony inherits by nature (but which Lear had to earn by hideous rebirth struggles). All the components are here, in one form or another. Like Adonis, Antony becomes a 'dragonish' cloud that fades into nothing. But his blood, instead of flowing into a flower, flows back into his Osirian/Dionysian self – the serpent, dying simultaneously on to the tragic plane (in the nets of Roman history, as a failed hero) and on to the transcendental plane (as a divinity, nestled at the breast of the Goddess of Complete Being). (Serpent and Flower are one, and both are Antony.)

Considered from the point of view of its position in the evolutionary tragic series, *Antony and Cleopatra* therefore, as I have said, occupies a special place in Shakespeare's steady advance towards his solution of the Tragic Equation. It marks the point of substantial transformation between those plays in which man destroys himself and his world through his misunderstanding and rejection of Divine Love, and those in which Divine Love redeems him in spite of his misunderstanding and its consequences.

In a sense, of all the plays, again (perhaps) because of Cleopatra's historical divine role, it is the most religious in substance. The other thirteen dramatize the tragedy of the man forced to perform and attempt to repair the delusions of the morally tyrannous god that he has created in the image of his own rationality. But *Antony and Cleopatra* is the tragedy of the God of Love himself, the tragedy of Eros, compelled to suffer not only the cruel moral tyranny of that other god, but also the inescapable tragedy of being an Immortal, the God of 'immortal longings', the God of Life itself in the mortal body.

This makes the play (rather like *Macbeth*) a hugely magnified examination of one particular moment in the Tragic Equation. When the 'total, unconditional' Divine Love of the idyllic Adonis, who is blissfully happy with his Divine Beloved, encounters the exacting demand of his own Puritan ego, then the dolphin falls into the hands of the fishermen. But though they carve up the living body, with suffering in every stroke of the blade, they cannot touch the divine nature – they can only liberate it.

At the same time, it could be said that the play's overall pattern once again follows the Tragic Equation. Caesar, as an Adonis, rejects the world of Cleopatra (by implication, the Roman world rejects it). Antony, as the Boar of Cleopatra, attempts a Macbeth-style coup, infusing Caesar with the 'madness' which brings him, as a Tarquin, against them both and which ends – as all the other tragedies proper end – by the Goddess (and her consort) being destroyed. This pattern, on this level, is obviously only a controlling outline in the worldly perspective (in which Goddess and love god must always die), but it is visible enough.

PART III

The Transformation of
the Tragic Equation
in the Last Plays

INTRODUCTION

The impossible thing

In *Othello*, the question is left hanging: how if Desdemona had survived and returned to Othello after he had come to his senses? Given the relentless emphasis of that play, the question might seem irrelevant. Yet it interested Shakespeare. And in *King Lear*, he produces his most formidable work trying to answer it.

I described the reunion in the Lear/Cordelia story as a mutation of the old-style Equation. It is a mutation in seeming to have been wrung out of the plot, by sheer pressure of necessity. Lear seems to have no alternative. And the key factor in the mutation is that when Lear repents, Cordelia is still alive.

At the corresponding point in *Hamlet*, Ophelia is dead. At the corresponding point in *Othello*, Desdemona is dead. For those heroes, the Tragic Equation concludes in a dead end, and they find no way to break out beyond it. So they die, corrected but unredeemed, in the cul-de-sac of the Equation, like the caterpillar in the cabbage. But in *King Lear*, Cordelia's survival opens that dead end and gives Lear power to spread wings beyond it, into his rebirth and transformation.

This discovery rescues the hero (only temporarily, in Lear's case) from the tragic deadlock. The impossible has happened. For the time of his reunion with Cordelia, Lear seems to have undone the mechanism behind the Tragic Equation, and separated the loved and the loathed. Shakespeare has rescued the hero from his tragic destiny by giving him the very thing the Tragic Equation denied: his true self reborn – reunited with his beloved who is also reborn.

Shakespeare did not forget this, though he seems to have all but lost sight of it during the next two plays. But then, in the final group of dramas, the 'romances', he took up that mutation again, and thereafter made its development the centre of his concern.

Isolating it (from the momentum of the events that overwhelm it in *King Lear*), one can see that it did not just pop up out of nowhere. It had been reached, so to speak, by logical steps. I argued that he divined the double vision quite early, in the *Sonnets* and *Venus and Adonis*, but even then his compass needle quivered a steady direction. He was finding ways to steal the impossible happiness in his comedy weddings. Though maybe what he snatched there barely escaped what gave him the *Sonnets* and narratives. Those bedevilled courtships, the perverse ultimatums and mistakings, the pixilations and mischievous plottings that bewilder the courting lovers in their mazes, and tangle them in their briers, are playful premonitions – as I describe elsewhere – of the tragic pattern slowly rising from the depths (cf. pages 488–97). But when the Tragic Equation finally sprawls on to the stage, the matrimonial instinct of his imagination becomes even more apparent. It is still able to master the impetuosity of *All's Well*, and even the stifled explosion of *Measure for Measure*.

Those logical steps obey Shakespeare's stubborn ethical compulsion, which in *As You Like It* and *All's Well* determined the ritual controls of their plot structure. They materialized, briefly, in the penitential first steps of the converted Duke Frederick, who was accompanied by his amanuensis Melancholy Jaques into the Underworld, and in Bertram's first 'reborn' steps from the 'fount' of Saint Jaques. And they committed Shakespeare to that almighty struggle with the ultimate enigma – from which he emerged in *King Lear* with this solution.

It could be said, remembering Duke Frederick and Jaques, that Lear's reunion with Cordelia is Frederick's first glimpse of the *Paradiso*. Or, if the seven tragedies (from *Hamlet* to *Antony and Cleopatra*) are likened less to the circles of Dante's *Inferno* and *Purgatorio*, and more to the seven valleys crossed by the thirty birds in Attar's *Conference of the Birds*, then Lear's last dazzled moments of bliss (like Macbeth's misinterpreted vision) are a proleptic encounter with the *Simurgh* – the egoless revelation of the true and divine self.

But in *King Lear*, Lear's happiness is not only the impossible thing, denied by every demon power on the tragic plane, it is also ephemeral. And this is where one sees with great clarity the distinction that now becomes essential to his drama. The Tragic Equation operates on the tragic plane and can never escape it. But the mutation is a breakthrough on to that new plane: the transcendental plane.

The tragic plane is the realistic plane, where the divided Goddess will always recombine, with some tragic result or other. The transcendental plane is a subjective plane, where the intolerable tragic laws of the realistic plane can be sublimated, transformed, experienced otherwise, within a 'spiritual space' inaccessible to the cruelty of those tragic laws.

In *King Lear*, Shakespeare's marvellously full objectification of the relationships between those two planes is felt as a superior and terrible realism, a Job-like realism. In Job, those laws of the indivisibility of the Goddess appear as the inscrutable mystery of the almightiness of God (not to be divided into Good and Evil, but to be altogether accepted and worshipped as glorious). Job's joyful acceptance (beyond the divisive judgement of Shakespeare's tragic heroes, beyond the double vision, that is) transcends the intolerable. In *King Lear*, the question is whether Lear gets to that point. After the tyrannous confined ego that created his tragedy has disintegrated, one might say, he attains a condition where the intolerable ceases to matter – so long as Cordelia is alive.

It is an emergency solution and, in the circumstances, the best available. It is presumably an emergency solution for Shakespeare himself. (Presumably in these works he was fighting towards his own salvation and inner survival.) He had a personal motive, inevitably, to secure the gains of this mutation. But he had a purely dramatic one, too, precisely in this: one feels not that Lear's impossible happiness is unreal (in any sense), but that it is the ultimate refinement, almost an apotheosis, of the most harrowing aspect of the tragic situation: the hero's mismanagement of the divine opportunity.

In spite of this, Shakespeare did nothing further with it immediately. After *King Lear*, things looked more hopeless than ever. From the audience's point of view, that germinal new mutation of the tragic fate, in which the hero's victim survives to redeem him, seemed to have died with the old mad King. Yet it reveals its quietly working presence behind the next two plays in a striking way, as I remarked earlier.

Timon is the first play of the tragedies in which the hero's madness fails to result in the death of the Female (surrogate – Athens). And then, in *Coriolanus*, the Female survives absolutely.

This survival of the Female tracks Shakespeare's hidden direction, which is confirmed in the transcendental deaths of Cleopatra and Antony. By the time he comes to compose *Cymbeline*, it is evident that he has salvaged the mutation, and formalized it distinctly. And here he gives it a play all to itself. Keeping the hero's victim alive, until the hero returns to his senses, now occupies all Shakespeare's dramatic imagination and skill.

Root meanings of the Equation

To digress a little: it is not hard to see this gruelling development in a wider perspective, and in a more 'natural context'. Earlier, I remarked that Shakespeare had shifted the religious terms of the Goddess religion and the Goddess-destroyer back into 'psychological terms, or rather back into the psycho-biological human mystery from which these religions and myths sprang in the first place'. The word 'psycho-biological' indicates a territory none too well defined. It begs fewer questions, maybe, to talk about the root meanings of the Mythic Equation – as if the Equation were a word. The drama of woman's fertility then becomes a root meaning. The Goddess's double nature takes on biological actuality in the light and dark of the womb's lunar cycle,* the anabolic and catabolic phases of the egg's life which dominate the immediate subjective being of all women and are watermarked (blood-printed) into the feminine component (and the original body mass) of all men. As the ideal image of her consort (the inseminator) and as the ideal image of her child (the crown of her divine activity), Adonis lives the full possibility of her monthly phase of creative life. As the sacrificed god he dies her monthly destruction. This most sacred and impassioned of all biological paradigms is projected, fittingly, on to the annual cycle of plants and creatures. The divine life of Adonis is thereby identified with the elemental germ of all organic life. This too becomes a root meaning. And one can see that Shakespeare makes full use of this meaning in particular. In each work of the tragic sequence, his crucial dramatic event is a death and a magical rebirth, where the Flower, flushed with blood, combines the Underworld power of the Goddess (and her avatar the Boar) with Adonis, to create Tarquin, hero and sufferer of the tragedy, which thereby becomes a parable of the heroic doom of all conscious organisms (no matter what the genus). In this sense, the Equation turns out to be the 'plot' of the drama of organic life: life itself is what terrifies living things and possesses them with their various forms of madness, and exhausts them with their struggles to control and contain it and to secure its subjective essence of joy.

*Extensively discussed in Penelope Shuttle and Peter Redgrove, *The Wise Wound*, London: Gollancz, 1978 and Peter Redgrove, *The Black Goddess and the Sixth Sense*, London: Bloomsbury, 1987.

As this little family of root meanings emerges into human consciousness, they become more distinctly formulated, and the problem of containment emerges as a moral problem. At the same time, the drama suffers a characteristic distortion. The peculiar division of the sexes, which bestows on woman the miraculous power to create man out of her blood, while it deprives man of any such ability, and which deposits the infant male, through his helpless, formative years, into the possessive control of the Female, injects a peculiar conflict into the situation – and this peculiarity, the implication of this conflict, might be called a root meaning of the Equation.

In the simplest terms, the sequence of the growing boy's attitudes towards his mother becomes a root meaning in that it parallels so closely the tragic hero's attitudes, in the Equation, towards the Female. (The myth of tragedy, like the myth of religion, magnifies the extreme case.) I have traced the other parallel to this sequence: the succession of phases in the Goddess religion, where the adoring, adored Divine Child grows up into a Marduk (or Jehovah, or Reformation Jehovan Christ) whose act of suppressive, severing violence against the former beloved (the Goddess) can never be violent enough (witness Holy Writ) simply because her possessive love power, though overthrown and rejected once, is, like life, indestructible, and will always threaten to resume control. This religious parallel, as I have said, is also a root meaning of the Equation and inseparable from it.

But Shakespeare goes further when he divines the psycho-biological consequences of that Marduk/Jehovah/Puritan innovation, and shows how Adonis's attempt to consolidate his adolescent, precarious independence from the Mother Goddess in a once-and-for-all act of severing violence against the occult power of her paralysing love is simultaneously commandeered and redirected by the uncontrollable new sexual energy which is searching for union with the unknown Female (see page 180 and page 220): the act of ultimate, suppressive violence becomes inextricably fused with the act of supreme sexual union. This single 'madness', of the two simultaneous, contradictory, elemental needs, which provides the plot pattern of *Lucrece* and the 'tragic' second half of the prototype Equation, can also be regarded as a root meaning.

The spontaneous, universal, archaic nature of this conflict is even more nakedly apparent (as a root meaning of Shakespeare's Equation) in the fundamental myth of the ritual life among aboriginal Australians.

That drama begins where Goddess religion begins, with woman as the Mother of Life, possessing the greatest magic of all – that power to create men and women out of her blood. It can be imagined how the fact of this ability confronted the primate male mind at the dawn of speculation. And what a profound shock it must have delivered to the primate male ego. The mythic action starts here, where the men (who realize that they are without the only thing that seems to matter, the power to create new life) steal the women's creative magic.

They do this by creating a world of ritual, a world of manipulated imagination, in which they take possession in artificial form (the gash and blood of sub-incision, sacred songs, secret myths, dances, etc.) of all the magical, creative powers of the women. They exclude the women from this world, and at the same time suppress and fragment their community, isolating them from each other and from the tribe, particularly at the great, feared magical moments of menstruation and parturition, while convincing them that these acts are unclean. In the mass of myths and stories that incorporate this violent expropriation, this war of conquest, in which the Female's magical, terrifying reproductive powers are stolen and transformed into a new ritual world ruled over by the men, a world in which the women are powerless, the whole strange business is encoded in literal, primary detail.

The same conflict, same ritual takeover, even the same compulsive details of behaviour and symbolism, can be traced through other traditions all over the globe. The battle between Marduk and Tiamat, in which the god creates his universe out of the magical Tiamat's remains, is like an Australian story from this matrix.* And when Prospero solemnizes a betrothal that is almost hysterically hedged with sexual taboos and observances, in a magical world and with magical powers that are stolen (effectively, in Ariel) from the original Great Witch Sycorax, he re-enacts and reaffirms that conquest by which the powerless, deprived aboriginal male fought his way clear of the womb's magnetic mystery, and asserted his dominance over the incomprehensible powers of the Creatrix, the Goddess of Complete Being.†

*The theft of woman's ultimate magic appears here in the baldest terms: in Marduk's (and Jehovah's) new universe, mankind is 'created' not out of the blood of the Female (the Goddess), but out of that of her 'champion' (her son and consort), Kingu (or Christ). As in the aboriginal mythos, man is properly born (the youth is initiated, reborn) only out of the male blood of circumcision (sub-incision): the Son of Man.

†In an article in *Man* (March 1983, Vol. 18), Chris Knight excavates this basic pattern from the Australian myths and rituals – incidentally identifying the main features – the storm, the coalescence of the 'monster' (of rejected female sexuality) with the male

Taken strictly, this 'parallel' confines Shakespeare's tragedies to the domestic drama surrounding adolescence. Likewise it confines the Catholic and Protestant religions to the metaphysics of infancy and adolescence – which one might hesitate to accept. Still, it seems that both situations could be helped by a third myth. What both Reformation Christianity and Shakespearean tragedy seem to lack is a bridging initiation rite, a mythic or symbolic passage, into a third phase.

The Reformation failed to find the myth of this third phase. But Shakespeare did find it, for his hero and heroine, in the last plays. His discovery of the missing third myth introduces the final phase of his work. His seven great tragedies brought him to it, almost as if they alchemized it out of their own intensities. And in fact, they brought him beyond it. In *Antony and Cleopatra*, the last of the seven, he opened a myth beyond that third myth, one in which his tragic hero embraced the whole nature of the Goddess, Queen of Hell specifically included, but only by becoming a god. After that it was sheer realism that returned him to a more practicable pattern of the transcendental solution – a human rather than a divine solution, a love union, in what turned out to be a Gnostic pattern, which, however aware of the perilous odds against it, was nevertheless (with enough self-control and understanding) workable as well as sacred.

In retrospect it can be seen that this third myth evolved partly from the Adonis myth itself, particularly from the double death of Adonis, in which he became a flower that was simultaneously the Boar-possessed Tarquin and the Divine Child at the breast of the Goddess. And partly, as I have said, it evolved from Shakespeare's own mystique of marriage. Later on I will show how this third myth relates to the Gnostic myth of Sophia (cf. pages 356–7). It is both an extra myth added to the two constituent myths of the Equation, and simultaneously a transformation of them. The muddy, dragonish tragic larva has suddenly split – and this shimmering nuptial insect rises out of it, in a halo.

The magician's task

The romances, then, are concerned with lifting the hero and heroine from the tragic plane, which has the weight of realism, to the transcendental plane, which has only the authority that subjective

—

hero, etc. – in a way that illuminates its family links to Shakespeare's Tragic Equation.

confidence can give it. Perhaps this explains the different specific gravity of the two groups of plays.

Coincidental influences on this sudden change in style of play might have been decisive. If the plays that dramatize the Tragic Equation are viewed as a suite of diagnostic variations on the result of the divisive religious policy of Henry VIII and his daughter Elizabeth, then the romances adapt equally well to the religious policy of James, which seemed potentially more fluid and even reconciliatory. A more immediate factor, perhaps, was that in 1608, which most likely saw the first of these last plays, Shakespeare's company acquired the lease of the Blackfriars Theatre, where the comparatively exclusive audience and different stage conditions (and the box office takings which, per performance, were double those at the Globe) prompted a different kind of drama. The same year brought another no doubt (to Shakespeare) seismic event – the death of his mother. As it happened, these 'external' factors, especially the requirements and opportunity of the Blackfriars stage, combined to push his inner world the way it was going. But they did so, maybe, a little more abruptly, and at a slightly different angle, than he might have moved without them. The radical change, from tragedy-centred to theophany-centred drama, reveals the shift of his attention from the tragic madness and suffering of the doomed hero to the happy rescue of the hero's beloved (and himself) from his homicidal violence. Basically, this means that the centre of dramatic interest is transferred from the inner life of the doomed male to the inner life of the surviving female. Never again does Shakespeare allow his heroine to be killed. On the contrary, at each opportunity he now gives her a dazzling new life. The whole purpose of the last plays, one could believe, is to give her a dazzling new life.

Simultaneously, he delivers his final judgement against the 'crime' that formerly deprived her of her old one. Posthumus Leonatus, in *Cymbeline*, is the first of the tragic heroes to survive, and the first to undergo the full consequences, evil and good, of his delusion and attempted murder. Then in *The Winter's Tale*, after being judged and condemned in the very court where he, as judge, was judging and condemning ('look for no less than death') his wife and baby daughter, Leontes survives likewise, to experience the full consequences (the suffering, the remorse, and the spiritual transformation) of the Tragic Equation's 'crime'. With the bald (albeit divine) legalism of this trial and conviction, it could be said that Shakespeare's ethical purpose declares itself, almost obtrusively. In each of these dramas, *Cymbeline*, *Pericles* and *The Winter's Tale*, the denouement is idealized, transcendent, and lifts into a music that does seem unearthly, and that does attempt, as the hero in each case might say, with King Lear, to

> redeem all sorrows
> That ever I have felt.
> *King Lear*, v. iii. 268–9

But they precipitate, like a corrective, the disturbingly reopened questions of *The Tempest*.

Shakespeare's own attitude to his task as a dramatist seems to have changed in this final group of plays. From being a prophetic visionary, swept along in the dam-burst of historical forces, nakedly exposed to the glories and terrors of creation and human events, which puts *King Lear* in a category not far from the Book of Job, he seems, with *Cymbeline*, to step out of that and become more like a kind of Noah among the rising waters, the magus of a Gnostic, Hermetic ritual, or perhaps an ageing Berowne, staging for the surviving Dumaine and Longaville and surviving fellow initiates of that 'little academe' in *Love's Labour's Lost* the salvation of Love, rescuing that lost Female from the torrential, benighted, diabolized world of Jaldabaoth – which puts these desperate rituals in a category closer to *The Chemical Wedding of Christian Rosenkreutz*.

CHAPTER 5

THE TRAGIC HERO BROUGHT TO JUDGEMENT:
Cymbeline, Pericles, The Winter's Tale

The mutant emerges

Cymbeline: the tragic hero reborn

Pericles and the Gnostic myth of Sophia

The Tragic Equation in court

The Winter's Tale: the cry and the silence

The Winter's Tale: Leontes as the tragic error

The Winter's Tale:
the Tragic Equation becomes a theophany

The pattern of the Gnostic Coda in *The Winter's Tale*

Hermione's plea as the voice of Heaven and Earth

The mutant emerges

Among these four last plays, the first three separate themselves into a single distinct development which might be called the emergence and nuptial flight of Shakespeare's Theophany. In one sense, this development culminates in *The Winter's Tale*. In another sense, it is Shakespeare's preparation for what he reveals – or for what is revealed to him – in *The Tempest*. In this chapter, I trace this ultimate phase in the evolution of the Tragic Equation from *Cymbeline*, through *Pericles*, into *The Winter's Tale*. In *Cymbeline*, midwife-like, he eases it out of its larval armour, letting it emerge, a little stiffly, into the full, clear light. In *Pericles*, he nurses the strange form, still rather tentative, stretching out the surprising, perfect legs, uncrumpling the damp wings and unfurling the antennae. Finally, in *The Winter's Tale*, he lifts it into perfect flight. After that, in my closing section, I will attempt to show how, in *The Tempest*, he returns this last word of the Tragic Equation to Earth – or rather to the cup, or crucible, of a water lily, the ciborium of a lotus, perhaps, and zooms in, as it were, on the eyeball, the living, compound, prismatic window of this miraculous creature's inner world. Within that rainbow-fringed magnification the whole evolution of the tragedy of Divine Love, the long, convulsive history from Aaron onwards, can be seen folded into a single consummate design, like an Elizabethan knot-garden maze, with Venus and Adonis, glistening and pulsating, as the divine clue (or Minotaur), figured, as in a fountain sculpture, at the centre.

Cymbeline: the tragic hero reborn

In *Cymbeline*, Shakespeare's approach is new but his basic material is old. He begins with a simplified statement of the Tragic Equation. For this purpose, as in *The Winter's Tale* a little later, he requisitions the prototype basic model: the story of Othello's jealousy. The familiar features hurry past, as he squeezes this rehabilitated plot into two and a half acts, with a geometry of motivation so stark it seems perfunctory. The outline is simple.

The action takes place in Britain at approximately the time of Christ's birth. The British King Cymbeline's daughter, Imogen, has married Posthumus, her father's foster child, whose parents were Roman. Since the couple have managed to do this without Cymbeline's consent, the King, in a rage, has banished Posthumus to Italy (i.e. back to Rome).

Posthumus is an Adonis in the idyllic, innocent phase. Boasting of his wife's chastity, he excites the interest of Iachimo (as Collatine's boast – and proof – of his wife Lucrece's chastity excited Tarquin). On a wager with Posthumus, Iachimo visits England and attempts to seduce Imogen. Failing, he steals evidence enough to persuade Posthumus that he has succeeded. That is, like Iago, Iachimo deceives the hero into seeing the 'double vision'.

In his 'madness', Posthumus delivers a great tirade against Woman and orders his servant Pisanio to kill Imogen.

In England, Pisanio gives to Imogen a letter from Posthumus, which informs her that her husband has landed at Milford Haven in Wales. She sets out with Pisanio to meet him there. This should be Pisanio's opportunity to kill her. Instead, he confesses his errand to her, and to protect her, in the Welsh mountains, disguises her as a boy.

The Tragic Equation ends here, with Posthumus's Tarquinian 'madness', his intent to murder his wife Imogen, thwarted. But at this same point a Coda begins: the 'mutation' takes over.

In *Cymbeline*, Shakespeare seems to be fitting the pieces together tentatively. There is something token and rudimentary about all the characters except Imogen. His cool deliberation is very evident in the mechanism by which he contrives the necessary event that opens the Coda – the rebirth of Imogen and the rebirth of Posthumus.

He is particularly cool with Posthumus. Here again, he resorts to the Tragic Equation's kit of variants. If a redeemed Posthumus is to be reborn, the Tarquinian Posthumus must die. To facilitate this, Shakespeare divides him into his three main constituents, which are:

(i) The pre-Puritan Adonis, Imogen's loving consort – who is violently displaced at the Shakespearean moment of Iachimo's lie, when the Boar takes possession of him to create the Tarquin who condemns Imogen to death.

(ii) The Boar, externalized in the person of Cloten.

(iii) The true self, the redeemable Posthumus, knowing his first error and able to suffer for it.

Externalized in Cloten, the nature of Posthumus's animalized shadow – that second self – is clearly a primitive type of Tarquin. He is also a primitive type of usurping Rival Brother, a true *doppelgänger* who will be mistaken, by Imogen, for Posthumus himself.

As inferior Rival Brother, Cloten is (almost inevitably) motivated by a Queen of Hell, his mother the Queen. This unnamed witch plots to secure her stepdaughter Imogen as wife for Cloten, whose succession to the throne would then be assured (displacing Posthumus).

Cloten's role as Posthumus's Tarquinian self is carefully designed in ritual style. Dressed in Posthumus's own clothes, he follows Imogen to Milford Haven, intending to do the Tarquinian thing and rape her, and also intending to fulfil his destiny as Rival Brother by murdering Posthumus, seizing the 'soul' figure Imogen, and ravishing her on Posthumus's dead body.

This is the most regressive, merely brutish Boar figure that Shakespeare has created so far in the sequence. As the secret nature of Posthumus's tragic error and Tarquinian madness, he corresponds, contrapuntally, to that new spiritual refinement into which Shakespeare is lifting the Lucrece figure, Imogen. The more idealized the one, the more brutalized the other. And maybe this Cloten reveals how the Tarquin/usurping brother complex is shrinking back, within Shakespeare's imagination, towards its naked, nuclear form – Caliban.

Up to this point the Tragic Equation has provided all the material and motivation in the play. But here the pattern of the mutation takes control, and all negative energies are converted to positive, as the Coda begins to work on them.

Everything follows from the transformation that accompanies the death and rebirth of Imogen. First, Posthumus's attempt to murder her is converted, with the help of his servant, Pisanio, into her temporary sex change. She conceals her identity as a wife in the form of a pre-pubertal boy. This in itself is like a return to pre-birth, and it is interesting, remembering what happens in the other three romances, that from this point she gives the impression of being a child as well as an adult, and returns to Posthumus, eventually, almost as a daughter as well as a wife. As a boy, she is now adopted by the outlaws, who turn out (unknown to her) to be the King's long-lost sons – her two real brothers – and all live together in a cave.

The Witch Queen's attempt to deal real death now becomes the occasion of Imogen's mythic rebirth. The Queen has given Pisanio a poison, persuading him that it is a medicine, which he passes to Imogen as part of her first aid in the wilderness. Imogen drinks this and falls into a sleep like death. But the Queen had herself been deceived by the doctor who supplied her with the ingredients, and the potion is a sleeping draught merely. Nevertheless, Imogen's sleep appears like death to her brothers, who hold a funeral over her and mourn her. It is during this apparent death of Imogen that Cloten, searching for her, arriving like a belated, dogged golem projected from Posthumus's Tarquinian intent to murder her, is killed and beheaded by one of the brothers.

Both Imogen and, somewhere offstage, Posthumus are now reborn into different worlds. Posthumus, convinced by a bloody cloth that Pisanio has fulfilled his command and killed Imogen, resolves to die, fighting against the invading Romans whose ships have brought him, as a Roman, to Britain. He is reborn, that is, into a world beyond Imogen's death, seeking to punish his crime by his own penitential death. But Imogen (like Cordelia) has survived the Tarquinian frenzy, so his salvation (like Lear's) is possible.

Imogen wakes as virtually a prisoner of the Romans, who have arrived to chastise the King, her father – for refusing the tribute due to Rome. Having mourned over what she imagines to be Posthumus's headless body, she is born into a world beyond his death, and now merely survives in the power of the enemy, albeit as a favoured servant.

The Romano-British war, which moves across the background, gives an impression of unwieldiness to the play, until one views it as a metaphor of what is happening on the level of the Tragic Equation and the new Coda. It can then be seen to be a matrix of larger meanings, closely integrated with the relationship of Imogen and Posthumus. (The unwieldiness also has something to do with what certainly seems to be there: the external allegory, in which the plot, as a political-religious fantasia, celebrates the ideal reconciliation of the Roman and the English Churches, Imogen being the soul of England, her two brothers James's two sons, etc.)

But looking at this pattern purely from the point of view of the Tragic Equation, one sees that behind the British King's defiant rejection of the Roman Empire there lies the basic pattern in which the Puritan Adonis rejects the Great Goddess, or, to come even closer to Shakespeare's parable, the pattern in which Coriolanus, the furious proud warrior, rejected Rome and the Great Mother and the Sacred Bride. In this case, Cymbeline's rejection of Roman rule coincides, in time, with the overthrow of the rational by the irrational in Posthumus (the moment at the end of Act Two, in which his Tarquinian madness takes possession of him and he rejects Imogen) and its mouthpiece is accordingly Cloten. Cloten is therefore not only the *doppelgänger* of Posthumus's Tarquinian phase, he is the incarnation of the Tarquinian phase of the kingdom of Britain itself.

This double role of Cloten's works consistently up to his death. His beheading coincides with Posthumus's rebirth into sanity and repentance, and with Imogen's rebirth, and with the arrival of the Roman force which takes Britain back into the Empire.

Britain's rejection of Rome coincides, likewise, with the Princess Imogen's becoming a fugitive, hidden within Britain. When Rome reinvades, the lost 'soul' of Divine Order and of the Crown (being reborn, as I say) emerges as the personal servant of the Roman commander. And so on. Using the chemistry of the broader international recombination of (Protestant) Britain and (Catholic) Rome, Shakespeare works out the real physical reunion of Posthumus and Imogen. (Most curious of all, perhaps, in this reconciliation, are the implications of Cymbeline's letting

> A Roman and a British ensign wave
> Friendly together.
>
> *Cymbeline*, v. v. 481–2

If this is read as a gloss on Shakespeare's verbal device, that I discussed earlier (pages 148–9), whereby Roman and native British lineages are married, it opens another view into the relationship between Shakespeare's 'double' language and the psychological drama behind it.)

In this way Imogen and Posthumus are finally united beyond their utmost hope, and, as if beyond death, in the new reign of 'the understanding heart', where hostilities are resolved and enemies forgiven (except the Witch Queen, whose death, like Cloten's, has removed all impurities).

The ingenious symmetry of harmony and counterpoint in this intricate design can be followed into every detail. Several clues suggest that here too the drama can be read as the alchemical transformation of a single soul. Very much as *As You Like It* works as the purgation and remaking of Orlando, *Cymbeline* can be read as the sin and redemption of Posthumus, and the play gains, in coherence and consistency, if it is read in this way. Apparent superfluities become potent glands within the organism.

To a casual reading, the two brothers, Arviragus and Guiderius, seem rather redundant – though one can see that Imogen's great death and rebirth scene needs somebody out there in the Welsh mountains. But the details reveal the vital roles of this pair.

The first scene of the play, into which all the necessary exposition is packed, contains only seventy lines. About two-thirds of this is a condensed biography of the play's hero, Posthumus, in which the background of Britain's conflict with Rome, the King's fostering of the Roman orphan Posthumus, his banishment of Posthumus and why, and Posthumus's own special qualities, are clearly set forth as is necessary for the subsequent action. But tucked away into the middle of all this are four and a half lines concerning Posthumus's two brothers, both (Romans born) killed fighting against Rome.

These brothers are never heard of again until their ghosts appear, in Posthumus's dream, with the ghosts of their mother and father, where all rebuke Jupiter for allowing Posthumus to be deceived into rejecting Imogen, and call for him to be forgiven, and to be made happy.

Even there, the two brothers do no more than swell the ghostly chorus. Accordingly, in this first speech one might suppose them nothing more than odd ends of realistic detail thrown in to give biographical ballast to Posthumus's peculiar name. But a listener who remembers that fleeting mention of Jaques, the clever brother in the second sentence of *As You Like It*, might notice how the dialogue now steps directly from Posthumus to the two lost brothers of Imogen. These two brothers of hers take up the rest of the scene – fourteen lines.

Confident, by now, that tiny clues are as important in these plays of Shakespeare as in any much longer and much wordier detective story, one takes note that both Imogen and Posthumus, by some strange coincidence, have each of them two older brothers – Posthumus's being certainly dead, Imogen's being certainly lost, possibly dead.

Stepping back and surveying the wallchart of the whole play, one sees how Imogen's brothers emerge from the cave, like a graph line rearing up from the base line of the chart (below which everything is dead, unknown or unconscious). When Imogen is rejected, and as it were cast into the wilderness (by one appointed to murder her) and hunted by one who intends to rape her, these two brothers suddenly appear. They save her and administer her magical death and rebirth. Similarly, when Posthumus, in despair, searches for death in battle, again these brothers appear beside him, and together they turn the tide of the battle against the Romans. Finally, they reappear at the grand reconciliation scene, where they are recognized as the King's sons and Imogen's true brothers, and where, in the only remark they address to him, they claim Posthumus with the words:

> You holp us, sir,
> As you did mean indeed to be our brother,
> Joy'd are we that you are.
>
> v. v. 423–5

The suspicion occurs, naturally, that Imogen's living but lost brothers and Posthumus's dead brothers are perhaps not 'brothers' at all, but something else. And that they are not two pairs but one and the same pair (it is a curious fact, for instance, that Imogen's two brothers have four names) and that they belong – obtrusively – to a level on which the play is a symbolic ritual. Experimentally, one could suppose that they are two beings who somehow manifest themselves to both Posthumus and Imogen. In Posthumus, at the beginning of the action, they are 'dead'. They are 'dead' because they cannot help him. And they cannot help him, because he carries the potential – the blindness of that tragic error – to become a Tarquin and kill his own soul.

This 'imperfection' in his apparently total and unconditional love for Imogen is what brings about the whole 'tragedy' of the first part of the play and the suffering of the second. It is a barrier between himself and Imogen, i.e., between himself and the soul which he will try to kill. This 'self', with its imperfect love, is therefore in some way a 'dead self', or at least a doomed self, and therefore the reflections of these two brother figures, which it carries, appear to be dead.

This 'imperfection', again, is symbolized by Cymbeline's raging refusal to consecrate Posthumus's marriage to Imogen. Whatever Cymbeline's reasons, the marriage cannot be consecrated by the Crown of Divine Order because Posthumus is 'imperfect'. Banishing Posthumus, the King converts that psychological barrier – that 'imperfection' –

[341]

into geographical distance, where it promptly matures into the 'double vision' with Iachimo's help, and proceeds to the tragic crime.

Only after he has gone through the Tarquinian frenzy, committed the crime, and repented, will that 'imperfection' be exorcized. Accordingly, at that point, when he sincerely repents, seeking to punish himself by death in battle, the two 'dead' brothers will suddenly appear beside him – *alive*.

For Imogen, the brothers are merely lost. They are alive in that her love is perfect and alive and her loving self is alive (in the sense that Posthumus's love is conversely imperfect and his loving self therefore in some way dead). But the two brothers are inaccessible to her, because the flowing electrical power of her love is arrested – blocked by that insulating 'imperfection' in Posthumus's love for her.

Before Imogen can become aware of her brothers, therefore, Posthumus has to go through his Tarquinian madness, that Tarquin self has to die, and the 'insulation' be removed. The current of her love will then be able to flow, and the brothers who minister to her 'death' will minister to his 'rebirth'.

This interplay of the living and dead brothers only makes sense if Imogen and Posthumus are regarded as two halves of one being, like the soul and the ego, divided and essentially inaccessible to each other, though they belong only to each other, and strive only to become a single new self together.

The correspondence of one brother to Imogen and one to Posthumus (though both appear to both) is indicated by a detail: in all the tragic sequence only Imogen and Guiderius are identified by a mole – hers on her breast, his 'a sanguine star, a mark of note' on his neck. And the 'active' role of her love, in Posthumus's rebirth, is symbolized by the fact that it is Guiderius who beheads Cloten.

The death and rebirth of Posthumus and Imogen are in this way simultaneous. The soul dies from its separateness as a soul, the ego from its separateness as an ego, and both are reborn into the single self, though this reunion takes time to work out on stage through the inertia of characterization and plot.

The two brothers can now be seen to resemble the two figures familiar in accounts of paranormal experience as the guardian angels, and throughout religious systems – the Dioscuri: the spirits of the polarity of being – who appear in the most fundamental crises of existence.*

Here they are the two spirits of the duality of the wholeness which is Imogen–Posthumus, who:

> Neither two nor one was called
>
> Reason, in itself confounded,
> Saw division grow together;
> To themselves yet either neither,
> Simple were so well compounded
>
> That it cried: 'How true a twain
> Seemeth this concordant one!
> Love hath reason, reason none,
> If what parts can so remain.'
> *The Phoenix and the Turtle*, 40–8

And within Shakespeare's basic patterns (Tragic Equation and Rival Brothers), just as the usurpation of one brother by another symbolizes the overthrow of the Puritan Adonis (the strict ego) by the enraged Boar (the Goddess of rejected being), so the mutual love and loyalty of these two brothers of Imogen's symbolizes something new in Shakespeare, namely, the mutual love and loyalty of the reborn criminal hero and his reborn victim: a vision of the ultimate union and sacred peace. Shakespeare goes on to use them again, with exactly this meaning, in *The Winter's Tale*, where the two 'brothers' Leontes and Polixenes, having gone through the 'murderous' usurpation of rational by irrational, rediscover their mutual love and loyalty, when a reborn couple unite in consecrated love.

This approach helps to explain the name of the hero as an algebraic term in the mutation of the Tragic Equation. *Cymbeline*, after all, is the first play which Shakespeare devotes to the rebirth of his hero. It is, and it is obviously intended to be, just this: the story of the tragic one reborn – of his posthumous and redeemed life. Being the story of what survives the crime and violent death of a false self, it becomes, inevitably, the story of the survival of the 'soul' of the true self, in this case Imogen: the story of the mutation – Posthumus Leonatus: the one born a lion, now reborn simply as 'after death'.

*Christ's two thieves, the Dadaphors, the two torchbearers who accompanied Mithras; the Vedic Nasatya or Ashvins, etc., the binary symmetry of brain and of body.

In these Theophanies, Leo personifies the same kind of creature that Orlando had to drive from his elder brother in the Forest of Arden, at the mouth of the Underworld. In *Pericles*, Leonine is the Witch Queen's hired murderer. In *The Winter's Tale* Leontes is a Tarquinian tyrant of the most surpassing ferocity and cruelty. Here, in *Cymbeline*, it is that original hero of imperfect love, who in a frenzy ordered Imogen to be killed. The lion, in other words, is like a preliminary phase of the Boar, representing that explosive murderous pride, a savage susceptibility to possession by the Boar.

Leonatus's lion nature, beheaded in the person of Cloten, becomes a lion-bloodied cloth in the hands of the new-born Posthumus – much as it did in the hands of the 'new-born' Oliver in *As You Like It*. In this sense, Leonatus incorporates all previous Tarquinian heroes. His madness and crime recapitulate all theirs, and his rebirth (when Shakespeare invented him, as I say, Posthumus was the only tragic hero who had managed to get this far) is all of them reborn.

Shakespeare must have viewed this new invention of his, this death and rebirth into redeemed life of all his inexorably doomed heroes, with some excitement. It amounts to a whole new technical process for dealing with the 'uncontrollable', the Tarquinian madness. That surge from the rejected Queen of Hell, the elemental power of the Boar, like a lump of uranium, or rather like a controlled nuclear explosion, is now suddenly contained within the power-station technology of the Gnostic-style Theophany, which converts it to human warmth and enlightenment.

At the same time, viewed from another angle, this death and rebirth is a magnified image of his inspirational moment, the death of Adonis as a repressive legalist, and his rebirth as a flower – the moment where the Goddess, as the Muse, drives through the pulses.

Pericles and the Gnostic myth of Sophia

Pericles lies just a little aside from the main route through the series: Lear/Cordelia, *Antony and Cleopatra*, *The Winter's Tale*, *The Tempest*. But it belongs to them, according to the Equation. The uncertainty concerns the first two acts. Since the last three acts are a fully developed dramatization of the Theophany, his Gnostic Coda, one looks for the Tragic Equation, from which it ought to have sprung.

At first glance, the connection between the first two acts and the last three appears to be so slight that it might be supposed the last three could be performed separately, getting rid of two acts that few seem willing to attribute to Shakespeare. Whatever may seem necessary for the plot could be given in a few lines of exposition, in the beginning of Act Three, which would then become Act One. The Coda, which opens there (where Shakespeare begins in earnest, in his ripest late manner, and at times mightily inspired), could then be a self-contained brief play, a theophany of a kind, starting in a tempest. Maybe it gave him an idea.

In spite of that, Shakespeare kept those first two acts, as if he needed them. Picking up seventeenth-century stage gossip, Dryden believed *Pericles* to be Shakespeare's earliest play, presumably his ugliest apprentice work, dug up from the pre-*Titus Andronicus* strata of foul papers (in one of those great trunks that he probably left in the Mountjoys' attic, in Silver Street, to be destroyed in the Great Fire), and now rewritten under pressure for a new kind of play for the Blackfriars stage.

That would explain the familiar juvenilian ring of several passages in the first two acts. He seems to have copied the whole thing out afresh, slashing and condensing, and yet in an absorbed way – suddenly taking off, apropos of nothing, and for no easily discernible dramatic purpose, into the involuntary arabesque:

> The blind mole casts
> Copp'd hills towards heaven, to tell the earth is throng'd
> By man's oppression; and the poor worm doth die for 't,
>
> *Pericles*, I. i. 100–2

and adding the fishermen's storm scene.

But most interestingly of all, it would explain how the first scene comes to be such a point-blank presentation of the hero's pure Shakespearean moment of 'double vision'.

> Pericles, a royal candidate hoping to solve the riddle that will give him the King of Antioch's beautiful daughter if he answers correctly (and a gruesome death if he fails), discovers, in the riddle, that the Princess is her father's whore. That is to say, Pericles, in the first seventy-five lines of the text, confronts the double vision in brute simplicity and high definition: the virgin, the royal bride and the incestuous whore in the one body.

Since he has not invested any love, any vulnerability, in this Princess, he does not recoil into Tarquinian madness, but he does recoil in a way that determines his subsequent fate. And as he recoils, the Equation, in its way, pursues him.

Assuming (correctly) that Antioch's King will now try to assassinate him, Pericles hides in the wide world.

If that double vision had in fact detonated the Tragic Equation here, Pericles should now be in his Tarquinian phase, and his wandering flight could be called the weakest possible variant of the Tarquinian madness. But he shows no familiar symptoms, and one might suppose the Equation, after that rudimentary, crude spasm, has gone to sleep, and that other dramatic laws have taken control, if they could be found. At last, it seems, Shakespeare has turned to a plot that breaks the mould of the Equation. If the Tragic Equation were indeed awake, Pericles should be showing at least some flash of the Tarquin, and he should find himself confronting, somehow, a Lucrece (a Diana), for whom the meeting should be fatal.

Sure enough, Pericles is suddenly climbing into an armour. And with a demonstration of martial prowess he defeats all contenders at a jousting contest (a variant of the earlier contest) and wins Thaisa, the Princess of Pentapolis, who, in contrast to the loathed Princess of Antioch, wears 'Diana's livery', and has vowed 'never to break her virgin honour', except for her true beloved – who now turns out to be Pericles.

Obviously, to the Equation-sensitized eye, the Equation has wakened up with a smiting of falchions and Thaisa is clearly in some danger. Though the familiar mechanism seems to be operating rather sporadically, the pattern is unmistakable. As in *All's Well*, the plot has fallen back into two parts, virtually into the two poems. In the first part, the Adonis has rejected the Princess of Antioch's Venusian promise of love, because of her 'lust'. And now in the second part, the martial hero, the same who rejected that Queen of Hell, has a Lucrece in his possession. The second part may well look very different in most respects from that of *All's Well* and the other earlier examples, but the Equation, one knows by now, moves in a mysterious way, to reach the same old conclusions. Though the Goddess is divided into two different individuals, on the mythic plane they are one. And if the Princess of Antioch was rejected, then Thaisa must die. Or at least, in the earlier Tragedies, she would have had to die. After *Coriolanus*, and certainly *Cymbeline*, she might escape with the skin of her teeth. She might, that is, if the Equation is fully in control. Since everything on the level of the characters and the plot is happening in such a haphazard, arbitrary tumble of accidents, without any visible thread of cause and effect, or the slightest show of dramatic necessity, one cannot be sure what the Equation is up to. Nevertheless, its shape continues to emerge.

And suddenly it is all there, at the opening of Act Three, where Shakespeare's 1608–9 goose quill enters with a magnificent flourish. In a few minutes Pericles has had to cast overboard his living wife in a tempest. This would be a Tarquinian act even more decisive than the indirect way in which Hamlet caused Ophelia to drown, if he had done it in a Tarquinian frenzy. But no such frenzy has touched him. Indeed, he was trying desperately to save her life. He simply believes her to be dead, in childbirth, and is forced to throw her overboard, in a sealed chest, by the superstitious sailors, against his will and in grief.

Immediately afterwards, he gives away his new-born daughter to be fostered. As it turns out, he hands her to the one who will now try to destroy her. In other words, in spite of his grief, his reluctance, his best intentions, Pericles has in effect cast his living wife into the tempestuous sea and his new-born daughter into the witch-ridden wilderness, like the blindest Tarquin. One now realizes that the shaky but remorseless Tragic Equation, like a steady will bearing on the bouncing dice, has completed its logic without ever showing its hand: the tragic hero is bereft, and the Goddess seems to have been destroyed (Antioch's Princess has been consumed in another storm by a fire from Heaven).

That is to say, in spite of the apparent structural incoherence of these first two acts, they launch Shakespeare into the third act, and the Theophany, from an unorthodox but firmly complete (except for that mutilated tail segment) Tragic Equation. Shakespeare can now concentrate all his attention on what evidently interests him: the survival of Thaisa, and the rescuing of her new self (and of Pericles's new soul) in Marina.

It is clear why Shakespeare needed those two acts. Rough as they are, they provide the tough old radical stock from which he can now grow his sophisticated blossom. It is as if those last three acts were some particular biological response, a conditioned reflex, that could never be triggered without at least a simulated replay of the physical preliminaries. Or as if they were a chemical precipitate that could never materialize without the real basic ingredients, even in the crudest form, being dropped into the crucible.

In an odd way, the very uncertainty of the course taken by the Equation now turns to the play's advantage. As currents of cause and effect sink and run underground, the attention comes to rest on a different topography of relationships, less self-evidently connected, more purely those of pattern and music, more readily opening into orders of experience that transcend the natural.

From this point, Pericles's career proceeds on two levels that seem self-contradictory. At the surface, on the level of character and plot incident, he is a tragic hero of a new kind: the innocent man guilty simply of existing, guilty simply of loving (trying to love the Princess of Antioch, definitely loving Thaisa and his daughter) the Goddess. The basic accidents that befall him are therefore suggestive (on stage immensely suggestive) of inscrutable divine laws in operation, a justice of ordeals, trials and eventual rewards, before which his baffled innocence is helpless, and to which at each point he merely submits.

But on the deeper level, the mythic level of the Equation, he is of course truly guilty: he rejected the Goddess 'in loathing' (imposing his own judgement of good and evil). On that level, he must take the consequences, like the other tragic heroes, of a guilt that he has managed to suppress, a guilt that he has managed not to suffer (as guilt). This mystery, of a man being mythically punished, transformed and redeemed, on account of a crime and a guilt that (like Oedipus's) never enters his awareness, is part of the fascination of *Pericles*.

The real coherence of this superficially chaotic drama rests, therefore, quite secure in that completed pattern of a Tragic Equation which develops into the Gnostic Coda and Theophany. Having rejected the Goddess, and therefore incurred the guilt, Pericles is the cause of the apparent death of his beloved (his wife and new-born daughter: alias his own soul). And that is the mythic crime for which he will be punished in real terms, and from which his wife and daughter, as if resurrected, will redeem him in reunited love. This is the iron logic of the Equation and its mutation (however some factors may appear in a variant, less painful form). And on this level, the integrity of the play is strong and clear.

Several features of the last three acts – what I have called the Coda – suggest a direct influence of Gnostic ideas, in particular of the Gnostic myth of Sophia, perhaps combined with the Gnostic myth of the Pearl, which is a variant of the same.

Very like the Christian conflict of the two old myths in the Reformation (and in the Tragic Equation), Gnosticism incorporated the myth of the Goddess as the divinity, the Goddess fallen into evil, and the Goddess all but destroyed by the madness of a Goddess-destroyer. Its mythology dramatized a situation in which rational intelligence had been separated from and set in murderous opposition to the *Gnosis Kardias*, the original divine unity of the 'understanding heart'. Unlike Reformation theology, Gnosticism (though not its Manichean variant) went beyond that opposition (as Occult Neoplatonism also attempted to do), and with a true theophany redeemed it, returning the Goddess to a union with the Divine.

Even in this sketch, one can see how the Gnostic Goddess myth recapitulates both the tragic phase of Shakespeare's dramatic myth and its mutated development, the Coda, the Theophany, which he invented in *King Lear* and now develops in *Cymbeline* and *Pericles*.

In *King Lear* he seemed to be drawing this transcendental solution out of his own entrails. But in *Cymbeline*, and certainly in *Pericles*, one could believe that he has recognized where it belongs in the tradition, and how the tradition itself (that rejected, subterranean, heretical tradition) can be incorporated into his own dramatic liturgy, as if he were writing not only as a Blackfriars entertainer, but also as an incognito Occult Neoplatonist creating a subliminal but ritualized (i.e. effectively influential) mythology, producing a visionary solution to religious conflict, for a select group.

The parallel between the Gnostic myth and Shakespeare's dramatization of both the conflict and its solution should be clear in the following very simplified outlines of the myths of the Pearl and of Sophia.

In the myth of the Pearl the child of splendidly wealthy parents in the East is divested of his royal robe, equipped, and sent down into Egypt to find the one pearl which lies in the depth of the sea, guarded by the encircling serpent. If he returns successfully, he will be robed again in glory and made heir to the kingdom.

He goes (accompanied by two royal helpers), descends through perils into the land of Babel, thence alone into the depths of Egypt, finally taking up lodgings in an inn, close to the serpent. Disguising himself as one of the 'unclean ones', in spite of his vigilance, drinking and eating with them he becomes one of them, forgets his mission, and sinks into a deep torpor.

His father, the King of Kings, sends him a letter to remind him of his task. The letter flies as an eagle, lands beside him and becomes a voice. Waking, he finds it a letter, reminding him of what he is about, and who he is.

Having conquered the serpent, by reciting over it the names of his father and mother (and brothers), he takes the pearl, and returns home. He dons his divine robe (described as the mirror image of his divine, true self, which is also the image of the King of Kings, quivering with the movements of the Gnosis) and mounts in glory to his father.

Though details of this myth peep through the four plays, as a dramatic parallel to Shakespeare's myth its form is veiled. Shakespeare's Tragic Equation appears simply as the separation from the divine home, the descent into Egypt, and the sleep close to the serpent, neglecting the pearl. As a theological gloss of one view of *Antony and Cleopatra* that is perhaps quite close. But not so patently close to any of the other tragedies in narrative shape. In spirit, however, the parallel holds with them all: the searcher's 'sleep' corresponds to the tragic hero's condition of insane delusion, which prevents him from seeing his beloved for what she is: so it corresponds to Hamlet's banishing of Ophelia and raging castigation of his mother, to Othello's murdering of Desdemona (casting 'a pearl away/Richer than all his tribe'), Macbeth's murder of Duncan, Lear's banishing of Cordelia, Timon's inability to find one redeeming thing in Athens, Coriolanus's will to destroy Rome and everybody in it.

Likewise, the searcher's sudden awakening to his true purpose corresponds closely in spiritual feeling to the Coda of the mutated Tragic Equation in the late plays. There is a suggestion in the myth of the Pearl, as everywhere in Gnostic variants of this phase of the basic idea, that the Pearl (the soul, the Sacred Bride) is the active one in the searcher's eventual redemption of both the Pearl and himself. In other words, in this latter part of the myth she can be portrayed as the dominant partner, the initiator of the action, through her resolute will to be redeemed.

She is so in Shakespeare's Theophany. So the arrival (in thunder) of the eagle letter corresponds to Lear's realization that Cordelia alone is his salvation, while Cordelia herself is already actively marching towards him. In *Cymbeline*, Posthumus's awakening occurs when

Imogen is reborn, in her struggle towards him, though he does not actually open his eyes until after the dream, in prison, when he reads, in the book delivered by Jupiter as an eagle, as it were, the whole reconciliation scene of the denouement, as if his awakening were an instantaneous return to the robe of his true self and reunion with sacred love. This reunion is symbolized, in the action, by the reunion, for Cymbeline, of all the lost limbs of his family, and Britain's reunion with Rome. In *Pericles*, the letter is, so to speak, incorporated in the active pearl, in Marina. It begins its flight when she leaves the brothel. It arrives and awakens Pericles (from his depressive torpor of dumbness) when she sings.

Likewise, in *The Winter's Tale*, the eagle starts its flight at the nadir of Leontes's insensibility, his lethal accusation of Hermione, and his casting away of the new-born Perdita. Its wing beats are the storm that sinks the ship that has brought Perdita to the shepherds. It arrives where Hermione moves on the pedestal. But, as I say, except for the details, the myth of the Pearl is more like a musical accompaniment than a felt, structural pressure in the play.

The myth of Sophia, however, vastly more complicated, and existing in many variations, in simplified essentials presents several specific points of resemblance, as in the following outline.

From the primordial, ineffable divine pair (Depth – masculine; Silence – feminine) emanate thirty Aions, which are imagined as divine beings arranged in male–female couples.

The youngest of the Aions is Sophia. She is separated from her divine partner Aion, generally known as Will.

The actual cause of the separation has to be divined from what follows. In her lost state, Sophia begins to seek for Gnosis (Divine Understanding, Divine Union) with a distorted (because separated) intelligence.

The distorted intelligence manifests itself as Pride – Conceit in the infallibility of her intellectual powers – which impels her to search out the Divine Mystery of Depth and Silence using the intellect alone.

This act of 'hubris' proves to be the tragic crime. It corresponds to the act of rational discrimination and judgement behind Adonis's 'double vision'.

As a result of it, Sophia falls from the realm of Divine Unity into the world of suffering and darkness.

This part of the myth corresponds to Shakespeare's Tragic Equation, if Sophia is imagined as Adonis: or if Adonis is imagined, rather, as the masculinized, *distorted* intelligence of Sophia, and Sophia therefore as the soul who must suffer for his crime, and suffer as he suffers. For instance, in the last scene of *Othello* both Othello (the distorted intelligence) and Desdemona (the Sophia) are suffering the consequences of that distortion of the intelligence (Iago), that separation of the critical intelligence from the divine loving unity of *Gnosis Kardias*, the 'understanding heart'.

Or, in *The Winter's Tale*, at the height of the trial scene, in Act Three, both Leontes and Hermione are suffering the consequences of the distorted intelligence to the point where Hermione, the Sophia, seems to die.

At this juncture, in the Sophia myth, Sophia splits into two.

The higher Sophia floats back into provisional relationship with the partner from whom she separated, Will. But the lower Sophia continues with the dramatic consequences of the distorted intelligence.

In the horror of the outer darkness, the lower Sophia begins to produce demonic monsters. Her successive states of mind – grief, fear, ignorance, bewilderment, and her constant passion to return to Divine Union – materialize as the elements of the created world. A demiurge, Jaldabaoth, likewise materializes to take tyrannical possession of the new creation of agonized materials, in which Sophia (actually the creatress of the whole thing) is now a prisoner. So, in a sense, Jaldabaoth, who imprisons and makes her suffer, is her son.

The antithesis of Jaldabaoth, the Aion Jesus (like a spiritual angelic brother of the material titanic daemon), comes into being and descends into the world of terror, to find Sophia in her prison.

He rescues her, lifts her out of her debasement among the demons, and becomes her 'Sacred Bridegroom', both together marrying into a reunion with the Divine Fullness of Heaven.

This is the broad highway driven through an immense jungle of variants, correspondences, and further developments of each possiblity and other directions, a theological and metaphysical world of inexhaustible variety, ramifying at every point into sophisticated abstractions that are ingenious, perverse or philosophically profound and fertile, according to one's point of view. However, one can see how this generalized narrative, as I have given it here, parallels the sequence of episodes in the myth of the Pearl, and anticipates the sequence of episodes in Shakespeare's Tragic Equation and Theophany.

The tragic section of Shakespeare's myth corresponds, as I say, to Sophia's fall and sufferings, up to her imprisonment in the material, daemonized prison of Jaldabaoth. The crucial detail is that intellectual sin, which is the *cause* of the tragedy, and fundamental to both. The fact that the demonic world of Sophia's suffering is created (i) by that sin, and (ii) by what that sin makes of her 'son' (i.e. of the created world of her incarnate life of sufferings), corresponds to the fact in Shakespeare that the Tarquin (who will try to destroy the Female) is created out of Adonis, by that sin (and that in so far as she is the Goddess, he was originally her son).

The fundamental point, common to both is that the entire, all-inclusive hell of the drama is a consequence of that intellectual sin. Likewise, the implication in both is that if the sin could somehow 'not happen', existence would be a bliss of perpetual Divine Union (as if the promises of those deities in the betrothal Masque in *The Tempest* could come true). At the same time, in both, in the Sophia myth and in Shakespeare, there is no doubt that the sin, somehow or other, has to happen: it is symbolic of something built into the very existence of (in Shakespeare) 'such stuff/As dreams are made on', and (in Gnosticism) the Depth and the Silence.

The next odd point of similarity occurs where Sophia splits. This, or something similar, occurs in *Pericles*, obviously where, at the nadir, Thaisa produces Marina in the tempest at sea. Thaisa then floats away, out of the drama, like the higher Sophia, to be preserved and saved for Pericles near Heaven, in Diana's temple, while Marina plunges deeper, towards the assassin, the pirates and the brothel, as the lower Sophia plunges into the dark world of Jaldabaoth.

Again, the Jesus Aion, who will find, rescue and redeem the Sophia, is, in a sense, the spiritual brother, the equal but antithetical self, of the 'hot tyrant'. So Posthumus's false or inferior self, who tried only to kill Imogen/Sophia, corresponds to Jaldabaoth.

In *Pericles*, Lysimachus, who finds Marina/Sophia in the brothel, is the Jesus Aion. The world of Jaldabaoth (of the cruel one, the assassin Leonine, the pirates and the brothel) is not specifically linked to Pericles, but it is, as I argued earlier, a consequence of his role in the Tragic Equation, i.e. of his original rejection of the Goddess.

In *The Winter's Tale* the pattern is more fully objectified. There the Sophia splits into Hermione and Perdita. Hermione floats off, as did Thaisa, to be preserved, for Leontes, unspoiled, by Paulina (the votaress of Apollo?). Meanwhile the lower Sophia plunges into a strange episode, where a ship is wrecked and her guard is devoured by a bear, while she is rescued by rough shepherds. In this case, the 'world of Jaldabaoth' is compressed into these symbols (an event projected from the frenzy of Leontes's distorted intelligence). But Florizel, as the Jesus Aion, is an emanation of Polixenes, who is in turn the true self of Leontes, the self driven out when his demented Jaldabaoth self took over. In that sense Florizel is to the self-deluded tyrant Leontes exactly as the Jesus Aion is to Jaldabaoth.

There are other odd links. I pointed out another clue to the symbol of the lion in the tragic myth, where the lioness in *As You Like It* gave a name to the savagely wilful and to-be-redeemed element in Posthumus Leonatus, and in Leontes. In both those plays, that lion name is a synonym of the Jaldabaoth figure. In *Pericles*, the world of Jaldabaoth takes hold of Marina, her first shock, with the hands of the assassin Leonine. In the Gnostic myth, Jaldabaoth is known as 'the lion-faced'.

Much of the bizarre ritual of reunion, and the denouement of *Pericles*, where the King addresses his new-found daughter as:

> Thou that beget'st him that did thee beget
>
> *Pericles*, v. i. 197

while the music of the spheres resounds, and where he asks the gods to let him dissolve into Thaisa, and her be buried in him:

> That on the touching of her lips I may
> Melt and no more be seen. O come, be buried
> A second time within these arms,

while Marina recites that extraordinary mantra of self-identification:

> My heart
> Leaps to be gone into my mother's bosom,
>
> v. i. 44–5

[354]

so that all three become a single fluid or gaseous composite being, delaying only for the marriage with Lysimachus, when presumably he, too, will join the spiritual union – much of that makes more sense if it is seen as a dramatization of the Gnostic marriage of lower Sophia and the Jesus Aion, as they are reabsorbed into the higher Sophia and the Will, within the Divine Fullness. It is certainly very easy to see that particular pattern of spiritual necessity behind that particular choreography, in that form of resolution. The Gnostic interpretation can also explain the exalted, spiritualized feeling of the whole finale, as it helps to explain the mystically enraptured abstractions with which Pericles tries to define Marina's 'divine' nature, after she has sung him out of his penitential silence.

This view of the second half of Pericles, as a roughly but artfully dramatized Gnostic liturgy, also sets the play in a category that again helps to explain certain things about it. The sophisticated theological myth sits easily with the almost primitive polarization of lust and chastity, in so far as the very basis of the Gnostic drama (hypertrophied in the Manichean branch of it) is the antithesis between the goodness of the soul, considered as a female from Heaven, and the evil of the incarnation, considered as a demon tyrant in Egypt. At the same time, this simplified polarity of lust and chastity (just as nakedly delineated and opposed here as in *Venus and Adonis*) suits the apparent crudity of the dramatic treatment – the rough-cut tableaux of a miracle or morality play. Paradoxically, the abbreviated, magnified code of the puppet dialogue in this style of drama communicates the hieratic quality of mystical events far more suggestively and movingly than anything more realistic ever could. At various points it comes very close to symbolic religious drama, and powerfully transmits the unearthly music peculiar to these last plays.

There is one last coincidence, as interesting as it is odd. If Shakespeare was as much an Occult Neoplatonist magus as Prospero, he could hardly have been ignorant of the Sophia myth and of a good deal else in connection with it. He would surely have been intrigued by the biography of the most celebrated father of Gnosticism, Simon Magus, whom the Christian Church Fathers regarded as the father of all heresy. Contemporary with the Apostles, Simon Magus was one of many Messiahs, and one of the more successful in impressing his personality and ideas on the religious turmoil of the first centuries after Christ. His version of the Sophia myth was simplified – but dramatic. And he dramatized it. The Sophia (for him, God's 'thought', or *epinoia*, the bearer of the 'creative powers' separated from the source) lost control of her own creation, and became its victim and prisoner. Even Simon Magus was a syncretizing mythographer: for him, Sophia was also Helen of Troy, over whom Greeks and Barbarians had fought. So his Sophia passed through descending incarnations till she became a whore in a brothel. Here, Simon Magus himself found her, in 'a brothel in Tyre'. He recognized her as the fallen 'thought of God', and redeemed her. Thereafter, she accompanied him in his preaching, and he called her Helena. Or, he called her Selene, avatar of the Moon Goddess, and of the Great Goddess in general, drawing on the same pool of mystery that had made Mary Magdalene the closest to Christ and his best beloved. Simon Magus was known as the Magician (but he called himself Faustus, 'the favoured one').

This tale must have had a lively career in Shakespeare's imagination, perhaps long before Pericles entered as a 'King of Tyre', or before Cerimon, the magician and master of ceremonies at the temple of the Moon Goddess, found Thaisa in the sea chest and released her (just as her new-born self, Marina, Princess of Tyre, would be released from the brothel).

All this is to say: by the time Shakespeare comes to compose *Cymbeline* and *Pericles*, the Tragic Equation has become the larval phase of a theophany which closely parallels the intricate redemptive pattern of the Gnostic myth.

This becomes, as I have suggested, even more explicit in *The Winter's Tale*, though at the same time the atmosphere becomes less Gnostic, more integrally and, as it were, more inwardly Shakespearean, gathering up all the currents of the tragic myth into a single, concentrated, culminating event.

The Tragic Equation in court

As in *Cymbeline*, the first half of *The Winter's Tale* presents the Tragic Equation in almost classic form: highly charged – but slightly and purposefully modified, and developed through the death–rebirth episode into Shakespeare's most comprehensive model of the Sophia-like Coda.

In the next play (and last of the series), *The Tempest*, he takes the Coda further but also, by a virtuoso snakes and ladders rearrangement of the algebra of the Tragic Equation and the Rival Brothers and the Sophia myth, turns it into something else.

Here in *The Winter's Tale*, as before, the theme of the Rival Brothers appears entwined with the Tragic Equation, illustrating once more just how the two stories are different aspects of the same event: The usurpation of one extreme state of mind by another.

A brief outline is enough to isolate the relevant patterns:

For his basic plot, as with *Cymbeline*, Shakespeare seems to have once again requisitioned his prototype Tragic Equation: the story of Othello's jealousy. Obvious differences (from the *Othello* story) include: the quality of Leontes's love for his wife, the fact that he fails to kill her, that he does not kill himself even though he thinks he has succeeded in killing her, and the absence of an Iago. But clearly enough, Iago is active from the first moment inside Leontes's own head.

From the first moment, also, the Rival Brothers are prominent. The first scene and some of the second is devoted to establishing that King Leontes and King Polixenes, his guest, have always been, from earliest boyhood, 'like twinned lambs'. Their mutual love is described as both separate from and in some ways superior to the love of their wives (who, they suggest, disrupted it as 'devils' with their 'temptations').

After his nine-month visit, King Polixenes wishes to leave. Leontes seems to want him to stay, and prompts Hermione, who is nine months pregnant, to persuade him. Exerting all her charms, Hermione succeeds.

Watching this act of feminine persuasion (as an image of seduction), Leontes sees, in Hermione, the double vision and is suddenly insane with jealousy.

Leontes gives orders for the assassination of Polixenes, who flees back to his own kingdom, Bohemia, thereby confirming Leontes's confidence in his own accusations against Hermione.

At that point, the rivalry of the brothers looms into position. Leontes imagines that he is in the situation, cast out from possession of his true crown (Hermione as his Lucrece), that the murdered King Hamlet was in, long ago, and that Prospero will be in, again, in the next play. Like

King Hamlet rising from the grave and giving the order of assassination to Prince Hamlet (but asking him to spare the sinful Queen), Leontes now orders the assassination of Polixenes, and (pitiless, unlike King Hamlet) sets about convicting the Queen. (Observing these patterns, one might wonder: what happened to Prospero's wife? What role did she play? Or what role ought she to have played? This question duly turns up in the catacombs of *The Tempest*.)

Here, in *The Winter's Tale*, these echoes of the seesaw of the Ghost and Claudius in *Hamlet*, and of Macbeth and Banquo, are potent electromagnetic waves, in Leontes's motivation. But they remain secondary to the dominant form of the Tragic Equation, in which Leontes rejects and attempts to condemn Hermione to death. They reflect and re-enforce the essential event: King Leontes's attempted murder and successful ejection of Polixenes is a shadow play of the eruptive takeover, within Leontes's psyche, by the Queen of Hell's Boar/'hot tyrant', which will now attempt to murder the rejected Hermione.

Having failed in his immediate attempt to kill the Rival Brother, Leontes resumes his role in the Tragic Equation as the Goddess-destroyer. Sending to the Delphic Oracle for a judgement, which he never doubts will confirm his own, he charges Hermione with adultery, convinced that her child, about to be born, was sired by Polixenes, and determined to execute both it and her.

If this court-room confrontation was intended to be Shakespeare's ultimate dramatization of the Tarquinian act against the Female, it is hard to imagine how her predicament could have been objectified more powerfully, or with more analytical focus on every aspect of Leontes's cruelty and injustice.

Hermione is dragged from the bed of childbirth to defend herself in public against the charge of adultery and sentence of death pronounced by the King her husband, whom she faithfully loves, and on whose love she depends, and who is insanely deaf to her plea and her suffering.

She defends herself at length, and everything that for some scruple or other she does not say is given amplified voice by her companion Paulina.

When her appeal is utterly exhausted, and Leontes, indifferent to all of it, seems triumphant, the judgement of the Delphic Oracle arrives, declaring Hermione innocent, and Leontes a jealous tyrant.

At this moment of apparent vindication, Hermione receives the final blow, in the news that her young son has died, suddenly, of sheer distress at the humiliation and grief heaped on his mother by his father. She collapses, and is carried out, and Paulina soon after announces her death.

As I say, this is the ultimate account, in fully articulated form, of the Tarquinian crime against the Female.

At this point, according to the old-style Tragic Equation (as obeyed by his predecessor Othello), Leontes should kill himself. But since this is the Tragic Equation new-style, with the Coda now well under way, where shepherds save the baby girl from death in the wilderness, and Hermione is not dead but smuggled away alive by Paulina, Leontes stays alive, only vowing to make a daily pilgrimage to the grave of his wife and his son for the rest of his life.

The Coda, launched in a sea storm, is an advance on that of *Pericles* and *Cymbeline*, and a sketch for that of *The Tempest*.

Looked at from a slightly different angle, the story reveals its resemblance to the Sophia myth, as a story of the intellectual sin, and the hero and heroine's suffering and redemption, which begins at the very opening of the play. Within this larger five-act unity, the Tragic Equation of the first two and a half acts is already something other than itself, and in its 'otherness' has taken the odd form of a case argued in court.

The last time the rights and wrongs of the Tragic Equation were argued in legal terms was in *Measure for Measure*. Other reminiscences of that play indicate how *The Winter's Tale* opens more directly back into the theological bitterness, the naked religious crime, behind the Tragic Equation than any of the intervening parables. One of these reminders is the fact that Leontes condemns Hermione, and Angelo condemns Juliet, for the same fault: that of becoming pregnant. The other is that Leontes is the first tragic hero since Angelo who lacks the preliminary vulnerability (in the text or on stage) of idyllic love for what he then proceeds to condemn.

One can argue that Leontes obviously loved Hermione at some time in the past, but this is as irrelevant to what shows of his inner life in the first half of the play as was Angelo's long-ago liaison with Mariana at the Moated Grange. The point here is that the apparent absence of love, in Leontes, decides the trajectory of dramatic development. It controls the investment of the audience's sympathy, and so enables Shakespeare to set at the centre of the play the inner life, the sufferings, the innocence and the redemption not of the tragic hero but of his victim. In other words, it enables Shakespeare to make this play a final court case, in which the tragic hero receives his ultimate conviction, condemnation and punishment, while his victim is absolved, and her innocence consecrated and all but canonized, as a martyr, by the God of Truth.

The Winter's Tale: the cry and the silence

I had thought of omitting any account of the Tragic Equation's presence in *The Winter's Tale* simply to relieve the reader of my tour guide's observations for at least one of the temples in the complex, and confident that the ritual plan – the 'double vision', rejection of the Female, insane attempt to destroy the Female, roofed, so to speak, with an overarching variant of the Rival Brothers – would leap out of its own accord, as the basic structural idea, to claim its place in the tragic sequence.

I have resisted the impulse because in this drama, it seems to me, the whole Tragedy of Divine Love culminates. *The Tempest* then follows not quite as a satyr-play, but as a summary comment on the entire sequence, returning it, in a fashion, back to its beginnings: as if *Venus and Adonis* should be rewritten with its conclusion corrected and yet encapsulating everything that had been endured, throughout the dramas, projected from the wrinkles and folds of the harrowed mask of Prospero worn by Adonis.

The technical advance of *The Winter's Tale* makes the forensic purpose of Shakespeare's Theophany much more apparent. In *Cymbeline*, the subordination of the tragic hero's imperious career to the sufferings of the Female, the robing of the stubborn, strenuous attitudes of the Tragic Equation in the curves of the Sophia myth, had hardly begun. And in that play, Posthumus's love for Imogen, his banishment, Iachimo's wager and deception, Posthumus's frenzy, the indirect operation of Posthumus's hit-man Pisanio, the mountain episode with the brothers, produce a bulk of action with a busy, diffusive life of its own.

Though the first two and a half acts launch Imogen's patient course of devotion, as a rocket launches its space capsule, the impression remains that the whole of *Cymbeline* is a lumpishly hybrid form. In *The Winter's Tale*, however, Hermione's glowing ascent surges through the Tragic Equation with such perfect economy that it is not easy to delineate the one except in terms of the other.

The features that best illustrate what has happened, maybe, are Hermione's oration in her own defence, and the fact that she delivers it in court. Here in *The Winter's Tale*, the heroic victim's confrontation with her persecutor might be thought a useful and even lucky *donnée*, provided by his source, that Shakespeare simply exploits. But as dramatic devices go, both have vivid precedents in the previous plays.

If one sets Hermione's defence in the series of great speeches by the female victims of the Equation, one sees immediately that it arrives as the logical climax of a long process.*

There are perhaps five occasions of this sort, where the Female has her full exhaustive say, in her own defence, against the hero. Out of sixteen large works (including the two long poems), in each of which the hero either violently rejects the Female, condemns her to death, or somehow kills her, more of that kind of eloquence might be expected. On the other hand, the silence, or the near silence, of most of these heroines is at least as effective, in condemning the action of the hero, as any speech. Even so, the great declarations of those who do raise their voices follow an orderly development of sorts, which interprets what is going on in the silence of those others.

The first of these occasions comes at the very beginning, in *Venus and Adonis*, where Venus pours her 'total, unconditional love' over Adonis for some 760 lines, in a vain attempt to thaw his resistance – before he rejects her absolutely. She calls on great Nature, and on the complete, necessary cycle of life, to witness the truth of her words and to support her, but in vain. One could say that this outburst erupts, as it were, from the Goddess in sheer incredulity, as she meets that Puritan denial for the first time.

*The same plea is taken up again, for the last time, by the rejected Queen Katharine in *Henry VIII*, who produces the most prolonged lament in the dramas – for the first time to no avail. In spite of the historical role of this particular queen in the formation of Shakespeare's Equation, I give reasons in Appendix I for setting that play outside the tragic sequence.

The second runs to even greater length, in the second long narrative, *Lucrece*, where the chaste, faithful, ravished wife pleads her case, one way or another, for over a thousand lines, calling on the gods and all noble Romans to witness her words, before she kills herself. This floodburst, again, could be regarded as the Goddess's outrage – her sheer, despairing incredulity – meeting the Tarquinian madness for the first time.

Looked at in this way, these two long poems (which eventually combine to make the Equation) become basically two terrible howls from the Female: the first, of the undivided Divine Love's baffled passion, the second, of sacred and true love's mortal injury. And in each case the reason for her outcry is blindingly clear. For length, mythic scope and intensity of Woman's grievance, one would have to look a long way in subsequent literature to find anything remotely like these. Having howled, Shakespeare's Female falls silent for a few years. But as soon as the Equation emerges into the plays, she starts up again.

I have excluded Helena's long, intermittent lament (*All's Well that Ends Well*) from the group of five, because though it is a more human, more modest (but at the bottom no less violent) harmonic of Venus's appeal, she fails to make a legal grievance of it, in so far as she never touches on her rights or Bertram's wrongs (or she touches on her rights only as far as Bertram has granted them to her at the very end). The scald of real injury claiming to be heard in a court burst out like the blast of a geyser in the following play, *Measure for Measure*. Here, the hero's action against the Female is understood clearly to be a crime (Puritan suppression equals Tarquinian onslaught), and is argued and proved to be such in a legal context. Isabella's accusative appeal goes a whole psychological revelation beyond Venus's rebuffed and suffering passion, but it is a response to the same 'crime' – to the dehumanized, prohibitive external rigour and inner corruption of the same ideal. Speaking for Juliet and Mariana, she wins her case. She proves the real hypocrisy and criminality of Adonis/Angelo's Puritan 'virtue', simply by revealing (by releasing) the Hell of 'perjured, murderous, bloody, savage, extreme, cruel', treacherous 'lust' behind it. By exposing and demonstrating, as I tried to show in the pages about *Measure for Measure*, just how Adonis's Puritan condemnation of lust conceals, and in a moment is overwhelmed by and becomes, Tarquin's assault.

Shakespeare's Female is stunned by what that Hell becomes as it explodes through the next seven plays. While the author gives full freedom of speech and action to the tragic hero who attacks her, the victim herself becomes virtually speechless under the pressure, until, in Cordelia's 'Nothing', her silence crystallizes into a kind of supernatural prism, where what cannot be heard becomes dazzling.

But then, in *Coriolanus*, she pulls herself together. That crystal becomes a flame of eloquence, and she speaks. Or at least, half of her speaks. Coriolanus's mother Volumnia states the victim's case with such exorcizing, relentless clarity and force that the hero's madness, his possessing daemon, flees from him, while he collapses and is destroyed. But even though Volumnia speaks to such devastating effect, her words become irresistible only by being refracted through that silence of her other half, the Cordelia beside her, Coriolanus's wife, Virgilia, his 'Sacred Bride', who 'bent her head and signed but spoke no word' – or hardly a word. As if the decisive magic power of the sufferer were still a silence. Or as if Volumnia, while she declaimed, held up, instead of her fingers twisted in a silent, divinely powerful mudra, the actual silent icon of Virgilia. As a dramatic fable, the infinite eloquence of the Mother, combined with the ineffable silence of the Wife, is a marvellously expressive invention, a marvellously complete image of Shakespeare's conception of inexpressible (albeit voluble) truth, and with it he seemed to find, at last, a means of saving the Female.

I made mention of the fact that this is the first and only time in the tragedies (as a scene coming at the end of *Coriolanus*, the last of them) where the heroine survives absolutely. Moreover, Volumnia's victory in court (and her appeal for mercy and humane justice, before witnesses, moving even the hostile Aufidian jury to pity, is virtually a speech by the condemned from the dock) is such a victory for the Female that she never has to die again, in any of the plays. It heralds, perhaps establishes, that final shift of Shakespeare's concern from the Male to the Female. In Volumnia's speech for herself and Virgilia (and for Rome) the dying 'hot tyrant' of the Tragic Equation is displaced from centre stage, for good, by the surviving heroine.

Even so, on the fifth and last occasion Shakespeare takes it further. Hermione's self-defence, here in court, supported as it is by Paulina, is the most comprehensive and unanswerable statement of the case in the series as a whole. This speech recapitulates them all. Venus's uncomprehending wail, the fatally crushed Lucrece's haemorrhage of accusation, Isabella's hectic exposé of the crime and her raging crusade for justice, Volumnia's triumphant conviction of the criminal in the very act and her forcing him to confess, and repent, before being destroyed, all resound together in this multiple chord of Hermione, Paulina and Perdita — where the new-born Perdita brings that silent component to a new focus of precision.

The effect is that the complex of ethical attitudes, already fully developed there in the beginning, behind the confrontation of Venus and Adonis, and operating so expansively through all the oblique parables of the tragic drama, has finally stepped into the open to state the case in its own direct, plain terms, not only in the High Court, but in the highest court of all, where the justice of Heaven, literally in the voice of God, judges the justice of Earth. The situation has a stunning universal finality and economy. King Leontes, the tragic hero, is not only the great criminal — the destroyer of the Female and of his own soul — he is the plaintiff, the plaintiff's advocate, the judge and the representative of God on Earth. The tyrannical injustice of the situation could hardly be made more absolute. Meanwhile, Hermione, his victim, the falsely accused, the defendant, has only her own prejudged eloquence, her new-born, already condemned, castaway daughter's silence, and a bare hope – that God himself will step from Heaven into court to defend her, and judge this judge.

This is what I mean by *The Winter's Tale* being the logical culmination of a long process. If the tragic series is regarded as the court hearings of Shakespeare's investigation into the crime that Adonis, it seemed, almost got away with, then *The Winter's Tale* is the summation and judgement.

From this angle one can see how the Tragic Equation has become something else. This is the furthest point attained by a graph which swings from psychic struggle as entertainment pure and simple, as in the early comedies, away from the 'dancing measures' of *As You Like It*, then through and beyond tragic realism, into this last phase — the emergency ritual of salvation, which is technically a theophany, where the primal rage and pain behind the whole irrepressible vision is redeemed and transformed by the God of the Revelation of Hidden Truth, Apollo himself, who now (virtually) steps into court to deliver judgement.

But it is curious to see, in this play, how slight an adjustment of the Tragic Equation enables Shakespeare to transpose it so perfectly into the terms of Hermione's Sophia-like destiny, and realign it to the priorities of his Theophany.

The Winter's Tale: Leontes as the tragic error

Throughout the tragedies, the Equation unfailingly concentrates the audience's interest and sympathy on the inner life of the tragic hero. Its mechanism reduces the heroine, even when she is a considerable figure, to a passive or at least helpless co-victim of his self-destruction. The only plays of the sequence in which the hero fails to hold the centre of gravity are *All's Well* and *Measure for Measure*, introducing the series, and *Cymbeline, Pericles* and *The Winter's Tale*, which usher it to a close. In each case there is at least one prominent reason why the failure occurs.

In *All's Well*, Bertram is without inner life. The play is, in some sense, a study of Helena's inner life. The parable as a whole concerns the transformation of Bertram. But he is transformed only by having Helena added to him: by waking up to Helena's inner life as if it were his own. The question is: why does Bertram lack inner life of his own? Part of the answer, as I have suggested, is that he is invulnerable, he has nothing to lose. From the beginning of the play he merely asserts a narrow petulant will, subject to a bad influence, and one cannot feel any apprehension for him, except perhaps a certain curiosity about just how Shakespeare will correct him. He moves unconsciously, along a track of unexamined selfishness, and one's dislike of him is converted automatically to sympathy for Helena, who suffers his moral blindness as an affliction. But the key to his unconsciousness is his security: he has nothing to be apprehensive about.

Angelo in *Measure for Measure* is similar in that he too has little inner life: he moves unconsciously, a legal/moral abstraction, along a narrow, unexamined principle of ideal behaviour, incapable of self-awareness, and so devoid of interest. When inner life arrives, in the form of Tarquinian lust, it brings only momentary illumination. Then it substitutes one unconscious, unquestioned, obsessive condition for the other.

Troilus is the first of the sequence whose inner life takes centre stage. I made the point earlier that, unlike Bertram and Angelo, Troilus is a potenially tragic figure because Shakespeare has planted in him that 'bomb of vulnerability' – the 'total, unconditional love' (which turns out after all to have a condition). Thereafter, each hero's tragic potential is exactly proportionate to the vulnerability of his inner life. And to that degree he dominates centre stage.

[365]

When Shakespeare turns to the inner life of the victim, which he does in *Cymbeline*, he finds that the hero is a problem. He has to curtail the audience's sympathies for Posthumus, if Imogen is to monopolize them. He does this by various means that are all unsatisfactory. He keeps Posthumus out of sight. He makes the cause of his double vision and madness so perfunctory, so arbitrary, that it seems inane rather than inevitable or terrible, based on a foolish wager and a single lie from an unscrupulous acquaintance. He reduces his madness, in dramatic terms, to a brief order for Imogen's murder, accompanied by a single frenzied tirade against women in general. The result is, his role seems large but comparatively empty. If his feelings had been dramatized in more detail, in sharper close-up, at greater length, if they were more enmeshed with circumstance, as they would have had to be if Shakespeare had revealed more of them, then Posthumus's inner life would have begun to engross the audience's sympathy, inevitably, simply because he has everything to lose. He has invested in Imogen his 'total, unconditional love'. And his crime, murdering his beloved, is truly tragic. In trying to deprive him of his inner life, without depriving him of his love, Shakespeare has to throttle back one engine in a play that is trying to go beyond certain limits.

If Shakespeare carefully planned *The Winter's Tale* as the story of Hermione's suffering and triumph, then he had once again to be sure that the tragic hero did not steal centre stage, and monopolize the audience's interest. He was presumably aware of the somewhat vacuous impression made by Posthumus's bulky but necessarily underpowered presence. In the so-many-ways perfect situation of *The Winter's Tale*, Leontes could not, like Posthumus, be edited into the background: his raging presence throughout the first half of the play is vital. The problem is to deprive him of inner life without neutralizing his inescapable, dangerous, frenzied presence.

Shakespeare solved this in the simplest way, with a slight adjustment to the Tragic Equation. He remembered *Measure for Measure* and simply removed from Leontes that first phase of the Tragic Equation – the pre-Puritan, idyllic phase of 'total, unconditional love'.

He manages this cleverly, because there is a general assumption – in Hermione, for instance – that Leontes's love for her is, say, as secure as Othello's was for Desdemona before Iago spoke, and it turns out eventually, at the end of the play, that in fact he did love her as his own soul. Yet Shakespeare so manipulates the audience that nowhere in the opening of the play can Leontes's love for his wife be believed; and in fact one is readier to suspect a latent hatred of some kind, that suddenly explodes.

The Winter's Tale: the Tragic Equation becomes a theophany

Leontes's madness is as sudden and as absolute as was Lear's when he confronted the 'double vision' in Cordelia. But what Leontes lacks, very clearly, is Lear's love. Lear reveals this great love, on which the power of that tremendous first act and indeed the whole play depends, in a very few lines. Shakespeare grants Leontes not one word. When Hermione has prevailed with Polixenes, and persuaded him to stay, Leontes's curt: 'at my request he would not' is followed by the only endearment or tender of affection, of any kind, in this first half of the play:

> Hermione, my dearest, thou never spoke'st
> To better purpose,
>> *The Winter's Tale*, I. ii. 88–9

which is nothing if not an opportunity for the actor to suggest the first icy waft of Leontes's homicidal rage against her. After that, his four lines or so, describing her first vow to him, of her eternal love, sound like the bubbles of something long ago drowned. And his next step after four innocent lines from Hermione takes him over the brink into the 'icy current and compulsive course' (*Othello*, III. iii. 455) which carry him away.

Deprived of the subjectivity of a tragic hero, Leontes has become something else. One sees what in comparing him with Othello, whose jealous frenzy has the same cause, and ought to be of the same kind but obviously is not. In *Othello* Iago has to work hard, throughout much of the play, persuading the hero that his wife is a whore. And one never thinks of Othello as a madman, only as one whose 'total, unconditional love' struggles in agony against an imminent madness, succumbs to it in a sort of swoon, then recovers completely.

But in Leontes, within the first moment, the Iago factor has triumphed one hundred per cent. The history of Othello's pathological frenzy is played out on stage: it is the play. But the history of Leontes's is over, a closed book, before the play begins. The ultimate madness, the double vision, rejection of and homicidal intent against Hermione, are

[367]

simply there, as if they had been there in a covert form for some time, and might even have prompted him to ask her to make the advances to Polixenes in the first place. And now they emerge less like suffering than like a rapture of righteousness.

Remembering the myth behind the two long poems, one can see that Leontes states the case of the Goddess-destroying god in large simple capitals. Because she radiates erotic magic (in her quasi-seduction of Polixenes) and is pregnant, she serves the female reproductive system, has surrendered herself to it, must therefore be a whore and must therefore be destroyed. In this way Hermione has become an incarnation of the fact that the female reproductive system is regarded, after *All's Well*, by the Tarquinized hero, as an impersonal, 'possessing', insatiable appetite, an evil deity (the organism of the Queen of Hell) quite distinct from (and far more powerful than) the human personality of the woman in whom it lives. And here the Goddess-destroyer has this elemental creature, at last, in his own court.

This reveals very clearly what I mentioned in passing in my pages about the two long narratives (cf. page 82). Those two poems, the two halves of the Equation, are linked not only as cause (in Heaven, in theology) and effect (on Earth, in secular life) and not only as inverted opposites, but as two simultaneous images of the same thing: Adonis's rejection of the Goddess is the same act, on another plane, as Tarquin's rape and Othello's murder.

Leontes, as the accuser, is now like Angelo in *Measure for Measure*, the embodiment of the Divine Right of this double act. No longer suffering the Equation, as a lover of the Goddess, like the true tragic hero, he simply embodies the cruel severity of it, as her destroyer.

He is very like the relentless chemical chain reaction of the tragic myth considered as those 'Cyclops' hammer' – the sword of Pyrrhus in the Player's speech – descending now on Hermione as it descended on old Priam's 'milky head', while Hecuba screamed through the burning palace. But since Leontes is also the husband she loves (Shakespeare makes that clear) and the father of her son, and her new-born child (Shakespeare multiplies the love bonds), the elemental vertigo of his madness is instantly converted into the illumination of her helpless inner life.

What Leontes has lost in inner life and potential tragic stature, Hermione has gained in inner life and Sophia-like mythic depth of self-awareness. What he has lost by becoming the embodiment of Angelo's

Puritan capital punishment for adultery (for creating new life, as I say, in both plays), Hermione has gained in radiant pain, luminous truth to the soul, that blaze of her near canonization.

Without ceasing to be itself, the Tragic Equation has become part of Sophia's story. No longer a hero at the centre of his own tragedy, Leontes has become a form of Jaldabaoth, the personification of Hermione's afflictions. The deluded world and possessed violence of the Tragic Equation have become an image of the diabolical realm into which the Sophia figure falls. The Tragic Equation, that is, has become more than the incubator of Shakespeare's new mutation, it has become the tortures and the martyred torso of the higher organism of the Theophany.

From this point of view *The Winter's Tale* consummates the shamanic, biological response (the need to fathom the reality of the injury, then to heal it – or find some way of living with it), as it was projected into Shakespeare's activity and as it was projected, further, into his embroilment with the forces of the Reformation. In this play he attempts to complete his public rescue of the soul, in the form of his Sacred Bride, in the form of the Goddess, in the form of the Divine Love, in the form of the divine creative power of Nature – his life and his Muse. (But then, as if he knew that time and the Reformation were about to destroy all these, he rescued them, so to speak, provisionally, for himself, in a leaky boat and on an island.)

The pattern of the Gnostic Coda in *The Winter's Tale*

Since these fundamental myths, like the lines on the palm, rise out of the biological foundations, the fact that the Goddess myth, descending through Asia into Christianity, and the myth of the Goddess-destroyer, dependent on the first myth, and descending likewise, should emerge combined in the Egyptian myth of the Eye, which then descended into Gnosticism as the dominant formative influence on the Sophia myth, is natural. And it is just as natural that Shakespeare's imagination, grappling with the two myths of the Reformation, and by the very impasse of that conflict being forced back into earlier sources and resources (as usually happens when the way forward is blocked) should recover the same synthesis and the same route of transcendence that had evolved before the Judaeo-Christian schism broke the whole complex into fragments.

The Gnostic pattern followed in *Pericles* is developed even more carefully, and is completed, in the second half of *The Winter's Tale*, as follows.

In *Pericles*, Thaisa splits into two at the moment of her apparent death in the sea storm, and the two parts are separated from each other (mother separated from daughter, in a sea storm) and both from Pericles. In *The Winter's Tale*, similarly, Hermione, at the moment of her apparent death, splits into two, and the two parts, mother and daughter, are separated from each other (the daughter rescued from a sea storm) and both from Leontes. Thaisa is preserved alive in Diana's temple until her daughter is grown: Hermione is preserved alive by Paulina, until her daughter is grown. In each play all are restored, against every hope, as if beyond death, to each other, wife to husband and daughter, daughter to father and mother and new husband simultaneously. Thaisa is restored from being a nun of Diana, and Hermione from being a 'statue' (protected, as it were, by Apollo's votaress, Paulina). This choreography makes perfect sense when it is interpreted according to all three algebraic systems: of the Equation, of Sophia, and of the Eye.

If Hermione is the Goddess as the Eye, Leontes is the Set figure (the Boar). Polixenes is the Horus figure (cf. the Egyptian mythic complex behind *King Lear*, page 270). Having torn Hermione (the Eye) from (as he thinks) Polixenes, Leontes (like Set) throws her away into the sea. In the terms of Shakespeare's secularization of this myth into the theme of the Rival Brothers, Leontes has torn the Crown (the Eye, the Lucrece) from his 'brother' and cast away the soul of it. In other words, he has seized the power of the Crown (it is very clear that in his own reckoning he had lost it) but has lost the inner sanctity of it. Just as, in *As You Like It*, Duke Frederick seized the ducal crown from his brother but banished his brother's daughter, Rosalind, who was its sanctity. And just as, in *The Tempest*, Antonio will tear the ducal crown from his brother Prospero but banish his brother's daughter, Miranda, who is its sanctity.

In all three plays, *As You Like It*, *The Winter's Tale* and *The Tempest*, the Horus figure, having lost the 'Eye', is banished.* The Duke is banished into the Forest of Arden, Polixenes is banished in that he flees for his life, Prospero is banished to the island. And in each of these

*Shakespeare's Egyptian sense of the Eye is already well developed in *Lucrece* – 'The eye of heaven is out' – lines 356 and 372–8.

[370]

plays, the soul of the Eye — Rosalind, Perdita, Miranda — ends up with the banished one, which is to say that the soul's truth, Justice, ends up with the defeated, blinded 'brother' (thereby in some way restoring his sight — and eventually his rule).

The common factor is the Lucrece figure who, as the soul of the rational, is the (sexual) victim of the irrational, and is also, as ever, the soul of the Crown — the soul of Divine Order and Truth. In the dimension of the Tragic Equation, she is an aspect of the Goddess Aphrodite/Persephone. In the mutated Equation, she is Sophia. And in the Egyptian myth behind the myth of Sophia, she is the Eye. These levels operate simultaneously, turning, as all the plays of the tragic sequence turn, on the multivalent role of the Female. The presence of this tiered stack of metaphysical levels, in these last plays, and their congruence within the unifying myth of the Eye, is maybe responsible for the logic of their mysterious wholeness, and for the teasing sense of their many-layered richness as symbols of transcendence — which is not to be explained on the level of character and local event.

The new factor in the Coda of *The Winter's Tale* is Polixenes's son, Florizel. This innovation becomes more significant when it throws its shadow forward into *The Tempest*. Of the two 'brothers' the rational Polixenes is the defeated and blinded Horus, who is the banished Duke, who is the Prospero. From this it is clear that, according to the myth, Justice, the soul of Order, which has been hurled into the wilderness in the form of Hermione and new-born Perdita, must now return to Polixenes — and so it does. Perdita has become an unknown shepherdess in his country.

Since she is the sanctity of his rule as the unjustly deposed brother (as Rosalind was Duke Senior's and as Miranda will be Prospero's), Perdita must be brought into close relationship with Polixenes. And this is effected by his duplicate new-born self, Florizel.

When these two are married, Perdita, daughter of Leontes, becomes also daughter (-in-law) to Polixenes, while Florizel becomes also son (-in-law) to Leontes.

And, since they are the two new-born selves of the divided brothers, when these two are married on the mythic plane, the brotherhood of Leontes and Polixenes is automatically healed on the real plane, the plane that was formerly tragic, in the world of time and memory, where crimes have to be forgiven, though they cannot be undone or forgotten, while wrinkles accumulate on the faces. This healing on the formerly tragic, now simply natural, plane is made real by the seemingly miraculous return, as from the dead, of Hermione, to the regenerate Leontes.

At the same time, this marriage of Florizel and Perdita, these two faultless, brand-new souls, by restoring the idyllic and thereby Divine Love of Venus and Adonis (before the double vision), heals the crime against the Female, returning love to a point in time before the crime has occurred, on a level where, perhaps, it cannot occur again. On the natural plane, this healing, too, is made real by the return of Hermione from beyond the death dealt to her by the crime (as if her return made the crime 'un-happen').

All are reunited simultaneously, as if into a single love, reconsecrated by Apollo's (in this play the God of Truth, the Sun God, the High God) validation of Hermione's Divine Truth, and in a new reign of *Gnosis Kardias*.

I should say again, I do not pretend to claim that Shakespeare was doing more, in articulating this pattern, than giving a rationale to the dance of his materials. Yet there is a strong suggestion that he is bent on working out an esoteric ritual (either giving these figures their conventional mythic significance, as I have done, or some other) with almost pedantic thoroughness. If his heart had been inside the box office exclusively, he would hardly have taken such theatrical risks as the self-enclosed, prolonged monotony of Leontes's frenzy and accusation, which he could easily have made more intriguing dramatically. And he would perhaps have presented Perdita's recognition scene as a spectacle, rather than hand it, as he does, to a report between casual strangers. It is easier to justify such things if one grants these last plays a role in religious propaganda – at a time when national religious policy, during Shakespeare's life, seemed ready to flow into a new mould. But the justification finds more evidence if one accepts that these plays have a crypto-ritual dimension, where Shakespeare's taste and aptitude for an almost perverse ingenuity of coded pattern-making served an esoteric audience watching over the shoulders of his popular audience, a scattering of initiates for whom the real pleasure and gratification, like Shakespeare's, was the secret meaning of the public statement.

Hermione's plea as the voice of Heaven and Earth

I suggested that *The Winter's Tale* was the last of the tragic series, and also the culmination. That play recapitulates Adonis's original crime, his rejection of the Goddess, and brings it to judgement and condemnation by Apollo – Apollo the God of Truth, the God of Poetry, the divine harpist of the seven vowels, and the God of Healing. Apollo, as I mentioned before, is the original father of the Craneskin Bag. He is the Europeanization of the Egyptian Horus, as the keeper of the Eye, who in turn is an aspect of Re, the father of the Eye.

Shakespeare's choice of this god is as pointedly functional as his other mythical devices. Apollo's shrine at Delphi was originally the shrine of the great serpent, Python. The oracular priestess, the Pythia, spoke literally with the voice of the Earth as the original serpent – the great serpentine Goddess as Total, Unconditional Being. When the protestation of Hermione and her new-born daughter is validated by the chthonic word of this priestess, it becomes virtually the word of the Earth, pronounced in the 'thunderous' speech of the god. Just as Venus had attempted to do in *Venus and Adonis*, Hermione therefore speaks with the voice of the Goddess as the living Earth. Shakespeare could hardly have hoped to find a more powerful and concise image of the Divine Authority of the truth of his heroine's suffering, and of the culpability of his hero.

'The Pythia, with raving mouth, uttering her unlaughing, unadorned words, reaches us over a thousand years with her voice – through the inspiration of the god,' says Heraclitus. It is worth a glance, just in passing the shrine at Delphi, to see that Dionysus, the archetypal dying and resurrected god, was buried here and that the Delphic priesthood regarded him as the cyclic, or dying and reborn, inner being of Apollo.

The Athenian tragic drama of the fifth century BC was composed for the Dionysia, the annual festival of this god. The instinct of later observers has been to suppose that the tragic hero evolved from ritual dramatic presentations of Dionysus himself, but scholars point out that the association between tragic drama and Dionysus was accidental. Dithyrambic choruses, originally sung to celebrate Dionysus, were apparently in the course of time adapted to heroic monologues and dramatic narratives. Aeschylus invented the tragic mode and introduced it in developed performances that no longer had any connection with the god, except that they continued to be presented at the Dionysia. The story that Aeschylus, as a young man, was visited by Dionysus in a dream and asked to compose a tragedy is dismissed as a legend.

Aeschylus was a native of Eleusis, the great cult centre of the Mysteries of Demeter, and is thought to have been connected with the priesthood there before becoming known as a tragic dramatist. In the almost total absence of other religious allegiances, the Demeter Mysteries were the foundation of Athenian spiritual life. The revelatory moment of these Mysteries at Eleusis was the magical nativity of Demeter's son, the god Brimus, or Iacchos, a form of Dionysus.

The hypothesis that tragedy appears wherever primal Dionysiac forces, moving in the ecstatic wave of a Goddess mystery religion, encounter head on a secularizing, rational, pragmatic morality is, as I suggested earlier, as good a way as any other of accounting for the conflict between rational and irrational in Greek tragedy. And it does not seem incongruous that the very last of the great tragedies, the *Bacchae*, produced in 405 BC, after Euripides's death, dramatizes exactly that situation in its own naked terms: the head-on collision of the god, among his possessed women, with Pentheus, the rational ruler.

Dionysus's father was the High God (like Christ's). His mother was Semele, whose sister, Agave, was the mother of Pentheus, King of Thebes. This is the first Shakespearean pre-echo in the story: Dionysus is the wild, 'irrational' kinsman of the reigning King Pentheus.

King Pentheus rejects Dionysus's ecstatic religion (and so, at first, does his mother Agave), whereupon Dionysus sends all the women into a worshipping frenzy. Pentheus tries to imprison Dionysus, but prison cannot hold him. And when Pentheus attempts to spy on the rites of the Maenads, his own mother mistakes him for a bull calf, or maybe a lion, and tears off his head.

In other words, the deity, rejected by Pentheus, goes mad and destroys him – but not before the 'madness' has become his own mother. This pattern replicates the death of Hippolytus – where Aphrodite, rejected in the form of his mother (his mother possessed by Eros/Aphrodite – as Agave is possessed by the rejected Dionysus), destroys him. In the same way, it obviously replicates the death of Adonis – in the long poem and on through the succession of the Tragic Equation.

In the *Bacchae*, the relationship of the Rival Brothers – usurpation of the one by the other – to the death of the Adonis figure is exactly as in Shakespeare. Pentheus is destroyed by an elemental figure composite of a Queen of Hell (his mad mother) and the irrational ego, the 'hot tyrant' or Boar – which is simultaneously his 'inferior brother' and the self-renewing, all-renewing god, the saint-maker.

At bottom of both the Greek tragedy and Shakespeare's Tragic Equation is the same thing: 'total, unconditional' Divine Love rejected. The *Bacchae* ends, and *Hippolytus* ends, where *Venus and Adonis* ends. Again, only Shakespeare took the next step and discovered the second part of the Equation, in which Pentheus and Hippolytus, surviving the terrors of the Goddess, and having atoned, would be, like Leontes, spiritually transformed by their sufferings and her love.

This inner link between the dying, reborn 'god' within Shakespeare's tragic hero, and the dying, reborn 'god' within the religious imagination of the Greek tragedians and their public, is made with even more literal immediacy in *The Tempest*. I say more about this when I come to that play – where the nativity of Brimus provides clues to the natures of both Caliban and Ariel.

CHAPTER 6

THE DISMANTLING OF THE TRAGIC EQUATION:
The Tempest

========

The beginning in the end

The Tempest as a Gnostic coda

The Storm

The evolution of the Storm up to *Macbeth*

The two selves of the Flower

The Storm changes planes: Macbeth's vision

The Storm passes to the Female

The Storm and the Flower

The Tragic Equation in *The Tempest*

Prospero's tripartite brother

The Tempest and Dido

Miranda as Dido reborn

The Gnostic pattern in *The Tempest*

Ulysses and the mythic background of *The Tempest*

Circe

The Tempest: a precarious moment in the alchemy

Ariel and the Harpy

The Masque in *The Tempest*: the defeat of Venus

The beginning in the end

Though *The Winter's Tale* completes the long investigations into the hero's 'original sin', *The Tempest* comes in no way as an anticlimax. And though so many of its features relate to the sequence, nevertheless it seems to stand apart as a radically different work from any that have gone before. There is something about Prospero's role that makes it easy to believe that with *The Tempest* Shakespeare is not so much adding another play to his repertoire, as making a retrospective summary, almost a philosophical revaluation of his long obsession.

Looking at the play through the optics of the Tragic Equation provides one explanation, or set of explanations, for this difference. Besides performing all the other functions which it inexhaustibly continues to perform, *The Tempest* turns out to be a virtuoso *Grosse Fuge* of the themes of Shakespeare's tragic myth.

As I have followed it, the Equation develops step by step from the two long poems to the mutation in *King Lear*, and from there, step by step, to the full Theophany in *The Winter's Tale*, where it arrives at a kind of completeness. In that completeness, however, the redemption of the tragic crime is lifted right off the Earth.

In *The Tempest*, Shakespeare makes the great, final necessary adjustment: he anchors his Theophany back to the Earth. And in doing so, in bringing his work to an end in this way, he finds himself facing the beginning.

The Tempest as a Gnostic coda

What seem like the two most striking innovations in the structure of *The Tempest*, and which have an enormous influence on the effect that the play makes, are both in fact established Shakespearean patterns. One is the overall form of the plot, the other is again that role of Prospero.

All the preceding works of the tragic sequence share, as a basic common factor, some replay of the Tragic Equation, as I have shown, right up to *The Winter's Tale*. In *King Lear*, what I have called the Sophia myth came to life briefly, as a sort of phantom pregnancy, or rather like an embryo reabsorbed in the frightful womb of the Equation. In *Cymbeline, Pericles* and *The Winter's Tale*, it was born out of the Tragic Equation's formerly fatal bite, somewhere in the third act, escaped the Tragic Equation, and grew up, so to speak, through the rest of the play. But here in *The Tempest* that Sophia story (the Coda) has suddenly expanded to become the entire play, all five acts. And the Tragic Equation has shrivelled away, like an umbilicus.

It has not disappeared entirely. But in its essential role, as power and blood supply for the Gnostic myth, it appears here in even more vestigial form than in *Pericles* – knotted and tucked, belly-button fashion, into Prospero's narrative exposition during the second act. And here, once again, it takes the classic simple form: a story of the Rival Brothers. But it reappears in the rest of the play, which, as I say, is a fugue of teeming larval shapes of the Tragic Equation and Rival Brothers, as if a child should be born already pregnant with quadruplets.

The other no less consequential novelty is related to this first one. Prospero is the only tragic hero, in the whole tragic sequence, who does not go through the madness and the Tarquinian crime. He is an Adonis figure, a standard potential tragic hero: he has seen the double vision rejected the Queen of Hell (Sycorax) to a great distance, and now he confronts her emanation the Boar (Caliban). But he stands his ground – *and overpowers the Boar*. Unlike any of the others, where Adonis is more or less agonizingly demolished and supplanted by Tarquin, this play ritualizes Adonis's victory – as he stops the Boar in mid-air, mid-charge, magically spellbound. He resists the Tarquinian madness. From beginning to end he remains vigilant Adonis. This explains the play's comparative lack of drama, since all the action, throughout the tragic sequence, erupts from that impact of the Boar, and Adonis's transformation. This also gives the play its unique centre of gravity and point of view, in so far as they are now determined by one who is, from beginning to end, in fact Adonis.

There are other ways of accounting for that special structure of *The Tempest*, but this is how it appears in terms of the Equation. Like all its predecessors it begins with Adonis confronting the Boar, but what drama there is now plays around Prospero's control as he gently undoes the mechanism of the double vision and fits together a sacred marriage, blessed by the Great Goddess, in which a new idyllic Adonis is united to a new reborn Venus/Lucrece, who is what Adonis in the long poem wanted her to be – like a Diana.

Once *The Tempest* has been shown in this light, as I say, it can be seen that Shakespeare has gone right back to the beginning, as if he would now (if there were time) start afresh. An itemizing of the main moves of the plot, in the light of the Tragic Equation, shows what this entails.

Antonio who, with the help of Alonso, King of Naples, usurped his brother Prospero and cast him away to sea, is a Macbeth-type Rival Brother who fails to kill. More obviously, he is a duplication of Duke Frederick who, in the tragic overture, *As You Like It*, usurped and banished Duke Senior, as if the Devil's Island where Prospero now finds himself were what remained of the Forest of Arden after the holocaust of the tragedies.

(Perhaps one should not make light of the fact that the Mother Forest of those lyrical days, when Shakespeare answered the call, *in mezzo del cammin*, has become the rocky, storm-beaten island of a terrible dead witch and her devil-god. Or that Prospero numbers off rather precisely the twelve years between the composition of *As You Like It* (when Jaques set out on the inward journey following the convertite Duke) and the composition of *The Tempest*, when Prospero, so much older, seeing the chance to settle the account, lifts his head from his books.)

Prospero escapes with his baby daughter, Miranda, just as in *As You Like It* the banished Duke lives (finally) in the forest with his daughter, Rosalind. Both these Lucrece figures, according to the Equation, correspond to the soul of the ducal crown, which cannot remain with the illegal usurper, but must live in exile with the rightful ruler.

Arriving on the island, Prospero finds it occupied by Caliban, son of the Great Witch Sycorax (said now to be dead) and (it is suggested) of the devil-god, Setebos. Prospero usurps this (demi-devil) Caliban's rule and, after attempting to educate him and failing, makes him his slave.

So Prospero becomes, like his brother Antonio, a usurper, and Caliban becomes, like Prospero himself, the usurped.

The 'rejected' Caliban nurses revenge, planning to murder Prospero and rape Miranda, and retake possession of the island in the name of his mother Sycorax. That is to say, he is now a usurper-in-waiting. In this role, as the 'inferior' brother, he has the credentials of the Boar and 'hot tyrant', who emerges from the penumbra of the Queen of Hell, as he emerges from the suppressed witch Sycorax, his mother.

Prospero, meanwhile, is also waiting, working towards the moment when he can depose his brother – counter-usurp him, and retake his ducal crown. So Caliban's counter-coup develops as a shadow and metaphor of Prospero's.

Prospero's fraternal relationship to Caliban, which this symmetrical pattern more or less imposes on him, is obviously adjusted with some care. A degree of *identity* with Caliban, imposed by the same pattern, is no less so. In the case of Prospero, the persona of Boar and 'hot tyrant', very like the magic mantle, is something he puts on and off fairly lightly – as if his magic were a mantling shadow of the Queen of Hell.

His magic is largely, of course, the magic of Sycorax, in so far as it operates, in the play, entirely through Ariel. Sycorax, the ultimate Queen of Hell, is still everywhere, like the natural pressure of the island's atmosphere. Prospero's statement that she died is little more than a figure of speech: the island, on which Prospero and Miranda have lodged for their twelve years, and on which all the action unfolds, is hers. Prospero's world – physical and metaphysical – seems to be fashioned out of her remains, rather as in the original myth of the Goddess-destroyer Marduk's was fashioned out of Tiamat's. The music and magic of Ariel was hers. And Prospero's alchemy, in which he uses the borrowed Ariel to transform his enemies, his fortunes, and even his soul in the sacred marriage of his daughter, is possible only within the crucible of Sycorax – her island.

Most potently of all, she lives on in her son, Caliban, as intact as in any of the Boar-possessed Tarquins of earlier plays: she is there in his endless contriving: to kill Prospero, to ravish Miranda and repossess the island – the Boar on the point of becoming the 'hot tyrant'.

The Storm

The opening storm is the last of a long series. It secretes a precise and fascinating etymology, evolved through the action of the earlier plays. The use to which the Equation puts it, play by play, reveals this quite clearly.

The Storm enters the drama – in functional form – in *Richard III.** By the time it reaches *Macbeth* its meaning is clear. But there are two storms in *Macbeth*. In the second storm the meaning has changed. This becomes evident retrospectively. After that, though the Storm reappears regularly, right up to *The Tempest*, it remains attached to this second meaning – and never again reverts to the first.

What is happening here becomes fully understandable only when the Storm's relationship to two other factors is taken into account. The first of these is its relationship to the charge of the Boar. The second is its relationship to the two planes, the tragic plane and the transcendental.

But at this point it is also clear that the mid-career change in the meaning of the Storm, and the relationship between the two planes themselves, can only be defined properly if one has a distinct idea of the two meanings – antithetical meanings – of the charge of the Boar. And these two meanings of the Boar's charge can only be distinguished if one has some idea of the meaning of the Flower.

The relationships between these glyphs are actually simple. And since both Storm and Flower burst with all their accumulated fullness of meaning into *The Tempest*, where the two planes are also brought to a moment of perfect but uneasy balance, this is the place to suggest an interpretation of their meanings.

The evolution of the Storm up to *Macbeth*

Remembering always that the charge of the Boar is – outside *Venus and Adonis* – a psychological event, a shock wave of death–rebirth, and that the polaroids of the Tragic Equation are to be worn in this argument at all times, one can say that the Storm, the Flower, the two planes, and the charge of the Boar all enter Shakespeare's oeuvre as active mythic components of his architectonic design – attain a functional degree of definition, that is – at about the same time, around 1592–3, in two works. The Boar's charge, the Flower, and the two planes are introduced and integrated by *Venus and Adonis*. The Storm is introduced by *Richard III*.

Both these works revolve around the charge of the Boar. *Venus and Adonis* presents the archetypal analysis, in mythic terms, of the dynamics behind the death–rebirth event: the rejected Goddess in her

---

*Though its eventual role was adumbrated, quite clearly, in *The Comedy of Errors* (page 491).

wild boar form charges – and Adonis is transformed. *Richard III* presents a parallel event in political terms as Richard murders his way to the crown, destroying his sole rival contender and brother, Clarence. Here, Clarence is the Adonis figure and Richard the Boar becomes a Tarquin by destroying him. Richard's credentials as the Boar (his crest) are established on every level, not least in the recurrent descriptions of him.

> Thou elvish-mark'd, abortive, rooting hog!
> Thou that wast seal'd in thy nativity
> The slave of nature and the son of hell!
>
> *Richard III*, I. iii. 228–30

His infinitely vengeful ambition, and deformity, are one of Shakespeare's most powerful symbols of that ectoplasmic entity – the elemental – emerging from the rejected, enraged Goddess.

The long poem, it should be said, is precise, and confines itself to the mythic analysis of the essential event. The play is far less coherent on the mythic level, dislocated by the exigencies of the recalcitrant and yet comprehensive historic plot.

The relevant episode in the play is the death of Clarence. This first dramatically functional storm – the sea storm in the nightmare that Clarence narrates just before he is drowned in the Butt of Malmsey* – seems to be the seminal episode. Richard trips him off the ship's hatches:

> Into the tumbling billows of the main.
> Lord, Lord! methought what pain it was to drown:
> What dreadful noise of water in mine ears!
> What sights of ugly death within mine eyes!
> Methought I saw a thousand fearful wracks . . .
>
> I. iv. 20–4

The dream is extended into the afterlife, the sea storm becomes Hell itself, till finally Clarence hears: 'Seize on him, Furies, take him unto

*Shakespeare's system of symbols, the imaginative lexicon that simply enriched itself magnetically there, inside his head, was consistent for every kind of use. That black joke of Clarence's premonitory dream, where his death in the Butt of Malmsey becomes a drowning in a roaring sea, and an epic visit to the Underworld, crops up again in *The Tempest*, where the same Butt comes bobbing ashore, after the sea storm, with Stephano (the would-be king of the island) astride it, full of the 'unearthly liquor' that will make Caliban drunk, and precipitate his Tarquinian bid to supplant Prospero and seize Miranda and the island.

torment . . .' (I. iv. 57). Richard then emerges as a Tarquin and turns his savage attentions on to Clarence's widow (gradually thereafter accumulating the curses of all the women in the play).

The next storm appears in *Measure for Measure* (in the evolutionary sequence, the second play of the Tragic Equation). Essentially the most intense (and admired) passage of poetry in the play, Isabella's speech to Angelo is virtually a storm:

> Could great men thunder
> As Jove himself does, Jove would ne'er be quiet,
> For every pelting, petty officer
> Would use his heaven for thunder; nothing but thunder.
> Merciful heaven!
> Thou rather with thy sharp and sulphurous bolt
> Split'st the unwedgeable and gnarled oak
> Than the soft myrtle; but man, proud man,
> Dress'd in a little brief authority,
> Most ignorant of what he's most assured,
> His glassy essence, like an angry ape,
> Plays such fantastic tricks before high heaven
> As make the angels weep; who, with our spleens,
> Would all themselves laugh mortal.
>
> *Measure for Measure*, II. ii. 110–23

In this speech, Isabella is calling Angelo to surrender his Puritan authority, and humble himself to Heaven, though the effect of the speech on the distorted uncorrected Angelo is to trigger the Boar's charge. His next words are the bewildered:

> Why do you put these sayings upon me?
>
> II. ii. 133

and then:

> She speaks, and 'tis
> Such sense that my sense breeds with it . . .
>
> II. ii. 141–2

whereupon his animal transformation begins. The moment she leaves him, he confronts that image.

> . . . it is I,
> That, lying by the violet in the sun,

Do as the carrion does, not as the flower,
Corrupt with virtuous season.

II. ii. 165–8

I connected this violet to the equivalent juncture in the hidden working of the Equation, where the Flower springs up through the 'carrion' Adonis, interpreting the Flower as Angelo's rebirth into Tarquin, the Flower symbolizing not spiritual rebirth on the upper plane, as the redeemed one, but rebirth into the Tarquin who dreams that his Heaven lies in violently taking sexual possession of Isabella (the votaress, the almost-nun), on the lower, the tragic plane.

The Flower here resembles a sort of retinal after-image of Adonis's redeemed rebirth as a flower in the poem, still lingering, as a double exposure, on his rebirth as Tarquin in the Tragic Equation.

What has happened in this case, as can be seen, is that the Storm (the thunder of Jove, speaking through Isabella, as thunderous Apollo will speak through Hermione) has been even more tightly integrated with the death of Angelo/Adonis and emergence of Angelo/Tarquin. In other words, the heavenly thunder accompanies the charge of the Boar-as-the-enraged-Goddess, just as, here, Isabella is the mouthpiece of the rejected, enraged Goddess.

After the brief but overwhelming 'hurricane' that delivers his new Tarquinian self to Troilus (page 193), the next storm flickers across the opening of *Hamlet* as prodigious happenings in Heaven, making a backdrop for the Ghost's bituminous pronouncement, which starts the transformation of Hamlet – and opens his hand-to-hand grappling fight with the Boar (which he maintains throughout the play, till it overcomes him, though not entirely, in Ophelia's grave).

The significant storm in *Hamlet* is brief and stunning, and occurs in the speech that Hamlet calls for from the Player: the description of Pyrrhus (the image of King Hamlet's murderer, Claudius, but more urgently of Claudius's murderer, Prince Hamlet himself) has just knocked the old Trojan King Priam over – 'with the whiff and wind of his fell sword' (II. ii. 503). At this moment, as if in sympathy, Ilium itself,

Seeming to feel this blow, with flaming top
Stoops to his base, and with a hideous crash
Takes prisoner Pyrrhus' ear.

II. ii. 505–7

In the circumstances, the whole city, like its king, kneels, and with the din of its ruin assails Pyrrhus's conscience – bellows for mercy, so to speak. And like Tarquin, torch on high, over Lucrece's bed, appalled at what he is about to do (like Adonis's horrified snapshot vision of the Boar the moment before it strikes him), Pyrrhus hesitates. His hesitation is described at length:

> for lo, his sword,
> Which was declining on the milky head
> Of reverend Priam, seemed i' the air to stick:
> So, as a painted tyrant, Pyrrhus stood,
> And like a neutral to his will and matter,
> Did nothing.
> But, as we often see, against some storm,
> A silence in the heavens, the rack stand still,
> The bold winds speechless and the orb below
> As hush as death, anon the dreadful thunder
> Doth rend the region; so, after Pyrrhus' pause,
> Aroused vengeance sets him new a-work;
> And never did the Cyclops' hammers fall
> On Mars's armour, forg'd for proof eterne,
> With less remorse than Pyrrhus' bleeding sword
> Now falls on Priam.
>
> II. ii. 507–22

Tarquin has arrived, as it were, with a bang – but again in a panoply of mythic definition. Cyclops (the monster in the cave, whom Ulysses escaped only with ruthless cunning) lays a strong lineal claim on Caliban, who, as I have said, and as I hope to show later (cf. page 465), in more detail, is more markedly the Boar than any other character in Shakespeare except the Boar itself. And since Mars was also, as Venus's jealous lover, the Boar who killed Adonis, Pyrrhus is, as it were, three times over the Boar in the process of dealing the death blow and becoming a Tarquin. That thunderclap, in other words, is the death of Adonis (just as the sea roaring in his ears was the death of Clarence) and the eruptive burst of Tarquin.

The next storm occurs in *Othello*, but here it is thunderless and has only a premonitory function, delivering the three innocents, Desdemona, Cassius and Othello, into the hands of Iago who, in his role of 'inferior' brother or cold reflection of the 'hot tyrant', works from this moment to introduce Othello to the Boar.

In *Macbeth* the storm is full blown and freakishly violent:

> Lamentings heard i' the air; strange screams of death,
> And prophesying with accents terrible
> Of dire combustion and confus'd events
> New hatch'd to the woeful time.
>
> *Macbeth*, II. iii. 62–5

This is the same storm striking Duncan with the lightning of Macbeth's dagger as struck Priam with Pyrrhus's sword. But it rolls its words throughout Macbeth's horrified transformation, and divine things are revealed in the livid, fiery openings as he sees it approaching:

> . . . this Duncan
> Hath borne his faculties so meek, hath been
> So clear in his great office, that his virtues
> Will plead like angels trumpet-tongu'd against
> The deep damnation of his taking-off;
> And pity, like a naked new-born babe,
> Striding the blast, or heaven's cherubim, hors'd
> Upon the sightless couriers of the air,
> Shall blow the horrid deed in every eye,
> That tears shall drown the wind . . .
>
> I. vii. 16–25

where Duncan is like a projection of the rational Adonis self that is being toppled within Macbeth by the tusks of the Boar (which are the words of the three Witches and his Hecate wife).

This storm is the climax of the storms that accompany the overpowering of Adonis and the emergence of Tarquin. Macbeth, as it turns out, has brought the fury to a point of psychological melt-down – that not even a Tarquin can withstand. The 'pity, like a naked new-born babe,/Striding the blast' is the proleptic image of a new kind of agonizing transformation, which I will come back to (cf. page 394).

At this point, in other words, the meaning of the Storm changes. The second storm in *Macbeth*, described by Macbeth when he goes back to consult the three Witches, will have quite a different meaning, will mean, in fact, the very opposite of what it has meant so far. But before that can be made clear, something has to be said about the two planes and the Flower. Another look has to be taken at *Venus and Adonis*.

The two selves of the Flower

In the pre-Shakespearean myth of Venus and Adonis, as Ovid simplified it, the meaning of the Flower, into which the slain Adonis was transformed, is quite clear. In the Flower the loving Adonis, beloved of the Goddess, has been reborn — as the same loving Adonis, beloved of the Goddess. The fact that he dies as a demi-god or god, and is reborn as a flower, is merely a way of expressing a primeval fact that he is at all times the god of the vegetative cycle, both god and flower, and always the beloved of the Goddess.

When Shakespeare disrupts this happy arrangement, making Adonis reject the Goddess, reject her as if he feared and hated her, he still keeps the old myth's ending, where the slain Adonis becomes a flower that the Goddess tucks between her breasts and kisses all the way back to Paphos.

Inevitably, this radical change in the story changes the meaning of the Flower, or rather complicates it. Adonis no longer dies as the Goddess's lover. He now dies in the full flush of his crime against her (his rejection of her Divine Love). He dies, apparently, with his tragic crime on his head, still unredeemed, still unreconciled, in his will, to the total demand of Divine Love, the immense offer of Complete Being.

In that case, when Venus plucks the flower that springs from his blood and tucks it between her breasts and kisses it, as she flies off, it can only mean that for some reason she has forgiven him. That is to say, by his violent death, Adonis must have atoned. The Goddess, as the fatal Boar, has forced him to atone.

The Goddess-rejector, compelled in this way to atone, in a violent death, now absolved and redeemed, has resumed his nature as the beloved of the Divine Being and has been gathered into reunion with Divine Love.

A single diagram makes this clear:

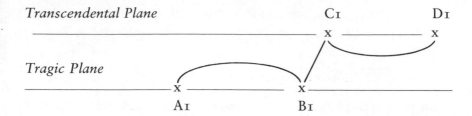

Transcendental Plane .... C1 .... D1

Tragic Plane .... A1 .... B1

A1 Adonis rejects Venus and becomes a Tarquin (Goddess-rejector = Goddess-destroyer).
B1 The Goddess, in the form of a Boar, compels Adonis to atone in violent death.
C1 Absolved and redeemed, Adonis is reborn as a Flower.
D1 Gathering him into reunion with her Divine Love, Venus flies off with him between her breasts.

What this diagram also makes clear is that *Venus and Adonis*, within itself, not only anticipates the complete shape of the Tragic Equation (in the first half A1, B1) but the final completed shape of the Tragic Equation plus Theophany, (A1, B1, C1, D1). It anticipates, that is, the full future evolution of Shakespeare's tragic idea. From this one can see just how the poem serves as his Rosetta Stone: it provides a key, within Shakespeare's oeuvre, to its own meanings, the Equation's meanings, and the mythic meanings of the *Complete Works*.

This interpretation of the tragic and transcendental planes would hold good if nothing but the poem existed, since the basic meanings are supplied by the old religious myth. When Shakespeare introduces his variation, here in the poem, where Adonis rejects the Goddess instead of loving her with 'total, unconditional love', his meaning is still strong, precise and clear, because he has reversed it so exactly against the old, expected meaning. And because his innovation is itself an application of mythic law (as in the Hippolytus myth, as in the Jehovah myth).

However, when he went on to write *Lucrece*, and then several years after that put the two poems together in the Tragic Equation, those two planes, the tragic and the transcendental, with their firm, single, contrapuntal meanings, found themselves incorporated into the bigger system – bigger but not different. And in this new system, the meanings of the death of Adonis were modified in the following way:

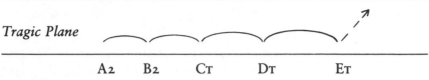

Tragic Plane

A2   B2   Ct   Dt   Et

Here,

A2 Adonis rejects Venus on moral principle.

B2 The enraged Goddess, as Boar, attacks and kills Adonis (takes possession of him).

Ct Possessed by the enraged Goddess, Adonis is reborn as a Tarquin.

Dt Tarquin assaults the Goddess.

Et Tarquin dies, understanding his error.

This diagram reveals just how the second poem (completing the Equation) has in fact been drawn like a telescopic section from the first, which has had the effect of dismantling certain simultaneous, compound meanings in the first into sequential, isolated meanings, symbolized by different narrative episodes. Mainly, the implications of the essential act, the rejection of the Goddess, have been, as it were, analysed into a whole sequential drama. A1 has become A2, B2, Ct, Dt and Et.

From one point of view, Shakespeare has zoomed in on that essential act and the Tragic Equation is a close-up of its psycho-biology, projected into sequential form.

One effect of this has been to close off the transcendental plane, or rather to remove the death-by-the-Boar atonement and rebirth as a flower to the very end of the Equation, where it will now, for a long time, receive only perfunctory attention. At the end of *All's Well*, the first play of the Mythic Equation, Bertram, reconciled to Helena, gets a glimpse of the transcendental possibility – though he hardly dies for it. And in the next play, *Measure for Measure*, Angelo likewise (though in his case Ragozine's bloody head suggests that a worser self has indeed been killed), at the moment of his redemption. Through the Tragedies proper, the hero, just before death, breathes the air of that transcendental plane, maybe, in those resonant, exalted pronouncements, as he looks back over his own tragedy under a greater light. But throughout the subsequent developments of the tragic idea, that last moment is waiting in vain for Shakespeare to find his way back to the Flower of rebirth on the upper plane (though Macbeth sees it in a vision, and Lear levitates into it briefly, before being knocked back).

The larger effect of the Mythic Equation, there, where Adonis dies not into the Flower but into Tarquin, is to shut everything darkly into the tragic plane, as under a dead fall. The emergence of Tarquin obliterates or rather supplants the Flower. Or rather suppresses it, as I described it, to the role of a recessive gene.

What this second diagram reveals is that in *Venus and Adonis*, Adonis dies, as it were, twice. The Boar attacks him twice. This is another aspect, another geometrical element, of the process just examined, where that compound image of Adonis's rejection of the Goddess is then dismantled into a narrative sequence *in the same story*. Adonis dies as Adonis, and becomes Tarquin, as I say, the moment he rejects the Goddess. And becoming Tarquin he incurs the inevitable, enforced atonement in a violent second death. Everything in the story happens in that flash: by the simple act of rejecting her Adonis brings about his own death, and his own correction, by her, instantaneously.

The whole action of *Lucrece*, or, to be more explicit, the whole crime of *Othello* – the murder and his own death – has to be imagined happening, invisibly, behind Adonis's simple words of rejection. In other words, Adonis's rejection, visible and clearly phrased, is the 'outside' of an event of which the 'inside', invisible but implied, is his fatal-seeming assault against her, which results in his own death. When this inside aspect of the event is developed in linear, sequential fashion, it becomes the Tragic Equation, where the hero's death happens twice: first as a compound, half-hidden psychological event, in which the shock wave of the Boar-madness transforms Adonis to Tarquin, and second as a literalizing of that 'madness' and 'death', where the same consequence, externalized and objectified in the Boar, transforms Tarquin, forcing him to atone by killing him (with the possibility of transcendence and rebirth into sainthood beyond).

This 'exploding' of the immensely rich and fateful act of rejecting the Goddess into this two-phase narrative is simply a way of dramatizing the two possibilities of the single event.

That single 'double' event is the fundamental human challenge: confronting the Goddess of Divine Love, the Goddess of Complete Being, the ego's extreme alternatives are either to reject her and attempt to live an independent, rational, secular life or to abnegate the ego and embrace her love with 'total, unconditional love', which means to become a saint, a holy idiot, possessed by the Divine Love. The inevitability of the tragic idea which Shakespeare projects with such 'divine' completeness is that there is no escape from one choice or the other. Man will always choose the former, simply because once he is free of a natural, creaturely awareness of the divine indulgence which permits him to exist at all, he wants to live his own life, and he has never invented a society of saints that was tolerable. In other words, always, one way or another, he rejects the Goddess. This is the first phase of the tragedy. Then follows his correction: his 'madness' against the Goddess, the Puritan crime (the fallen Sophia's 'intellectual' depravity) which leads directly to his own tragic self-destruction, from which he can escape only after the destruction of his ego – being reborn through the Flower rebirth, becoming a holy idiot, renouncing his secular independence, and surrendering once again to the Goddess. From the human point of view, obviously the whole business is monstrous: tragic on a cosmic scale, where the only easements are in the possibilities of a temporary blessing from the Goddess (an erotic fracture in the carapace of the tragic ego) or of becoming a saint. There is a third possibility, in some degree of self-anaesthesia, some kind of living death. But man has no more choice in the basic arrangement than the blue-green algae.

That is to say, at every phase of the Commedia, Shakespeare's Tragic Equation, and Theophany, applies.

What this means for the Equation, as I say, is that the Boar charges twice. Adonis, rejecting the Goddess, sees the underbrush shake and feels the hoofbeats under his foot-soles as a vibration through all his skeleton. Tarquin (Macbeth and after) at the height of his madness, as he commits his crime, sees the clouds in a turmoil, lightning scattering, and hears the hoofbeats coming across the Heaviside layer.

From this dismantling of *Venus and Adonis* into the full form of the Equation, and recalling the 'storm' that I followed through from Clarence's premonitory dream to the first storm in *Macbeth*, one can now say that the two planes are clearly distinguished, at least up to that mid-point in *Macbeth*, by certain tokens.

The poetic tokens of Adonis's rebirth into the doomed Tarquin on the tragic plane are: the charge of the Boar (symbolized by the Storm), and the sequence of actions, madness against the Goddess, etc., which I have already described exhaustively.

The poetic tokens of Tarquin's rebirth into a flowering, redeemed one on the transcendental plane are: the charge of the Boar (in some form), the Flower, and the waiting embrace of the forgiving Goddess.

What needs to be clear, in this long digression, is that *up to the mid-point of* Macbeth, the charge of the Boar is common to both events. On the tragic plane it is symbolized by the Storm. On the transcendental plane one only knows that it was symbolized by the actual charge of the real Boar – since up to the mid-point of *Macbeth* it has happened only the once, in *Venus and Adonis*, where the existence of that plane was first established.

In the middle of *Macbeth*, however, things changed, and the flowering, reborn one suddenly peers through at Macbeth – from the transcendental plane – out of the Storm.

The Storm changes planes: Macbeth's vision

At the opening of Act Four, after the murder (and ghostly return) of Banquo, Macbeth, trapped in his career as a murderous butcher, fearful of the future, comes back to the three Witches to hear 'by the worst means, the worst' of what is to come.

This spectacular short scene consists of his opening request, followed by exchanges with three apparitions that are conjured by the Witches out of the cauldron. Each apparition makes a prophecy about his fate. The cauldron then sinks and Macbeth is finally shown a vision of future Scottish kings, all descended from the Banquo he has just murdered.

The language of this scene is double in a particular way. Each speech, or image, contributes directly and powerfully, in the external, immediate plot, to the bitterness of Macbeth's tragic doom. But at the same time it reveals a change in the Tragic Equation, a development which is absolutely new. (The apparitions are, so to speak, images in Shakespeare's dream of *Macbeth*. Their significance has its roots beneath the immediate plot of the play, in the substratum of Shakespeare's tragic myth. They bring news, that is, of what is happening to his myth, as well as their more immediate meanings for this play in particular.)

The final apparition in the succession – the parade of future kings – relates simply to the immediate plot (and to the external context of the play, in which James I watched it and found it a supportive salute to himself, in his role as a sacred king who might repair the terror of the Reformation nightmare). But the other images speak a deeper, opposite language.

Macbeth's opening request anticipates dreadful revelations, which he describes as a short, world-ending storm:

> answer me:
> Though you untie the winds and let them fight
> Against the churches; though the yesty waves
> Confound and swallow navigation up;
> Though bladed corn be lodg'd and trees blown down;
> Though castles topple on their warders' heads;
> Though palaces and pyramids do slope
> Their heads to their foundations; though the treasure
> Of Nature's germens tumble all together,
> Even till destruction sicken; answer me
> To what I ask you.
>
> *Macbeth*, IV. i. 51–61

Superficially this is one more storm like the earlier one that blew down chimneys and drove maddened horses to eat each other, and was the most severe of the storms that have accompanied the emergence of a Tarquin. But the three prophesying apparitions reveal that this is a storm of a new kind. The imagery is different in kind from the earlier storm in *Macbeth* – less local and specific, more global, cataclysmic and general, with masked, anticipatory features of the storm in *King Lear*, which is a further development of this new kind of storm.

The first apparition is the image of an armoured head, which tells Macbeth that he needs to beware the Thane of Fyfe, Macduff. This mild warning, which Macbeth takes as a warning of danger rather than of anything else ('Thou hast harp'd my fear aright') is, of course, if Macbeth only knew it, the open identification of his executioner. Moreover, the head is a meaning in itself. It is not only the traditional guarantee of the completed execution, but is also his own. This foregone conclusion of Macbeth's cornered, criminal death, trapped on the dead-end tragic plane, is a powerful dramatic stroke, intensifying the sense of his doom.

But in retrospect one sees that the head actually appears on the mythic plane where it holds other meanings. And the two apparitions, which follow it, confirm these other meanings.

Throughout mystical tradition, beheading signifies 'removing carnal consciousness, replacing it with spiritual consciousness'. In general, beheading means to be reborn with a new, other consciousness. This meaning is constantly refreshed and re-enforced by recurring as a common, archetypal event in ordinary dream life. In each of the beheadings of the tragic sequence (there are only three) Shakespeare uses the idea, as if quite consciously, in this sense. Ragozine's in *Measure for Measure* (Angelo's rebirth); Macbeth's (an anticipation of the tragic hero's rebirth, from his Tarquinian to his redeemed nature, which will be fully realized in *King Lear*, the next play); and Cloten's (Posthumus's rebirth from his Tarquinian nature to his redeemed nature). In other words, this first apparition is saying: 'Tarquin will be slain, but reborn.'

The next apparition is a bloody child, who tells Macbeth that 'none of woman born/Shall harm Macbeth'. This extraordinary statement heartens Macbeth, but again, as throughout the play, Fate is winning him with 'honest trifles' to betray him 'in deepest consequence'. The audience knows that this apparent assurance of Macbeth's immunity from any man's hand identifies the executioner with even more sinister precision than did the man's name. In the contingent world of the plot the phrase serves as an ironic metaphor for the executioner's Caesarean birth. And again it is a powerful dramatic stroke, warping another diabolical twist of delusion into Macbeth's imminent death.

But once again, looking through the plot into the mythic plane, the audience sees that, in the world of metaphoric myth, and particularly in the world of Shakespeare's Tragic Equation, at this momentous point of its transformation – the point at which it mutates and evolves its own theophany – birth not of woman can only be spiritual rebirth. Adonis killed and reborn as a blood flower is not born of woman. The whole purpose of those later plays – *Cymbeline*, *Pericles* and *The Winter's Tale*, and indeed *The Tempest*, one might say – is to produce, with the most elaborately devised accouchements, heroes and heroines reborn not of woman.

And after Macbeth's beheading, of course, in the very next play, after terrific travail, this bloody child,

> like a naked new-born babe,
> Striding the blast

I. vii. 21–2

will appear actually on stage, tempest-soused rather than blood-washed King Lear himself, tumbling out on the transcendental plane, with his memories of wauling and crying, in infantile, saintly helplessness, crowned with flowers, into Cordelia's arms – reborn, but not of woman.

What this second apparition is saying, then, is: 'Tarquin will be reborn of the spirit, on the transcendental plane, harmless as a child, the beloved of the Goddess, like the bloodied Adonis flower.'

The third apparition to rise from the cauldron is a crowned child with a tree in its hand, who tells Macbeth that he is safe until 'Great Birnam wood to high Dunsinane hill/Shall come against him'. Macbeth is heartened again, ignoring most of the image, and assuming that the tree in the child's hand relates to the strange, apparent impossibility of a forest marching like an army, as an army, against him.

In this image, the Tragic Equation, on the mythic plane, has delivered its third and final fiat. The Divine Child Adonis is born from a tree, Osiris is resurrected from a tree, Attis and Christ are sacrificed on trees: the tree is the Goddess. Appearing here, like a blazing sign out of the storm that Macbeth invoked as the scene opened, lit by a fiery crack in 'the frame of things', it is the equivalent of the lightnings on the heath in *King Lear* compelling the hero to atone. The tree is also the Flower, that original 'double' flower of Adonis's death, which is both the doomed, Boar-possessed Tarquin on the tragic plane, which Macbeth now is, and the reborn Adonis at the breast of the Goddess on the transcendental plane, which he can never be – but which King Lear, in the next play, finally will be, albeit briefly. Here it pushes through, exactly where the violet lifted through the text of *Measure for Measure*, immediately after the death of Adonis (immediately after the death of Macbeth's Adonis self in Duncan is completed in the death of Banquo) and just before Macbeth's emergence into Tarquin's absolute tyranny, and his assault on Scotland's wives and mothers. This is the same child that Macbeth glimpsed, earlier in the play, 'striding the blast' – as if from the first throes of his own birth travail. The same that had fallen, as the 'bloody child', as if into real birth, in the previous apparition. But now it is secure in the embrace of the Divine Love, symbolized by the Crown (the restoration of Sacred Order) which is also, again, the Flower, and which, in the next play when King Lear wears it, will be a crown of flowers. All this can be said confidently because of what the following plays deliver, as Shakespeare's imagination is transformed.

In other words, for the first time in the tragedies proper, the second death of the *Venus and Adonis* poem is beginning to happen. Having been driven mad in the first death (Adonis to Tarquin), the hero will now be forced to atone (Tarquin into the reborn, flowering redeemed one) in the second one. This is what I meant by saying that the three apparitions open (as the heavens did to the dreaming Caliban) to Macbeth from the transcendental plane.

The 'transcendental' meaning of this third vision, at this point in the tragic hero's spiritual evolution, is identical with the meaning of a tree and a child in the following medieval legend about the wood of Christ's cross:

When Adam has lived there for 923 years, in the Hebron valley, he is struck down with a fatal illness, and sends his son Seth to ask the angel at the gate of Paradise for the Oil of Mercy. Seth follows Adam and Eve's footsteps, where the grass has never grown, and comes to Paradise. There he makes Adam's request to the archangel. The archangel asks Seth to look three times into Paradise. The first time Seth sees the water from which four rivers flow and a dried tree above it. The second time, a serpent coils around the tree's trunk. The third time, and he sees the tree has risen to heaven, its roots have reached down through the Underworld, and in its crown is a new-born child. The archangel then explains that a Redeemer is to come. He gives to Seth three seeds from the fruit of the fatal tree that his parents tasted, and tells him to place them on Adam's tongue, whereafter, in three days, Adam will die. Hearing Seth's story, Adam laughs for the first time since he left Paradise, realizing that man will be saved. After his death, three trees rise above his grave, living till the time of Moses. Moses, knowing their origin, transplants them to Horeb – the centre of the world. After a thousand years, King David, on Divine Command, transplants them to Jerusalem (the new centre of the world). The three become one, and the wood of Christ's Cross is eventually made from that tree. The blood of Christ, crucified at the 'centre', falls on the skull of Adam, redeeming him from his sin, and baptizing the Father of Mankind.

After the vision of the kings, the whole scene ends in music with a dance of witches. Apart from formal, ceremonial 'hautboys' this is the only music in the play: the scene has moved from the storm that revealed the vision of transcendental flower rebirth to music and a dance: virtually the storm has been turned to music. In this dance, the Witches divulge (it is their last appearance) that they are, in fact, the triple Goddess herself, and that whatever the mystery of her tragic methods, they have achieved her ultimate purpose: the hero has been reborn, on the transcendental plane, as a redeemed one restored to her Love.

At least, in the Tragic Equation, deep in the matrix of the operation behind this play, he has been redeemed. Macbeth himself, too laden with blood and guilt to take advantage of the little window that has opened in his 'terrible dreams', unaware of what has happened, rushes towards worse murders, in defiance of the revelation, and is soon killed in despair – aware that his life has become empty, blind automatism, a tale 'told by an idiot, full of sound and fury,/Signifying nothing'.

In a real way, this little climactic scene, a play within the play, is a curious anticipation of the Masque in *The Tempest*. It is staged likewise by three supernatural women, it solemnizes a union with Divine Love on the transcendental plane, and it enacts a nativity – a sacred birth. The fact that for Macbeth himself this carries the certain literal meaning of physical death by beheading intensifies its real meaning, and intensifies again the damnation of this hero who has broken through to the crisis of his spiritual rebirth only by diving through the very bottom of Hell – where he is stuck, as it were, half-way.

The inner meaning of these three apparitions – corroborated by the future career of Shakespeare's tragic hero, and by the future development of the Equation – reinterprets, as I say, the meaning of the storm that induced them.

Whereas all earlier storms have accompanied the death of Adonis and the emergence of Tarquin, as if the pains and terrors of the one were actually the birth pangs and labour that delivered the other, this new storm clearly accompanies the death of Tarquin and the emergence of the redeemed one, who is also a flower and a child. And here, too, the pains and terrors of the one seem to be the birth pangs and labour that deliver the other.

What this means is that somewhere between the two thunders, in *Macbeth*, the Storm itself has changed planes. It has shifted from the blood-boltered, hellish atmosphere of the tragic plane and Tarquin's doom to a radiant higher plane where the 'fingers of the powers above' tune it to a music of transcendental peace, showering flowers on the spiritually reborn.*

*An intriguing parallel to this occurred in the experience of Jonathan Edwards, who recorded: 'After this, my sense of divine things gradually increased, and became more and more lively and had more of that inward sweetness. The appearance of everything was altered; there seemed to be, as it were, a calm, sweet cast, or appearance of Divine Glory, in almost everything. God's excellency, his wisdom, his purity and love, seemed to appear in everything; in the sun, moon and stars; in the clouds and blue sky; in the grass, flowers and trees; in the water and all nature; which used greatly to fix my mind. And scarce anything, among all the works of nature, was so sweet to me as thunder and lightning; formerly nothing had been so terrible to me. Before, I used to be uncommonly terrified with thunder and to be struck with terror when I saw a thunder-

Somewhere between the two storms, in other words, Macbeth has begun to atone. His supreme suffering of his own guilt, the most gripping and horrifying in all the plays, has begun to change him, as it were, chemically, biologically. And so it is Macbeth and not Lear who actually makes the first breakthrough on to the spiritual plane – without understanding it. He is the Moses, who glimpses the Promised Land that he himself will never enter.

To summarize: in *Richard III*, the external storm appears as the violent accompaniment of Adonis's death and Tarquin's emergence. It rumbles and flashes along the tragic plane, through *Measure for Measure*, *Troilus and Cressida*, *Hamlet*, *Othello* and the first part of *Macbeth*. In each case its eruption coincides with that 'first' death, and symbolizes the cosmic dimension of the charge of the Boar, producing Tarquin on the tragic plane.

Somewhere in Act Three of *Macbeth*, under the abnormal stress, the sleeping mythic genes of Adonis's redemption are awakened, and the transcendental plane opens – as an escape route from the intolerable, mortal circumstances of the tragic plane. The Storm thereupon crosses over to the transcendental plane and the flower child rises from the cauldron, to show Macbeth not his personal future, but the future of Shakespeare's tragic hero, whom he too briefly incarnates.

From that point, all of Shakespeare's storms are of the new type and perform the new function, roll their thunders along the transcendental plane, violently force the Tarquin to atone in the second death, induce his rebirth into the arms of the waiting Goddess, and fade in music.

Once established on the higher plane, the Storm is modified slightly by other developments. But before I follow those through to *The Tempest*, a few words should be said about the first death that continues to occur, and the Tarquin that continues to emerge, after the Storm has abandoned the tragic plane.

Noticeably, Lear's explosion into Tarquin, in Act One, where he rejects Cordelia, occurs without external storm. Already (in *Macbeth*) the Storm has gone over on to the transcendental plane. There it waits for him, and will later force him through his prolonged, agonized atonement.

Similarly, Timon explodes into Tarquin without the visible trembling

---

storm rising, but now, on the contrary, it rejoices me.' (Quoted in William James, *Varieties of Religious Experience*, Harmondsworth: Penguin, 1983.)

of any leaf. Coriolanus the same. Posthumus the same. Leontes the same. In each case it becomes apparent, later in the play, that the thunder has been stolen from all these external explosions – by the second death, by the Tarquinian death-in-atonement and his rebirth redeemed.

Far more noticeable, however, in these fine-weather Tarquins, is the extreme violence of what might be called their internal storm.

And now, maybe, it becomes obvious that, right from the 'beginning', there tended to be two sides to the Storm: external and internal. Clarence's storm, though it is described as an event in nature, is manifestly a storm of internal agitation opening into a vision of damnation and Hell. Likewise, in *Measure for Measure*, the storm described by Isabella – the heaven full of Jove's or men's thunders – finds an echo in the following soliloquy, a muffled reverberation. In *Troilus and Cressida*, the sudden explosion of the war, which accompanied Troilus's frenzy, is a metaphor, in its way, of his internal storm, and dramatizes his transformation (see page 193). But his actual tirade culminates in

> Not the dreadful spout
> Which shipmen do the hurricano call,
> Constring'd in mass by the almighty sun,
> Shall dizzy with more clamour Neptune's ear
> In his descent than shall my prompted sword
> Falling on Diomed
>
> v. ii, 168–73

who is the substitute for Cressida's faithlessness – the real culprit.

In *Hamlet* the heavenly disturbances are internalized in Hamlet's raging speeches against Ophelia, against his mother and against himself, and are projected, as if from Hamlet himself, in the one shocking flare, in the Player's set piece about Pyrrhus, as if the whole electrical potential of the play were trying to earth itself in the downstroke of Pyrrhus's sword, but failing. Failing, in so far as Hamlet's tirades carry on for as long as the death and rebirth struggle of Tarquin emerging from Adonis is protracted.

Again, in *Othello*, Othello's tirades against Desdemona discharge an internal storm of Tarquin's emergence more violent than the external storm that 'bang'd the Turks' – and delivered him into the hands of

Iago, on the Island of Venus. Macbeth's internal and external storms are hardly to be separated.

But then, after the storm has crossed over, when Lear banishes Cordelia, his internal thunderflash is spectacular – though the weather stays fine. His subsequent thunderbolts against Goneril and Regan, before it dawns on him that the way of the Tarquin is blocked, are again stunning in their verbal power and poetic intensity, but explode without heavenly orchestral accompaniment.

Timon's tirades are the ultimate expression of a storm that cannot find an echo in Heaven. He endures the last two acts suspended – writhing and fulminating – in the internalized storm of an arrested birth into Tarquin, unable to perform the climactic crime (destroy Athens) and unable to atone and die as a redeemed one (because he has not managed to commit the crime for which he could atone).

Coriolanus's internal storm takes a unique form. His tirades – against the Roman mob – are shattering and brief thunderblasts, but his effective meteorological manifestation is to become himself a thunderbolt – a monumental missile that 'moves like an engine, talks like a knell' and 'his hum is a battery'.

Posthumus's transformation into Tarquin is also internalized – a single, storming tirade. But the external thunderstorm on the transcendental plane ignores him, until he is ripe for atonement, when Jove himself descends with thunder and lightning, hurling thunderbolts, and releasing Posthumus, reborn, as it were, from the prison and the sentence of death and returning him to Imogen in the same moment.

In a similar way, Leontes's prolonged internal storm delivers its lightning without any disturbance of the heavens, until the moment is ripe, and the 'ear-deafening voice' of Apollo's Oracle, 'kin to Jove's thunder', breaks him to pieces, and initiates his atonement.

This clean distinction between the suffering agitation of the internal storm which accompanies the death of Adonis and emergence of Tarquin, and the punishing external storms which force Tarquin to atone, indicate the decisive shift in Shakespeare's own inner development. Up to the mid-point in *Macbeth*, the tragic error, and the subsequent tragic crime, were themselves an evil of cosmic significance – in other words the error, whatever its origins or metaphysical status (whether it was biological and inevitable, or merely theological, accidental, historical), had cosmic implications in its disastrous consequences. Therefore, the emergence of Tarquin was accompanied by the upheaval of Heaven, Earth and Hell.

But once the hero has broken through on to the transcendental plane, the tragic error and crime become the earthly norm. Now it is the redemption of the hero, the atonement of the tragic criminal, that has cosmic implications, and involves the intervention of Heaven.

From *Hamlet* to *Macbeth*'s mid-point, the crime is a cosmic cataclysm, because the soul is destroyed without possibility of salvation. After *Macbeth*'s mid-point, the crime is a human tragedy, but no longer a cosmic cataclysm, because the soul now has a hope of salvation (Athens survives completely, Rome, Volumnia, Virgilia, etc., survive, the Female now survives). What is of cosmic concern now is precisely that – the soul's salvation: the criminal's atonement and rebirth into reunion with Divine Love.

The Storm which arrives at *The Tempest*, then, is of this kind and it initiates the ordeal of atonement – for the Tarquinian criminals involved: the transcendental solution of the Tragic Equation.

But it is no longer attached exclusively to the hero. I mentioned a further development, to be undergone by the Storm, once it arrived on the transcendental plane.

The Storm passes to the Female

This final modification seems natural. In *Cymbeline* Shakespeare's gradual promotion of his heroine, first to survival, then to centre stage, was complete, but the Tragic Equation lagged a little. It still insisted, in the form that he still used in that play, on trying to keep the play's centre of gravity within the hero. This seems evident in Shakespeare's efforts to edit Posthumus down into a secondary, maimed sort of role. And also in the fact that the Storm of atonement is still attached exclusively to the hero – as in Lear.

In *Pericles* he finds a simpler, more radical way of bringing his heroine into the foreground: he deprives the hero of tragic passion. At this point, the Storm becomes the accompaniment of the rebirth not only of the hero but of the heroine – and in fact moves almost wholly to her.

The logic of this seems to be, as I say, natural.

At bottom, the argument runs: if the hero destroys his soul, he and his world are doomed: both the hero and his world can be saved only if his soul is saved. The hero who murders his soul can be saved if his soul can be reborn. The whole endeavour, in that case – the emergency operation – is to bring the soul back to life. In this way the drama of the hero saved by a spiritual rebirth comes to be a drama about the rebirth of the heroine. Once she is reborn, his rebirth follows simply and automatically, as a consequence, as a silver echo of her golden note.

In all this, the female element is the active, the male the passive. This is consistent throughout the tragic sequence, from the time Venus tries to engage Adonis in a total response. He precipitates the tragedy not by acting, but by refusing to act, by refusing to engage. His obduracy is then broken down by the Divine Love (enraged) that he has excluded, and his atonement enforced, at which point, she, his soul, can be reborn to him, offering him new life.

In this way, the Storm that forces atonement on him becomes the Storm that induces rebirth for her. And as the fact of her rebirth becomes more urgent than what he feels about the pains of atonement so, without altogether leaving his death-in-atonement, the Storm concentrates its more spectacular demonstrations on her rebirth.

Pericles contains two storms. The first, with a stray flash or two from *King Lear*: 'Wind, rain, and thunder, remember, earthly man' (II. i. 2) with other molten surprises trickling through the cruder ores typical of the first two acts, seems, as I have suggested, to be part an early play (or play by another hand) rewritten. It would not be surprising, therefore, to find it only loosely linked to the story of the tragic sequence. As it happens, it has features of the later type of storm.

It comes well after Pericles's rejection of the Princess of Antioch, and just before his discovery of the woman whom he will love and who will love him – Thaisa. Indeed, the storm brings the two together – throwing him up on her shore, as fishermen drag from the sea his own lost armour with which he will win her. It is a weak, almost rudimentary form of the storm that tosses up Lear into the arms of Cordelia, and of the thunderclap dream that brings Posthumus to Imogen. Then again, paradoxically, it fits Pericles out with Tarquin's birthday suit – complete martial armour in which he will do the Tarquin thing, take possession of a Diana. These shadows of the first type of storm, playing so sharply over the later type, illustrate again the high fidelity of the Shakespearean hieroglyph – 'storm' – even in such a low-relief instance.

The first storm here, interestingly enough, seems to have been the only episode in the first two acts that prompted Shakespeare to fresh invention. But now with the third act, as if he were bursting with it, he enters with the new-style storm – the Storm on the transcendental plane, locked on to the Sophia:

> Thou God of this great vast, rebuke these surges,
> Which wash both heaven and hell;
>
> *Pericles*, III. i. 1–2

and a minute or so later, after her apparent death:

> A terrible child-bed hast thou had, my dear;
> No light, no fire. The unfriendly elements
> Forgot thee utterly . . .
>
> III. i. 57–9

This moment is the beginning of Pericles's rebirth, but only in the sense that it is, maybe, the moment of conception, following the earlier storm, which was merely the consummation – of his self-surrender to rebirth. His actual rebirth, his coming into the air, to see and recognize Marina (the silver echo) is deferred almost to the end of the play. Meanwhile, this is the 'golden note', the death-before-rebirth of Thaisa, and the rebirth of Thaisa's new soul: the moment of Sophia's division.

In so far as Pericles shares it – as he should share the most painful moment of the rebirth of his own soul – the Storm still adheres to the hero. But it has clearly moved with larger consequences into the fate of the double Sophia, mother and daughter.

In *The Winter's Tale*, this is even more apparent. Leontes's atonement, as I mentioned, begins with the distant thunderclap of the Oracle, but the authentic storm centre puts the new-born Perdita into the hands of the shepherds, as the ship that carried her is wrecked.

> O the most piteous cry of the poor souls! Sometimes to see 'em, and not to see 'em; now the ship boring the moon with her mainmast, and anon swallowed with yeast and froth, as you'd thrust a cork into a hogshead.
>
> *The Winter's Tale*, IV. iii. 91–6

It is intriguing to see how this marvellous shot has cannibalized various components of Shakespeare's signs and sigils for his tempest. The mainmast boring the moon is a throwaway hyperbole – casual speech – yet it fits into the tragic myth like a three-point plug: it is the maddened hero's (the tossed ship's) assault on his Sacred Bride – on the Lucrece or Diana aspect of the Goddess, for which, throughout

Shakespeare, the moon is the first title. The cork thrust into the hogshead is a comic reminiscence of Clarence/Adonis going head first into the Butt of Malmsey. As if that were not specific enough, suddenly, in the very next sentence, a bear (almost a boar, and in fact associated with the earliest Great Goddess at Delphi. The appropriate alternative form of the Boar for this play) plunges across the scene to tear out the shoulder bone of Perdita's guardian. Storm and bear co-operate, as everywhere else Storm and Boar have combined, to break up the vessel of Leontes's crime of rejection.

Perhaps these later dramas play on a further refinement of the Storm – distinguishing between the thunderclap advent of a deity and the sea tempest. The former type comes to the Tarquinized hero – as in Posthumus's eagle dream, the Oracle's answer to Leontes, and, perhaps, in Ariel's pronouncement of Fate's, Destiny's and Nature's verdict against the courtiers. The latter type launches the Sophia into new life. Both types are combined in *Pericles* and in the overture of *The Tempest*. On the other hand, these extremes are perhaps no more than different manifestations, adapted to specific situations, of the same rage: the convulsive upheaval and corrective violence, of the Divine Order disturbed. In both, the Divine Love enforces its laws, where Jove, Apollo and the other figurative deities are simply ancillary aspects of what Job called God and what Shakespeare was careful not to set a name to, except provisionally, in that he seems to embody it in the rejected or otherwise afflicted woman, or the woman and her child.

The most peculiar aspect of the Storm is its relationship to the Flower. This is soon delineated, though maybe not so readily followed.

The Storm and the Flower

The flower that Venus plucked reappears in Lear's coronal, when his old white head breaks through into the transcendental plane. It seems to have regressed a little, physically. It is now:

> rank fumitor and furrow weeds,
> With burdocks, hemlock, nettles, cuckoo flowers,
> Darnel, and all the idle weeds that grow
> In our sustaining corn.
>
> *King Lear*, IV.iv. 3–6

But at this moment, Lear is not quite born. He still has his blackest moment to come. Also, he is not going to be allowed more than a few moments in this region. 'All the idle weeds' contain some pretty species anyway. And the rough, humble prickles have the virtue of being the natural, flowering thing. They take account of a birth labour (Lear's) that has been in equal measure painful, miraculous and elemental.

Nevertheless, the formally rejected one embraces them. And the flower that Venus nestled between her divine breasts carried its own complication (as I will show, cf. pages 473–4).

These flowers of death and rebirth next appear in the great funereal rebirth scene of Imogen in *Cymbeline*.

When she seems to die in the cave, the brothers bury her in flowers (not earth). When she wakes, she finds herself in the same posture as Venus at the end of the long poem. The components of this hieratic tableau are deftly assembled. In the long poem, Venus mourns the corpse of the one who rejected her, and holds the flower of his rebirth, redeemed into her love. In *Cymbeline*, Imogen mourns the corpse of Cloten, who is, as I showed (page 337), the Tarquinized golem of Posthumus – the externalized form of the Boar madness that possessed him when he rejected her. The flowers in her hands are her own rebirth, that signify more materially the fact that Posthumus has been reborn, in his redeemed self, to her love.

Posthumus is the first Tarquinized Adonis since the long poem (sixteen years earlier) to be reborn into secure reunion with the Divine Love. So it is fascinating to see how faithfully and in what literal detail Shakespeare has resuscitated the same image. Lear's rebirth, it might be said, precedes this one: but there too the same image has been assembled: all its components the same, though in a slightly different arrangement. King Lear is obviously not yet a corpse. He is, as it were, less fully analysed than this combination of dead Cloten, flowers, and Posthumus-reborn-elsewhere. Yet, in a clear sense, Lear is once again the corpse of Adonis from which the Flower is springing, both dead and alive. The Cordelia-rejector is dead, symbolized by his prostration and amnesia, while the new, infantile person, crowned with petals, is alive, but, like a new-born baby, only just – symbolized also by his helplessness and amnesia.

What is missing, perhaps, in Imogen's flower birth, is the stormy thunder of the atonement from which it should spring. That is still tightly attached, as I noted, to the death–rebirth of Posthumus, where Jupiter will descend in thunder, mounted on an eagle, to his sleep in the prison, from which he will rise – to liberty and reunion with Imogen. Conversely, what is missing from Posthumus's rebirth is – the flowers.

One could say that Imogen's scene is complete: the three essential constituents are present: as they appeared in *Venus and Adonis* and *King Lear*. The essential image, the soul reborn, is intact. The only disorienting circumstance is that the component of the flower rebirth, and the component of the thunder as the atonement from which it springs, are separated by several scenes.

The flowers appear again in *Pericles*. After the storm at sea, and Sophia's rebirth, one looks for the flowers. They arrive promptly with Marina's next appearance. She enters in her early teens, on her way to lay flowers on the grave of her nurse, Lychorida, who was last seen on Pericles's tempest-tossed ship as the maid of Thaisa and who has only now died.

This new grave is a composite grave, having claimed three women. The body of Lychorida, Thaisa's surrogate, is also Thaisa buried afresh. The body of Thaisa, from whose death Marina was born (like Thaisa herself new-born), is also Marina's. This is familiar Shakespearean thinking, as any bystander, watching Marina at the grave with her arms full of flowers, could easily now say to explain her grief: burying her nurse, she buries her mother over again; and burying her mother again, she has buried herself. And it would be a straightforward Shakespearean remark.

The structural point is clear, however: standing at this grave of Lychorida-Thaisa-Marina, Marina herself, holding her flowers, has just risen from it (we see her for the first time) and is in the same situation as Imogen, holding her flowers, standing at the grave from which she has just risen, in which her brothers buried her with flowers. In other words, Marina is only now reborn:

> No, I will rob Tellus of her weed,
> To strew thy green with flowers; the yellows, blues,
> The purple violets, and marigolds,
> Shall as a carpet hang upon thy grave,
> While summer days do last. Ay me! Poor maid,
> Born in a tempest, when my mother died,
> This world to me is like a lasting storm,
> Whirring me from my friends.
>
> *Pericles*, IV. i. 13–20

This speech is a solid plaque of signs from the Equation and its mutation. Tellus (or Gaia) is the High Goddess herself in a form which combines (anticipating the Masque in *The Tempest*) Demeter (Ceres) and the High Goddess Hera (Juno). Her 'weed' is of course her robe — her flowers as a garment, the emanation of her divinity and her power to resurrect. The same garment, as 'unusual weeds', appears in the first line addressed to Sophia/Perdita, reborn in the next play, *The Winter's Tale*. And the flowers drape this grave of Marina's death–rebirth in a way so like the flowers which draped the grave of Imogen's death–rebirth (in the preceding play), that the same phrase, with only a slight metrical rebore, serves for both ('while summer days do last' instead of 'while summer lasts').

Marina then makes the connection between the storm and the flowers that *Cymbeline* failed to make:

> Ay me! Poor maid,
> Born in a tempest, when my mother died.
>
> IV. i. 17–18

In the next play, *The Winter's Tale*, in the same way, Perdita is 'born in a tempest when [her] mother died'. (Antigonus, committing the baby Perdita to the 'desert' as the storm breaks, calls her 'blossom'. His next remark is: 'The storm begins', and then 'The day frowns more and more', followed by:

> I never saw
> The heavens so dim by day. A savage clamour!
>
> *The Winter's Tale*, III. iii. 54–5

This 'savage clamour', which we assume to be thunder, is in fact the Bear: the Storm has become the Bear. Whereupon her new father finds Perdita, the 'blossom' lying on the seashore, as if tossed up there by the storm.) Perdita will make her next appearance as Flora (sixteen years later) in what is virtually a flower ceremony. And the scene opens when she is greeted:

> These your unusual weeds to each part of you
> Do give a life; no shepherdess, but Flora
> Peering in April's front.
>
> IV. iii. 1–3

These words are spoken by Florizel, her beloved. Imogen rising from her grave in flowers, and Marina rising from her grave in flowers, both encountered many ordeals before they found the redeemed one reborn into the flesh – a transformed Posthumus and an ecstatic Pericles. The process in *The Winter's Tale* has been foreshortened. Perdita has, as it were, foresuffered her Sophia-like ordeals in the bear's attack and her orphaned upbringing among shepherds. Now Florizel is himself the redeemed one (the reborn self of Polixenes), who springs, so to speak, from the flowers, which are the reborn nature of Perdita. Perdita and Florizel are reborn, therefore, only now and simultaneously in the flowers, that 'give a life to each part' of them.

Instead of mourning a slain one, but cherishing him new-born in the form of a flower, Perdita is rejoicing in the new-born one in the Flower and in the flesh. She is the Goddess as Flora, and one of the petty gods. Their drama is already completed. Both are united in Divine Love. The only drama now possible is for their inevitable marriage to meet difficulties. (Or for Florizel to see the double vision and start everything over again.)

Perdita performs the amplest floral ritual that Shakespeare has produced so far. She distributes herbal flowers of winter, and flowers of summer. She rejects hybrid autumnal flowers, though she acknowledges them 'the fairest flowers o' the season', and wishes she had spring flowers for Florizel and the girls of the feast:

> I would I had some flower o' the spring that might
> Become your time of day; and yours, and yours,
> That wear upon your virgin branches yet
> Your maidenheads growing: O Proserpina!
> For the flowers now that frighted thou let'st fall
> From Dis's wagon! daffodils,
> That come before the swallow dares, and take
> The winds of March with beauty; violets dim,
> But sweeter than the lids of Juno's eyes
> Or Cytherea's breath; pale primroses
> That die unmarried, ere they can behold
> Bright Phoebus in his strength, a malady
> Most incident to maids; bold oxlips and
> The crown imperial; lilies of all kinds,

The flower-de-luce being one. O these I lack
To make you garlands of, and my sweet friend,
To strew him o'er and o'er!

IV. iii. 113–29

This consummate passage secretes the sinister event, the ravishing of Proserpina, Ceres's daughter, by the 'hot tyrant' Dis, who dragged her into the Underworld. This myth of Proserpina's 'death' (and ultimate rebirth) parallels the bloody death of Adonis, when Proserpina herself (as Queen of Hell), in the shape of the wild Boar, slew him and snatched him into the Underworld. As *Cymbeline*, *Pericles* and *The Winter's Tale* demonstrate, the woman killed and reborn has now displaced Adonis's death from centre stage, in the tragic sequence, with the myth of Sophia. Proserpina, ravished by Dis, is a pagan parallel (historically a formative precedent) to the lower Sophia seized by Jaldabaoth.

In this way, Perdita's idyllic rhapsody of her rebirth, replays, subliminally, her death – from which she is being now reborn.

The tidal wave of the hidden myth carries right on through the end of this speech with the ominous phrase: 'To strew him o'er and o'er!' which Florizel immediately recognizes with: 'What, like a corpse?' (IV. iii. 129) Perdita, perfectly programmed, instantly translates this into an anamnesis of the death–rebirth of the redeemed one – right back to *Venus and Adonis*:

No, like a bank for love to lie and play on;
Not like a corpse; or if – not to be buried,
But quick and in mine arms . . .

IV. iii. 130–2

gathering up, on the way, the purely formal flowers of Desdemona (the willow, the plucked rose that cannot be returned to life), and of Ophelia, but also reaching forward, into *The Tempest*, to the culmination of all the flower festivals, in the betrothal Masque.

In retrospect, one sees that the flower in *Venus and Adonis* was the 'reborn, redeemed soul' simply. In *Macbeth* the tree in the child's hand was the first germinal root fibre of the reborn, redeemed soul, glowing in the dark, attended by three dancing witches, where the three supernatural women and the tree were also the Goddess herself, cradling the child. In *King Lear* the crown of prickly flowers was the hazardously reborn soul, clinging to the lightning-singed pate of the old transfigured

[411]

King, and was a symbol, again, of Cordelia herself, precariously embracing him. In *Cymbeline*, the flowers were the rich robes of the reborn soul itself – flowers and Imogen are each other, and are Posthumus's reborn soul. In *Pericles*, the same – flowers and Marina are each other, and are her father's and Thaisa's reborn souls. And in *The Winter's Tale* the same – Perdita and her flowers are each other, and are Leontes's and Hermione's reborn souls.

But in each case the flowers were reborn out of that 'fatal' storm of atonement: the storm, in a sense, became the flowers. As if the enraged Goddess, charging in the form of the Boar, struck the soul of the Goddess-rejector, like thunder and lightning,* and ransacked her way through it, transforming it, fusing with it – as Divine Love and soul should be fused – and emerging through the tattered remains of the old Goddess-rejecting destroyer of the human soul as the soul redeemed and reborn – in a flower. As if the Boar, that became the Storm, had become the Flower.

So, this is the storm that arrives at the opening of *The Tempest*.

The Tragic Equation in *The Tempest*

Prospero (like Shakespeare) has produced the storm and shipwreck magically. As he waits for this first phase in his plan to be completed (managed by his executive spirit Ariel) he explains to his daughter Miranda who the best passengers in the ship are, and why he has shipwrecked them.

This exposition encapsulates that matter of the Tragic Equation which, in the three preceding dramas, occupied the whole first half of the action, and in the works before that, within the tragic sequence, occupied the entire play. Prospero resurrects it here in both its forms.

His account of his own displacement from his dukedom of Milan by his brother Antonio (prompted and aided by King Alonso of Naples), which supplies the motive for his present action, constitutes a classic example of the Rival Brothers' 'crime'.

But then, having sent Miranda off to sleep, he summons his master/

*The Storm's double nature, as the Boar and the Goddess, is there, perhaps, in the very beginning: in Golding's Ovid, Shakespeare's source, Venus warns Adonis: 'The cruell Boares bear thunder in their crooked tushes', and in Shakespeare's description of Venus's grief, before she plucks the flower, 'earth's foundation shakes' (1047), and her passions are, 'Like many clouds consulting for foul weather' (972), and in Adonis's death, 'black chaos comes again' (1020).

mistress (androgynous*) spirit Ariel, and, so to speak, continues the exposition in another key. He introduces this episode with a markedly artificial pretext:

> I must,
> Once in a month, recount what thou hast been,
> Which thou forgets't . . .
>
> *The Tempest*, I. ii. 261–3

and then proceeds to give what is virtually a modified and yet highly mythicized account of the double vision. His description of the Great Witch Sycorax, of her

> Mischiefs manifold and sorceries terrible
> To enter human hearing,
>
> I. ii. 264–5

of her banishment, of her being abandoned in a wilderness (an island) by sailors, of her evil doings there, of her consorting with the devil, of her producing in her banished, rejected wickedness a murderous, lustful, half-animal, half-demon son, Caliban (which, as the product of a swine-crow (Sycorax) is presumably, in some way, a black Boar) – all this is a richly developed portrait of the creature that Adonis rejected: a typical Queen of Hell.

Prospero closes in on this portrait, obviously with Shakespeare's fullest and most fascinated collaboration, when he dismisses Ariel, wakes his daughter (as if Ariel belonged to her dreaming) and calls in Caliban. That is to say, having identified Caliban (on the mythic plane) as the male representative of the rejected Queen of Hell, Prospero now zooms in on him for a close-up.

Stepping from description to materialization of the thing itself, he apostrophizes Caliban as a 'poisonous slave', the offspring of the 'devil himself' and the Great Witch, who responds only to floggings, not kindness, who is 'filth' that repaid Prospero's human care with an attempt to rape Miranda, who is an 'abhorred slave' incapable of 'goodness', 'being capable of all ill', one of a 'vile race' that 'good natures could not abide to be with', who is 'hag-seed', and 'malice' and again a 'slave'.

---

*For convenience I will refer to Ariel henceforth as 'her' or 'she' – though my ontological genealogy (see page 471) finds 'her' male/female.

[413]

If it were more explicitly declared that Caliban is a black Moor (his mother was from Algiers), there would be no difficulty in recognizing Aaron's descendant, and his direct link to Othello might be queried. Even at this first meeting he might evoke the memory of every other 'Boar', those revolutionary projectiles of 'lust', the champions of the rejected Queen of Hell.

The wealth of converging tributaries in this last lap of the journey is distracting, but I shall try to keep my course narrowly to that of the tragic myth. So it is enough to say, about this second scene, that by the time Prospero has dismissed Caliban, Shakespeare has made as full and carefully delineated a formulation of the theme of the Rival Brothers and of the opening of the Tragic Equation as in any of the plays.

At this point, he lifts (out of the tempest) a new-born Adonis into position. He sets him in front of Miranda as if the Adonis of the long poem, before he ever met Venus, now saw descended from Heaven the ideal love that had 'fled' there to escape 'sweating Lust'. Or to bring things into sharper close-up, as when Florizel first met Perdita.

Instantly, Ferdinand and Miranda fall rapturously in love.

Within the strict confines of the Equation, Shakespeare has done here exactly what Adonis himself in the long poem wanted to do, which is to separate the chaste, ideal, Diana-like beloved from the overwhelming and promiscuous Venus. And he has dedicated his new hero (a new Adonis) to her, as if that other Venus did not exist.

It posed an impossible problem then, fifteen years before in the long narrative poem. Is it any more possible now?

By the end of the first act, *The Tempest* has restated the opening situation of the long poem *Venus and Adonis* as if setting chess pieces into the same positions, but with a difference, and with a bold declaration (in other words, taking full account of the experience of all the intervening tragedies) that this time Sycorax, the Queen of Hell, shall be helpless, the Boar shall be powerless to attack, and Adonis shall marry Miranda/Diana, his Goddess, his true beloved. Prospero, the undefeated veteran of his thirteen gruesome defeats (or draws after a defeat), plays the game, with Ferdinand as the image of his young Adonis self.

This first meeting of Miranda and Ferdinand turns certain keys in the Equation that open some startling inner vistas.

Believing that his father, King Alonso of Naples, is drowned, and all aboard with him, the survivor Ferdinand is led to Miranda by the music of Ariel. Their love at first sight is of a peculiar kind. Almost every phrase they speak sets it on the transcendental plane: Miranda, at first sight of him, thinks him a spirit – a supernatural, disembodied figment of her father's magic. When Prospero corrects her, she still calls him 'a thing divine'.

Ferdinand then addresses her as the Goddess – on whom Ariel's supernatural music attends. He follows this (before she has replied) with a strange 'prime request' (or, perhaps, after so long in the world of the Tragic Equation, not so strange) which is to ask her:

> O you wonder,
> If you be maid or no?
>
> I. ii. 423–4

When Ferdinand next addresses Miranda, after Prospero's interruption, he repeats the same inquiry, coupling it with a promise that, if she is a virgin, he will make her Queen of Naples.

The intriguing aspect of this frank opening of marital proceedings is not that it is a stereotype of romance conventions, which are the norm through the whole relationship of these two, but that Shakespeare has knit them so intrinsically into his own myth, as if he drew these threads only from his own earliest sources.

Ferdinand's plight, coming ashore as a castaway and addressing a strange girl, in those genteel, artificial terms, as a goddess who seems a Diana, is the first turning of that key – which trips tumblers in other locks, particularly in the birthplace of Sycorax, in the etymology of her name, and in the biography and secret life of Dido, Queen of Carthage. As these open, they reveal the Tragic Equation lying in a rich and strange cradle – the oldest story of all the sacred stories, as I shall attempt to sketch briefly when I come to look at those two women more closely.

In the simplest, immediate terms, Miranda is a maiden Lucrece, or, as I say, an embodiment of that love which in *Venus and Adonis*

> to heaven is fled,
> Since sweating Lust on earth usurp'd his name.

The difference here, of course, is that Miranda is on earth, not in heaven, and she has not yet been usurped by 'sweating Lust', while Ferdinand, the Adonis who worships her, has not yet seen any 'double vision' or felt any shiver of the Tarquin. And Prospero, who is watching over them, as over the chemicals in his crucible, is determined that their holy purity shall be 'fixed', in a sacred marriage, proof against Sycorax and the Boar, and that the tragedy of the double vision shall never happen again.

Prospero's tripartite brother

The shipwrecked courtiers come ashore, hermetically undamaged. Alonso (the King of Naples), his brother Sebastian, Antonio (Prospero's usurping brother, now Duke of Milan) and Gonzalo – the one man of the court who had earned Prospero's gratitude by supplying him, in his 'rotten carcass of a butt', with food, water, rich robes, necessaries and, most vital of all, his magic books.

This scene is divided into two parts. The second part is largely a re-enactment of the theme of the Rival Brothers, as follows:

When all the courtiers but Antonio and Sebastian are suddenly put to sleep by Ariel, the opportunity prompts Antonio to reveal his evil bent. In other words, he falls into the trap set by Prospero, and obligingly – as if automatically – demonstrates the wickedness that justifies Prospero's undiminished rage and the whole action of the play.

Antonio urges and successfully persuades Sebastian to usurp his reigning brother, Alonso, by allowing him, Antonio, to kill the King as he sleeps. Though they are frustrated for the moment, Sebastian, it seems, resolves to do it. This electrical unfolding of the past crime into the present moment, conjured out of Antonio's nature by Prospero's cunning, is more than a simple time warp, or a means of conducting the high voltage of Antonio's original crime against Prospero, twelve years ago, directly into the already supercharged atmosphere of the island. It subtly shifts relationships – towards the resolution.

King Alonso, as instigator and abetter of Antonio's usurpation of Prospero, is naturally as guilty as Antonio – in the eyes of Prospero. But when Alonso becomes the sleeping victim of his brother Sebastian's and Antonio's plot, threatened by Antonio's own dagger, 'three inches of it', he is dislodged from his own culpability, and is identified, by his brother's usurping will and Antonio's dagger, with Prospero himself. This has its effect on his son Ferdinand's credentials – as Prospero's prospective son-in-law – and frees the drift (inevitable, as part of Prospero's plan) of the Neapolitan crown towards the joyful coronation of Prospero's own daughter Miranda, which will also seal the forgiving reconciliation between Alonso and Prospero, and return Prospero to his dukedom.

This is straightforward, but what is interesting to see is how Shakespeare engineers the process through his jugglery with algebraic factors, in the relationship between the two brothers. In effect, Prospero's brother is not Antonio – but Antonio/Alonso/Sebastian: a composite, of which one component is merely opportunist in a shallow way (Sebastian), one is irremediably evil and will always push the knife home (Antonio), and one is wicked but capable of remorse (Alonso). These three are essential to Shakespeare's choreography. When they are looked at in this way, various additions (such as the brief surfacing of Antonio's 'brave' son) can be seen to be necessary harmonic touches in the algebra (the inevitability) of the musical key change, which in turn is required by the resolution of the Tragic Equation and the Sophia myth. I will attempt to say more about that a little later.

Meanwhile the first half of this scene, superficially more relaxed and even chaotic, while it develops the play's larger themes, seems to engage with the Tragic Equation hardly at all.

But the sensitized antennae of the Equation-seeker are alerted by the North African wedding of Alonso's daughter, Ferdinand's sister – from which the whole court were returning when the tempest caught them.

Inquiry into this can go far. But a few steps to the first signposts are all that are necessary to show how much of the hinterland belongs, almost exclusively, to the Tragic Equation.

The Tempest and Dido

Gonzalo's mention of Alonso's daughter's marriage to an African king of Tunis strikes two echoes: a sombre one, from Desdemona's marriage to Othello, which foundered on the Venusian isle of Cyprus, and a lighter, less ominous one from Florizel's recent announcement, in *The Winter's Tale*, to Perdita's father, Leontes, that his betrothed, Perdita herself, is the daughter of a Libyan 'war-like lord'.

These might remain no more than teasing echoes if the courtiers did not immediately begin to worry at the real identity of Tunis, determined to confuse it with Carthage and to entangle the newly married Queen Claribel with its former widowed Queen Dido.

At this point, where Ferdinand's sister Claribel is seen to be sitting on Dido's throne, the Occult Neoplatonist's image theatre of mnemonic correspondences lights up. The figure of Dido gradually brightens until quite suddenly the whole of *The Tempest* swings into a different light. As it dawns, every vibrant detail of Dido's story becomes relevant to this play.

Dido was a pervasive presence in the Elizabethan imagination, through her passionate, tragic, major role in the first four books of Virgil's *Aeneid*. As with all writers of the Renaissance, and especially the comparative newcomers of the upstart Elizabethan theatre, this work lay under the foundations of Shakespeare's dramatic imagination. The first part, in particular, had an immense, obviously early influence on him. It is something of a primer for recurrent images and situations throughout his plays. It could well have had more than a little to do with the main configuration and colouring of the Tragic Equation itself. One need not be surprised to find *The Tempest* so rich in allusions to it, especially, as I say, to those first books which concern Dido, and which open, like the play, in a sea storm, with storm-beaten mariners and a heroic prince coming ashore in a strange land.

Dido's story, as Shakespeare knew it, begins with Aeneas fleeing from the sack of Troy (and on his way – though he is not aware of it – to found Rome and the Holy Roman Empire), escaping a tempest by coming ashore in Carthage, where Dido is creating her new state.

As he climbs inland, the first person he meets is his own mother – the goddess Venus. The peculiarity of her appearance on this occasion is that she is disguised as a votaress of her counterpart Diana – the goddess of chastity and hunting. Diana, of course, like Lucrece in Shakespeare's tragic myth, is one aspect of the Great Goddess – of whom Venus is another. So Venus is merely appearing, to her son, in one of her aspects: as 'total, unconditional, elemental love', but in its 'chaste' mode.

She introduces herself as one of Dido's subjects, a girl from Tyre, and asks if he has seen one of her sisters, dressed like herself as a huntress, following a wild boar. He suspects that she is divine, and assumes that she is, in fact, Diana herself.

Venus then tells him Dido's biography. After extricating the theme of the Rival Brothers from the plays of the tragic sequence, there is no difficulty in recognizing a stark specimen of it here.

Dido was the daughter of a king of Tyre. Her brother murdered her wealthy husband – who was also their uncle. The dynastic imagination that concocted the tragedies can hardly have missed the possibilities. The family likeness to Hamlet's mother and to Ophelia (Virgil's description of the ghost of Dido's husband, returning to tell all, must be the original of King Hamlet's), to Lady Macbeth, to Antony's wife (Caesar's sister), Octavia, to Cloten's half-sister Imogen, are clear and strong. Other points of kinship touch various other females in the Rival Brothers series. And Dido's brother, the usurper of the uncle, is, as far as Shakespeare goes, a classic prototype.

Dido then fled to Libya. In terms of Shakespeare's Equation and Theophany, she fell into the abyss, into the wilderness, as Rosalind fled to the Mother Forest of Arden, as the rejected Cordelia was banished south to France, as the cataleptic Thaisa was cast away at sea, as the new-born Marina was given away to a witch, as Hermione vanished beyond the grave, as the new-born Perdita was cast away (to be found, in Florizel's untruth, where Aeneas found Dido, in Libya). One might add, as Claribel was cast 'ten leagues beyond man's life' to Libya, and as Sycorax was banished from Libya, to an even wilder place – the Devil's Island. And as new-born Miranda herself was cast away to the Devil's Island. This might be thought an arbitrarily coincidental posy of variants if Shakespeare had not picked out the most incongruous and oddest one of them all – Claribel's joyful, royal marriage to the King of Tunis – to reveal the common tap-root, Dido.

In Libya, as a landless refugee, Dido persuaded King Iarbas to give her as much soil as could be squeezed into an ox hide. She then cut the skin into a long thread of leather and, stretching it across a promontory, acquired a sort of island. Here she is building her new city when Aeneas arrives.

He entertains her with a narration, in truncated form, of the Trojan view of the *Iliad*, and with the adventures of his sea journey, where it becomes clear that he incorporates more than a little of Odysseus – of his experiences, if not his character. She falls desperately in love with him and he becomes her lover. Eventually his destiny (as Rome's founder) calls, and he abandons her. Hurling terrible curses after his fleeing ships, she kills herself on a pyre.

A central mythic feature of this story, in Virgil's telling, is that Dido's fatal passion is dramatized as the goddess Venus's victory over the goddess Juno, while her actual death is described as a ritual ministered by Juno, Iris and Proserpina.

She needs only one more attribute – known to any of Shakespeare's contemporaries who knew the writings of St Augustine* – Dido was

De Civitate Dei, II, 4.

originally a Libyan goddess of the Ishtar/Aphrodite type, and her temples were places of ritual prostitution: Dido was a Venus, that is, in her orgiastic phase.

The potential, in this narrative of Dido's tragedy, for some major variant of the Tragic Equation, is almost obtrusive. The basic Shakespearean crime – the fatal rejection of the Venusian female – is there: the greatest and best-known classic example of it. And Aeneas is like an epitome of the Adonis type: he is the son of Venus, like the sacrificed god himself, precursor of Christ, and founder of Rome. And at the same time he is the rejector of the lustful Venus. By comparison, Antony was a parochial figure, and so was Coriolanus. As for Dido, though she might not inherit the mythic watershed of the Nile like Cleopatra, nevertheless, when one looks into her more narrowly, her qualifications, as the actual Queen of Hell, are even better.

It could be that her story was too well known, its details too fixed in the learning of the learned, among Shakespeare's audience, to allow him the latitude that his drama would need. Marlowe's version is comparatively faithful to the source. But one can hardly doubt that, over the years, Shakespeare must have often revolved it. Certainly from the time that Adonis rejected Venus in 1592. Well before Bertram abandoned Helena, around 1600. And as it happens, apart from Shakespeare's pages in the play of *Sir Thomas More*, the only other dramatic fragment, unquestionably by Shakespeare, but outside the canonical titles, is from the 'excellent play' that Hamlet admired, and so judiciously praised, which contained the Player's speech, and which must have been, as Hamlet all but confirms, a tragedy of *Dido and Aeneas*. This long narration of Pyrrhus's butchering of King Priam, a terrific development of the original account in Virgil (*Aeneid*, Book II), belongs to Aeneas's story of the sack of Troy and of 'the dangers [he had] passed', which he tells to Dido as Othello told his story to Desdemona, and with which, like Desdemona, Dido falls in love. Obviously Shakespeare was more than capable of improvising a speech wherever a play needed it, and this particular passage does not prove the existence of some play that he had scrapped, some unfinished draft that he rather liked, the torso of some attempt that failed to get as far, say, as *Timon of Athens*, or some sequel to *Troilus and Cressida* that, like *Troilus and Cressida* itself, 'was never acted; or, if it was, not above once; for the play . . . pleased not the million; 'twas caviare to the general . . .' (*Hamlet*, II. ii. 464–6). But it proves how blazingly alive, in Shakespeare's imagination, back there at the opening of the tragic series, the dramatic theme of Dido and Aeneas already was, and how impatient to shove all alternative plots aside and burst on to the stage (even interrupting some other play).

In fact, scrutinizing *The Tempest* from this angle prompts a question: whether that strange first 'crime' (whatever went wrong long ago when the male rejected (abandoned) the female) is not, in this last play of the tragic series, given its ultimate reparation. Does *The Tempest* lack an overtly dramatized enactment of the Tragic Equation (such as takes up the first half of the preceding three plays and the whole of each of the tragic plays before them) because it is the Theophany of an unwritten, life-long-pondered tragedy that is hidden behind or within the text – the tragedy of Dido and Aeneas?

Miranda as Dido reborn

The threads drawn from Virgil's poem and woven into *The Tempest* are visible enough, for the most part. But many others are drawn from elsewhere, that enrich Dido's portrait in the play.

As I mentioned, in Virgil's account, Dido was the daughter of a king of Tyre, as was Pericles's daughter, Marina. Marina, I suggested, was maybe Shakespeare's first measured attempt to assimilate the metaphysical persona of the fallen Sophia to the 'new-born' Female of his mutated Equation.

Pericles is something of a sketch for Prospero. In the play *Pericles*, the vivid figure, Cerimon, is a magician of the power of flowers, a laborious turner-over of 'authorities' in the 'secret art', of herbals. He is the one who raises Pericles's castaway as-if-dead wife, Thaisa, from her coffin-chest (as Prospero released Ariel from the pine), preserved her as a priestess in Diana's temple and eventually presided over her reunion with her husband. If one can imagine Pericles (as the father of Sophia/Marina) combined with the flower-magician Cerimon, one would have a single character beginning to resemble Prospero – the magician of Ariel's flower-spirit magic, preserving a Tyrian Sophia/Miranda within his pentacle of chastity (very like a temple of Diana).

In this way, through that King of Tyre and through Marina's lineal reincarnation in Miranda, Dido takes shape as a shadow of Miranda (whose very name is an anagram of Marina with the 'd'). If this connection seems tenuous and forced, others strengthen it.

I mentioned the ways in which Dido's role as the wife of the usurped one, and sister of the usurper, associates her with the two lineages of Shakespeare's women, one of which might be called the fallen Sophia lineage (from Rosalind to Miranda) while the other might be called the Queen of Hell or Hecate (of which Lady Macbeth is the most celebrated, and Sycorax the last). I also mentioned the ways in which Dido's role as the rejected Venusian beloved associates her, painfully but most emphatically, with Shakespeare's great female plaintiff, whose lineage (voluble or silent) runs from Venus in the first long narrative poem, through Helena, Mariana, Juliet, Ophelia, Desdemona, Cordelia, Volumnia/Virgilia, Imogen, Thaisa/Marina, Hermione/Perdita to Miranda (and perhaps, stepping outside the magic circle, one might include Shakespeare's wife/mother/daughter). But the same role (according to the remorseless mechanics of the Tragic Equation) also associates her with what the rejecting heroes incur from their rejection of each of these women; the vision of the Queen of Hell and the assault of the Boar. In other words, it associates her with the Boar in the long poem, and thereafter with the Venusian goddess of 'sweating Lust', the vision of the Queen of Hell execrated by Hamlet (in Ophelia and his mother), with the hallucinatory 'foul toad' that drove Othello out of his mind, with the 'sea monster' that Lear saw when he heard Cordelia's 'Nothing', and with the 'sulphurous pit' that he saw at his blackest moment, with the 'half-workers' that sent Posthumus mad, with the 'hobby-horse' that demented Leontes, and with 'the damned witch Sycorax' – who was banished from Arghier, and produced the Tarquinian Boar Caliban.

That is to say, once Dido's name has entered the play, her biography alone, apart from any use that Shakespeare makes of it, binds her naturally into the secret persona of Miranda, and no less closely into the persona of Sycorax, and through this birfucated figure closely into the text and meaning of the whole work. Details in the text adjust the role she plays there, tightening the relationship between her story and Prospero's, between Carthage and the island.

After the opening tempest, the first moment one becomes aware that the characters are perhaps inhabiting two places simultaneously occurs when Ferdinand, as a castaway wandering inland, meets Miranda.

When he addresses her as a goddess, and falls in love with her, while insisting that she reassure him of her virginity, he gives her effectively the role that Venus took, when Aeneas, wandering inland as a castaway, encountered her. In other words, he sees her as the Goddess of Love in the aspect of Diana.

The mythic instinct of Shakespeare's imagination (and its superiority in this respect to Virgil's) is very evident here. Though Virgil makes so much of the fact that Aeneas's mother is Venus, he has no interest, apparently, conscious or unconscious, in his hero's potential as an avatar of the sacrificed god. So far as he is concerned, Aeneas's founding of Rome is simply an imperial legend: a political asset. The prophetic aspect of the poem, inevitably misunderstood by the author, is another matter. But by presenting Virgil's poem and his own island play simultaneously, as a double exposure, by superimposing Miranda as an apparent goddess in the form of Diana on the form of Aeneas's mother, Venus, and by superimposing Ferdinand, as her adoring lover, on the form of Aeneas himself, Shakespeare sets his hero, on the mythic plane, in the perilous double role and infinite perspective of the archaic dying god, who is both son and lover of the Great Goddess, a role obviously far weightier than that of either Aeneas or Ferdinand on the 'realistic' plane.

At the same time, in a more limited sense, he sets him within the workings of the Tragic Equation, placing him at that idyllic point of the pre-'double-vision' adoration of the Female – corresponding to that point in the tragedies just before she reveals herself, or the hero sees her, as the Goddess (as well as of ideal love) of terrible life, the Queen of Hell.

Again, because the play's Ferdinand/Aeneas is meeting, after all, not only the Goddess, his mother, on the mythic plane, but his beloved, Miranda/Diana, on the real plane, and because both these figures (in Virgil's poem) are simply the preliminary, and, so to speak, introductory aspect of Dido, then inevitably, once again, Miranda is set within the aura of Dido, as the love of Aeneas/Ferdinand. That is to say, Miranda is the living hologram formed by the converging identities of Venus (as the Goddess of Love), of Diana (as the ideal beloved), and of Dido (as the tragic unknown figure for whom she, Miranda, has been reborn – as Perdita had been reborn from the unknown, to her, Hermione).

This same identification is reaffirmed, here and there, lightly but powerfully. The smouldering presence of that previous life, in which Miranda was Dido, seems to become more and more the secret, poignant, smothered tragedy of this play.

[423]

It breaks through again, almost nakedly, in the bantering exchange of the courtiers about 'widow Dido' and 'widower Aeneas'. This is arresting and yet thematically at home in a play that completes a series of four, of which the first three have bent their whole plot and energy to restoring – in near-miraculous fashion – an apparently dead, fatally rejected wife to her mourning 'widower'.

Where, one might well ask, is the corresponding figure, the mourning 'widower', of the rejected woman in this play, the one who fills the special place, roughly, of Posthumus in *Cymbeline*, or, more precisely, of Pericles in *Pericles*, and Leontes in *The Winter's Tale*. The father of the daughter of the lost wife. Clearly, the widower here is Prospero and, according to the circumstantial evidence, in the imagination of the play – this dream shaped and manipulated by Prospero and Shakespeare – the lost wife has become Dido.

The 'circumstantial evidence' goes on accumulating.

A delicate link made by that first association – Claribel's crowning in the Tunis that has to be Carthage – turns out, first of all, to be only one thread in a mesh. Since Claribel has been identified as Dido, as the Queen on Dido's throne, Miranda finds herself once again identified with Dido, through her relationship to Claribel.

Where Claribel is Ferdinand's sister, Miranda is his future wife: i.e. Miranda's closest female relative (since she lacks a mother) becomes the Queen on Dido's throne.

Where Claribel is King Alonso's daughter and (as Sebastian suggests, since Ferdinand is presumed drowned) the heiress now to the Neapolitan throne, Miranda is his future daughter-in-law and (as Sebastian actually says) the heiress to the Neapolitan throne: in other words, Miranda will sit on the throne that is not Dido's throne, but that belonged to the one who sits on Dido's throne – almost as if she were Dido's daughter.

Ferdinand comes ashore as an Aeneas (as Shakespeare carefully ensures) and meets that composite being, Venus/Diana/Dido/Miranda (again as Shakespeare carefully ensures), which is like a reprise, up to a point, of the adventure he has just completed – his visit to the throne of Dido in the Tunis that ought to be Carthage, where he has left the woman closest to him, the Queen on Dido's throne, as surely as if he had abandoned her 'ten leagues beyond man's life', as surely as if she had immolated herself. And that Queen, abandoned in Africa, is – to the degree I have suggested – identified with the one whom he now meets for the first time as Venus/Diana/Dido/Miranda.

These are spectral flickerings of interconnection that juggle the identities and feed each word spoken, for instance, by Ferdinand, into an endless cycle of Tragic Equations, and set each word spoken by Miranda between the lips of Dido, in ways that are more clearly heard by the imagination than by the tape recorder. And they all combine to open the whole play to the echo chamber of Dido's tragedy – and to the bigger chambers beyond that.

The full relationship between Carthage and the island, and Dido and Miranda, becomes clearer, however, when the play is fitted back into the sequence of *King Lear*, *Pericles*, and *The Winter's Tale*, where the Tragic Equation finds its Theophany in the Sophia story – or in the particular choreography by which Shakespeare dramatizes what resembles the Sophia story. And remembering that throughout the whole tragic series the hero's crime is always the same – the rejection of the Goddess of Complete Being, who is Divine Love – we can fill in some of the lacunae between Prospero's island and the world behind Dido.

The Gnostic pattern in *The Tempest*

The 'geometry' or 'choreography' of the Theophany develops from *King Lear* to *The Winter's Tale* in a definite and orderly way, as a brief résumé makes clear.

In *King Lear* the hero's crime, rejection, is directed against his daughter. And the Theophany, such as it is, reconciles and reunites the two.

In *Cymbeline* the hero's crime is directed against his wife – but there is a strong sense that the child component is pushing to make itself felt.

In *Pericles* the hero's crime is directed against both his wife and daughter simultaneously. The reconciliation becomes more elaborate, more of a square dance, but also more psychologically and metaphysically comprehensive, and yet it is still simple – in a theophany administered this time by Diana. The wife, Thaisa, as if from beyond the grave, is reunited with Pericles. His daughter, who is his wife's self reborn (without memory of the crime), is united to a new husband, Lysimachus, who is (roughly) like a reborn Pericles (without memory of his woes) – governor instead of king.

These tentative explorations snap into masterful action in *The*

Winter's Tale. Again the crime is directed against both wife and baby daughter, but also — a new element — simultaneously against the 'rational brother' Polixenes. This 'new element' makes the whole pattern complete, in that it takes account of both Shakespeare's templates for the essential 'crime': the Tragic Equation and the Rival Brothers.

The reunion in *The Winter's Tale* can now resolve the multiple violation in a perfect, symmetrical pattern. In a theophany supervised by Apollo, the wife, Hermione, as if from beyond the grave, is reunited to Leontes. Their daughter, Perdita, who is Hermione reborn (without any memory of her father's crime or her mother's suffering), is united to Florizel, who is Polixenes reborn likewise (without any memory of the crime committed against him). This reunion of the reborn Polixenes and the reborn Hermione/Leontes, reunites Leontes and Polixenes, the rational brother and the irrational. The original binary crime of Tragic Equation and Rival Brothers is not only healed (in Leontes, Hermione and Polixenes), it is made to un-happen (in Florizel and Perdita). This spotlights the weakness of the pattern in *Pericles*, where Lysimachus had to be roped in — as something of a loose horse — to make up the full team, whereas in *The Winter's Tale* his equivalent, Florizel, is tightly one of the stable.

Aligned thus, as a developing approximation to the main moves of the Sophia myth, this series of simple patterns makes two things clear. The first is that this latest elaboration of the Shakespearean heroine into wife and daughter was inherent in the mythical nature that she revealed at the very beginning of the Tragic Equation — where she was the triple Goddess.

In discussing *Venus and Adonis*, I compared it with Euripides's *Hippolytus* and mentioned how, once the Queen of Hell component had been split from the Goddess (to become the avenging beast), a double figure remained. In *Hippolytus* this was Phaedra as stepmother and Phaedra as maiden in love. In *Venus and Adonis* it was Venus as a mother (that image of the 'hurrying doe') and Venus as a maiden in love. This dual mother/maiden nature of his heroine appeared again in *All's Well*, in *Hamlet*, and in *Coriolanus* as two different women. Now, in *Pericles* and *The Winter's Tale*, Shakespeare requisitions the same benign pair, with a slight adaptive shift, to the Sophia-like extra segment of his Tragic Equation, which I have called a theophany, and where they still appear as what remains after the Queen of Hell has been rejected.

Second, this consistently developing pattern produces a certain expectation. One turns to *The Tempest* confident of seeing the same organism – modified a little further.

Superficially, perhaps, *The Tempest* defies expectation in all kinds of ways. The new perspective, refracted through Prospero, is partly responsible for this impression of an unfamiliar kind of play.

After fourteen consecutive dramas centred on the usurping brother, or the Tarquin, the disorienting effect of Shakespeare centring his drama on this usurped brother, the defeated rational ego, throws everything awry. It is as if Polixenes had been made the central figure of *The Winter's Tale*.

As the eyes adjust, fragments of the ur-pattern come into view. But now, through the lens of the Tragic Equation, one can see that the old pattern glows through, at one level or another, almost completely intact, and what seems to be absent in specific detail Shakespeare delivers by subterfuge or sleight of hand.

In so far as that essential power generator, the Tragic Equation based on the rejection of the principal female, is hidden in Dido, as I have suggested, and is openly present in the ubiquitous Medusa ghost of Sycorax, Shakespeare links his five-act Theophany to its tragedy. But the square dance of this Theophany, too, manages to complete itself.

The symmetry that he had arrived at in *The Winter's Tale*, where irrational brother/reborn daughter parallels the rational brother/reborn son, has been switched. It now appears as rational brother/reborn daughter in parallel to (almost) irrational brother/reborn son. That 'almost' indicates the snag in the circuit. The reborn son, Ferdinand, belongs not to the 'irrational brother' Antonio, as he would if the pattern were perfect, but to the King, Alonso, who is not related to Prospero at all.

Or rather, as I noted a little earlier, he *is* indirectly related – as co-usurper with Antonio. Shakespeare's ingenuity and tenacity at this point enable him one way to intensify Antonio's culpability, another way to give to the ultimate blessed reunion of the reborn selves a royal crown, and another way to balance the transcendental solution (for the first time since *King Lear*) with sinister realism.

According to the newly established 'law' of the Theophany, if

Prospero and Antonio are usurped and usurper, and if Prospero has the daughter, then Antonio must have the son.

Accordingly, Ferdinand ought to be Antonio's son. The love union of these two reborn selves, Ferdinand and Miranda, would then – by sympathetic magic, as in *The Winter's Tale* – reconcile Prospero and Antonio. This is the ur-pattern of the Theophany pressing to be realized.

And this pattern is so strong, and so necessary to Shakespeare's satisfaction, that Antonio's, the Duke of Milan's, 'brave son' does show his back above the waves, briefly. Ferdinand mentions him. And when he does so, Shakespeare asterisks the reference with Prospero's retort about the Duke of Milan's braver daughter – a remark that has no other function but to point again to Antonio's son.

Once the impression of Antonio's 'brave son' has registered, he is absorbed into Ferdinand. The metamorphosis of this is again typical of Shakespeare's algebra.

As far as Prospero is concerned, Ferdinand's father King Alonso, who instigated the usurpation and profited by it, is as guilty as Antonio, who committed it. Together they are a two-headed (actually, as I pointed out, with Sebastian, a three-headed) usurper – Prospero's enemy, who surfaced there at sea for a moment with two sons, but actually on dry land only has one, Ferdinand.

By making Antonio Prospero's real brother, Shakespeare brings his crime to the maximum intensity. As with Claudius's crime against King Hamlet, for the usurpation of the rational by the irrational self to induce, of itself, the full spiritual consequence of the crime against the self, they need to be real brothers.

But real brothers cannot be fitted into the nuptial dance of the Theophany, because the union of their children, far from sublimating the fathers' crime in forgiveness and understanding, would introduce the direst of Shakespeare's horrors – incest.

Shakespeare has solved all this by the single stroke of doubling Antonio, and giving him a second royal self, Alonso, whose treachery to Prospero, though it initiated his fall, was not uterine, and who, as I say, unlike Antonio, is capable of remorse. Antonio's necessary son, therefore, can elide into Alonso's, producing Ferdinand, who has no blood tie to Miranda, and can bestow on their marriage a sacred royal crown.

The pattern of the Theophany is now complete: Antonio/Alonso is reborn in Ferdinand, and Prospero in Miranda: the transcendental love union of the two selves can reunite Prospero and Alonso – leaving Antonio as an irredeemable fact of a brutally real universe in which transcendental subjectivity rises only precariously, and against the odds, from the tragic plane.

The only missing person in this final floral dance of the consecrated betrothal is the wife from beyond death.

That strange composite Libyan woman – Dido/Sycorax – howling in the previous incarnation of Claribel/Miranda, cannot resurrect. The clenched (and now lonely) face of Prospero tells it plainly: she cannot be resurrected. A closer look might suggest why not.

Ulysses and the mythic background of *The Tempest*

There are certainly other ways to dismantle *The Tempest*, but approaching it, from whatever starting point, with the kit provided by the Tragic Equation and the Theophany, one finds that the three nodes of the feminine qualities are Miranda, Dido and Sycorax. If Miranda occupies the centre of the Lucrece qualities (corresponding, say, to Ophelia), and if Sycorax occupies the centre of the Queen of Hell qualities (corresponding to the lustful, incestuous, murder-condoning aspect of Hamlet's mother), then Dido occupies the middle range, the apparently culpable, rejected woman who is – like Hermione – innocent (corresponding to Hamlet's mother, bewildered by what her beloved son accuses her of, utterly contaminated by it, but susceptible to remorse and open to redemption).

Since Dido remains a floating, unconfessed and unfocused centre of guilt in the supercharged, tempest, background currents of the play, she is never distinctly separated from that other North African – Sycorax. Very much as the 'innocent' yet rejected and accused mother of Hamlet is not distinguished from the fratricidal Claudius's lustful incestuous colluding sexual mate – until Hamlet tries to dissect her nature in her bedroom.

Since the tunnel vision, the stage spotlight, of busy consciousness is deflected from these two, Sycorax and Dido, they have liberty, like a suppressed crime, to gather the 'dark backward and abysm' of the hidden world into the tingling webs of their complex. The result registers, as on flickering dials, in Ariel and Caliban throughout, but also in Shakespeare's entire conception. As if the hidden fermenting abyss of Dido/Sycorax were the dangerous ocean on which the island floats, like some kind of lotus. If this sounds exaggerated, one only has to look into the play, into the bacteriology of the play, so to speak, through the two lenses – Dido and Sycorax. Even a brief look is enough.

This dimension of *The Tempest* is brought into focus by the figure which Shakespeare so carefully places as a key to Ferdinand and Prospero – Aeneas.

Virgil's Aeneas, as I mentioned before, inherits the mantle of Ulysses and Jason. His sea journey recapitulates in abbreviated form a grander, fuller, more archaic, more authentically mythic sequence of the sea tempests, shipwrecks and encounters with monsters or supernatural or idyllic women on islands, who try either to devour him, transform him or nurse him, that Ulysses survived on his way home from the sack of Troy. On his way to and from the Golden Fleece, Jason encountered some of the same ordeals and terrific personalities. Behind all three epics is a common corpus of myth – though it is differently orchestrated in each case.

The three heroes belong to the lineage of universal, archetypal Gilgamesh-like heroes. Those magical islands, underworlds of the dead, supernatural antagonists, interested participation of Heaven and Hell, death, rebirth and transmogrification, are all the classical trappings of the story of stories, which in its most sophisticated form is the religious quest (Attar's *Conference of the Birds*, Dante's *Commedia*), in its secular barbaric form the quest epic, in its popular, vernacular form one of the most common folktales, and in its biological, elemental, spontaneous form, the shaman's emergency flight to the source of healing, illumination and renewal.

I mention this well-known link between the human mind's primal sacred experience and these three epics only to bring the shamanic type of vision into alignment, at this point, with the forms of Aeneas, Jason and Ulysses that stand behind Ferdinand/Prospero and *The Tempest* (which is to say, once again, behind the Adonis who encounters the Goddess of Complete Being, in Shakespeare's tragic myth).

In *Troilus and Cressida* Shakespeare indulges his special interest in Ulysses. That name, Ulysses, was derived from his identifying mark: the 'thigh wound', made by the tusk of a boar. When he returns home to Ithaca, incognito, his old nurse recognizes him by that famous scar. In any computer such as Shakespeare's, such a wound would automatically bring up the ninth poem of *The Passionate Pilgrim*, where Venus tells Adonis:

> 'Once,' quoth she, 'did I see a fair sweet youth
> Here in these brakes deep-wounded with a boar,
> Deep in the thigh, a spectacle of ruth!
> See, in my thigh,' quoth she, 'here was the sore.'
>
> *The Passionate Pilgrim*, Sonnet 9

(whether he himself wrote it or not), and behind Venus the gored Adonis himself. Like the heroes of Shakespeare's late Theophanies, Posthumus, Pericles and Leontes, but more like the epitome of them all, Prospero (that battered relic of his devotion to Diana, the goddess of the hunt), Ulysses was an Adonis who had survived the impact of the Boar.*

---

*Not the least notable member of Shakespeare's sacred order of thigh-wounded heroes is of course the original Jaques – the patriarch Jacob, Esau's God-protected brother, who became Israel (whose altar flame was Ariel). God's help did not save Jacob from a crippled thigh when he fought all night at the river Jabbok (before crossing into his brother's territory) with the daemon who had to break off the fight at dawn – and who is sometimes argued to have been God himself, sometimes Samael (Satan), sometimes the Archangel Michael (who gathered the dust with which God made Man), and sometimes Jacob's brother Esau. (If he had been the thigh-crippling Boar, he would have been all these: Great Goddess, daemon of the Goddess's correction, the Goddess's infernal consort, and the irrational brother.)

A lineal descendant of Jacob's, resurrected in medieval Spanish Christianity, was the patron saint of Shakespeare's heroine – St Jaques le Grand (cf. page 122), alias St Iago of Compostela, who was traditionally depicted with a wound in the thigh. In this post-Saracen Catholicism, such a wound (like that of Adonis himself, like that of the original of them all, paradoxically the god of potency, Dionysus – whose name means 'lame god') is related to that of Amfortas, the Fisher King in the legend of the Grail. This same association – between the Fisher King, the pierced saint and the sacrificed god (where the arrow-riddled St Sebastian equals the dismembered St Narcissus equals the representative of the sacrificed god) is the dramatic, mythic basis of Eliot's *The Waste Land*: all these figures carry the same

wound. The sexual wound (piercing both thighs) that made the Grail King impotent and laid the land waste was inflicted by a pagan knight's spear, on the blade of which was inscribed 'The Grail'. The submerged but tightly interconnected circuitry of these apparently separate mythic complexes can be glimpsed in this metaphor of the Boar (the spear blade) emerging from the estranged (lost) Goddess (the Grail cauldron) as itself a form of the Goddess (bearing her name, The Grail), and simultaneously an alien warrior. This is not a fortuitous association but lineally authentic, and indicates just how vitally Shakespeare's oeuvre is linked to the vast matrix of the medieval Grail tradition.

Other links between the two can be seen at many points in the greatest rendering of the Grail legend – Wolfram von Eschenbach's *Parzival*. This immense poem shaped the colliding and fermenting inexhaustible mix of materials and religious passions that coursed through Europe in the eleventh and twelfth centuries – a fusion of the Arthurian mythos and the Islamic/Indian Ocean of Story, Persian, Buddhist and Christian Gnostic ideas, that found concentrated expression particularly in the 'heretical' Albigensian culture of the south of France, and through the sensibility of the troubadours. Perhaps the otherwise mysterious polarization of Shakespeare's imagination between the Christian and the 'Moorish', his pervasive dialectic of the black and the white, and his gradual resolution of the oppositions in a Gnostic union of love, has its literary source here, in Wolfram's contrapuntal patterns of the Christian and the Islamic, which turn up

By this route also, the *Odyssey*, via Aeneas, flows into the story of Ferdinand/Prospero.

In Jason's epic quest for the Golden Fleece, the component of divine hero detached itself into Hercules — another shamanic astronaut who carried the Boar's wound in his thigh.

Apart from that immediate localization of *The Tempest*'s action in the setting of Dido's Carthage, various other specific features from Jason's *Argosy*, as well as from the *Odyssey* and the *Aeneid*, are alive in the underside circuitry of *The Tempest*. All conduct current to the composite identity of Dido/Sycorax.

When the cave-dwelling cannibal Cyclops, Polyphemus, imprisons Ulysses and his crew and begins to devour them, Ulysses identifies himself to the monster as 'Nobody'. Ulysses then blinds him 'with a stake' and escapes with his remaining companions. When the other Cyclops ask the groaning monster who blinded him, he can only answer 'Nobody', while Ulysses jeers at him from his departing ship. Aeneas heard this story from one of Ulysses's crew, and he recounts it to Dido in Carthage. Apart from the strong identification with this Polyphemus that the Virgilian undercurrent lifts into Caliban, Shakespeare introduces the clue, in his own style, in a single word. When Ariel provides the teasing, airy music for the catch about 'freedom of thought' that

—

even in Parzival's own family. Parzival has a Moslem stepmother, and his half-brother, her son Feirefiz, is half-black, piebald. When Feirefiz, as a gorgeously caparisoned knight, finally challenges Parzival to battle, his armour — like Edgar's in *King Lear* when he challenges Edmund — hides his identity. As they struggle to kill each other, Wolfram laments their enmity (in words that speak as much for Shakespeare's vision as for *Parzival*: 'I cannot refrain from speaking up: I mourn for this, that one flesh and one blood are doing each other such harm . . . One could say that "they" were fighting, if one wished to speak of two. They are, however, one. "My brother and I" is one body.'

Again, in the depth of the rich amalgam Wolfram's Grail, the vessel that had received Christ's blood, is identified not only with the cauldron of the British god Bran (who was Llud, who was Lear) that restored slain men to life (the cauldron, after some slight mythic drift, from which 'damned' Macbeth's new-born self rose, as he watched it,

to a transcendental life that he would never share), but with the stone begging bowl of the Buddha. Lifting the Shakespearean veils from this particular image, the Equation watcher will recognize Wolfram's Loathly Damsel, the Grail Messenger Cundrie, with her Boar snout and tusks and her Boar's bristly hair: she is Kali, the Great Goddess of India in her 'terrible' form, the original of the angered Boar Goddess that all Shakespeare's heroes have to meet.

After the genocidal Albigensian Crusade, launched in 1209, and the Inquisition's suppression of the Templars, Wolfram's world disappeared underground. But it emerged again in the Occult Neoplatonism of the sixteenth century, with a changed religious emphasis and a more sophisticated philosophical superstructure but with the same proclivity for Dervish-like, Templar-like, secret, 'anonymous' orders (such as the Masons and eventually the Rosicrucians) that nursed the esoteric doctrines and kept the keys to such 'mysteries' as *Parzival*.

Caliban calls for, it arrives mysteriously, like the mockery of Prospero/ Ulysses, and is promptly recognized by Trinculo as:

> the tune of our catch, played by the picture of Nobody,
> *The Tempest*, III. ii. 137–8

whereupon both drunkards are terrified, till Caliban heartens them again with his purpose – to destroy 'with a stake' the Prospero who has imprisoned him.

Polyphemus claims descent from an international species, the cannibal cave ogre, child of a witch, like Beowulf's Grendel, whose terrible mother lives under deep water. He is also close to the ogre-king, from whom the hero stole the royal rams. That itself is a variant of the folktale where the ogre-king is also the one-eyed Sun, or the High God, and the animals are the solar animals – the golden creatures of fire. This comes close to the variant theft of fire on one side (a pure shamanic raid on the 'Promethean heat' at the source of life) and on the other to the even commoner story of the ogre-king from whom the hero – after magical tasks – wins the daughter and the magical treasure, which is an archetype behind both the *Argosy* and *The Tempest*. So, along this lineage also, Caliban, by being a Polyphemus, was formerly a king and a Prospero.

Scylla and Charybdis appear in the immediate family tree of Sycorax. Charybdis, as daughter of the sea god and Mother Earth, had been flung into the sea (like Sycorax, like Miranda) by Zeus. And Scylla, once the beautiful daughter of Diana in her Underworld aspect of Hecate, was now a sea monster, attended by savage dogs, and known by her yelp (maybe responsible for Caliban's 'puppy-head').

The Harpies, like Scylla and like many another Shakespearean female whose virgin 'face between her forks presageth snow', were beautiful maidens down to their waists, beneath 'all the fiend's', and were emissaries of Persephone, the death goddess, flying on whirlwinds and (in Virgil) rising from the very waves of the Styx. When Ariel assumes this Sycorax-like form of the rejected, infernalized Goddess and accuses Alonso, Antonio and Sebastian of their crime, pronouncing the judgement against them, in thunder, it recalls very clearly Apollo and the Python, speaking in thunder through the Pythia, and pronouncing the judgement against Leontes.

All these female monsters are one way or another an aspect of Persephone or Hecate, or some form of the Goddess in her Underworld phase. And of all of them the most impressive and perhaps, as far as *The Tempest* goes, the most influential, was Circe.

Circe

Circe's island was populated by swine, wolves and lions, formerly men but now transformed by her witchcraft. Ulysses – a Prospero before his time – neutralizes her spells with the help of a magic herb, a flower, and becomes her lover. In the interlude she directs him through the Grove of Persephone (the Mother Forest) to the Underworld. There he meets Tiresias (who tells him how to complete his journey home safely) and his own mother. (In the same place, Aeneas found Dido; Dante, after the terrors of Hell, found Beatrice and the Mother of Heaven; and Shakespeare, after entering that 'cave' in the Mother Forest of Arden, in *As You Like It*, and after the terrors of the tragedies, found . . .)

The assimilation of Circe's island, where the thigh-wounded hero overcomes the bestializing magic of the witch, using the power of a flower, to the island of Sycorax, where a veteran scarred Adonis overcomes a son of the swine-crow witch, making her flower magic (Ariel) his own, and with it restoring bestialized men to their human selves, finally repairing his own stricken life in a heavenly marriage, is thoroughly apt, and rich. But the link is more historical.

Circe's original home was Colchis, in the land of the Coraxi. Her shrine in Colchis, planted with willows, was sacred to Hecate. In the *Odyssey*, her attendant swine and her role as guide to the Grove of Persephone identify her as a death goddess, a surrogate of Persephone herself. (The same Persephone who, in the Adonis myth, emerged in the form of a boar, to claim him.)

Ulysses was protected from Circe's magical power by the herb Moly – given to him by Hermes (the guide to the Underworld). This flower connects him to an earlier god, confronting an earlier great witch-goddess. In the Sumerian prototype of the Tarquin story, the pre-Jehovan Jehovah, Marduk, made himself immune to the thaumaturgic superpower of Tiamat, during their world-creating battle, by sniffing at a magic flower.

This lineage – Marduk–Ulysses–Prospero – paralleled by the lineage Tiamat–Circe–Sycorax (Dido) – comes the whole way on the magic of a flower spirit, which in Prospero's case turns out to be Ariel.

Or it comes another way: Marduk–Jehovah–Adonis/Tarquin–

Prospero, gathering on the way, from that death–rebirth of the Tarquinized Adonis on the transcendental plane, the Shakespearean flower of resurrection and redemption, the violet or blood-spotted cowslip (in which Ariel lives). Parallel to that is the lineage: Tiamat–Astarte–Venus–the Queen of Hell/Persephone–Sycorax (Dido).

By either route, all the infernal witch-goddesses of the archaic pagan world (including the Dido who conjured Hecate to curse Aeneas) flock into the island of Sycorax and roost in her name, like bats in a cave, and identify her, in her every reincarnation, as the Female rejected, and now defeated, by Prospero.

Besides being the land of the Coraxi, Circe's Colchis was the home of the Golden Fleece – the sacred treasure that drew Jason on his quest with the Argonauts.

In Jason's epic, the semi-supernatural chatelaine of the Golden Fleece was Medea. Falling in love with the hero at first sight (as Miranda falls in love with Ferdinand) and helping him to accomplish the impossible tasks set by her murderous father the King, Medea hypnotized the dragon serpent that guarded the Fleece (shades of the Gnostic Pearl) and let Jason carry off herself and the Fleece together: she and the Fleece were his prize, as Miranda and her chastity are Ferdinand's.

These two double prizes are suggestively interrelated, as if somewhere hidden behind Miranda and her chastity were Medea and the Golden Fleece. The paradox of Jason's prize is that while the Fleece was the miraculous trophy, Medea was the most diabolically savage and dangerous woman in classical tradition. In other words, the Fleece is related to Medea, as Miranda's chastity, sanctified for the betrothal Masque (administered by Heaven), is related to the matrix of Dido/Sycorax, the enraged tempest, from which she has been lifted, and which does inherit the witch-goddess lineage of Medea.

In the many examples of the shamanic flight recorded in the literature and folklore, the prize can be almost anything – stolen fire, a flask of the water of resurrection, the herb of immortality, a fruit from the Tree of Life, the tongue that cannot lie, a supernatural bird, a vision of the true self, a hair from the sun god's beard – any image of the healing mana that infuses the hero returning from his encounter with the source. But almost always his success is mediated by a woman, who either guides him, or is herself the keeper of the treasure, or is herself the treasure, and who returns with him. But the shaman's problem lies in bringing his prize back into the world. It is as if the prize, the object, the woman, were some image of that Complete Being. When he re-enters the world, human life cannot accept what he brings — his own waking consciousness cannot accept it. Or rather, can accept only part of it. The rest he has to reject. That is presumably one origin of the rejected, enraged, diabolical half of the Goddess. Jason hangs on to the Golden Fleece, but the rejected Medea becomes a homicidal witch. Prospero wakes up protecting Miranda with a kind of desperation, but looking back in horror towards Sycorax/Dido.

Medea was the niece of Circe. In effect, Medea and Circe are two faces of the figure that absorbed so much of Shakespeare's imaginative energy — the hero's beloved as Hecate, in this case the Hecate of the Coraxi, Sycorax, whose other face was Dido.

Prospero has come back from his encounter with Divine Love, bringing Medea/Circe/Dido/Sycorax/Miranda: the total Goddess of Complete Being. But then, having arrived in the sublunary world of men, he has examined his prize with the double vision. The question is, having divided the indivisible Divine Love, the Complete Being, into Miranda cherished and the remainder rejected, how does he arrest the mechanism of the Tragic Equation? Having rejected that terrific assemblage, how does he stop the inevitable assault of the Boar?

Because it is a fact, as I remarked earlier, Prospero does stop it — mid-charge, mid-air. Adonis's Boar-spear, that failed in *Venus and Adonis* and failed again in *Troilus and Cressida*, and in every play since, has suddenly, in *The Tempest*, become a magic staff. Against this staff the elemental fury of the Goddess, incarnate in the Boar Caliban, is impotent. And what the Boar's *doppelgänger*, the inferior brother, managed to do in the past, is now magically undone, by its power. At the same time, Prospero has succeeded at last in halting the oscillation of the two women, the loved and the loathed, in the one body. He has separated the two halves of the double vision, as if forever. And holding them fixedly apart, and dismantling the crooked wiring behind Adonis's eyes, he now marries a Diana-like Miranda to an uncorrupted, idyllic Ferdinand. That is to say, he has solved the never-before-solved tragic problem of the Mythic Equation. But he has done all this through Ariel. Just as Ulysses did, he has brought the island under control, and transformed the evil on it, with Ariel's flower-magic. And it is Ariel who stages the ritual betrothal, and raises the magic ramparts encircling Ferdinand and Miranda, patrolled by the benign powers of Heaven — in the Masque.

The undivulged tragedy of the former Astarte, Dido, which crackles at all these points throughout the text, makes its fullest, simplest self-revelation here in the Masque. A crucial feature of Dido's story, as Virgil tells it, is, as I mentioned before, that her fatal passion is described as Venus's victory over Juno – the result of a power struggle in Heaven. Dido's death then follows as a ritual directed by Juno, and managed by Iris and Proserpina. In *The Tempest*, in the betrothal Masque of the fourth act, which is the moment of Theophany, where Prospero reverses that old disaster of the Tragic Equation, the new-born Dido (Miranda) is married to the new-born Aeneas (Ferdinand) under the blessing and protection of that same Juno, Iris, and Ceres (Proserpina's mother). Most curiously of all, the drama within the drama of the Masque is a window glimpse of an activated tableau, presenting at last the defeat and repulse of Venus.

The Tempest: a precarious moment in the alchemy

In Act Two, Scene One, Caliban, carrying logs for Prospero and cursing him, encounters the two clownish sailors. Drunk on Stephano's 'celestial liquor', Caliban adores Stephano as a new kind of god, offering to serve him and show him all the secrets of the island.

Ferdinand, like a Caliban compelled by Prospero to carry logs, now encounters Miranda for the second time. What was love at first sight now becomes mutual adoration and promise of eternal love. Prospero, eavesdropping, and nursing this along as if it truly were happening, as I say, inside his sealed crucible, nevertheless helps to introduce the taint of the decomposing Adonis, saying of his daughter pityingly:

> Poor worm, thou art infected,
> *The Tempest*, III. i. 31

which insinuates itself into Ferdinand's startling comment that he would

> no more endure
> This wooden slavery than to suffer
> The flesh-fly blow my mouth . . .
> 61–3

picking up the word 'fly' in his next sentence, to settle, pullulating, ominously, into Prospero's:

Heavens rain grace
On that which breeds between them!
75–6

Caliban quickly coerces Stephano and Trinculo to his will, seeing in them a means to fulfil his ambition: to destroy Prospero as he sleeps (though he is now willing to leave the ravishing of Miranda to his new master Stephano). This lower-case replay of Antonio's prompting of Sebastian to kill King Alonso as he sleeps, which is in itself a replay of Alonso and Antonio's usurping of Prospero, brings to Caliban the role of 'tortoise' bearing the grand three-tiered complex of variants of the Rival Brothers which is now carrying the play.

Just as Ariel observed the plot of Antonio and Sebastian, she observes this one also.

Ariel and the Harpy

It is now the mid-point of the play. Lost in the maze, the courtiers are brought to a standstill, perplexed and exhausted – removed from every reassurance, and King Alonso is in despair. Only Antonio and Sebastian maintain their purpose – to kill the King.

As in a sensory-deprivation chamber, the world of the castaways begins to dissolve into a phantasma. Strange shapes enter to 'a solemn and strange music', bearing in a banquet, dancing about it with 'gentle actions of salutation', inviting them to eat. Their bewilderment, deepening since they were so strangely preserved from the tempest, becomes amazement: which is to say, they become susceptible to correction.

When Lear entered a similar process of self-estrangement, and deepening bewilderment, his old Tarquinian ego was violently and convincingly shattered, whereupon his true self emerged new-born – the saintly Lear, united to Cordelia.

A more controlled and formal version of a similar process is working on the courtiers here in *The Tempest*. When Ariel enters, in a crash of thunder as a Harpy, sweeping the banquet away with a clap of his wings, and accusing them, out of the thunder, of crimes that make them 'most unfit to live', it has the effect on them that the storm culminating in Edgar's suddenly erupting from the hovel had on Lear. One must take Ariel's word seriously and accept that the guilty courtiers are suddenly mad:

And even with such-like valour men hang and drown
Their proper selves.

III. iii. 59–60

It is a moment of judgement, corresponding to the moment in *The Winter's Tale* when Apollo's word came to Leontes. But here, Ariel, in the form of a creature from the Underworld, speaks through all the powers of Nature – the 'seas and shores' and 'all the creatures' – with the voice of 'Destiny'. This is not Jupiter, or Apollo, or Diana, but the Great Goddess herself, whose magic, as Prospero's later invocation reveals, is also that of Medea – who is Circe and Hecate. It is, in fact, the voice of the violated one, the victim, the rejected – who is both Miranda (as the 'outcast', new-born one) and Sycorax/Dido (who is the condemned, banished one). It is the voice, again, of Hermione, who though Leontes's double vision divided her, and rejected her as a Queen of Hell, in fact remained whole, and spoke the divinely revealed truth out of her undivided being. It is the voice of the Pythia, in which the thunder voice of the Python speaks, with the words of Apollo: an image of Shakespeare's Apollonian poetry as the voice of the Dionysiac Kundalini of the organism in crisis. The deity of this Theophany, in other words, is the deity behind Shakespeare's vision: the undivided Complete Being, Goddess of Creation, the Goddess as the three Fates – the Moeriae, to whom Jupiter himself is subject.*

*It is not impossible that Shakespeare knew, through the Occult Neoplatonist route, the legend of Buddha's enlightenment. When Buddha found the 'immovable place', at the foot of the Bodhi (wisdom) Tree, and sitting there in meditation commenced his great siege, refusing to move until the Truth of Creation had revealed itself, he was confronted by the Antagonist, the King of Delusion. This near-Almighty Being appeared to him first as Kama, the Lord of Desire, assailing him with the Lusts, Pleasures, Gratifications (and Regrets) of the physical worlds; next as Mara, the Lord of Death, assailing him with all the Terrors of the demonic worlds; finally as Dharma, the Lord of Social Duty, commanding him to return to the responsibilities of his princely throne. The meditating Buddha was so perfectly detached from ego that he remained unmoved by all this. At last he stretched the fingertips of his right hand to touch the earth – whereupon the Goddess of the Earth, and of that Cosmic Tree (the Serpent in the Tree) and of the enclosing Heavens, spoke *in Thunder*, declaring that the unmoved and immovable Prince, the Lord of Compassion, was the true inheritor of this seat under the Tree of Wisdom. This thunderbolt pronouncement crushed the powers of the Antagonist, the Ruler of the World, and that night Buddha achieved enlightenment. As a metaphor for Prospero's triumph, this legend sets the Masque and the transcendental 'stuff of dreams' sermon, (Shakespeare's 'Fire Sermon'), and also the hero's confrontation with the world of the Boar (throughout the entire history of the Equation) in a context consistent with the strange 'egolessness' of Shakespeare's creation and final attainment.

So it is quite fitting that Ariel, who is the daemon of the Goddess's transcendental positive magic, should pronounce the judgement of the total Goddess through the Harpy, the most loathsome form of her negative magic, descended directly from Tiamat, the beautiful-faced monster, whose coils were the ocean.

This revelation of judgement, conjured and supervised by Prospero, is almost entirely successful. Alonso lurches away, apparently ready to drown himself, while Sebastian and Antonio follow him, slashing at imaginary devils, and Gonzalo observes:

> their great guilt,
> Like poison given to work a great time after,
> Now gins to bite the spirits.

III. iii. 104–6

When next they appear, though they will not have progressed anything like so far as Lear did in his transformation, they will be changed (except for Antonio) and eager to repent and be forgiven.

The Masque in *The Tempest*: the defeat of Venus

According to the Tragic Equation, and the Sophia-style Theophany, the heart of *The Tempest* should be the Masque.

If it is as I have argued, if the Tragic Equation beginning back there in *Venus and Adonis* is the story of the fundamental crime, where the secularizing, moralizing, defensive ego rejects the primeval Goddess of Divine Love, which is to say the Goddess of 'total, unconditional' Love, and if that rejection implicates the ego in a simultaneous rejection of its own soul (is in fact the same thing) and if the tragic sequence of dramas is a coherent investigation into that crime, a methodical analysis of the evidence (which Shakespeare traces into every detail of what the criminal ego thinks, feels, says and does), and is also the judgement, pronounced in that court case in *The Winter's Tale*, under the eye of Apollo, as the god of poetic inspiration and revealed oracular truth, and if the Theophany which develops (as I have traced) out of Shakespeare's ethical determination (his sacred shamanic mission) to heal the crime, redeem the criminal, and reconsecrate his victim (the human avatar of Divine Love, the beloved, the incarnation of the 'soul') is the whole purpose of the last four 'romances' (as I have argued), and if these dramas achieve this atonement, redemption and reconsecration in a sacred marriage of 'new-born' souls, and if, finally, the sequence of four Theophanies culminates in *The Tempest* then . . .

The sacred nuptial ceremony in *The Tempest* ought to be the consummation of the whole tremendous labour. It ought to be the crowning illumination of the entire oeuvre.

I have tried to indicate the evidence which more than suggests, to my mind, that the ur-tragedy behind *The Tempest* is the story of Dido, the beloved rejected by Aeneas – who is the classic shamanic figure, composite of all his predecessors, son and beloved of the Great Goddess (rejector of the Great Goddess as Dido), founder of the Roman Empire. If this is so, it can be seen how this play does reinterpret all the plays of the tragic sequence (right back to *Venus and Adonis*) and presents them again as metaphors, variations, in a grand fourteen-drama disclosure of the tragedy of Dido – the Tyrian Queen abandoned in Libya by the warlike hero who was himself the prisoner of a different, as if divine, historical imperative.

We can expect to see, therefore (it would be logical if what I say has any consistency) that the sacred betrothal in *The Tempest* should repair, in some quite specific way, that crime of Aeneas/Adonis, and in particular the suffering and death of Dido. The brief Masque, those few lines spoken by deities, conjured by Ariel, at Prospero's command, has somehow to accomplish this.

It is curious to see how far it does literally succeed in the task, and how far it qualifies its own triumph.

The overture of the Masque is a dialogue between Prospero and Ferdinand, in which Prospero ratifies 'afore heaven' his giving of Miranda to Ferdinand, and declares afresh her infinite virtues.

Ignoring Ferdinand's ominous response:

> I do believe it
> Against an oracle,
> *The Tempest*, IV. i. 11–12

as if some oracle might just have contradicted his 'boast', Prospero goes on to reformulate the sole condition on which he makes this 'rich gift': it is, of course, the old proviso of chastity:

> If thou dost break her virgin knot before
> All sanctimonious ceremonies may
> With full and holy rite be ministered,

No sweet aspersion shall the heavens let fall
To make this contract grow.

IV. i. 15–19

This is like the preparation before a holy vision, the ritualizing of 'purity' before a magical operation. But it is also the ultimate statement of Adonis's requirement: that true religious love must be chaste. Ferdinand duly vows chastity, as at a shrine, and Prospero summons Ariel to bring in the Masque, but then (perhaps alarmed by Ariel's parting words: 'I conceive') returns, Polonius-style, to the perils of affection:

Look, thou be true; do not give dalliance
Too much the rein: the strongest oaths are straw
To the fire i' the blood; be more abstemious,
Or else goodnight your vow!

IV. i. 51–4

And again Ferdinand swears that the animal ardour of his liver is abated under whole mountain ranges of Diana's virgin snow, inadvertently suggesting what an unpredictable sort of creature his liver might turn out to be when he shakes those snows off.

The Masque which follows is an incantatory magical spell, a Hermetic ritual in the active mode. Its purpose in terms of the Tragic Equation (which it sticks to closely) is to ensure that the event is a flowering on that upper plane, where Male and Female are reborn, as Sophia and her Jesus Aion, in a reunion 'in heaven'. As algebraic factors of Shakespeare's mythic system, the poetic terms operate with engineered, economic precision to repair what happened to Adonis. At the same time the dramatis personae reveal that the rite is also carefully reversing what happened, in particular, to Dido.

In Dido's original story, as Virgil tells it, Juno accuses Venus of tripping Dido into 'total, unconditional' love for Aeneas (as Desdemona loved Othello for telling the story of the dangers he had passed). But Juno then tries to turn this love to her own account, by arranging the marriage of the pair.

The 'marriage' of Dido and Aeneas, in Virgil, is a striking antithesis to Adonis's rejection of Venus in Shakespeare's long poem. The setting is a hunt, the same. The splendour of a stallion (as in Shakespeare's poem) is celebrated, and lions and boars are searched for (prayed for). Juno now contrives a terrific thunderstorm that drives Dido and Aeneas into a cave, where, with Juno's and the Earth's help, Dido's passion proves irresistible (unlike Venus's in the poem) and the act is consummated in peals of thunder, while the nymphs cry out on the mountain peaks.

By folding this 'marriage' around Dido's hopeless passion, Juno had intended to secure Aeneas's residence in Carthage, his help in building the city and establishing the state, and his future protection for Dido. The goddess had hoped to secure, in fact, in primitive fashion, what Prospero is hoping to secure in the Masque for Miranda (though the possibility of the ideal new state, in a new world, has detached itself, and fallen into the fantasy and banter of the befuddled, bewitched courtiers). But Juno (goddess of marriage) underestimated (to Venus's amusement) the primordial ferocity of the energies released by Venus, nor did she take any account of Aeneas's higher destiny, which was to found Rome.

At Jove's bidding, Mercury calls Aeneas away – to his destiny – and Juno can do nothing to defend Dido from her sexual despair.

This 'marriage' which Juno had so optimistically staged, with divine accompaniments, now turns into an awesome, orgiastic death: Dido's funeral service is a witch-priestess's invocation of the goddess Diana as Hecate, Chaos and Hell, while Dido delivers a prolonged curse against Aeneas and all his hopes, once more calling down Hecate and the Furies, after which she stabs herself on a pyre of his belongings.

Against this explosion of infernal passions, Juno is helpless. The most she can do is to send down her messenger, Iris, to minister to Dido's actual parting moment, and to ease her passing into the hands of Proserpina, Queen of the Underworld.

Considering again that Prospero (in so far as he is the original Aeneas) is the survivor of that explosion and of those curses, one can see, maybe, what trauma has sensitized him to the character of Sycorax, and what has conditioned his whole nervous system to react so violently against any hint of her reincarnation: what has mobilized his whole life, one might say, to achieve a mastery of protective magic, of which this marriage of his daughter is now to be the masterpiece.

So it comes about, as I say, that this betrothal Masque is a corrected replay of the nuptial ceremony of Dido and Aeneas, reborn as Miranda and Ferdinand. It has to undo what Venus did, and invert all the values of Dido's death, employing, as before, Juno and Iris, and replacing Proserpina, who took Dido down into the Underworld, with her mother

Ceres (who had eventually won Proserpina herself back into the upper world, for the nine flowering and fruiting months of each year).

What this ritual must forcibly exclude, therefore, using all magical means, is what threatens it: the mischief of Venus, which is simultaneously, in this play, the mischief of the Queen of Hell as Sycorax and her Boar.

The dramatis personae of the Masque – Juno, Ceres and Iris – conscripted from Dido's marriage and death, are three benign faces of the Great Goddess. Juno is the Great Goddess as consort of Jupiter, goddess of marriage; Ceres is the Great Goddess as Earth Mother, the goddess of the bounty of growing things, who is also the divine instructress of bride and bridegroom in the secrets of the bride bed (and who was present, as the Earth, with Juno, at the nuptials of Aeneas and Dido in the cave); Iris is the messenger of Juno, but is also the 'sweet aspersion' that 'the heavens let fall' to make the flowering earth fruitful, and marriage contracts to grow: the Goddess in her aspect of actually blessing the fertile Earth.

The Masque opens with Iris, at Juno's command, calling Ceres to celebrate and bless 'with some donation' this betrothal of Ferdinand and Miranda. Her conjuration is the last in line of the death–rebirth flower passages – trimmed into couplets which have a touch of the mummers' play jobbery about them, but with the true sap flowing through their syllables nevertheless. It is an invocation of the Earth as a garden, both wild and cultivated. As Iris speaks, great Juno descends through the rainbow, drawn by her peacocks. This apparition of the Great Goddess, in her highest protective form, drawn by rainbow-coloured birds, descending in the full spectrum of rainbow light on to a garden altar heaped with every flowering and fruiting plant, is in part an alchemical vision – where the prismatic colours dissolve into the white light, as Male and Female are united in a glory of divine being, in the Divine Presence. So the Masque opens.

But into this oratorio of heavenly favours the action of the Masque intervenes as a distant dramatic scuffle watched through a telescope. Or as the report, rather, of an assault frustrated – which is (and this is the whole point of it) a disaster averted. Averted, that is, from the couple whose happiness is being secured in the spirit of Theophany, by these authorities from Heaven.

The drama frustrated is none other than the 1593 death of Adonis and the rape of Lucrece: the Tragic Equation in its primal, naked, original, pre-dramatic terms.

Ceres asks for this bulletin – as if it had been some threatened attack that all still feared:

> Tell me, heavenly bow,
> If Venus or her son, as thou dost know
> Do now attend the queen? Since they did plot
> The means that dusky Dis my daughter got,
> Her and her blind boy's scandal'd company
> I have forsworn.
>
> IV. i. 86–91

Dusky Dis – Lord of the Underworld – is the 'hot tyrant', who is the archetypal figure that possesses Tarquin. As Ceres's daughter, Proserpina was the virgin form of the Goddess, originally a Lucrece. Overwhelmed and carried into the Underworld by Dis, she was there assimilated to the Queen of Hell, but in a form that could be reborn as a goddess of the flowering spring (a virgin Lucrece, Marina, Perdita, etc.).

Ceres is here alluding to Venus in the form of the goddess of lust: the very form that Adonis rejected, in the poem. She is alluding, that is, not to Venus in general, but to that particular aspect of the Goddess who becomes the daemon of the Tragic Equation, and who, as the one who possessed Dido, is the one who, when rejected, transformed Adonis into Tarquin. In other words, she is alluding to the specific mythic enemy of this ultimate Shakespearean marriage.

Iris's reply is the magical conclusion of this ritual as a spell:

> Of her society
> Be not afraid: I met her deity
> Cutting the clouds towards Paphos, and her son,
> Dove-drawn with her. Here thought they to have done
> Some wanton charm upon this man and maid,
> Whose vows are that no bed rite shall be paid
> Till Hymen's torch be lighted; but in vain;
> Mars's hot minion is returned again;
> Her waspish-headed son has broke his arrows,
> Swears he will shoot no more . . .
>
> IV. i. 91–100

In other words, Venus's assault on Adonis in the long poem has been repulsed, has been un-made, in fact, as if it never happened. Her waspish-headed son who was also the Boar, whose attack would transform Ferdinand into Tarquin, repulsed, has broken his weapons. (That 'waspish-headed son' was also, of course, the 'hot tyrant'.)

This snapshot of Venus flying away is a carefully modified recycling, and a carefully positioned reversal of the end of the long narrative poem, which after all, at the time of Shakespeare's writing *The Tempest*, lay probably not three paces from his elbow, and was still the favourite long poem of many of those who would be watching this play in the theatre. The phrase:

> Cutting the clouds towards Paphos
>
> IV. i. 93

splices the penultimate line of the long poem:

> Holding their course to Paphos
> *Venus and Adonis*, 1193

into the very fabric of the Masque. But in this case, the image is presented as a successful active ritual of magical enforcement. In the immediate world of the play it presents, as a *fait accompli*, Prospero's triumph over Sycorax and her son Caliban. They are reeling away defeated. In the mythic world of the Tragic Equation, this is the guarantee that the goddess of lust and the Boar are finally neutralized and rebuffed – the guarantee that Prospero has repaired what happened to Adonis, and has undone what happened to Dido. Up to this point, then, in this episode, Prospero has managed to accomplish what no other potential tragic hero before him had managed to do: he has separated the loved (Miranda) and the loathed (Sycorax/Dido, and all that comes with her). He has controlled the double vision and, carefully taking the wiring apart, has defused the 'bomb of vulnerability', the madness that explodes in the returning Boar, as the spark leaps between the two points.

The result is a betrothal as de-eroticized as heavenly help can make it. At least from Prospero's point of view, according to the contract he has drawn up with Ferdinand and Miranda, and witnessed by these deities, it is. But, according to the Ainu proverb, 'At the end of the ritual, up comes a goblin', the Masque itself produces its own destruction.

To begin with it has to be asked whether Juno and Ceres, in this ritual, can promise more to Ferdinand and Miranda than they formerly promised to Dido and Aeneas, when they presided at those embraces in the cave near Carthage, during the thunderous drench.

More dangerously, Shakespeare embeds the news of the repulse of the goddess of lust and her terrible son in a particular ritual which, by its very nature, contradicts it.

The Masque as the nativity of a god

The poetry of *The Tempest* is a strange substance. It gives the impression of being the final product of long alchemical labour. The impression seems to be almost palpable, even where the language is manifestly perfunctory and constrained – in the Masque, for example.

The Masque, in fact, is in some way almost like a source for this peculiar diffused effect. When this episode is aligned, as I have tried to align it, with the toiling evolution of the Tragic Equation, it can focus an illumination which is actually not easy to contemplate. As the lens of that long perspective, it can generate almost a kind of fear in the reader – like the end of the *Paradiso*. It precipitates one passage, in particular, which in spiritual tone, in resonance within the oeuvre, seems like Shakespeare's ultimate word. These are the lines, of course, which begin:

> Our revels now are ended. These our actors,
> As I foretold you, were all spirits and
> Are melted into air, into thin air;
> And, like the baseless fabric of this vision,
> The cloud-capp'd towers, the gorgeous palaces,
> The solemn temples, the great globe itself,
> Yea, all which it inherit, shall dissolve
> And, like this insubstantial pageant faded,
> Leave not a rack behind. We are such stuff
> As dreams are made on, and our little life
> Is rounded with a sleep.
>
> *The Tempest*, IV. i. 148–58

The common interpretation of this speech, that it is Shakespeare's own summary of his activity as a dramatic poet – as the mouthpiece, that is, of a Siva-like mystery whose dramas are the incessant creation and dissolution of the world and its life – touches a feeling that does set it apart from his other pronouncements, which are as a rule squeezed from the crowding contingencies of action. Also the speech seems to emerge here, in the play that consummates Shakespeare's poetic vision, in its natural, proper place.

A curious thing about it, though, is precisely this: its occasion and timing. Its contemplative, elegiac, god's-eye survey of existence comes at a crisis, when urgent, particular business would seem to make it inopportune. That such an essential statement (essential to all Shakespeare) should have been simply inserted as a 'good block', without very special dramatic justification, seems unlikely — considering how subtly and economically trimmed everything else is. So it is tempting to look for some explanation for this uniquely radiant passage.

The most obviously suggestive circumstance is that it follows the Masque. The Masque, as I have noted, is written in the equivalent of puppet language — stilted and quaintly formal, concentrated yet homely: the weak pipe and little drum music of an artificially restored archaic rite. And then, after a few more lines, comes this spectacular effortless effulgence — one of the high moments in all poetic literature.

Perhaps this is not so strange. If a priest were able for ten minutes or so after the Mass to heal the seriously ill, but for no longer and never at any other time, it would automatically be assumed that the rite of the Mass had somehow released in him some inexplicable power, which expressed itself in this way, as an abnormal brief access of supernatural ability. The same would be assumed if the rite were only a reinvented ancient cult mystery, performed by a private society of eccentrics, and the priest were normally a comedian. Everybody accepts cause and effect of this kind, where religiously toned rituals produce peculiar but real changes (even if they are put down to hypnosis) in those who take part.

Authors of imaginative literature are familiar with something similar: certain fantasies, particularly those concerning ritualized, religiously toned events, can have startling psycho-biological consequences on the fantasist's immediate life — sometimes very like the brief effect of a consciousness-changing drug. A crude but well-known example is the violent physical effect, on Flaubert, of composing the scene of Madame Bovary's poisoning.

Having said that, it seems reasonable to ask whether this 'ultimate word' of Shakespeare's could possibly be related to the rite dramatized in the Masque which has just preceded it. And whether anything else might be concealed there.

After that little mime of the defeated Venus, which is like a play within the play (which in turn makes Ferdinand, wondering at the art of the father who produced it, think himself in the garden – the calyx – of Paradise), there comes a pause.

> Juno and Ceres whisper seriously:
> There's something else to do.
>
> IV. i. 125–6

What follows is Iris's invocation of 'the nymphs of the brooks' and the reapers: she summons them to help in celebrating 'a contract of true love'. This formal Elizabethan call to a picturesque dance finale is also a clue.

It has often been remarked that the principal deity in this Masque, Ceres, is the form taken by the Goddess in the Eleusinian Mysteries, where she was known as Demeter. These particular Mysteries were regarded then (and still are) as the living source of spiritual life in the Greece of the period of the great tragedies and for long after (in all for 2,000 years). Partly because of this, they have always held a special fascination for inheritors of the classical tradition and for the Occult Neoplatonist movement in particular.

It has been suggested that the myth of these same Mysteries is behind *Pericles* and *The Winter's Tale*. Obviously the Sophia story – the descent of the lower Sophia (the daughter, like Proserpina, daughter of Ceres) into the Underworld of Jaldabaoth, and her 'redemption thence' to reunion with the upper Sophia (the mother, like Demeter) is a variant of the Demeter myth. There can hardly be much doubt about the historical connection. Shakespeare was aware of this myth's relevance to his own ideas, as his various purposefully placed references to it indicate. He was well aware, too, of its specific relevance to this Masque, where he fuses the ravishment of Proserpina with the death of Adonis. In doing this he was being quite orthodox. The two myths are like the male and female of the annual descent of the vegetative spirit into the Underworld. In the Masque, while Ceres evokes that long-ago assault of Venus on Adonis – which cost Adonis his life (an episode identified by Iris's linking phrase, 'Cutting the clouds towards Paphos') – she does so in terms of Dis's assault on her daughter, accusing Venus of prompting Dis to the act, and plotting:

> The means that dusky Dis my daughter got.
>
> IV. i. 89

The cast of those particular goddesses in this rite – Juno and Iris, as well as Demeter – also indicates, as I have suggested, that she is evoking Venus's role in the Virgilian death of Dido, where the Love Goddess plotted the tragedy that snatched the Libyan Queen into the Underworld. Ceres (with Iris) is by implication accusing 'lustful Venus' of being the villain in all three deaths.

As it happens, the Eleusinian Mysteries celebrated a birth, as well as a death. Besides Proserpina's 'flower-death' descent into the Underworld, the Ceres/Demeter myth incorporates a flower rebirth – like the myth of Adonis. Or, if not a flower rebirth, a rebirth of vegetative life.

The rebirth of Proserpina thrived in folk custom (even in England, well past Shakespeare's day, where she was buried in the field as a corn dolly, to be reborn as corn). Her rebirth never became a large-scale religious event – presumably because it was assimilated to the more successfully promoted rebirth of her male equivalent. Ceres/Demeter, who mourned and searched so famously for her lost daughter, was also the mother of a divine male child. In the Eleusinian Mysteries, Ceres/Demeter bore this god, thought to have been symbolized by an ear of corn growing and ripening instantaneously in a miraculous fashion, but anyway a child who was not the reborn Persephone but male and known as Brimus – 'the mighty one'. In other words, Ceres/Demeter's Mysteries, in this respect, were another form – the classical Greek form – of the nativity of the god.

This straightforward happening, in the rite that therefore incorporated Shakespeare's seminal sacred myth – the death and rebirth of this peculiar god – leads straight into the sacred event of *The Tempest*, if one approaches the Masque with an imagination even partly formed, as Shakespeare's certainly was, by the previous fifteen works of the tragic sequence.

According to the many contemporary witnesses, the actual ceremony, and especially this moment of the birth of the god, permanently transfigured all who took part. It was the great 'revelatory' religious experience of the classical world, for Cicero as for Aeschylus five hundred years before him. Something of that mode of ecstatic adoration, which these Mysteries developed, as well as the mystical concepts and specific details of the myth, have survived, maybe, in the Gospels. It is hardly surprising, then, to find some trace of it here.

Up to that point, in the Masque, where Juno and Ceres 'whisper seriously', the ritual 'death' (of Adonis and Proserpina and Dido) has been accounted for (not by any re-enactment, but by the repulse of Venus from her mischievous assault on Ferdinand and Miranda, i.e. by a magical reversal and undoing of her fatal act). The 'serious' whispering of the two goddesses indicates that what is now going to happen is the real thing. And at that moment, the entry of the reapers reveals what has been missing so far.

The finale of this Masque – the dance of the nymphs and the reapers – is the most important part of the rite. As these petty goddesses and rustics enter, Shakespeare dissolves the betrothal ceremony of Ferdinand and Miranda into the most primeval nativity cave drama: the rebirth, from earth, of the god. In other words, the alchemical marriage of the two redeemed ones, of 'widower Aeneas' and 'widow Dido' – the archetypal Shakespearean hero and heroine reborn and reunited – is symbolized by the birth of the divine self, the god Brimus. But where in this Masque is the god?

The Masque as the twin birth of Tragedy and Transcendence

Shakespeare distributes simultaneous components of the nativity into a dramatic sequence.

In the original ceremony the birth of the Divine Child of Ceres was the ecstatic culmination of the ritual. It burst on to the worshippers with a 'thunderous' shouting as the priests entered, dressed as shepherds, bearing the god in a winnowing fan. Brimus was better known as Iacchos – and the shattering, ecstatic yell 'Iacchos' became legendary. (Before the battle of Salamis, when the defeat of the Persian fleet freed Greece for its great century, a dust cloud 'as of thirty thousand men' was seen rolling from the direction of Eleusis, and out of the cloud came the great cry 'Iacchos' – taken to be a portent of the Greek victory.) This shout echoes in the Gospels, perhaps, as the shout of the angels in Heaven that announced the 'glad tidings' to the shepherds near Bethlehem.

Shakespeare inflects the whole ritual more tightly, to fit his own system. By converting the shepherds to reapers, he takes the logical step that the Eleusinian Mysteries themselves never seem to have taken.

Presumably the god was originally a 'lamb', which changed to an ear of corn when the nomads became settled agriculturalists and updated the winnowing-fan cradle of the god but failed to update the shepherds who carried it. Shakespeare also naturalizes the event to local harvest custom – familiar from his own background. English reapers celebrated this death–rebirth, in English cornfields, but shepherds did not.

Iacchos was clearly associated (to a degree identified) with Dionysus – the generalized, elemental form of the Divine Child/sacrificed god. And just as the reapers alias shepherds nursed the infant Brimus, the water nymphs in this context are the nymphs who nursed the infant Dionysus, and became the rain-makers, the Hyades (the piglets). These nurses of the god were also known, like the shepherds of Brimus, as the 'roaring' ones (the shouting angels). In other words, they and the reapers are the Graeco-Latin and the English, the female and the male, the ancient and modern, dancers revolving about the single concept or event – the birth of divine life, the delivery of the 'word within a word', the Redeemer. Reapers and nymphs, in a way, are near synonyms, and in this way these Warwickshire reapers, in fact, linked as they are here with the classical 'nymphs of the brooks' obey that habitual Shakespearean reflex which combines the Graeco-Latinate term with the native English, in his verbal icons.

Reapers and nymphs dance gracefully to music: i.e. without any shattering yell, as everywhere in these later plays the 'thunder' of rebirth on the higher plane modulates to the music of a divine peace, or, ideally, the music that reconciles Earth and Heaven and all opposites in a dance. But there is something missing, obviously: the god in person. Maybe Prospero is pondering this absence when he suddenly remembers Caliban.

Instead of a shouting of angels or ecstatic priests, there is a kind of thunder – 'a strange, hollow and confused noise' – and the dancers 'heavily vanish', as Prospero cries:

> I had forgot that foul conspiracy
> Of the beast Caliban, and his confederates
> Against my life –

IV. i. 139–41

This shocking moment, it seems, disrupts the ritual – with a violent intrusion from another world. But, keeping in mind the terms of the Tragic Equation, this episode flashes out as a dazzling expression of the

Equation's most fundamental idea. In announcing the rebirth of the divine one, Brimus, 'the mighty one', the dancers have disclosed to Prospero (this veteran Adonis of all those earlier disastrous-for-him encounters) the latest charge of the Boar. The Boar, he suddenly realizes, is almost upon him. This awareness bursts directly out of the spectacle of the dancing nymphs and shepherds.

The situation is dramatic but also deeply disturbing and well worth analysing.

✱ The Masque has just consummated that long labour of Shakespeare's tragic sequence: the betrothal of the new-born couple, on the transcendental plane, radiantly focused. Literally, he has produced the solution of his Tragic Equation, symbolized in the birth of the god as the god himself, the Divine Child of Ceres/Demeter.

But apparently, here on the stage, that birth of the god on the transcendental plane coincides with the shocking, headlong emergence of the Boar – on the tragic plane.

And then, before one can properly recover from the lobbed bomb of this surprise, it is gathered up, as it were, into another and greater surprise: the serene, all-dissolving light of the great speech.

This confusion of effects needs to be examined step by step.

Prospero is frequently irascible – with Caliban, with Ariel, even making a show of it with Ferdinand – and his long-nursed vengeful rage against his usurpers is evident enough. But his fury at remembering Caliban – in the very moment of the birth of the new self, in this alchemical wedding of the Masque – is so extreme that Miranda exclaims:

> Never till this day
> Saw I him touched with anger so distempered.

> IV. i. 144–5

This seems dramatically apt not only because Prospero has such a short time (measured in minutes) to reverse the tragic failure of all the heroes before him, as well as his own misfortune. If the drama is to be galvanized, with a serious urgency, at this moment, one might expect an upheaval – everything tossed aside in the emergency, just as the heavenly pageant is dismissed. But Prospero recovers instantly, and in the blink of an eye he is reassuring Ferdinand, whom he now addresses as his 'son':

                    be cheerful, sir:
                        IV. i. 147

and then climbs straight into:

                Our revels now are ended . . .
                        IV. i. 148–58

that most exalted of cruising flights through nirvana. This sudden
exhalation, arrives, as I said before, apropos of nothing – merely
informing Ferdinand and Miranda that the show is over, and was
created by spirits. The actual inspiration of the speech, however, seems
far away beyond any apparent dramatic requirement of the moment.
The last thing the action needs, one might think, is a trance of poetic
vision. What it does need is for Prospero to do something, and quickly,
about this goblin Caliban – the elemental lump of *sangsara* that has
somersaulted in, like a clown through a paper hoop, through these veils
of 'such stuff/As dreams are made on'.

Looking at this speculatively, and a little fancifully, it could be
supposed that this is the only occasion in all the plays when the process
of the redemptive rebirth is reversed. That is to say, the process that
passes from storm on the transcendental plane (the opening tempest and
its after-grumblings) into the musical accompaniment of the flower
rebirth of the redeemed one (the Masque dance, at the birth of the god)
is suddenly reversed. The music of the dance disintegrates in a kind of
thunder (the hollow din) and out tumbles Caliban as a Tarquin bent on
usurpation and murder.

But then, to go on in the same fanciful vein, along with Caliban,
delivered with him like an Abel to his Cain, comes the divine speech –
the philosopher's stone of all Shakespeare's alchemical labours. This
speech could be considered, swelling as it does out of the nativity, here
behind Caliban, as the unaborted birth of the redeemed one. As if it
were, in some sense, the transcendental form of Caliban. In other
words, as if Caliban and the speech were metaphysical twins, the two
possible forms of the god's rebirth – the tragic and the transcendental.

Brimus and Proserpina/Persephone are ambiguous figures. Brimus,
'the mighty one', was associated, as I say, with Dionysus, the one
capable of terrible frenzies, who proved as fatal to the repressive
Pentheus (in the *Bacchae*) as the Boar did to Adonis. I mentioned above
that the nativity of Brimus also incorporated the rebirth of Proserpina/

                        [454]

Persephone. But her animal form was the Boar – the form in which she had come to claim Adonis, in his myth. In that way, just as the emergent Tarquin was possessed by the Queen of the Underworld in the form of a boar, Brimus contains the dark Persephone as a boar. That is to say, the betrothal ceremony of Ferdinand and Miranda, symbolized as the nativity of the redeemed self, the reborn divine self, is simultaneously, inevitably, the rebirth of Tarquin. And Brimus, it seems, is the perfect and precise image of Shakespeare's reborn hero: born simultaneously on the transcendental and tragic planes.

And now, of course, having followed the fortunes of the Tragic Equation through the plays, one recalls that this simultaneity was always there – in the very form of the Tragic Equation. The Flower and Tarquin were always the transcendental and the tragic aspects of the reborn divinity – like the wave and particle forms of the wave particle. As the Divine Child was always the transcendental form of the Tarquin, and the Tarquin the tragic form of the Divine Child. This is a fundamental paradox of Shakespeare's tragic idea, and the eruption of Caliban from this sacred nativity is his most condensed, supreme image of it.

So it is not surprising that the speech should follow Caliban into the world, or that it would thrust itself into the action at this point, as Shakespeare's response to the hypnotic requirement of the ritual nativity. It objectifies the divine birth promised by the rite, the Horus to Caliban's Set, the Jacob to his Esau. It objectifies, both as representation and description, the essential condition of the transcendental state of mind, beyond opposites, united with divine being at the source of creation before creation. Meanwhile Caliban objectifies the opposite – the Goddess as the Boar, incarnate in the sexual body, baffled and trapped in all the limitation of existential being, mortal but possessed by the fury of immortal appetite.

This sequence of nativity/Caliban/speech can be extended. What follows is: entrance of Ariel, with news of how Caliban's plot – the charge of the Boar – is already under control, whereupon the fourth act, and the last of the play's real action, concludes with Caliban and his confederates being hunted across the island by spirit hounds. This is the first hunt fully dramatized in the tragic sequence since *Venus and Adonis*, but now Adonis is alive and the Boar is in full flight (another view of what Iris had reported in the Masque).

The suggestive feature of this sequence is that, in relationship to the eruptive Caliban, the transcendental speech and Ariel are linked – though it would be premature to imagine Ariel as the active personification of the spirit of the speech.

All this makes clear my earlier statement that Prospero's ritual of consecration – of the new-born couple – produces its own antithesis.

From a slightly different angle this great passage, 'Our revels now are ended . . .' is in place, also, as the evolved response which the Adonis figure (Prospero) now (at the close of Shakespeare's career) makes to the irruptive entry of the Boar. In earlier plays, as the Tragic Equation shows, the Adonis figure *always* succumbs to the Boar, is possessed by it, becomes a Tarquin – and thereupon delivers a 'tirade'. As if the arrival of the Boar, as well as being everything else that it is, were a terrific surge of poetic oratorical energy. Or, if the Tarquin does not deliver that speech, Shakespeare does. Shakespeare too, inevitably, experiences this bolus of Goddess energy as a surge entering into his own brains – ritually invoked by his written invention. So it happens, in *Measure for Measure*, at the close of Act Two, when, for the very first time (in the three preparatory 'problem' plays) the Boar enters Adonis full tilt and transforms him into an uncontrollable Tarquin. Angelo orders Isabella:

> And now I give my sensual race the rein:
> Fit thy consent to my sharp appetite . . .
>   . . . redeem thy brother
> By yielding up thy body to my will,
> Or else he must not only die the death,
> But thy unkindness shall his death draw out
> To lingering sufferance . . .
>
> *Measure for Measure*, II. iv. 162–8

and then immediately, at the opening of Act Three, Shakespeare delivers one of the most magnificent speeches in the *Complete Works*, through the mouth of the Duke:

> Be absolute for death . . .
>
> III. i. 5–41

as if Angelo had swallowed the magic mushroom and this were the terrific vision, coming a little after, in a poetry far more evolved and new

[456]

than those lines above. It shoulders the action aside, and lifts a volcanic cone high above the whole play.

In a similar way, one might look through all the plays of the tragic sequence and find the poetic response, to the arrival of the Boar, in a major speech, usually the high point – as prolonged, passionate, poetic speeches go – in the play. As I say, this speech releases the influx of tragic passion in the hero – naturally, since the arrival of the Boar is the arrival of the madness. But one could say it also releases the poetic energy in Shakespeare – as that invocation of the triumphant Boar, operated by the ritualized fantasy of his text, triggers the psycho-biological charge of the inspiration, in so far as the Boar is, as I described it, the shock wave of the Muse's advent, in her most savage, tragic form, from the depths of his nervous system.

But in *The Tempest* for the first time the situation is different. The text docs not ritualize the invocation of the Boar into that triumphant Adonis-transforming, Tarquin-creating assault. Instead, it invokes the Boar – Caliban – to meet its match in the magically invulnerable Prospero, and to be not only stopped in mid-charge, not only arrested, as I said, in mid-air, but *sublimated* into its transcendent form.

In this way, as all the earlier Boar-impact speeches express the Boar's victory and the Tarquinian madness, this speech expresses the Boar's defeat and transubstantiation into its opposite self – not into the condition of Tarquinian madness but into the condition of transcendent peace and the bliss of the sacred vision, the verbal form of the transcendent god. Caliban is volatilized in mid-stride. That is (to be clear), the speech expresses not what the doomed Tarquins have to say about the Boar's assault – but what the supreme alchemist Prospero/ Shakespeare has to say about it: the Boar's arrival has become simply the opportunity and the energy for transcendence.

In other words, the relationship between this speech and the threat of Caliban corresponds to the relationship between this whole play, this crowning work (as a theophany) and the tragic world that it transcends (or rather, transcends and recreates) – the world of Dido and the Tragic Equation. So this sequence: nativity/Caliban/speech, is a condensed, essentialized emblem of the whole play.

It is likewise a condensed, essentialized emblem of the long psycho-logical process, within Shakespeare, that produced this ultimate, transcendental poetry, this strange substance, out of that first, long-ago 'rape-and-murder' irruption of Caliban's Moorish uncle, Aaron.*

The triumph of the lame hunter

With the hunt of Caliban the action of *The Tempest* is virtually over. Nothing remains but to bring to some kind of balanced resolution the developments that are all now completed. Back in *Venus and Adonis* the action of the tragic sequence began with a hunt. But here at the very end it rounds itself off with a hunt. It is the same hunt, Adonis's boar hunt, but, as I say, reversed. Between Adonis's fatal hunting accident and Prospero's hallooing of his spirit hounds, the only glimpse of hunting in

*Robert Graves, in *The White Goddess* (a rich primer for the genetic tributaries that enrich the bloodstream of Shakespeare's Goddess and hero), though he is well aware of the other possible sources, points out that the situation and main dramatis personae of *The Tempest* are anticipated in the early Welsh Romance (mythic material slightly domesticated) of the birth of Taliesin, the miraculous child and poet. Cerridwen (the great Sow Goddess) lived on an island with her two children, the most beautiful girl in the world (Creirwy – related to Cordelia through Creir, meaning 'heron'), and the ugliest boy, Afagddu. Her husband, Tegid Voel, a form of the god Llew, the Welsh Hercules, is related to Apollo and thereby to the great British god Bran (and thereby to Lear): the bird of Apollo was a white crow, the bird of Bran a black crow or raven (hence the ravens on Tower Hill, where Bran's oracular head was buried). The name Sycorax combines the totems of Cerridwen and Bran. To compensate Afagddu for his ugliness, Cerridwen decided to make him intelligent, and boiled up a cauldron of inspiration and knowledge – a compost of herbs reminiscent of Medea's. A cauldron, one might think, reminiscent of the Witches' in *Macbeth*. She set little Gwion (a mere local lad) to watch over the simmering. Three burning drops (not three revelatory apparitions) flew out and scalded his finger. When he sucked the burnt finger he instantly understood all things, past, present and future, including Cerridwen's plan to kill

him at the completion of the work. He fled and she came after him as 'a black screaming hag'. By his new-found magical powers he became, in succession, a hare, a fish, a bird and a grain of wheat on the floor of a barn. She followed as a greyhound, an otter, a hawk and finally a black hen, that swallowed the grain, whereupon returning to her own form she found herself pregnant. Eventually she bore a child of such radiant beauty that she could not bear to kill him, so (instead of incarcerating him in a pine tree) she tied him in a leather bag (reminiscent of the Craneskin Bag) and threw him into the sea. Carried to a weir, and rescued, he was called Taliesin – 'radiant brow' – and immediately began to recite magical poetry. Cerridwen's cauldron had produced, indirectly, the miraculous child much as, in Shakespeare's tragic myth, the three burning 'drops' from the cauldron of the Witches produced the miraculous, 'naked new-born babe' (see page 398), the hero's rebirth, the uterine twin of what was contained in the Craneskin Bag of poetry, and also, as I shall show, of Ariel. If Shakespeare had (as Graves suggests) heard this story as a boy from his Welsh schoolmaster, and if he had also heard the (related) myth of Llyr and Creiddylad, it would help to explain how this Celtic complex comes to lie so richly and strangely in the deep strata of his Tragic Equation, and how Cordelia (as Miranda) comes to be so closely related (again as I shall show) to Ariel and to Caliban.

the entire sequence comes where King Lear, after banishing Cordelia, returning from the hunt meets the first rumour of Goneril's anger. In the beginning, Adonis was killed by the Boar. And here – at exactly the mid-point of the sequence – King Lear, hearing the Boar coming through the undergrowth (his rage against Goneril, rejecting her, registers the animal's approach) braces himself for the fight with the Boar which he will actually win (the first Tarquinized Adonis to be redeemed). And finally, here at the very end, omnipotent in magical power, Prospero, a Boar-proof, Tarquin-proof Adonis, hunts the Boar out of Shakespeare's life. It is a strangely symmetrical business.

Shakespeare's psychic preoccupation with the survivor of a shock arrest by the Underworld, the hero 'deep-wounded with a Boar,/Deep in the thigh', casts an odd light on the recurrent theme of his own lameness in the *Sonnets*. The four references, in poems notable (if taken seriously) for their plain-spoken directness, are generally dismissed as figurative. Yet:

> Speak of my lameness, and I straight will halt
>
> Sonnet 89,3

coming after the particularly down-to-earth, confrontational separating of the facts from the falsehoods of:

> Say that thou didst forsake me for some fault,
> And I will comment upon that offence
>
> 1–2

in what is a particularly heartfelt, naked statement, sounds (at least to me) like a touchstone, pointed reference to an accepted, in-the-bone, and indeed self-evident personal flaw. No less so is the carefully literal comparison of:

> As a decrepit father takes delight
> To see his active child do deeds of youth
>
> Sonnet 37, 1–2

to:

> So I, made lame by fortune's dearest spite,
> Take all my comfort of thy worth and truth . . .
>
> 3–4

This 'lameness' appears later as the chief of three grievous complaints when Shakespeare contrasts his patron's plainly itemized 'beauty, birth, wealth, wit' – the unfigurative roll call of the young Lord's undoubted and again self-evident advantages – with his own condition of being just as self-evidently 'lame', 'poor', and 'despised'. In Sonnet 66, the list of pitiable cases of Fate's injustice that have exhausted his will to live (by the age of thirty-one or so) begins by picking over the social scene:

> Tir'd with all these, for restful death I cry:
> As to behold desert a beggar born,
> And needy nothing trimm'd in jollity,
> And purest faith unhappily forsworn,
> And gilded honour shamefully misplac'd,
> And maiden virtue rudely strumpeted . . .
>
> 1–6

and then, following the rhyme inward, he comes inadvertently to:

> And right perfection wrongfully disgraced,
>
> 7

which cannot easily refer to anything but an act of skill or a work of art, and which immediately precipitates:

> And strength by limping sway disabled,
>
> 8

followed by the further intimate disclosures, bursting to be aired, of:

> And art made tongue-tied by authority,
> And folly – doctor-like – controlling skill,
> And simple truth miscall'd simplicity . . .
>
> 9–11

If his 'simple truths' are to be entertained only with a willing suspension of disbelief (and these sonnets relegated to a less remarkable order of art), then speculation need go no further. But if Shakespeare's manifest effort to record a few straightforward truths is to be taken seriously, then the meaning of these lines is also straightforward enough: they make a plain declaration of the burdensome subjective side of his life as a professional dramatic artist beleaguered by police-state censorship (as we know all dramatists were), by officious pedants (as we know he was, with Ben Jonson on record among them), and by a super-sophisticated elite (at that time infatuated with rhetorical convolution and wordplay). It is particularly interesting as the only direct comment he makes that reflects his opinion of his own art's special quality and his patient sufferance (though they are wearying him to death) of critical experts who never entered the arena: and interesting, too, for that testament of his dogged loyalty to misunderstood, against-the-stream, true simplicity (recalling

> While others fish with craft for great opinion
> I, with great truth, catch mere simplicity).
> *Troilus and Cressida*, IV. iv. 103–4

If, as I say, one takes these remarks seriously, this exasperated, half-stifled, private cry is released by the line that touches lameness. And comes from an actor who is now limited, perhaps, to such parts as the only two he is recorded as having played: the Ghost in *Hamlet*, who passed majestically by 'with martial stalk', and Adam in *As You Like It*, who, as the anecdote goes, 'appeared so weak and drooping and unable to walk, that he was forced to be supported and carried by another person'. If his words could be believed, that he was indeed lame, it would awake another nerve in his myth, and would hardly contradict the ranging alacrity of his mind. (A curious arabesque on this feint at a conjecture is the fact that the sole object still claimed by his descendants – the Hart family, who preserve it – to be his, is a stout, knob-handled walking stick, curved as if by heavy use, though this again stands only slightly clear of the rings, swords, books, etc. that at various times have made a bid for his ownership.)

The Boar has charged in every work of the tragic sequence. On each occasion it has overpowered Adonis and created a Tarquin – on its first assault. But now, in *The Tempest*, for the first time, it has failed. Since that first bloody collision the Boar has never again appeared as a boar – only as a shock wave of transforming, spectral madness, emerging from the same place, under the same provocation. But now, where Prospero's magical armour rebuffs the shock wave, the Boar reappears, materializes, so to speak, in stunned, half-animal form, shaking its head from the impact – the baffled, 'demi-devil' Caliban. The Tarquinian madness has been, as it were, externalized – in this hog-backed, bristly offspring of the Moorish witch and the devil-god Setebos. And Prospero, calling up his astral hounds, does what Adonis failed to do – he hunts it out of the *Complete Works*, and brings the tragic sequence to an end.

The Tempest as a keyboard for playing the *Complete Works*

If *The Tempest* is a keyboard, each key reduced to a minimal sign, then the actual instrument is the entire oeuvre. The entire massive stack of organ pipes resounds, as Prospero, or Caliban, or Antonio, or Ferdinand, or Miranda, lightly touches the words. At least, that is the impression of a devout member of Shakespeare's congregation. As Mozart was said to hear a whole completed work as a single simultaneous sound.

When Miranda greets the courtiers with 'O brave new world' and Prospero mutters, almost aside, "tis new to thee', Prospero is plainly hearing the truth about this brave new world in the terms with which the earlier tragedies defined it – since Alonso, Antonio and Sebastian are 'words' with etymological histories. In this way, Antonio was formerly Claudius who murdered King Hamlet, Macbeth who murdered Duncan and Banquo, Edmund who usurped Edgar, and the insurgent Oliver and Duke Frederick. In so far as he prompted Sebastian, he carries the Iago factor, and comes of the same family as Lady Macbeth. Antonio stands in front of Miranda, therefore, virtually in the dock, guilty of the perennial crime against the rational self, and of the tragedy that followed whenever Tarquin emerged. His each word and move, or lack of word or move, echoes among those affiliations. In a similar way, Prospero himself is 'thicker than himself' with previous incarnations. Because he is the first hero to remain, beginning to end, an Adonis immune to the Tarquinian madness, whereas all his predecessors succumbed and sank into the tragic flames, Prospero may seem unfamiliar, and *The Tempest* may seem, as I noted, like a different kind of play altogether from all that came earlier in the sequence, but his proper context identifies him.

It seems to be the case that Shakespeare's final hero attracts little sympathy. Though he survives to preside at the Theophany, where his reborn self, his daughter, is betrothed, he has nothing of the recently shattered, only-just-repaired, spiritualized stature even of Leontes at his reunion, or of Posthumus at his, and certainly nothing like Lear's at his. He seems to have arrived at this ceremony of transcendence without having visibly paid any price for it. Where Lear's love of his daughter is saintly and stricken, Prospero's can seem merely possessive, manipulative, imperious, crabbed.

This is a difficulty in the play – until one accepts that *The Tempest* is only half a play. Until, that is, one countersinks Prospero in the broader, deeper, total context of Dido's submerged tragedy, of which, as I have argued, these five acts are the battered reef, where the survivors reaffirm the mutilated coda, the Theophany, against the odds.

That is where Prospero properly lives – in that past. That past is, of course, Shakespeare's tragic imagination, shaped and inhabited by all the previous works. Prospero is the surviving rational ego of all the usurpations, all the Shakespearean moments. That is to say: not only has he paid the price, he has paid it in every mythic work since *Venus and Adonis*.

In that context he begins to look different, and his air of rheumatic petulance, his vigilant, testy severity becomes largely an optical illusion – an effect of the play's technical foreshortening. His case-hardening, it now appears, is scar tissue. He is the survivor of some fifteen encounters with the Boar out there in the stadium, every one of which, up to now, was for him a gruesome if not a final defeat.

He was the gored young hunter looking up numbed at the mourning Goddess, the mater dolorosa, and no less the shamed, painfully corrected, headstrong adventurer Bertram. He was the shamed, painfully corrected judge within Angelo too, and the despairing, embittered idealist in Troilus. The Prince aghast at his own fate in Hamlet, the mesmerized-against-his-will murderer in Othello, the appalled self-witness in Macbeth, the broken, reborn King in Lear, the failed *imitatio Christi* in Timon – and the rest. And beyond them, he is the Aeneas who sailed away from Carthage, the Shakespeare who (perhaps) rode away from Stratford with the acting company, the storm-ravaged Ulysses, who is now telling his tale (to a virgin bride and an assembled court) just before he returns home to his wife after twenty years.

In this long perspective, one can see Prospero not only as the Adonis who suffered all those deaths, now resurrected with the lessons learned, but also as the surrogate Adonis who stepped in at the end of each play to restore order. These inheritors of the finale are not merely less interesting poetically and dramatically than the Adonis who succumbs to the Boar and goes mad, they are in a sense not poetic or dramatic at all. They are of two types: either the monument of clinker and ash after the volcanic event – cold and fixed, but a foundation for new human settlement (with enriched soil for quiet farmers), or they contain the volcanic effect, the Tarquinian madness and crime, transformed into a spirituality that salamander-like or lotus-like can live in the flames.

The first type corresponds to those externalizations or projections of the hero's rational self who survive and resume control after his actual death: the combination of Lodovico, Gratiano and Cassio in *Othello*, or Macduff and Malcolm in *Macbeth*, Fortinbras in *Hamlet*, Edgar in *King Lear*, Alcibiades in *Timon*, the combination of Roman Senate and Aufidius in *Coriolanus*, and Octavius in *Antony and Cleopatra*. One can also include the healed French king from *All's Well* and the Duke from *Measure for Measure*: the equivalent figure is absent only from *Troilus and Cressida*, where Troilus, as the first 'tragic' hero (in the series) has entered his madness but has not yet had time to commit the crime – making this the only play that ends in the first moments of the explosion rather than after the last, as if it were the introductory scene (the autobiographical prelude) to the seven great tragedies that constitute the explosion proper. Prospero has something of all these – the aridity and judgemental rigour of one who never met, or was somehow by nature immune to, the Boar, one who never attracted the passion of the Goddess or who somehow managed to fortify his rejection of her. If these plays are opened by an Adonis who succumbs and becomes a Tarquin, resembling the young Shakespeare, then the Adonis who stalks on when the drama and poetry are over, the terrible problem solved, and the play at an end, resembles the young Milton, or perhaps the old Milton. Prospero is the palimpsest of all these possession-proof, authoritarian, sober administrators, and that is the aspect of him, perhaps, that seems repellent.

The second type corresponds to the Tarquinized Adonis who has been transformed by his crime and punishment, and is now reborn to his soul: Posthumus, Pericles and Leontes. These, too, have accumulated in Prospero, and they are dominant. In *The Tempest*, he reformulates and analyses, in slow motion, and with the security of controlled ritual, exactly what happened to him confusedly and unconsciously in the three preceding plays, and he now integrates it into his real, worldly existence. In this aspect he is a mystery and inherits, as I say, the lives of the tragic heroes whom the Boar overwhelmed and who, suffering everything, had to die in earnest. And it is in this aspect that Prospero has not only learned all the lessons: he has earned his vision of the abyss – the daemonic stuff of dreams – and the magical technology required to subjugate it and to protect himself and Miranda.

Caliban's genetic make-up

Caliban too is in one way a compound of his earlier incarnations. On page 87, I quoted an account of a shamanic initiation dream in which the Goddess appeared as different animals. In the Adonis myth (as in the Attis and Thammuz and related Celtic myths) she appears as a boar, but in that wider complex of Goddess myths on which Shakespeare draws directly she also appears:

as a lion
as a serpent which may also be a poisonous snake
as a serpent which may be a dragon
as a serpent which may be an oracular earth spirit
as a fishy sea monster (which may be part serpent)
as a dolphin (or porpoise)
as a horse
as a bull or a cow
as a wolf or a dog
as a bear.

This does not exhaust her cult animals nor Shakespeare's animal references, but these are the masks that she seems to wear most identifiably in the tragic sequence. The lion manifestation appears very definitely in the Leo figures of *Cymbeline*, *Pericles* and *The Winter's Tale*, as well as in straightforward animal form in *As You Like It*. The poisonous snake appears, specifically identified, in *Macbeth* and *King Lear*, but most overtly in *Antony and Cleopatra*, where it is assimilated to the earth spirit which is also a divine river ('serpent of Old Nile'), and which reabsorbs Cleopatra back into itself. In *The Winter's Tale*, the serpent as oracular earth spirit plays the central role as the thunder (delivered through the Sybil, in the voice of Apollo) of the truth of Hermione's 'sanctity'. The sea monster figures largely in *King Lear* – nakedly as the mermadonna in the King's vision of woman's sexuality as the 'terrible' source of life. In Tarquinized, possessed form, both King Lear and Coriolanus become dragons. Wolves and dogs appear passim, either as the Queen of Hell's attendants or as her representatives, in minor functions, though the wolf takes on a major role, maybe, in Timon. The bear enters *The Winter's Tale* almost as *ex machina* as the

Boar in *Venus and Adonis*. In his 'divinely possessed' form – as consort of the Goddess – Antony appears as a dolphin. And in so far as the story of Hippolytus is secreted within the mythic plot of *Venus and Adonis*, the monstrous sea bull and the uncontrollable horse can be regarded as the Boar's second nature. Other appearances, more or less fleeting, of these particular creatures recur in image and reference throughout the sequence, obviously, but in each of the instances that I cite the creature has a heraldic or rather a totemic presence in the drama powerful enough to be functional on the poetic and mythic level.

It is Caliban's distinction to be identified at one point or another with each of these creatures. One is tempted to say, and only with these. In fact, he also finds his reflection, subliminally, in a beehive, an ape, a barnacle – the shellfish that was thought to be the embryo form of a certain wild goose – and a hedgehog. Rather than blurring and weakening the mythic integrity of the main cast, as characterized above, these four extras actually sharpen and strengthen it. The first of them, the beeswarm that will pinch him as 'thick as honeycomb', is a classic materialization of the Goddess, in this image punishing herself (she is both the bees and the honeycomb). The ape, which appears twice, once 'mowing and chattering' and again with a forehead 'villainous low', is the traditional consort of the virgin in Hell (mentioned elsewhere by Shakespeare). The third, 'barnacles', are, as both shellfish and bird, classic forms of the Goddess. Finally, the hedgehog or 'urchin', that Caliban twice complains about as one of Prospero's favourite petty tormentors, is (as the 'hedge-pig') a miniaturized goblin distortion of himself as the Boar.

Prospero calls him up, out of his cave, with three abusive terms: 'thou earth, thou', 'thou tortoise', and 'thou poisonous slave, got by the Devil himself/Upon thy wicked dam'. This little impressionistic sketch conjures up a venomous kind of primeval reptile only just poking out of its egg – its shell – which is the Earth itself. The tortoise as a symbol of the Earth, or supporter of the Earth, a snake-headed, snake-skinned creature, in fact a snake with legs, carrying the Earth, recurs wherever there are tortoises. And so when Prospero sees this creature in Caliban, he sees him as the primal child of Earth's creatress and her consort – regarded as demons. In other words, he sees him purely and simply as the child of the rejected Goddess. At the same time, Shakespeare knew the tortoise as the very first musical instrument. When the baby god Hermes stole Apollo's cattle, killed a pair, and strung their twisted guts in the shell of a tortoise, he made the first 'lute' and invented music. He then gave this instrument to Apollo, as compensation. This was the very 'lute' that entertained the gods on Olympus ever after, and made Apollo the god of music and song. And throughout his plays and poems, this very same lute was Shakespeare's most prized mythic possession, as if it were an heirloom handed down to him personally, and it tends to resound wherever he refers to his preoccupation with music. Bringing Caliban on to the stage as a 'tortoise', therefore, Shakespeare is presenting him, according to one of his own most cherished ideas, as the naked 'daemon' of music, the humanoid form of the 'bowels of the earth'. That Prospero calls him 'poisonous' merely connects him that much more directly, as if by family name, to the Macbeth who was 'the serpent' under the innocent flower, and to the 'asp' which was the spirit of the fig, the sexual divine nature of Cleopatra, the elemental form of the Goddess which drew her back into itself, as it was also the divine infant form of Antony which sucked her asleep.

Caliban's Boar nature, the compendium of all these other forms, is innate in his role in the Equation and the Rival Brothers, but Shakespeare touches it in more graphically with the 'sty' in which Prospero keeps him, and the fact that the most delectable food he can think of – the first natural delicacy that occurs to him – is 'pig-nuts'. And whenever he looks into what he most fears from Prospero, he sees that distorted mirror image – the 'hedge-pig'. His 'monster' nature is obtrusive enough to provide him with his nickname 'monster', and its fishy side is pronounced, at the same time associated with the sea storm, the tempest, mistaken perhaps for a dolphin washed up, or rather a 'porpus' (a 'sea-pig') – like the one that the fisherman saw before the storm (so recently) in *Pericles*: '. . . how he bounced and tumbled! They say, they're half fish half flesh. A plague of them! They ne'er come but I look to be washed.' (II. i. 26–9). That same storm washed up not a monster, but Pericles from his 'watery grave' to meet Thaisa, and that same 'porpus', maybe, was the great fish that the fisherman thought hung in the net before it 'turned to a rusty armour' (II. i. 129) – with which Pericles won Thaisa for his wife – and that Trinculo seems to be remembering when he describes Caliban as 'half a fish and half a monster'. And when he calls this 'drunken monster' a 'deboshed fish' he is (surely!) remembering the ocean of yeast and froth, of Malmsey perhaps, into which the ship that had brought Perdita was 'thrust' like a cork 'into a hogshead', and in which, maybe, the 'porpus' 'bounced and tumbled' like Bacchus himself. Caliban is also addressed as 'cat', and then hunted like the 'spotted [like Tarquin's soul, and like the blood flower] pard or cat o' mountain' – both lions of a kind sacred to the Goddess and to Dionysus in particular, this following immediately after his occult Masque rebirth as Iacchos-Dionysus. His hell-dog or sea-wolf forebears are acknowledged in that 'puppy-head'. And he is repeatedly addressed as 'moon-calf' – child of the Queen of Hell who sent her tidal wave sea bull to overwhelm Hippolytus. Again, Ariel leads him and his calibanized confederates, Trinculo and Stephano, with a drum:

> At which, like unback'd colts, they prick'd their ears,
> Advanc'd their eyelids, lifted up their noses
> As they smelt music
>
> *The Tempest*, IV. i. 176–8

(like that stallion in *Venus and Adonis* smelling the 'breeding jennet, lusty, young and proud' (line 260)) into the 'filthy-mantled pool' of 'horse-piss' (on an island where the only horse is mythic and inhabits Caliban). Finally, if the seventeenth-century tradition is correct, Shakespeare's own stage Caliban wore a bear-skin as if it were his own pelt.

The curious thing about this list of specifications is its economical completeness. None of them comes as a surprise in the play-world of what has developed as a tightly systematized code. But to find the whole lot together, each one touched in with such mythic precision and suggestive colour, is yet another indication of that summarizing tendency in *The Tempest*, where Shakespeare seems to be recapitulating in essential, compacted form all that has gone before.

Prospero dismantles the Tragic Equation

So now with great deliberation – and extraordinary stubbornness – Prospero goes back to the beginning, and for one last time steps into the arena. Once again he sets his young self, Adonis/Ferdinand, to meet the Goddess – exactly as in the first long poem. He starts where he always started, by splitting Venus. The lustful Queen of Hell (as Sycorax) and the overwhelming Dido figure are banished from the action.

This should be the beginning of a tragedy. As in all his previous lives, he should now succumb to the Tarquinian madness. But with his raised magician's staff, he halts the tragic consequences. The shock wave of Tarquinian madness, which surges towards him from the double vision, meets the impassable barrier. Prospero brings the whole daemonic, dramatic machinery of the Equation to a dead stop. And proceeds to take it apart.

The Tempest, therefore, is not merely the Theophany of the hidden Dido tragedy. It is also a replay of it – aborted. *The Tempest* is what happens when Adonis, by Hermetic mastery of supernatural powers, refuses to let the Tragic Equation take its course, and when he enforces his idealism, with a will now magically omnipotent, on to the convulsed mass of Complete Being.

The Equation does try to happen – it writhes its legs and contorts its abdomen. But Prospero has pinned it to the wall. Caliban's attempt to usurp him, and take possession of Miranda, and Antonio's attempt to persuade Sebastian to usurp Alonso, are pinned there from the start. They move only with Ariel's permission.

So, the action of the play seems perfunctory. Yet it exerts tremendous suggestive power. It could be called not so much action, as the dismantling of action – but what is being dismantled is the mythic dynamo of the entire tragic sequence. In this way, the undoing of action becomes momentous.

Again, to summarize the process:

He dismantles the crime of the usurping brother by bringing Alonso and Antonio ashore helplessly at his mercy, by the power of magic.

He dismantles the double vision. By sealing Sycorax/Dido, apparently dead, twelve years into the past, under the island, and by enclosing Miranda within the pentacle tower of his magic, he has separated the loved and the loathed and has sealed their separation, by the power of magic.

He has purged himself of any shadow of the Boar – of the slightest taint of it. And having stopped it, out there in the open, mid-stride, and rendered it impotent to harm either his own rationality or Miranda's virginity, he has subjugated it to slavery, as Caliban, excluding him from any foothold in civilized life, with the power of magic.

Though Prospero has not contrived it personally, yet for his sake Shakespeare has contrived to appease the cry of the rejected one – Queen Dido on the African shore – by marrying her surrogate,

Claribel, to the King of the Tunis that ought to be Carthage, in a marriage evidently happy. By stilling that agonized howl in the background, and making that woman happy, this marriage also serves to disconnect the Tragic Equation from its detonation.

And again, by sealing the betrothal of Miranda and Ferdinand within the Masque, protected by Heaven, he seems to have ensured that the double vision shall not detonate the Tarquinian madness for Ferdinand, and that the Boar shall not topple them into the inferno of the Equation. He seems to have guaranteed that their future will be secure from it, by the power of magic.

The question of how far Prospero succeeds, of how final and complete the dismantling process is, depends on how far this magic extends – on whether it can, in fact, provide any guarantees.

Obviously, the limits are plain to see – the magic, as Shakespeare makes clear, is far from omnipotent.

The earlier Theophanies – *Pericles, Cymbeline, The Winter's Tale* – ended as if sealed within the sacred guarantee of the divine reunion. No dissident voices sour the final chorus, no discords disrupt the harmony tuned by 'the fingers of the powers above'. But the end of *The Tempest* is a chord of dissonance. It ends, as the tragic sequence started, with the transcendental love confronted by the tragic potential. Prospero has disabled the will of Caliban and Antonio, but only temporarily. He has, at best, acknowledged Caliban as his own 'thing of darkness', but Caliban's:

> I'll be wise hereafter,
> And seek for grace
> *The Tempest*, v. i. 294–5

is in character with his naive, irrepressible craving for love (which Prospero disappointed), which learns nothing from experience, and is innate in the 'heat' of his darkness, part of his being a lump of the rejected Queen of Hell, that half of the Great Goddess, whose passion is simply to return, somehow, into life.

At the same time, Prospero's grudging forgiveness of Antonio:

> whom to call brother
> Would even infect my mouth,
> v. i. 130–1

which sounds more like a curse, recognizes in the unmoved, unanswering usurper the cold reflection of the hot danger – the Iago-esque malignity which I described as the intellectual, playful, cold-fish-eyed reflection of the terrific, elemental, sea-pig hot power within Caliban.

So these two emissaries of that Queen of Hell, which Shakespeare's hero has confronted from the beginning, confront him still at the end, unmodified.

And the magical power that controlled them, the transcendental spirit, Ariel, is about to vanish. All Prospero's achievements, it would appear, are precarious, provisional. Ferdinand and Miranda, when they return to Milan, will presumably have as little protection there as anybody else from the whisper of an Iachimo.

And those 'finger of the powers above' that tune the 'harmony of this piece', in 'paradise', will hardly be heard, after Prospero's retirement, in the Gadarene, possessed rush down the hill into the Civil War.

Ariel's ancestry

The identification made in historical myth, where the Boar is either the enraged form of the rejected Goddess (as in the story of Phaedra, and Shakespeare's *Venus and Adonis*), or is the animal form of Persephone (the Underworld form of the Goddess, as in the original Greek myth), holds good, as I have tried to show, through every play of the sequence, right down to *The Tempest*, where the animal appears as Caliban, the child of the African witch Sycorax (swine-crow) and a devil-god.

The evolutionary history of the Tragic Equation, it seems, supplies a distinct lineal descent of etymological meaning, just as consistent as Caliban's, for Ariel.

Like Caliban, Ariel formerly lived with Sycorax, not as her child but her servant, an agent of her magical power.

Ariel served Sycorax only up to a point – then jibbed:

> too delicate
> To act her earthy and abhorred commands,
> Refusing her grand hests.
> *The Tempest*, I. ii. 272–4

Ariel's magic, that is, belonged to that end of the register opposite to the black. And when Sycorax ordered her to shift her operations towards the black, then somewhere in the middle, grey range, she jibbed.

Her magic, it seems, was less powerful than the black. As Prospero reminds her, Sycorax – thrown into a 'most unmitigable rage' by Ariel's purism –

> did confine thee,
> By help of her more potent ministers. . .
> Into a cloven pine.
>
> I. ii. 274–7

'Too delicate' and 'less potent' than other daemons, Ariel turns out, as we saw, to be a flower spirit:

> Where the bee sucks, there suck I,
>
> v. i. 88

who lives in the bell of a cowslip. That is one definite thing she tells us about herself.

Yet, somehow, this delicate flower spirit enters the *Complete Works* managing a sea tempest. She conducts the terrific electrical storm overture in the likeness of a tongue of St Elmo's fire, the 'nimble corposant':

> now on the beak,
> Now in the waist, the deck, in every cabin,
> I flamed amazement: sometime I'd divide,
> And burn in many places; on the topmast,
> The yards, and bowsprit, would I flame distinctly,
> Then meet, and join.
>
> I. ii. 196–201

She then goes on to reveal herself as the spirit that rides the Shakespearean lightnings, as if they were horses, and describes herself finally as 'the fire and cracks/Of sulphurous roaring' that terrified the whole ocean and the god of the sea himself:

> Jove's lightnings, the precursors
> O' the dreadful thunder-claps, more momentary
> And sight-outrunning were not: the fire and cracks
> Of sulphurous roaring, the most mighty Neptune

Seem to besiege and make his bold waves tremble,
Yea, his dread trident shake.

I. ii. 201–6

This combination of storm spirit and flower spirit is suggestive enough after what the Tragic Equation has revealed of the curiously related lineages of the Storm and of the Boar. This storm which opens *The Tempest* is clearly created by Ariel, controlled and concluded by Ariel, and (one could think, from her own description) consisting entirely of Ariel. Later on in the play, Ariel appears in another burst of thunder, and speaks out of it so tremendously that the courtiers are frightened out of their wits, and reduced – as the earlier storms have reduced the 'criminal' – to that point of final breakdown and atonement. Can it be that Ariel's power and purpose has been operating within this metaphysical storm from the beginning?

The lineal descent of the Flower can be traced, as I say, parallel to that of the Storm, but it is more revealing maybe to start with Ariel's flower and go backwards.

Ariel's bed, the cowslip bell, has a predecessor.* The most dramatic other appearance of a cowslip comes in *Cymbeline* – on the breast of the sleeping Imogen, when Iachimo lifts back the coverlet and spies:

> On her left breast
> A mole cinque-spotted, like the crimson drops
> I' the bottom of a cowslip.

Cymbeline, II. ii. 37–9

This flower is reminiscent of that spectacular earlier flower. Shakespeare does not name the flower of the slain Adonis. He prefers to assemble it from algebraic components:

> A purple flower . . . chequer'd with white;
> Resembling well his pale cheeks, and the blood
> Which in round drops upon their whiteness stood.

Venus and Adonis, 1168–70

He has it both ways. This is a purple flower spotted with white, and a white flower spotted with purple. Already, one might say, he has anticipated the fact that this flower has a double life – as a redeemed

---

*For the role of this cowslip in *A Midsummer Night's Dream*, see page 496.

Adonis gathered into reunion with the divinity he formerly rejected (white spotted with purple) and as a Tarquin possessed by the Boar but torn with conscience (purple spotted with white).

Even on this lower plane, however, the Flower is holy – in an unholy way. Those algebraic components maintain their precision. On both planes, the Flower is both an image of the rejected Goddess (her milk) and of the slain Adonis (his blood) mingled together – and at the same time (as I noted before) an image of the Boar's actual face, after the killing:

> Whose frothy mouth bepainted all with red,
> Like milk and blood being mingled both together.
>
> 901–2

On either plane, then, this flower is not simply Adonis 'changed'. It is Adonis transformed by being suffused with the Goddess in the form of the Boar. On the higher plane, the redeemed Adonis flower is suffused with the Boar as the punishing Goddess that forced him to atone. On the lower plane, with the Boar as the excluded, enraged Goddess, who simply took possession of him. But since, in either case, the Boar is a form of the Goddess, the Flower is Adonis suffused, one could say, simply with the Goddess: the supernatural, magical element in this flower of rebirth is the Goddess.

Since that other blood-spotted flower, on the cheek of Imogen's left breast,* is in that obvious physical respect linked to the blood-spotted

*This blood-spotted cowslip on Imogen's breast, which is also the Adonis death-flower, which is also Tarquin's birth-flower, which is the face of the Boar, lifts through the plot, and, so to speak, 'flowers' into action, at exactly the same point, in the Equation, as the 'violet' pushed up through the text of *Measure for Measure* (see pages 173–4). And it corresponds exactly, in its nature and its dramatic function, to the handkerchief that destroyed Desdemona and that first opened into action, again, at exactly the same juncture of the Equation in *Othello*. Iago described this napkin as 'spotted with strawberries'. And according to Othello:

> That handkerchief
> Did an Egyptian to my mother give;
> She was a charmer, and could almost read
> The thoughts of people; she told her,

> while she kept it,
> 'Twould make her amiable and subdue
> my father
> Entirely to her love . . . She dying gave it
> me;
>
> *Othello*, III. iv. 56–64

This supernatural item already combines the three components of the Goddess: the Mother (of Othello), the Sacred Bride (of his father), and the Queen of the Underworld (the Egyptian woman who as a clairvoyant 'charmer' was something of a witch and who produced the handkerchief in the first place as a double-natured, love-bringing, death (utter loss of love) -bringing piece of juju). These three aspects then coalesce into one triple figure: the Mother who was the Bride, now at the point of death descending into the Underworld, i.e. on the threshold of the Underworld, takes the Egyptian's place flower between the breasts of Venus, one might suspect that it carries potentially the same two opposite meanings – for Posthumus. With the inevitability of Shakespeare's algebra, so it turns out.

This cowslip is the single item responsible for transforming Posthumus into a Tarquin. In Iachimo's lying account of his sexual conquest, the flower-mole convinces Posthumus that Imogen has given her body, and is therefore a Queen of Hell:

> If you seek [says Iachimo]
> For further satisfying, under her breast,
> Worthy the pressing, lies a mole, right proud

---

and gives the handkerchief to Othello. He then describes it, analyses it, more closely:

> there's magic in the web of it;
> A sybil, that had numbered in the world
> The sun to course two hundred
>   compasses,
> In her prophetic fury sew'd the work;
> The worms were hallow'd that did breed
>   the silk,
> And it was dy'd in mummy which the
>   skilful
> Conserv'd of maidens' hearts
>   III. iv. 70–6

That 'mummy' is an even more compact image of the Goddess who is the Mother ('mummy' simply), but also the Sacred Bride (made of 'maidens' hearts'), and also the Death Goddess or Queen of Hell (made from mummified dead hearts). And the whole handkerchief is like a full chord of harmonics of the same compound image: it is part white (the benign half of the Goddess, Mother and Sacred Bride together), part red (the Venusian or venous red of the Goddess's rejected lust, that will be Queen of Hell), and *in toto* the life–death magical work of a High Priestess of the Queen of the Underworld (a 'sybil' – oracular mouthpiece of the Queen of the Underworld – so preternaturally old that she is herself the nightmare Life-in-Death). The 'dye' from those 'conserv'd' hearts evidently provides the red of the strawberries. In other words, the 'blood-spots', growing on the handkerchief's whiteness, like the blood-spots on the Adonis flower, are in this case the inflamed (tumescent – 'inflamed with Venus' (cf. page

192)) fruits of the Love Goddess (in all European tradition). That is to say, the white strawberry flower has turned into a red fruit, and each strawberry, on that white napkin (strawberry fruits and flowers come together, 'like milk and blood being mingled') is a little Tarquin in his bloodswollen (Boar-congested) 'flower' form. Shakespeare's algebra opens effortlessly into deeper, more intricate precisions. The leaf-eating 'worms', hallowed by a witch, are the same creatures that appeared, promptly on cue, at line 798, in that crucial stanza of *Venus and Adonis*:

> Call it not love, for Love to heaven is fled,
> Since sweating Lust on earth usurp'd his
>   name;
> Under whose simple semblance he hath
>   fed
> Upon fresh beauty, blotting it with blame;
>   Which the hot tyrant stains and soon
>   bereaves,
>   As caterpillars do the tender leaves . . .
>   793–8

where Adonis sees them as swarming doubles of that 'hot tyrant' emerging from the lust of Venus. This composite symbol, of a strawberry-embroidered, silken handkerchief, which knocks Othello foaming and unconscious to the ground, is constructed entirely of intricately nested fractals of Adonis's death-flower in that moment at which it becomes Tarquin's birth-flower, image within image, like a sort of Russian doll, making a perfect Shakespearean hieroglyph of the Boar's tragically fatal and redemptive face.

Of that most delicate lodging: by my life,
I kiss'd it, and it gave me present hunger
To feed again, though full. You do remember
This stain upon her?

Cymbeline, II. iv. 133–9

to which Posthumus replies:

Ay, and it doth confirm
Another stain, as big as hell can hold,
Were there no more but it.

II. iv. 139–41

Imogen's cowslip has become a 'stain', a darkness 'as big as hell can hold', and now explodes, inside Posthumus, as a classical Tarquinian storm, in the great tirade:

Is there no way for men to be, but women
Must be half workers?

II. v. 1–2

This storm then whirls him to the Tarquinian crime, the assassination of Imogen.

Without stepping outside the currents of association that carry the traffic of the play, it could be said that this cowslip asserts its higher role in Imogen's own flower death and flower rebirth. But even in its Tarquinian role, it lifts Posthumus finally on to the higher plane. The storm, which becomes his Tarquinian murder, becomes thereby the storm of remorse (equivalent to the storm in *King Lear*), which forces him to atone, and finally brings him to transcendental rebirth in the thunderclap dream of Jupiter's eagle and book.

The whole process, in a tightly logical sequence, sprang from the cowslip on Imogen's breast. And the end of the process is to return Posthumus to Imogen's breast redeemed, as if he were simply the human form of that flower, having suffered through its tragic meaning, to emerge into its transcendental meaning.

Here again, the Flower is like a daemon of the Goddess – moving (like God's will) in a mysterious way, to accomplish her ends. Which is to say, moving in a mysterious way to break down the one who rejects her, and force him to atone, finally returning him to Divine Love.

These same flowers that graced the death and rebirth of Imogen reappeared, as I followed through, in the death and rebirth of Marina and of Perdita. Earlier, as seemed unmistakable, the same flowers were Lear's crown, which sprang directly from the flower that rose from the blood of Adonis, and became the tree that Macbeth saw in the hand of the child. On the way it spilled other flowers for the deaths of Desdemona and Ophelia – where rebirth failed.

Again, in each case, wherever the flowers appear, they tend to be associated with passages of verbal poetry that challenge and eventually surpass the passages of storm poetry.

It seems likely that this poetic phenomenon has something to do with the fact that the Flower and Storm episodes are, in every case, an epiphany of the Goddess. They are episodes in which she breaks up the tragic order* that prevails at the beginning of the play, and

*This thunderstorm of Shakespeare's, which is both the charge of the Boar and the activity of the cowslip-flower-spirit Ariel, is echoed in other pantheons, as well as in private, spontaneous experiences of religious conversion. I mentioned how an 'uncommon terror' of thunder preceded Jonathan Edwards's spiritual awakening, but was transformed to an especial delight in thunderstorms ('And scarce anything, among all the works of nature, was so sweet to me as thunder and lightning') once his spirit was fully awake, fully aware of the wisdom, purity and love of God's presence in nature herself, visible in herbs and flowers, that 'used greatly to fix [his] mind'. It could easily be supposed that in Jonathan Edwards's hidden mind the thunder represented (as in Part V of The Waste Land) the voice of the Divine Source, of Almighty God in his case, terrifying and threatening annihilation when it battered at the unregenerate ego that protected his spiritual sleep, but revelatory and 'rejoicing' after he woke. Standard Freudians diagnose this neurotic dread of thunder (as in the Roman emperor Caligula) as terror of conscience based on fear of Father apotheosized as God, but it can just as easily be based on fear of the rejected Mother (as perhaps in James Joyce). I mentioned, in passing, the cataclysmic 'storm' in which the monster that emerges from the alien, magically creative blood of female sexuality (the rainbow serpent) swallows the hero (takes possession of him) and initiates his heroic rebirth, in the ur-myth of

aboriginal man. The Sioux shaman Black Elk was caught up by the Thunder-Beings, who revealed to him his great vision of the cosmos they ruled, and a series of further revelations. In his words: 'When a vision comes from the Thunder-Beings of the west, it comes with terror, like a thunderstorm. But when the vision has passed, the world is greener and happier.' This was in his case a spontaneous facility for the spirit-renewing, world-renewing theophany that the Sioux (and many other native American groups) sought painfully and laboriously in their spirit quests – notably in their solitary fasting ordeals that operated like brainwashing, by actually breaking down the old personality and mental 'set', possibly by physical destruction of parts of the cortex (by extreme exhaustion: as the Eskimo shaman Isjugarjuk described his initiatory ordeal: 'I died a little'). Black Elk was drawing on the same Asiatic tradition, via the Bering Straits, that gave to the ancient gods of India and Mesopotamia the weapon that became, in the hand of Buddha, the 'vajra' (in shamanic Tibetan Buddhism, the 'dorje') – the thunderbolt of irresistible enlightenment that shatters the illusory appearances of this world and reveals reality, the spiritual truth. This was the very weapon of Jehovah. In Cabbala, a lightning flash of irresistible enlightenment descends through the Tree of Life, from the Divine Source, piercing each of the Sephiroth in turn, until it enters and transfigures the lowest. The Christian Cabbala of the Occult Neoplatonists, as I

[477]

re-establishes the new, transcendental order, which becomes possible at the end.

So the Storm and the Flower become the daemons of a spiritual alchemy by which the Goddess transforms the conflicting, resistant, hostile elements of the tragic plane into the consecrated elements of the transcendental plane – her own plane.

But both poetic daemons, it appears – both the one descending from the sea tempest that drowned Clarence, and the one descending from the bloody flower – unite their operation in the function of Ariel.

This suggests how Ariel is related to Caliban.

The evolution of Shakespeare's poetry: the Boar, the Storm and the Flower

I have suggested that the passages of verse either describing or addressed to the external storm, or expressive of the reverberations and flames of the internal storm, account for most of the spectacular and sustained outbursts of verbal poetry in the plays of the tragic sequence, and that these are equalled by those (very different) passages which attend the moment of flowering rebirth.

That is to say, the great poetic moments – poetically eloquent in a sustained grand manner – tend to be clustered quite tightly around, and to be thematically linked quite tightly with, one or other type of the

---

explained, shifted the God-centred emphasis of Hebrew Cabbala to a Christ-centred emphasis. On the Tree of Life of Christian Cabbala, Christ is identified as the sixth Sephirah (in descending order), Tiphareth, the mid-point through which the supernal powers of the upper five Sephiroth descend, by a kind of self-sacrifice, a kenosis, into the 'human' powers of the lower four. It corresponds to the Heart and to the Rose on the Cross. In Hebrew Cabbala the highest Sephirah, the Divine Source, from which the lightning flash of creative power enters the structure of materialization, is both God and his female form, the Shekinah. A title of the Temple in Rabbinical literature was Ariel – as if the executive power of God (and the Shekinah) should be the spirit of Israel. Ari-el, literally 'Lion of God', the 'roarer of Judah', but also 'Flame of God', the thunder and lightning of the Divine Source. In the

Christian Cabbala (especially that of an originally Catholic Occult Neoplatonist), the Shekinah becomes the Great Goddess (also) of the sacrificed god (Tiphareth/Christ/ Adonis). Ariel thereby becomes the thunder of the Temple of the Goddess, her creative power and law, her irresistible enlightenment, the lightning flash descending through her Tree of Life (her Temple, of which the masts and yard-arms of a ship make a good image), in a tremendous storm of corrective revelation ('What care these roarers for the name of King?'). Hence, the ship in *The Tempest* is also the Tree of Life undergoing revelatory correction, and Ariel, as Shakespeare literally tells us, is the tempest itself, the executive lightning flash of the Goddess, which becomes a flower, just as her thunderbolt Boar (ridden by the lightning flash), having shattered the illusory, false ego of Adonis, resurrects his soul in a flower.

death–rebirth episodes: Adonis's transformation into Tarquin or Tarquin's transformation into the redeemed one.

An odd circumstance which I mentioned is that the poetic release is not confined to the character actually undergoing the change. He often does deliver the great speech, but in *Measure for Measure*, for instance, the supreme poetic illumination flares out just before Angelo's change, almost as the cause of his change, in Isabella's speech (see page 385): 'Could great men thunder . . .' (II. ii. 110–23), and immediately after his change is completed in the Duke's great meditation on death in life: 'Be absolute for death . . .' (III. i. 5–41). The passage has no direct connection with Angelo's transformation, and yet it springs directly from the crisis of death–rebirth through which Angelo has just passed. As I remarked earlier in a different context, the explosive poetic release of this event has obviously been felt primarily by Shakespeare himself – by the mind putting itself through this self-transformation in a way that induced real psycho-biological consequences.

That this should be so, that the poetry should seem to debouch into the plays from this particular *fons et origo*, is not surprising. The secret of Shakespeare's unique development lies in this ability (in most departments of life it would be regarded as a debility) to embrace the inchoate, as-if-supernatural actuality, and be overwhelmed by it, be dismantled and even shattered by it, without closing his eyes, and then to glue himself back together, with a new, greater understanding of the abyss, all within the confines of a drama, and to do this once every seven months, year after year for twenty-four years.

The point here is that though every play is made up, to some degree, of an amalgam of his earlier styles, each one opens a core of poetry, in the death–rebirth episode, that is absolutely new.

In other words, the episode of death–rebirth that the Equation formulates, and that each play of the sequence dramatizes, is the systole–diastole of Shakespeare's poetic life, the fundamental rhythmic event of his perpetual inspiration and his perpetual, convulsive growth. This is another way of saying that the shamanic dream, in which the Goddess, as a boar, overwhelmed his intellectual ego, must have been an in-built, recurrent event in his psychic life.

I suggested that the poetry which expresses this event in immediate terms, the Storm poetry and the Flower poetry, is associated, from beginning to end, with a daemon that reveals itself, finally, in *The*

Tempest, as Ariel. At the same time, according to the Tragic Equation, the death–rebirth does not happen without the charge of the Boar.

On each occasion, in fact, the death and rebirth event can be reduced to two separable active components, and a third passive one. The passive component is the hero. He simply rejects the Goddess, who cannot be rejected with impunity.

The active components then appear as, first, the shock wave of the Goddess's divine, infernalized rage, the irresistible substance of it, which is mythically the Boar; and, second, the *ethical purpose* of her rage.

This ethical purpose is evident in every word of the passages which express, directly or indirectly, the destruction of Adonis and the emergence of the monster Tarquin. That is the moral and even 'divine' aspect of their poetry. The charging Boar carries a rider – a 'naked new-born babe' of some kind, howling and crying, in great torment, but overpoweringly audible and compelling.

The first death and rebirth, then, is accomplished by the physical mass of the Boar, which is the dark, maddened body mass of Tarquin, plus a high ethical purpose that flickers around him as a black sort of lightning, in which now and again that babe can be glimpsed, and in which its thrilling voice can be heard.

The second death and rebirth, where Tarquin dies into the Flower, happens where the Boar's fury, as a prolonged ordeal (Lear's prolonged madness in the storm) exhausts and breaks down the physical mass of Tarquin to a condition resembling death. At that point, the flickering black lightning condenses into the form of the Flower, which turns out to hold the new-born babe, which turns out to be the hero's soul reborn and transfigured by that higher ethical purpose of the Goddess, lifted into reunion with Divine Love. This is the babe that Macbeth saw in the 'blast' and rising from the cauldron, and that Lear became, and that is inseparable from the Flower.

The two different kinds of death are both composed of the Boar combined with the Goddess's high purpose. In the first death, the Boar is dominant, and the purpose simply suffers through it, as that divine quality in the voice of Adonis's suffering, and in the voice of Tarquin's madness – which eventually glows into Macbeth's vision of the new-born child. In the second death, the Flower is dominant (as the hero's soul reborn into the purpose of Divine Love, which brings him back to life redeemed – in *Cymbeline* and after), and the Boar, the passion of enraged, rejected Divine Love, is transformed now simply to Divine Love, within the body of the reborn hero.

The whole operation is driven by the nature of the Boar (in its striving to reclaim Adonis) and the nature of the Flower, which has condensed out of the ethical spirit that always rode the Boar, and that bears the child.

That is to say, it was always driven by the two entities that in *The Tempest* become Caliban and Ariel.

Another way to see the relationship between these two, remembering that until *The Tempest* they were never separated, is to imagine the relationship of the tragic hero's poetry to his acts, where his poetry is

> too delicate
> To act [the] earthy and abhorr'd commands
> *The Tempest*, I. ii. 272–3

of the acts of the Boar. Instead, it rides on them, tormented and crying out – harrowing all listeners. As if the acts of the Boar were the directed commands of Sycorax, the Queen of Hell, which of course they are. And the poetry, too, knows that those acts are inevitable, even if it despairs because it has to be present at their performance. The poetry has to suffer the acts of Tarquin, so to speak, as that vision of the bloody babe has to suffer the fate of Macbeth. Both are manifestations of the extreme poles of the single process – which is the ethical purpose of Divine Love.

Or, in the rebirth on the trancendental plane, the Flower radiates the sexual passion of the Boar, spiritualized, rooted in the earth but consecrated and blossoming in the spirit. (Throughout the mythic plays the Boar is identified as being itself Hell, or the son of Hell. This is orthodox: the Boar always was Hell: Phorcus (pig) became Orcus, the Underworld. Which is to say that Shakespeare's opus transforms 'Hell' into the Flower of Paradise, as Dante's did.)

Heraclitus made the observation 'Hell and Dionysus are the same.' The apparent implication of this is: better stay clear of both. As if the Israelite reformers might say: 'Hell and Baal (Thammuz, Adonis) are the same – i.e. Baal brings with him the evil of the Goddess, and is therefore to be abolished with her. By co-opting the Adonis myth, Shakespeare took full account of the boar's identification with Hell and with the reborn god of frenzy. But while he analysed the manifestations of that frenzy within a world of suppressive (Puritan) order, he reintegrates the results of his analysis within the world of Complete

Being, where the reborn god of frenzy became – as it was Adonis's original nature to become – a flower. The Boar that he found, in the Puritan world, as the son of Hell became, because of his skilful husbandry, in the world of Complete Being, a flower.

He managed this not by philosophical, moral or religious abstraction, but by a slow, laborious transformation of himself. This is attested by the phenomenon of his poetic development. Each phase of his psychic illumination produces a 'physically' new poetic substance of steadily increasing value.

I mentioned the two radical transformations of this style. I also matched the mythic stages of the Boar's career to the mythic stages of the Storm's development, and both to the mythic stages of the development of the Flower. This is not difficult, since all three lineages are aspects of the one developing myth – the one evolving psychic organism – inside Shakespeare's head. It is to be expected, then, following the arguments I have used, if the distinct stages in the development of his poetic style synchronize in some way with the same sequence of crises in the myth.

That first radical transformation of his poetry, that sudden doubling of his language in *All's Well*, arrives with the first emergence of the tragic myth into his drama – in other words, it appears with the first instance of the Adonis-into-Tarquin mythic death–rebirth.

The second radical transformation, in which his language became once more essentially simple and which happened, as I remarked, at a very particular point, promptly happened with the first instance of the Tarquin-into-saint rebirth – in *King Lear* – where the new poetry is heard clearly for the first time in: 'Come, let's away to prison . . .' etc. (v. iii. 8–19). That is to say, the language 'doubled' where the hero was reborn to his tragic fate by the double vision, but dissolved its binary elements into a new singleness when the hero was reborn to reunion with Divine Love.

Taking these two changes as the major divisions, it can then be seen that each episode of death–rebirth – of either kind – within the divisions, tends to signal a discernible transformation, enlargement and reintegration of his means of poetic expression within a 'new' poetry. I noted where this occurred in *Measure for Measure*, with Isabella's 'Could great men thunder'.

The effect is not so marked in *Troilus and Cressida*, as if that fearful, constant deferment of Troilus's death–rebirth filled the play with an anticipatory dribbling lava of the new substance without an eruptive explosion. When that explosion does come, though the verse is magnificent, it would be a very subjective business to decide whether it was any newer than what went before.

The verse of *Othello* is fresh, full, supple, free of immaturities (as that of *Measure for Measure* and *Troilus and Cressida* is not), all of a piece, yet the poetry swells to a weightier authority, an ampler resonance, an orchestration of tones and imagery unique in itself, quite suddenly, in Othello's own language, as his transformation begins and he slides towards the 'destiny unshunnable', the revelation of the Queen of Hell, in his

> if I do prove her haggard,
> Though that her jesses were my dear heart-strings,
> I'd whistle her off and let her down the wind,
> To prey at fortune. Haply, for I am black,
> And have not those soft parts of conversation
> That chamberers have, or, for I am declin'd
> Into the vale of years – yet that's not much –
> She's gone, I am abus'd; and my relief
> Must be to loathe her. O curse of marriage!
> That we can call these delicate creatures ours,
> And not their appetites. I had rather be a toad,
> And live upon the vapour of a dungeon,
> Than keep a corner in the thing I love
> For others' uses. Yet, 'tis the plague of great ones;
> Prerogativ'd are they less than the base;
> 'Tis destiny unshunnable, like death:
> Even then this forked plague is fated to us
> When we do quicken.
>
> *Othello*, III. iii. 260–77

And he sustains this to the very last speech in the play.

The same might be said for *Hamlet*, though here the new poetry in Hamlet's soliloquies wells more identifiably and directly from his fight with the Boar – his secular resistance to it, his paralysis between the mythic commands. The much maligned Player's speech, which explodes as a vision of the Tarquin struggling to be born, is an unforgettable and tremendous verbal *tour de force* in itself and immediately brings the best

[483]

out of Hamlet, as does the parallel vision of Fortinbras marching without a qualm as if Tarquin could be reborn painlessly.

The convulsively new poetry in *Macbeth* bursts from Lady Macbeth, as the first birth pangs of the Boar, and from both of them as Macbeth is delivered as a Boar-Tarquin (his birth cry could be: 'If it were done when 'tis done . . .' etc.).

In *King Lear*, a change in emphasis seems to occur. His Tarquinian speeches, in the first two acts, are tremendous – but it could be questioned whether they have the internality of Macbeth's. They are perhaps more brilliantly machined. Every line of 'Hear, Nature, hear! dear goddess, hear!' etc. (I. iv. 299–313), seems more splendidly fashioned, more cruelly finished, than anything in *Macbeth*. But the recognizably new Tarquinian poetry is felt, rather, in the storm scenes – which are already the birth pangs of Tarquin's rebirth as a saint. This seems to be a transitional phase culminating in: 'I pardon that man's life . . .' etc. (IV. vi. 112–35), which is maybe the ultimate poetry of Tarquin's utterance. After that, the generically new poetry of the saintly rebirth clears itself, until 'Come, let's away to prison . . .' etc. (V. iii. 8–19) runs pure and whole.

This progression suggests one reason why *Timon*'s status as 'poetry' (like its status as drama) should seem confused. If at this point Shakespeare has himself psychologically passed beyond the unregenerate or dead-end life of Tarquin, into the possibilities of saintly rebirth, then the theme of *Timon* precludes what the writer now has to give – namely, the poetry of transcendence – and demands instead the old staple: Tarquin's 'unmitigable [and doomed] rage'. In spite of the many powerful currents that flow into this play, and in spite of the fact that Timon's Adonis-into-Tarquin speeches contain a massively hewn poetry, with new fusions of strange precious metals veined in the ore, the total effect is of an agglomeration, something baffled and static, a burning mountainous structure amassed, almost from surplus stock, rather than of an organism living its essential life eliminating the obsolete, casting out 'all that is not itself' (which one feels, for instance, with *Antony and Cleopatra*). The truth is, perhaps, that the living organism of Shakespeare's perpetually new, exploratory poetry – reborn in *King Lear* – had no real role in *Timon*, which thereby became the dumping place, the spoil heap, of everything that had accumulated in Tarquin's frenzied 'doomed' life and could now no longer be used. As if *Timon* were the purgation of the new, saintly birth, the heap of placenta and bloody cloths, the echo of birth howls: everything the saint left behind.

The same circumstance would help to explain the bare, hard-edged poetry of *Coriolanus*. As I suggested, in this play Shakespeare shifts his attention to the survival of the Female. Coriolanus's Adonis-into-Tarquin rebirth already has the slightly perfunctory quality of a demonstration (much more pronounced, again, in Posthumus and Leontes). The 'newness' of the very distinctive verse of his drama is a combination of the doubled complexity of the old Tarquinian language, with the driving, executive, *impatient* efficiency of a monstrously wilful ego whose inner life is simplified, headlong, functional – is, in fact, almost numbed. Tarquin is by definition partly numbed, he must numb himself, to the inner life, the vast distress, of his victim: this, after all, is his crime. As Shakespeare defined and clarified his conception of his hero's criminality, he progressively deprived him of inner poetic complexity, directing illumination instead towards his possibilities for sainthood and the life of his victim. This new simplicity and, perhaps, purity of the Tarquin idea may be what burnishes the peremptory gleam of newness on Coriolanus's language. But since the theme of *Coriolanus*, like that of *Timon*, precludes the possibility of sainthood, or of inner divinity, it precludes again that genuinely new phase of Shakespeare's living poetry. Maybe he planned both these plays before his own poetic organism, changing at such speed (two years probably covers *King Lear*, *Timon* and *Coriolanus*), rendered them, in a sense, obsolete for his poetic needs.

He caught up with himself in *Antony and Cleopatra* where the new Tarquin-into-saint poetry flows unconstrained from Antony's Osirian love for Cleopatra and her Goddess love for him. Since the whole play is a slow-motion birth of this divinity, a four-act parturition with a fifth-act ascent by Cleopatra into a Goddess-like embrace of the new-born god on that plane of transcendence (out of this world), this new poetry, heard here for the first time since the end of *King Lear*, floods all their love exchanges and the world of their love.

But it is absent from the Roman world. The *Tarquinian* poetry of Antony himself borrows something from this divine world. His tirade against Cleopatra is mingled with the voice of the mortified god and this is certainly part of its novelty – that it borrows the authentic newness of the reborn voice.

The new Tarquin-into-saint poetry undergoes another transformation, or perhaps it would be more accurate to say that it completes its transformation when it abandons Tarquin's rebirth into sainthood and begins to accompany the death–rebirth of the Female – which it does with startling freshness and intensity in *Cymbeline*, at the funeral–rebirth scene of Imogen:

> With fairest flowers
> While summer lasts and I live here, Fidele,
> I'll sweeten thy sad grave; thou shalt not lack
> The flower that's like thy face, pale primrose, nor
> The azur'd harebell, like thy veins, no, nor
> The leaf of eglantine, whom not to slander,
> Outsweeten'd not thy breath: the ruddock would,
> With charitable bill – O bill! sore-shaming
> Those rich-left heirs, that let their fathers lie
> Without a monument – bring thee all this;
> Yea, and furr'd moss besides, when flowers are none,
> To winter-ground thy corse.
>
> *Cymbeline*, IV. ii. 218–29

It reappears in *Pericles* at the death–rebirth scene of Thaisa/Miranda – in the storm (see page 405). In *The Winter's Tale* it emerges again in the rebirth scene of Perdita (a flower ritual after a storm, see pages 410–11). Finally, in *The Tempest*, which is a four-act rebirth of the Female (rebirth to the world) culminating in the Masque, which is the rebirth of the soul, the entire play is suffused with the new transcendental poetry, as the ritual of a lotus opening in a stormy sea. In this way, at each stage, the quality of the poetry validates the actuality of the psychic progress, which is more discernibly symbolized in plot form by the development of the Equation and the Gnostic Coda.

Meanwhile, through these last plays, the poetry of Adonis-into-Tarquin continues to change in a way which suggests that Shakespeare had chosen one of two alternative routes. In *Cymbeline*, the Adonis-into-Tarquin rebirth is clearly no longer the main source of poetic growth. Posthumus's tirade against Imogen is a superb set piece, but part of its novelty lies in certain qualities that it shares (has perhaps borrowed) from the new simplicity of the death–rebirth poetry of the Female. No longer a double language in the old style, it is made up of brutally direct plain statements in simple words, a flexible, brilliant prose, a swift musical interplay of ideas, in rhythmical sequences of sinuous, tensile strength. Yet that directness, the plain and simple language (with a rich, often exotic effect), the flexible, intricate music – these are the physical qualities of the flower passages. This is even more evident, perhaps, in those speeches – borrowed from Tarquin's outlook – by which Iachimo describes Posthumus's behaviour in Rome.

Again, the long Tarquinian tirades of Leontes create their fascinating effect from a further deployment of the same means – the direct, fluid simplicity at the service of an insane rage. But in both cases – Posthumus and Leontes – there is something routine, or rather controlled: Shakespeare is exploiting, rather than exploring, the feeling behind these outbursts. In fact it seems obvious that he deliberately turns the flame off from that source, from Adonis's agonized death–rebirth into Tarquin, and subjects the burnt, suffering hero to the healing light from the other source, the death–rebirth illumination of the Female who is also the soul. At the same time, as the poetry proves and as the shifting ethical centre of gravity of Shakespeare's development seems to have made natural and inevitable, this other source is now the poetry's living core of growth.

Nevertheless, a question remains open. Though the Tarquinian speeches of Posthumus and Leontes are, as I say, controlled and exploitative rather than exploratory, still the feeling behind them is far from diminished in ferocity since the old days of Othello, Lear and Timon. In some ways it is more alarming, more absolute and savage, and somehow more personal, than in the Tragedies proper. Those late speeches are doorways, maybe, into the rapidly darkening real world where the weaponry of the Civil War was being cleaned and primed, and where, for a while, all outcomes would be pitiless, all worst fears would be realized. Shakespeare tries to accommodate what they reveal in his Neoplatonist determination to rescue the human soul, but their flame is acetylene and laser. In spite of his control, jets of it burn raw and frightful holes in the spiritualized fabric of these 'romances'. His new power-station technology was not entirely successful. There was more behind the Boar and Sycorax, in other words, than *The Tempest* communicated. Perhaps if fashion, politics and health had gone differently, beyond *Antony and Cleopatra* there were tragedies, of a kind that can hardly be guessed, waiting to be written.

Yet Shakespeare seems no longer to have felt the need or the inclination to explore them. This close down of his dramatic enterprise is stated in plain terms by Prospero. And when the character of the irrational self, Duke Frederick, in *As You Like It*, where the tragic sequence began, is contrasted with the character of the irrational self which corresponds to the same, namely the combination of Antonio and Caliban, in *The Tempest*, where the sequence comes to a close, the prognosis seems to be confirmed. In the case of the latter, Antonio, confronted by his criminal life, receives Prospero's quasi-curse forgiveness in a 'hard and fastened' silence. One can almost hear the pinioned Iago's: 'From this time forth I never will speak word' (*Othello*, v. ii. 303). Throughout this entire last act of general reconciliations Antonio's only reaction is a solitary, derisive remark, like the sudden flick of a motionless reptile, about Caliban (the elemental force of all Shakespeare's heroes, the enigma from which in a sense he had wrestled his whole creation): 'a plain fish, and no doubt marketable' (*The Tempest*, v. i. 266).

And even Caliban's own: 'I'll be wise hereafter,/And seek for grace' (v. i. 294–5) does no more than introduce the possibility of an unlikely hope — almost certainly a vain hope, nothing more really than a resolution to pray without hope. But in the former case, twelve or so years before, when Shakespeare could still imagine his protagonist as a young man with his serious life ahead, Duke Frederick, brought to face his own irrational being and the Caliban in himself, had undergone a violent religious conversion, entering the holy life and the search into the Underworld of his own soul, that had opened all the circles of the tragic sequence.

The Equation in five early plays

Though I have concentrated on what happened once the tragic myth arrived and took possession of the drama in *All's Well*, I have referred, here and there, to the striking fact that the two forms of the myth in these later plays — the Tragic Equation and the Rival Brothers — are anticipated by the plot schemata of Shakespeare's very earliest works (in particular, the comedies).

Recurrent patterns in those early comedies, and their anticipation of patterns in the late romances, have been noticed often enough, from various points of view. But the precision of the symbolic language of the myth, as it operates in the tragic sequence, casts an unexpected and even a mythic light, retrospectively, into some of their features. The farcical choreography of the Rival Brothers (the Equation behind it) in *The*

Comedy of Errors, and the bravura variant of the Equation in *The Taming of the Shrew*, reveal a different kind of coherence, I believe, when they are connected directly to the mythically supercharged Tragic Equation and Rival Brothers that open the depths of the mature plays.

In *The Two Gentlemen of Verona*, one of the very earliest works, the plot is a classic if rudimentary combination of Rival Brothers and Equation – though only roughly wired and at low voltage. Proteus (at home) and Valentine (at court), sworn to mutual trust and affection, are the two brothers who will soon be rivals. At the same time, Proteus is the Adonis in the first part of the Equation. He loves Julia, who seems to reject him. In fact, she loves him. Her belated declaration of her love is overtaken by Proteus's father's decision to send him off to court, to join Valentine. Proteus thereupon leaves the loving Julia, and the first part of the Equation has groped into place. The feelings here are more complicated (in a mechanical sense) than in the similar situation in *All's Well*, where Bertram (who knows nothing of her love) abandons Helena and goes off to court. And Proteus's departure is not intensified to outright face-to-face rejection as Bertram's is after his forced marriage, though outright rejection is implicit in his sudden pursuit of a new love. But like Helena, Julia (though more faintly) is now under the shadow of the Venus rejected by Adonis. And like Helena she sets out after her man.

At court, Valentine and Silvia are in love. Silvia is a Lucrece, chaste and (because sworn to his friend Valentine) inaccessible to Proteus, who promptly becomes infatuated with lust for her. Deciding to possess her, even against her will, in true Tarquinian style, he enters the second part of the Equation. By an act of treachery against his friend, he separates Silvia from him, pursues her and (magnetized by the future pattern) actually tries to rape her. His attempt dissolves into a denouement that returns him to his true love, Julia. This completes the second half of the Equation in a way that anticipates the pattern in *All's Well* and *Measure for Measure*, but at the same time is supported by what they lack, a complementary form of the theme of the Rival Brothers. Proteus, true to his name, is the unreliable, irrational one, whose carefully planned treachery usurps Valentine from his courtship of Silvia. Like Duke Senior, the usurped Duke in *As You Like It*, and like Prospero in *The Tempest*, Valentine falls into the wilderness – in this case the forest. Like Rosalind in *As You Like It*, and like Miranda in *The Tempest*, Silvia goes with the usurped one. In the play as a whole, there is little of the essential action that is not supplied by these two close prefigurings of the alternative patterns of Shakespeare's myth.

The Comedy of Errors is generally thought to have been composed close in time to *The Two Gentlemen of Verona*, though in structure it seems more sophisticated. Once again, the Rival Brothers and the Equation supply almost everything. What they do not supply is largely provided by a first faint rehearsal of the Gnostic Coda. The Rival Brothers is dominant and seems to be testing its possiblities, still in the primary phase of mutual love and parity of virtue between the two brothers. For much of the play it is clear that they inhabit different worlds, in that they are invisible to each other and ignorant of each other, only taking turns to occupy the one persona of Antipholus; but they are not in different moral worlds. The doubling of the twins, and the fact that Antipholus of Ephesus is local, well known and married, enables Shakespeare to wring a good deal of antic bewilderment out of this. But gradually, with sinister extras, the pattern of usurpation asserts itself. The visitor, Antipholus of Syracuse, turns out to be the usurper. The resident Antipholus of Ephesus is displaced, briefly, from his wife, from his secure public status and from the recognition of his friends, falling into the wilderness (the prison, where he is assumed to be mad) under the condemnation of a prostitute and a gratuitously mischievous mountebank. These two operate as the usual agents (Queen of Hell and cold reflection of the 'hot tyrant') for the 'evil' aspect of the usurper. Meanwhile the usurper, who is innocent (and knows nothing of the metaphysical powers of the theme of the Rival Brothers, which can apparently animate prostitute and mountebank even when the usurping brother refuses to co-operate by playing his wilfully usurping part), enters the precinct of the Gnostic Coda. He is 'redeemed' in the priory (temple of chastity),* by an abbess (high priestess) who is revealed as the long-lost mother of the two brothers.

At this point, another event, crucial to the plot, becomes recognizable: the sea-storm wreck, with the description of which the play

*This would be the temple of the Virgin Mary in which she was first proclaimed the Mother of God (AD 431), whence her cult spread throughout the world. But she supplanted, there in Ephesus, the most famous Artemis of classical times, whose Roman bronze and alabaster statue, with black face, feet and hands, multiple breasts, her crown a tower, her dress emblazoned with images of bulls, goats, deer and a bee, combines the goddess of the wild beasts and chastity (in whose fount Actaeon/Bertram of *All's Well that Ends Well* was reborn) with the lunar Queen of the Underworld, and the orgiastic goddess of reproduction.

opened, and in which the twin brothers were parted, their twin servants parted likewise with them, while their mother and father were parted from the four and from each other, is a prototypical opening of Shakespeare's Gnostic Coda, where the old order is dissolved, in a kind of baptismal sousing, that sets all parts free for a rearrangement in the new order and the new life. The new order here comes into being with the mother resolving the misunderstandings of her own sons and saving her long-lost husband's life, reuniting all in happy, enlightened love.

Other standard features — of the Equation — rise to be recognized. For the first time (in what may have been only his second or third play), Shakespeare embeds his 'usurpation' in a background of witchcraft which is also the world of Hecate — the city of Ephesus, the great cult centre of Diana, where events seem to be under the control of devilish spirits, culminating in what will eventually be (later in the Equation's evolution) that climactic episode — the 'madness' of the usurped. In classical style (as if he were an Edgar), the madness and its associated suffering are foisted on to Antipholus of Syracuse by others (by that 'Queen of Hell' prostitute and the mountebank, specifically).

It is curious to see how the whole 'theorem' of action, in this work, is a benign rehearsal, in simple and (as far as the Equation is concerned) fragmentary form, of the theorem that will shape the romances, and how it is already assembled almost entirely, as I say, from the kit of the Rival Brothers, the Equation and the Gnostic Coda. The possibility of Shakespeare finding in one of his own old plays from this period the basic structure for *Pericles* seems not at all far-fetched.

The Taming of the Shrew, another very early play, makes a brilliantly dramatic situation out of what is a comic metaphor of the Equation. Kate's unmanageable shrewishness is a variation on the unacceptable (frightening) demand of 'total, unconditional love'. She is more than men can handle, and their rejection — in routine Equation style — has distorted her 'love' into aggressive rage. But Petruchio sees through this distortion. On the mythic level (in so far as it exists at this early stage) ordinary men have seen in her the 'double vision'. Following the Equation's law (as if it were already dictating these moves by remote control), Petruchio becomes a representative of these rejectors and suddenly decides to bring this uncontrollable spirit under control — by forcing his love on to her. His taming of her is not only the enforcement of his love, but a feigned 'madness', which altogether is a comic image of the Tarquinian 'madness' and sexual assault. So he subdues her to the accompaniment of astonished, admiring laughter, as Othello brings his deluded idea of Desdemona under control to the accompaniment of horror and fear. Because Kate's shrewishness is a devilish or infernal distortion of 'total, unconditional love' it reveals, once corrected, a nature that amazes those who misunderstood her. And because Petruchio's 'madness' is shrewdly put on and managed, and is in fact the active wisdom of genuine love, or of a capacity both for love and for recognizing the capacity for love in Kate, the whole play demonstrates the returning to health (by extreme curative measures) of love, and therefore, though it uses the dynamics of the Equation that will be tragic, it remains comic – and even more than comic: it prefigures the total pattern of the tragic sequence, which could be called the forcible returning to health of suicidally distempered 'total, unconditional' love.

Much Ado about Nothing, moving towards Shakespeare's maturity, finds a sharper definition of the Equation – though still without breaking through into the mythic reality of its substrata. The love match between Benedick and Beatrice is like a double echo of *The Taming of the Shrew*. In each, the capacity for excessive love is defensively distorted to aggression against the other. The distortion has to be removed by a trick. In other words, that foreground display of two virtuosos is dramatically galvanized by a fragment of the Equation (the vengeful distortion of the rejected) on the comic wavelength. Meanwhile, the action of the play is a serious and full-length sketch of the Equation (almost tragic) and the Rival Brothers. The brothers are incisively drawn: the bastard, Don John, is the irrational inferior, while Don Pedro (his true brother) and Claudio *combined* are the rational. The figures in the Equation are likewise cleanly and economically projected. Claudio and Don Pedro *combined* are the Adonis (Don Pedro does the courting, Claudio the loving, then both, as one, see the double vision and react in Equation style). Malignant Don John is the Iago figure who injects them with that double vision. Hero is the undivided Goddess whom they, Don Pedro and Claudio, having as one man rejected, assault so cruelly and violently, in the church, at the marriage service (with a prototype tirade:

> Would you not swear,
> All you that see her, that she were a maid,
> By these exterior shows? But she is none:

She knows the heat of a luxurious bed;
Her blush is guiltiness, not modesty . . .)
Much Ado about Nothing, IV. i. 38–42

that she 'dies'. The denouement, where this Tarquin Claudio/Don Pedro learns his error (only after penitential self-castigation, in which Claudio relinquishes his ego and submits his life to the will of Hero's father), is again a rehearsal of what will emerge, when Shakespeare has earned it, as the full Gnostic Coda, where the beloved returns from the dead. Once more, Shakespeare finds all the components of his basic power drive, that lifts this play off the runway, in the patented kits of his Equation, Rival Brothers and Gnostic Coda.

A Midsummer Night's Dream marks a new phase in his vision of the rejected woman, and therefore in the evolution of the Equation, since for the first time this play breaks through into the mythic plane, and floods the text and action with that 'supernatural' light which becomes, eventually, the vital 'substance', so to speak, of the plays of the tragic sequence. Presumably this work was written not too long after *Venus and Adonis*, and reveals how that poem and its myth were ripening in his imagination, suffering through their sea change into something even stranger and richer.

Fragments of the Equation and Rival Brothers vitalize the square dance of the lovers as follows:

Demetrius and Lysander are Rival Brothers much as were Proteus and Valentine in *The Two Gentlemen of Verona*, without the mutual trust. Demetrius attempts to displace, 'usurp', Lysander from possession of Hermia, as Proteus attempted to usurp Valentine from possession of Silvia.

Lysander, displaced from the rational world of moral, legal approval, flees to the forest (as did Valentine), accompanied by the desired Hermia (the 'crown' in question between the two 'brothers') as Valentine was joined by Silvia.

The Equation supplies much of the rest:

Demetrius rejects the infatuated Helena who pursues him (following the steps of the first half of the Equation). He tries to take possession of Hermia against her will (by force) and like

Proteus pursues her into the forest (following the steps of the Equation's second half).

The lovers, Lysander and Hermia, flee towards a transcendental plane of earthly happiness (beyond moral tragic opposition) as Romeo and Juliet flee (but towards tragic deaths), and as Antony and Cleopatra flee (also towards tragic deaths), which is to say, towards the Gnostic Theophany – the union (blessed by Heaven) in redeeming love.

   Likewise, Pyramus and Thisbe, fleeing towards the transcendental plane of their love, fall into tragic death, albeit in burlesque mode.

The Equation (dominant) and the Rival Brothers (rudimentary) also determine the intermingled action of the Fairies and Bottom:

The Goddess appears in her own person as Titania, alias Mab (alias Medb, the great triple Goddess of the Irish Celtic pantheon). Oberon (the Adonis figure, her consort) has rejected her – as if her love for the Indian boy were an infidelity of 'sweating Lust'. Since he, too, loves the Indian boy, and rejects and punishes her specifically to force her to hand over the loved object to him, the motive for his anger is double – exactly as was Shakespeare's against his mistress when she seduced and appropriated his patron, in the *Sonnets*. In other words (though through a fairyland rainbow), Oberon has seen the 'double vision' in Titania, his Queen, and rejects her. His 'revenge', a grotesque fairyland nightmare for Titania, becomes a form of assault, i.e. a form of Tarquinian 'madness', or irrationality at least, in that he makes her now wholly a Queen of Hell. She experiences what it is to be a Queen of Hell, in the sense that Desdemona, during Othello's jealous frenzy, experienced what it was to be regarded as a Queen of Hell.

   As a result she is revealed as the consort of the Lord of Hell – who is always the gross inferior brother, Set, who is the Boar, or alternatively (in Egyptian terms) the Ass. The vision of Titania voluptuously entwined with Ass-head Bottom becomes a Saturnalian tableau of the Queen of Hell with that figure which Adonis saw in Venus's 'sweating Lust' – the 'hot tyrant'.

   Translated to the terms of *Antony and Cleopatra*, Bottom in his

Ass-head is Antony in his (false) Boar phase, luxuriating in Cleopatra's lust (as Queen of Hell). It is Shakespearean high fidelity once again, then, when within *A Midsummer Night's Dream*, in the 'tedious brief scene of tragical mirth', Bottom reappears as Pyramus who, translated into the terms of *Antony and Cleopatra*, is Antony in his true Osirian phase, dying (by suicide at the tomb) into his transcendent love.

Titania is a goddess of flowers – as Venus is of the flowers of Adonis. She is introduced, in the play, by a description of her special flower, portrayed in six intense little lines: it is the blood-spotted cowslip – which will later (in *Cymbeline*) be the flower of Adonis's death and rebirth and (in *The Tempest*) Ariel's home. Curiously, a fairy describes this flower (in the opening of the first fairy scene) to Puck. This fairy, as a composite (unnamed) of all the servant fairies, anticipates Ariel. At the same time, Puck serves Oberon much as Ariel serves Prospero. Fairy and Puck, like two aspects of Ariel, are divided between Titania and Oberon, as the obedient spirits for running magical errands. Just as in *The Tempest* Ariel at one time served the Goddess as Queen of Hell (Sycorax whose consort was the devil-god Setebos) but now serves Prospero (as the Adonis who has rejected that Goddess), so here in *A Midsummer Night's Dream* the fairy serves Titania in her Queen of Hell nightmare of lust with Bottom as Ass-head Typhon (or Set), while Puck serves Oberon in rejecting and controlling her.

A different but equally natural association connects Puck and the Indian boy. The result suggests Caliban: Puck as the potentially dangerous, slightly infernal goblin, who is also attractively comical, and the Indian boy as the love god in his Divine-Child phase who is also black. Fused together, these two become Shakespeare's primordial figure, Venus's 'waspish-headed son', Cupid or terrible Eros, who is love in its unacceptable (to mortal egos), uncontrollable phase, alias (in *The Tempest*) Caliban, alias the Boar. So here too the occult relationships between Caliban and Ariel, and the Boar and the Flower, emerge intact.

The Flower appears again in Oberon's famous lines:

> That very time I saw, but thou coulds't not,
> Flying between the cold moon and the earth,

Cupid all arm'd: a certain aim he took
At a fair vestal throned by the west,
And loos'd his love-shaft smartly from his bow,
As it should pierce a hundred thousand hearts;
But I might see young Cupid's fiery shaft
Quench'd in the chaste beams of the watery moon,
And the imperial votaress passed on
In maiden meditation, fancy-free.
Yet mark'd I where the bolt of Cupid fell:
It fell upon a little western flower,
Before milk-white, now purple with love's wound,
And maidens call it, Love-in-idleness.
Fetch me that flower . . .

            A Midsummer Night's Dream, II. i. 155–69

This fully qualified candidate for the Flower from Adonis's blood
here again operates as in the Tragic Equation.

When the flower's juice is applied to the eyes of Lysander, he
rejects Hermia and fastens his passion instantaneously (like
Tarquin) on Helena who loves Demetrius (and truly belongs to
Demetrius, as Lucrece belonged to another). On Demetrius it has a
similar effect, of rousing an instantaneous, uncontrollable, sudden
desire for Helena – who actually does and will belong to him.
These spasms of Tarquinian delusion from the mere juice of the
flower nevertheless serve – as the Flower eventually does in the
complete evolutionary pattern of the Equation – to bring the souls
to their senses and secure the final love unions on the
'transcendental' plane (which, in the early plays, is marriage
simply).

Via Titania's deluded infatuation, that same juice converts
Bottom to a latent Tarquin in comic mode (the 'hot tyrant', the
Set, the usurping brother, consort of the Queen of Hell – *before* he
emerges to make his assault), and simultaneously it nestles him in
the bosom of the Goddess, as if he were the Flower itself being
carried back to her transcendental love heaven in Paphos, in an
unearthly dream of Divine Love.

In these early plays, Shakespeare can be seen like some archaeologist,
making tentative interpretation of the new system of hieroglyphs that
somehow he has unearthed. He is still far from the full meaning of the

symbols, and from the ordered, timeless, metaphysical world that will open within the meanings, but he has already felt out the gist and much of the syntax.

Caliban's blackness

Prospero's first reference to Caliban in the final act of *The Tempest* is:

> this thing of darkness I
> Acknowledge mine.
> *The Tempest*, v. i. 275–6

In every play, each one dramatic just to the degree that the struggle is intense, Prospero – as one form or other of Adonis – has fought to make sense of this monstrously difficult being whom he now, in this grand denouement to the tragic sequence, acknowledges to be his own, something in himself. Just as Alonso, Antonio and Sebastian are brought to admit and face their crime, Prospero has been brought to confess *Caliban*, the protagonist of all the crimes.

On the other hand, in spite of Prospero's triumphant restoration of civilized behaviour, Caliban remains the real figure, the attractive and even fascinating bearer of the life of the play, and of uncontainable life itself. This creature who was ready to love Prospero as much as he lusted for Miranda, and for whom the heavens open (and who weeps when they close), and who speaks the poetry of the natural world, possesses a sensibility and a nature that makes his master's seem stale and sour. Yet his complexity, his comprehensive being and appeal, are to be expected: after all he is the daemon in the mechanism of the Tragic Equation, who is also the daemon within the usurping brother. And he is therefore made of the dark divine substance of the rejected Goddess.

If it seems strange that Shakespeare's final play should revolve around Caliban, and should leave him in possession of the stage (the island), it is equally strange that his first 'tragic' play, *Titus Andronicus*, one of the most monstrous of all Elizabethan plays, should revolve around the even more demonic Aaron the Moor.

Since Shakespeare invented her, he could just as easily have brought Caliban's mother from Lapland. But bringing her from Algiers he chose to make her what he would call a Moor. He chose her to be black. As black, at least, as Aaron and Othello.

Likewise, Claribel could have been married anywhere else in the

Mediterranean. Shakespeare chose to marry her, like Desdemona, to a Moor, and to put her on the throne of Dido – the high priestess of Venus as the black Goddess in Libya.

The marriage between Claribel and the Moorish King of Tunis is an image of the marriage between Ferdinand and Miranda. Claribel and Ferdinand, the Italianate, sophisticated brother and sister, represent the white side of this *conjunctio*, which leaves the Moorish King (like the warrior-king Iarbas, whom Dido rejected) to share the black side with Miranda (who is the reborn Dido). Both marriages are symbols of the old conflict resolved, the antagonists reconciled, their past histories and earlier lives redeemed (the conflict of the Tragic Equation – between 'white' Adonis and 'black' Queen of Hell, and between 'white' Lucrece and 'black' Tarquin).

In spite of these ideal events, solemnized and consecrated in the heavenly Masque, *The Tempest* ends with Prospero as the white Adonis (albeit cripplingly, darkly scarred by his previous Tarquinian incarnations) confronting an alarmingly fresh, unregenerate black Boar – Caliban.

Caliban's 'blackness', his semi-supernatural (his father a devil-god) 'African-ness', is like the blackness of Dionysus, or the blueness of Krishna, a token of his absolute 'otherness', of his origins in the depths of what has been excluded from the ego's life. In this case, the depths of the rejected Divine Love, the Goddess of Complete Being. According to the Equation, then, his 'black' Moorish matrilineal descent is precisely the sign of his divinity. As the emissary of that part of the Goddess which cannot be assimilated, through each play of the tragic sequence his 'invasion', as a usurping madness, has forced a kind of assimilation, a partial assimilation. Up to *Coriolanus*, the Boar's possession of each of the tragic heroes – uncontrollable, disastrous – created parables of the tragic predicament, shattering the orthodox mind, compelling it to suffer and die for its limitations, followed by a wiser, enriched rebirth, reassembly on a larger scale, in the next play. In *King Lear* and *Antony and Cleopatra*, though it was, as ever, shattering, the Boar's possession broke through to full spiritual awakening and transcendence. From *Cymbeline* onwards, the heroine's and the hero's survival of the assault is a measure of the hero's success in assimilating the Boar, in assimilating rejected Divine Love and greater being, and is expressed in the plays as rebirth into transcendence. Aaron/Caliban the Boar, the unrecognizable avatar of the missing component of Complete Being, distorted and depraved in the conditions of human life, becomes the sole means of greater being and spiritual transcendence.

But the process works for only one individual at a time, in only one place – in this case Shakespeare, for a decade either side of the turn of the sixteenth and seventeenth centuries. The *Complete Works* are the record of what it entails. Elsewhere, in every other individual, the rejection continues to be made, the Boar charges, the madness erupts.

Which is to say that this act of transcendence can never be more than provisional, a possibility to be sustained, if achieved, only by containing that high ethical purpose of the Goddess within ritual, 'religious', quasi-magical procedures.

Otherwise, the Boar is at large, seething with undiminished potential, full of visions and attended by that crying voice, but full, also, of 'jealous' fury, the rage of the rejected Goddess, who continues to whisk her sea-monsterish tempest tails around the island stage.

POSTSCRIPT

The Boar with a Flower in its Mouth

According to my argument, this lineage of the Boar (taken together with the Storm, that comes with it, and the Flower in the hand of the babe that rides it) is the key to Shakespeare's ethical system.

The two united divine figures with which I began – the Great Goddess behind Venus and the god behind Adonis – became, in the plays, three separate dramatis personae, one of them 'mortal'. Adonis became a type of rational, moral intelligence, which split the Goddess into the Queen of Hell (the Boar) and Lucrece, and rejected both.

This 'big bang' style of beginning to Shakespeare's cosmos created a situation resembling that of a fractured sun, the three reglobed chunks now spinning on a common centre of gravity (located in the space somewhere between them), with terrific centripetal force (the original and still-surviving magnetic field of Divine Love) pulling them together, while a temporarily equal but opposite centrifugal force (Adonis's divisive moral will) drives them apart.

In this arrangement, the Adonis fragment is, so to speak, content. He merely wants to perpetuate his judgemental system of right love and wrong love (like Angelo's 'strict statutes and most biting laws') by annihilating or neutralizing the Queen of Hell and by preserving Lucrece in a nunnery (or its equivalent – 'married chastity').

Lucrece contains all the light of the broken, furiously active system, but no physical power. In so far as she is powerless to force her love on to the one who rejected it, and unable to declare it in words that he can hear, she is helpless and speechless, and can only endure her fate. But she is not entirely passive. Her love has a positive energy, a real effect, since so long as she can stay alive she embodies that ideal of 'total, unconditional', unaltering love, and this offer remains perpetually available to the hero, radiating a beam of redemption through the darkness towards him, like the female firefly's coded strobe, which does successfully guide him and in the end redeem him. Shakespeare dramatizes this as-if-telepathic potency of the inactive, ineffable love in several ways – by Helena's ingenuity in her circumvention of Bertram's attempt to forsake and forget her, by the phenomenon of parallel rebirths (as with Imogen and Posthumus, where the brothers play the part of Imogen's pheromones, synchronizing Posthumus's rebirth with hers), and by the consequences, for the hero, of the love choice of his daughter (as for Leontes and Prospero).

The Queen of Hell's Boar, meanwhile, embodies the system's entire regenerative power – all the elemental, magnetic, physical power of the reunion, as well as the molten heat that can still fuse and reintegrate the other two, if it can recapture them. Since its whole nature is the will to recombine at any cost, this third heavenly body moves first to repossess the source of disruption and disunion, and after that the source of the light, the repository of the light. Which is to say, the Boar has only one metaphysical purpose: to repossess Adonis, and, having recombined with him (albeit in violence, creating that fourth dramatis persona Tarquin), then to reclaim, in violence again, Lucrece, so restoring (though violently, scattering the human puppets) the Divine Union. The final state, therefore, like the first, is perfect union in Divine Love. (For a further simplification of the dynamics of the Tragic Equation, see Appendix II.)

One can see that the linear form of the Tragic Equation takes full account of this disintegration of primal matter and order (by the 'double vision' and 'rejection') and of the reunion in violence (the Tarquin's rape, murder or usurpation, the crime of his 'madness'). Explosion to implosion – like a supernova.

When this cycle of 'repossession' is completed in violence (*Hamlet, Othello, Macbeth, King Lear, Coriolanus*) it is Tragedy pure if not simple. When Shakespeare finds a way of nursing the hero and heroine through that implosion, bringing them out 'reborn' into the new wholeness, it does turn out that they are back in the union of Divine Love (with some earthly qualifications), which is Tragedy redeemed by Theophany (briefly in *King Lear*, subjectively in *Antony and Cleopatra*, substantially in the last four plays).

This is another way of putting what I described at the end of the discussion of *Othello* as the *perpetuum mobile* of the Tragic Equation. This formula maps the full cycle within which Divine Love is first made to destroy itself in its human vessels (the tragic hero and heroine), and then by destroying the aberrant form of human vessel (the limiting, 'Puritan' ego) to create for itself a greater form of containment (the heroine's redeeming love, the redeemed hero). But the main point here is that throughout these dramas the active Divine Love enters the action, according to the Equation, in the form of the Boar.

The implications of this are curious, but also large. Given that the divine energy source (in that distorted opening situation of the dramatic action) is within the Boar, and the divine ethical source (towards which the Boar, with its Flower and Babe, strives blindly) is within Lucrece, and given that these two exist in unarguable, inspired poetic reality within Shakespeare's works, then it can be said that he created these works (there cannot have been any other way) out of a mystical self-identification with both: with the ineffable 'word within a word', in Cordelia, and with the daemonic entity within the Boar.

Plenty has been said about Shakespeare's steadfast bearing and advance under that 'ever-fixed mark', 'Whose worth's unknown, although his height be taken' (Sonnet 116), which shines from the love of the tragic heroine: the crown of the axis of his universe. Not so much has been said about that dark being which, in the body of the possessed Tarquin hero, drives these mature plays. Even less has been said about the very odd fact that this self-identification with a creature partly from the blood sea, partly from the tree of nerves, partly straight out of the astral (which, according to the Equation – it cannot be said too often – incarnated that omnipotent 'lust' for recombination, the primal, creative power, of the rejected Divine Love), took a form which the plays present as the Moorish Aaron at the beginning of his career, the Moorish Caliban at the end, and the Wild Boar of Persephone within all the tragic heroes between.

Without too much difficulty Shakespeare can be granted that first self-identification with the speechless truth of the all-suffering woman dedicated to Divine Love. It is peculiar enough – it suggests an extreme and even afflicted degree of spiritual isolation – but at least it is understandable, since it belongs traditionally where Shakespeare repeatedly puts it, in the ascetic life of a saintly nun, or in her perfectly loving marriage to a redeemed (and therefore Christ-like) man.

It is not so easy, perhaps, to accept his simultaneous self-identification with the most alien, outcast and inimical figure of the Elizabethan Christian world, the black Saracen, the 'Blackamoor'. A Blackamoor moreover who, in Lear's and Timon's madness, revealed himself as he did (with Shakespeare's ultimate eloquence), as the naked, essential man, before language and even against language, the 'bare, forked animal' – all but the Boar itself, hovelled 'with swine', rooting in the earth. In his punished but primordial and indomitable truth to nature (his deity, the creative power and substance of the Goddess of Complete Being herself) this figure is a strange twin brother to Cordelia in her punished but primordial, indomitable truth to the soul (her deity, the spiritual axis of the Goddess of Complete Being), and who is, like him, 'before language and even against language'.

Even more ominously than Goethe's Mephistopheles, or the vengeful, pitiless, lonely hatred behind Dante's *Inferno*, Shakespeare's misfit, in its elemental otherness and ferocity, suggests an almost pathological psychic alienation from the culture within which his plays triumphed, a radical estrangement that sits oddly with the traditional idea of the 'gentle Shakespeare', the benign senior citizen of an English country town. But not when the Boar is translated, according to the Equation, back into its true being.

As he embodies the rejected Divine Love, and as he strives to recombine with its lost light and its fallen consort, and as he is the power unit and vital protagonist of Shakespeare's entire dramatic, tragic, transcendental, poetic creation, this Blackamoor, alias the Boar with the Flower in its mouth, can be translated, word for word, like the last lines of Dante's *Paradiso*:

> Already my Desire and Will were rolled –
> Even as a wheel that moveth equally –
> By the Love that moves the sun and the other stars.

APPENDIX I

The Tragic Equation in *Henry VIII* and *Two Noble Kinsmen*

Though Fletcher wrote a large proportion of both *Henry VIII* and *Two Noble Kinsmen*, the acts and scenes supplied by Shakespeare, and the actual plots of these plays, suggest that Shakespeare proposed both subjects. In so far as Henry's rejection of the Papal Authority introduced the Reformation to England, his 'divorce' from the Catholic Church was the act which begot the Tragic Equation within the English psyche. As such it became the creation story – in its immediate, non-mythic, realistic terms – of Shakespeare's dramatic universe. That being so, it seems understandable that at some point, especially after he had so thoroughly worked through those mythic consequences, Shakespeare should have a go at the historical event itself, in the direct style of his pageant-sagas.

One can see why the subject was taboo in Elizabeth's reign – at least, in the form which only Shakespeare could give it, as the ur-parable of the Tragic Equation. But even in 1611 it ran him headlong towards political quicksands, from which he deftly backed off – leaving them to Fletcher.

His hand can be seen in the design of the basic situation, and in the direction given by the opening two scenes (which are his). Buckingham is strongly characterized as the external rational self of the King (the doomed Adonis self, or the rational brother). Wolsey is just as firmly drawn as the irrational self (and in fact as the painstakingly identified Boar, the 'butcher's cur' 'from hell' who was 'a new hell in himself'). Wolsey's violent displacement of Buckingham is a classic usurpation in the Rival Brothers pattern, which is then interiorized, within Henry, and translated to Tragic Equation terms as Wolsey (having liquidated Buckingham) becomes the King's voice in his rejection of the true and loving (Catholic) Queen, Katharine.

This is a bold, clear opening of the Tragic Equation, not that far from the opening of *The Winter's Tale* (though at much lower temperature). But at this point Shakespeare's political difficulty appears. Katharine's prolonged defence and lament is in several ways reminiscent of Hermione's in *The Winter's Tale*. But there is no way in which Henry can come to his senses about her, annul the divorce, and reunite with her in enlightened love and understanding – as Leontes did with Hermione. History denies Shakespeare, and the Equation, that course. History requires, rather, that Henry confirm his rejection of Katharine, which is to say that in terms of the Equation he affirms his irrational action – somewhat as Antony affirmed his when he abandoned Octavia and committed himself to Cleopatra.

And now Anne Boleyn emerges, from behind Henry/Wolsey's rejection of Queen Katharine, as the exotic (dark-skinned, black-eyed, six-fingered) woman behind the hero's irrational self. In terms of the Equation, that is, Anne Boleyn stands in the role of a Queen of Hell.

In Shakespeare's imagination, the guiding precedent for this situation, perhaps, was Macbeth's renunciation of the world of Duncan and the true Crown (Katharine is repeatedly described as the perfect, most holy Queen), and his self-submersion in the 'lust' of Lady Macbeth. The design of the Equation, within the pattern of the plot of *Henry VIII*, casts the mother of Queen Elizabeth I, therefore, in the role of the Great Witch, and Henry himself, in his marriage to here, as the Boar, quite simply.

In history, Katharine's fate followed the Tragic Equation as it shaped the plot of *The Winter's Tale*. The King's treatment of her and her daughter Mary (eventually Bloody Mary, the Catholic fanatic) resembles nothing so much as Leontes's pitiless persecution of Hermione and their daughter Perdita, making virtual criminals of both and separating them absolutely from each other as well as from himself, in a sustained cruelty that Katharine failed to survive.

That Shakespeare did regard Elizabeth as the daughter of the Great Witch can be argued. His mythicization of her is an obscure business. It is far easier to identify her, in the plays, on that mythic level, with the Queens of Hell (Cloten's mother, etc.) of the tragic sequence, right up to Sycorax, than with that 'Fair vestal throned by the west . . .' in *A Midsummer Night's Dream* (II.i.158), where Shakespeare was still going around his myth on tiptoe.

His prudent withdrawal from full imaginative involvement in the story of Henry VIII's divorce and marriage to Anne Boleyn and the birth of Elizabeth presents an image, a sort of involuntary portrait, perhaps, of his true religious allegiance, antithetical to the show of orthodoxy. He revealed his secret, in the code of his Equation, and left the show of orthodoxy to Fletcher. This internal non-participation in the overall business of the play has a curious effect on the verse. The combative, massively knitted physique of the syntax and ideation is there (so distinct from Fletcher's repertoire of etiolated, second-hand, lyrical attitudes) but strangely empty of blood – circulating salt solution maybe. He was evidently quite happy to see Fletcher (who knew nothing of the Equation, whose whole talent had evolved as an evasion of the demonic and actual in the spiritual struggle of the times, and whose popularity reveals an audience that was beginning to make the same escape) to turn his outline into a pageant that actually inverted its mythic implications, glorifying Henry's tragic 'error' and its offspring, Elizabeth I.

If one accepts that Shakespeare's (Apollo-like) judgement of Henry VIII's tragic error was the explosive political-religious secret of his dramatic phantasmagoria, then it is fitting that this naked, final disclosure should be concealed behind Fletcher's 180 degree reversal of its meaning, and that his thunderous condemnation (like Delphi's judgement against Leontes), converted to a cannon's dummy fireball salute, should burn down the Globe Theatre (built in 1599 just in time for *As You Like It* and the opening of Shakespeare's relentless investigation into that very crime).

In a similar way, his designing hand can be seen in *Two Noble Kinsmen* – Chaucer's classic story of the Rival Brothers. Inevitably, this well-known plot had attached itself, in Shakespeare's imagination, to his own Rival Brothers theme. Knowing the original from his earliest reading, he must often have toyed with its dramatic potential. The ardent dedication of the two brothers to Mars and Venus respectively, and of Emilia to Diana, and the fact that the action revolves around the peculiar gratifications of these three deities, must have made it even more attractive – once his Rival Brothers/Tragic Equation schema had entered its fully integrated mythic phase.

Yet – though Arcite and Palamon are 'Rival Brothers', ready to fight to the death – something vital is missing. Drama is missing, obviously. The plot, such as it is, becomes a succession of static tableaux. The rivalry of the 'kinsmen' is disabled somehow. According to the laws of Shakespeare's dramatic mechanism, this symptom suggests a particular failure: and there it is. The necessary hostility of the one (the irrational usurper) lacks the daemonic dimension. He is not connected, that is, to that bottomless power supply, the enraged Queen of Hell.

Both love Emilia with noble love, and she loves both – equally. As she sighs (while they try to kill each other for possession of her):

> Were they metamorphosised
> Both into one – O why? there were no woman
> Worth so composed a man!
>
> *Two Noble Kinsmen*, v. iii. 84–6

As a result, at the 'usurpation', when Mars's warrior Arcite (who should be the Boar) overthrows Venus's warrior Palamon (who should be Adonis), no depths contribute, and none is stirred. Two noble gentlemen, noble kinsmen, have agreed, nobly, to settle their blameless rivalry for the blameless woman by duelling nobly to the death, and whichever wins, it seems, will please this jewel of chastity. What is missing, as I say, is that mythic 'infernal' world of the demonic, from which Arcite should emerge, uncontrollable and pitiless, with dreadful consequences for Emilia and himself, as well as for Palamon.

The likely seeming plot, therefore, has a fatal flaw, from the dramatic point of view. That equal nobility of the brothers, which is the main point of the original knightly romance, has resisted the temperatures and chemical solvents within Shakespeare's mythic crucible, and remains essentially what it was in Chaucer. This archetypal, statuesque assemblage of Mars's champion deadlocked with Venus's champion, for the prize of Diana's high priestess, who watches with impartial, patient acceptance, strikes a mythic and even a primeval chord (in the animal kingdom), but unless the personality of one of the two combatants is radically altered, no drama can flow, at least none of Shakespeare's kind.*

*On the other hand, that absence of drama can be seen as an incidental effect of what is also, from Shakespeare's point of view, the image of a desirable spiritual achievement. If the painful drama of the Tragic Equation/ Rival Brothers mechanism sprang from the alienation of the Adonis mind from the Queen of Hell mind, and if Shakespeare's artistic evolution, as I have followed it through, was a laborious process of bringing these two minds (the Rival Brothers), within himself, to mutual understanding, forgiveness, and unity in love, then inevitably real success in attaining such a state of ultimate wholeness (as a genuine inward fact) would mean the end of conflict in fantasies projected from it. Shakespeare had always entertained an image of this ultimate wholeness as a perfect, final resolution of conflict: two brothers who love each other and are in love with, and marry, two sisters who love each other. This image gave him the solution to *The Comedy of Errors*, when he first confronted the 'problem' of his own genius. The same image resolved the complications of *As You Like It*, when he eventually stood at the beginning of the tragic sequence. And now it appears before him as the substantial symbol of his imagination, of the real condition of his nature on the mythic plane, in the drama that ends his work. What was formerly the idealized situation that unfailingly brought dramatic conflict to a peaceful close, now stands, slightly modified, as the opening situation in which he has to find, somehow, drama. If he had hoped to galvanize things as at the opening of *The Winter's Tale*, he is soon forced to realize that essential factors have changed. The plotted quarrel of the two noble kinsmen seems stagey, unreal,

The result of that absence of the rejected Queen of Hell has a serious effect on Shakespeare's verse. His grasp of the mythic aspects of the situation has involved him with it poetically. The verse has the moulded luminosity of his latest phase, and in some registers of the composition one can detect quite new tones. In the first scene, one of three queens, wives of kings slain at Thebes, whose bodies lie unburied by order of Creon, entreat Theseus for help:

> He will not suffer us to burn their bones,
> To urn their ashes, nor to take offence
> Of mortal loathsomeness from the blest eye
> Of Holy Phoebus, but infects the winds
> With stench of our slain lords. O pity, Duke,
> Thou purger of the earth, draw thy fear'd sword
> That does good turns i' th' world, give us the bones
> Of our dead kings, that we may chapel them . . .
>
> I. i. 43–50

and then, appealing to his wife, Hippolyta:

> dear glass of ladies,
> Bid him that we, whom flaming war doth scorch,
> Under the shadow of his sword may cool us,

———

factitious, non-mythic, in that it is like a mere memory, recollected in tranquillity, of the earlier, deadly combats. It cannot disturb what seems to be the basic mythic actuality that the two now love each other and have, in fact, become like one. This is reflected in Emilia, the living image of the new wholeness. The resolution of the Goddess's former duality emerges now from Emilia's description of the perfect love ('more than in sex dividual') that had existed between her and her childhood friend, Flavinia, who mirrored her every move, until she died: as if Lucrece and the Queen of Hell – in a blessed absence of the double vision – had now become inseparably, benignly one. But in the middle of her reminiscence, Emilia produces the surprising nest of metaphors:

> The flower that I would pluck
> And put between my breasts (O then
>   beginning

> To swell about the blossom), she would
>   long
> Till she had such another, and commit it
> To the like innocent cradle, where phoenix-
>   like
> They died in perfume.
>
> I. iii. 66–71

In these lines her greater role suddenly swirls up at her from the depths of her earlier incarnations, sharply glimpsed through that lodging of the flower, the 'hollow cradle' (from the finale of *Venus and Adonis*), and through that further mythicization of the flower as a phoenix. Her phoenix dies 'in perfume' but (though she does not go on to say it), being a phoenix, is simultaneously – out of its perfumed death and in that cradle – reborn. Before the battle Palamon puts himself in the care of Venus but Arcite, neglecting the shrine of Venus, puts himself in the care

[509]

Require him he advance it o'er our heads;
Speak't in a woman's key — like such a woman
As any of us three; weep ere you fail;
Lend us a knee;
But touch the ground for us no longer time
Than a dove's motion when the head's plucked off,
Tell him if he i' the blood-sized field lay swollen,
Showing the sun his teeth, grinning at the moon,
What you would do.

I. i. 90—101

———

of Mars. While the victor's prize is Emilia, the loser's penalty is death. Having conquered Palamon, Arcite finds that his horse, a black stallion given to him by Emilia, now becomes uncontrollable, rears up and, whining 'pig-like', falls backward on top of him, crushing him to death (see page 73).

    your cousin,
Mounted upon a steed that Emily
Did first bestow on him — a black one, owing
Not a hair-worth of white, which some will
                    say
Weakens his price, and many will not buy
His goodness with this note; which super-
                   stition
Here finds allowance — on this horse is Arcite
Trotting the stones of Athens, which the
                 calkins
Did rather tell than trample; for the horse
Would make his length a mile, if't pleas'd his
                 rider
To put pride in him. As he thus went counting
The flinty pavement, dancing as 'twere to th'
                 music
His own hoofs made (for as they say from
                 iron
Came music's origin), what envious flint,
Cold as old Saturn, and like him possess'd
With fire malevolent, darted a spark,
Or what fierce sulphur else, to this end made,
I comment not — the hot horse, hot as fire,
Took toy at this, and fell to what disorder
His power could give his will, bounds, comes
                 on end,
Forgets school-doing, being therein train'd,
And of kind manage; pig-like he whines
At the sharp rowel, which he frets at rather
Than any jot obeys; seeks all foul means

Of boist'rous and rough jad'ry, to disseat
His lord that kept it bravely. When nought
                 serv'd,
When neither curb would crack, girth break,
             nor diff'ring plunges
Disroot his rider whence he grew, but that
He kept him 'tween his legs, on his hind hoofs
. . . . on end he stands,
That Arcite's legs, being higher than his head,
Seem'd with strange art to hang. His victor's
                 wreath
Even then fell off his head; and presently
Backward the jade comes o'er, and his full
                 poise
Becomes the rider's load. Yet is he living,
But such a vessel 'tis that floats but for
The surge that next approaches.

v. iv. 47—83

Arcite dies, therefore, somewhat like Adonis himself, but also — as a warrior of Mars who has taken the ideal of chastity 'by force' — somewhat like a Tarquin. Simultaneously Palamon, condemned to death by Arcite's victory, is reborn, out of that double death of Arcite, as a redeemed Adonis/Tarquin — restored to his place on the breast of the Goddess-as-Emilia. In fact, as a compendious, brilliantly condensed recapitulation of both Adonis's and Tarquin's deaths and rebirths, this intricate double death/rebirth is as algebraically precise, in the literal, mythic terms of the Equation, as anything in the plays — though it lacks the tragic dimension. And here in Emilia's speech, just as in Angelo's speech in *Measure for Measure*, Adonis's death-flower pokes through the plot to tell us just where everybody stands.

Or Arcite, after first seeing Emilia (in the background 'Noise and hollowing, as people go a-Maying'):

> This is the solemn rite
> They owe bloom'd May, and the Athenians pay it
> To the heart of ceremony. O Queen Emilia,
> Fresher than May, sweeter
> Than her gold buttons on the boughs, or all
> The enamell'd knacks o' the mead, or garden! Yea
> We challenge too the bank of any nymph
> That makes the stream seem flowers! Thou, O jewel
> O' the wood, o' the world, has likewise blest a place
> With thy sole presence . . .
>
> III. i. 2—11

All this is rich, and new. And yet it lacks something essential, that Shakespeare normally puts there. And in the play, where quite a few similar passages occur (Fletcher imitated the scoring as well as he could, and produced some of his most haunting lines), one sees that for all its density this music lacks inner momentum. It is psychologically static. Not so much flowing blood as (like Stravinsky's, as he complained) coagulating clots of rubies. The sense of inner challenge and dramatic confrontation, which electrifies the comparable passages in *The Winter's Tale*, or *Pericles*, is oddly absent. Perhaps what is absent too is that phrase-by-phrase refraction of the working themes of the play – which can only happen, presumably, where the composing imagination is revolving the whole play as a single organic and complete system. Here, where Shakespeare has sketched an outline, with guiding scenes, and left the rest to Fletcher – probably sending his own contribution from Stratford in fulfilment of a contract – that total process could not happen. As a result, the tremendous athlete, resting under his mulberry, never even got into condition for the job. (Even Dickens, after all, every bit as fluent as Shakespeare, in his way, if he missed one day at his desk could not get back into 'form' in less than a week of steady writing.)

APPENDIX II

The *Perpetuum Mobile*

Setting aside everything to do with religion and history, to construct the simplest possible working psychological model of the Tragic Equation it can be imagined taking shape within the mind of one man. This, it should be emphasized, is nothing more than a metaphor. At one pole is the rational ego, controlling the man's behaviour according to the needs and demands of a self-controlled society. At the other is the totality of this individual's natural, biological and instinctual life. It has to be accepted (for the sake of the Equation) that from the point of view of the rational ego this totality appears to be female, and since it incorporates not only the divine source of his being, the feminine component of his own biological make-up, as well as the paranormal faculties and mysteries outside his rational ego, and seems to him in many respects continuous with external nature, he calls it the Goddess. Obviously, this is only a manner of speaking, or of thinking, but it is one that has imposed itself on man throughout his history.

The rational ego can apprehend this Goddess as a totality, but he cannot express the fullness of her life while at the same time remaining a rational ego. The nearest he can come to that is to relinquish his command (as controller of the individual's behaviour) to a state of mind corresponding to that of an infant, or of an ecstatic worshipper, or of a saint – and with this kind of surrender (as a Puritan of the Reformation, an idealist of rational control) he has difficulty. Nevertheless, the Goddess, being his own nature, insists with constant pressure that the fullness of her life be somehow expressed. If he is to preserve the equilibrium and control required of him by society, it is obvious what that rational ego has to do, so he does it. He splits the Goddess into the part that supports and confirms his rational existence, and the part that would disrupt it. He makes a sacred, binding contract with the one, and suppresses the other.

According to the Equation, this act of suppression is the beginning of the dramatic consequences. The rejected part of the Goddess, angered, so to speak, by the suppression, defies it, and works to find some way back into life. Inevitably, she separates herself into an alternative existence, inimical to the rational ego, whose regime she now threatens. Since her successful breakthrough into the behaviour of this male individual would have to take a male form, she creates a male beachhead, a front man midway between her Underworld and the world of the rational ego. This new personality becomes a secondary ego, as irrational as the Underworld half of the Goddess who has created him, and, like her, suppressed by the rational ego. He is not only her subordinate, and the commander of her powers. He serves as a rallying point, a recruiting officer, for every malcontent impulse that the rational ego continues to reject or suppress.

As can be seen, there are now four dramatis personae, and all four are linked together with dynamic tensions within the divided individuality of the one man. Just to go over them again:

The first is the rational ego, who controls the individual's attempt to live an ordered, prudent life. In the case of the Equation, the near-fanatic definition of the Puritan ideal (any thoroughgoing system of rational control) has supercharged this ego with fundamentalist-style severity. He is the Equation's Adonis.

The second is that part of the Goddess which confirms and supports this rational ego's ideals and well-being. This can be imagined as that half of his instinctive life, the half of the Goddess, which has assimilated all the supportive love he ever experienced from his creatrix (his mother) and which incorporates the absolutely reliable (i.e. faithful), unconditionally devoted, all-giving sustenance of his being, centred presumably on the heart itself, which is, biologically, the electrical source of his minute-by-minute life and is, at the same time, spiritually, his assurance of the truth and, to some degree, miraculous fact and actuality of his existence. This composite creature is therefore 'one flesh' with him and can be projected on to the image of a mother and a perfect wife, or perhaps on to a perfect wife and a daughter, and he gives her the general name 'soul'. This soul is therefore an integral part of the Goddess but not co-extensive with her totality. In the Equation, she is the Lucrece, who on occasion splits into wife and daughter (who becomes a bride), mother and ideal bride (*Hamlet*), or mother and perfect wife (*Coriolanus*).

The third is the other part of the Goddess, that 'dark', separated part which not only includes the orgiastic, amoral and even non-human biological drive for reproduction (the faithless promiscuity feared by the Adonis), but associates herself, being forbidden, with everything forbidden, uncontrollable, naturally or supernaturally hostile, thereby uniting the world of death with the world of elemental sexuality, animality and the daemonic. This other composite creature obviously inhabits the same organism as the soul, and in countless ways is inseparable from the psycho-biological continuum of the soul. To that extent, this darker part of the Goddess and that other acceptable part of the Goddess are indivisible. No matter how they are temporarily split apart by the rational ego's perspective, they will always recombine as the Great Goddess. The rational ego's intuition, Adonis's intuition, concerning this hidden unity of the two halves of the Goddess, is the basis of his fear, which amounts to an assumption, that the acceptable soul will prove treacherous, and which prompts the double vision on the slightest hint that his intuition is about to be proved correct. In the Equation he sees this darker half of the Goddess as the Queen of Hell.

The fourth character in the drama is that irrational ego, the other 'self' created by the Queen of Hell to lead her incessant, secret campaign for control of the individual: the inferior, usurping brother.

This theorem of basic possibilities explains the kind of relationship that has to exist between (a) the rational ego and the soul; (b) the rational ego and the Queen of Hell; (c) the Queen of Hell and the irrational ego; (d) the irrational ego and the rational ego; and (e) the irrational ego and the soul.

And, just to go over the 'mythic' law behind each of these relationships, one can therefore expect to find the following:

In (a) the natural relationship between rational ego and soul is 'total, unconditional love' both ways. This 'love' has the force and divine rightness of a cosmic or biological law, and therefore the individual who errs from it is heading for a 'divine' correction (humbling, in the case of Bertram and Angelo; tragic in the case of Hamlet, Othello, Macbeth, Lear, Timon, Coriolanus; tragic and redemptive in the case of Posthumus, Pericles and Leontes).

In (b) the natural relationship between rational ego and the Queen of Hell can only be one of mortal terror on the part of the rational ego and inexhaustible hunger to overpower and wholly possess on the part of the Queen of Hell. Her advance can only be experienced, by the rational ego, as a threat to his survival. Her triumph can only mean his death, which in the Shakespearean moment becomes a sort of suspended, horrified awareness of the madness which then takes possession. This madness arrives as the enraged passion of the Queen of Hell in the form of the irrational self.

In (c) the natural relationship between the Queen of Hell and the irrational ego is so close that it amounts again to a psychic continuum. He, as I described him, is in a sense her 'son', the commander of her powers, and in him her enraged passion is given the form of some kind of 'jealousy'. This expresses the original 'Hell' of the Queen of Hell, which is one of deprivation – forbidden life in the world, denied love, loathed and feared. She is deprived, also, of her natural unity with the other half of the Goddess, the soul. The ambition of the irrational self, therefore, is to seize all these lost things in a single coup, and always takes the path of usurping the rational ego and attempting to seize the soul by force. In this way, when the usurpation takes the form of the Rival Brothers, the Queen of Hell has become the usurping, irrational brother, and when it takes the form of the Tragic Equation, the Queen of Hell has become the irrational ego (the Boar who is also the 'hot tyrant') who combines with the rational ego to produce a Tarquin.

This last sentence explains (d) and also (e). The irrational ego's relationship to the soul introduces the peculiar *frisson* that characterizes Shakespeare's tragic idea, where the soul has become the victim of Hell itself. The irrational self is, as it were, in love with the soul from which, by definition, both it and its controller, the Queen of Hell, have been separated. The situation has enormous dramatic power. In so far as the irrational self is the representative of the Queen of Hell he is the infernal self, the damned self. The idea of the damned self rising to steal the beloved woman, who is the soul, from the rational self gives another perspective to the rational self's double vision – when his soul's apparent treachery is a secret love affair with his own damned and infernal other self.

It should be said again, this is only a metaphor. From the point of view of woman, everything is different, in the sense that the 'tragic error' belongs exclusively to the psychology of the man (except where woman imitates man). That division of the loved and the loathed woman in the one body, which precipitates the Tragic Equation, is projected on to her (involving her in its real consequences) by the man. And he projects it on to her in so far as his rationality is separated from nature, is therefore insecure, is therefore autocratically jealous of power and fearful of what he suppresses: i.e. in so far as he fights against her maternal control, fears her reproductive mystery and is jealous of her solidarity with the natural world. Within her own mind, woman alternates between the Aphrodite of the positive half of her menstrual cycle and the Persephone of her negative half (in her one body). She lives the psycho-biological totality of that cyclic alternation which is (and which she in her bones understands to be) inseparable from the organic cycle and vital sympathies of the natural world, and from the electrical character of matter in the laws of time and space. In this sense, Shakespeare's Tragic Equation is an aberration that man has to live and suffer, and that woman has to endure and redeem him from (reuniting him to the natural world and to total life and being). On top of this, menstrual woman and rational man, as a sexual pair, have to deal with the psychological reality that the man secretes three women (maiden, mother and crone – roughly centred on the internalized image of his mother: a Lucrece, a Divine Mother and a Queen of Hell), while the woman secretes three men (sacred lover, demonic tyrant and holy father – roughly centred on the internalized image of her father: idyllic Adonis, rampant, fatal Tarquin and saint). These four (the male and his internalized, composite female, the female and her internalized, composite male) produce the four characters (potentially ten) of the Tragic Equation and the infinite problem of their living together in love as 'one flesh'.

APPENDIX III

The Equation in *The Merchant of Venice*

Apart from the conventional role given to the Jew by medieval Christianity (as by Marlowe, in *The Jew of Malta*), the Reformation developed a special relationship with Biblical Israel. This relationship included a proprietary feeling for the land itself, for its resonant complex of sacred locations. In England this preoccupation was acute, and continued to grow more so, right into this century, culminating, perhaps, in the restoration of Israel as a nation state. The fact that the Holy Bible became our national sacred book, and the shrine and sacred model of our language, had a decisive influence on the English imagination. The irresistible propaganda for Omnipotent Jehovah's triumph (in the Old Testament) and for the Terrible Lamb His Son's victory (in the New Testament and particularly in *Revelations*) over 'Mystery, Babylon the Great, the Mother of Harlots and of the Abomination of the Earth' made every English man and woman to some degree an honorary Israelite, who lived and spoke from that prophetic dream-time scenario. Hence Milton's *Paradise Lost* and *Samson Agonistes*. Hence Blake, and the curious fact that even today one of the most popular English hymns (and a good candidate for the unofficial National Anthem) is Blake's song 'Jerusalem', in which the Holy City is to be built again in modern industrial England. Though he made his own interpretation, inverting the Puritan values (as Shakespeare had done two hundred years before him), Blake drew on what was still – perhaps even more pervasively – the national dream. Just as the Australian aboriginal peoples imprint the map of their dream-time happenings on to the actual territory they inhabit, Blake superimposed his visionary map of the Holy Land on Britain's real landscape. What Blake envisaged in his *Prophetic Books* Methodism made in a sense actual, superimposing that dream-time map of Biblical Israel on Britain's topography (and on the imagination of rural and industrial workers) with the dense plantation of chapels.

This odd development was already well under way in the sixteenth century. Combined with the fact that Occult Neoplatonism, too, was preoccupied with Israel – specifically with Jewish mystical tradition – it should prepare us to find Shylock, in *The Merchant of Venice*, not merely at the centre of Shakespeare's mythos, but occupying it in a paradoxical fashion – the despised and apparent villain carrying, nevertheless, the most sacred and human quality (in a work written not long after the narrative poems).

Sure enough, in this drama the parts of the Equation can be seen pushing towards the surface, though still not too well coordinated. Just as in *Macbeth* King Duncan, Banquo, Macduff and the others made up a composite Adonis, here the Venetians fulfil the same role. Rejecting Shylock (in their contempt for him), in effect they reject the Divine Source of the biblical revelation. That is implicit in their rejection (as if the rejection of Divine Love were simply a fundamental component of anti-Semitism). Retrospectively, it appears that Shakespeare has equated this Divine Love with the Goddess: the Venetians reject not so much Shylock, or Israel, as the Shekinah. This can be said because Shylock emerges into the play, in typical style, as if from the rejected Goddess. He emerges, that is, making his bloodthirsty demand for his pound of flesh, and is addressed by the Venetians as 'a cruel devil', and, more pointedly, in a revealingly structured image, as a 'damn'd, inexecrable dog' whose

> currish spirit
> Govern'd a wolf, who, hang'd for human slaughter,
> Even from the gallows did his fell soul fleet,
> And whilst thou lay'st in thy unhallow'd dam,
> Infus'd itself in thee, for thy desires
> Are wolfish, bloody, starved and ravenous.
> *Merchant of Venice* IV. i. 133–8

This metamorphosis of a man, by 'infusion' of a ferocious animal, vividly parallels that of Adonis into Tarquin, in the Equation. And here it is given as the precise explanation for the savagery of one who, like Tarquin, is attempting to overpower the woman of exemplary virtue (Portia). The basic situation of the play – in other words, the dramatic design – is a rough charcoal sketch of the two long poems considered as one sequence and adapted to the stage.

In this play (the Equation being still so tentative) the Boar fails to push its charge home. As in *The Tempest*, it is stopped in mid-career. Adonis is not killed, and so no Tarquin emerges into the full completion of his crime, in that sense. The weddings are secured, as at the end of

The Tempest, without the Puritan Adonis figures having been transformed in any way.

At the same time, the pattern of Tarquinian transformation is prefigured, to a degree, within Shylock himself. He, too, incorporates an Adonis, as Macbeth will. His austerity, his hatred of frivolities, his Puritan control of his daughter Jessica, are the flexing tensions of an Adonis' latent 'double vision'. His attack on the Venetians, therefore, like Macbeth's attack on Duncan and Banquo, is two things: it is primarily the attack of the Boar / irrational Brother against the composite (Venetian) Adonis, but at the same time an externalized image of the collision, within Shylock himself, of Boar and rational Adonis.

According to the Equation, this moment of impact should coincide with the moment at which the Adonis in him sees the 'double vision' bold and clear. Promptly on cue, there it is: the two faces of the female. The legalist Portia (a militant form of Lucrece) confronts his 'Murderous, bloody, full of blame, / Savage, extreme, rude, cruel' assault, while the lustful Jessica confirms his worst, most cynical suspicions and abandons him, preferring the love of another. So both combine to drive him mad, or to make him in some sense 'mad'. In this way, with highly dramatic effect, the Equation presents both the 'double vision' of the female and the hero's – Shylock's – response to it. But the play misunderstands, slightly. Portia has not quite surrendered to her mythic role. Nevertheless, Shylock does in a real sense attack her, in that the combat consists of her resisting, and finally outwitting, his homicidal effort to claim his bond. But he turns his response most violently against the treacherous one, his daughter Jessica, the loved one who must now be loathed, and he does not fail to deliver the obligatory tirade: 'I would my daughter were dead at my foot, and the jewels in her ear'.

In all this, the mechanism of the Equation can be seen wrestling with materials that still have miscellaneous wills of their own, and cannot quite hear the etheric instructions. Yet behind Shylock's charge against the armoured virtue of Portia, and his rage against the apparent perfidy of Jessica which precedes and seems quite unconnected with it, lies the chemistry of the Equation's inevitable single chain reaction, in which these two are the products of the hero's having divided one female. This pattern comes clearer when Shylock's rage against Jessica is compared to Lear's against Cordelia, but clearer still when his rage against Portia and Jessica combined is compared to Leontes' rage against Hermione in *The Winter's Tale*. As Leontes' rage against Polixenes is deflected against Hermione (and as Macbeth's usurping act of bloodthirsty violence against Duncan, Banquo and Macduff is deflected against the wives and mothers of Scotland), Shylock's rage against the Venetians finds itself, in effect, deflected against Portia and Jessica. And just as far as Shylock shares that pattern he shares the fate, and something of the stature, of the tragic figures, and attracts the same kind of interest. These mythic shadows are comparatively weak, though their influence on the action is decisive, as appears well enough. The play clearly adumbrates the full form of the Equation and draws its weird energy, its grotesque yet compelling situation, from the myth trying to emerge. This being the case, it is the presence of the myth which enables us to identify the real nature of Shylock, and to explain something of the strange power and complexity of his role.

Being the Boar who is almost a Tarquin, Shylock carries – just like all the later tragic heroes, and like Caliban – the true humanity, the living divine spark, the authentic self, in the play. He is the only one able to suffer, and his cause – like Caliban's – is just: he has been deprived of his sacred birthright (as the Chosen One of Divine Love), rejected and given the status of an outlaw. But since the Adonis in him is so ill-defined, his Tarquinian, tragic dimension remains uncertain, not fully achieved. He is chased out as the Boar rebuffed and wounded (rather as Caliban will be chased out), while the Venetians pass on laughing and unscathed towards their nuptials.

Properly speaking, what has been described as the anti-Semitism in this play corresponds, exactly, to the autocratic (and cruel) Calvinism in, say, *Measure for Measure* – or indeed to the hysterical rejection of the Goddess by any of the heroes just before the Boar hits him. In Shakespeare's total Court Case, therefore, this anti-Semitism of the Venetians is presented as a form of the 'tragic error', that first phase of the tragic crime which, throughout the tragedies, is hideously punished, and throughout the 'romances' convicted, punished, corrected and finally redeemed in saintly transcendence. In this sense, the sense in which the whole tragic cycle is a single judgemental (and healing) drama, *The Merchant of Venice* becomes a profoundly pro-Semitic, profoundly anti-anti-Semitic work, where Israel equals the Goddess of Complete Being, the undivided form of the Divine Love as worshipped by Job.

If this characterization of Israel as the Divine Love sounds like an unorthodox conclusion, it is nevertheless, as I indicate above, deeply